www.wadsworth.com

www.wadsworth.com is the World Wide Web site for
Thomson Wadsworth and is your direct source to dozens
of online resources.

At *www.wadsworth.com* you can find out about supplements, demonstration software, and student resources.
You can also send email to many of our authors and pre-
view new publications and exciting new technologies.

www.wadsworth.com

Changing the way the world learns®

Readings in World Politics

A New Era

STEVEN L. SPIEGEL
University of California at Los Angeles

JENNIFER MORRISON TAW
Occidental College

FRED L. WEHLING
Monterey Institute of International Studies

KRISTEN P. WILLIAMS
Clark University

THOMSON ™
WADSWORTH

Australia • Canada • Mexico • Singapore • Spain
United Kingdom • United States

THOMSON

WADSWORTH

Publisher: Clark Baxter
Executive Editor: David Tatom
Assistant Editor: Rebecca F. Green
Editorial Assistants: Reena Thomas and
    Cheryl Lee
Technology Project Manager: Michelle
    Vardeman
Marketing Manager: Janise Fry
Marketing Assistant: Tara Pierson
Advertising Project Manager: Kelley McAllister
Project Manager, Editorial Production:
    Megan E. Hansen
Art Director: Maria Epes

Print/Media Buyer: Emma Claydon
Permissions Editor: Kiely Sexton
Production Service: Leah McAleer,
    G&S Book Services
Copy Editor: Frances Andersen
Cover Designer: Jeanette Barber
Cover Images: Clockwise from top:
    © REUTERS/Eskinder Debebe;
    © REUTERS/Radu Sigheti; © REUTERS/
    Jorge Silva
Compositor: G&S Book Services
Printer: Courier Corporation/Stoughton

For more information about our products,
contact us at:
**Thomson Learning Academic
Resource Center
1-800-423-0563**

For permission to use material from this text
or product, submit a request online at
http://www.thomsonrights.com.

Any additional questions about
permissions can be submitted by email to
thomsonrights@thomson.com.

Library of Congress Control Number:
2004107247

ISBN 0-15-506055-4

**Thomson Wadsworth
10 Davis Drive
Belmont, CA 94002-3098
USA**

Asia
Thomson Learning
5 Shenton Way #01-01
UIC Building
Singapore 068808

Australia/New Zealand
Thomson Learning
102 Dodds Street
Southbank, Victoria 3006
Australia

Canada
Nelson
1120 Birchmount Road
Toronto, Ontario M1K 5G4
Canada

Europe/Middle East/Africa
Thomson Learning
High Holborn House
50/51 Bedford Row
London WC1R 4LR
United Kingdom

Latin America
Thomson Learning
Seneca, 53
Colonia Polanco
11560 Mexico D.F.
Mexico

Spain/Portugal
Paraninfo
Calle Magallanes, 25
28015 Madrid, Spain

Contents

Acknowledgments

Aall, Pamela. From "Guessing the Rules: Conflict Resolution in the Post–Cold War Era," *Peace and Conflict: Journal of Peace Psychology,* vol. 8, no. 3 (2002): 277–280. Copyright © 2002 by Lawrence Erlbaum Associates, Inc. Reprinted by permission.

Bean, Richard. From "War and the Birth of the Nation State," *The Journal of Economic History,* vol. 33, no. 1 (March 1973): 203–221. Copyright © 1973 Economic History Association. Reprinted by permission of The Cambridge University Press.

Berkowitz, Bruce D. From "Who Won the Cold War—and Why It Matters," *Orbis,* vol. 40, no. 1 (Winter 1996): 164–171. Copyright © 1996. Reprinted with permission from the Foreign Policy Research Institute.

Byman, Daniel L., and Kenneth M. Pollack. From "Let Us Now Praise Great Men: Bringing the Statesman Back In," *International Security,* vol. 25, no. 4 (Spring 2001): 107–146. Copyright © 2001 President and Fellows of Harvard College and the Massachusetts Institute of Technology. Reprinted by permission of the MIT Press Journals.

Christensen, Thomas J. From "Perceptions and Alliances in Europe, 1865–1940," *International Organization,* vol. 51, no. 1 (Winter 1997): 65–97. Copyright © 1997 IO Foundation and the Massachusetts Institute of Technology. Reprinted by permission of the MIT Press Journals.

2003): 2–7. Copyright © 2003 by the Council on Foreign Relations. Reprinted by permission.

Gilpin, Robert. From "A Postscript to the Asian Financial Crisis: The Fragile International Economic Order," *Cambridge Review of International Affairs,* vol. 16, no. 1 (April 2003): 79–88. Copyright © 2003 by Taylor and Francis, Ltd. (www.tandf.co.uk/journals). Reprinted by permission of the author and the publisher.

Green, Duncan, and Matthew Griffith. From "Globalization and Its Discontents," *International Affairs* (London), vol. 78, no. 1 (January 2002): 49–68. Copyright © 2002 the Royal Institute of International Affairs. Reprinted by permission of Blackwell Publishers, Ltd.

Guéhenno, Jean-Marie. From "Globalization and the International System: The Post–Cold War World," *Journal of Democracy,* vol. 10, no. 1 (1999): 22–35. Copyright © 1999 National Endowment for Democracy and the Johns Hopkins University Press. Reprinted by permission.

Harkavy, Robert E. From "Images of the Coming International System," *Orbis,* vol. 41, no. 4 (Fall 1997): 569–590. Copyright © 1997. Reprinted with permission from the Foreign Policy Research Institute.

Heisbourg, François. From "A New Security Landscape: The End of the Post–Cold War Era," *Asia-Pacific Review,* vol. 10, no. 1 (May 2003): 52–63. Copyright © 2003 by Taylor and Francis, Ltd. (www.tandf.co.uk/journals). Reprinted by permission.

Holsti, Ole R. "Theories of International Relations," from *Explaining the History of American Foreign Relations,* 2nd ed., eds. Michael J. Hogan and Thomas G. Paterson. Cambridge University Press. Copyright © 2004 by Ole R. Holsti. Reprinted by permission of the author.

Huntington, Samuel P. From "The Clash of Civilizations?" *Foreign Affairs,* vol. 72, no. 3 (Summer 1993): 22–49. Copyright © 1993 by the Council on Foreign Relations. Reprinted by permission.

Kindleberger, C. P. From "The Rise of Free Trade in Western Europe, 1820–1875," *The Journal of Economic History,* vol. 35, no. 1 (1975): 20–55. Copyright © 1975 Economic History Association. Reprinted by permission of The Cambridge University Press.

Kortunov, Sergei. From "Is the Cold War Really Over?" *International Affairs* (Moscow), vol. 44, no. 5 (1998): 141–154. Copyright © 1998 East View Information Services, Inc. Reprinted by permission.

Lukacs, John. From "The Coming of the Second World War," *Foreign Affairs,* vol. 68, no. 4 (Fall 1989): 165–174. Copyright © 1989 by the Council on Foreign Relations. Reprinted by permission.

Raymond, Susan. From "Foreign Assistance in an Aging World," *Foreign Affairs,* vol. 82, no. 2 (March/April 2003): 91–105. Copyright © 2003 by the Council on Foreign Relations. Reprinted by permission.

Roberts, Adam. From "From San Francisco to Sarajevo: The UN and the Use of Force," *Survival,* vol. 37, no. 4 (Winter 1995–1996): 7–28. Copyright © 1995 Oxford University Press. Reprinted by permission.

Skidelsky, Robert. From "Imbalance of Power," *Foreign Policy* (March/April 2002): 46–55. Copyright © 2002 Robert Skidelsky. Reprinted by permission of the author.

Sofka, James R. From "Metternich's Theory of European Order: A Political Agenda for 'Perpetual Peace,'" *The Review of Politics,* vol. 60, no. 1 (Winter 1998): 115–149. Copyright © 1998. Reprinted by permission of the Review of Politics.

Van Evera, Stephen. From "The Cult of the Offensive and the Origins of the First World War," *International Security,* vol. 9, no. 1 (Summer 1984): 58–107. Copyright © 1984. Reprinted by permission of the MIT Press Journals.

Walt, Stephen M. From "International Relations: One World, Many Theories," *Foreign Policy,* vol. 110 (Spring 1998): 29–44. Copyright © 1998 by Stephen M. Walt. Reprinted by permission of the author.

Wolf, Martin. From "The Morality of the Market," *Foreign Policy* (September/ October 2001): 47–50 (www.foreignpolicy.com). Copyright © 2001. Reprinted by permission.

❋

Introduction

With this reader we seek to provide students with a range of articles on topics important to the study of world politics. Some of the foremost scholars in the fields of political science, history, and economics wrote the articles included in this collection, the overarching themes of which are globalization and fragmentation. Neither of these dynamics is particularly new or novel; in fact, students will find that they both predate the post–Cold War, 9/11 period. What is particularly interesting for students, however, is how each dynamic appears to have increasing influence not only on economic and security decisions internationally, but also on how states and the global community respond to environmental dilemmas, changing ethical codes, and other evolving social issues.

PART I

This reader complements our textbook, *World Politics in a New Era* (Third Edition) in both approach and structure, yet it can stand alone as an independent text for students and teachers alike. (For example, the articles can be read in sequence [paired with the textbook] or mixed and matched according to the course content and structure.) The reader thus begins with articles dealing with "world politics in theory and history," introducing, at the outset, the themes of globalization and fragmentation. These preliminary articles are followed by a series of readings examining the various theories used to explain world politics (realism, liberalism, Marxism, and constructivism) in terms of both their main components and the most relevant critiques. After reading these initial articles, students should have a better sense of how theory can be used to focus analysis, narrow down a question into a more manageable format, and identify key actors and factors in how world politics unfold.

Complementing the theory articles are historical readings that begin with the origins of the modern international system (the rise of the nation-state as the primary actor in world politics), then turn to the European states' efforts of the early nineteenth century to establish, through the Concert of Europe, a formalized system to ensure peace following the French Revolutionary and Napoleonic Wars, and then conclude with analyses of the causes of World War I and World War II, the Cold War, the end of the Cold War, and the evolution of the world economy. These historical articles set a context for understanding more current global events and demonstrate the relevance of the theories discussed in the reader's earlier articles.

The theoretical and historical articles are far from comprehensive, but represent a useful cross-section of viewpoints and approaches, topics, and issues, all intended to bring an added richness to the study of world politics. At the end of the first part of the reader, students should have an appreciation for how authors choose their topics, formulate their questions, and approach their research. They should be able to recognize an author's assumptions and points of view, and they might also be able to identify alternative applicable theories or research methods. In fact, each article offers students the opportunity to consider exactly how the complexity and cacophony of world politics have been simplified, parsed, categorized, and focused in order to arrive at a specific question or issue and means of addressing it.

PART II

The articles in the second part of the reader have several commonalities, though they deal with a variety of topics relevant to contemporary world politics, including the current state of international economics, the potential for effective conflict prevention, and emerging social issues (from environmental degradation to aging populations). The issue of globalization, in particular, ties the readings together, whether being addressed directly, as in the first couple of articles, or more indirectly, as an issue influencing the shape of the coming international system, the growth of a universal code of ethics, or changing demographics.

Globalization is defined in these articles, variously, as "the integration of everything with everything else"; "the integration of markets, finance, and technology in a way that shrinks the world from a size medium to a size small"; "the increasing interconnectedness of individuals, groups, companies, and countries"; and, least pithily, "Westernization, secularization, democratization, consumerism, and the growth of market capitalism, represent[ing] an onslaught to less privileged people in conservative cultures repelled by the fundamental changes that these forces are bringing—or angered by the distortions and uneven distributions of benefits that result."

Clearly, there is some debate about how best to define globalization, and there are also disputes about whether it is a new phenomenon, about the role of technology in fomenting it, and about whether it does more harm or good. In the 1990s and early twenty-first century, globalization has become part of the equation in discussions about states' sovereignty, balance-of-power politics, ethical obligations to intervene in crises or to provide humanitarian aid, international entities' appropriate roles and responsibilities, the influence of ethnicity and nationality, not to mention the amazing effects of technology on communication, economic interactions, demographics, and even conflict. Indeed, one way to approach the articles in the second part of the reader is to consider them in terms of some of the following questions.

In terms of *security:*

- Does globalization facilitate terrorism?
- Does it facilitate the fight against terrorism?
- Does it augur well in terms of collective security?
- Does it increase the likelihood of the proliferation of weapons of mass destruction?
- On the other hand, is it fragmentation that is the chief cause of issues such as terrorism and proliferation because of the tensions and hostilities it generates?
- Are there military means of bringing fragmentation under control?
- Does outside intervention accelerate or dampen forces of fragmentation?
- In the end, how destabilizing are forces of fragmentation in various parts of the world?

In terms of *economics:*

- Does globalization create the situation, as some claim, in which "all boats rise," or are its benefits disproportionate?
- Who are the winners and losers in the globalization of the world economy, within as well as across state boundaries?
- What are the primary causes of fragmentation?
- Can the causes of fragmentation be overcome mainly by economic means?

In terms of *social and legal issues:*

- Are we sharing cultures or homogenizing?
- How related are urbanization and globalization? Urbanization and fragmentation?

- Does globalization translate into increased personal freedoms?
- Is fragmentation associated with human rights abuses and opposition to democracy?
- Is globalization leading to a new acceptance of a universal code of ethics?
- Is fragmentation leading to the "same old world of conflict" that predated the contemporary rapid pace of globalization?

And, of course, some questions *span the categories,* including:

- Does globalization decrease the possibility of war by increasing economic interdependence as some liberal theorists claim?
- If fragmentary forces are localized, can globalization still expand elsewhere?
- Is globalization reversible? If the United States, for example, as hegemon, rejects international economic, security, social, and legal institutions, will that slow or even end the process?
- Does fragmentation mean that globalization will never be fully realized?
- How important are the processes, mechanisms, and institutions of globalization? Will it progress even if these are flawed?
- How different are globalization and Americanization?
- Does globalization make states more or less influential?
- What role do states' policies play in determining the benefits or costs of globalization? What policies help a nation benefit; what policies are costly?
- How costly and destructive are the forces of fragmentation in thwarting the development of new international economic, security, social, and legal systems worldwide?

Students would also benefit from comparing and contrasting across the articles, rather than examining the unifying theme. For example, each security article identifies a different security-related theme and then proceeds down entirely different analytical paths. Pamela Aall summarizes some big-picture thinking in her book review, raising important questions about the role of states in the international system, sovereignty, and conflict resolution. Audrey Kurth Cronin, in contrast, focuses very specifically on the practical requirement to recognize the relationship between globalization and terrorism. And Brian Frederking's challenging article comes from an entirely different perspective, employing constructivist theory to better understand the potential for improved collective security. Each author has focused in on one specific security-related question out of the vast realm of security issues, applied a certain logic to the research and analysis, and offered tentative results. If we consider, furthermore, that these select security issues are influenced by other security considerations, as well as interrelated economic, political, ethical, and cultural issues (to name a few), the challenge of truly understanding the full scope of international relations becomes quickly evident. That said, this reader is intended to help students precisely by providing them with articles that span theories, viewpoints, and approaches, so that students can benefit not only from the articles' content, but from their comparison.

Finally, each article also deserves to be read on its own merit, independent of any broader consideration of globalization/fragmentation or heuristic exercises. These articles represent some of the best thinking that's been done on global security, economics, and legal and social issues, and stand as strong examples of compelling scholarship. For students anxious to know more about contemporary world political issues, these articles provide a solid foundation.

GENERAL GUIDANCE

In reading each of the articles, students should ask themselves several questions. What argument is each author making? What perspective is each author coming from? Do any of them examine the same issue, but with entirely different assumptions? Are some authors more convincing in their arguments? If so, why and how? Does an author rely more on a descriptive examination of empirical evidence or on the application of theory? Is an author attempting to account for one or more particular events in world politics or for broader trends? Is the author explaining policy options or the flux of international relations? Is he or she describing the actions of individuals, the roles of states or nonstate actors, or the dynamic of the international system?

It is our hope that this reader will help students become more confident in identifying key issues; determining what factors influence outcomes in global interactions; considering how best to approach a world politics question historically, theoretically, and practically; and recognizing authors' biases, approaches, and assumptions so that every article can be understood as part of a story, rather than the story itself.

1

Introduction to World Politics

Reading 1-1

Globalization and the International System
The Post–Cold War World
Jean-Marie Guéhenno

The "international system" is a comforting expression which assumes that international relations can be described according to a single unifying logic which inspires the actions of well-identified actors. This assumption may have been valid when the Cold War provided a defining issue; the world was divided into two camps, and non-alignment was itself a by-product of alignment. After the end of the Cold War, however, this assumption has become much more problematic. Is there still a defining issue that brings the world together and explains how human communities interact with one another? Do we need enemies?

The idea of "us" versus "them" may well be the defining force of any human community, which begins to exist when it can draw a line between those who belong and those who do not. What specifically belongs to the Western political tradition is the idea that we need enemies to overcome our own political divisions. The ancient Chinese thought of non-Chinese not as enemies, but as inferior people who were expected

SOURCE: From "Globalization and the International System: The Post–Cold War World" by Jean-Marie Guéhenno, *Journal of Democracy*, vol. 10, no. 1 (1999): 22–35. Copyright © 1999 National Endowment for Democracy and the Johns Hopkins University Press. Reprinted by permission.

to pay tribute to the emperor; the Middle Kingdom existed by itself, and had no need for any external challenge. (Actually, it died of that excess of self-confidence.) But ever since the Greeks invented the "barbarians," the reality of political divisions between rival states has echoed the divisions of the rival cities of ancient Greece. We dream of a unity that would be achieved against a common enemy, and the Roman Empire provides us with a nostalgic model of a political unity that would match our universalistic tradition.

This may explain why we in the "West" are so desperate to find new enemies after the end of the Cold War. The communists were convenient "barbarians"; for a short while, we could speak of the "West" in a way that would have been familiar to the citizens of Athens. We would like to find a similar threat, global enough in its scope to unify our uncertain communities. But where can we find it? Where is the convenient fault line that will give us new certainties?

Today, there is no such obvious fault line, and nothing has the potential to give shape to the post–Cold War world in a way comparable to the East-West divide. But we still want to think in normative terms. We want to have an enemy that defines us. With the end of the Cold War, we have often been tempted to build up the new opposition between globalization and fragmentation as if it were a substitute for the old East-West divide. According to this logic, history is a battle of good against evil. Globalization and the triumph of the market are the economic consequences of the victory of democracy. The global market will give economic freedom to billions of consumers and producers in the same way that political freedom has given millions of individuals new rights. And it is tempting to see nationalism, ethnicity, and fragmentation as obstacles to that bright global future. They are all relics of the past, and as such, easy to dismiss.

But we must go beyond that analysis. The proliferation of intrastate wars today suggests that fragmentation may be a product of globalization rather than a remnant of the past, and that instead of viewing these two phenomena as opposed to each other, we should consider them linked. Moreover, we should recognize their ambiguity, acknowledging both the limits and risks of globalization and the virtues, if not of fragmentation, then of smaller entities.

What is globalization, and is it really global? Is fragmentation always negative? How is stability best achieved, and war avoided? The experience of the Cold War has led us to believe that the world is a safer place when left to the supervision of a couple of superpowers acting as enforcers and stabilizers. Is that model still valid when there is no unifying issue and no enemy, and are we right to consider the evolution toward ever bigger political entities not only as inevitable but also as desirable?

GLOBALIZATION AND FRAGMENTATION

Although one of its versions was defeated when the Soviet Union and the communist system collapsed, scientism is still very much alive. We tend to understand globalization as the outcome of a linear pattern of progress, largely determined by economic forces. As technological evolution makes possible (and requires) economies of scale, human communities are expected to form increasingly larger political entities. The city-state was replaced by the nation-state, which has itself been overtaken by the new dimensions of industry and information technology. According to this functionalist view, the only relevant debate now is whether, in a world economy, even the continental state makes sense. Some would actually argue that the global firm does better when its action is not impeded by the localism of states. Producers as well as consumers should be able to meet freely in the global marketplace. Political institutions are just a nuisance, which will soon be sidestepped by self-regulating authorities and transnational organizations that blur the distinction between private and public and are making public institutions increasingly irrelevant.

According to this interpretation of globalization, the world is becoming an apolitical place, in which politicians are relegated to a sideshow: The reality lies elsewhere, in financial markets that get rid of Indonesia's Suharto, force Russia to reform its economy, and are transforming even China.

In fact, of course, markets only function properly if contracts are enforced, and if peacekeepers and policemen ensure that a state of law prevails over violence and brute force. The global economy can work only if the world is a predictable place in which individuals and corporations know their rights and can enforce them. In other words, the apolitical world of globalization can prosper only under the aegis of a political entity, its guarantor, the United States. That is why globalization is increasingly understood to be a synonym of Americanization. Globalization has become a euphemism for a unipolar world of which Washington would be the capital.

This identification between globalization and Americanization deserves further analysis because it is a source of ambiguities, misunderstandings, and resentment. Does it mean that the United States is the benevolent servant of market forces that are much stronger than any political strategy that could emerge in Washington, and that the world should be grateful to have such a benign cop? Or does it mean that globalization is an instrument of U.S. power, a new ideology that supports an imperial design, just as communism supported Soviet ambitions? Is the new science of the market merely a cover for political ambitions of the most traditional type?

In developing countries, as well as in a rich country like France that prides itself on having a universal message, many people harbor this suspicion, and they resent what they see as a U.S. imperialism that threatens the identity of existing communities. But anybody who watches the United States today cannot fail to notice how unimperial this allegedly imperial power really is. The pervasive influence of the United States is evident in eating habits, entertainment, and clothing, as well as in the more traditional tokens of power, from Okinawa to Naples. Yet the United States is the first power in history whose imperial reach has been achieved not through a concerted design, but almost unwittingly. The Americanization of the world often seems to result from a reaction to external events or a spillover of domestic forces rather than a projection of power and political will. In fact, the more "American" the world becomes, the less interested in "foreign" affairs American citizens seem, and the more difficult it becomes for the U.S. government to get public support for its "imperial" interests.

This also is unprecedented. No previous empire has been a democracy. The American "empire" depends upon the support of its citizens, and that support, when it is forthcoming, is given for very domestic reasons, because the United States, having become an empire unknowingly, does not see itself as an empire. Actually, its foreign policy looks increasingly like the sum of the special interests promoted by specific internal groups, and the transnational nature of its influence and power means that its links with the rest of the world are increasingly formed through those particular groups. This may strengthen these links and prevent U.S. isolation, but it also presents an obstacle to any global vision. Washington may be the capital of a global empire, but it is an empire without an emperor.

Yet much of the rest of the world perceives that an American empire is indeed being built, and watches it with a mixture of envy and resentment. These feelings exist in spite of the absence of any grand design on the part of the United States, and perhaps even because of that absence. What fascinates and irks at the same time is the way in which Americans can reduce politics to a clash of interests, and yet maintain the vitality of the American polity. How can one reconcile the fact of globalization, which ignores borders and destroys the old social structures that mediate between the individual and the global marketplace, with this other reality, the American nation, which seems to resist globalization better than most communities? The answer probably lies in the unique history of the United States, which sees itself not as an inherited community but as a community of choice, built on a contract. American patriotism is institutional; it is less linked to a particular territory and is more global than that of most other nations, which have been shaped by the contingent forces of history, not by the free choice of their citizens.

This uniqueness of the U.S. experience explains why globalization can be equated with Americanization. It also reveals the limits of globalization. Globalization is much more than the projection of U.S. influence, but it is linked to America's particular historical experience. The attempt to present it as a universal model triggers powerful reactions from those who feel that their own community is built on more than functional choices, that its roots go beyond the free will of its citizens. This reaction is strongest in poor countries, but it is present even within the United States. It is a reaction of religion against science, one which expresses the need for a truth that is not determined by the utilitarian logic of individuals.

THE RESURGENCE OF RELIGION

The collapse of scientistic ideologies has brought with it a new longing for religion (taken in its etymological meaning of that which "binds" human beings together). Both rich and poor want their lives to be determined by something more than the contingent necessities of the market and of the individual choices that it provides. The extreme freedom of the market is seen by many as an unbearable burden. Individuals long for a framework that they can interpose between themselves and the global market. They want to belong to a particular community that is not functionally determined. And this longing is not primarily determined by class considerations. It is quite striking to observe how the American Right's insistence on "family values" parallels the moralistic claims of Jewish or Islamic fundamentalists. Retired Americans who have done well on Wall Street and feel comfortable in a California "gated community" are indeed quite different from the uprooted young men from the slums of big Third World cities who join some radical movement. The second group resents the fact that market forces have left them behind, while the first would like to believe that their success is based on a set of values that the market may reflect but does not create. But both groups, albeit for opposite reasons, maintain that values cannot be grounded in a purely functional logic.

That belief is widely shared, and likely to get stronger. The driving force behind today's revival of religion is not what Marx expected it to be—consolation for all those who feel they have missed their chance in this world and hope for a better life in the next. It goes much deeper, and should be understood as a reaction against the functionalism of the age of progress and science. The first stage of that reaction was the collapse of communism, which could not deliver on its claim that it would scientifically improve society. A second stage may be coming, and the growth of rightist movements in highly developed capitalist societies is a symptom of that impending crisis.

Unlike communism, capitalism *has* delivered on its promises; the increase in wealth over the past two centuries is unprecedented. But that economic success is not enough. Having won the scientific argument over communism, capitalism now has to convince people that a society can be based on science. The more that people question this, the more precarious capitalism's triumph will be.

This new emphasis on values and religion carries with it a great potential for violence. History teaches us that contrary to the conventional wisdom, human beings are much more willing to die for their ideas than for their interests; interests can be bargained for, but ideas are the foundations of identities, and nobody wants to compromise his identity. The diplomats of the seventeenth century who negotiated the treaties of Westphalia understood this well when they confirmed the principle *cuius regio, eius religio;* after decades of religious wars, they decided that religion should not and could not be the organizing principle of international relations. It had to be the other way around. Princes might be able to accommodate their conflicting interests, provided that religious affiliations gave way to political considerations.

We are now in the process of reversing that position. We are putting ideas, beliefs, and values first. But this does not mean that we should expect religious states to replace ideological states, or religious interstate conflicts to replace the ideological interstate conflicts of the twentieth century.

The fault lines of religion are quite different from the fault lines of ideology, and their impact on the "international system" will not be the same. The growth of ideologies paralleled the growth of the modern state; the resurgence of religion is a sign of its weakening. We would like to believe, however, that religion provides us with a new defining issue that does not call into question the state system as we know it, but only changes the reasons for conflict.

In Europe, the ideas presented by Samuel Huntington in *The Clash of Civilizations and the Remaking of World Order* have found their caricature in the fear that Islamic fundamentalism is the threat of tomorrow. A North-South divide in the middle of the Mediterranean is viewed as the new front line between a tired Judeo-Christian civilization and an Islamic world on the offensive. The Bosnian conflict, the Turkish-Greek rivalry in Cyprus and the Aegean, and the Israeli-Palestinian conflict are the flashpoints of this new strategic conflict. In South Asia, the "Islamic bomb" of Pakistan is the answer to the "Hindu bomb." According to this theory, each great religion needs to have its own instruments of mass murder.

This vision is based on some objective facts, but it misses the reality of tomorrow's world. To draw such conclusions, we have to assume that political institutions will remain strong enough to transform these huge civilizational communities into coherent actors in the international system, and that the existing nation-states within these religious-cultural areas will overcome their differences and develop compatible policies.

The rise of religion, ethnicity, and nationalism is a reaction against the abstract functional world of globalization. But it is an illusion to expect these powerful forces to consolidate existing states, let alone groups of states. Their logic is not territorial, and they cut across existing borders. The Cold War did not question existing states; it even consolidated them, because the East-West confrontation made "internal" disputes secondary. But today, the land-for-peace negotiations between Israel and the Palestinians, the conflict over Kashmir between India and Pakistan, and the Dayton agreement all involve difficult negotiations over maps. The definition of the polity is at stake. Geography remains a central issue, because most people feel their personal safety begins with political control of a territory, but the definition of the territory is no longer an uncontested starting point; it is itself an object of negotiation. The political settlement cannot be separated from the geographic settlement. In other words, existing states cannot be taken for granted anymore. What is being contested is not just the nature of a specific regime that will rule a specific territory; it is the nature of its borders, and eventually the definition of the polity.

These are new questions for traditional geopolitics; they erase the convenient separation between domestic and international affairs and undermine the assumption that geopolitical analysis consists in identifying the interests of existing states. The interests of states can be no more permanent than states themselves. The Cold War provided a framework that consolidated the traditional interstate system. Its end may expose previously hidden weaknesses, introducing more flexibility but also more uncertainties into the international system. Today, no issue can be deemed a defining issue, and no state can be assumed to be a permanent actor. The new forces at work—religion, ethnicity, nationalism—are symptoms of the precariousness of existing states in a world where no community can be deemed invulnerable.

Religions are not creating the foundations of new continental states; on the contrary, the divisions that they reveal within existing states make superstates look even more utopian. In Europe, for instance, the attitude toward Muslims varies so much from one country to another, depending on the importance of its Muslim minorities, that this issue divides rather than unites Europeans. Confronted with the abstraction of the global economy, human communities search for closer, more concrete relationships. Even when they find them in transnational religious belief, the eventual result is fragmentation, narrower horizons that provide the reassuring proximity of a more tightly knit community, rather than the broader horizons that one might expect of new transnational solidarities.

THE CHALLENGES OF THE POST–COLD WAR SYSTEM

Fragmentation is the product of globalization, and the international system cannot expect to find stability by denying the increasing demands for identity, the need of human beings for belonging to a particular community. The vision of even larger communities eventually creating a concert of "continental states" that would play the same stabilizing role played by the concert of nation-states in nineteenth-century Europe is neither realistic nor desirable. Such a change of scale would make the international system very rigid and eventually unstable. On the other hand, if every ethnic group were to achieve statehood, the proliferation of states would also be a source of instability, and would make the world unmanageable.

These tendencies will coexist in the post–Cold War system. The real issue is to make this coexistence dynamic rather than destructive, to reconcile the need for global management of global issues with the need for identity and differentiation. The international system will remain stable only through increased flexibility. Diffusion of power, if it is accompanied by the strengthening of cooperative procedures, may be a much more effective answer to globalization than the concentration of power in oversized institutions, which would progressively become incapable of managing complexity and lose the capability for global leadership.

Three issues may soon test this balance between global leadership and local identities, and between the need for cooperation and the need for autonomy and self-reliance. They will decide whether the passive stability of the Cold War will be replaced by a new proactive stability, and whether the coming devolution of power will effectively preempt conflicts or will lead to uncontrolled violence. These issues are: (1) the capability of Europe and the United States to share the burden and responsibilities of global management; (2) the capability of the United States and Europe to integrate China into the international system and to stabilize Asia; and (3) the capability of the United States and Europe to prevent the development of a new type of post-nation-state anarchy.

Geopolitics is a very cyclical "science." A decade ago, nobody would have predicted the present supremacy of the United States, the quick collapse of the communist system, or the Asian economic crisis. Today, it is accepted wisdom that Europe has lost its centrality. Many pundits, after having predicted that the Euro would never become a reality, have cut their losses and are now confident that it will eventually fail economically and politically. Europe, in their view, has the wrong agenda, and is headed for permanent decline.

My own view is that the European model, messy as it is, still has something to teach the rest of the world, and that its success or failure is of strategic importance. Europeans have been learning how to reconcile democracy and interdependence. They are trying to come to terms with the ideas that national sovereignty cannot be the ultimate goal of democracy, that a decision is legitimate only if it takes into consideration the concerns of one's neighbors, and that limiting power may sometimes be more important than giving power to the people. This is a painful process, one that entails permanent negotiations and reduces the scope of politics because it strikes a new balance between experts and politicians. It is far from perfect and often frustrating, but ultimately efficient.

The advent of the Euro, which will require even closer coordination between the United States and Europe, opens a new phase in this process and raises new questions. Can the organized interdependence that has been achieved within Europe be extended beyond its borders? For only by combining their power and influence can the United States and Europe hope to shape the twenty-first century according to their democratic and universalist values.

There is no obvious answer to this question. The European tradition and the American tradition are very similar, but also very different. The United States is indeed a "European power," shaped by the philosophy of the Enlightenment and sharing with Europe the same fundamental values. Yet it was built in opposition to the corruption of old Europe, and rejected the cynical compromises of traditional diplomacy. It cherishes the sovereignty of the American people, and contemplates with reluctance the prospect of submitting its legal order to an external authority, whether it be the UN Security Council, the World Trade Organization, or an international court. The compromises on which contemporary Europe is building its institutions have little in common with the power politics of the eighteenth and nineteenth centuries, but the Americans remain suspicious. They expect European institutions to be either weak and ineffective or a cynical camouflage for traditional balance-of-power arrangements. According to this view, American patriotism is the only true institutional patriotism. The Europeans will never be able to combine old-style national patriotism, based on history, with a European patriotism based on institutions and the democratic ambition of Europeans to be interdependent rather than dependent.

These doubts are understandable, but they are based on a mistaken analysis. A long-term view of European integration shows that it has been more resilient than most of its critics expected. The real issue of the future is whether the United States will be able to develop a new post–Cold War framework for relations with the European Union that would borrow some features of the European experience. This issue is of strategic importance because Europe is the only continent with which the United States shares both a historical relationship and a moral sense of kinship. If the United States is ever to accept a more collegial management of world affairs, based on interdependence rather than sovereignty, it will be through its European connection. And continued effective involvement of the United States in world affairs is a realistic prospect only if it can share the burden—and the leadership—with like-minded countries. A unilateralist America will eventually become an isolationist America.

The transatlantic relationship therefore epitomizes the tensions between globalization and fragmentation. Political will exists only when citizens maintain a sense of belonging to a particular community they can identify with, but effective action requires going beyond one's particular community, joining forces, and managing multiple identities. The Europeans have started that process, but they have to go further, and broaden it to a transatlantic dimension that cannot be limited just to NATO and security issues. The question whether the United States is prepared to join Europe on the path of interdependence remains open. If they do join forces, their combined influence may shape the next century; if they fail to do so, the major challenges looming on the horizon may trigger either a catastrophic return to power politics on a global scale or a period of retrenchment, which would eventually lead to chaos.

THE INTEGRATION OF CHINA

The biggest challenge for the post–Cold War international system is Asia and the integration of China. The management of power in a country of a billion people could not follow the same patterns as in a traditional nation-state in any case, but the challenge of sheer size becomes even more pressing with transnational economic forces pulling apart the old fabric of Chinese society. The Chinese leadership will find it increasingly hard to maintain its central control while encouraging economic initiative; the temptation will arise to use ethnic nationalism to resist pressures for democratization and to shore up a weakened center.

In the coming years, China's weight and the resources its government can mobilize to strengthen its military power will significantly increase. Although the model of a huge nondemocratic continental state does not provide a credible answer for the long-term development of the country, it is the easiest answer, and the one most likely to extend the power of the existing leadership. Inventing a Chinese democracy, which would necessarily be quite different from traditional forms of democracy, would bring the country onto an unknown path that its leaders may be reluctant to take.

The integration of China into a global order that fosters stability and predictability on the basis of law and common norms is by no means assured. It is not clear whether China will accept in its external relations legal and procedural disciplines that it does not yet accept in its internal organization. Will it contribute to a global legal order, or will it act as a destabilizer, capitalizing on the discontent of all those who are not satisfied with the status quo? Some of China's high-technology exports, the support it has given to Pakistan, its maritime conflicts with most Asian countries, and its ambiguous trade practices suggest that a clear choice has yet to be made.

The present Asian economic crisis gives China a temporary and superficial advantage, because it is not bound by the constraints of domestic public opinion or volatile financial markets, and thus appears to be a haven of stability. This may encourage its leaders to believe that the balance of power is shifting in their favor, as Japan remains in recession, ASEAN is in disarray, and India is ostracized and incapable of reforming its economy. In fact, the lack of accountability and the "crony capitalism" that have plagued other Asian economies are even worse in China, but they are hidden behind a political façade of stability; if that façade were to crumble, the economic crisis would be combined with a political crisis that would make the Indonesian crisis look minor.

China's economic and political integration into the international system are therefore closely linked. The effective management of global interdependence will be achieved only through the strengthening of a state of law that blurs the distinction between domestic and international affairs. The Europeans, the United States, and the rest of Asia share the same interest—to avoid having either to contain or to appease China. China has to be integrated, not isolated, but its integration requires some fundamental changes in its political order. These changes can be peaceful only if they are not postponed indefinitely. The Chinese leadership must be under no illusion that it will be allowed to postpone them by playing off Europe against the United States.

If these powers fail to develop a coordinated policy on this issue, China's emergence is likely to be the first major test of the post–Cold War international system. China has enough concentrated power to resurrect the traditional world of power politics; at the same time, power within the democracies and postnational entities has been so diluted that it would be difficult to achieve a stable balance. The emergence of a Chinese superstate playing the traditional game of power politics would certainly trigger a chain reaction throughout Asia. Other states—India, Korea, and eventually Japan—would follow the same pattern, in a context of nuclear proliferation.

PREVENTING ANARCHY

The challenge of China points to a more general feature of the post–Cold War order: Globalization brings together societies and political entities that are governed by different logics. People look beyond the nation-state only when they feel confident enough about their national community, but globalization makes many people less confident, and therefore more attached to their particular community and less willing to build the overarching structures that might reconcile their need for an identity with the need for democratic management of interdependence. People who are comfortable with postnational entities will therefore have to coexist with people for whom the nation-state can still mobilize passions much more effectively than the international bureaucratic structures that try to manage globalization. This coexistence of people with widely differing historical experiences may eventually degenerate into paralysis and anarchy.

The postnational structures that are being built are still weak and are not designed for crisis management; their logic is slow and procedural, better suited for incremental changes than for big decisions. At the same time, frustration grows when globalization is not matched by institutions that can convincingly manage it. The feeling of dependence creates a longing for independence, rather than the acceptance of interdependence. A race has started between the diffusion of power (which will eventually make the international system more flexible) and the development of a global institutional framework that can prevent this devolution of power from creating new obstacles. The more autonomy that smaller communities gain, the greater is the need for globally negotiated norms to define and regulate their relations.

Without such institutions, we may feel the negative impact of globalization without enjoying its benefits. Traditional state structures will be further weakened, while international institutions, whose strength is ultimately based on the strength of their member states, will not grow stronger. New actors will occupy the resulting vacuum without being accountable to anybody, and their influence will be increased by the multiplying power of money and modern technology. Weak states will be hijacked by criminal gangs, as the emergence of a global marketplace in the absence of a global community creates new opportunities for manipulation and crime. In Russia, we can already see the links that are developing between corrupt bureaucracies and criminal gangs; where legitimate political communities are lacking, the state itself is sometimes "privatized." It is naive to expect the free play of market forces and "global democracy" to exert an effective countervailing influence against such dangers. Both the market and democracy need strong institutions to function in a transparent and orderly way. The disappearance of structures able to mediate between the individual and the global setting will jeopardize the market as well as democracy.

In the Middle East, a weak and divided transatlantic community, unable to develop a coherent and balanced strategy, will give local actors more leverage, and make them more unpredictable. This will happen at the worst possible moment, as local actors react to the forces of globalization by redefining their national identity. The challenge that Hamas represents for the traditional nationalism of Arafat is paralleled by the redefinition of Israeli domestic politics and the new forces that have weakened the reformist and secular ideology of the old Labor party.

In many other parts of the world, particularly in Africa, post-colonial nationalism is a spent force, and democratic structures have not created a new legitimacy to replace it. The weakening or quasi-disappearance of the state creates vast areas that are becoming the new *terrae incognitae* of a postnational world. We still believe that they can be insulated with a *cordon sanitaire,* but this is a double illusion. Territorial containment becomes meaningless in the world of globalization. Diseases, weapons, and people can move freely. We will find relatively high-tech weaponry in low-tech countries and low-tech poor people in high-tech countries. Eventually, terrorism will show the vacuity of a policy that would limit its ambitions to containing anarchy. Furthermore, the globalization of information means that we can no longer pretend to ignore what is happening in those areas of anarchy. While we may temporarily appease our conscience with cosmetic operations, in the long run a cynical policy of nonintervention will destroy democracies from within by destroying their self-respect.

The more advanced parts of the world must be proactive if the dynamics of globalization and fragmentation are to be managed in a positive way. The risks of such proactive policies will be accepted only if they are broadly shared. In this respect, also, the relationship between the United States, its European allies, Russia, and Japan will determine our future. If regions that require a concerted effort from these powers, involving the whole range of policy instruments, are seen either as unimportant (Africa) or as arenas of competition (the Middle East), we will fail, and the balance between order and chaos will gradually tip toward the latter.

This does not mean that the answer lies in a single unified "Western" policy. On the contrary, a truly multipolar but integrated system would be able to accommodate differences and varying degrees of involvement among its component parts. But this useful diversity must find its limits in the understanding that all actors share some fundamental interests, and thus should engage in an organized and continuous negotiation and abstain from unilateral actions. This would require political habits rooted in a tradition of cooperation that has to be built gradually over time.

THE WORST CASE IS NEVER THE MOST LIKELY SCENARIO

There are many ways in which the post–Cold War system could go wrong, and the conditions that must be present to strike the right balance between the need for global leadership and the legitimate aspiration to local identities are unlikely to be met. These conditions are: (1) a constructive involvement of the United States government (and not just of its corporations) in world affairs through a continuing and deepening relationship with Europe, and the acceptance by the United States of the constraints of multilateralism; (2) a European Union capable of reconciling democracy with interdependence and of becoming an effective partner of the United States; (3) a China that manages a transition toward a new form of democracy and is successfully integrated in the global order; (4) a Russia capable of inventing a postimperial regime that organizes a true devolution of power without destroying its political institutions; (5) a Middle East in which the failing logic of the nation-state is not replaced by a new form of fundamentalism; (6) a successful policy of nonproliferation; and (7) a consolidation of the many human communities that, in the aftermath of the Cold War, have to confront the question of their own identities.

The age of nation-states was born when the primacy of political institutions over religion was asserted by the treaties of Westphalia. This period is coming to an end, and the pessimists will argue, with good reason, that we may be entering a period comparable to the one that immediately preceded the Westphalian settlement—a time of great violence and religious wars, now made even worse by weapons of mass destruction.

But the worst case is never the most likely scenario. Rather than returning to a model of the past, we may be at the beginning of a new paradigm of international relations. Most of the conditions of a stable international order depend on the invention of new political institutions. The post–Cold War world will achieve stability only if it is postnational, able to combine the leadership that traditionally has been associated with nation-states with an organized interdependence based on a global rule of law that evokes the Roman Empire rather than the modern multiplicity of national polities. This reconciliation of democratic ambitions with imperial logic brings us into uncharted territories. Shall we be able to find our bearings in this new world?

There is one reassuring thought. The logic of the emerging world weakens intermediate structures and gives increased leverage and influence to individuals and non-state actors. This new freedom is for some a source of anxiety that can lead to religious fundamentalism and fanaticism. But it also opens new ground for the initiative of free individuals and tremendously increases the flexibility of the global system. There are many more actors, making competing small decisions, which are then sorted on a global scale in a huge trial-and-error process. At the very moment when we have been deprived of the big issues of the Cold War, we may now be deprived of the big actors as well. And that may not always be as bad as we think.

Reading 1-2

Imbalance of Power
Robert Skidelsky

The 1941 Japanese attack on Pearl Harbor created the Grand Alliance against fascism, just as the September 11, 2001, attacks on the World Trade Center and the Pentagon created the global coalition against terrorism. The leaders of the Grand Alliance were the United States, Great Britain, and Russia, with China a somewhat distant

SOURCE: From "Imbalance of Power" by Robert Skidelsky, *Foreign Policy* (March/April 2002): 46–55. Copyright © 2002 Robert Skidelsky. Reprinted by permission of the author.

fourth. Today's chessboard has not changed that much. With his historical debt to the 19th-century Austrian statesman Klemens von Metternich, former U.S. Secretary of State Henry Kissinger has talked about a new "concert of great powers" to keep the peace in the new century.

The parallel can be taken further. In each case it was an attack on the United States that brought the global coalition into existence. Before 1941, the United States was isolationist; before September 11, the Bush administration was "unilateralist." Each attack forced Americans to engage more strenuously with a world from which geography and history had shielded them. The questions regarding that engagement remain as before: On what terms, with what aims, with what permanence, and with what friends?

To answer these questions, it may be helpful to look back on the politics of the original Grand Alliance. Here the protagonists were not only British Prime Minister Winston Churchill and U.S. President Franklin Roosevelt but John Maynard Keynes (who virtually ran Britain's wartime external financial relations), U.S. Secretary of the Treasury Henry Morgenthau Jr., and Assistant Secretary of the Treasury Harry Dexter White. While the two government leaders concentrated on how to fight the war, Keynes and his U.S. counterparts negotiated on who was to pay for it. As Keynes wrote of Churchill's visit to President Roosevelt soon after Pearl Harbor: "It has been a question of buddies sitting around writing large numbers of tanks and planes on paper . . . [with] no financial matter . . . given a minute's consideration."

What kind of alliance was it? For many Americans, it has been forever embalmed in the warm glow of Churchill's memorable prose: a union of the two great democracies fighting fascism, a union cemented not just by shared values but by an unparalleled act of generosity by the United States in the form of the military aid provided through the Lend-Lease Act. These memories have merged almost seamlessly into the start of the Marshall Plan, the creation of NATO, and the struggle against communism.

SPOILS OF VICTORY

Reality and myth are related, but not as closely as memory has made them. What has been forgotten is the bitterness of wartime Anglo-American rivalry. Churchill was fighting to preserve the British empire. Keynes's war aim was "the retention by us of enough assets to leave us capable of independent action," a necessary condition of Great Britain's survival as a Great Power. And the United States? It was far from being in accord with either of these objectives. It wanted the war to end with Great Britain cut down to size—no longer in a position to oppose U.S. plans for a postwar order. Behind the facade of the Grand Alliance, an intense jockeying for postwar position was taking place.

In this struggle, the United States had a huge weapon in its hand in the form of lend-lease. Lend-lease had a double aim. The first was to keep Great Britain in the war, partly for the protection of the United States itself, by keeping Adolf Hitler out of the Atlantic. The Lend-Lease Act became law in March 1941, nine months before the Japanese attack on Pearl Harbor, when it was by no means clear when, or even whether, the United States would enter the war. It was a brilliant political ploy by Roosevelt to bypass the Neutrality Acts, which forbade U.S. government loans to belligerents. In principle, however, it was no different from Great Britain's policy of subsidizing other countries to fight France in the continental wars of the 18th century.

But the U.S. administration also realized that lend-lease could be used as a lever to pressure London to sign on to Washington's plans for the postwar world—a world without the British empire, sterling area, or imperial preference system (which discriminated against American goods). Keynes's wrangles with the Americans were so fierce that he was driven to write: "I always regard a visit [to the United States] as in the nature of a serious illness to be followed by convalescence." The lesson for today is that the politics of any wartime alliance is concerned not just with how to achieve victory but with how to share the sacrifices and allocate the spoils of victory.

This brings us to a second theme from the past: how to make peace. A good settlement of a war is one that results in a durable peace. The Treaty of Vienna that ended the Napoleonic wars and set up the Congress system is one such example. The earlier Treaty of Westphalia, which ended the Thirty Years' War and is generally recognized as the first conscious application of "balance of power" theory to international relations, is another example. But it also might be argued that the physical destruction of Carthage by Rome in 146 B.C. was a good settlement because it brought to an end the century-long cycle of Punic Wars.

In his famous 1919 polemic, *The Economic Consequences of the Peace,* Keynes took the classic view that either you crush your enemy or you conciliate it. The worst outcome was a settlement that was too harsh to conciliate and not harsh enough to crush. This, he thought, exactly described the Treaty of Versailles, which is why he predicted a war of revenge by Germany. In particular, he attacked the policy of reparations because it maximized the irritation of the defeated with minimum benefit to the victors.

The planning for peace in the Second World War took a Carthaginian turn with the Morgenthau Plan, which aimed to pastoralize as well as dismember Germany. When someone suggested to Morgenthau that an agrarian Germany bereft of industry would not be able to support its existing population, he casually suggested dumping the surplus in Africa.

In its stark form the Morgenthau Plan was never adopted, but there is little doubt that Germany was more harshly treated after the Second World War than after the first. Its structural capacity to wage a new war was drastically reduced by partition into two parts and by Allied reforms of its constitution and industrial structure. A similar policy was applied in Japan. It should not be forgotten that both Japan and Germany were physically occupied by the victors for several years after the war and that they were subsequently embedded in multilateral organizations controlled by the United States and (in East Germany's case) the Soviet Union. It was not until reunification in 1990, following the collapse of the Soviet empire, that Germany regained some room for maneuver in high politics—50 years after Hitler launched the European war.

However, despite these measures, the treatment of Germany after the Second World War does not really qualify as a Carthaginian peace, for Germany was given a series of positive incentives to break with its past that the Treaty of Versailles had not provided. The most important of these were Marshall Plan aid, the rapid integration of West Germany into the NATO alliance, and the deliberate commitment by the United States to maintain a recession-proof, free world order.

VIRTUOUS ISOLATIONISM

The relationship of the United States to the central traditions of European diplomacy has always been highly ambivalent. President George Washington's farewell warning that "there can be no greater error than to expect or calculate, upon real favors from Nation to Nation" was a call for isolationism that has echoed throughout U.S. history. Washington wanted the United States to steer clear of entangling alliances, because they would sully America's original virtue.

Of course, isolationism has long ceased to be an option for the most powerful nation in the world. But the isolationist legacy remains. It helps explain not just the somewhat intermittent attention the United States gives to foreign policy but the feeling that when Americans are engaged in foreign policy it is from a position of exceptional virtue.

Americans do not think naturally in terms of alliance politics. They either want to be uninvolved or masters of the situation. For example, the European notion of the balance of power has never had much resonance in the United States. Americans like to think that their own country is the uniquely godly power in a world of fallen angels and that their plans and their ways of thinking are genuinely good for everyone. They are startled and annoyed when others disagree. President Woodrow Wilson came to the Paris Peace Conference in 1918 trailing what French Prime Minister Georges Clemenceau called the Fourteen Commandments, and the Roosevelt administration, too, had extensive peace plans based on U.S. principles rather than contemporary reality. Wafting from isolationism to world supremacy, the United States has never comfortably occupied the intermediate ground of international relations, in which there is no white or black, only many different shades of gray. Americans want partners who play supporting roles, not allies, because Americans believe they alone have the best plans.

It is too easy to douse this New World idealism with Old World cynicism. The power to do good is very seductive and not always illusory. An Atlantic Community (which in some ways might be thought of as an extension of the United States), united by a shared value of freedom, resolute in its defense, and gradually extending its boundaries, is a noble vision.

Moreover, for the first time in history there is, in the United States, a genuine world power, one that cannot be effectively challenged by any other combination of powers. This supremacy, it could be argued, makes possible a quantum leap in international organization from the old politics of competitive imperialism and balance of power to a new universalist world order based on liberty, democracy, and the rule of law. Are we not, for the first time, in a position to overcome the limitations that kept the world warlike and poor for so long? This vision is bewitching, but utopian. The world history of the future cannot be written according to an exclusive American script. The United States will continue to be the paramount leader in international affairs, but the new world order, if it is to flourish, will have to be a negotiated one.

This point brings us back to the Grand Alliance that won the Second World War. Today it is commonly believed that at its core was the Anglo-American "special relationship." Yet if one goes through the history, one discovers that this relationship was special mainly in its difficulties. These difficulties only waned as British power declined and the Soviet threat became paramount.

There has been a systematic misreading of Anglo-American relations—a projection backward in time of a partnership that was only fully consummated after the Second World War. The root idea is that of a natural union of what Churchill called the "English-speaking peoples," which disclosed itself in two world wars, and the leadership of which was gradually transferred from Great Britain to the United States.

This perspective opens with the Anglo-American rapprochement of 1898–1906, in which a number of vexatious Anglo-American disputes ranging from Alaska to Venezuela were settled on largely U.S. terms. During this period, Great Britain excluded the possibility of war with the United States so as to be better able to meet more pressing challenges to the British position in Europe, South Africa, and Southern Asia. There is a lot in this view, notably propounded by Canadian diplomat Lionel Gelber in his

1938 book, *The Rise of Anglo-American Friendship: A Study in World Politics, 1898–1906.* What it leaves out is that Great Britain was simultaneously seeking to ensure itself against a potentially lethal combination of enemies by forging alliances with both Germany and Japan, only the second of which came to fruition.

Much more important, the conventional view omits the fact that the First World War was followed by a wave of U.S. isolationism, driven largely by Anglophobia. U.S. public discourse in the interwar years was dominated by the view that the British had inveigled the United States into a war that served not the interests of the American people but a small group of financiers and arms manufacturers. This sentiment led to the Neutrality Acts.

The roots of Anglophobia lay in the American War of Independence itself, but it was nourished by the Irish and German immigrations, the existence of the British empire, global financial and commercial competition, and cultural insecurities. Anglophobia encompassed both political parties. It tended to make Republicans isolationist, despite some East Coast Anglophilia. The Democrats were more interventionist. But from Roosevelt downward there was the conviction that while the United States might need to go to war to rid the world of Nazism, it should not do so to defend Great Britain's world position. As late as October 9, 1945—after the war was won—a British Treasury official in Washington wrote: "The pro-British line always needs defending in this country; the anti-British never."

In the 1930s, the financial and commercial rivalry between the two countries peaked. Great Britain may have been the "going" and the United States the "coming" power, as Harry Dexter White put it with brutal frankness, but Great Britain had a lot of assets left to keep it going. Among these assets was the British empire, which in the Ottawa agreements of 1932 started to discriminate against U.S. goods. Cordell Hull, then U.S. secretary of state, described the agreement, which set up the imperial preference system, as a "grievous injury" to U.S. commerce.

There was thus nothing inevitable about Anglo-American partnership in the 1930s. Indeed, it was only the impossible character of the Hitler regime that prevented an Anglo-Franco-German understanding, which would have led to a substantial consolidation of European power in the world. The thinking behind European unity goes back long before the birth of the European Economic Community in 1957. Originally seen as a counterweight to the United States, the European Union grew up as an American protectorate only because of the Second World War.

When Keynes and British Ambassador Lord Halifax first came to Washington in 1941 as begging plenipotentiaries of "plucky" Britain, they were soon made aware of the strength of Anglophobia. Halifax was regularly shouted down as he traveled around the United States trying to rally support for Britain. It was not until August 1941, when he faced down an egg-throwing crowd in Detroit with the unflappable remark, "You are lucky to have eggs to throw," that his relations with the American public and press started to thaw.

Keynes did not encounter outright hostility in Washington so much as deep suspicion of British motives, which his reputation for cleverness did nothing to dispel. When he first arrived at the U.S. Treasury, one of Morgenthau's officials asked Keynes's private secretary, "Where is your lawyer?" When the British official explained he had none, he got the reply, "Who does your thinking for you?" Keynes, of course, was perfectly capable of doing his own thinking. But the very speed of his thinking and the subtle quality of his plans inflamed the suspicion that he was trying to pull a fast one, as indeed he was. "He's one of those fellows that just knows all the answers, you see?" U.S. presidential advisor Harry Hopkins told Morgenthau.

The Americans knew the British were in a hole. At one point in the Octagon conference at Quebec in 1944, Churchill expostulated to Roosevelt: "What do you want me to do . . . stand up and beg like Fala [the president's dog]?" Groveling was not Churchill's style, and it was also not Keynes's. As a British Treasury official stationed in Washington perceptively wrote: "[Keynes] thinks we are a great [and] independent nation, which on the financial side is patently not true. . . . I think he is inclined to ask as of right what they are only prepared to give as a favour."

The British fought hard to retain some room for maneuver in the Grand Alliance, short of using the unthinkable sanction of making a separate peace with Nazi Germany. Churchill refused to discuss the future of the British empire with Roosevelt. When forced to do so, he agreed to pious declarations like the Atlantic Charter in 1941. In financial and economic negotiations, the British inserted or tried to insert escape clauses into every commitment they signed. On the whole it was a losing battle. On his last financial mission to Washington in 1945, Keynes wrote to his mother, "May it never fall to my lot [again] to have to persuade anyone to do what I want, with so few cards in my hand." The fact that the postwar world turned out to be worse than the Americans hoped and better than the British feared was the achievement of that third pillar of the Grand Alliance, the Soviet Union.

Here I come to a more controversial point: Many members of the Roosevelt administration, including Roosevelt himself, expected the Soviet Union, not Great Britain, to be the United States' chief postwar partner. This inclination was partly a matter of power wanting to talk to power. Only the Soviet Union could match the United States in raw resources. The American expectation of a U.S.-Soviet partnership existed partly because there was no commercial and financial rivalry to sour relations. But most importantly, it was a matter of ideological illusion. Odd as it now seems, the "democratic," "socialist," and "peace-loving" Soviet Union of Uncle Joe seemed a much more attractive partner to the American left than did "imperialist," "semi-fascist," and (with Churchill as its symbol) "bellicose" Great Britain. In fact, hardly anyone in Washington knew anything about Russia except for its heroic resistance to Nazism. And most of the information filtering through was largely the work of Soviet spies, communists, and fellow travelers in Roosevelt's administration. Britain was not only not part of this heady vision of American-Soviet condominium but also was a positive obstacle. Here then was another reason for cutting Britain down to size.

Disillusion with the Soviets came slowly, but when it arrived it came like a thunderclap. At the end of 1944, Keynes had comforted himself with the thought that the United States was now committed to the restoration of Great Britain as a Great Power. American illusions about its other allies were fading: "There is nothing to be found reliable or homely in the habitable globe outside Britain and the British Commonwealth. This, today, is America's deepest, least alterable conviction—a sure rock upon which, whatever may appear on the surface, we can build with safety." It took the Cold War to make Keynes's prophecy come true.

FROM ALLIES TO PARTNERS

History is not a good basis for prediction, since every historical event is unique and since, despite all our backsliding, we do make progress in understanding the world and dealing with its problems. Nevertheless, used with care, history can teach important lessons and alert us to the possibilities and limits of successful action.

The first lesson is that, in thinking about foreign policy, we need to distinguish between partners and allies. Of the four countries that made up the Grand Alliance, two (the United States and Britain) became partners, and the other two (Russia and China) ceased even to be allies. Allies are for temporary objectives; partners are for the long haul. Wars between partners are unthinkable; future wars between allies remain possible.

What converts allies into partners? Shared values and past associations are obviously important. But they are not enough. The argument that democracies never go to war with each other should be treated skeptically. Nor does free trade automatically guarantee international amity, as 19th-century liberals fondly believed. As long as there are nation-states, there will be conflicts of national interest, and therefore the possibility of war.

Just as important as shared values in converting allies into partners—and this is the second lesson suggested by the wartime alliance—is asymmetry of power. Great Britain did not really become a "reliable" partner of the United States until it was no longer powerful enough to be a serious rival. To adapt Harry Dexter White's phrase, the "going" powers have to be "gone" before they become partners in a joint enterprise. The relationship between the United States and Western Europe had reached this point by the end of the Second World War. The partnership was consolidated in the NATO treaty during the Cold War and is now unbreakable. Talk of setting up Europe as a "third force" between the United States and the Soviet Union after the Second World War was never realistic. The historical moment had passed.

Asymmetry of power does not negate the need for partners to be treated with consideration. They must believe they have some influence over the partnership. Otherwise, the full value of the partnership is lost. Partners can also be very useful as intermediaries or go-betweens. Such was the role played by British Prime Minister Margaret Thatcher in her shuttles between U.S. President Ronald Reagan and Soviet President Mikhail Gorbachev in the mid-1980s. Today, British Prime Minister Tony Blair has been playing the same kind of role in Europe, the Middle East, and Asia.

In any partnership, there will always be an awkward member. In the Western alliance, this part has been played by France with great elegance and to the frequent irritation of the United States, but with some benefit to the partnership as a whole by making it appear as not wholly subservient to U.S. wishes.

Russia and China were allies in the Grand Alliance and are allied with the United States in the coalition against terrorism today, but they are not partners of the United States, though perhaps Russia would like to be. But Russia is still very different from the West and is right to think of itself as a coming, not going, power. Both of these things are even more obviously true of China. There is no reason to anticipate that either country will become actively hostile to the United States. But they are, or will soon be, in a position to bargain their place in the international order, and therefore to shape its future. The same will be true of India. In its relations with these powers, the United States will be much more in that intermediate area of international relations—more like a balance-of-power situation—in which it has never been comfortable.

This argument is admittedly "state-centered." Many people have argued that globalization is putting the nation-state out of business and that the new units of decision making are regional or supranational bodies (or, if you are against globalization, multinational corporations). "Governance" is supposed to have replaced "government." The events of September 11, 2001, have shown that however true this may be of soft politics, it is not true of hard politics. The crucial decisions to act in the wake of September 11 were taken by Bush, Blair, and Russian President Vladimir Putin, just as in the Second World War they had been by Roosevelt, Churchill, and Soviet leader Joseph Stalin—that is, by the heads of national governments, and there are no governments that are not national. September 11 has shown the distance the European Union still has to travel before it can make life-and-death decisions on behalf of its members.

What about the Islamic world? It has less of a permanent interest in working with the United States than Russia or China does, and it has many serious grievances against it, not least in connection with Palestine. On the one hand, the facts of power are overwhelmingly in favor of the United States. This imbalance destroys any notion that Islam might be in a position to mount a serious challenge to the West. The asymmetry of power is simply too great. Even if the West is as decadent as Islamic fundamentalists claim, unlike the decadent civilizations of the past, it has hugely superior firepower (much more so than between the 7th and 17th centuries when Islam mounted a serious challenge to Christianity). The ease and speed with which the United States destroyed the Taliban in Afghanistan is a much more convincing demonstration of power than was Osama bin Laden's suicide mission of September 11.

On the other hand, unsettled Islamic grievances can keep terrorism in business. The events of September 11 have brought clarity to the problem of peacemaking in the Middle East. Everyone agrees that things cannot be allowed to drift on as they have for many years, in face of the latest Palestinian uprising. But are we driven to the choice between a Carthaginian peace and what is opprobriously called appeasement of Palestinian terrorism?

If we examine the Israeli-Palestinian conflict in these terms, it surely becomes clear that the Carthaginian solution on its own is a non-starter, whoever tries it. The West would not tolerate a Palestinian attempt to destroy Israel. There would be more support, perhaps, for a permanent occupation of the West Bank by Israeli forces, backed up by the West. However, on closer inspection, this solution, too, loses its allure. It is not just contrary to the ethics of our time, but it really would lead to a "clash of civilizations." Every Islamic state would be host to terrorists. They could not overthrow the West, but they could inflict much damage on its way of life. Nor can the United States and its allies restore a vanished imperium over the Islamic world.

The classical alternative to conquest is appeasement. The Palestinians are to be given a "viable" state in the occupied territories. Israel's security is to be guaranteed within the agreed international frontiers. This formula is the basis of the "land for peace" process. The idea that a settlement along these lines was almost clinched at Camp David in 2000 is an illusion. There never was enough "land" available to satisfy the passionate possessiveness of all those with claims to it. And "land for peace" never made economic sense. The last thing the Middle East needs is a new state, with a new set of obstacles to trade and migration in an area that is essentially a single economic space.

The solution of the German problem after the Second World War suggests an alternative approach. Germany was not only deprived of the structural capacity to wage aggressive war; it was given positive incentives to renounce the methods of the past. Hitherto the political incentives given to the Palestinians to abandon armed conflict have been far too weak, and the economic incentives almost nonexistent.

So should we not try to restart the search for peace on a new tack? The occupied territories might be declared a U.N. mandate, with de jure NATO-U.N. occupation replacing de facto Israeli control. The enforced peace should be accompanied by a new Marshall Plan for the occupied territories and the Palestinian diasporas, supplied jointly by the United States and the European Union. It should aim at building a regional business infrastructure, getting the million or so Palestinians out of camps and into jobs, and helping reopen the clogged channels of trade and migration. The economic area thus established could in turn become the nucleus of a Middle Eastern Common Market. Further down the road, moderate leaders on both sides might come to accept the advantages of a political federation, resulting in a new entity, Israel-Palestine, self-governing in its component parts. There are many possible variations on this approach. But such orthogonal thinking, I suggest, is needed to lift the peace process out of its present rut.

To sum up: the chief difference between now and then is that power has become more asymmetrical. This imbalance allows alliances to become partnerships and gives the United States more scope to fashion a world to its own liking. But there are limits. Over much of the world, the older principle of the balance of power is still the best guide to the conduct of foreign policy. And in some parts of the world, such as in the Middle East, it may still be necessary to impose peace by power—and back it up by "economic appeasement."

2

Levels of Analysis: Approaches to Studying World Politics

Reading 2-1

Let Us Now Praise Great Men
Bringing the Statesman Back In
Daniel L. Byman and Kenneth M. Pollack

In January 1762, Prussia hovered on the brink of disaster. Despite the masterful generalship of Frederick the Great, the combined forces of France, Austria, and Russia had gradually worn down the Prussian army in six years of constant warfare. Austrian armies had marched deep into Saxony and Silesia, and the Russians had even sacked Berlin. Frederick's defeat appeared imminent, and the enemy coalition intended to partition Prussia to reduce it to the status of a middle German state no more powerful than Bavaria or Saxony. And then a miracle occurred. The Prusso-phobic Czarina Elizabeth unexpectedly died, only to be succeeded by her son Peter, who idolized the soldier-king. Immediately Peter made peace with Frederick and ordered home the Russian armies. This reversal paralyzed the French and Austrians and allowed Frederick to rally his forces. Although Peter was soon ousted by his wife, Catherine, the allied armies never regained their advantage. In the end, Frederick held them off and kept Prussia intact.[1]

SOURCE: From "Let Us Now Praise Great Men: Bringing the Statesman Back In" by Daniel L. Byman and Kenneth M. Pollack, *International Security*, vol. 25, no. 4 (Spring 2001): 107–146. Copyright © 2001 President and Fellows of Harvard College and the Massachusetts Institute of Technology. Reprinted by permission of the MIT Press Journals.

Frederick's triumph in the Seven Years' War was essential to Prussia's eventual unification of Germany and all that followed from it. Conceiving of European history today without this victory is impossible. It is equally impossible to conceive of Prussian victory in 1763 without the death of Elizabeth and Peter's adoration of Frederick. In the words of Christopher Duffy, "It is curious to reflect that if one lady had lived for a very few weeks longer, historians would by now have analyzed in most convincing detail the reasons for a collapse as 'inevitable' as that which overtook the Sweden of Charles XII."[2] In short, had it not been for the idiosyncrasies of one man and one woman, European history would look very, very different.

The story of Prussia's reprieve is, admittedly, an extreme example of the role that individuals play in international relations, but such influence is by no means exceptional—far from it. How can we explain twentieth-century history without reference to Adolf Hitler, Joseph Stalin, Vladimir Lenin, Franklin Roosevelt, Winston Churchill, Mahatma Gandhi, or Mao Zedong? Nor would any policymaker in any capital try to explain the world today without recourse to the personal goals and beliefs of Bill Clinton, Vladimir Putin, Jiang Zemin, and Saddam Hussein, among others. Indeed the policymaking community in Washington takes it as an article of faith that who is the prime minister of Great Britain, the chancellor of Germany, or the king of Saudi Arabia has real repercussions for the United States and the rest of the world. As Henry Kissinger remarked, "As a professor, I tended to think of history as run by impersonal forces. But when you see it in practice, you see the difference personalities make."[3]

For these reasons, the tendency of scholars to ignore the role of personalities in international relations is particularly troubling. Most political scientists, when pressed, will admit to the importance of personal idiosyncrasies and human error in determining the course of international relations. Most will further concede that because they do not attempt to explain the roles of either human error or personality in international relations, they cannot explain all of the variance in the affairs of nations.

However, political scientists most frequently have argued that they must set aside both *fortuna* and *virtú,* and instead focus only on impersonal forces as the causes of international events. Their reasons for doing so fall under three rubrics. First, many political scientists contend that individuals ultimately do not matter, or at least they count for little in the major events that shape international politics. Instead they argue that the roar of the anarchic system, domestic politics, and institutional dynamics drown out the small voices of individual leaders. Second, other political scientists posit that although individuals may matter from time to time, their influence does not lend itself to the generalizations that political scientists seek. Simply put, individuals are too individualistic. Third, several leading international relations theorists have raised a number of specific objections that they argue render the study of individuals theoretically hopeless.

We believe that political scientists are simultaneously too modest and too arrogant in these claims. Too modest because political scientists need not throw up their hands and believe that they have nothing useful to say about the role of individuals in international relations. The theoretical objections raised over the years do not stand up under closer examination and should not prevent us from mining this rich ore. Too arrogant because too many political scientists imply or assert that the impersonal forces on which they focus their attention explain the vast majority of events in international relations. In so doing, they marginalize the crucial impact of individuals on war and diplomacy and neglect the extent to which social science can tease out useful generalizations regarding the role played by individuals.

It is time to rescue men and women, as individuals, from the oblivion to which political scientists have consigned them. This article is not intended as a comprehensive account of the importance of individuals—such an effort would require the work of many lifetimes—but it is intended to question scholars' current assumptions about international politics and show the plausibility of analyzing international relations by focusing on the role of individuals.

What is the impact of individuals on international relations? What aspects of state behavior do they affect? Under what conditions are they influential? These are the questions this article seeks to answer. We contend that the goals, abilities, and foibles of individuals are crucial to the intentions, capabilities, and strategies of a state. Indeed individuals not only affect the actions of their own states but also shape the reactions of other nations, which must respond to the aspirations, abilities, and aggressiveness of foreign leaders. Of course, individuals matter more to international relations under certain circumstances. Individual personalities take on added significance when power is concentrated in the hands of a leader, when institutions are in conflict, or in times of great change. Individuals also shape many of the drivers identified by other theorists, such as the balance of power, domestic opinion, and bureaucratic politics. These paradigms suffer when individuals are ignored.

This article has four parts. We first rebut the specific, theoretical arguments denigrating the utility of theories of the impact of individuals on international relations. We then counter the argument that individuals do not have a significant impact on international events by examining five historical cases that show that the role of individuals was crucial to the outcome of each. We next refute the argument that it is impossible to generate hypotheses regarding the role of individuals, by teasing out plausible, testable hypotheses from the cases in the previous section. We conclude by noting how the study of individuals enriches our understanding of international relations.

REBUTTING THE THEORETICAL OBJECTIONS

The study of individuals has not been attacked so much as ignored by international relations theorists. This is not to say that no work has been done on this topic. At least since the time of Aristotle, scholars have tried to explain politics in terms of individual behavior. Indeed classical realist thinkers such as Thucydides, Niccolò Machiavelli, and Hans Morgenthau all explicitly acknowledge the impact of individual personalities on international relations. Since then, however, work on individuals in political science has generally been left to psychologists, historians, and area studies specialists.[4] These scholars have produced many excellent studies on the importance of individuals, but they have not treated the subject in a systematic fashion that would help answer the general questions of when and how individuals affect international relations. These works provide a foundation on which to build, but as they are, they remain incomplete.[5]

One exception to political scientists' neglect of individuals is Kenneth Waltz's seminal work, *Man, the State, and War.* Waltz famously outlines three levels of analysis, calling them "images" of international relations. In the first image, the behavior of nations springs from the behavior of individuals. Waltz's second image considers the behavior of nations to be driven by their internal organization, positing that different kinds of governments and social structures produce different kinds of international behavior. Finally, the third image contends that the behavior of nations is driven by their relative position—in terms of both power and geography—in an anarchic international system.[6]

Although Waltz is unusual in even considering the first image, he nonetheless rejects it. Waltz, and those following in his tradition, believe that the third image best explains international relations—or the most important elements of it, such as the causes of great power wars and alliances.[7] Champions of the third image have many critics. Nevertheless, even scholars who challenge Waltz's focus on the third image generally do so in the name of second-image factors, such as bureaucracy, culture, and political systems. Thus even Waltz's critics neglect the first image.[8]

Objection 1: The First Image Cannot Provide an Adequate Explanation for International Relations Because Human Nature Is a Constant, Whereas International Relations Vary

In *Man, the State, and War,* Waltz argues that if human nature is constant, the behavior of nations—the example he employs is war making—should also be constant. That is, nations should always be at war. Because nations are not always at war, Waltz claims that human nature cannot possibly explain why nations go to war.[9] On this point, Waltz is simply mistaken: Human nature is not a constant; it is a variable. By defining the first image solely in terms of an ineffable quality shared among all humans, Waltz has constructed a straw man. Not all men and women are entirely evil, aggressive, greedy, or vainglorious. A few are, but a few others are wholly generous, humble, and restrained. The vast majority of humans, however, possess a mix of traits. Thus "human nature" entails a tremendous range of variance. Properly understood, the first image should generate theories derived from the distribution of these traits across the population and their impact on international relations.

As soon as one recognizes that personalities vary widely, Waltz's criticism of the first image becomes unconvincing. Because personalities differ, it is entirely possible that variance in the traits of individuals explains differences in international relations. For instance, although not all wars have been caused by aggressive, risk-tolerant, greedy, or vainglorious leaders, those leaders who did manifest these traits regularly went to war—often for seemingly absurd reasons, and often more than once. Indeed leaders most notorious for these traits, such as Louis XIV, Peter the Great, Frederick the Great, Napoleon Bonaparte, Napoleon III, Wilhelm II, Benito Mussolini, and Hitler, have fomented some of the greatest conflicts in modern European history.[10]

Objection 2: Theories Focused on the Influence of Individuals in International Relations Cannot Be Parsimonious

In his book *Theory of International Politics,* Waltz claims that parsimony must be an important criterion for judging the value of a theory.[11] He argues that the more closely a model approximates reality, the more variables it will include; therefore a realistic theory will be less parsimonious and thus less useful.[12] First, we contend that it is possible to derive elegant theories from the first image—a challenge we answer in the third section of this article. Of greater relevance, however, we dismiss the contention that parsimony is somehow more important than accuracy when deriving political science theory. The field of international relations is an effort to explain the interaction of states and, ultimately, predict their behavior. Consequently, realism (with a small "R") is the best, and perhaps the only, determinant of the utility of a theory: How well does the theory actually explain behavior and allow us to predict future actions? Creating parsimonious models may be useful for illustrative or heuristic purposes, but this is, at best, several steps removed from the actual goals of the discipline. A massive model with hundreds of variables that took a month to run but predicted international behavior perfectly would be far more useful by any measure than a model with only a single variable that could illustrate only occasional tendencies and only in badly underspecified circumstances.[13]

Objection 3: State Intentions Are Not Germane to Theories of International Relations

Many proponents of the third image acknowledge that individual leaders often have a heavy influence on state goals.[14] Because they believe that state intentions are not necessary to the construction of a theory of international politics, however, any impact that individual personalities may have in this sphere is likewise irrelevant. Instead they claim that all states are functionally equivalent, and therefore their intentions are irrelevant because they all have the same primary or "dominant" goal, namely their own security.[15] Even the most benign state is not certain how other states will act, either now or in the future, and thus must take steps to defend itself.[16]

The assertion about the essential irrelevance of actor preferences is empirically weak and (again demonstrating the danger of overly parsimonious models) analytically misleading. For example, Stephen Walt's work on alliance formation demonstrates that, by omitting state intentions, Waltz's argument that alliance formation is based purely on the distribution of power poorly predicts actual alliance patterns.[17] Other scholars have established the importance of the distinction between "status quo" states—those nations content with the state of affairs as they are—and "revisionist" states—those unhappy with the current state of affairs and willing to change it. Revisionist states want more territory, influence, prestige, or other objectives that are not always directly related to their security. They may go to war or otherwise disrupt the international system even when they are secure. At times, they may even jeopardize their security to pursue these aims.[18] On the other hand, status quo states are able to assure potential rivals of their benign intentions—thus preventing uncertainty and misunderstanding from escalating into war. This allows status quo states to take steps, such as keeping their defense budgets low, even though this would endanger their security in a world that followed structural realist precepts. In short, state intentions are a critical factor in international relations and, to the extent that individual personalities shape those intentions, they too must be considered important.

INDIVIDUALS MATTER: LESSONS FROM HISTORY

Individuals play a central role in shaping international relations, including the causes of war, alliance patterns, and other areas that international relations scholars consider important. To demonstrate this claim—and to provide the historical foundation on which we build testable hypotheses in the next section—we draw on five cases: (1) Germany under Hitler; (2) the contrasting impact of Chancellor Otto von Bismarck and Kaiser Wilhelm II on European politics; (3) France under Napoleon Bonaparte; (4) a comparison of Iraq under Saddam Hussein and Syria under Hafiz al-Asad; and (5) the behavior of Iran in its war with Iraq under Ayatollah Ruhollah Khomeini.

We chose these cases according to several criteria. They demonstrate the importance of individuals regardless of political system, period of time, or region of the world. They highlight particular aspects of the impact of individual leaders on international relations. Each case also suggests theories derived from the first image related to some of the most fundamental questions of international relations theory of the last thirty years: the causes of war, the formation of alliances, and the likelihood of cooperation under anarchy, to name only a few.[19]

Adolf Hitler

The personal characteristics and idiosyncrasies of Adolf Hitler led to the deaths of millions and changed the history of the world. Hitler's unique pathologies were the single most important factor in causing both World War II in Europe (at least in the sense of the continent-wide total war that ensued) and Germany's eventual defeat. Hitler defied both domestic opposition and systemic logic in igniting World War II, leading Germany to astonishing victories, visiting unimaginable misery on the world, and then causing the collapse of the empire he had built. Understanding international relations during the 1930s and 1940s is impossible without grasping the impact of Hitler himself.

Germany after World War I was clearly a revisionist state, but Hitler's ambitions far exceeded those of the people he led. The German people detested the terms of the Treaty of Versailles. Most believed that Germany should rearm, regain its pre-Versailles territory in the east, and demand integration with Austria and the German-populated Sudetenland.[20] However, though revisionism was the *Zeitgeist* in interwar Germany, European hegemony and global domination were not. The vast majority of Germans had lost any inclination toward military expansion after living through the horrors of World War I. Although many Germans wanted to revise the Treaty of Versailles, few were willing to wage another major war to do so.[21] Indeed, on September 27, 1938, when Hitler mobilized the German army to attack Czechoslovakia, the Berlin crowds turned their backs on the German troops marching through the streets of the capital.[22]

Nor were most German elites sympathetic to Hitler's aspirations. Even most of the mainstream nationalist parties and the army high command—among the most bellicose groups in Germany—wanted only to restore their country to its pre-1914 status. Although they were probably more willing than the average German to use force to achieve these goals, the great majority were equally chary of another major war and had no aspirations to continental mastery.[23] On the uniqueness of Hitler's aspirations, Gordon Craig has written: "Adolf Hitler was *sui generis,* a force without a real historical past . . . dedicated to the acquisition of power for his own gratification and to the destruction of a people whose existence was an offence to him and whose annihilation would be his crowning triumph. Both the grandiose barbarism of his political vision and the moral emptiness of his character make it impossible to compare him in any meaningful way with any other German leader. He stands alone."[24]

For their part, Britain and France did not want war with Germany and were prepared to make considerable sacrifices (in terms of both their own relative security and other people's territory) to appease Berlin. Public opinion in Britain during the interwar years was sympathetic to Germany, believing that the terms of the peace had been overly harsh. Moreover, the possibility of a World War I–like bloodbath terrified Britain, and London was willing to write off considerable portions of Eastern Europe to avert another one.[25] Although the French were less sympathetic to German aspirations, they were equally afraid of another continental war and thus were willing to give in to at least some German demands for revisions to the Versailles treaty, including demands for territory in the east. In addition, to the extent that France contemplated using military force against Germany, it was unwilling to do so without Britain's full participation.[26] For these reasons, the French and British acquiesced to German rearmament after 1933, the remilitarization of the Rhineland, the *Anschluss* with Austria, and the occupation of *Sudeten* Czechoslovakia. Moreover, the evidence indicates that Britain and France would not have gone to war to prevent German reoccupation of the Polish corridor.[27] In short, Britain and France were willing to swallow hard and accept virtually any German demands—short of granting Berlin a hegemonic position in Europe or ceding their own territory—as long as they believed that by doing so they could avert a war. Consequently, Germany should have been able to achieve the moderate revisionist goals espoused by most Germans without sparking a general European war. Only Hitler's personal ambitions made such a conflict unavoidable.

Thus World War II, at least in the sense of the global conflagration that eventually ignited, was caused by the unique aspirations of Adolf Hitler, not by the widespread German desire to revise the order established at Versailles in 1918. The outbreak of World War II was prompted by the German invasion of Poland—a country that few Germans were willing to risk war with Britain and France to remove from the map of Europe. Moreover, the British and French did not go to war for Polish sovereignty per se, but only because they saw the German attack on Poland (and the earlier occupation of Bohemia in violation of the 1938 Munich agreement) as incontrovertible proof that Hitler would not be satisfied with modest revisions of the postwar peace, but instead was determined to make himself master of all Europe.[28]

Hitler's personal role in the course of world politics did not end with the start of war between Germany and the Western Allies. Instead he relentlessly pushed Germany down the road to annihilation. Every step of the way, the decision to act was effectively Hitler's alone, taken despite the opposition of whatever independent voices still existed. Indeed the army high command consistently opposed Hitler's foreign adventures until it was ultimately battered into submission. Hitler also made sure that all other opposing voices were stilled or subverted. Thus the opposition parties, the foreign ministry, and ultimately even the army were all brought under his control, leaving German decisionmaking entirely in his hands.[29]

Hitler's decision to invade France in 1940 propelled Germany and the world further down the road to total war. Given the terror of the British and French of becoming involved in another major war with Germany, it is not clear what they would have done had Germany not attacked France. The stalemate that prevailed along the Rhine from October 1939 to May 1940 suggests that they might ultimately have acceded to Germany's conquest of Poland.[30] Hitler, however, was determined to destroy France to remove it as an obstacle to his plans for expansion in the east.[31] Once again, he was opposed by the senior army leadership, who believed that German troops would be unlikely to achieve the same success against the French army, then considered the most powerful force on the continent.[32] But Hitler insisted on attacking and turning "phony war" into total war.

Hitler's next, and most self-destructive, step was attacking Russia. Once again, this was essentially his idea alone, taken over the opposition of his generals (including even his most pliant lackeys such as Hermann Göring, Wilhelm Keitel, and Alfred Jodl), who unanimously believed that Germany should not attack Russia—and certainly not until Britain had sued for peace.[33] The attack on Russia marked the beginning of the end for Hitler's *Reich*. Although there is still much debate over whether Germany could have defeated Russia had the German generals been given a free hand to fight the war as they wished, there is no dissent that it was the Red Army that eventually destroyed the *Wehrmacht* and sealed Hitler's fate.

Here as well, it is interesting to consider what might have happened had Germany not attacked Russia in 1941, which would likely have been the case (given the unanimous opposition of the general staff) had Hitler not been in charge. Even assuming that the United States had joined the war that December, it is at best unclear whether the Anglo-Saxon powers could have found a way to get ashore and defeat the *Wehrmacht* in Western Europe without the Red Army pinning down two-thirds of the German military.[34] Against a German *Reich* possessing most of the resources of continental Europe, a Cold War between Britain and Germany seems the most likely outcome, leaving Germany the hegemon of Europe.

Just as Hitler was the most important cause of World War II, and the most important factor in the vast, sudden expansion of the German *Reich,* so too was he the most important cause of Germany's defeat.[35] As recent work such as Richard Overy's superb analysis of Allied victory makes clear, German strategic- and operational-level defeats were the decisive factor in the destruction of the *Wehrmacht.* Allied material strength—and the growth in the ability of the Allied armed forces to wield that strength—played an important role, but only the German failures at Moscow, Stalingrad, and Kursk made it possible for the Allies to bring that material strength to bear. In each of these instances, Hitler deserves the lion's share of the blame for defeat.[36] Even after Hitler lost these crucial battles, he insisted on retaining command and greatly hastened Allied victory by leading superb German armies to defeat after defeat. Despite a never-ending stream of revisionist work on World War II, the evidence and scholarly analysis remains compelling that Adolf Hitler's "generalship" crippled the German army and so was the principal cause of Nazi defeat and Allied victory.[37]

Summarizing Hitler's importance is difficult given the magnitude of his influence. Hitler determined the intentions of the German state, shaping its decisions to go to war, its choice of enemies, and the extent of its ambitions. Hitler also meddled directly in Germany's strategy for achieving its goals—interference that led to the *Wehrmacht*'s defeat and his own undoing. Hitler's aggressiveness and malevolence also inspired a strong anti-German coalition, leading even such anticommunist stalwarts as Winston Churchill to ally with the Soviet Union.

Otto von Bismarck and Wilhelm II

Germany's Chancellor Otto von Bismarck, through sheer force of genius, created a diplomatic structure that kept peace in Europe from 1871 to 1890. Kaiser Wilhelm II, who dismissed Bismarck in 1890, brought Bismarck's architecture crashing down through sheer force of idiocy. The nature of the threat to Germany, bureaucratic interests, and other impersonal factors remained roughly constant during the period before and after 1890. Yet Germany veered from being the pillar of Europe's status quo states to the leader of its revisionist camp. Clearly changes in the balance of power played an important role. A comparison of the two periods, however, reveals the key role that individuals play in forging and maintaining alliances, guiding bureaucracies, and paving the road to war.

A brilliant diplomatic tactician, Bismarck forged a complex series of alliances to strengthen Germany's position as a status quo power and preserve the peace in Europe. Bismarck's alliances were designed to prevent Germany from falling victim to a coalition of great powers on both its borders—a German nightmare later realized in World War I. To ease other powers' security concerns, Bismarck tried to portray Germany as a sated power.[38] Bismarck also sought to keep his allies from fighting one another, recognizing that Germany could easily become involved if conflict flared. Thus he forged alliances with Austria and Russia that were explicitly defensive.[39] Bismarck also sought to maintain Britain's goodwill and to placate French opinion on every issue except Alsace-Lorraine.[40]

Bismarck defied the systemic logic of balancing in forging his coalitions. He succeeded in crafting alliances despite the growing industrial might of the Ruhr and Germany's evident military prowess, as demonstrated by its decisive victories over Austria in 1866 and France in 1870–71. Indeed rather than balance against Berlin, other European powers looked to Germany for diplomatic leadership.[41] When Bismarck left office in 1890, France and Britain were competing bitterly for colonies in Africa, while Russia and England were rival players in the Great Game. The idea that these three powers would ally was almost unthinkable.[42]

By championing the status quo and refusing further expansion in Europe after 1871, Bismarck also defied the wishes of the German people and bureaucracies. Bismarck, as A. J. P. Taylor notes, "stood outside party or class, a solitary figure following a line of his own devising."[43] Bismarck alone restrained Germany. As one contemporary noted in 1888, "All the world is really pro-war here. . . . With the almost exclusive exception of His Excellency [Bismarck], who exerts himself to the utmost for the maintenance of peace."[44] Germany's military leadership in particular harbored aggressive goals and repeatedly considered preemptive war against both France and Russia. Bismarck killed these ideas. Even though most Germans disliked allying with Russia and favored Austria's position on the Eastern Question, Bismarck tried to keep close to Moscow and prevent Vienna from expanding in the Balkans. Unlike his successors, he recognized that Germany could not afford problems on both borders and, given France's unrelenting hostility, Germany's eastern border had to be secure.[45]

Indeed critics have faulted Bismarck for devising a strategy so individual dependent that only a diplomatic genius could carry it out. Henry Kissinger, for example, notes that "where Bismarck failed was in having doomed his society to a style of policy which could only have been carried on had a great man emerged in every generation."[46] Yet in truth we will never know whether it was inevitable that Bismarck's successors should have chosen to substitute rigidity for flexibility and bullying for conciliation.[47] His successors did not fail to maintain his intricate system; they simply never tried.

The year 1890 is rightly seen as a turning point in German foreign policy, but this can be explained only by the change in German leadership. Germany's social and bureaucratic structures remained unchanged, as did its trade patterns. No great technological leap radically altered the nature of military might or national wealth. Of course, German power did rise steadily following German unification. But this gradual rise cannot explain the radical disjuncture between the Bismarckian and Wilhelmine foreign policies. Although Germany's power rose gradually, in the few short years after Bismarck's demise Germany went from a champion of the status quo to its greatest challenger. Only the change in leadership can explain this sudden transformation.

Once settled on his throne, Kaiser Wilhelm II ousted the aging chancellor, and Germany quickly shed Bismarck's policies. Bismarck's successors abandoned his alliance strategy of restraint, abruptly ended their alliance with Russia (much to St. Petersburg's dismay), and blindly lashed themselves to Austrian policy in the Balkans, disregarding its potential to provoke a war with Russia.[48] Understanding Wilhelmine Germany is difficult without focusing on the role of Wilhelm II himself. As Paul Kennedy has argued, a structuralist approach "tells us why Wilhelmine Germany was expansionist at a certain time, but it has much less explanatory power when we move on to the equally important questions of what sort of expansionist policies were chosen, and why, and with what effects."[49]

As if alienating St. Petersburg was not enough of a blunder, the kaiser's pursuit of a fleet in the face of British opposition drove London into anti-German alliances and bought Germany little in return. The naval program indicates how individuals shape bureaucratic politics and even domestic economic interests. Without Kaiser Wilhelm II, there would have been no naval program. As Kennedy further observes, "From the beginning to the end of the *Flottenpolitik,* the kaiser played a critical and fatal role."[50] Only after the naval program got into high gear did the kaiser find a domestic base for it.[51]

Not surprisingly, after 1890 the kaiser's misguided policies and alarming behavior destroyed the protective web of alliances that Bismarck had created and drove the three former adversaries—Britain, France, and Russia—into a Triple Entente opposing Berlin. Most foreign governments and populaces saw Wilhelm's rhetoric as German policy.[52] Where Bismarck had tried to downplay the image of German power, the kaiser swaggered. At the Congress of Berlin in 1878, Germany under Bismarck had sought to promote peace among the European powers and demonstrate that Germany was a satiated power. Wilhelm II, on the other hand, was an incorrigible jingoist who, rather than reassure other capitals, regularly frightened them by rattling Germany's saber and demanding more "respect" for Berlin. True, Wilhelm's *Weltanschauung* was shared by many of his countrymen. However, though the kaiser may have been closer to the norm than Bismarck, he was hardly normal. Wilhelm showed an uncanny knack for stampeding Germany's erstwhile allies into anti-German coalitions while cajoling his ministers into policies that they knew were foolish. Just before World War I, Chancellor Theobald Bethmann-Hollweg lamented this turn of events: "A Turkish policy against Russia, Morocco against France, fleet against England, all at the same time— challenge everybody, get in everyone's way, and actually, in the course of all this, weaken nobody."[53] Given the growth in German power by the turn of the century, even Bismarck might have been hard-pressed to avoid an anti-German *entente,* but his successors worsened rather than helped the problem.

The comparison between Bismarck and Wilhelm II reveals several points about the importance of individuals. With the shift from Bismarck to Wilhelm II came a change in Germany's alliances and foreign policy posture. This shift did not reflect a new strategic environment or domestic pressures, but rather the different visions of the individuals at the helm of the state. Bismarckian Germany sought to preserve the status quo; Wilhelmine Germany sought to become Europe's hegemon. Not only did the choice of alliance partners change, but so too did the nature of the alliances: Under Bismarck, Germany's alliances were defensive and intended to restrain its allies; under Wilhelm II, they encouraged Austria and others toward aggression. Similarly, the face that Germany presented to the world went from the reassuring peacemaker of the Berlin Congress to the bellicose expansionist of the two Moroccan crises (and numerous others) provoked by Wilhelm II. As a result, the nations of Europe banded together to oppose German expansionism. The comparison of Bismarck with Wilhelm II also demonstrates the role that individuals play in the success or failure of diplomacy. Balances of power are created by individuals, not fostered solely by power politics.

Napoleon Bonaparte

Napoleon Bonaparte's impact on nineteenth-century European affairs demonstrates that an individual leader can determine not only the intentions of his state but also its capabilities and the reactions of other states. Like the personalities of Hitler and Wilhelm II, Napoleon's was a major impetus to war. Napoleon's unique role in shaping European politics in the early nineteenth century encompassed more than just his megalomaniacal pursuit of glory, however. Napoleon not only profoundly shaped French intentions; he was also a crucial component of French power. Napoleon's military skills were so great that, as an individual, he affected the balance of continental power and so helped force the other states of Europe to move against him as much as to move against France.

One cannot blame Napoleon entirely for the wars that bear his name. Even if Bonaparte had never taken power, there is an argument to be made that revolutionary France might still have launched a crusade to liberate the world from the chains of absolute monarchy even after the cannonade of Valmy ended the threat to the new republic in 1792.[54] The philosophy of the revolution demanded that its blessings of "*Liberté, Egalité, et Fraternité*" be spread to the benighted peoples of the rest of Europe.[55]

But the French Revolution explains only part of the story. The War of the First Coalition (1792) was the only conflict France fought in the age of Napoleon that was unequivocally defensive. Thereafter French motives were increasingly aggressive. Defending, or even spreading, the revolution became less and less relevant and, especially after 1807, France's wars were fought largely to sate the personal demons of the emperor. As early as the War of the Third Coalition (1805), Austria and Russia sought only to compel France to disgorge its conquests since 1791, whereas Napoleon fought this campaign as much to establish his control over central Germany as to end any threat from the Third Coalition.[56] Reflecting on Napoleon's aggressive nature, David Chandler has conceded that "there can be no denying that many of these attacks were, in the last analysis, provoked by the Emperor."[57]

Following the Battle of Friedland in 1807, Czar Alexander I and the king of Prussia, Friedrich Wilhelm III, signed the Peace of Tilsit, leaving Napoleon the hegemon of Europe. After Tilsit, the tatters of the argument that his wars were defensive or the result of the unstoppable tide of revolution disintegrate. The French people were satisfied by the glories they had won and grew increasingly disenchanted with the costs of Napoleon's constant war making.[58] Prince Metternich (then Austria's ambassador to Paris) wrote in December 1808 that "it is no longer the French people who are waging war, it is Napoleon alone who is set on it. . . . Even his army no longer wants this conflict."[59] Despite the vast conquests he had achieved at Tilsit, however, Napoleon was not content. In the words of Alistair Horne, "The trouble was that, for all his new, consolidated power, Napoleon had to go on. . . . As he himself had written as a youth, 'Ambition is never content, even on the summit of greatness.'"[60] Thus Napoleon, because of his overweening ambition and ego, was as much the cause of the wars of 1796–1815 as were the forces unleashed by the French Revolution. Indeed Napoleon's ego may have been the most important of the forces unleashed by the revolution.[61]

One telling commentary on the increasingly idiosyncratic nature of French war making was the reaction of Charles-Maurice de Talleyrand-Périgord, Napoleon's brilliant but despicable foreign minister. As the years passed, Talleyrand steadily distanced himself from the emperor because he concluded that Napoleon's ambitions could lead only to disaster. After Austerlitz, Talleyrand urged Napoleon to offer Austria generous terms to win it over as an ally (precisely the course Bismarck would pursue so successfully sixty-one years later), but Napoleon's ego demanded that Austria be humiliated. The peace he inflicted on Vienna ensured the undying enmity of the Hapsburgs. Talleyrand ardently opposed Napoleon's subsequent invasions of Portugal (1807), Spain (1808), and Russia (1812) as dangerous and unnecessary adventures. By 1812, Talleyrand had effectively abandoned Napoleon and was working for the czar because he recognized that Napoleon's unquenchable ambition would condemn everyone around him to certain doom.[62]

Napoleon's personal ambition was not the only facet of his personality that made him a crucial factor in the international relations of his time. Napoleon was also a military genius, one of the greatest generals in history. At the beginning of the nineteenth century, France was the wealthiest and the second most populous nation in Europe. In addition, the manpower furnished by the *levée en masse* combined with the military re-

forms of the late eighteenth century gave France formidable military power. These factors alone suggest that revolutionary France would have been a tougher foe for the
other European powers to contain than Louis XIV's France. Nevertheless, Napoleon
himself was a "force multiplier" of tremendous value.[63] The Duke of Wellington remarked that Bonaparte's presence on the field of battle was worth 40,000 men.[64] His
skills as a general were repeatedly showcased in virtuoso performances such as the
Marengo, Austerlitz, Jena/Auerstadt, Friedland, and Wagram campaigns—where he
scored colossal successes although regularly outnumbered by his adversaries. When
Napoleon was at his best, he could achieve almost anything as a general, regardless of
the forces arrayed against him. At his worst, he still inspired his troops to superhuman
efforts and terrified even his most able opponents. Ultimately, Napoleon proved so
uniquely important to French aggressiveness and power that the other European powers broke with centuries of tradition and made his removal a principal war aim.[65]

Saddam Hussein and Hafiz al-Asad

Although Saddam Hussein and Hafiz al-Asad faced many similar problems as leaders,
their preferred solutions were very different. They were both Arab dictators ruling il-
legitimate regimes who feared they would be overthrown. They both ruled in countries where domestic institutions were feeble and therefore did not significantly constrain policymaking. They both ruled fairly weak Arab states bordering considerably
stronger neighbors (Israel, Turkey, and Iran) as well as weaker ones (Jordan, Kuwait,
Lebanon, and Saudi Arabia). They were both members of minority groups in the countries they ruled and were both challenged by the majority communal groups, whom
they suppressed in bloodthirsty fashion. For both, their own continued rule was their
preeminent concern. To stay in power, they centralized decisionmaking in their own
hands, created divided and competing bureaucracies, and ruthlessly quashed any individual or group that appeared to be gaining independent power for fear that it could become a rival.

Despite these similarities, the two leaders—and as a result the two states they led—
had very different intentions and strategies. Although both sought to aggrandize the
power of their respective states (and so their own power), Asad's ambitions were more
limited than Saddam's. Whatever Asad's early aspirations to a "greater Syria" comprising the entirety of the Levantine littoral, for the last eighteen years of his life his primary foreign policy goals were regaining the Golan Heights from Israel, institutionalizing Syrian suzerainty over Lebanon, and perhaps regaining the Hatay/Alexandretta
province from Turkey. On the other hand, Saddam has repeatedly sought to don Gamal
Abdel Nasser's mantle of "leader of the Arab world." Saddam's invasions of Iran and
Kuwait, his pursuit of all manner of ballistic missiles and nonconventional weapons, his
efforts to build a massive Iraqi military, and his various diplomatic gambits have all been
explicitly pursued—at least in part—in the name of making himself and Iraq the voice
of the Arabs in regional and global affairs.[66] Even when such goals were clearly secondary to more immediate concerns (such as the threat from revolutionary Iran in
prompting his decision to attack in September 1980), Saddam has never failed to re-
mind his people of the larger stakes he always believes are involved.[67]

An even greater difference between these two despots lay in how they pursued their
goals. To say that Saddam is risk tolerant would be a gross understatement.[68] Even when
his motives are defensive, his course of action is usually offensive. Whenever he has confronted a difficult situation, Saddam has frequently chosen the most reckless of all available options. When faced with the threat from Syrian Ba'thism and Syria's damming of
the Euphrates River in the mid-1970s, Saddam was ready to attack Syria had Asad not
moved to defuse the situation.[69] Fearing the threat from Ayatollah Khomeini and the

Islamic Revolution in the late 1970s, Saddam attacked Iran.[70] To avoid economic hardship, Saddam attacked Kuwait in 1990.[71] Confronted by a thirty-nation coalition led by the world's only superpower, Saddam gambled that he could ignore the coalition's air forces, stalemate its armies, and force the rest of the world to accept his annexation of Kuwait.[72] Three years later, while Iraqi society slowly suffocated under international sanctions, Saddam refused to give up the remnants of his nonconventional weapons programs and instead tried to attack Kuwait once again. Nor have the recurrent crises with Baghdad since then given any indication that Saddam has learned his lesson: He continues to bully, threaten, and provoke. Indeed even the decline of Iraqi power appears not to have affected the aggressiveness of Baghdad's foreign policy. Undeterred by the loss of three-quarters of his military power to the U.S.-led coalition in 1991, Saddam has continued to provoke Washington as if Desert Storm meant no more to him than a weather forecast.

Asad, on the other hand, was one of the most cautious leaders in the Middle East. Asad agonized over difficult decisions, only choosing a course of action long after it had become imperative for him to do so. He alone among the Syrian leadership opposed Syria's invasion of Jordan in September 1970 for fear that it was too risky.[73] Asad agonized over his own coup, delaying it until long after it could not possibly fail.[74] He did not invade Lebanon until 1976, after every other course of action had failed him and he realized that further hesitation could undermine the stability of Syria.[75] He threatened to attack Jordan several times in the early 1980s but drew back every time.[76] He tried hard to avoid a war with Israel in 1982 and fought back only when the Israelis attacked him despite his efforts.[77] Similarly, he moved against his brother Rif'at only after Rif'at tried to seize control of the government in 1984, even though the rest of Syria's top leadership had been urging him to defang Rif'at for years.[78]

Perhaps the best indication of the differing approaches of these two Arab dictators to foreign policy was their divergent responses to the collapse of the Soviet Union. Asad adopted a policy of appeasement, while Saddam assumed a policy of aggressive expansion. Both concluded that the loss of the Soviet Union as a counterweight to the United States would allow Washington and Israel to bring greater pressure to bear on them. Saddam's response was offensive: Seize Kuwait to secure its economic resources, overawe the other Arab states, and demonstrate Iraqi military might.[79] Indeed many experts suspect that Saddam consciously sought to challenge the United States to demonstrate its (relative) weakness and Iraq's strength.[80] The fact that this action threatened to provoke war with the United States (something that considerable evidence indicates Saddam fully understood) was an acceptable risk to him.[81] On the other hand, Asad reacted to the Cold War's end by moderating many of his more aggressive policies. He curbed Syria's involvement in international terrorism, joined the U.S.-led coalition against Iraq, and, in his own dysfunctional and dithering manner, showed a surprising—albeit painfully cautious and unrealistic—willingness to actually consider a peace treaty with Israel.

Comparing Saddam Hussein and Hafiz al-Asad, two of the most brutal tyrants of the Arab world, demonstrates that the course of despotic regimes can, to a considerable extent, be predicted by the personality of their leaders. Despite all of their similarities, Saddam and Asad shared a crucial difference: Where Saddam is aggressive, reckless, and extremely expansionist, Asad was defensive, cautious, and only modestly expansionist.

Ayatollah Ruhollah Khomeini and the Iran-Iraq War

Hitler and Napoleon are hardly history's only leaders who extended wars beyond what systemic, domestic, and bureaucratic pressures might dictate. Although Saddam Hussein may have started the Iran–Iraq War, its duration beyond 1982 can largely be blamed on the determination of Ayatollah Ruhollah Khomeini, the charismatic Iranian leader. In 1982 Iranian forces had recovered the territory lost in the initial Iraqi invasion of 1980, but Khomeini kept the war going for six more years in the hope of removing Saddam from power. Khomeini insisted on conducting fruitless offensives to try to break the Iraqis. During this time powerful allies cast their lot against Iran, leading elites began to oppose the war, and the Iranian people became increasingly disgruntled. Yet the fighting dragged on. To the Imam, the dictates of his revolutionary Islamic credo mattered more than military and economic realities.[82] Only the complete collapse of Iran's armies along the front in 1988 led the Imam to "drink the bitter cup of peace," in his own words. As William Quandt laments, hundreds of thousands of Iranians and Iraqis died as a result of "this old man's intransigence."[83]

Khomeini, like Napoleon, was himself a source of fear. This fear affected the reactions of other states, particularly within the Middle East. State borders did not limit the draw of his charisma, which amplified the strength of his revolutionary credo. In Lebanon, Iraq, Bahrain, and elsewhere in the Muslim world, Shi'a radicals and Islamist militants of all sects were drawn by the commanding image that Khomeini presented. It was in part this threat that led the traditional monarchies of the Persian Gulf to form the Gulf Cooperation Council and work with Iraq against Iran.[84]

HYPOTHESES ON THE ROLE OF INDIVIDUALS IN INTERNATIONAL RELATIONS

The final charge we have left to fulfill is to demonstrate that the first image can produce plausible, and testable, hypotheses about international relations. Ideally, future research would test and elaborate on these hypotheses to develop a more comprehensive set of theories regarding the role of individuals in international relations. The very existence of these credible hypotheses, however, demonstrates the value of the first image: It can be used to derive important theories that scholars can test and refine.

Below we present thirteen hypotheses on the role of individuals in international relations. The first set of hypotheses describes the most general ways in which individuals shape the behavior of nations. The next set delves down to a deeper level of analysis, presenting hypotheses that detail how specific personality traits of leaders may cause certain patterns of outcomes in international affairs. The third set of hypotheses examines the conditions under which leaders have the most influence. The fourth and final group suggests how the first image interacts with the other two—simultaneously shaping them and being shaped by them in turn.

The Basics: Foundational Hypotheses on the Impact of Individuals
The first four hypotheses presented below address how individuals can shape the broadest contours of international relations. At the most basic level, the core question of this article is, Do individual personalities matter to the affairs of nations? Our conclusion is a resounding "yes." These four hypotheses are intuitive, obvious (we hope), and perhaps even commonsensical. Their obviousness should not detract from their value, however—quite the opposite. In Aristotelian fashion, sometimes it is important to catalogue knowledge—even that which after having been articulated seems obvious—in search of new insights.

Hypothesis 1: Individuals Set the Ultimate and Secondary Intentions of a State One of the most important roles of individuals is to shape, if not determine, a

state's intentions. At times, the influence of individuals can be so great as to transform a defender of the status quo into its greatest nemesis. Bismarck fought for the status quo in Europe, whereas Wilhelm II fought to overturn it. Even when a country's people and leaders already oppose the existing order, a leader can greatly magnify the extent of the state's revisionist ambitions. The German people and their generals sought only a greater Germany, but Hitler would be satisfied with nothing less than the enslavement of Europe. Similarly, Napoleon's ego, not the aspirations of the French people, drove *la grande armée* to destruction on the steppes of Russia and the mountains of Spain. A prescient leader also can direct foreign policy toward important long-term goals that are often ignored by demagogues, bureaucrats, and the general populace. Bismarck recognized the danger of alienating Russia even though most German officials were hostile to the czar.

Of course, a country's strategic position, domestic politics, culture, and other factors—both systemic and domestic—also shape a state's intentions. The cases presented above, however, suggest that individuals can often transcend these factors, play them off against one another, or otherwise exercise a direct and decisive influence on a state's behavior.

Hypothesis 2: Individuals Can Be an Important Component of a State's Diplomatic Influence and Military Power Just as individuals can determine a state's intentions, so too are they often an important aspect of a state's capabilities. Sterile, quantifiable measures such as industrial output and orders of battle are only part of a country's military power: The competence or ineptitude of its leaders also weighs heavily in the balance. By itself, France was a formidable military power, capable of matching, or even besting, any of its rivals. With Napoleon leading its armies, France could be defeated only by the combined forces of all of Europe. Hitler, in contrast, diminished Germany's military power: His foolish strategies and amateurish orders destroyed Germany's superbly led and trained armies. Great leaders also can strengthen a country's diplomatic power. It is individuals who build the alliances, and create the threats, that maintain or destroy balances of power. Bismarck forged alliances where others would have failed: Absent the Iron Chancellor, it is hard to imagine a defeated Austria aligning with Prussia after the humiliations of Sadowa and Königgrätz. Similarly, it is equally hard to imagine a leader other than Wilhelm II repeatedly antagonizing Britain for so little purpose. This emphasis on the impact of individuals on state power is not to belittle geography, resources, state capacity, or other vital factors. But political scientists must recognize that these factors alone often fail to account for a state's overall military might or political influence.

Hypothesis 3: Individual Leaders Shape Their State's Strategies Leaders shape not only a state's goals and capabilities but also the manner in which the state employs its resources in pursuit of its goals. Napoleon was a soldier first and last. All too often, the emperor ignored Talleyrand's sage advice to solve his foreign policy problems at the bargaining table, preferring to solve them instead on the battlefield. Whereas Asad dithered in response to challenges, Saddam invariably reached for the sword.

One particular manifestation of this role is the influence that individuals have in making and breaking alliances. The idiosyncratic preferences of leaders often cause them to ally with one state over another even in the face of strong systemic or domestic pressures. Because of his animus against the House of Windsor, Wilhelm II would consider allying with Britain only if London would grovel before him. Moreover, Wilhelm II demanded simplicity in Germany's alliances and thus let relations with Russia and Britain deteriorate. Bismarck could juggle many balls, Wilhelm II one on a good day. As scholars often forget, balances of power are not inevitable: They rest on the shoulders of individuals.[85]

Hypothesis 4: Individual Leaders Affect the Behavior of Opposing States That Must React to Leaders' Idiosyncratic Intentions and Capabilities

Leaders not only influence the actions of their states; they also shape the reactions of other states. At times the mere presence of charismatic, moronic, bellicose, or puissant figures alters how other international actors behave toward the state. Napoleon's overweening ambition coupled with his overwhelming military prowess convinced the rest of Europe that the emperor himself had to be deposed. The Gulf oil monarchies, fearing both revolution and invasion, banded together to oppose the threat from Islamic Iran led by the charismatic Khomeini. Incompetence, as well as ability, can force other states to react. Wilhelm II's erratic diplomacy and provocative swaggering led other European leaders to see him—and thus Germany—as untrustworthy and dangerous. And we will not even mention Hitler.

Building on the Obvious: Foundational Hypotheses and the Future of China

The above four hypotheses can be faulted as obvious, but if true, international relations scholars must change their analytic approach. Consider any assessment of the future of China—a vital question for the coming years. Neorealists might stress China's ability to generate power and the relative power of its rivals. Second-image theorists would add a discussion of how the communist legacy shapes Beijing's behavior and the relative power and agendas of the People's Liberation Army (PLA) party apparatchiks, and other institutions. Still other scholars might weigh China's strategic culture, the existing offense-defense balance, or the presence of important domestic interest groups, such as farmers and factory workers.

If our hypotheses above are true, however—even to the point of being obvious—then scholars cannot understand the future impact of China on international relations without also understanding the mix of skills and abilities of China's leaders, such as Jiang Zemin. Does Jiang, like Mao Zedong and Deng Xiaoping before him, exert tremendous influence over China's overall policies? How will he pursue China's foreign policy objectives? Is Jiang a skilled diplomat, or will he transform China's potential friends into real enemies? If Beijing goes to war, will he shape the PLA's strategy, or, like so many leaders, tragically overreach? How do China's neighbors and other key states view Jiang: as a dangerous warlord, a man of peace, or some uneasy mix? The answers to these questions do not, by themselves, provide a perfect guide to China's future behavior. But ignoring the particular qualities of Jiang's personality risks courting disaster.

How Individuals Matter: Hypotheses on Personality Traits

Of course, it is not enough to speculate merely on whether individuals "matter" to the course of international relations. What is necessary to demonstrate the utility of the first image is to show that it can generate specific, testable hypotheses regarding how individuals affect international relations. As we argued earlier, the first image should be able to generate testable hypotheses in which the variance in the distribution of personality traits among leaders is said to cause states to act in particular ways. The hypotheses listed below are hardly exhaustive, but drawing on the case studies presented above, they demonstrate the kind of hypotheses that can be inferred regarding the correlation between the distribution of leaders' personality traits and international relations outcomes.[86]

Hypothesis 5: States Led by Risk-Tolerant Leaders Are More Likely to Cause Wars Some leaders are more willing than others to tolerate high levels of risk, and this willingness to accept risk often determines how aggressive a state is. Hitler and Napoleon stand out as leaders willing to take risks to gain resources, glory, or other objectives. Hitler's invasion of France was a daring venture, to say nothing of his foray into Russia. Napoleon repeatedly rolled the dice, risking his empire in the pursuit of further conquests. A more cautious man might have opted to consolidate his power rather than trust in his star so absolutely. The contrast between Saddam Hussein and Hafiz al-Asad highlights the importance of risk tolerance. Saddam's willingness to accept high risks led him to attack Iran, Kuwait, Saudi Arabia, Bahrain, and Israel—and to repeatedly provoke the United States. Asad, on the other hand, generally sought to avoid risky undertakings: He intervened reluctantly in Lebanon only after exhausting all other options; he backed down from confrontations with Jordan and Iraq in the 1970s and 1980s; and after 1982 he challenged Israel only indirectly, preferring to work through proxies rather than risk a direct confrontation. Faced with similar circumstances, Saddam saw opportunities where Asad saw dangers. This different perspective has often meant the difference between war and peace in the Middle East.

Hypothesis 6: States Led by Delusional Leaders Start Wars and Prolong Them Unnecessarily Some leaders view the world through cracked lenses. Their ideology or their pathology clouds their vision, leading them to ignore reality and to overestimate their chances of success. A variety of work on decisionmaking shows that individuals interpret information in different ways, with certain fallacies being common but present to different degrees. Delusional individuals are particularly likely to ignore or misinterpret systemic imperatives, and domestic constraints, causing them to overestimate their chances of victory in war or to underestimate the value of an alliance. Delusional leaders see threats that do not exist. They miscalculate balances of power. And they imagine alliances where none are possible.

Needless to say, words such as "crazy" and "delusional" are overused. Saddam Hussein, although certainly evil and often foolish, is not insane. Rationality is a spectrum: Some leaders follow a hyperrational course, whereas others are more prone to wishful thinking. But leaders such as Hitler and Khomeini have clearly slipped over the edge. Hitler believed that his German *Übermenschen* could defy the entire world, and continued to believe this even as armies of Russian *Untermenschen* approached Berlin. Khomeini refused to countenance any peace with Iraq's government of heretics, even after the impossibility of military victory became obvious to everyone around him.

Delusional leaders and the security dilemma interact in particularly pernicious ways. In its classic depiction, Robert Jervis explains that in an anarchic world system, a state's actions to defend itself often cause a counterreaction by its rivals, which in turn leaves all states less secure. It is not always the anarchic system that imposes the security dilemma. A delusional or foolish leader can create one through his or her actions. Wilhelm II saw Germany as surrounded by hostile powers (including several that had been Germany's diplomatic partners until the kaiser dismissed Bismarck) and believed that their militaries and alliances threatened German ambitions, indeed Germany's very survival. In turn, Wilhelm's own actions, most notably his development of a fleet, spurred the British and French to see him as a threat. Delusional leaders can create security dilemmas where none previously existed, or cause precarious situations to spiral into calamity.

Hypothesis 7: States Led by Leaders with Grandiose Visions Are More Likely to Destabilize the System It is difficult for the international system to accommodate the outsized dreams of leaders. The status quo has great difficulty with leaders who cannot be sated with minor concessions and modest territorial transfers. These leaders often overreach in a desperate attempt to realize their ambitions. Triumphs that would have been the crown jewels for Louis XVI were disdained as cut-glass baubles by Napoleon. Similarly, Hitler's ambitions soared beyond those of other German leaders. In both cases, their ambitions exceeded not only the capabilities of their states, but also the ability of the international system to contain them without massive dislocation. The determination of Napoleon and Hitler to rule all of Europe (and dominate the world) sparked wars and upheaval that changed the face of the continent. Nor is vast military power a necessity: Saddam Hussein and Ayatollah Khomeini had dreams of similar proportion, and even without commensurate military power, both managed to radically shake the international affairs of the Persian Gulf, and to some extent, the world. Had their dreams been less ambitious, history books and atlases would look very different.[87]

Vast dreams also produce numerous enemies. By attacking all of Europe, Hitler and Napoleon turned all of Europe against them. Iran's modest power made it little threat to any state beyond its neighbors. Yet by seeking to export Iran's revolution throughout the Islamic world, Khomeini even made enemies of distant Indonesia and Morocco. Seeking to lead the Arab world, Saddam instead alienated it by attacking five Middle Eastern states and threatening a half dozen others.

Hypothesis 8: States Led by Predictable Leaders Will Have Stronger and More Enduring Alliances A state whose behavior can consistently be predicted is one that can be trusted—trusted to do good or trusted to do evil, but trusted nonetheless. States may forge alliances with states whose behavior they do not trust, but they are unlikely to adhere to these ties for long or place much weight on them for the achievement of their goals. Furthermore, such alliances are unlikely to realize their full potential because their cohesion will be weak and their actions disjointed. In many of these cases, it is the predictability of leaders that is at issue. For example, although Hitler and Mussolini had many goals that were either shared or complementary, each repeatedly surprised the other, destroying any trust between them with the result that their actions often ran at cross purposes, and their alliance was as often a source of weakness as of strength.

Indeed the personal relationships among leaders often overcome systemic dynamics or other factors. As Hans Morgenthau notes, "The smooth and effective operation of an alliance, then, depends in good measure upon the relations of trust and respect among its military statesmen."[88] Churchill deliberately cultivated a "special relationship" with Roosevelt, which paid off with unswervingly close cooperation, even when the United States and Britain had diametrically opposed ideas about the conduct of World War II. Observers of the Middle East have often remarked that Iraq and Syria should have been natural allies—they shared an ideology, common internal problems, common external enemies, and generally compatible aspirations—yet they detested each other. As a result, Syria, the self-proclaimed champion of Arab nationalism, was the only Arab state to back Persian Iran against Iraq.

It may be that one contributing factor to the democratic peace is that democracies are more likely to produce leaders whose behavior can be predicted and thus trusted, especially by other democratic leaders. Trustworthiness and consistency are qualities rewarded by voters in democratic systems. In addition, modern democracies tend to have a range of institutional checks on leaders, which makes it difficult for them to push their countries too far from their preexisting course. Consequently, it may be that the success of democratic alliances and the easier ability of democratic leaders to avoid wars when their interests clash come in part from the fact that democratic systems select for the kind of behavior that foreign leaders find predictable and trustworthy.

Critics may contend that characteristics such as risk tolerance and a proneness toward delusions are impossible to operationalize. Such criticisms, however, were once also applied to culture, ideology, ideas, and norms, but scholars over time developed methods to measure and weigh these concepts, greatly enriching the study of international relations. Psychologists have a wide range of measures for determining degrees of rationality. Scholars of decisionmaking have identified situations such as a desire to preserve one's political position or make good on sunk costs that steer individuals toward risky behavior.[89] International relations scholars must draw on these studies in their own work. Just because we lack analytic measures today does not mean we should assume we always will.

When Individuals Matter: Enabling Factors

Leaders do not have the same impact on foreign policy in all situations. No matter how delusional, egocentric, or risk acceptant, some leaders are unable to gain popular support, whereas others are overwhelmed by bureaucratic, systemic, cultural, or other factors. Below we present three hypotheses that suggest when individuals have a greater impact on international relations, and consequently under what conditions theories derived from the first image should most likely have the greatest explanatory power.

Hypothesis 9: The More Power Is Concentrated in the Hands of an Individual Leader, the Greater the Influence of That Leader's Personality and Preferences

Individuals are only one of many factors that determine a state's actions. In vying to set policy, leaders often must contend with a bewildering array of institutions and actors, such as a nation's military, parliament, bureaucracy, political opposition, elites, and people. When other institutions are strong, the ability of any individual leader to shape policy is correspondingly diminished. If a soldier of Napoleon's ability entered the French army today, it is unlikely that he would shake the foundations of Europe. On the other hand, when institutions are weak or unformed, the impact of leaders increases. Consequently, individuals generally matter most in authoritarian regimes with weak institutions. As Bismarck's adviser Friedrich von Gentz described the czar's position, "None of the obstacles that restrain and thwart the other sovereigns—divided authority, constitutional forms, public opinion, etc.—exists for the Emperor of Russia. What he dreams of at night he can carry out in the morning."[90]

Nevertheless, an exceptionally charismatic leader can overcome even strong institutions. Figures such as Hitler and Napoleon—and other modern giants such as Mustafa Kemal Ataturk, Mao, Simon Bolívar, Nasser, and Gandhi—are able to defy the wishes of pragmatic elements around them and succeed in having their followers follow. Ayatollah Khomeini, of course, represented almost an ideal-type of the Weberian charismatic leader. As Max Weber noted, the charismatic authority can defy convention and standard arguments: Such a leader is able to note, "It is written . . . but I say unto you."[91] Thus Khomeini's grip on the Iranian people allowed him to ignore the opposition of other leading figures to the war with Iraq. The hundreds of thousands of Iranians slaughtered on the battlefields of al-Basrah, al-Faw, and Kurdistan testify to the force of his charisma.

Individuals, however, still matter even when strong institutions shape their behavior and limit the impact of their personal idiosyncrasies. As former presidential adviser Clark Clifford once noted, "The executive branch of our government is like a chameleon. To a startling degree it reflects the character and personality of the President."[92] Even in a democracy with well-established checks and balances, recognizing the strengths and weaknesses of the leader is essential.

Hypothesis 10: Individuals Are More Important when Systemic, Domestic, and Bureaucratic Forces Conflict or Are Ambiguous

At times institutional, systemic, and domestic factors may be strong, but their interaction leads to vague or conflicting pressures on policymaking. In these circumstances, the preferences of individuals assume greater importance. Although not one of the historical cases we examined, an excellent example of how individuals can choose among equally viable options is British Prime Minister Margaret Thatcher's decision to confront Argentina over the Falkland Islands. Today many analysts chalk up Thatcher's attack on the Falklands as a (successful) attempt to restore her government's flagging popularity. At the time, however, what path Britain would choose was not so clear. The Foreign Office counseled against any provocation and urged Thatcher not to send a task force.[93] Defense officials doubted that Britain could retake the Falklands, and the treasury feared the impact of the cost of war on Britain's struggling economy.[94] A narrow majority of public opinion polls taken before the fighting began indicated that the British public felt that the Falklands were not worth British casualties. The United States also pushed for a diplomatic solution.

Thatcher, however, played down voices urging restraint and led her nation to war. As Max Hastings and Simon Jenkins note: "The figure of Margaret Thatcher towers over the Falklands drama from its inception to the euphoria of the final triumph. . . . Each of the participants interviewed for the war made similar remarks. 'It was Mrs. Thatcher's war. She held us to it. She never seemed to flinch from her conviction about its course. She took the risks on her shoulders and she won. She emerged as a remarkable war leader.'"[95] Without the Iron Lady, Britain might well have chosen negotiation over confrontation, and the Falklands War—for better or for worse—would never have occurred.

Hypothesis 11: Individuals Are More Important when Circumstances Are Fluid

In times of tremendous change, individuals often assume greater importance. Individuals, in contrast to large bureaucracies or unwieldy parliaments, can act decisively and purposefully. There was a good reason why the Roman Republic transferred the powers of the Senate to a dictator in times of crisis: A single person can react quickly to rapidly unfolding events, seizing opportunities and fending off calamities. In the 1930s, Europe was in chaos. The dramatic political changes resulting from World War I, the emergence of communism and fascism, and the dislocation caused by the worldwide depression threw the power structure of Europe into disarray. Hitler skillfully exploited this disorder. He played Britain, Italy, France, and Russia off one another, effectively paralyzing them as he remilitarized the Rhineland and gobbled up Austria, Czechoslovakia, and Poland. Hafiz al-Asad also took advantage of the fluid circumstances created by the end of the Cold War and the Iraqi invasion of Kuwait to secure Syria's suzerainty over Lebanon even while moving closer to the United States.

The Interacting Images

It is ultimately impossible to explain all of international relations by resort to only one of the three images. None can effectively explain all of the variance in the world. Furthermore, none of the images is entirely discrete—each shapes the others. Thus their impact is felt both directly on events and indirectly through the influence they exert on the other images.[96] The first image is no exception. At least some of its utility as a predictor of international relations lies in the indirect influence it exerts through the other two images.

Hypothesis 12: Individuals Can Shape the Second Image Domestic opinion, bureaucratic politics, and other second-image factors are not independent of individuals. In bureaucratic politics, it is *not* inevitable that where you stand depends on where you sit, especially if where you sit is determined by the leader. The German military was a hindrance to Hitler's machinations only until he was able to oust the strong, independent generals running the army and replace them with pliant lackeys who owed their positions to his beneficence. Likewise the public opinion that guides states is often created by the deliberate actions of leaders who can employ charisma, propaganda, or other means to twist public opinion into an enabling factor. Hitler, Stalin, Saddam, and other dictators have adeptly incited nationalist fervor, created specious *casus belli,* and otherwise played their publics like violins to support their policies. Khomeini's messianic appeal created a mass following for whatever policies he enunciated. If the Imam wished it so, then his followers wanted it too.

Nor are interest group politics independent of individuals. In the early 1900s, an aggressive coalition of German industrialists and naval officers championed Germany's "risk fleet," making it difficult for Berlin to back away from the hostile spiral it was fostering with London. This coalition, however, came into being only after the kaiser had decided to begin the *Flottenpolitik.* Without his ill-conceived first effort, the interest group never would have become so strong.

Leaders also build institutions.[97] Khomeini, for example, created a bizarre system of overlapping administrative bodies—governmental, religious, and parastatal—that functioned adequately during the Imam's life because he had the requisite blend of political power, charisma, and religious learning to control the system. Khomeini's legacy lives on in the institutions he created to suit his rule. Today, without the Imam, the system he created is fractious and chaotic, with power diffused among a multitude of competing organizations—a direct legacy of a system created for a unique man.

Nor do all leaders lead equally well. Some inspire their subordinates, getting the most out of their governing teams, military staffs, and diplomatic corps. Napoleon's officers were fiercely devoted to him, making superhuman efforts to carry out his grandiose vision. Similarly, as Fred Greenstein notes, some leaders create a climate of tolerance that allows dissent and creativity to flourish.[98] Other leaders, however, are bad at receiving advice from their subordinates. Saddam has created a system where fear and sycophancy are necessary for survival. Not surprisingly, he seldom receives objective or useful advice.

Hypothesis 13: Individuals Can Shape the Third Image To the extent that third-image theories rest on the assumption that the distribution of power is a key moving force in international relations, then individuals must be counted when measuring the distribution. As noted in hypothesis 2, the skills of individual leaders are often key components of national power. When judging the balance of power between France and its rivals in the early nineteenth century, scholars must recognize that Napoleon's military genius multiplied the value of sterile production figures and orders of battle.

Hypothesis 8, the impact of a leader's trustworthiness and reliability, posits another influence of the first image on third-image considerations. A key component of cooperation under anarchy appears to be the willingness of leaders to trust one another. In the absence of a common threat, cooperation becomes quite difficult. For cooperation to survive, leaders must feel able to predict one another's behavior and trust them to act in a mutually beneficial manner.

The role of individuals extends beyond merely serving as an input into a third-image model. For instance, a key aspect of some third-image theories is that the uncertainty and imperfect information inherent in the anarchic international system fosters certain patterns of behavior in states. As we noted above, this geopolitical fog is frequently the creation of individual leaders. Often it is not a lack of information that leads to miscalculation, but self-deception on the part of leaders. Few human beings are perfectly objective processors of information, and many of the world's most important figures have lived in deep denial, even psychosis. For this reason, proponents of the third image are adamant that even if the future brings perfect information, it will not eliminate these long-standing systemic pressures because the problem is not necessarily in the quality or quantity of information, but in its interpretation. In other words, the fault lies not in our stars but in ourselves.

CONCLUSIONS

Giants still walk the earth. International relations cannot be understood if the role of the individual is ignored. Critics may still contend that we have focused on exceptions. And indeed we have. Yet such exceptional individuals knit the tapestry of history: Explaining international relations while ignoring Hitler, Bismarck, Napoleon, and other monumental figures is like trying to understand art or music without Michaelangelo or Mozart. Thus policymakers and politicians are right to pay attention to the goals, abilities, and idiosyncrasies of the world's leaders. It is time for scholars to play their part, helping us better understand when and how individuals can make a difference.

Recognizing the importance of individuals is necessary to explode one of the most pernicious and dangerous myths in the study of international relations: the cult of inevitability. Just because a particular event occurred does not mean it was fated to do so. Scholars often fail to acknowledge that common international behavior—balancing against a threat, choosing a grand strategy, or marching off to war—results from decisions made by individuals. It was not inevitable that Germany became bellicose in the late nineteenth century: Without Bismarck, it might have happened earlier, and without Wilhelm II it might not have happened at all. Scholars are too quick to dismiss individuals' behavior with reference to "Cleopatra's nose," but—as the hypotheses we present above suggest—scholars can deduce useful generalizations about the role of individuals.

We hope that our work spurs a renewal in the study of the first image. Although the range of issues to explore is vast, several suggest themselves immediately. First, although we argue that the first image has an impact on military and diplomatic power, clearly individuals do not shape all elements of power equally. For example, leaders can affect important factors such as strategy and training, but have less of an impact on the tactical level during the conduct of operations. A more complete assessment of how individuals influence the factors that make up military and diplomatic power would be highly useful. Second, we barely scratch the surface of when individuals matter. The autocratic political systems that allowed individuals far more freedom are (fortunately) becoming fewer in number. Institutions in all their variety should be assessed for the latitude they allow individuals and the particular policy areas that are most and least affected. Third, scholars should explore the role of individuals on issues other than war and alliances, which has been the focus of this initial foray. Individuals may be important to such tragedies as ethnic conflict, mass killing, the perpetuation of tyranny, and other wrongs (and of course rights) whose understanding is basic to the study of politics. Fourth, work on the impact of individuals outside the role of state leader is essential. The personalities of generals, diplomats, religious authorities, and other shapers and implementers of policy cannot be ignored. Fifth, scholars should examine whether different political systems routinely produce certain types of leaders.

Like other approaches to international relations, the first image does not provide all the answers. Within the discipline of international relations, the study of individuals can be only one part of a larger whole. Ignoring their role is foolish, but so too is ignoring the influence of other forces such as systemic factors, domestic politics, and bureaucratic pressures.[99] International relations are complex and cannot be understood by focusing on any one aspect of politics alone: A foolish parsimony is the hobgoblin of small minds. Of course, recognizing the role of individuals will make the job of scholars and analysts more difficult. Political scientists will have to employ biography and psychology in addition to traditional tools such as economics and history. Such additions, however, will result in a far richer product that is better able to explain our world and anticipate coming challenges.

NOTES

1. Christopher Duffy, *Frederick the Great: A Military Life* (New York: Routledge, 1985), pp. 226–243; and Dennis E. Showalter, *The Wars of Frederick the Great* (London: Longman, 1996), pp. 309–320.

2. Duffy, *Frederick the Great,* p. 233.

3. A background talk with reporters in January 1975, as quoted in Walter Isaacson, *Kissinger* (New York: Simon and Schuster, 1992), p. 13.

4. Other useful work for understanding the role of individuals in international relations comes from historians and area studies experts. Fred I. Greenstein has published an exemplary work demonstrating how the personality traits of postwar presidents have shaped U.S. foreign policy. See Greenstein, *The Presidential Difference: Leadership Style from FDR to Clinton* (New York: Free Press, 2000). See also James M. Goldgeier, *Leadership Style and Soviet Foreign Policy: Stalin, Khrushchev, Brezhnev, Gorbachev* (Baltimore, Md.: Johns Hopkins University Press, 1994); and David Shambaugh, ed., *Deng Xiaoping: Portrait of a Chinese Statesman* (New York: Oxford University Press, 1994). Daniel Markey has written an interesting study of how individuals' desire for prestige affects international relations. Markey, "The Prestige Motive in International Relations," Ph.D. dissertation, Princeton University, 2000.

5. Political psychologists and political scientists drawing on their insights also devote considerable attention to the biases and perceptions that may shape human behavior, paying particular attention to the behavior of leaders and elites in general. See Robert Jervis, *Perception and Misperception in International Politics* (Princeton, N.J.: Princeton University Press, 1976). Three valuable examples of works on leaders and perceptions are Yuen Foong Khong, *Analogies at War* (Princeton, N.J.: Princeton University Press, 1992); Paul Hart, Eric K. Stern, and Bengt Sundelius, eds., *Beyond Groupthink: Political Group Dynamics and Foreign Policy-making* (Ann Arbor: University of Michigan Press, 1997); and Alexander L. George, *Presidential Decisionmaking in Foreign Policy: The Effective Use of Information and Advice* (Boulder, Colo.: Westview, 1980). For an interesting work comparing the role of new leaders on the formulation of public policy, see Valerie Bunce, *Do New Leaders Make a Difference?* (Princeton, N.J.: Princeton University Press, 1981). A good summary of literature on leadership can be found in Robert J. House and Mary L. Baetz, "Leadership: Some Empirical Generalizations and New Research Direction," in L. L. Cummings and Barry M. Staw, eds., *Leadership, Participation, and Group Behavior* (Greenwich, Conn.: JAI Press, 1990), pp. 1–84. Other important works include Harold D. Lasswell, *The Analysis of Political Behaviour: An Empirical Approach* (London: Kegan Paul, 1947); Alexander L. George and Julliette L. George, *Woodrow Wilson and Colonel House: A Personality Study* (New York: Dover, 1964); and Harold D.

Lasswell and Daniel Lerner, eds., *World Revolutionary Elites: Studies in Coercive Ideological Movements* (Cambridge Mass.: MIT Press, 1965). For a sample of more recent interesting works on individual decision making, see Scott Plous, *The Psychology of Judgment and Decision Making* (New York: McGraw-Hill, 1993); and Herbert C. Kelman, *International Behavior: A Social-Psychological Analysis* (New York: Holt, Rinehart, and Winston, 1965). For an interesting assessment of different views of the individual throughout history, see Janet Coleman, ed., *The Individual in Political Theory and Practice* (New York: Oxford University Press, 1996). For works that assess when personality factors should be examined to explain political outcomes, see Fred I. Greenstein, *Personality and Politics* (Chicago: Markham, 1969); Fred I. Greenstein, "The Impact of Personality on Politics: An Attempt to Clear Away the Underbrush," *American Political Science Review,* Vol. 61, No. 3 (September 1967), pp. 629–641; Margaret Hermann, "When Leader Personality Will Affect Foreign Policy: Some Propositions," in James Rosenau, ed., *In Search of Global Patterns* (New York: Free Press, 1976), pp. 326–333; and Margaret Hermann, "Leaders and Foreign Policy Decision-Making," in Dan Caldwell and Timothy J. McKeown, eds., *Diplomacy, Force, and Leadership* (Boulder, Colo.: Westview, 1993), pp. 77–94.

6. Kenneth N. Waltz, *Man, the State, and War* (New York: Columbia University Press, 1959), especially pp. 16, 80–81, 159–165.

7. In his words, only a theory drawn from the third image can offer a "a final explanation because it does not hinge on accidental causes—irrationalities in men, defects in states." Ibid., pp. 231–232. See also pp. 224–238; and Kenneth N. Waltz, *Theory of International Politics* (New York: McGraw-Hill, 1979), pp. 60–68.

8. For example, the world system, domestic politics ("second image"), and other mainstream approaches also slight the importance of individuals. See Immanuel Wallerstein, *The Modern World-System I* (New York: Academic Press, 1974); and Immanuel Wallerstein, *The Politics of the World Economy* (Cambridge: Cambridge University Press, 1984). For an example of the second image as related to democracies, see Michael Doyle, "Liberalism and World Politics," *American Political Science Review,* Vol. 80, No. 4 (December 1986), pp. 1151–1169.

9. Waltz, *Man, the State, and War,* pp. 27–30. As an example, on page 28, he claims that

human nature cannot explain the outbreak of war in 1914 because the same human nature that conceived World War I must have caused peace in, for example, 1910.

10. We recognize a likely selection bias in this claim: It may be that there were leaders who did possess these traits but did not go to war, and therefore the fact that they did possess these traits was not well known beyond their intimates, and perhaps their biographers. We believe that a more rigorous analysis of this claim is warranted.

11. Waltz, *Theory of International Politics,* especially pp. 19–20. We note that Waltz has retreated from his earlier defense of parsimony in his more recent work. For instance, in 1997 he observed that "the explanatory power of a theory, not its parsimony, is the criterion of a theory's success." Kenneth N. Waltz, "International Politics Is Not Foreign Policy," *Security Studies,* Vol. 6, No. 1 (Autumn 1996), p. 57.

12. Waltz, *Theory of International Politics,* pp. 19–20, 61–68.

13. This is not to suggest that parsimony is not desirable. Undoubtedly, a parsimonious theory is better than a complicated theory, all other things being equal. When all other things are not equal, as is usually the case, we prefer an accurate complexity over an inaccurate parsimony.

14. In his defense, Waltz himself recognizes this. See, for example, Waltz, *Man, the State, and War,* p. 218.

15. Again, the best statement of these views is Waltz, *Theory of International Politics,* pp. 91–101; and Kenneth N. Waltz, "Evaluating Theories," *American Political Science Review,* Vol. 91, No. 4 (December 1997), p. 915.

16. The definitive expression of this is Robert Jervis, "Cooperation under the Security Dilemma," *World Politics,* Vol. 30, No. 2 (January 1978), p. 168. Joseph M. Grieco argues that cooperation will fail as a result of these dynamics. See Grieco, *Cooperation among Nations* (Ithaca, N.Y.: Cornell University Press, 1990), p. 45.

17. Stephen M. Walt, *The Origins of Alliances* (Ithaca, N.Y.: Cornell University Press, 1987).

18. Randall L. Schweller, "Bandwagoning for Profit: Bringing the Revisionist State Back In," *International Security,* Vol. 19, No. 1 (Summer 1994), pp. 72–107; Randall L. Schweller, "Neorealism's Status Quo Bias: What Security Dilemma?" *Security Studies,* Vol. 5, No. 3 (Spring 1996), pp. 90–121; and Arnold Wolfers, "The Balance of Power in Theory and Practice,"

in Wolfers, *Discord and Collaboration: Essays on International Politics* (Baltimore, Md.: Johns Hopkins Press, 1962), especially p. 124.

19. A caveat is in order regarding our case selection. This article does not seek to *test* first-image theories of international relations. Instead it seeks to generate testable hypotheses to demonstrate that the first image is a valid line of inquiry for international relations scholars. Consequently, we have chosen "easy" cases—cases in which the individual's influence is self-evident, even to the point of obviousness—rather than "hard" cases or a random sample.

20. Most Germans had accepted the loss of Alsace-Lorraine because they recognized that these territories could not be recovered without fighting a major war with France. Gordon A. Craig, *Germany: 1866–1945* (New York: Oxford University Press, 1978), p. 674; Klaus Hildebrand, *The Foreign Policy of the Third Reich*, trans. Anthony Fothergill (Berkeley: University of California Press, 1973), pp. 29–37; and Donald Kagan, *On the Origins of War and the Preservation of Peace* (New York: Doubleday, 1995), pp. 309–310.

21. Kagan, *On the Origins of War*, pp. 328, 403; Kenneth Macksey, *From Triumph to Disaster: The Fatal Flaws of German Generalship from Moltke to Guderian* (London: Greenhill, 1996), pp. 72–75; Ernest R. May, *Strange Victory: Hitler's Conquest of France* (New York: Hill and Wang, 2000), pp. 15–110; Richard Overy, *Why the Allies Won* (New York: W. W. Norton, 1995), pp. 9–10, 298–305; Richard Overy with Andrew Wheatcroft, *The Road to War*, rev. and updated ed. (London: Penguin, 1999), p. 41; A. J. P. Taylor, *The Origins of the Second World War* (New York: Atheneum, 1983), pp. 58–59; Donald Cameron Watt, *How War Came: The Immediate Origins of the Second World War, 1938–1939* (New York: Pantheon, 1989), pp. 30, 33, 38–39, 105; and Gordon Wright, *The Ordeal of Total War, 1939–1945* (New York: Harper Torchbooks, 1968), p. 7. We have purposely included citations from Taylor not despite, but because of, his apologies for Hitler to demonstrate the strength of our arguments.

22. Alan Bullock, *Hitler: A Study in Tyranny*, abridged ed. (New York: Harper Perennial, 1991), p. 268.

23. Ian Kershaw provides the definitive contemporary assessment of how Hitler's foreign policy diverged from the revisionist aspirations of other German elites in Kershaw, "Nazi For-

eign Policy: Hitler's 'Programme' or 'Expansion without Object'?" reprinted in Patrick Finney, ed., *Origins of the Second World War* (London: Arnold, 1997) pp. 129–135. See also Bullock, *Hitler: A Study in Tyranny*, pp. 176, 233–240, 258–259, 268; Craig, *Germany*, pp. 679, 693, 697–699; Hildebrand, *The Foreign Policy of the Third Reich*, pp. 24–37; Kagan, *On the Origins of War*, p. 339; Macksey, *From Triumph to Disaster*; May, *Strange Victory*, pp. 15–110, 215–232; Overy with Wheatcroft, *Road to War*, pp. 40–41, 48–49, 53, 71; Wright, *Ordeal of Total War*, p. 7; Watt, *How War Came*, pp. 104–105; and Corelli Barnett, ed., *Hitler's Generals* (New York: Quill/William Morrow, 1989).

24. Craig, *Germany*, p. 543. Craig's view is the consensus among contemporary historians. Both the Taylor/Fischer revisionist school (Hitler was no different from other German statesmen) and the functionalist school (Nazi foreign policy stemmed from domestic pressures) have been effectively discredited. See Patrick Finney, "Introduction: History Writing and the Origins of the Second World War," and "Commentary," in Finney, *Origins of the Second World War*, pp. 4–7, 41–42; the response by Richard Overy to Tim Mason, reprinted in "Debate: Germany, 'Domestic Crisis,' and War in 1939," in ibid., pp. 99–109; and especially Kershaw, "Nazi Foreign Policy," pp. 121–144.

25. Sidney Aster, "'Guilty Men': The Case of Neville Chamberlain," in Finney, *Origins of the Second World War*, pp. 62–64, 66–70; Bullock, *Hitler: A Study in Tyranny*, pp. 269, 293; David Dilks, "'We Must Hope for the Best and Prepare for the Worst': The Prime Minister, the Cabinet, and Hitler's Germany, 1937–1939," in Finney, *Origins of the Second World War*, pp. 52–53; Finney, "Introduction," pp. 13–16; Kagan, *On the Origins of War*, pp. 290–307, 340–342; May, *Strange Victory*, pp. 169–212; Overy with Wheatcroft, *Road to War*, pp. 52, 73–120; R. A. C. Parker, "Alternatives to Appeasement," in Finney, *Origins of the Second World War*, pp. 211–220; Taylor, *Origins of the Second World War*, pp. xi–xii, 34, 45–46, 58, 68, 74–77, 94–95, 99–100, 135–136, 160, 165, 189, 227–228; and Watt, *How War Came*, pp. 27–29, 83–84, 168, 385–386.

26. Anthony Adamthwaite, "France and the Coming of War," in Finney, *Origins of the Second World War*, pp. 78–90; Kagan, *On the Origins of War*, pp. 269–298; May, *Strange Victory*, pp. 6, 113–160; Stephen A. Schuker,

"France and the Remilitarization of the Rhineland," in Finney, *Origins of the Second World War,* pp. 224–227, 238–239; Taylor, *Origins of the Second World War,* pp. 73–76, 91, 98–100, 155, 188; and Wright, *Ordeal of Total War,* p. 8. Taylor concludes that ultimately "the French were therefore willing to surrender everything [to Germany] except their own security." Taylor, *Origins of the Second World War,* p. 188. See also Finney, "Introduction," pp. 17–20.

27. Beginning at Locarno in 1925, British and French statesmen repeatedly made clear that they would not go to war over the Polish corridor per se. Right up to the German invasion, they continued to believe that the "question of Danzig" should not be a *casus belli*—and encouraged Polish concessions to Germany on Danzig in hope of forestalling a war. The British and French guarantees to Poland in 1939 had committed the Allies to fight for Polish independence, but neither London nor Paris had guaranteed every inch of Polish territory, specifically meaning Danzig. Their decision to go to war to defend Poland in September 1939 was not based on any change of heart regarding Danzig. Rather it was a reaction to Germany's invasion of all of Poland, demonstrating that Hitler was determined to make Germany the hegemon of Europe under his leadership. See Bullock, *Hitler: A Study in Tyranny,* p. 293; Anna M. Cienciala, "Poland in British and French Policy, 1939: Determination to Fight—or Avoid War?" in Finney, *Origins of the Second World War,* pp. 414–415, 417–426, 428–429; Dilks, "'We Must Hope for the Best and Prepare for the Worst,'" p. 53; Kagan, *On the Origins of War,* p. 311; May *Strange Victory,* pp. 198–212; Overy with Wheatcroft, *Road to War,* pp. 14–17, 113, 119; Taylor, *Origins of the Second World War,* pp. 38, 54, 59–60, 194–199, 207–212, 213–221, 238, 249–252, 264–265, 270–273; and Watt, *How War Came,* pp. 59, 69, 186, 320–321. In Taylor's words, during the August 1939 crisis, "[Britain, France, and Italy] were convinced that Danzig was not worth a war; all three were agreed that it should return to Germany, with safe-guards for Polish trade." Taylor, *Origins of the Second World War,* p. 252.

28. Adamthwaite, "France and the Coming of War," pp. 84–7; Aster, "'Guilty Men,'" pp. 64–65, 72–73; Cienciala, "Poland in British and French Policy," pp. 418–421; Dilks, "'We Must Hope for the Best and Prepare for the Worst,'" p. 53; Kagan, *On the Origins of War,* p. 410; May, *Strange Victory,* pp. 291–308;

Overy; *Why the Allies Won,* p. 9; Overy with Wheatcroft, *Road to War,* pp. 15–17; Taylor, *Origins of the Second World War,* pp. 205–214, 249–252, 264–265, 270–273; and Watt, *How War Came,* pp. 168–169, 186, 385–386, 509–510.

29. Bullock, *Hitler: A Study in Tyranny,* pp. 233–240, 258–259, 268, 321–325; Kershaw, "Nazi Foreign Policy," pp. 121–144; and Watt, *How War Came,* pp. 20–21, 24–25, 255, 441. In particular, on the army's efforts to oppose Hitler's foreign policies and his ultimately successful efforts to subvert the officer corps, see Barnett, *Hitler's Generals;* Matthew Cooper, *The German Army, 1933–1945* (Lanham, Md.: Scarborough House, 1990); Macksey, *From Triumph to Disaster,* pp. 65, 79–80, 132–134; and Overy, *Why the Allies Won,* pp. 23–24.

30. Even after declaring war in September 1939, there was no discussion in Paris of an offensive against Germany. Overy with Wheatcroft, *Road to War,* p. 15; May, *Strange Victory,* pp. 271–336; A. J. P. Taylor, *Bismarck: The Man and the Statesman* (New York: Vintage, 1967), pp. 264–266; and Watt, *How War Came,* pp. 330–332. The German general staff was also convinced that the French and British would not take the offensive and would eventually accede to the German conquests if Berlin refrained from attacking France. See Cooper, *The German Army,* p. 180.

31. Bullock, *Hitler: A Study in Tyranny,* pp. 204, 296, 319; Craig, *Germany,* p. 677; Hildebrand, "The Foreign Policy of the Third Reich," p. 88: Eberhard Jäckel, *Hitler's World View* (Cambridge, Mass.: Harvard University Press, 1982), pp. 37–38; Taylor, *Bismarck,* pp. 131–132; Wright, *Ordeal of Total War,* p. 6; and Watt, *How War Came,* pp. 42–43.

32. On German army opposition to the invasion of France, see Bullock, *Hitler: A Study in Tyranny,* pp. 233, 321–325; Cooper, *The German Army,* pp. 178–182; Craig, *Germany,* pp. 716–717; Macksey, *From Triumph to Disaster,* pp. 79–80; and May, *Strange Victory,* pp. 15–27. Indeed Cooper notes that even Keitel—Hitler's worst lackey among the generals—objected to the attack on France.

33. Cooper, *The German Army,* pp. 246–258, 286; Kenneth Macksey, "Guderian," in Barnett, *Hitler's Generals,* pp. 451–452; Macksey, *From Triumph to Disaster,* pp. 132–134; and Bernd Wegner, "The Road to Defeat: The German Campaigns in Russia, 1941–1943," in John Gooch, ed., *Decisive Campaigns of the*

Second World War (London: Frank Cass, 1990), pp. 107–108. There were some German generals, including the chief of staff, who were not opposed to the idea of attacking Russia in the abstract, but only after the war with Britain had been won. See Cooper, *The German Army,* pp. 252–256.

34. Accounts of the Normandy invasion, such as Overy's superb analysis, make clear just how dicey an operation it was, and how much harder it would have been if the *Wehrmacht* had been able to concentrate its forces in France. See Overy, *Why the Allies Won,* pp. 134–179.

35. In October 1941, Stalin put out diplomatic feelers to see what surrender terms he might get from Germany. Hitler brushed these entreaties aside because nothing short of the destruction of the Soviet state and the enslavement of the Russian people would satisfy his objectives. We do not know what concessions Stalin might have been willing to make, but given the military balance at the time and the German advances up to that point, the two sides might have agreed on a settlement similar to the 1917 Brest-Litovsk treaty, in which Lenin conceded the Ukraine, Belarussia, and the Baltic states to Germany. If Germany had accepted such terms from Stalin, it would have "won" the war. Only Hitler could have considered such a victory inadequate. See Overy, *Why the Allies Won,* pp. 14, 19.

36. Cooper, *The German Army,* pp. 260–287, 316–325, 340, 423–428, 437–441, 456–460; Macksey, "Guderian," pp. 452–456; Macksey, *From Triumph to Disaster,* pp. 135–136; Martin Middlebrook, "Paulus," in Barnett, *Hitler's Generals,* pp. 366–367; Overy, *Why the Allies Won,* pp. 2–7, 67, 98–100; R. H. S. Stolfi, *Hitler's Panzers East: World War II Reinterpreted* (Norman: University of Oklahoma Press, 1993), 82–89; and Wegner, "The Road to Defeat," especially pp. 111–123.

37. For recent historical work concurring that Hitler's leadership was the most important of a range of factors leading to the defeat of the German army, see Paul Adair, *Hitler's Greatest Defeat. The Collapse of Army Group Centre, June 1944* (London: Arms and Armour, 1995), especially pp. 23, 66–67, 84, 104, 168; Corelli Barnett, "Introduction," in Barnett, *Hitler's Generals,* pp. 2–7; Cooper, *The German Army,* especially pp. 246, 304, 316–325, 400, 406, 423–428, 437–441, 456–484, 491, 510–511, 518, 528–531; Overy, *Why the Allies Won,* pp. 67, 87–88, 175, 198–207, 274–281; Macksey, *From Triumph to Disaster,* p. 225; Albert Seaton, *The*

Russo-German War, 1941–1945 (Novato, Calif.: Presidio, 1971), especially pp. 113, 404, 459, 529–535; Stolfi, *Hitler's Panzers East,* especially pp. 72–73; Wegner, "The Road to Defeat," pp. 105–127; and Joachim Wieder and Heinrich Graf von Einsiedel, *Stalingrad: Memories and Reassessments,* trans. Helmut Bolger (London: Arms and Armour, 1993), pp. 16–22.

38. Kagan, *On the Origins of War,* p. 101.

39. For example, in the 1887 Reinsurance treaty, Germany and Russia promised neutrality if the other engaged in a war against a third country unless Germany attacked France or Russia attacked Austria. In other words, as long as the countries had defensive goals they would be allied. Henry Kissinger, *Diplomacy* (New York: Simon and Schuster, 1994), p. 165. Bismarck also used their alliance to rein in Austria. He repeatedly reminded Vienna of the alliance's defensive character and refused to support it in its Balkan ambitions. In 1882 Bismarck brought Italy into its alliance with Austria. Kagan, *On the Origins of War,* p. 108.

40. Kissinger, *Diplomacy,* p. 160. To distract Paris, Bismarck urged the French to engage in colonial adventures. Bismarck also pushed the British and the Austrians to work together to preserve the status quo in the Mediterranean. The result, the "Mediterranean agreement" of 1887, led Britain to become associated with the Triple Alliance and thus deter Russian and French adventurism. Craig, *Germany,* p. 131.

41. Craig, *Germany,* p. 116.

42. Kissinger, *Diplomacy,* p. 171.

43. Taylor, *Bismarck,* p. 53.

44. Friedrich von Holstein, as quoted in Kagan, *On the Origins of War,* p. 115. At the time Holstein worked in the German Foreign Office.

45. Taylor, *Bismarck,* p. 210. During the Congress of Berlin, the German parliament urged Bismarck to take a stronger stand vis-à-vis the Eastern question. Kissinger, *Diplomacy,* p. 156. Moreover, in 1887 some leading German military figures urged a preemptive war on Russia—an idea Bismarck rejected out of hand.

46. Kissinger, *Diplomacy,* p. 138.

47. Kissinger notes that the removal of Bismarck's genius did not by necessity usher in a policy of idiocy. Ibid., p. 169. Similarly, Craig notes that even when the Germans had solid grounds for their actions, their interventions were often menacing, insulting, and violent. Craig, *Germany,* p. 243.

48. Kissinger, *Diplomacy,* p. 179; and Paul M. Kennedy. "The Kaiser and German *Weltpoli-*

tik: Reflections on Wilhelm II's Place in the Making of German Foreign Policy," in John C. G. Rohl and Nicolaus Sombart, eds., *Kaiser Wilhelm II: New Interpretations* (Cambridge: Cambridge University Press, 1982), p. 164. Bismarck's successor as chancellor, Leopold von Caprivi, confessed that he wanted to simplify foreign policy because he lacked Bismarck's ability to keep eight balls in the air at once. Russia, to preserve the alliance, offered several concessions with regard to Germany's position with Austria, but Caprivi still refused to renew the alliance. Kagan, *On the Origins of War,* p. 122.

49. Kennedy, "The Kaiser and German *Weltpolitik,*" p. 151. See also Robert G. L. Waite, "Leadership Pathologies: The Kaiser and the Führer and the Decision for War in 1914 and 1939," in Betty Glad, ed., *Psychological Dimensions of War* (Newbury Park, N.J.: Sage, 1990), pp. 143–168.

50. Kennedy, "The Kaiser and German *Weltpolitik,*" p. 162.

51. Blaming German industry, as some scholars do, does not explain the German decision to build a large fleet. As Kennedy notes, it cannot have mattered to Krupp whether the government spent millions on infantry divisions or on battleships, as the giant arms manufacturer would have supplied the guns for either. Ibid., p. 152.

52. Ibid., p. 160.

53. Kurt Riezler, *Tagebücher, Aufsätze, Dokumente,* ed. Karl Dietrich Erdman (Göttingen, Germany: Vandenhoeck and Ruprecht, 1972), p. 188, as quoted in Craig, *Germany,* p. 337.

54. David. G. Chandler, *The Campaigns of Napoleon* (New York: Scribner, 1966), pp. xxix–xxx.

55. Such expansionary behavior is typical of revolutionary states. Stephen M. Walt, *Revolution and War* (Ithaca, N.Y.: Cornell University Press, 1996).

56. Alistair Horne, *How Far from Austerlitz? Napoleon, 1805–1815* (Armonk, N.Y.: St. Martin's, 1996), p. 69; and Alan Schom, *Napoleon Bonaparte* (New York: HarperCollins, 1997), p. 400.

57. Chandler, *Campaigns of Napoleon,* p. xxix.

58. Horne, *How Far from Austerlitz?* pp. 296–297; and Schom, *Napoleon Bonaparte,* pp. 305, 434, 478, 482–495.

59. Schom, *Napoleon Bonaparte,* p. 400.

60. Horne, *How Far from Austerlitz?* p. 235.

61. See also Felix Markham, *Napoleon* (New York: Signet New American Library, 1963), pp. 55–56.

62. Horne, *How Far from Austerlitz?* pp. 237–240; and Schom, *Napoleon Bonaparte,* pp. 248–250, 417–418, 478. Schom also notes that Napoleon's secret police chief, Joseph Fouché, perhaps the third most powerful man in the empire, also constantly sought peace despite the emperor's compulsive war making. See Schom, *Napoleon Bonaparte,* pp. 271–272.

63. Perhaps the best examples were the campaigns of 1813 and 1814. By then, Napoleon had lost the advantage of superior military effectiveness because most of his best-trained combat veterans had been slaughtered in Spain and Russia, while his enemies had reformed their own militaries along French lines. Likewise his adversaries had adopted their own versions of the *levée en masse,* and so the French were badly outnumbered as well. Nevertheless Napoleon nearly won each of these campaigns, and his conduct of the 1814 campaign in defense of France was nothing short of astonishing. See Chandler, *Campaigns of Napoleon,* pp. 865–1004.

64. Markham, *Napoleon,* p. 141. This in an era when 100,000 men was considered a large field army.

65. Chandler, *Campaigns of Napoleon,* pp. 899, 947, 994, 1001; and Schom, *Napoleon Bonaparte,* p. 414. Schom contends that the allies recognized that Napoleon had to be removed because of his bellicosity and martial skills as early as 1805 after the Battle of Austerlitz. Chandler argues that the Austrians were convinced of the necessity of this course only after the Battle of Leipzig in 1813.

66. See, for example, Ofra Bengio, *Saddam Speaks on the Gulf Crisis: A Collection of Documents* (Tel Aviv: Dayan Center for Middle Eastern and African Studies, 1992), pp. 14–17.

67. F. Gregory Gause III, "Gulf Regional Politics: Revolution, War, and Rivalry," in W. Howard Wriggins, ed., *Dynamics of Regional Politics: Four Systems on the Indian Ocean Rim* (New York: Columbia University Press, 1992), p. 52; and Phebe Marr, *The Modern History of Iraq* (Boulder, Colo.: Westview, 1985), p. 245.

68. For an interesting analysis of Saddam's decisionmaking, see Jerrold M. Post, "The Defining Moment of Saddam's Life: A Political Psychology Perspective on the Leadership and Decision-Making of Saddam Hussein during the Gulf Crisis," in Stanley A. Renshon, ed., *The Political Psychology of the Gulf War. Leaders, Publics,*

and the Process of Conflict (Pittsburgh, Pa.: University of Pittsburgh Press, 1993), pp. 49–66.

69. Christine Moss Helms, Iraq: Eastern Flank of the Arab World (Washington, D.C.: Brookings, 1984), pp. 45–46, 149–150; Majid Khadduri, Socialist Iraq: A Study in Iraqi Politics since 1968 (Washington, D.C.: Middle East Institute, 1978), pp. 68, 161–164; and Marr, Modern History of Iraq, pp. 230–231.

70. Helms, Iraq: Eastern Flank of the Arab World, pp. 151–162; Dilip Hiro, Lebanon: Fire and Embers (New York: St. Martin's, 1992), pp. 25–39; and Marr, Modern History of Iraq, pp. 292–294.

71. Amatzia Baram, "The Iraqi Invasion of Kuwait: Decision-Making in Baghdad," in Baram and Barry Rubin, eds., Iraq's Road to War (New York: St. Martin's, 1993), pp. 6–9; Lawrence Freedman and Efraim Karsh, The Gulf Conflict, 1990–1991: Diplomacy and War in the New World Order (Princeton, N.J.: Princeton University Press, 1993), pp. 38–41, 45–47; and F. Gregory Gause III, "Prospect Theory and Iraqi War Decisions," paper presented at the 1997 annual meeting of the American Political Science Association, Washington, D.C., August 28–31, 1997.

72. On Saddam's aggressive grand strategy beginning in early 1990, see Baram, "The Iraqi Invasion of Kuwait," pp. 5–28; and Bengio, Saddam Speaks on the Gulf Crisis, pp. 11–34.

73. Neville Brown, "Jordanian Civil War," Military Review, September 1971, p. 45; Alasdair Drysdale, "The Syrian Armed Forces in National Politics: The Role of the Geographic and Ethnic Periphery," in Roman Kolkowicz and Andrej Korbonski, eds., Soldiers, Peasants, and Bureaucrats: Civil-Military Relations in Communist and Modernizing Societies (London: George Allen and Unwin, 1982), pp. 68–69; Derek Hopwood, Syria, 1945–1986: Politics and Society (London: Unwin Hyman, 1988), pp. 51–52; Fred H. Lawson, Why Syria Goes to War: Thirty Years of Confrontation (Ithaca, N.Y.: Cornell University Press, 1996), p. 68; Moshe Ma'oz, "The Emergence of Modern Syria," in Ma'oz and Avner Yaniv, eds., Syria under Assad (New York: St. Martin's, 1986), p. 26; and Nikolaos Van Dam, The Struggle for Power in Syria: Sectarianism, Regionalism, and Tribalism in Politics, 1961–1978 (New York: St. Martin's, 1979), pp. 84–88.

74. Ma'oz, "The Emergence of Modern Syria," p. 28; Patrick Seale, Asad of Syria (London: I. B. Tauris, 1988), p. 171; and Van Dam, The Struggle for Power in Syria, pp. 87–92.

75. Reuven Avi-Ran, The Syrian Involvement in Lebanon since 1975 (Boulder, Colo.: Westview, 1991), pp. 3–22; Robert Fisk, Pity the Nation: The Abduction of Lebanon (New York: Atheneum, 1990), pp. 80–91; Hiro, Lebanon: Fire and Embers, pp. 33–44; Hopwood, Syria, pp. 60–62; Moshe Ma'oz, Syria and Israel: From War to Peacemaking (London: Oxford University Press, 1995), pp. 160–165; Itamar Rabinovich, "The Changing Prism: Syrian Policy in Lebanon as a Mirror, an Issue, and an Instrument," in Ma'oz and Yaniv, Syria under Assad, pp. 179–184; Itamar Rabinovich, The War for Lebanon, 1970–1985 (Ithaca, N.Y.: Cornell University Press, 1985), pp. 36–37, 47–56, 85–88, 201–236; Seale, Asad of Syria, pp. 267–289; and Naomi Joy Weinberger, Syrian Intervention in Lebanon (New York: Oxford University Press, 1986), pp. 95–213.

76. Joseph Nevo, "Syria and Jordan: The Politics of Subversion," in Ma'oz and Yaniv, Syria under Assad, p. 145.

77. Avi-Ran, Syrian Involvement in Lebanon, pp. 132–136; Anthony H. Cordesman and Abraham R. Wagner, The Lessons of Modern War, Vol. 1, The Arab-Israeli Conflicts, 1973–1989 (Boulder, Colo.: Westview, 1990), p. 83; Ma'oz, Syria and Israel, pp. 174–175; Ze'ev Schiff and Ehud Ya'ari, Israel's Lebanon War, ed. and trans. Ina Friedman (New York: Simon and Schuster, 1984), pp. 117–118, 155–156; and Seale, Asad of Syria, p. 380.

78. The best account of Rif'at al-Asad's fall is Michael Eisenstadt, "Syria's Defense Companies: Profile of a Praetorian Unit," unpublished manuscript, Washington Institute for Near East Policy, 1989, pp. 8–12.

79. For Saddam's analysis of the new world order and aggressive prescriptions for Iraq and the other Arab states, see his address to the Fourth Summit of the Arab Cooperation Council, Amman, February 24, 1990, reprinted in Bengio, Saddam Speaks on the Gulf Crisis, pp. 37–49.

80. Baram, "Iraqi Invasion of Kuwait," pp. 10–11; Bengio, Saddam Speaks on the Gulf Crisis, p. 15; and Lawrence Freedman and Efraim Karsh, The Gulf Conflict, 1990–1991: Diplomacy and War in the New World Order (Princeton, N.J.: Princeton University Press, 1991), p. 31.

81. The best known of Saddam's statements implying that he understood the risk that the United States might intervene if Iraq attacked Kuwait was his warning to U.S. Ambassador

April Glaspie that American society "cannot accept 10,000 fatalities in one battle," in their infamous meeting on July 25, 1990. See Micah L. Sifry and Christopher Cerf, eds., *The Gulf War Reader: History, Documents, Opinions* (New York: Random House, 1991), p. 125. However, Iraqi officials restated this after the war. See, for example, "Aziz Interviewed on Outbreak of Gulf War," *Milliyet,* May 30, 1991, in Foreign Broadcast Information Service—Near East—South Asia-91-107, June 4, 1991, pp. 13–14; and Milton Viorst, "Report from Baghdad," *New Yorker,* June 24, 1991, pp. 66–67.

82. See Sandra Mackey, *The Iranians: Persia, Islam, and the Soul of a Nation* (New York: Penguin, 1996), pp. 322–328, for statements on Khomeini's ideology as it relates to the war's continuation. A good overview of Khomeini's theology can be found in Hamid Dabashi, *Theology of Discontent: The Ideological Foundation of the Islamic Revolution in Iran* (New York: New York University Press, 1993), pp. 409–484.

83. William Quandt, "The Middle East on the Brink: Prospects for Change," *Middle East Journal,* Vol. 50, No. 1 (Winter 1996), p. 13. See also R. K. Ramazani, *Revolutionary Iran* (Baltimore, Md.: Johns Hopkins Press, 1988), p. 74.

84. Jacob M. Landau, *The Politics of Pan-Islam: Ideology and Organization* (Oxford: Oxford University Press, 1994), pp. 259–260. On the formation of the Gulf Cooperation Council, see David Priess, "Balance-of-Threat Theory and the Genesis of the GCC," *Security Studies,* Vol. 5, No. 4 (Summer 1996), pp. 143–171; Lenore G. Martin, *The Unstable Gulf: Threats from Within* (Lexington, Mass.: Lexington Books, 1984), pp. 24–27; and Emile A. Nakleh, *The Gulf Cooperation Council: Policies, Problems, and Prospects* (New York: Praeger, 1986).

85. Indeed Henry Kissinger—one of the premier realists—devotes much of his early work to examining how such a balance was created in nineteenth-century Europe. See Kissinger, *A World Restored: Metternich, Castlereagh, and the Problems of Peace, 1812–1822* (Boston: Houghton Mifflin, 1957), for a superb example.

86. We recognize that there is a selection bias in the cases from which we generated several of these hypotheses. For example, we note the correlation between risk tolerance and war, but our cases focus largely on instances of war. Additional testing of these hypotheses using cases of peace is necessary, as are tests using leaders who are not risk tolerant, egotistical, and so on.

87. See Greenstein, *The Presidential Difference,* pp. 192–198.

88. Hans Morgenthau, *Politics among Nations,* 3d ed. (New York: Alfred A. Knopf, 1960), p. 201.

89. Jack Levy, "Prospect Theory, Rational Choice, and International Relations," *International Studies Quarterly,* Vol. 41, No. 1 (March 1997), p. 93; and Jack S. Levy, "Loss Aversion, Framing, and Bargaining: The Implications of Prospect Theory for International Conflict," *International Political Science Review,* Vol. 17, No. 2 (April 1996), p. 189. A leader's proneness toward risk could be measured by examining how he or she responded to similar circumstances before assuming power.

90. Friedrich von Gentz, "Considerations on the Political System in Europe" (1818), in Mack Walker, ed., *Metternich's Europe.* (New York: Walker and Co., 1968), p. 80. Quoted in Kissinger, *Diplomacy,* p. 140.

91. Max Weber, *Economy and Society* (Berkeley: University of California Press, 1978), p. 243 (ellipsis in the original).

92. Quoted in Greenstein, *The Presidential Difference,* p. 189.

93. Max Hastings and Simon Jenkins, *The Battle for the Falklands* (New York: W. W. Norton, 1983), p. 66. Throughout the conflict, key cabinet officials, such as Foreign Secretary Francis Pym and Home Secretary William Whitelaw, urged compromise over confrontation. The Sunday Times of London Insight Team, *War in the Falklands: The Full Story* (New York: Harper and Row, 1982), pp. 177–178.

94. The military contingency file for an invasion of the Falklands stressed the logistical problems of operations so far from British shores. It also noted that Britain might not be able to meet its NATO commitments if it were engaged in a conflict in the Falklands. Most ominously, it argued that not even the largest task force could retake the islands after an Argentine invasion. Hastings and Jenkins, *Battle for the Falklands,* p. 56.

95. Ibid., pp. 335–336.

96. For a similar study of interacting images, see Philip Gourevitch, "Second Image Reversed: International Sources of Domestic Politics," *International Organization,* Vol. 32, No. 4 (Autumn 1978), pp. 881–911.

97. Harry Truman and Dwight Eisenhower, for example, created a national security structure that has lasted for decades after their terms ended. Greenstein, *The Presidential Difference,* p. 195.

98. Ibid., pp. 195–196.

99. Favoring one level of analysis at the ex-

pense of the others is perhaps the most pernicious form of "reductionism." See Charles A.
Kupchan, *The Vulnerability of Empire* (Ithaca,
N.Y.: Cornell University Press, 1994), p. 7.
Likewise, we echo Fareed Zakaria's plea for
scholars to "develop a tolerance for more limited—but more accurate—generalizations," by

developing theories of international affairs that
draw on both internal and external factors to explain state behavior. See Zakaria, "Realism and
Domestic Politics: A Review Essay," *International
Security*, Vol. 17, No. 1 (Summer 1992),
pp. 178–179.

Reading 2-2

Theories of International Relations
Ole R. Holsti

Universities and professional associations usually are organized in ways that tend to
separate scholars in adjoining disciplines and perhaps even to promote stereotypes
of each other and their scholarly endeavors. The seemingly natural areas of scholarly
convergence between diplomatic historians and political scientists who focus on international relations have been underexploited, but there are also some signs that this may
be changing. These include recent essays suggesting ways in which the two disciplines
can contribute to each other; a number of prizewinning dissertations, later turned into
books, by political scientists that effectively combine political science theories and historical materials; collaborative efforts among scholars in the two disciplines; interdisciplinary journals such *as International Security* that provide an outlet for historians and political scientists with common interests; and creation of a new section, "International
History and Politics," within the American Political Science Association.[1]

This essay is an effort to contribute further to an exchange of ideas between the two
disciplines by describing some of the theories, approaches, and "models" political scientists have used in their research on international relations during recent decades. A brief
essay cannot do justice to the entire range of theoretical approaches that may be found in
the current literature, but perhaps those described here, when combined with citations
of some representative works, will provide diplomatic historians with a useful, if sketchy,
map showing some of the more prominent landmarks in a neighboring discipline.

The most enduring "great debate" among students and practitioners of international relations has pitted realism against various challengers. Because "classical realism"
is the most venerable and persisting theory of international relations, it provides a good
starting point and baseline for comparison with competing models. Robert Gilpin may
have been engaging in hyperbole when he questioned whether our understanding of
international relations has advanced significantly since Thucydides, but one must acknowledge that the latter's analysis of the Peloponnesian War includes concepts that are
not foreign to contemporary students of balance-of-power politics.[2]

Following a discussion of classical realism, an examination of "modern realism" or
"neorealism" will identify the continuities and differences between the two approaches.
The essay then turns to several models that challenge one or more core premises of both

SOURCE: "Theories of International Relations" by Ole R. Holsti, from *Explaining the History of American Foreign Relations*, 2nd ed.,
eds. Michael J. Hogan and Thomas G. Paterson. Cambridge University Press. Copyright © 2004 by Ole R. Holsti. Reprinted by permission of the author.

classical and modern realism. The first three challengers focus on the system level: global society/complex interdependence/liberal institutionalism, Marxist/world system/dependency, and constructivism. Subsequent sections discuss several "decision making" models, all of which share a skepticism about the adequacy of theories that focus on the structure of the international system while neglecting political processes within units that comprise the system.

Several limitations should be stated at the outset. Each of the systemic and decision-making approaches described below is a composite of several models; limitations of space have made it necessary to focus on the common denominators rather than on subtle differences among them. This discussion will pay little attention to the second "great debate," centering mostly on methodological issues; for example, what Stanley Hoffmann called "the battle of the literates versus the numerates." [3] Efforts of some political scientists to develop "formal" or mathematical approaches to international relations are neglected here; such abstract models are likely to be of limited interest to historians. [4] The "post-modern" challenge to all other theories and methodologies—the third "great debate"—will only briefly be described and evaluated. With these caveats, let me turn now to classical realism, the first of the systematic models to be discussed in this essay.

REALISM

There have always been Americans, such as Alexander Hamilton, who viewed international relations from a realist perspective, but its contemporary intellectual roots are largely European. Three important figures of the interwar period probably had the greatest impact on American scholarship: diplomat-historian E. H. Carr, geographer Nicholas Spykman, and political theorist Hans Morgenthau. Other Europeans who have contributed significantly to realist thought include John Herz, Raymond Aron, Hedley Bull, and Martin Wight, while notable Americans of this school include scholars Arnold Wolfers and Norman Graebner, diplomat George Kennan, journalist Walter Lippmann, and theologian Reinhold Niebuhr. [5]

Although realists do not constitute a homogeneous school—any more than do any of the others discussed in this essay—most of them share at least five core premises about international relations. To begin with, they view as central questions the causes of war and the conditions of peace. They also regard the structure of the international system as a necessary if not always sufficient explanation for many aspects of international relations. According to classical realists, "structural anarchy," or the absence of a central authority to settle disputes, is the essential feature of the contemporary system, and it gives rise to the "security dilemma": in a self-help system one nation's search for security often leaves its current and potential adversaries insecure, any nation that strives for absolute security leaves all others in the system absolutely insecure, and it can provide a powerful incentive for arms races and other types of hostile interactions. Consequently, the question of *relative* capabilities is a crucial factor. Efforts to deal with this central element of the international system constitute the driving force behind the relations of units within the system; those that fail to cope will not survive. Thus, unlike "idealists" and some "liberal internationalists," classical realists view conflict as a natural state of affairs rather than as a consequence that can be attributed to historical circumstances, evil leaders, flawed sociopolitical systems, or inadequate international understanding and education.

A third premise that unites classical realists is their focus on geographically based groups as the central actors in the international system. During other periods the primary entities may have been city-states or empires, but at least since the Treaties of Westphalia (1648), sovereign states have been the dominant units. Classical realists also agree that state behavior is rational. The assumption behind this fourth premise is that states are guided by the logic of the "national interest," usually defined in terms of survival, security, power, and relative capabilities. Although the national interest may vary according to specific circumstances, the similarity of motives among nations permits the analyst to reconstruct the logic of policymakers in their pursuit of national interests—what Morgenthau called the "rational hypothesis"—and to avoid the fallacies of "concern with motives and concern with ideological preferences."[6]

Finally, the state can also be conceptualized as a *unitary* actor. Because the central problems for states are starkly defined by the nature of the international system, their actions are primarily a response to external rather than domestic political forces. According to Stephen Krasner, for example, the state "can be treated as an autonomous actor pursuing goals associated with power and the general interest of the society."[7] Classical realists, however, sometimes use domestic politics, especially the alleged deficiencies of public opinion, as a residual category to explain deviations from "rational" policies.

Realism has been the dominant model of international relations during at least the past six decades because it seemed to provide a useful framework for understanding the collapse of the post–World War I international order in the face of serial aggressions in the Far East and Europe, World War II, and the Cold War. Nevertheless, the classical versions articulated by Morgenthau and others have received a good deal of critical scrutiny. The critics have included scholars who accept the basic premises of realism but who found that in at least four important respects these theories lacked sufficient precision and rigor.

Classical realism has usually been grounded in a pessimistic theory of human nature, either a theological version (for example, Saint Augustine and Reinhold Niebuhr) or a secular one (for example, Machiavelli, Hobbes, and Morgenthau). Egoism and self-interested behavior are not limited to a few evil or misguided leaders but are basic to *homo politicus* and thus are at the core of a realist theory. But because human nature, if it means anything, is a constant rather than a variable, it is an unsatisfactory explanation for the full range of international relations. If human nature explains war and conflict, what accounts for peace and cooperation? In order to avoid this problem, most modern realists have turned their attention from human nature to the structure of the international system to explain state behavior.[8]

In addition, critics have noted a lack of precision and even contradictions in the way classical realists use such core concepts as "power," "national interest," and "balance of power."[9] They also see possible contradictions between the central descriptive and prescriptive elements of realism. On the one hand, nations and their leaders "think and act in terms of interests defined as power," but, on the other, statesmen are urged to exercise prudence and self-restraint, as well as to recognize the legitimate interests of other nations.[10] Power plays a central role in classical realism, but the correlation between relative power balances and political outcomes is often less than compelling, suggesting the need to enrich analyses with other variables. Moreover, the distinction between "power as capabilities" and "usable options" is especially important in the nuclear age, as the United States discovered in Vietnam and the Soviets learned in Afghanistan. The terrorist attack on New York and Washington of September 11, 2001, even more dramatically illustrated the disjunction between material capabilities and political impact.

Although classical realists have typically looked to history and political science for insights and evidence, the search for greater precision has led many modern realists to look elsewhere for appropriate models, analogies, metaphors, and insights. The discipline of choice is often economics, from which modern realists have borrowed a number of tools and concepts, including rational choice, expected utility, theories of firms and markets, bargaining theory, and game theory.

The quest for precision has yielded a rich harvest of theories and models, and a somewhat less bountiful crop of supporting empirical applications. Drawing in part on game theory, Morton Kaplan described several types of international systems—for example, balance-of-power, loose bipolar, tight bipolar, universal, hierarchical, and unit-veto. He then outlined the essential rules that constitute these systems. For example, the rules for a balance-of-power system are: "(1) increase capabilities, but negotiate rather than fight; (2) fight rather than fail to increase capabilities; (3) stop fighting rather than eliminate an essential actor; (4) oppose any coalition or single actor that tends to assume a position of predominance within the system; (5) constrain actors who subscribe to supranational organizational principles; and (6) permit defeated or constrained essential actors to re-enter the system." [11] Richard Rosecrance, David Singer, Karl Deutsch, Bruce Russett, and many others, although not necessarily realists, also have developed models that seek to understand international relations by virtue of system-level explanations. [12]

Kenneth Waltz's *Theory of International Politics,* the most prominent effort to develop a rigorous and parsimonious model of "modern" or "structural" realism, has tended to define the terms of a vigorous debate during the past two decades. It follows and builds upon another enormously influential book in which Waltz developed the Rousseauian position that a theory of war must include the system level (what he called the "third image") and not just first (theories of human nature) or second (state attributes) images. Why war? Because there is nothing in the system to prevent it. [13]

Theory of International Relations is grounded in analogies from microeconomics: international politics and foreign policy are analogous to markets and firms. Oligopoly theory is used to illuminate the dynamics of interdependent choice in a self-help anarchical system. Waltz explicitly limits his attention to a structural theory of international systems, eschewing the task of linking it to a theory of foreign policy. [14] Indeed, he doubts that the two can be joined in a single theory and he is highly critical of many system-level analysts, including Morton Kaplan, Stanley Hoffmann, Richard Rosecrance, Karl Deutsch, David Singer, and others, charging them with various errors, including "reductionism," that is, defining the system in terms of the attributes or interactions of the units.

In order to avoid reductionism and to gain parsimony, Waltz erects his theory on the foundations of three core propositions that define the structure of the international system. The first concentrates on the principles by which the system is ordered. The contemporary system is anarchic and decentralized rather than hierarchical; although they differ in many respects, each unit (state) is formally equal. A second defining proposition is the character of the units. An anarchic system is composed of sovereign units and therefore the functions that they perform are also similar; for example, all have the task of providing for their own security. In contrast, a hierarchical system would be characterized by some type of division of labor. Finally, there is the distribution of capabilities among units in the system. Although capabilities are a unit-level attribute, the distribution of capabilities is a system-level concept. [15] A change in any of these elements constitutes a change in system structure. The first element of structure as defined by Waltz is a quasi-constant because the ordering principle rarely changes, and the second element drops out of the analysis because the functions of units are similar as long as the system remains anarchic. Thus, the third attribute, the distribution of capabilities, plays the central role in Waltz's model.

Waltz uses his theory to deduce the central characteristics of international relations. These include some nonobvious propositions about the contemporary international system. For example, with respect to system stability (defined as maintenance of its anarchic character and no consequential variation in the number of major actors) he concludes that, because a bipolar system reduces uncertainty, it is more stable than alternative structures. Furthermore, he contends that because interdependence has declined rather than increased during the twentieth century, this trend has actually contributed to stability, and he argues that the proliferation of nuclear weapons may contribute to rather than erode system stability.[16]

Waltz's effort to bring rigor and parsimony to realism has stimulated a good deal of further research, but it has not escaped controversy and criticism.[17] Most of the vigorous debate has centered on four alleged deficiencies relating to interests and preferences, system change, misallocation of variables between the system and unit levels, and an inability to explain outcomes.

Specifically, a spare structural approach suffers from an inability to identify completely the nature and sources of interests and preferences because these are unlikely to derive solely from the structure of the system. Ideology or domestic politics may often be at least as important. Consequently, the model is also unable to specify adequately how interests and preferences may change. The three defining characteristics of system structure are not sufficiently sensitive to specify the sources and dynamics of system change. The critics buttress their claim that the model is too static by pointing to Waltz's assertion that there has only been a single structural change in the international system during the past three centuries.

Another drawback is the restrictive definition of system properties, which leads Waltz to misplace, and therefore neglect, elements of international relations that properly belong at the system level. Critics have focused on his treatment of the destructiveness of nuclear weapons and interdependence. Waltz labels these as unit-level properties, whereas some of his critics assert that they are in fact attributes of the system.

Finally, the distribution of capabilities explains outcomes in international affairs only in the most general way, falling short of answering the questions that are of central interest to many analysts. For example, the distribution of power at the end of World War II would have enabled one to predict the rivalry that emerged between the United States and the Soviet Union (as de Tocqueville did more than a century earlier) but it would have been inadequate for explaining the pattern of relations between these two nations—the Cold War rather than withdrawal into isolationism by either or both, a division of the world into spheres of influence, or World War III. In order to do so, it is necessary to explore political processes *within* states—at minimum within the United States and the Soviet Union—as well as *between them*.

Robert Gilpin shares the core assumptions of modern realism, but his study of *War and Change in World Politics* also attempts to cope with some of the criticism leveled at Waltz's theory by focusing on the dynamics of system change. In doing so, Gilpin also seeks to avoid the criticism that the Waltz theory is largely ahistorical. Drawing upon both economic and sociological theory, his model is based on five core propositions. The first is that the international system is in a state of equilibrium if no state believes that it is profitable to attempt to change it. Second, a state will attempt to change the status quo of the international system if the expected benefits outweigh the costs. Related to this is the proposition that a state will seek change through territorial, political, and economic expansion until the marginal costs of further change equal or exceed the marginal benefits. Moreover, when an equilibrium between the costs and benefits of further change and expansion is reached, the economic costs of maintaining the status quo (expenditures for military forces, support for allies, etc.) tend to rise faster than the resources needed to do so. An equilibrium exists when no powerful state believes that a change in the system would yield additional net benefits. Finally, if the resulting disequilibrium between the existing governance of the international system and the redistribution of power is not resolved, the system will be changed and a new equilibrium reflecting the distribution of relative capabilities will be established.[18]

Unlike Waltz, Gilpin includes state-level processes in order to explain change. Differential economic growth rates among nations—a structural-systemic level variable—play a vital role in his explanation for the rise and decline of great powers, but his model also includes propositions about the law of diminishing returns on investments, the impact of affluence on martial spirit and on the ratio of consumption to investment, and structural change in the economy.[19] Table 1 summarizes some key elements of realism. It also contrasts them to other models of international relations—global society/complex interdependence, Marxist/world system/dependency, and constructivism, to which we now turn.

GLOBAL SOCIETY, INTERDEPENDENCE, INSTITUTIONALISM

Just as there are variants of realism, there are several global society/complex independence/liberal institutionalism (GS/CI/LI) models, but this discussion focuses on two common denominators; they all challenge the first and third core propositions of realism identified earlier, asserting that inordinate attention to the war/peace issue and the nation-state renders it an increasingly anachronistic model of global relations.[20]

The agenda of critical problems confronting states has been vastly expanded during the twentieth century. Attention to the issues of war and peace is by no means misdirected, according to proponents of a GS/CI/LI perspective, but concerns for welfare, modernization, the environment, and the like are today no less potent sources of motivation and action. It is important to stress that the potential for cooperative action arises from *self-interest,* not from some utopian attribution of altruism to state leaders. Institution building to reduce uncertainty, information costs, and fears of perfidy; improved international education and communication to ameliorate fears and antagonisms based on misinformation and misperceptions; and the positive–sum possibilities of such activities as trade are but a few of the ways, according to the GS/CI/LI perspective, by which states may jointly gain and thus mitigate, if not eliminate, the harshest features of a self-help international system. The diffusion of knowledge and technology, combined with the globalization of communications, has vastly increased popular expectations. The resulting demands have outstripped resources and the ability of sovereign states to cope effectively with them. Interdependence and institution building arise from an inability of even the most powerful states to cope, or to do so unilaterally or at acceptable levels of cost and risk, with issues ranging from terrorism to trade, from immigration to environmental threats, and from AIDS to new strains of tuberculosis.[21]

Paralleling the widening agenda of critical issues is the expansion of actors whose behavior can have a significant impact beyond national boundaries; indeed, the cumulative effects of their actions can have profound consequences for the international system. Thus, although states continue to be the most important international actors, they possess a declining ability to control their own destinies. The aggregate effect of actions

Table 1. Four Models of the International System

	Realism	Global Society	Marxism	Constructivism
Type of Model	Classical: descriptive and normative Modern: deductive	Descriptive and normative	Descriptive and normative	Descriptive and normative
Central Problems	Causes of war Conditions of peace	Broad agenda of social, economic, and environmental issues arising from gap between demands and resources	Inequality and exploitation Uneven development	Content, sources, and consequences of state identities and interests
Conception of Current International System	Structural anarchy Structure conceived in terms of material capabilities	Global society Complex interdependence (structure varies by issue area)	World capitalist system Structure conceived in terms of material capabilities	Environment in which states take action is social as well as material; the social gives meaning to the material world
Key Actors	Geographically based units (tribes, city-states, sovereign states, etc.)	Highly permeable states *plus* a broad range of non-state actors, including IOs, IGOs, NGOs, and individuals	Classes and their agents	States with socially constructed identities and interests
Central Motivations	National interest Security Power	Security and a wider range of human needs and wants	Class interests	Different rather than uniform Interests based on identities rather than fixed by structures

Table 1. (*continued*)

	Realism	Global Society	Marxism	Constructivism
Loyalties	To geographically based groups (from tribes to sovereign states)	Loyalties to state may be declining. To emerging global norms, values, and institutions and/or to subnational groups	To class values and interests that transcend those of the state	To states, at least for the intermediate future
Central Processes	Search for security and survival	Aggregate effects of decisions by national and nonnational actors. How units (not limited to nation-states) cope with a growing agenda of threats and opportunities arising from human wants	Modes of production and exchange. International division of labor in a world capitalist system	Actors behave on the basis of socially constructed identities and interests
Likelihood of System Transformation	Low (basic structural elements of system have revealed an ability to persist despite many other kinds of changes)	Moderate in the direction of the model (owing to the rapid pace of technological change, etc.)	High in the direction of the model (owing to inherent contradictions within the world capitalist system)	Indeterminate; change in social identities is both possible and difficult
Sources of Theory, Insights, and Evidence	Politics. History. Economics (especially modern realists)	Broad range of social sciences. Natural and technological sciences	Marxist-Leninist theory (several variants)	Sociology. Social psychology. Anthropology/cultural studies

by multitudes of nonstate actors can have potent effects that transcend political boundaries. These may include such powerful or highly visible nonstate organizations as Exxon, the Organization of Petroleum Exporting Countries, or the Palestine Liberation Organization, and even shadowy ones such as the al Qaeda group that claimed to have carried out the 9/11 terrorist attacks. On the other hand, the cumulative effects of decisions by less powerful actors may also have profound international consequences. For example, decisions by thousands of individuals, mutual funds, banks, pension funds, and other financial institutions to sell securities on 19 October 1987 not only resulted in an unprecedented "crash" on Wall Street but also within hours its consequences were felt throughout the entire global financial system. The difficulties of containing economic problems within a single country were also illustrated by the international consequences of difficulties in Thailand, Mexico, and Russia during the late 1990s.

The widening agenda of critical issues, most of which lack a purely national solution, has also led to creation of new actors that transcend political boundaries; for example, international organizations, transnational organizations, nongovernment organizations, multinational corporations, and the like. Thus, not only does an exclusive focus on the war/peace issue fail to capture the complexities of contemporary international life but it also blinds the analyst to the institutions, processes, and norms that self-interested states may use to mitigate some features of an anarchic system. In short, according to GS/CI/LI perspectives, analysts of a partially globalized world may incorporate elements of realism (anarchy, self-interest, rationality, etc.) as a necessary starting point, but these are not sufficient for an adequate understanding.

The GS/CI/LI models recognize that international behavior and outcomes arise from a multiplicity of motives, not merely the imperatives of systemic power balances. They also alert us to the fact that important international processes originate not only in the actions of states but also in the aggregated behavior of other actors. These models enable the analyst to deal with a broader agenda of critical issues; they also force one to contemplate a richer menu of demands, processes, and outcomes than would be derived from realist models, and thus, they are more sensitive to the possibility that politics of trade, currency, immigration, health, the environment, or energy may significantly and systematically differ from those typically associated with security issues.

A point of some disagreement among theorists lumped together here under the GS/CI/LI rubric centers on the importance and future prospects of the nation-state. The state serves as the starting point for analysts who focus on the ways in which these self-interested actors may pursue gains and reduce risks and uncertainties by various means, including creation of institutions. They view the importance of the nation-state as a given for at least the foreseeable future.

Other theorists regard the sovereign territorial state as in a process of irreversible decline, partly because the revolution in communications is widening the horizons and thus providing competition for loyalties of its citizens, partly because states are increasingly incapable of meeting the expanding expectations of their subjects; the "revolution of rising expectations" is not limited to less developed countries. Theirs is a largely utilitarian view of the state in which national sentiments and loyalties depend importantly on continuing favorable answers to the question: "what have you done for me lately?" However, these analysts may be underestimating the potency of nationalism and the durability of the state. Several decades ago one of them wrote that "the nation is declining in its importance as a political unit to which allegiances are attached."[22] Objectively, nationalism may be an anachronism but, for better or worse, powerful loyalties are still attached to states. The suggestion that, because even some well-established nations have experienced independence movements among ethnic, cultural, or religious minorities, the territorial state is in an irreversible decline is not wholly persuasive. In virtually every region of the world there are groups that seek to create or restore geographically based entities in which its members may enjoy the status and privileges associated with sovereign territorial statehood. Events since 1989 in Eastern Europe, parts of the former Yugoslavia and Soviet Union, Palestine, Sri Lanka, Iraq, Quebec, Turkey, and elsewhere, seem to indicate that obituaries for nationalism may be somewhat premature.

The notion that such powerful nonnational actors as major multinational corporations (MNCs) will soon transcend the nation-state seems equally premature. International drug rings do appear capable of challenging and perhaps even dominating national authorities in Colombia, Panama, and some other states. But the pattern of outcomes in confrontations between MNCs and states, including cases involving major expropriations of corporate properties, indicate that even relatively weak nations are not always the hapless pawns of MNCs. The 9/11 terrorist attacks demonstrated once again that even the most powerful states that also enjoy a favorable geographical location cannot provide absolute safety for their populations. Perhaps paradoxically, these attacks and the resulting responses also reconfirmed the continuing importance of the state in world politics.

Underlying the GS/CI/LI critique of realist theories is the view that the latter are too wedded to the past and are thus incapable of dealing adequately with change. Even if global dynamics arise from multiple sources (including nonstate actors), however, the actions of states and their agents would appear to remain the major sources of change in the international system. The third group of systemic theories to be considered, the Marxist/world system/dependency (M/WS/D) models, further downplays the role of the nation-state even further.

MARXISM, WORLD SYSTEMS, DEPENDENCY

Many of the distinctions among M/WS/D theories are lost by treating them together and by focusing on their common features, but in the brief description possible here only common denominators will be presented. These models challenge both the war/peace and state-centered features of realism, but they do so in ways that differ sharply from challenges of GS/CI/LI models.[23] Rather than focusing on war and peace, these theories direct attention to quite different issues, including uneven development, poverty, and exploitation within and between nations. These conditions arise from the dynamics of the modes of production and exchange, and they must be incorporated into any analysis of intra- and inter-nation conflict.

According to adherents of these models, the key groups within and between nations are classes and their agents: As Immanuel Wallerstein put it, "in the nineteenth and twentieth centuries there has been only one world system in existence, the world capitalist world-economy."[24] The "world capitalist system" is characterized by a highly unequal division of labor between the periphery and core. Those at the periphery are essentially the drawers of water and the hewers of wood whereas the latter appropriate the surplus of the entire world economy. This critical feature of the world system not only gives rise to and perpetuates a widening rather than narrowing gap between the wealthy core and poor periphery but also to a dependency relationship from which the latter are unable to break loose. Moreover, the class structure within the core, characterized by a growing gap between capital and labor, is faithfully reproduced in the periphery so that elites there share with their counterparts in the core an interest in perpetuating the system. Thus, in contrast to many realist theories, M/WS/D models encompass and integrate theories of both the global and domestic arenas.

M/WS/D models have been subjected to trenchant critiques.[25] The state, nationalism, security dilemmas, and related concerns are at the theoretical periphery rather than at the core. "Capitalism was from the beginning an affair of the world-economy," Wallerstein asserts, "not of nation-states."[26] A virtue of many M/WS/D theories is that they take a long historical perspective on world affairs rather than merely focusing on contemporary issues. Yet, by neglecting nation-states and the dynamics arising from their efforts to deal with security in an anarchical system—or at best relegating these actors and motivations to a minor role—M/WS/D models are open to question, much as would be analyses of *Hamlet* that neglect the central character and his motivations.

Finally, the earlier observations about the persistence of nationalism as an element of international relations seem equally appropriate here. Perhaps national loyalties can be dismissed as prime examples of "false consciousness," but even in areas that experienced two generations of one-party Communist rule, as in China, Poland, Hungary, Czechoslovakia, or Estonia, there was scant evidence that feelings of solidarity with workers in the Soviet Union or elsewhere replaced nationalist sentiments.

The end of the Cold War and subsequent events have rendered Marxist theories somewhat problematic, but the gap between rich and poor states has, if anything, become more acute during the past decade. Globalization has helped some Third World countries such as Singapore, South Korea, and Taiwan, but it has done little for most African countries. This condition has given rise to two somewhat related explanations for disparities, not only between the industrial west and the rest of the world, but also among countries that gained their independence since 1945.

The first focuses on *geography*. One analyst notes, for example, that landlocked countries in tropical zones have serious disadvantages in coping with such health problems as malaria and in overcoming the high costs of land transportation for exporting their goods.[27] The second cluster of theories purporting to explain uneven development point to *cultural differences*.[28] Neither of these theories is new; Max Weber's *The Protestant Ethic and the Spirit of Capitalism* is a classic illustration of a cultural explanation for development.

While geographical and cultural theories have enjoyed some revival recently, they have also provoked spirited debates, in part because of highly dubious uses in the past.[29] Unlike Marxist theories, they also appear to place the primary responsibility for underdevelopment on the poor countries themselves, and they seem to offer limited prospects for coping with the problem because neither geography nor culture can easily be changed. Proponents of these theories respond that a proper diagnosis of the roots of under-development is a necessary condition for its amelioration; for example through aid programs that target public health and transportation infrastructure needs.

CONSTRUCTIVISM

Although the theories described to this point tended to dominate debates during the past century, "constructivism" has recently emerged as a significant approach to world politics. Unlike many "post-modernists" (discussed in [a later] section), most constructivists work within the theoretical and epistemological premises of the social sciences, and they generally seek to expand rather than undermine the purview of other theoretical perspectives. As with other approaches summarized in this essay, constructivists do not constitute a monolithic perspective, but they do share some key ideas, the first of which is that the environment in which states act is social and ideational as well as material. Money provides a good example of the construction of social reality. If money is limited to metals such as gold and silver, then it has value because the metal itself is valuable, and its use constitutes a form of barter. For reasons of convenience and to expand the money supply, modern governments have also designated bits of colored paper and base metals to serve as money although they have little if any intrinsic value; that they are valuable and can be used as a medium of exchange is the result of a construction of economic reality.[30]

In their emphasis on the construction of social reality, its proponents challenge the materialist basis of the approaches discussed above. Because the social gives meaning to the material, many core concepts, including anarchy, power, national interest, security dilemma, and others, are seen as socially constructed rather than as the ineluctable consequences of system structures. Moreover, interests and identities—for example, those who are designated as "allies" or "enemies"—are also social constructs, the products of human agency, rather than structurally determined. The title of a widely cited work by Alexander Wendt, "Anarchy Is What States Make of It," provides something of the flavor of the constructionist perspective. Wendt shows that because anarchy can have multiple meanings for different actors, it may give rise to a wider range of behaviors than postulated by realism.[31]

Constructivists have also shown that ideas and norms sometimes compete with, shape, or even trump material interests. Although not labeled as a constructivist analysis, an early study of John Foster Dulles' policies toward the USSR revealed that he constructed a model of the Soviet system, based largely on his lifelong study of Lenin's writings. Brutal Soviet foreign policies during the Stalin era provided ample support for Dulles' model, but the more variegated policies of those who came to power in the Kremlin after the Soviet dictator's death in 1953 were also interpreted in ways suggesting that Dulles' model was largely impervious to any evidence that might call it into question.[32] The end of the Cold War and disintegration of the Soviet Union have triggered off a lively debate among proponents of ideational and material interpretations of the acceptance by Mikhail Gorbachev of domestic reforms and collapse of the Soviet empire in Eastern Europe.[33]

At this point, constructivism is less a theory than an approach. It has been used to analyze the origins, development, and consequences of norms and cultures in a broad range of settings.[34] It might offer an especially fruitful contribution to the persisting debates, described below, on the "democratic peace" thesis. The constructivist approach is of relatively recent vintage, but it bears considerable resemblance to the venerable social science dictum that we all perceive our environment through the lenses of belief systems, and thus that, "It is what we think the world is like, not what it is really like, that determines our behavior."[35] This also illustrates the tendency for each generation of political scientists to reinvent, if not the whole wheel, at least some parts of it.

DECISION MAKING

Many advocates of realism recognize that it cannot offer fine-grained analyses of foreign policy behavior and, as noted earlier, Waltz denies that it is desirable or even possible to combine theories of international relations and foreign policy. Decision-making models challenge the premises that it is fruitful to conceptualize the nation as a unitary rational actor whose behavior can adequately be explained by reference to the system structure—the second, fourth, and fifth realist propositions identified earlier—because individuals, groups, and organizations acting in the name of the state are also sensitive to domestic pressures and constraints, including elite maintenance, electoral politics, public opinion, interest groups, ideological preferences, and bureaucratic politics. Such core concepts as "the national interest" are not defined solely by the international system, much less by its structure alone, but they are also likely to reflect elements within the domestic political arena. Thus, rather than assuming with the realists that the state can be conceptualized as a "black box"—that the domestic political processes are unnecessary for explaining the sources of its external behavior—decision-making analysts believe one must indeed take these internal processes into account, with special attention directed at policymakers.

At the broadest level of analyses within the "black box," the past two decades have witnessed a burgeoning literature and heated controversies on the "democratic peace," arising from the finding that, while democracies are no less likely to engage in wars, they do not fight each other.[36] The literature is far too vast to discuss in any detail in this brief essay. Some of the debate is about minutiae (does Britain's pro forma declaration of war on Finland during World War II constitute a crucial disconfirming case?), but parts of it engage such central issues as the role of institutions (transparent policymaking) in allaying fears of perfidy or of norms (the culture of compromise) in reducing or eliminating wars between democracies. Suffice it to say that proponents and critics of democratic peace thesis line up mostly along realist-liberal lines. The democratic peace thesis is especially troubling to realists for at least three reasons. It runs counter to a long tradition, espoused by Alexis de Tocqueville, Hans Morgenthau, George Kennan, Walter Lippmann, Henry Kissinger, and other notable realists, that depicts democracies as seriously disadvantaged in conducting foreign affairs. Moreover, the thesis democracies may behave differently directly challenges a core premise of structural realism. As Waltz notes, "If the democratic peace thesis is right, structural realist theory is wrong."[37] At the policy level, few realists are comfortable with espousal by the first Bush and Clinton administrations of "democracy promotion" abroad as a vital goal of American diplomacy, at least at the rhetorical level, usually denouncing it as an invitation to hopeless crusading, or as "international social work" worthy of Mother Teresa but not of the world's sole superpower.[38]

To reconstruct how nations deal with each other, it is necessary to view the situation through the eyes of those who act in the name of the state: decision makers and the group and bureaucratic-organizational contexts within which they act. Table 2 provides an overview of three major types of decision-making models, beginning with the bureaucratic-organizational models.[39]

Bureaucratic and Organizational Politics

Traditional models of complex organizations and bureaucracy emphasized the benefits of a division of labor, hierarchy, and centralization, coupled with expertise, rationality, and obedience. They also assumed that clear boundaries should be maintained between politics and decision making, on the one hand, and administration and implementation on the other. Following pioneering works by Chester Barnard, Herbert Simon and James March, and others, more recent theories depict organizations quite differently.[40] The central premise is that decision making in bureaucratic organizations is not constrained only by the legal and formal norms that are intended to enhance the rational and eliminate the capricious aspects of bureaucratic behavior. There is an *emphasis* upon rather than a denial of the political character of bureaucracies, as well as on other "informal" aspects of organizational behavior. Complex organizations are composed of

Table 2. Three Models of Decision Making

	Bureaucratic Politics	Group Dynamics	Individual Decision Making
Conceptualization of Decision Making	Decision making as the result of bargaining within bureaucratic organizations	Decision making as the product of group interaction	Decision making as the result of individual choice
Premises	Central organizational values are imperfectly internalized Organizational behavior is political behavior Structure and SOPs affect substance and quality of decisions	Most decisions are made by small elite groups Group is different than the sum of its members Group dynamics affect substance and quality of decisions	Importance of subjective appraisal (definition of the situation) and cognitive processes (information processing, etc.)
Constraints on Rational Decision Making	Imperfect information, resulting from centralization, hierarchy, and specialization Organizational inertia Conflict between individual and organizational utilities Bureaucratic politics and bargaining dominate decision making and implementation of decisions	Groups may be more effective for some tasks, less for others Pressures for conformity Risk-taking propensity of groups (controversial) Quality of leadership "Groupthink"	Cognitive limits on rationality Information processing distorted by cognitive consistency dynamics (unmotivated biases) Systematic and motivated biases in causal analysis Individual differences in abilities related to decision making (e.g., problem-solving ability, tolerance of ambiguity, defensiveness and anxiety, information seeking, etc.) Cognitive dissonance
Sources of Theory, Insights, and Evidence	Organization theory Sociology of bureaucracies Bureaucratic politics	Social psychology Sociology of small groups	Cognitive psychology Dynamic psychology

individuals and units with conflicting perceptions, values, and interests that may arise from parochial self-interest ("what is best for my bureau is also best for my career"), and also from different perceptions of issues arising ineluctably from a division of labor ("where you stand depends on where you sit"). Organizational norms and memories, prior policy commitments, inertia, and standard operating procedures may shape and perhaps distort the structuring of problems, channeling of information, use of expertise, the range of options that may be considered, and implementation of executive decisions. Consequently, organizational decision making is essentially political in character, dominated by bargaining for resources, roles and missions, and by compromise rather than analysis.[41]

An ample literature of case studies on budgeting, weapons acquisitions, military doctrine, and similar situations confirms that foreign and defense policy bureaucracies rarely conform to the Weberian "ideal type" of rational organization.[42] Some analysts assert that crises may provide the motivation and means for reducing some of the nonrational aspects of bureaucratic behavior: crises are likely to push decisions to the top of the organization where a higher quality of intelligence is available; information is more likely to enter the top of the hierarchy directly, reducing the distorting effects of information processing through several levels of the organization; and broader, less parochial values may be invoked. Short decision time in crises reduces the opportunities for decision making by bargaining, log rolling, incrementalism, lowest-common-denominator values, "muddling through," and the like.[43]

Even studies of international crises from a bureaucratic-organizational perspective, however, are not uniformly sanguine about decision making in such circumstances. Graham Allison's analysis of the Cuban missile crisis identified several critical bureaucratic malfunctions concerning dispersal of American aircraft in Florida, the location of the naval blockade, and grounding of weather-reconnaissance flights from Alaska that might stray over the USSR. Richard Neustadt's study of two crises involving the United States and Great Britain revealed significant misperceptions of each other's interests and policy processes. And an examination of three American nuclear alerts found substantial gaps in understanding and communication between policymakers and the military leaders who were responsible for implementing the alerts.[44]

Critics of some organizational-bureaucratic models have directed their attention to several points.[45] They assert, for instance, that the emphasis on bureaucratic bargaining fails to differentiate adequately between the positions of the participants. In the American system, the president is not just another player in a complex bureaucratic game. Not only must he ultimately decide but he also selects who the other players will be, a process that may be crucial in shaping the ultimate decisions. If General Matthew Ridgway and Attorney General Robert Kennedy played key roles in the American decisions not to intervene in Indochina in 1954 and not to bomb or invade Cuba in 1962, it was because Presidents Eisenhower and Kennedy chose to accept their advice rather than that of other officials. Also, the conception of bureaucratic bargaining tends to emphasize its nonrational elements to the exclusion of genuine intellectual differences that may be rooted in broader concerns, including disagreements on what national interests, if any, are at stake in a situation. Indeed, properly managed, decision processes that promote and legitimize "multiple advocacy" among officials may facilitate high-quality decisions.[46]

These models may be especially useful for understanding the slippage between executive decisions and foreign policy actions that may arise during implementation, but they may be less valuable for explaining the decisions themselves. Allison's study of the Cuban missile crisis does not indicate an especially strong correlation between bureaucratic roles and evaluations of the situation or policy recommendations, as predicted by his "Model III" (bureaucratic politics), and recently published transcripts of deliberations during the crisis do not offer more supporting evidence for that model.[47] Yet Allison does present some compelling evidence concerning policy implementation that casts considerable doubt on the adequacy of traditional realist conceptions of the unitary rational actor.

Small Group Politics

Another decision-making model used by some political scientists supplements bureaucratic-organizational models by narrowing the field of view to foreign policy decisions within small-group contexts. Some analysts have drawn upon sociology and social psychology to assess the impact of various types of group dynamics on decision making.[48] Underlying these models are the premises that the group is not merely the sum of its members (thus decisions emerging from the group are likely to be different from what a simple aggregation of individual preferences and abilities might suggest), and that group dynamics can have a significant impact on the substance and quality of decisions.

Groups often perform better than individuals in coping with complex tasks owing to diverse perspectives and talents, an effective division of labor, and high-quality debates on definitions of the situation and prescriptions for dealing with it. Groups may also provide decision-makers with emotional and other types of support that may facilitate coping with complex problems. Conversely, they may exert pressures for conformity to group norms, thereby inhibiting the search for information and policy options, ruling out the legitimacy of some options, curtailing independent evaluation, and suppressing some forms of intragroup conflict that might serve to clarify goals, values, and options. Classic experiments have revealed the extent to which group members will suppress their beliefs and judgments when faced with a majority adhering to the contrary view, even a counterfactual one.[49]

Drawing on historical case studies, social psychologist Irving Janis has identified a different variant of group dynamics, which he labels "groupthink" to distinguish it from the more familiar type of conformity pressure on "deviant" members of the group.[50] Janis challenges the conventional wisdom that strong cohesion among group members invariably enhances performance. Under certain conditions, strong cohesion can markedly degrade the group's performance in decision making. Members of a cohesive group may, as a means of dealing with the stresses of having to cope with consequential problems and in order to bolster self-esteem, increase the frequency and intensity of face-to-face interaction, resulting in greater identification with the group and less competition within it; "concurrence seeking" may displace or erode reality-testing and sound information processing and judgment. As a consequence, groups may be afflicted by unwarranted feelings of optimism and invulnerability, stereotyped images of adversaries, and inattention to warnings. Janis's analyses of both "successful" (the Marshall Plan, the Cuban missile crisis) and "unsuccessful" (Munich Conference of 1938, Pearl Harbor, the Bay of Pigs invasion) cases indicate that "groupthink" or other decision-making pathologies are not inevitable, and he develops some guidelines for avoiding them.[51]

Individual Leaders

Still other decision-making analysts focus on the individual policymaker, emphasizing the gap between the demands of the classical model of rational decision making and the substantial body of theory and evidence about various constraints that come into play in even relatively simple choice situations.[52] Drawing upon cognitive psychology, these models go well beyond some of the earlier formulations that drew upon psychodynamic theories to identify various types of psychopathologies among political leaders: paranoia, authoritarianism, the displacement of private motives on public objects, etc.[53] Efforts to include information-processing behavior of the individual decision maker have been directed at the cognitive and motivational constraints that, in varying degrees, affect the decision-making performance of "normal" rather than pathological subjects. Thus, attention is directed to all leaders, not merely those, such as Hitler or Stalin, who display symptoms of clinical abnormalities.

Many challenges to the classical model have focused on limited human capabilities for objectively rational decision making. The cognitive constraints on rationality include limits on the individual's capacity to receive, process, and assimilate information about the situation; an inability to identify the entire set of policy alternatives; fragmentary knowledge about the consequences of each option; and an inability to order preferences on a single utility scale.[54] These have given rise to several competing conceptions of the decision maker and his or her strategies for dealing with complexity, uncertainty, incomplete or contradictory information, and, paradoxically, information overload. They variously characterize the decision maker as a problem solver, naive or intuitive scientist, cognitive balancer, dissonance avoider, information seeker, cybernetic information processor, and reluctant decision maker.

Three of these conceptions seem especially relevant for foreign policy analysis. The first views the decision maker as a "bounded rationalist" who seeks satisfactory rather than optimal solutions. As Herbert Simon has put it, "the capacity of the human mind for formulating and solving complex problems is very small compared with the size of the problem whose solution is required for objectively rational behavior in the real world—or even a reasonable approximation of such objective rationality."[55] Moreover, it is not practical for the decision maker to seek optimal choices; for example, because of the costs of searching for information. Related to this is the concept of the individual as a "cognitive miser," one who seeks to simplify complex problems and to find short cuts to problem solving.

Another approach is to look at the decision maker as an "error prone intuitive scientist" who is likely to commit a broad range of inferential mistakes. Thus, rather than emphasizing the limits on search, information processing, and the like, this conception views the decision maker as the victim of flawed decision rules who uses data poorly. There are tendencies to underuse raw data in making judgments, believe in the "law of small numbers," underuse diagnostic information, overweight low probabilities and underweight high ones, and violate other requirements of consistency and coherence.[56]

The final perspective emphasizes the forces that dominate the policymaker, forces that will not or cannot be controlled.[57] Decision makers are not merely rational calculators; important decisions generate conflict, and a reluctance to make irrevocable choices often results in behavior that reduces the quality of decisions. These models direct the analyst's attention to policymakers' belief systems, images of relevant actors, perceptions, information-processing strategies, heuristics, certain personality traits (ability to tolerate ambiguity, cognitive complexity, etc.), and their impact on decision-making performance.

Despite this diversity of perspectives and the difficulty of choosing between cognitive and motivational models, there has been some convergence on several types of constraints that may affect decision processes.[58] One involves the consequences of efforts to achieve cognitive consistency on perceptions and information processing. Several kinds of systematic bias have been identified in both experimental and historical studies. Policymakers have a propensity to assimilate and interpret information in ways that conform to rather than challenge existing beliefs, preferences, hopes, and expectations. They may deny the need to confront tradeoffs between values by persuading themselves that an option will satisfy all of them, and indulge in rationalizations to bolster the selected option while denigrating others.

A comparison of a pair of two-term conservative Republican presidents may be used to illustrate the point about coping with tradeoffs. Both came to office vowing to improve national security policy and to balance the federal budget. President Eisenhower, recognizing the tradeoff between these goals, pursued security policies that reduced defense expenditures—for example, the "New Look" policy that placed greater reliance on nuclear weapons, and alliance policies that permitted maintenance of global commitments at lower cost. Despite widespread demands for vastly increased defense spending after the Soviet space capsule *Sputnik* was successfully placed in orbit around the earth, Eisenhower refused to give in; indeed, he left office famously warning of the dangers of the "military-industrial complex." The result was a period of balanced budgets in which surpluses in some years offset deficits in others. In contrast, President Reagan denied any tradeoffs between defense expenditures and budget deficits by positing that major tax cuts would stimulate the economy to produce increases in government revenues. The results proved otherwise as the Reagan years were marked by annual deficits ranging between $79 billion and $221 billion.

An extensive literature on styles of attribution has revealed several types of systematic bias. Perhaps the most important for foreign policy is the basic attribution error—a tendency to explain the adversary's behavior in terms of his characteristics (for example, inherent aggressiveness or hostility) rather then in terms of the context or situation, while attributing one's own behavior to the latter (for example, legitimate security needs arising from a dangerous and uncertain environment) rather than to the former. A somewhat related type of double standard has been noted by George Kennan: "Now is it our view that we should take account only of their [Soviet] capabilities, disregarding their intentions, but we should expect them to take account only of our supposed intentions, disregarding our capabilities?"[59]

Analysts also have illustrated the effect on decisions of policymakers' assumptions about order and predictability in the environment. Whereas a policymaker may have an acute appreciation of the disorderly environment in which he or she operates (arising, for example, from domestic political processes), there is a tendency to assume that others, especially adversaries, are free of such constraints. Graham Allison, Robert Jervis, and others have demonstrated that decision makers tend to believe that the realist "unitary rational actor" is the appropriate representation of the opponent's decision processes and, thus, whatever happens is the direct result of deliberate choices.[60]

Several models linking crisis-induced stress to decision processes have been developed and used in foreign policy studies.[61] Irving Janis and Leon Mann have developed a more general conflict-theory model that conceives of man as a "reluctant decision maker" and focuses upon "when, how and why psychological stress generated by decisional conflict imposes limitations on the rationality of a person's decisions."[62] One may employ five strategies for coping with a situation requiring a decision: unconflicted adherence to existing policy, unconflicted change, defensive avoidance, hypervigilance, and vigilant decision making. The first four strategies are likely to yield low-quality decisions owing to an incomplete search for information, appraisal of the situation and options, and contingency planning, whereas vigilant decision making, characterized by a more adequate performance of vital tasks, is more likely to result in a high-quality choice. The factors that will affect the employment of decision styles are information about risks, expectations of finding a better option, and time for adequate search and deliberation.

A final approach we should consider attempts to show the impact of personal traits on decision making. Typologies that are intended to link leadership traits to decision-making behavior abound, but systematic research demonstrating such links is in much shorter supply. Still, some efforts have borne fruit. Margaret Hermann has developed a scheme for analyzing leaders' public statements of unquestioned authorship for eight variables: nationalism, belief in one's ability to control the environment, need for power, need for affiliation, ability to differentiate environments, distrust of others, self-confidence, and task emphasis. The scheme has been tested with impressive results on a broad range of contemporary leaders.[63] Alexander George has reformulated Nathan Leites's concept of "operational code" into five philosophical and five instrumental beliefs that are intended to describe politically relevant core beliefs, stimulating a number of empirical studies and, more recently, further significant conceptual revisions.[64] Finally, several psychologists have developed and tested the concept of "integrative complexity," defined as the ability to make subtle distinction along multiple dimensions, flexibility, and the integration of large amounts of diverse information to make coherent judgments.[65] A standard content analysis technique has been used for research on documentary materials generated by top decision makers in a wide range of international crises.[66]

Decision-making approaches permit the analyst to overcome many limitations of the systemic models described earlier, but they also impose increasingly heavy data burdens on the analyst. Moreover, there is a danger that adding levels of analysis may result in an undisciplined proliferation of categories and variables. It may then become increasingly difficult to determine which are more or less important, and ad hoc explanations for individual cases erode the possibilities for broader generalizations across cases. Several well-designed, multicase, decision-making studies, however, indicate that these and other traps are not unavoidable.[67]

POST-MODERN CHALLENGES

The field of international relations has gone through three "great debates" during the past century. The first, pitting the venerable realist tradition against various challengers, was summarized above. The second, centered on disagreements about the virtues and limitations of quantification ("if you can't count it, it doesn't count" versus "if you can count it, that ain't it") and, more recently, on "formal modeling." Although those arguments persist in various guises, they have been bypassed in this essay.

The most recent debate, in many respects the most fundamental of the three, is the "post-modern" challenges to all of the theories and models described above.[68] The intellectual foundations of post-modernism are largely in the humanities, but the current debates extend well beyond issues of humanistic versus social science perspectives on world politics. They are rooted in epistemology: what can we know? Rather than addressing the validity of specific variables, levels of analysis, or methodologies, most post-modernists challenge the premise that the social world constitutes an objective, knowable reality that is amenable to systematic description and analysis.

Although realism has been a prime target, all existing theories and methodologies are in the cross-hairs of post-modern critics who, as Pauline Rosenau noted, "soundly and swiftly dismiss international political economy, realism (and neorealism), regime theory, game theory, rational actor models, integration theory, transnational approaches, world system analysis and the liberal tradition in general." [69] Nor are any of the conventional methodologies employed by political scientists or diplomatic historians spared.

Some versions of post-modernism label "evidence" and "truth" as meaningless concepts, and they are critical of categories, classification, generalization, and conclusions. Nor is there any objective language by which knowledge can be transmitted; the choice of language unjustifiably grants privileged positions to one perspective or another. Thus, the task of the observer is to deconstruct "texts" (everything is a "text"). Each one creates a unique "reading" of the matter under consideration, none can ultimately be deemed superior to any other, and there are no guidelines for choosing among them.

Taken at face value, the ability of these post-modernist perspectives to shed light on the central issues of world affairs seems problematic, and thus their contributions to either political science or diplomatic history would appear to be quite modest. Indeed, they appear to undermine the foundations of both undertakings, eliminating conventional research methods and aspirations for the cumulation of knowledge. Moreover, if one rejects the feasibility of research standards because they necessarily "privilege" some theories or methodologies, does that not also rule out judgments of works by Holocaust deniers or of conspiracy buffs who write, for example, about the Kennedy assassination or the Pearl Harbor attack?

Even more moderate versions of post-modernism are skeptical of theories and methods based on reason and Western logic, but works of this genre have occasionally offered insightful critiques of conventional theories, methodologies, and concepts. [70] The proclivity of more than a few political scientists for reifying a false image of the "scientific method" and for overlooking the pervasiveness of less elegant methodologies offers an inviting target. However, such thoughtful critical analyses are certainly not the unique province of post-modern authors; critiques of naive perspectives on scientific methods, for example, have abounded in political science and history journals for several decades.

Finally, most post-modernists are highly critical of other approaches because they have failed to come up with viable solutions for mankind's most pressing problems, including war, poverty, and oppression. Though some progress has been made on all these fronts, not even a modern-day Pangloss would declare victory on any of them. But what does post-modernist nihilism offer along these lines? Jarvis makes the point nicely:

> In what sense, however, can this approach [post-modernism] be at all adequate for the subject of International Relations? What, for example, do the literary devices of irony and textuality say to Somalian refugees who flee from famine and warlords or to Ethiopian rebels who fight in the desert plains against a government in Addis Ababa? How does the notion of textual deconstruction speak to Serbs, Croats, and Muslims who fight one another among the ruins of the former Yugoslavia? How do totalitarian narratives or logocentric binary logic feature in the deliberation of policy bureaucrats or in negotiations over international trade or the formulation of international law? Should those concerned with human rights or those who take it upon themselves to study relationships between nation-states begin by contemplating epistemological fiats and ontological disputes? [71]

Quite aside from the emptiness of its message for those with a concern to improving the human condition, the stylistic wretchedness of most post-modern prose ensures that it will have scant impact on the real world.

CONCLUSION

The study of international relations and foreign policy has always been an eclectic undertaking, with extensive borrowing from disciplines other than political science and history.[72] At the most general level, the primary differences today tend to be between two broad approaches. Analysts of the first school focus on the structure of the international system, often borrowing from economics for models, analogies, insights, and metaphors, with an emphasis on *rational preferences and strategy* and how these tend to be shaped and constrained by the structure of the international system. Decision-making analysts, meanwhile, display a concern for internal political processes and tend to borrow from psychology and social psychology in order to understand better the *limits and barriers* to information processing and rational choice. For many purposes both approaches are necessary and neither is sufficient. Neglect of the system structure and its constraints may result in analyses that depict policymakers as relatively free agents with an almost unrestricted menu of choices, limited only by the scope of their ambitions and the resources at their disposal. At worst, this type of analysis can degenerate into Manichean explanations that depict foreign policies of the "bad guys" as the external manifestation of inherently flawed leaders or domestic structures, whereas the "good guys" only react from necessity.

Conversely, neglect of foreign policy decision making not only leaves one unable to explain fully the dynamics of international relations, but many important aspects of a nation's external behavior will be inexplicable. Advocates of the realist model have often argued its superiority for understanding the "high" politics of deterrence, containment, alliances, crises, and wars, if not necessarily for "low" politics. But there are several rejoinders to this line of reasoning. First, the low politics of trade, currencies, and other issues that are usually sensitive to domestic pressures are becoming an increasingly important element of international relations. The George W. Bush administration came into office vowing to replace the "mushy" policies of its predecessor with "hard-headed realism" based on self-defined national interests. Yet its actions have shown a consistent willingness to subordinate those interests to those of such favored domestic constituencies as the energy, steel, and soft lumber industries and the National Rifle Association. Second, the growing literature on the putative domain par excellence of realism, including deterrence, crises, and wars, raises substantial doubts about the universal validity of the realist model even for these issues.[73] Finally, exclusive reliance on realist models and their assumptions of rationality may lead to unwarranted complacency about dangers in the international system. Nuclear weapons and other features of the system have no doubt contributed to the "long peace" between major powers.[74] At the same time, however, a narrow focus on power balances, "correlations of forces," and other features of the international system will result in neglect of dangers—for example, the command, communication, control, intelligence problem or inadequate information processing—that can only be identified and analyzed by a decision-making perspective.[75]

At a very general level, this conclusion parallels that drawn three decades ago by the foremost contemporary proponent of modern realism: The third image (system structure) is necessary for understanding the context of international behavior, whereas the first and second images (decision makers and domestic political processes) are needed to understand dynamics within the system.[76] But to acknowledge the existence of various levels of analysis is not enough. *What* the investigator wants to explain and the *level of specificity and comprehensiveness* to be sought should determine which level(s) of analysis are relevant and necessary. In this connection, it is essential to distinguish between two different dependent variables: foreign policy decisions by states, on the one hand, and the outcomes of policy and interactions between two or more states, on the other. Political scientists studying international relations are increasingly disciplining their use of multiple levels of analysis in studying outcomes that cannot be adequately explained via only a single level of analysis.[77]

A renowned diplomatic historian asserted that most theories of international relations flunked a critical test by failing to forecast the end of the Cold War.[78] The end of the Cold War has also led some theorists to look outside the social sciences and humanities for appropriate metaphors and models, but these are beyond the scope of the present essay.[79] This conclusion speculates on the related question of how well the theories discussed above might help political scientists and historians understand global relations in the post–Cold War world. Dramatic events since the late 1980s have posed serious challenges to several of the system-level theories, but we should be wary of writing premature obituaries for any of them, or engaging in "naive (single case) falsification." Further, in 2002, only a little more than a decade after disintegration of the Soviet Union and less than a year after the 9/11 terrorist attacks, some caution about declaring that major events and trends are irreversible seems warranted.

The global society/complex interdependence/liberal institutionalism theories have fared relatively better than either structural realism or various Marxist theories. For example, creation of the World Trade Organization and progress toward economic unification of Europe, although not without detours and setbacks, would appear to provide significant support for the view that, even in an anarchic world, major powers may find that it is in their self-interest to establish and maintain institutions for cooperating and overcoming the constraints of the "relative gains" problem. Woodrow Wilson's thesis that a world of democratic nations will be more peaceful has also enjoyed some revival, at least among analysts who attach significance to the fact that democratic nations have been able to establish "zones of peace" among themselves. Wilson's diagnosis that self-determination also supports peace may be correct in the abstract, but universal application of that principle is neither feasible nor desirable, if only because it would result in immense bloodshed; the peaceful divorces of Norway and Sweden in 1905 and of the Czech Republic and Slovakia in 1992 are unfortunately not the norm.[80] Although it appears that economic interests have come to dominate nationalist, ethnic, or religious passions among most industrial democracies, the evidence is far less assuring in other areas, including parts of the former Soviet Union, Central Europe, the Middle East, South Asia, and Africa.

Recent events appear to have created an especially difficult challenge for structural realism; although it provides a parsimonious and elegant theory, its deficiencies are likely to become more rather than less apparent in the post–Cold War world. Its weaknesses in dealing with questions of system change and in specifying policy preferences other than survival and security are likely to be magnified. Moreover, whereas classical realism includes some attractive prescriptive features (caution, humility, warnings against mistaking one's preferences for the moral laws of the universe), neorealism is an especially weak source of policy-relevant theory. Indeed, some of the prescriptions put forward by neorealists, such as letting Germany join the nuclear club or urging Ukraine to keep its nuclear weapons, seem reckless.[81] In addition to European economic cooperation, specific events that seem inexplicable by structural realism include Soviet acquiescence in the collapse of its empire and peaceful transformation of the system structure. The persistence of NATO, more than a decade after the disappearance of the threat that gave rise to its creation, has also confounded realist predictions that it would not long survive the end of the Cold War; in 1993, Waltz asserted: "NATO's days are not numbered, but its years are."[82] The problem cannot be resolved by definition: asserting that NATO is no longer an alliance because its original adversary has collapsed. Nor can the theory be saved by a tautology: claiming that the Cold War ended, exactly as predicted by structural realism, "only when the bipolar structure of the world disappeared."[83] These developments are especially telling because structural realism is explicitly touted as a theory of major powers. Although proponents of realism are not ready to concede that events of the past decade have raised some serious questions about its validity, as distinguished a realist is Robert Tucker has characterized structural realism as "more questionable than ever."[84]

More importantly, even though the possibility of war among major powers cannot be dismissed and proliferation may place nuclear weapons into the hands of leaders with little stake in maintaining the status quo, national interests and even conceptions of national security have increasingly come to be defined in ways that transcend the power balances that lie at the core of structural realism. The expanded agenda of national interests, combined with the trend toward greater democracy in many parts of the world, suggests that we are entering an era in which the relative potency of systemic and domestic forces in shaping and constraining international affairs is moving toward the latter. The frequency of internal wars that have become international conflicts—the list includes but is not limited to Somalia, Haiti, Bosnia, Afghanistan, Rwanda, Congo, and several parts of the former Yugoslavia—suggests that "failed states" may compete with international aggression as the major source of war.[85] Such issues as trade, immigration, the environment, and others, can be expected to enhance the impact of domestic actors—including legislatures, public opinion, and ethnic, religious, economic, and perhaps even regional interest groups—while reducing the ability of executives to dominate the process on the grounds, so frequently invoked during times of war and crises, that the adept pursuit of national interests requires secrecy, flexibility, and the ability to act with speed on the basis of classified information.

If that prognosis is anywhere near the mark, it should enhance the value of decision-making models, some of which were discussed above, that encompass domestic political processes. Whatever their strengths and weaknesses, these models seem less vulnerable to such major events as the end of the Cold War. Most policymaking will continue to be made by leaders in small groups, with supports and constraints from bureaucracies. Moreover, even if nation-states are having to share the global center stage with a plethora of non-state actors, decision-making concepts such as information processing, satisficing, bureaucratic politics, groupthink, and many of the others described above can be applied equally well to the World Trade Organization, NATO, OPEC, and the like.

Which of these models and approaches are likely to be of interest and utility to the diplomatic historian? Clearly there is no one answer: political scientists are unable to agree on a single multilevel approach to international relations and foreign policy; thus they are hardly in a position to offer a single recommendation to historians. In the absence of the often-sought but always-elusive unified theory of human behavior that could provide a model for all seasons and all reasons, one must ask at least one further question: a model for what purpose? For example, in some circumstances, such as research on major international crises, it may be important to obtain systematic evidence on the beliefs and other intellectual baggage that key policymakers bring to their deliberations. Some of the approaches described above should prove very helpful in this respect. Conversely, there are many other research problems for which the historian would quite properly decide that this type of analysis requires far more effort than could possibly be justified by the benefits to be gained.

Of the systemic approaches described here, little needs to be said about classical realism because its main features, as well as its strengths and weaknesses, are familiar to most diplomatic historians. Those who focus on security issues can hardly neglect its central premises and concepts. Waltz's version of structural realism is likely to have more limited appeal to historians, especially if they take seriously his doubts about being able to incorporate foreign policy into it. It may perhaps serve to raise consciousness about the importance of the systemic context within which international relations take place, but that may not be a major gain; after all, such concepts as "balance of power" have long been a standard part of the diplomatic historian's vocabulary.

The global society/complex interdependence/liberal institutionalism models will be helpful to historians with an interest in the evolution of the international system and with the growing disjuncture between demands on states and their ability to meet them, the "sovereignty gap." One need not be very venturesome to predict that this gap will grow rather than narrow. Historians of international and transnational organizations are also likely to find useful concepts and insights in these models.

It is much less clear that the Marxist/world system/dependency theories will provide useful new insights to historians. If one has difficulty in accepting certain assumptions as *true by definition*—for example, that there has been and is today a single "world capitalist system"—then the kinds of analyses that follow are likely to seem flawed. Most diplomatic historians also would have difficulty in accepting models that relegate the state to a secondary role. Finally, whereas proponents of GS/CI/LI models can point with considerable justification to current events and trends that would appear to make them more rather than less relevant in the future, supporters of the M/WS/D models have a much more difficult task in this respect. The declining legitimacy of Marxism-Leninism as the basis for government does not, of course, necessarily invalidate social science theories that draw upon Marx, Lenin, and their intellectual heirs. It might, however, at least be the occasion for second thoughts, especially because Marx and his followers have always placed a heavy emphasis on an intimate connection between theory and practice.

Although the three decision-making models sometimes include jargon that may be jarring to the historian, many of the underlying concepts are familiar. Much of diplomatic history has traditionally focused on the decisions, actions, and interactions of national leaders who operate in group contexts, such as cabinets or ad hoc advisory groups, and who draw upon the resources of such bureaucracies as foreign and defense ministries or the armed forces. The three types of models described above typically draw heavily upon psychology, social psychology, organizational theory, and other social sciences; thus for the historian they open some important windows to these fields. For example, theories and concepts of "information processing" by individuals, groups, and organizations should prove very useful.

Decision-making models may also appeal to diplomatic historians for another important reason. Political scientists who are accustomed to working with fairly accessible "hard" information such as figures on gross national products, defense budgets, battle casualties, alliance commitments, UN votes, trade, investments, and the like, often feel that the data requirements of decision-making models are excessive. This is precisely the area in which the historian has a decided comparative advantage, for the relevant data are usually to be found in the paper or electronic trails left by policymakers, and they are most likely to be unearthed by archival research. For purposes of organization this essay has focused on some major distinctions between theoretical perspectives. This should not be read, however, as ruling out efforts to build bridges between them, as urged in several recent essays.[86]

Perhaps the appropriate point on which to conclude this essay is to reverse the question posed earlier: ask not only what can the political scientist contribute to the diplomatic historian but ask also what can the diplomatic historian contribute to the political scientist. At the very least political scientists could learn a great deal about the validity of their own models if historians would use them and offer critical assessments of their strengths and limitations.

A NOTE ON SOURCES

Contributions to and debates about theories of international relations take place within both books and journals. While it is impossible to forecast the books that may, in the future, be useful in this respect, it may be helpful to identify some journals that are likely to be especially fruitful sources of theoretical developments and controversies. This list is limited to U.S.-based journals. Many others published in Europe, Japan, Israel, South Korea, and elsewhere may also include relevant articles.

The top mainline political science journals include *American Political Science Review, Journal of Politics,* and *American Journal of Political Science. APSR* has published some major articles in international relations and foreign policy, especially in recent years, and each issue has a section devoted to book reviews. However, all three of these journals tend to place greater emphasis on American politics. That is especially true of *JP* and *AJPS.*

International Organization, International Security, International Studies Quarterly, Journal of Conflict Resolution, Security Studies, and *World Politics* are the most important sources of articles that bear on theoretical issues. Many of the authors are political scientists, but diplomatic historians, economists, sociologists, and other social scientists are also frequently represented on their pages. These journals are indispensable for anyone interested in following theoretical developments and debates. Of the six, only *World Politics* regularly features extended book reviews.

Foreign Affairs and *Foreign Policy* are largely focused on current affairs, but on occasion essays in these journals have been authored by major contributors to current debates about theoretical issues. Both include book reviews, but they are often relatively brief.

The best source of book reviews is *International Studies Reviews,* which, along with *International Studies Quarterly,* is a publication of the International Studies Association. It features both extended review essays and shorter critical assessments of single books. *ISR* regularly includes reviews of books published in languages other than English.

NOTES

1. See, for example, John Lewis Gaddis, "Expanding the Data Base: Historians, Political Scientists, and the Enrichment of Security Studies," *International Security* 12 (Summer 1987): 3– 21; John English, "The Second Time Around: Political Scientists Writing History," *Canadian Historical Review* 57 (March 1986): 1–16; Jack S. Levy, "Domestic Politics and War," *Journal of*

Interdisciplinary History 18 (Spring 1988): 653–73; Deborah Welch Larson, *Origins of Containment: A Psychological Explanation* (Princeton, NJ, 1985); Timothy Lomperis, *The War Everyone Lost—and Won: America's Intervention in Viet Nam's Twin Struggles* (Washington, DC, 1987); Barry Posen, *The Sources of Military Doctrine: France, Britain, and Germany between the World Wars* (Ithaca, NY, 1984); Paul Gordon Lauren, ed., *Diplomacy: New Approaches to History, Theory, and Policy* (New York, 1979); Richard R. Neustadt and Ernest R. May, *Thinking in Time: The Use of History for Decision-Makers* (New York, 1986); Irving L. Janis, *Crucial Decisions: Leadership in Policymaking and Crisis Management* (New York, 1989); K. J. Holsti, *The State, War, and the State of War* (Cambridge, 1996); Graham Allison and Philip Zelikow, *Essence of Decision: Explaining the Cuban Missile Crisis,* 2nd edition (New York, 1999); Douglas C. Foyle, *Counting the Public In: Presidents, Public Opinion, and Foreign Policy* (New York, 1999); Colin Elman and Miriam Fendius Elman, eds., *Bridges and Boundaries: Historians, Political Scientists and the Study of International Relations* (Cambridge, 2000); G. John Ikenberry, *After Victory: Institutions, Strategic Restraint, and Rebuilding of Order after Major Wars* (Princeton, NJ, 2001).

2. Robert Gilpin, *Change and War in World Politics* (Cambridge, UK, 1981).

3. Stanley Hoffmann, "An American Social Science: International Relations," *Daedalus* 106 (Summer 1977): 54.

4. The British meteorologist Lewis Fry Richardson is generally regarded as the pioneer of mathematical approaches to international relations. See his *Statistics of Deadly Quarrels* (Pittsburgh, 1960); and his *Arms and Insecurity* (Chicago, 1960). These are summarized for non-mathematicians in Anatol Rappaport, "L. F. Richardson's Mathematical Theory of War," *Journal of Conflict Resolution* 1 (September 1957): 249–99. For more recent effort see Bruce Bueno de Mesquita, *The War Trap* (New Haven, CT, 1981); idem., "The War Trap Revisited: A Revised Expected Utility Model," *American Political Science Review* 79 (March 1985): 156–77; Bruce Bueno de Mesquita and David Lalman, *War and Reason* (New Haven, CT, 1992); a series of articles by Robert Powell in *American Political Science Review;* Michael Brown et al., eds., *Rational Choice and Security Studies: Stephen Walt and His Critics* (Cambridge, 2000).

5. Among the works that best represent their realist perspectives are E. H. Carr, *Twenty Years' Crisis* (London, 1939); Nicholas Spykman, *America's Strategy in World Politics: The United States and the Balance of Power* (New York, 1942); Hans J. Morgenthau, *Politics among Nations: The Struggle for Power and Peace,* 5th ed. (New York, 1973); John Herz, *International Politics in the Atomic Age* (New York, 1959); Hedley Bull, *The Anarchical Society: A Study of Order in World Politics* (London, 1977); Raymond Aron, *Peace and War* (Garden City, NY, 1966); Martin Wight, "The Balance of Power and International Order," in *The Bases of International Order: Essays in Honor of C. A. W. Manning,* ed. Alan James (London, 1973), 85–115; Arnold Wolfers, *Discord and Collaboration* (Baltimore, 1962); Norman A. Graebner, *America as a World Power: A Realist Appraisal from Wilson to Reagan* (Wilmington, DE, 1984); George F. Kennan, *American Diplomacy, 1900–1950* (Chicago, 1951); Walter Lippmann, *U.S. Foreign Policy: Shield of the Republic* (Boston, 1943); Reinhold Niebuhr, *The Children of Light and the Children of Darkness* (New York, 1945).

6. Morgenthau, *Politics,* 5, 6.

7. Stephen Krasner, *Defending the National Interest: Raw Materials Investment and U.S. Foreign Policy* (Princeton, NJ, 1978), 33.

8. For an excellent overview of the concept of system, see Robert Jervis, *System Effects: Complexity in Political and Social Life* (Princeton, NJ, 1997).

9. Inis L. Claude, *Power and International Relations* (New York, 1962); James N. Rosenau, "National Interest," *International Encyclopedia of the Social Sciences* (New York, 1968), 11: 34–40; Alexander L. George and Robert Keohane, "The Concept of National Interests: Uses and Limitations," in *Presidential Decision-Making in Foreign Policy: The Effective Use of Information and Advice,* ed. Alexander George (Boulder, CO, 1980), 217–37; Ernst B. Haas, "The Balance of Power: Prescription, Concept or Propaganda," *World Politics* 5 (July 1953): 442–77; Dina A. Zinnes, "An Analytical Study of the Balance of Power," *Journal of Peace Research* 4, no. 3 (1967): 270–88.

10. Morgenthau, *Politics,* 5.

11. Morton Kaplan, *System and Process in International Politics* (New York, 1957).

12. Richard Rosecrance, *Action and Reaction in International Politics* (Boston, 1963); idem., "Bipolarity, Multipolarity, and the Future," *Journal of Conflict Resolution* 10 (September 1966): 314–27; Kenneth Waltz, "The Stability of a

Bipolar World," *Daedalus* 93 (Summer 1964): 881–909; J. David Singer, "Inter-Nation Influence: A Formal Model," *American Political Science Review* 57 (June 1963): 420–30; Bruce M. Russett, "Toward a Model of Competitive International Politics," *Journal of Politics* 25 (May 1963): 226–47; Karl Deutsch and J. David Singer, "Multipolar Power Systems and International Stability," *World Politics* 16 (April 1964): 390–406; Andrew Scott, *The Functioning of the International Political System* (New York, 1967).

13. Kenneth Waltz, *Theory of International Politics* (Reading, MA, 1979); idem., *Man, the State, and War* (New York, 1959).

14. For a debate on whether neorealism may be extended to cover foreign policies as well as international politics, see Colin Elman, "Horses for Courses: Why *Not* Neorealist Theories of Foreign Policy," *Security Studies* 6 (Autumn 1996): 7–53; and a rejoinder by Waltz, "International Politics Is Not Foreign Policy," in the same issue of *Security Studies*, pp. 54–57.

15. Waltz, *Theory,* 82–101.

16. Waltz, "The Myth of National Interdependence," in *The International Corporation: A Symposium,* ed. Charles P. Kindleberger (Cambridge, MA, 1970), 205–23; idem., "The Spread of Nuclear Weapons: More May Be Better," *Adelphi Papers,* no. 171 (1981).

17. See especially Robert Keohane, ed., *Neorealism and Its Critics* (New York, 1986); David A. Baldwin, ed., *Neorealism and Neoliberalism: The Contemporary Debate* (New York: 1993); Charles W. Kegley, Jr., ed., *Controversies in International Relations Theory: Realism and the Neoliberal Challenge* (New York, 1995); John A. Vasquez, *The Power of Power Politics* (New Brunswick, NJ, 1988); Yale H. Ferguson and Richard W. Mansbach, *The Elusive Quest: Theory and International Politics* (Columbia, SC, 1988). A useful post–Cold War appraisal of realism may be found in "Realism: Restatements and Renewal," *Security Studies* 5 (Spring 1996): ix–xx, 3–423. The journal *International Security* is an indispensable source for the continuing debates on realism.

18. Gilpin, *War and Change,* 10–11.

19. Ibid., chap. 4. Gilpin's thesis appears similar in a number of respects to Paul Kennedy, *The Rise and Fall of the Great Powers: Economic Change and Military Conflict from 1500 to 2000* (New York, 1987).

20. Robert Keohane and Joseph S. Nye, Jr., *Power and Interdependence* (Boston, 1977); Edward Morse, *Modernization and the Transformation of In-*ternational Relations* (New York, 1976); James N. Rosenau, *The Study of Global Interdependence* (London, 1980); Robert Keohane, *After Hegemony* (Princeton, NJ, 1984); Richard Mansbach and John Vasquez, *In Search of Theory: A New Paradigm for Global Politics* (New York, 1981); James N. Rosenau, *Turbulence in World Politics* (Princeton, NJ, 1990). The journal *International Organization* is an indispensable source. See especially the 50th anniversary issue edited by Peter Katzenstein, Robert Keohane, and Stephen Krasner.

21. For an excellent overview of the challenges of creating effective yet non-oppressive institutions—the "Governance Dilemma"—to cope with such issues, see Robert O. Keohane, "Governance in a Partially Globalized World," *American Political Science Review* 95 (March 2001): 1–13.

22. Rosenau, "National Interest," 39. A more recent statement of this view may be found in Richard Rosecrance, *The Rise of the Trading State* (New York, 1986); Yale Ferguson and Richard Mansbach, *Polities: Authority, Identities, and Change* (Columbia, SC, 1996). See also John H. Herz, "The Rise and Demise of the Territorial State," *World Politics* 9 (July 1957): 473–93; and his reconsideration in "The Territorial State Revisited: Reflections on the Future of the Nation-State," *Polity* 1 (Fall 1968): 12–34.

23. James Cockroft, Andre Gunder Frank, and Dale L. Johnson, *Dependence and Underdevelopment* (New York, 1972); Immanuel Wallerstein, *The Modern World-System* (New York, 1974); idem., "The Rise and Future Demise of the World Capitalist System: Concepts for Comparative Analysis," *Comparative Studies in Society and History* 16 (September 1974): 387–415. Debates among advocates of these models are illustrated in Robert A. Denemark and Kenneth O. Thomas, "The Brenner-Wallerstein Debates," *International Studies Quarterly* 32 (March 1988): 47–66.

24. Wallerstein, "Rise and Future Demise," 390.

25. Tony Smith, "The Underdevelopment of Development Literature: The Case of Dependency Theory," *World Politics* 31 (January 1979): 247–88; Aristide Zolberg, "Origins of the Modern World System: A Missing Link," ibid., 33 (January 1981): 253–81.

26. Wallerstein, "Rise and Future Demise," 401.

27. Ricardo Hausmann, "Prisoners of Geography," *Foreign Policy* (January–February 2001); 44–53; David Landes, *The Wealth and Poverty of Nations* (New York, 1999).

28. Samuel Huntington has been a leading proponent of a cultural perspective on world affairs. Huntington, *The Clash of Civilizations and the Remaking of the World Order* (New York, 1996); Lawrence Harrison and Samuel Huntington, eds., *Culture Matters: How Values Shape Human Progress* (New York, 2000).

29. For example, the writings of Karl Haushofer were used (or misused) by the Nazis to justify German expansion into the "Eurasian Heartland"; and in *The Geography of Intellect,* Stefen Possony and Nathaniel Weyl propounded the racist thesis that intelligence is related to climate—the warmer the climate from which various racial groups originated, the lower their intellectual capacities.

30. This example is drawn from a study of the philosophical bases of constructivism, John R. Searle, *The Construction of Social Reality* (New York, 1995), 37–43.

31. *International Organization* 46 (Spring 1992): 391–425.

32. Ole R. Holsti, "Cognitive Dynamics and Images of the Enemy: Dulles and Russia," in *Enemies in Politics,* ed. David J. Finlay, Ole R. Holsti, and Richard R. Fagen (Chicago, 1967).

33. Stephen G. Brooks and William C. Wohlforth, "Power, Globalization and the End of the Cold War," *International Security* 25 (Winter 2000–01): 5–53; Jeffrey T. Checkel, *Ideas and International Political Change* (New Haven, CT, 1997); Robert D. English, *Russia and the Idea of the West: Gorbachev, Intellectuals and the End of the Cold War* (New York, 2000).

34. Some representative works include Alexander Wendt, *Social Theory of International Politics* (Cambridge, UK, 1999); Nicholas Onuf, *World of Our Making: Rules and Rule in Social Theory and International Relations* (Columbia, SC, 1989); Martha Finnemore, *National Interests in International Society* (Ithaca, NY, 1996); Peter Katzenstein, ed., *The Culture of National Security* (New York, 1996); Audie Klotz, *Norms in International Relations* (Ithaca, NY, 1995); Yosef Lapid and Friedrich Kratochwil, eds., *The Return of Culture and Identity in IR Theory* (Boulder, CO, 1996). Thoughtful but contrasting assessments may be found in adjoining articles in *International Security* 23 (Summer 1998): Michael Desch,

"Culture Clash: Assessing the Importance of Ideas in Security Studies," 141–70; and Ted Hopf, "The Promise of Constructivism in International Relations Theory," 171–200.

35. Kenneth Boulding, "National Images and International Systems," *Journal of Conflict Resolution* 3 (June 1959): 120. See also Robert Jervis, *The Logic of Images in International Relations* (Princeton, NJ, 1970), and some of the decision-making approaches described in the next section.

36. The debate was triggered by Michael Doyle, "Liberalism and World Politics," *American Political Science Review* 80 (December 1986): 1151–70. Some important contributions to the debate include: Bruce Russett, *Grasping the Democratic Peace* (Princeton, NJ, 1993); John Owen, *Liberal Peace, Liberal War* (Ithaca, NY, 1997); Spencer Weart, *Never at War* (New Haven, CT, 1998); Miriam Fendius Elman, ed., *Paths to Peace: Is Democracy the Answer?* (Cambridge, MA, 1997); James Lee Ray, *Democracy and International Conflict* (Columbia, SC, 1995); Edward Mansfield and Jack Snyder, "Democratization and the Danger of War," *International Security* 20 (Summer 1995): 5–38.

37. Kenneth Waltz, "Structural Realism after the Cold War," *International Security* 25 (Summer 2000): 13.

38. Michael Mandelbaum, "Foreign Policy as Social Work," *Foreign Affairs* 75 (February 1996): 16–32.

39. There are also models that link types of polities with foreign policy. Two of the more prominent twentieth-century versions—the Leninist and Wilsonian—have been effectively criticized by Waltz in *Man, the State, and War.* Although space limitations preclude a discussion here, for some research along these lines see, among others, Rudolph J. Rummel, "Libertarianism and Violence," *Journal of Conflict Resolution* 27 (March 1983): 27–71; Michael Doyle, "Liberalism and World Politics;" idem., "Kant, Liberal Legacies, and Foreign Affairs," *Philosophy and Public Affairs* 12 (Winter 1983): 205–35.

40. Chester Barnard, *Functions of the Executive* (Cambridge, MA, 1938); Herbert Simon, *Administrative Behavior: A Study of Decision-Making Processes in Administrative Organization* (New York, 1957); James G. March and Herbert Simon, *Organizations* (New York, 1958).

41. Henry A. Kissinger, "Conditions of World Order," *Daedalus* 95 (Spring 1960): 503–

29; Allison and Zelikow, *Essence;* Morton Halperin, *Bureaucratic Politics and Foreign Policy* (Washington, DC, 1974).

42. The literature is huge. See, for example, Samuel R. Williamson, Jr., *The Politics of Grand Strategy: Britain and France Prepare for War, 1904–1914* (Cambridge, MA, 1969); Posen, *Sources of Military Doctrine.*

43. Wilensky, *Organizational Intelligence* (New York, 1967); Theodore Lowi, *The End of Liberalism: Ideology, Policy and the Crisis of Public Authority* (New York, 1969).

44. Charles F. Hermann, "Some Consequences of Crises Which Limit the Viability of Organizations," *Administrative Science Quarterly* 8 (June 1963): 61–82; Allison and Zelikow, *Essence;* Richard Neustadt, *Alliance Politics* (New York, 1970); Scott Sagan, "Nuclear Alerts and Crisis Management," *International Security* 9 (Spring 1985): 99–139.

45. Robert Rothstein, *Planning, Prediction, and Policy-Making in Foreign Affairs: Theory and Practice* (Boston, 1972); Stephen D. Krasner, "Are Bureaucracies Important? (Or Allison Wonderland)" *Foreign Policy* 7 (Summer 1972): 159–70; Robert J. Art, "Bureaucratic Politics and American Foreign Policy: A Critique," *Policy Sciences* 4 (December 1973): 467–90; Desmond J. Ball, "The Blind Men and the Elephant: A Critique of Bureaucratic Politics Theory," *Australian Outlook* 28 (April 1974).

46. Alexander L. George, "The Case for Multiple Advocacy in Making Foreign Policy," *American Political Science Review* 66 (September 1972): 751–85, 791–95.

47. David A. Welch and James G. Blight, "The Eleventh Hour of the Cuban Missile Crisis: An Introduction to the ExComm Transcripts," *International Security* 12 (Winter 1987/ 88): 5–29; McGeorge Bundy and James G. Blight, "October 27, 1962: Transcripts of the Meetings of the ExComm," ibid., 30–92; James G. Blight and David A. Welch, *On the Brink: Americans and Soviets Reexamine the Cuban Missile Crisis* (New York, 1989); Ernest R. May and Philip Zelikow, *The Kennedy Tapes* (Cambridge, MA, 1997).

48. Irving L. Janis, *Victims of Groupthink: A Psychological Study of Foreign Policy Decisions and Fiascos* (Boston, 1972); idem., *Groupthink: Psychological Studies of Policy Decisions and Fiascos* (Boston, 1982); Charles F. Hermann and Margaret G. Hermann, "Who Makes Foreign Policy Decisions and How: An Empirical Inquiry," *International Studies Quarterly* 33 (December 1989): 361–88.

49. Solomon Asch, "Effects of Group Pressures upon Modification and Distortion of Judgement," in *Group Dynamics: Research and Theory,* ed. Dorwin Cartwright and Alvin Zander (Evanston, IL, 1953), 151–62.

50. Janis, *Victims;* idem., *Groupthink.* See also Philip Tetlock, "Identifying Victims of Groupthink from Public Statements of Decision Makers," *Journal of Personality and Social Psychology* 37 (August 1979): 1314–24; Paul 't Hart, Eric Stern, and B. Sundelius, *Beyond Groupthink* (Stockholm, 1995).

51. Janis, *Groupthink,* 260–76; idem., *Crucial Decisions,* 231–64.

52. For a review of the vast literature see Robert Abelson and A. Levi, "Decision Making and Decision Theory," in *Handbook of Social Psychology,* 3rd ed., vol. 1, ed. Gardner Lindzey and Elliot Aronson (New York, 1985). The relevance of psychological models and evidence for international relations are most fully discussed in Robert Jervis, *Perception and Misperception in International Politics* (Princeton, NJ, 1976); Robert Axelrod, *The Structure of Decision: The Cognitive Maps of Political Elites* (Princeton, NJ, 1976); Philip Tetlock, "Social Psychology and World Politics," in *The Handbook of Social Psychology,* 4th ed., ed. Daniel Gilbert, Susan Fiske, and Gardner Lindzey (Boston, 1998); Jerel Rosati, "The Power of Human Cognition in the Study of World Politics," *International Studies Review* 2 (Fall 2000). 45–75.

53. See, for example, Harold Lasswell, *Psychopathology and Politics* (Chicago, 1931).

54. March and Simon, *Organizations,* 113.

55. Simon, *Administrative Behavior,* 198.

56. Amos Tversky and Daniel Kahneman, "The Framing of Decisions and the Psychology of Choice," *Science* 211 (January 30, 1981): 453–58; Daniel Kahneman, Paul Slovic, and Amos Tversky, *Judgment under Uncertainty: Heuristics and Biases* (Cambridge, UK, 1982).

57. Irving L. Janis and Leon Mann, *Decision Making: A Psychological Analysis of Conflict, Choice, and Commitment* (New York, 1977); Richard Ned Lebow, *Between Peace and War* (Baltimore, 1981); Yaacov Vertzberger, *The World in Their Minds* (Stanford, CA, 1990).

58. Donald Kinder and J. R. Weiss, "In Lieu of Rationality: Psychological Perspectives

on Foreign Policy," *Journal of Conflict Resolution* 22 (December 1978): 707–35.

59. George F. Kennan, *The Cloud of Danger: Current Realities of American Foreign Policy* (Boston, 1978), 87–88.

60. Allison, *Essence;* Jervis, *Perception.*

61. Charles F. Hermann, *International Crises: Insights from Behavioral Research* (New York, 1972); Margaret G. Hermann, "Indicators of Stress in Policy-Makers during Foreign Policy Crises," *Political Psychology* 1 (March 1979): 27–46; Ole R. Holsti, *Crisis, Escalation, War* (Montreal, 1972); Ole R. Holsti and Alexander L. George, "The Effects of Stress on the Performance of Foreign Policy-Makers," *Political Science Annual* 6 (Indianapolis, 1975).

62. Janis and Mann, *Decision Making,* 3.

63. Margaret G. Hermann, "Explaining Foreign Policy Behavior Using Personal Characteristics of Political Leaders," *International Studies Quarterly* 24 (March 1980): 746.

64. Nathan Leites, *The Operational Code of the Politburo* (New York, 1951); Alexander L. George, "The 'Operational Code': A Neglected Approach to the Study of Political Leaders and Decision Making," *International Studies Quarterly* 13 (June 1969): 190–222; Stephen G. Walker, "The Motivational Foundations of Political Belief Systems: A Re-Analysis of the Operational Code Construct," *International Studies Quarterly* 27 (June 1983): 179–202; Stephen Walker, Mark Shafer, and Michael Young, "Presidential Operational Codes and Foreign Policy Conflict in the Post–Cold War World," *Journal of Conflict Resolution* 43 (1999): 610–25.

65. Integrative simplicity, on the other hand, is characterized by simple responses, gross distinctions, rigidity, and restricted information usage.

66. Peter Suedfeld and Philip Tetlock, "Integrative Complexity of Communications in International Crises," *Journal of Conflict Resolution* 21 (March 1977): 169–86; Philip Tetlock, "Integrative Complexity of American and Soviet Foreign Policy Rhetoric: A Time Series Analysis," *Journal of Personality and Social Psychology* 49 (December 1985): 1565–85; Karen Guttieri, Michael Wallace, and Peter Suedfeld, "The Integrative Complexity of American Decision Makers in the Cuban Missile Crisis," *Journal of Conflict Resolution* 39 (December 1995): 595–621.

67. Alexander L. George and Richard Smoke, *Deterrence in American Foreign Policy: Theory and Practice* (New York, 1974); Richard Smoke, *Escalation* (Cambridge, MA, 1977); Glenn H. Snyder and Paul Diesing, *Conflict among Nations: Bargaining, Decision Making, and System Structure in International Crises* (Princeton, NJ, 1977). Useful discussions on conducting theoretically relevant case studies may be found in Harry Eckstein, "Case Study and Theory in Political Science," in *Handbook of Political Science,* 9 vols., ed. Fred I. Greenstein and Nelson W. Polsby (Reading, MA, 1975), 7: 79–138; Alexander L. George, "Case Studies and Theory Development: The Method of Structured, Focused Comparison," in *Diplomacy,* ed. Lauren, 43–68; Gary King, Robert Keohane, and Sidney Verba, *Designing Social Inquiry* (Princeton, NJ, 1994).

68. This perspective is sometimes called "post-positivism" or "post-structuralism." Yosef Lapid, "The Third Debate: On the Prospects of International Theory in a Post-Positivist Era," *International Studies Quarterly* 33 (1989): 235–54; Andrew Linklater, "The Question of the Next Stage in International Relations Theory," *Millennium* 21, no. 1 (1992): 77–98; Chris Brown, "'Turtles All the Way Down': Anti-Foundationalism, Critical Theory and International Relations," *Millennium* 23, no. 2 (1994): 213–36. For overviews, see Pauline Rosenau, *Post-Modernism and the Social Sciences* (Princeton, NJ, 1992); Rosenau, "Once Again Into the Fray: International Relations Confronts the Humanities," *Millennium* (1990): 83–110; D. S. L. Jarvis, *International Relations and the Challenge of Postmodernism* (Columbia, SC, 2000).

69. Richard Ashley, "The Poverty of Neo-Realism," *International Organization* 38 (Spring 1984): 225–86. Rosenau, "Once Again," 84.

70. Prominent post-modern students of world affairs include Hayward Alker, Jim George, Richard Ashley, Michael Shapiro, James Der Derian, Christine Sylvester, and R. B. J. Walker.

71. D. S. L. Jarvis, *International Relations and the Challenge of Postmodernism* (Columbia, SC, 2000), 197–98. For both substance and clarity, reform-minded social scientists are urged to compare the writing of Ashley and his colleagues with Robert Keohane, "Governance in a Partially Globalized World," *American Political Science Review* 95 (March 2001): 1–13.

72. The classic overview of the field and the disciplines that have contributed to it is Quincy Wright, *The Study of International Relations* (New York, 1955).

73. In addition to the literature on war, crises, and deterrence already cited, see Richard Betts, *Nuclear Blackmail and Nuclear Balance* (Washington, DC, 1987); Robert Jervis, Richard Ned Lebow, and Janice G. Stein, *Psychology and Deterrence* (Baltimore, 1985); Ole R. Holsti, "Crisis Decision Making"; Jack S. Levy, "The Causes of War: A Review of Theories and Evidence," in *Behavior, Society, and Nuclear War,* vol. 1, ed. Philip E. Tetlock et al. (New York, 1989), 8–84, 209–333.

74. John Lewis Gaddis, "The Long Peace: Elements of Stability in the Postwar International System," *International Security* 10 (Spring 1986): 99–142.

75. Paul Bracken, *Command and Control of Nuclear Forces* (New Haven, CT, 1983); Bruce Blair, *Strategic Command and Control: Redefining the Nuclear Threat* (Washington, DC, 1985); Sagan, "Nuclear Alerts"; Alexander L. George, *Presidential Decision Making in Foreign Policy: The Effective Use of Information and Advice* (Boulder, CO, 1980).

76. Waltz, *Man, the State, and War,* 238.

77. See, for example, David B. Yoffie, *Power and Protectionism: Strategies of the Newly Industrializing Countries* (New York, 1983); John Odell, *U.S. International Monetary Policy: Markets, Power, and Ideas as Sources of Change* (Princeton, NJ, 1982); Jack Snyder, *The Ideology of the Offensive: Military Decision Making and the Disaster of 1914* (Ithaca, NY, 1984); Vinod K. Aggarwal, *Liberal Protectionism: The International Politics of Organized Textile Trade* (Berkeley, CA, 1985); Larson, *Origins of Containment; Posen, Sources of Military Doctrine;* Stephen Walt, *Alliances.*

78. John Lewis Gaddis, "International Relations Theory and the End of the Cold War," *International Security* 17 (Winter 1992–93): 5–58.

79. Rosenau's concept of "turbulence" is drawn from meteorology, and Gaddis finds some interesting parallels between the contemporary international system and "tectonics," a concept drawn from geology. Rosenau, *Turbulence;* and John Lewis Gaddis, "Living in Candlestick Park," *Atlantic Monthly* (April 1999): 65–74.

80. Although the concept of self-determination is generally associated with liberals, in the wake of civil wars within the former Yugoslavia, two prominent realists have suggested redrawing the map of the Balkans to reflect ethnic identities. John J. Mearsheimer and Stephen Van Evera, "Redraw the May, Stop the Killing," *New York Times* (April 19, 1999), p. A27.

81. John Mearsheimer, "Back to the Future: Instability in Europe after the Cold War," *International Security* 15 (Summer, 1990): 5–56. Rejoinders by Stanley Hoffmann, Robert Keohane, Bruce Russett, and Thomas Risse-Kappen, as well as responses by Mearsheimer, may be found in the same journal (Fall 1990): 191–99 and (Winter 1990/91): 216–22. Also, Mearsheimer, "The Case for a Ukrainian Nuclear Deterrent," *Foreign Affairs* 72 (Summer 1993): 50–66.

82. Kenneth N. Waltz, "The Emerging Structure of International Politics," *International Security* 18 (Fall 1993), 76.

83. Waltz, "Structural Realism after the Cold War," 19, 39.

84. Robert W. Tucker, "Realism and the New Consensus," *National Interest* 30 (1992–93): 33–36. See also Paul Schroeder, "Historical Reality vs. Neo-Realist Theory," *International Security* 19 (1994): 108–48.

85. Robert Kaplan, "The Coming Anarchy," *Atlantic Monthly* (February 1994): 44–76; K. J. Holsti, *The State, War, and the State of War* (Cambridge, 1996); Barbara Walter and Jack Snyder, eds., *Civil War, Insecurity, and Intervention* (New York, 1999).

86. Robert O. Keohane, "The Globalization of Informal Violence, Theories of World Politics, and the 'Liberalism of Fear,'" *Dialog-IO* (Spring 2002): 29–43; Theo Farrell, "Constructivist Security Studies: Portrait of a Research Program," *International Studies Review* 4 (Spring 2002): 49–72; Jennifer Sterling-Folker, "Realism and the Constructivist Challenge: Rejecting, Reconstructing, or Rereading," *International Studies Review* 4 (Spring 2002): 73–97.

Reading 2-3

International Relations
One World, Many Theories
Stephen M. Walt

Why should policymakers and practitioners care about the scholarly study of international affairs? Those who conduct foreign policy often dismiss academic theorists (frequently, one must admit, with good reason), but there is an inescapable link between the abstract world of theory and the real world of policy. We need theories to make sense of the blizzard of information that bombards us daily. Even policymakers who are contemptuous of "theory" must rely on their own (often unstated) ideas about how the world works in order to decide what to do. It is hard to make good policy if one's basic organizing principles are flawed, just as it is hard to construct good theories without knowing a lot about the real world. Everyone uses theories—whether he or she knows it or not—and disagreements about policy usually rest on more fundamental disagreements about the basic forces that shape international outcomes.

Take, for example, the current debate on how to respond to China. From one perspective, China's ascent is the latest example of the tendency for rising powers to alter the global balance of power in potentially dangerous ways, especially as their growing influence makes them more ambitious. From another perspective, the key to China's future conduct is whether its behavior will be modified by its integration into world markets and by the (inevitable?) spread of democratic principles. From yet another viewpoint, relations between China and the rest of the world will be shaped by issues of culture and identity: Will China see itself (and be seen by others) as a normal member of the world community or a singular society that deserves special treatment?

In the same way, the debate over NATO expansion looks different depending on which theory one employs. From a "realist" perspective, NATO expansion is an effort to extend Western influence—well beyond the traditional sphere of U.S. vital interests—during a period of Russian weakness and is likely to provoke a harsh response from Moscow. From a liberal perspective, however, expansion will reinforce the nascent democracies of Central Europe and extend NATO's conflict-management mechanisms to a potentially turbulent region. A third view might stress the value of incorporating the Czech Republic, Hungary, and Poland within the Western security community, whose members share a common identity that has made war largely unthinkable.

No single approach can capture all the complexity of contemporary world politics. Therefore, we are better off with a diverse array of competing ideas rather than a single theoretical orthodoxy. Competition between theories helps reveal their strengths and weaknesses and spurs subsequent refinements, while revealing flaws in conventional wisdom. Although we should take care to emphasize inventiveness over invective, we should welcome and encourage the heterogeneity of contemporary scholarship.

WHERE ARE WE COMING FROM?

The study of international affairs is best understood as a protracted competition between the realist, liberal, and radical traditions. Realism emphasizes the enduring propensity for conflict between states; liberalism identifies several ways to mitigate these conflictive tendencies; and the radical tradition describes how the entire system of state relations might be transformed. The boundaries between these traditions are somewhat fuzzy and a number of important works do not fit neatly into any of them, but debates within and among them have largely defined the discipline.

Realism

Realism was the dominant theoretical tradition throughout the Cold War. It depicts international affairs as a struggle for power among self-interested states and is generally pessimistic about the prospects for eliminating conflict and war. Realism dominated in the Cold War years because it provided simple but powerful explanations for war, alliances, imperialism, obstacles to cooperation, and other international phenomena, and because its emphasis on competition was consistent with the central features of the American-Soviet rivalry.

Realism is not a single theory, of course, and realist thought evolved considerably throughout the Cold War. "Classical" realists such as Hans Morgenthau and Reinhold Niebuhr believed that states, like human beings, had an innate desire to dominate others, which led them to fight wars. Morgenthau also stressed the virtues of the classical, multipolar, balance-of-power system and saw the bipolar rivalry between the United States and the Soviet Union as especially dangerous.

By contrast, the "neorealist" theory advanced by Kenneth Waltz ignored human nature and focused on the effects of the international system. For Waltz, the international system consisted of a number of great powers, each seeking to survive. Because the system is anarchic (i.e., there is no central authority to protect states from one another), each state has to survive on its own. Waltz argued that this condition would lead weaker states to balance against, rather than bandwagon with, more powerful rivals. And contrary to Morgenthau, he claimed that bipolarity was more stable than multipolarity.

An important refinement to realism was the addition of offense-defense theory, as laid out by Robert Jervis, George Quester, and Stephen Van Evera. These scholars argued that war was more likely when states could conquer each other easily. When defense was easier than offense, however, security was more plentiful, incentives to expand declined, and cooperation could blossom. And if defense had the advantage, and states could distinguish between offensive and defensive weapons, then states could acquire the means to defend themselves without threatening others, thereby dampening the effects of anarchy.

For these "defensive" realists, states merely sought to survive and great powers could guarantee their security by forming balancing alliances and choosing defensive military postures (such as retaliatory nuclear forces). Not surprisingly, Waltz and most other neorealists believed that the United States was extremely secure for most of the Cold War. Their principal fear was that it might squander its favorable position by adopting an overly aggressive foreign policy. Thus, by the end of the Cold War, realism had moved away from Morgenthau's dark brooding about human nature and taken on a slightly more optimistic tone.

Liberalism

The principal challenge to realism came from a broad family of liberal theories. One strand of liberal thought argued that economic interdependence would discourage states from using force against each other because warfare would threaten each side's prosperity. A second strand, often associated with President Woodrow Wilson, saw the spread of democracy as the key to world peace, based on the claim that democratic states were inherently more peaceful than authoritarian states. A third, more recent theory argued that international institutions such as the International Energy Agency and the International Monetary Fund could help overcome selfish state behavior, mainly by encouraging states to forego immediate gains for the greater benefits of enduring cooperation.

Although some liberals flirted with the idea that new transnational actors, especially the multinational corporation, were gradually encroaching on the power of states, liberalism generally saw states as the central players in international affairs. All liberal theories implied that cooperation was more pervasive than even the defensive version of realism allowed, but each view offered a different recipe for promoting it.

Radical Approaches

Until the 1980s, marxism was the main alternative to the mainstream realist and liberal traditions. Where realism and liberalism took the state system for granted, marxism offered both a different explanation for international conflict and a blueprint for fundamentally transforming the existing international order.

Orthodox marxist theory saw capitalism as the central cause of international conflict. Capitalist states battled each other as a consequence of their incessant struggle for profits and battled socialist states because they saw in them the seeds of their own destruction. Neomarxist "dependency" theory, by contrast, focused on relations between advanced capitalist powers and less developed states and argued that the former—aided by an unholy alliance with the ruling classes of the developing world—had grown rich by exploiting the latter. The solution was to overthrow these parasitic élites and install a revolutionary government committed to autonomous development.

Both of these theories were largely discredited before the Cold War even ended. The extensive history of economic and military cooperation among the advanced industrial powers showed that capitalism did not inevitably lead to conflict. The bitter schisms that divided the communist world showed that socialism did not always promote harmony. Dependency theory suffered similar empirical setbacks as it became increasingly clear that, first, active participation in the world economy was a better route to prosperity than autonomous socialist development; and, second, many developing countries proved themselves quite capable of bargaining successfully with multinational corporations and other capitalist institutions.

As marxism succumbed to its various failings, its mantle was assumed by a group of theorists who borrowed heavily from the wave of postmodern writings in literary criticism and social theory. This "deconstructionist" approach was openly skeptical of the effort to devise general or universal theories such as realism or liberalism. Indeed, its proponents emphasized the importance of language and discourse in shaping social outcomes. However, because these scholars focused initially on criticizing the mainstream paradigms but did not offer positive alternatives to them, they remained a self-consciously dissident minority for most of the 1980s.

Domestic Politics

Not all Cold War scholarship on international affairs fit neatly into the realist, liberal, or marxist paradigms. In particular, a number of important works focused on the characteristics of states, governmental organizations, or individual leaders. The democratic strand of liberal theory fits under this heading, as do the efforts of scholars such as Graham Allison and John Steinbruner to use organization theory and bureaucratic politics to explain foreign policy behavior, and those of Jervis, Irving Janis, and others, which applied social and cognitive psychology. For the most part, these efforts did not seek to provide a general theory of international behavior but to identify other factors that might lead states to behave contrary to the predictions of the realist or liberal approaches. Thus, much of this literature should be regarded as a complement to the three main paradigms rather than as a rival approach for analysis of the international system as a whole.

NEW WRINKLES IN OLD PARADIGMS

Scholarship on international affairs has diversified significantly since the end of the Cold War. Non-American voices are more prominent, a wider range of methods and theories are seen as legitimate, and new issues such as ethnic conflict, the environment, and the future of the state have been placed on the agenda of scholars everywhere.

Yet the sense of déjà vu is equally striking. Instead of resolving the struggle between competing theoretical traditions, the end of the Cold War has merely launched a new series of debates. Ironically, even as many societies embrace similar ideals of democracy, free markets, and human rights, the scholars who study these developments are more divided than ever.

Realism Redux

Although the end of the Cold War led a few writers to declare that realism was destined for the academic scrapheap, rumors of its demise have been largely exaggerated.

A recent contribution of realist theory is its attention to the problem of relative and absolute gains. Responding to the institutionalists' claim that international institutions would enable states to forego short-term advantages for the sake of greater long-term gains, realists such as Joseph Grieco and Stephen Krasner point out that anarchy forces states to worry about both the absolute gains from cooperation and the way that gains are distributed among participants. The logic is straightforward: If one state reaps larger gains than its partners, it will gradually become stronger, and its partners will eventually become more vulnerable.

Realists have also been quick to explore a variety of new issues. Barry Posen offers a realist explanation for ethnic conflict, noting that the breakup of multiethnic states could place rival ethnic groups in an anarchic setting, thereby triggering intense fears and tempting each group to use force to improve its relative position. This problem would be particularly severe when each group's territory contained enclaves inhabited by their ethnic rivals—as in the former Yugoslavia—because each side would be tempted to "cleanse" (preemptively) these alien minorities and expand to incorporate any others from their ethnic group that lay outside their borders. Realists have also cautioned that NATO, absent a clear enemy, would likely face increasing strains and that expanding its presence eastward would jeopardize relations with Russia. Finally, scholars such as Michael Mastanduno have argued that U.S. foreign policy is generally consistent with realist principles, insofar as its actions are still designed to preserve U.S. predominance and to shape a postwar order that advances American interests.

The most interesting conceptual development within the realist paradigm has been the emerging split between the "defensive" and "offensive" strands of thought. Defensive realists such as Waltz, Van Evera, and Jack Snyder assumed that states had little intrinsic interest in military conquest and argued that the costs of expansion generally outweighed the benefits. Accordingly, they maintained that great power wars occurred largely because domestic groups fostered exaggerated perceptions of threat and an excessive faith in the efficacy of military force.

This view is now being challenged along several fronts. First, as Randall Schweller notes, the neorealist assumption that states merely seek to survive "stacked the deck" in favor of the status quo because it precluded the threat of predatory revisionist states— nations such as Adolf Hitler's Germany or Napoleon Bonaparte's France that "value what they covet far more than what they possess" and are willing to risk annihilation to achieve their aims. Second, Peter Liberman, in his book *Does Conquest Pay?* uses a number of historical cases—such as the Nazi occupation of Western Europe and Soviet hegemony over Eastern Europe—to show that the benefits of conquest often exceed the costs, thereby casting doubt on the claim that military expansion is no longer cost-effective. Third, offensive realists such as Eric Labs, John Mearsheimer, and Fareed Zakaria argue that anarchy encourages all states to try to maximize their relative strength simply because no state can ever be sure when a truly revisionist power might emerge.

These differences help explain why realists disagree over issues such as the future of Europe. For defensive realists such as Van Evera, war is rarely profitable and usually results from militarism, hypernationalism, or some other distorting domestic factor. Because Van Evera believes such forces are largely absent in post–Cold War Europe, he concludes that the region is "primed for peace." By contrast, Mearsheimer and other offensive realists believe that anarchy forces great powers to compete irrespective of their internal characteristics and that security competition will return to Europe as soon as the U.S. pacifier is withdrawn.

New Life for Liberalism

The defeat of communism sparked a round of self-congratulation in the West, best exemplified by Francis Fukuyama's infamous claim that humankind had now reached the "end of history." History has paid little attention to this boast, but the triumph of the West did give a notable boost to all three strands of liberal thought.

By far the most interesting and important development has been the lively debate on the "democratic peace." Although the most recent phase of this debate had begun even before the Soviet Union collapsed, it became more influential as the number of democracies began to increase and as evidence of this relationship began to accumulate.

Democratic peace theory is a refinement of the earlier claim that democracies were inherently more peaceful than autocratic states. It rests on the belief that although democracies seem to fight wars as often as other states, they rarely, if ever, fight one another. Scholars such as Michael Doyle, James Lee Ray, and Bruce Russett have offered a number of explanations for this tendency, the most popular being that democracies embrace norms of compromise that bar the use of force against groups espousing similar principles. It is hard to think of a more influential, recent academic debate, insofar as the belief that "democracies don't fight each other" has been an important justification for the Clinton administration's efforts to enlarge the sphere of democratic rule.

It is therefore ironic that faith in the "democratic peace" became the basis for U.S. policy just as additional research was beginning to identify several qualifiers to this theory. First, Snyder and Edward Mansfield pointed out that states may be more prone to war when they are in the midst of a democratic transition, which implies that efforts to export democracy might actually make things worse. Second, critics such as Joanne Gowa and David Spiro have argued that the apparent absence of war between democracies is due to the way that democracy has been defined and to the relative dearth of democratic states (especially before 1945). In addition, Christopher Layne has pointed out that when democracies have come close to war in the past their decision to remain at peace ultimately had little do with their shared democratic character. Third, clearcut evidence that democracies do not fight each other is confined to the post-1945 era, and,

Waiting for Mr. X

The post–Cold War world still awaits its "X" article. Although many have tried, no one has managed to pen the sort of compelling analysis that George Kennan provided for an earlier era, when he articulated the theory of containment. Instead of a single new vision, the most important development in post–Cold War writings on world affairs is the continuing clash between those who believe world politics has been (or is being) fundamentally transformed and those who believe that the future will look a lot like the past.

Scholars who see the end of the Cold War as a watershed fall into two distinct groups. Many experts still see the state as the main actor but believe that the agenda of states is shifting from military competition to economic competitiveness, domestic welfare, and environmental protection. Thus, President Bill Clinton has embraced the view that "enlightened self-interest [and] shared values . . . will compel us to cooperate in more constructive ways." Some writers attribute this change to the spread of democracy, others to the nuclear stalemate, and still others to changes in international norms.

An even more radical perspective questions whether the state is still the most important international actor. Jessica Mathews believes that "the absolutes of the Westphalian system [of] territorially fixed states . . . are all dissolving," and John Ruggie argues that we do not even have a vocabulary that can adequately describe the new forces that (he believes) are transforming contemporary world politics. Although there is still no consensus on the causes of this trend, the view that states are of decreasing relevance is surprisingly common among academics, journalists, and policy wonks.

Prominent realists such as Christopher Layne and Kenneth Waltz continue to give the state pride of place and predict a return to familiar patterns of great power competition. Similarly, Robert Keohane and other institutionalists also emphasize the central role of the state and argue that institutions such as the European Union and NATO are important precisely because they provide continuity in the midst of dramatic political shifts. These authors all regard the end of the Cold War as a far-reaching shift in the global balance of power but do not see it as a qualitative transformation in the basic nature of world politics.

Who is right? Too soon to tell, but the debate bears watching in the years to come.

—S.W.

---

as Gowa has emphasized, the absence of conflict in this period may be due more to their common interest in containing the Soviet Union than to shared democratic principles.

Liberal institutionalists likewise have continued to adapt their own theories. On the one hand, the core claims of institutionalist theory have become more modest over time. Institutions are now said to facilitate cooperation when it is in each state's interest to do so, but it is widely agreed that they cannot force states to behave in ways that are contrary to the states' own selfish interests. . . . On the other hand, institutionalists such as John Duffield and Robert McCalla have extended the theory into new substantive areas, most notably the study of NATO. For these scholars, NATO's highly institutionalized character helps explain why it has been able to survive and adapt, despite the disappearance of its main adversary.

The economic strand of liberal theory is still influential as well. In particular, a number of scholars have recently suggested that the "globalization" of world markets, the rise of transnational networks and nongovernmental organizations, and the rapid spread of global communications technology are undermining the power of states and shifting attention away from military security toward economics and social welfare. The details are novel but the basic logic is familiar: As societies around the globe become enmeshed in a web of economic and social connections, the costs of disrupting these ties will effectively preclude unilateral state actions, especially the use of force.

This perspective implies that war will remain a remote possibility among the advanced industrial democracies. It also suggests that bringing China and Russia into the relentless embrace of world capitalism is the best way to promote both prosperity and peace, particularly if this process creates a strong middle class in these states and reinforces pressures to democratize. Get these societies hooked on prosperity and competition will be confined to the economic realm.

This view has been challenged by scholars who argue that the actual scope of "globalization" is modest and that these various transactions still take place in environments that are shaped and regulated by states. Nonetheless, the belief that economic forces are superseding traditional great power politics enjoys widespread acceptance among scholars, pundits, and policymakers, and the role of the state is likely to be an important topic for future academic inquiry.

Constructivist Theories

Whereas realism and liberalism tend to focus on material factors such as power or trade, constructivist approaches emphasize the impact of ideas. Instead of taking the state for granted and assuming that it simply seeks to survive, constructivists regard the interests and identities of states as a highly malleable product of specific historical processes. They pay close attention to the prevailing discourse(s) in society because discourse reflects and shapes beliefs and interests, and establishes accepted norms of behavior. Consequently, constructivism is especially attentive to the sources of change, and this approach has largely replaced marxism as the preeminent radical perspective on international affairs.

The end of the Cold War played an important role in legitimating constructivist theories because realism and liberalism both failed to anticipate this event and had some trouble explaining it. Constructivists had an explanation: Specifically, former president Mikhail Gorbachev revolutionized Soviet foreign policy because he embraced new ideas such as "common security."

Moreover, given that we live in an era where old norms are being challenged, once clear boundaries are dissolving, and issues of identity are becoming more salient, it is hardly surprising that scholars have been drawn to approaches that place these issues front and center. From a constructivist perspective, in fact, the central issue in the post–Cold War world is how different groups conceive their identities and interests. Although power is not irrelevant, constructivism emphasizes how ideas and identities are created, how they evolve, and how they shape the way states understand and respond to their situation. Therefore, it matters whether Europeans define themselves primarily in national or continental terms; whether Germany and Japan redefine their pasts in ways that encourage their adopting more active international roles; and whether the United States embraces or rejects its identity as "global policeman."

Constructivist theories are quite diverse and do not offer a unified set of predictions on any of these issues. At a purely conceptual level, Alexander Wendt has argued that the realist conception of anarchy does not adequately explain why conflict occurs between states. The real issue is how anarchy is understood—in Wendt's words, "Anarchy is what states make of it." Another strand of constructivist theory has focused on the future of the territorial state, suggesting that transnational communication and shared civic values are undermining traditional national loyalties and creating radically new forms of political association. Other constructivists focus on the role of norms, arguing that international law and other normative principles have eroded earlier notions of sovereignty and altered the legitimate purposes for which state power may be employed. The common theme in each of these strands is the capacity of discourse to shape how political actors define themselves and their interests, and thus modify their behavior.

Domestic Politics Reconsidered
As in the Cold War, scholars continue to explore the impact of domestic politics on the behavior of states. Domestic politics are obviously central to the debate on the democratic peace, and scholars such as Snyder, Jeffrey Frieden, and Helen Milner have examined how domestic interest groups can distort the formation of state preferences and lead to suboptimal international behavior. George Downs, David Rocke, and others have also explored how domestic institutions can help states deal with the perennial problem of uncertainty, while students of psychology have applied prospect theory and other new tools to explain why decision makers fail to act in a rational fashion. . . .

The past decade has also witnessed an explosion of interest in the concept of culture, a development that overlaps with the constructivist emphasis on the importance of ideas and norms. Thus, Thomas Berger and Peter Katzenstein have used cultural variables to explain why Germany and Japan have thus far eschewed more self-reliant military policies; Elizabeth Kier has offered a cultural interpretation of British and French military doctrines in the interwar period; and Iain Johnston has traced continuities in Chinese foreign policy to a deeply rooted form of "cultural realism." Samuel Huntington's dire warnings about an imminent "clash of civilizations" are symptomatic of this trend as well, insofar as his argument rests on the claim that broad cultural affinities are now supplanting national loyalties. Though these and other works define culture in widely varying ways and have yet to provide a full explanation of how it works or how enduring its effects might be, cultural perspectives have been very much in vogue during the past five years. This trend is partly a reflection of the broader interest in cultural issues in the academic world (and within the public debate as well) and partly a response to the upsurge in ethnic, nationalist, and cultural conflicts since the demise of the Soviet Union.

TOMORROW'S CONCEPTUAL TOOLBOX

While these debates reflect the diversity of contemporary scholarship on international affairs, there are also obvious signs of convergence. Most realists recognize that nationalism, militarism, ethnicity, and other domestic factors are important; liberals acknowledge that power is central to international behavior; and some constructivists admit that ideas will have greater impact when backed by powerful states and reinforced by enduring material forces. The boundaries of each paradigm are somewhat permeable, and there is ample opportunity for intellectual arbitrage.

Which of these broad perspectives sheds the most light on contemporary international affairs, and which should policymakers keep most firmly in mind when charting our course into the next century? Although many academics (and more than a few policymakers) are loathe to admit it, realism remains the most compelling general framework for understanding international relations. States continue to pay close attention to the balance of power and to worry about the possibility of major conflict. Among other things, this enduring preoccupation with power and security explains why many Asians and Europeans are now eager to preserve—and possibly expand—the U.S. military presence in their regions. As Czech president Václav Havel has warned, if NATO fails to expand, "we might be heading for a new global catastrophe . . . [which] could cost us all much more than the two world wars." These are not the words of a man who believes that great power rivalry has been banished forever.

As for the United States, the past decade has shown how much it likes being "number one" and how determined it is to remain in a predominant position. The United States has taken advantage of its current superiority to impose its preferences wherever possible, even at the risk of irritating many of its long-standing allies. It has forced a series of one-sided arms control agreements on Russia, dominated the problematic peace effort in Bosnia, taken steps to expand NATO into Russia's backyard, and become increasingly concerned about the rising power of China. It has called repeatedly for greater reliance on multilateralism and a larger role for international institutions, but has treated agencies such as the United Nations and the World Trade Organization with disdain whenever their actions did not conform to U.S. interests. It refused to join the rest of the world in outlawing the production of landmines and was politely uncooperative at the Kyoto environmental summit. Although U.S. leaders are adept at cloaking their actions in the lofty rhetoric of "world order," naked self-interest lies behind most of them. Thus, the end of the Cold War did not bring the end of power politics, and realism is likely to remain the single most useful instrument in our intellectual toolbox.

Yet realism does not explain everything, and a wise leader would also keep insights from the rival paradigms in mind. Liberal theories identify the instruments that states can use to achieve shared interests, highlight the powerful economic forces with which states and societies must now contend, and help us understand why states may differ in their basic preferences. Paradoxically, because U.S. protection reduces the danger of regional rivalries and reinforces the "liberal peace" that emerged after 1945, these factors may become relatively more important, as long as the United States continues to provide security and stability in many parts of the world.

Meanwhile, constructivist theories are best suited to the analysis of how identities and interests can change over time, thereby producing subtle shifts in the behavior of states and occasionally triggering far-reaching but unexpected shifts in international affairs. It matters if political identity in Europe continues to shift from the nation-state to more local regions or to a broader sense of European identity, just as it matters if nationalism is gradually supplanted by the sort of "civilizational" affinities emphasized by Huntington. Realism has little to say about these prospects, and policymakers could be blind-sided by change if they ignore these possibilities entirely.

In short, each of these competing perspectives captures important aspects of world politics. Our understanding would be impoverished were our thinking confined to only one of them. The "compleat diplomat" of the future should remain cognizant of realism's emphasis on the inescapable role of power, keep liberalism's awareness of domestic forces in mind, and occasionally reflect on constructivism's vision of change.

3

✳

Introduction to IPE

Reading 3-1

Bargaining, Enforcement, and International Cooperation

James D. Fearon

INTRODUCTION

A cluster of arguments referred to as "cooperation theory" or "neoliberal institutionalism" stands as one of the more interesting and important developments in international relations theory in the last fifteen years.[1] Focused on the problems of whether and how states might cooperate for mutual advantage despite the absence of supranational government (anarchy), these arguments may be summarized as follows.

Cooperation theorists argued that different international issues and issue domains—trade, finance, arms control, the environment, and so on—may have different strategic structures, and these crucially affect the prospects for international cooperation and the nature of the specific problems states must overcome to achieve it. The different strategic structures have typically been characterized by reference to simple 2 × 2 matrix games such as Prisoners' Dilemma, Chicken, Harmony, Deadlock, Stag Hunt, and Pure Coordination.[2] Analysts have focused primarily on Prisoners' Dilemma problems and, to a much lesser degree, on coordination problems.

Scholars working in the realist tradition had already suggested that cooperation may occur when states are "playing a coordination game" such as allying against a common threat or choosing telecommunications standards. They argued, however, that cooperation is more difficult in Prisoners' Dilemma–like situations, which they imply are more prevalent and more fundamental in international politics.[3] In response, cooperation theorists observed that if states interact repeatedly on a particular issue—which they typically do—cooperation in Prisoners' Dilemma–like situations might be sustained by mechanisms of conditional retaliation such as Tit-for-Tat. For example, mutually beneficial cooperation in satellite reconnaissance might be sustained by the implicit threat that "if you try to shoot down our spy satellites, we will shoot down yours." A key condition for such mechanisms to work is that the "shadow of the future" be long enough—the states have to care sufficiently about future payoffs and expect that future interactions are likely enough for the threat of retaliation to deter cheating. Cooperation theorists further suggested that international institutions might serve to extend the shadow of the future by regularizing interactions and to facilitate the information flows and monitoring necessary to make mechanisms of conditional retaliation work.

In this article I develop two main arguments bearing on these central propositions of cooperation theory. First, while conceiving of different issue domains in terms of different strategic structures may be heuristically useful for some purposes, doing so misunderstands the problem of international cooperation as state leaders typically face it. I argue that understanding problems of international cooperation as having a common strategic structure is more accurate and perhaps more theoretically fruitful. Empirically, there are always many possible ways to arrange an arms, trade, financial, or environmental treaty, and before states can cooperate to enforce an agreement they must bargain to decide which one to implement. Thus, regardless of the substantive domain, problems of international cooperation typically involve first a bargaining problem (akin to various coordination games that have been studied) and next an enforcement problem (akin to a Prisoners' Dilemma game). To specify and explore this conception analytically, I develop a game-theoretic model that depicts problems of international cooperation as having two linked phases. In the first phase, states bargain over the particular deal to be implemented in the second, "enforcement phase" of the game, which is modeled as a repeated Prisoners' Dilemma.

Second, using this model I show that the bargaining and enforcement problems can interact in an interesting way that cuts against the received wisdom of cooperation theory. Whereas cooperation theorists argued that a longer shadow of the future makes cooperation sustainable and so more likely, the analysis here suggests that though a long shadow of the future may make *enforcing* an international agreement easier, it can also give states an incentive to *bargain harder*, delaying agreement in hopes of getting a better deal. For example, the more an international regime creates durable expectations of future interactions on the issues in question, the greater the incentive for states to bargain hard for favorable terms, possibly making cooperation harder to reach. The shadow of the future thus appears to cut two ways. Necessary to make cooperative deals sustainable, it nonetheless may encourage states to delay in bargaining over the terms.[4]

These arguments and the model are presented in the second and third sections of the article. In the fourth section I briefly assess empirical implications of these theoretical claims, arguing in particular that the theory may make better sense of the early Cold

War arms competition than received cooperation theory can. The conclusion compares the bargaining problem to the relative-gains problem and notes some implications for understanding international regimes.

STRATEGIC STRUCTURE AND PROBLEMS OF INTERNATIONAL COOPERATION

Whether the goal is to control arms racing, reduce the risk of preemptive war, limit global environmental damage, stabilize exchange rates, or reduce protectionism in trade, state leaders need to coordinate state policies and the actions of the relevant state bureaucracies if they wish to gain various benefits of cooperating. Cooperation theorists proposed that such diverse problems might be usefully analyzed by focusing on the *strategic structure* of the decision problem faced by state leaders contemplating cooperation. As exemplified by the 1985 *World Politics* volume titled "Cooperation Under Anarchy," strategic structures were understood in terms of simple 2 × 2 games, which include a description of two policy choices available to each state (typically labeled "cooperate" and "defect"), an outcome associated with each of the four combinations of policy choices, and preferences for each state over the four outcomes.[5]

As noted earlier, the various arguments making up cooperation theory advance two, not entirely consistent, propositions. First, different issue domains have different strategic structures with different consequences for the likelihood of international cooperation. Second, many or even most domains have the structure of a repeated Prisoners' Dilemma and so may allow international cooperation by means of Tit-for-Tat-like regime if state leaders perceive a long enough shadow of the future. Because it more directly challenges the realist claim that cooperation under anarchy is very difficult, the second proposition has attracted the most attention and controversy, chiefly in the form of the relative-gains debate.[6] In addition, empirical work drawing on cooperation theory has generally attempted to characterize different international issue domains and problems as repeated Prisoners' Dilemmas,[7] while empirical instances of coordination problems have been relatively neglected.[8]

Despite the greater attention paid to the second argument, I would argue that the first set of propositions is integral to the way that cooperation theory envisions international politics. Further, the "different strategic structures" argument has (often unwittingly) shaped the major questions asked by scholars working in this research program.

Regarding the importance of the argument, two of the earliest theoretical articles in cooperation theory maintained that empirically, states face two types of problems of international cooperation, labeled "coordination versus collaboration" by Arthur Stein and "coordination versus Prisoner's Dilemma" by Duncan Snidal.[9] Both Stein and Snidal argued that differences in international regimes could be explained according to whether they focused on solving a problem of coordination or collaboration (Prisoners' Dilemma), which was held to depend on the nature of the issues in question. For example, Stein saw the Strategic Arms Limitation Talks (SALT) agreements, market-sharing arrangements like the International Coffee Agreement, and international "commons" dilemmas as regimes addressing Prisoners' Dilemma–like problems, whereas product standardization agreements and international radio and airplane traffic conventions were cited as instances of regimes focused on problems of coordination.[10]

The same thesis is very much in evidence in the "Cooperation Under Anarchy" volume, where Kenneth Oye and other contributors made the "payoff structure" in different 2 × 2 games one of their three major independent variables for explaining variation in cooperation across cases and issue domains.[11] Oye in fact ranged the several 2 × 2 games used by the authors on a rough scale reflecting the degree to which the strategic structure in question was hypothesized to favor cooperation.[12]

The idea that different international issues and issue domains have different strategic structures has had at least three important consequences for the evolution of research on international cooperation. First, by leading scholars to ask "Which 2 × 2 game best characterizes the specific empirical case that I am interested in?" the idea of different strategic structures inevitably led scholars to focus on the question "What are the preferences?" understood as how the states in question would rank the four outcomes deemed possible by the theoretical setup. But cooperation theory provided no guidance here, and the problem of how to assign preferences often seems so difficult or controversial as to render the exercise pointless—most of the "action" of the theory is loaded into the arguments about what the right preferences are and how exactly to characterize what "cooperate" and "defect" mean in a particular setting.[13] Mainly due to this problem of assigning preferences, analysis of problems of international cooperation in terms of different 2 × 2 games has not blossomed, although on the plus side the problem helped lead researchers to look more carefully at how multiple domestic actors with diverse goals interact to influence the foreign policy preferences and strategies of the "chief of government."[14] As I will argue, one reason that assigning preferences to define the "right" 2 × 2 game is so difficult as an empirical matter may be that such games are simply bad models of the strategic problem that leaders typically confront when they are contemplating international cooperation.

A second significant consequence of the "different strategic structures" idea has been a running debate over the relative empirical importance of Prisoners' Dilemma and coordination problems as obstacles to international cooperation. This is seen most clearly in Stephen Krasner's "Global Communications and National Power," where he argues that coordination problems such as the 2 × 2 game Battle of the Sexes are empirically more prevalent than problems of "market failure," a reference to Prisoners' Dilemma–like problems of cheating and enforcement.[15] This framing suggests an either/or choice in characterizing which strategic structure, coordination or Prisoners' Dilemma, is most common and important in international relations. The idea of "coordination versus Prisoners' Dilemma" also appears among proponents of the relative-gains argument, whom Krasner cites as providing supporting evidence for his thesis and who cite Krasner in turn, thus establishing a loose (and, as I later argue, dubious) association between coordination problems and the relative-gains argument.[16]

The third significant consequence of the "different strategic structures" idea is the most relevant for the argument of this article. By defining the realm of interesting possibilities as coordination and Prisoners' Dilemma games, cooperation theorists fostered considerable confusion about how international relations scholars should think about international *bargaining*. The confusion is due to the fact that bargaining problems are not well represented by any 2 × 2 game. Indeed, coordination games such as Chicken and Battle of the Sexes are such minimal models of the bargaining problem that in the international relations literature they generally are not understood as being about bargaining at all.[17] For this reason and because of the "either coordination or Prisoners' Dilemma" framing, many scholars using cooperation theory treated repeated Prisoners' Dilemma inappropriately as a model of international bargaining, when it is better understood as a model of the problem of enforcing a particular agreement given short-run incentives to renege.

In the classic theoretical sense elaborated by John Nash and Thomas Schelling, a bargaining problem refers to a situation where there are multiple self-enforcing agreements or outcomes that two or more parties would all prefer to no agreement, but the parties disagree in their ranking of the mutually preferable agreements.[18] As an empirical matter, a second characteristic feature of bargaining problems is that they are dynamic. They are resolved, if at all, through time, in sequences of offers and counteroffers or with one or both parties "holding out" in hope that the other will make concessions.[19] A final empirically significant aspect of bargaining problems is that they typically involve uncertainty or private information about what the other side's true "bottom line" is and thus possibilities for bluffing and misrepresentation.

Given this understanding of the nature of a bargaining problem, it is immediately apparent that virtually all efforts at international cooperation must begin by resolving one. Regardless of whether the specific domain is arms control, trade talks, exchange-rate coordination, or environmental regulation, there will almost invariably be *many* possible ways of writing the treaty or agreement that defines the terms of cooperation, and the states involved will surely have conflicting preferences over some subset of these various possibilities. Further, in practice the resolution of such a bargaining problem will take place, if at all, in a series of offers and counteroffers or with states holding out for their preferred option. And of course uncertainty about the minimum that the other side would accept is often important in international negotiations.[20]

At the same time, most efforts at international cooperation also involve issues of monitoring and enforcement. Once a deal is struck on the terms of cooperation—as at a GATT round or an IMF negotiation, for example—the next task is typically to implement, monitor, and enforce the agreement. A very few international agreements (such as air traffic control guidelines) may be largely self-implementing and self-enforcing without any special arrangements. But in the majority of cases, the parties involved recognize that there may be incentives for them to renege in various ways on aspects of the deal, and they set up governance structures—regimes—of varying complexity to cope with this.[21]

It follows, then, that the empirical problem faced by states contemplating international cooperation cannot be grasped by a theoretical apparatus that poses an either/or distinction between coordination and collaboration problems. In a broad range of empirical settings, getting to international cooperation involves first a bargaining problem and, second, issues of monitoring and enforcement. This simple observation is obscured by the theoretical apparatus of received cooperation theory. In the next section I consider a model in which the problem of bargaining (coordination with conflicting interests) and enforcement are combined in sequence in order to examine how they interact.[22]

Before developing this conception, a further distinction should be made, one that is also unclear in received cooperation theory. Empirically, problems of international cooperation may involve either (1) bargaining over the division of *new* or potential benefits; or (2) attempts to *renegotiate* an existing cooperative arrangement, where one party threatens to revert to noncooperation if the present terms are not adjusted. In the first class of cases, something happens to "open up" a set of deals that both or all parties would prefer to the status quo. For example, new ideas or more consensual scientific knowledge may lead state leaders to see potential benefits from cooperation on environmental problems, as with the Mediterranean Plan, the 1979 Convention on Long-Range Transboundary Air Pollution (LRTAP), the Montreal Ozone Protocol, or certain aspects of the Law of the Sea Treaty.[23] Alternatively, a change in domestic political circumstances may lead government leaders to see new potential gains from collaboration, as when a political party with stronger commitments to liberalizing trade comes to power or the costs of arms racing or agricultural price supports generate new domestic political pressures.[24] And, of course, technological and economic changes can produce new benefits obtainable by international cooperation, as when the globalization of capital markets creates gains for international macroeconomic and exchange-rate coordination, or when satellite technology makes possible arms control monitoring that in turn makes mutually beneficial arms treaties newly feasible.

In the second type of problem the states involved have already negotiated, tacitly or explicitly, a cooperative arrangement, and some change leads one or more to want to renegotiate the terms. In recent years, threatened trade wars among the OECD countries provide the most striking examples—one state (typically the United States) threatens to begin a mutually damaging trade war by unilaterally imposing tariffs or other protective measures unless the others renegotiate more favorable terms of market access.[25] In terms of strategic structure, problems of this sort are similar to cases of international crisis bargaining in which one state threatens military action and war (mutually costly noncooperation) in the event of failed efforts at renegotiation.[26] It should be noted, however, that once the phase of "trade war" or costly noncooperation has begun, problems of international renegotiation are structurally similar to problems of dividing up new benefits. Although the model developed in the next section depicts the first type of problem—bargaining over newly available benefits—it can also be understood as a model of renegotiation once the "trade war" or other costly conflict has begun. In addition, note that after an initial agreement is reached, bargaining problems may recur as circumstances change or relative power shifts, leading to efforts at renegotiation. Indeed, some international regimes build in formal arrangements for periodic renegotiation of prior agreements, and to an extent they might even be identified with these institutions of renegotiation.[27]

Saying that diverse international issue domains can be productively viewed as having a common strategic structure does not imply that bargaining and enforcement issues arise in the same manner in all issue areas if these are considered at a lower level of generality. My point is simply that reflection on the empirical problem faced by states wishing to cooperate suggests that, taken as dichotomous alternatives, coordination games and Prisoners' Dilemma–type games are misleading theoretical models. Almost regardless of the substantive domain, states will face *both* a bargaining problem *and* problems of enforcement, and it is natural to expect that the two problems will interact. To ask "which is more common empirically?" or to treat a model of enforcement (repeated Prisoners' Dilemma) as a model of bargaining is to start with a theoretical apparatus ill-suited for the empirical matter at hand.

A MODEL IN WHICH STATES BARGAIN TO DETERMINE WHICH AGREEMENT TO ENFORCE

I will consider a model in which two states must bargain to decide which of two possible deals they will implement before they can begin cooperating. The states are assumed to have conflicting preferences over the two deals. Both would prefer coordinating on either one of the two packages to noncooperation, but they differ over their most preferred package. Once the states reach agreement in the bargaining phase, they begin the enforcement phase, in which the deal they agreed to establishes the payoffs for mutual cooperation. In the enforcement phase the states have a short-run incentive to defect, to renege on the agreement while the other side cooperates. Thus in the enforcement phase the states engage in a classical repeated Prisoners' Dilemma.

By restricting attention to the simplest case of two possible cooperative deals, I can model the bargaining phase as a war of attrition, a simple bargaining model that has a number of appealing features. In the classical war of attrition, two parties choose lengths of time to hold out for the prize in question (here, the better cooperative deal), and holding out is costly. The first player to quit the contest cedes the prize to the other side. As an international politics example, we might think of the United States and France each refusing to back down over whether the French will make a specific trade concession.[28] Delay is costly here for two main reasons. First, delay means more time spent without the benefits an agreement would bring; second, as time passes there may be some growing risk that one side will break off negotiations entirely and look for other trading partners (for example, drop GATT in favor of a regional trade bloc).

As an empirical matter, international bargaining often takes the appearance of a war of attrition—two sides holding out, waiting in the hope that the other will make some significant concession first. This holds true at least for international crises, U.S.-Soviet arms control bargaining, and bargaining in GATT rounds; so there is some justification for using a war-of-attrition model for the bargaining phase.[29] However, it should be stressed that the issues states bargain over are typically divisible in many more ways than two. Something more like "continuous offer" bargaining is normally possible in principle, and if states do not make smooth sequences of offers (as in, say, bargaining over the price of a car), this is because for some reason they choose not to. For example, states are not really unitary actors, and the need to forge a domestic consensus among relevant bureaucracies and interest groups may make it very costly for state leaders to generate new offers. I will discuss the possible consequences of allowing for continuous-offer bargaining at the end of the section.

The Model

There are two states, 1 and 2, that attempt in the first phase of the game to select a particular cooperative deal from a set of possible deals. Let the interval $X = [0, 1]$ be the policy space, with each point in X representing the terms of a particular cooperative agreement. Let state 1's utility for the deal $z \in X$ be z, while state 2's is $1 - z$. Thus the states have conflicting preferences over the deals in X. State 1 likes deals closer to 1, state 2 likes deals closer to 0. For concreteness we could think of $z \in X$ as some measure of state 2's trade openness to state 1's products.

As discussed earlier, I will assume that for whatever reason only two deals in X can actually be implemented or that coming up with alternative proposals is prohibitively costly. Let this set of feasible agreements be $A = \{x, y\}$, where $x > y$. Thus state 1 prefers agreement x, whereas 2 prefers y. To illustrate, we could take x to be a trade deal in which state 2 lowers its barriers to a particular product produced mainly by state 1, and y to be the same deal without this concession.

The enforcement phase of the game will be described first. If the states manage to agree on a particular deal $z \in A$ in the bargaining phase, they will play a continuous time Prisoners' Dilemma with payoffs per unit of time represented in Figure 1.[30] The deal agreed to establishes the per-unit-time payoffs for the mutual cooperation outcome. $a > 1$ is the per-unit-time gain from defecting while the other player cooperates, and $b > 0$ is the per-unit-time cost of being "the sucker."[31] c_1 and c_2 are the states' per-unit-time costs for mutual defection (assume that b is greater than both c_1 and c_2). Finally, in order to make it possible for a state to gain by defecting, assume that if a state switches strategies at time t, the other state is unable either to detect or to respond to this switch for a length of time $\Delta > 0$. The term Δ represents the *detection lag*. If states could instantaneously detect and respond to defection by another state, there would be

	Cooperate	Defect
Cooperate	$z, 1 - z$	$-b, a$
Defect	$a, -b$	$-c_1, -c_2$

Note: $a > 1$, $b > c_i$ ($i = 1, 2$), $z \in [0, 1]$, and $a - b < 0$.

FIGURE 1. Per-unit-time payoffs in the enforcement phase (a prisoners' dilemma)

no short-term gain from reneging and so no problem of enforcement. Thus Δ is naturally interpreted as a measure of how easy or difficult it is to monitor the terms of an agreement, with smaller Δ's implying greater efficacy of monitoring arrangements.

I now describe the bargaining phase that precedes the enforcement phase. The game starts at time $t = 0$. A pure strategy for a state in this phase is a choice of a "quit time" $t_i \geq 0$ ($i = 1, 2$). This is the time at which state i will concede the better deal if the other side has not already done so.[32] Thus a state's quit time t_i determines how long it will incur the costs of noncooperation, holding out in hope of getting the better deal. For example, if $t_1 < t_2$, the states will move at time t_1 to the enforcement phase with y as the cooperative deal to be implemented—state 2 gets its preferred deal because state 1 "caved in" first. It is natural to say that the longer a state plans to hold out (the bigger t_i), the tougher its bargaining strategy.

While the states hold out in the bargaining phase, they incur per-unit-time costs c_1 and c_2. The idea is that before they reach an agreement about how to cooperate, both suffer the costs of noncooperation. Finally, in both phases the states discount payoffs according to a constant discount rate $r > 0$. When r is close to zero, the states discount future payoffs very little so that the shadow of the future is long. The greater r, the more states discount future payoffs, and the shorter the shadow of the future.

Thus there are *two* costs for delay in the bargaining phase. First, there is the usual discount rate, or shadow of the future, assumed to affect both players. Second, there is the opportunity cost of living with the status quo relative to a cooperative agreement, which varies with the cost terms c_1 and c_2. Differences in costs for noncooperation can be thought of as reflecting the *states' relative power* on the specific issue in question. It is natural to say that the state with lower costs for noncooperation is more powerful, because it has less to lose from not cooperating.

Analysis

Clearly, expectations about what will happen in the enforcement phase will affect how the states bargain. Suppose, for example, that the states expect that neither agreement (x or y) would be enforceable, so that the "both defect" outcome would prevail in the second phase. Then there is no incentive to bargain seriously. A state may as well hold out forever or concede the better deal at any time with no intention of observing the agreement. An interesting substantive implication follows. If states anticipate that obstacles to monitoring and enforcement would make any cooperative agreement in an issue area unstable, they have no incentive to negotiate or to negotiate seriously. Thus there is a potentially important *selection effect* behind cases of international negotiations aimed at cooperation. We should observe serious attempts at international cooperation in cases where the monitoring and enforcement dilemmas are probably resolvable.

Other obstacles to cooperation, such as bargaining inefficiencies, may then *appear* to be the more significant constraints in the cases we actually observe.[33]

Under what conditions will a particular agreement $z \in X$ be enforceable? The answer depends on the specific "punishment regime" that states expect to govern relations in the enforcement phase. Of many possibilities (Tit-for-Tat is a well-known example), for the rest of the article I will use the simple and severe "grim trigger" regime. In this strategy profile, if during the enforcement phase either player is ever observed to have defected for any length of time, both then defect forever afterwards. This regime is employed purely for convenience—no substantive results depend critically on its choice.[34]

I show in the appendix that an agreement $z \in X$ will be enforceable by trigger strategies when the following condition holds:

$$r\Delta \leq \min\left\{\ln\frac{a + c_1}{a - z}, \ln\frac{a + c_2}{a - (1 - z)}\right\}. \tag{1}$$

Loosely, this means that it is more likely that an agreement will be enforceable the longer the shadow of the future (that is, smaller r); the better the technology for monitoring and response to violations (smaller detection lag Δ); the lower the short-run benefits of defection, a; and the greater the costs of noncooperation, c_1 and c_2.

These results are familiar and unsurprising. Greater interest attaches to the nature of the agreement, z, about which two points emerge. First, it is easily shown that the longer the shadow of the future (the smaller r), the larger the set of enforceable agreements. Second, consider the case of two "equally powerful" states that have the same fixed costs for delay ($c_1 = c_2$). Then condition (1) is more easily satisfied the more symmetric the agreement—that is, the closer z is to $1/2$. Asymmetric agreements are harder to enforce because the state getting the raw end of the deal is more tempted to renege. This temptation is less, of course, the greater the costs of noncooperation for this state (that is, the less powerful it is). Thus the less powerful a state is, the more it is willing to live with relatively asymmetric deals that disadvantage it because the option of noncooperation is relatively worse.

For a given pair of feasible agreements x and y, condition (1) determines which of three cases is relevant, namely, whether both, one, or neither of the two agreements is enforceable in the second phase of the game. The case where neither agreement can be enforced has just been discussed; here, the states have no incentive to bargain seriously. Similarly, in the case where only one of the two agreements is enforceable there is in effect nothing to bargain over. If the preferred deal of state i is the only enforceable one, in any efficient equilibrium state j will concede this immediately at time $t = 0$. Relative power may matter in this case, however. Greater power means lower costs for noncooperation, and condition (1) implies that the lower c_i, the less willing state i is to abide by an asymmetric agreement that disadvantages it. Thus the lower a state's costs for noncooperation, the more likely it is that only agreements favoring this state will be enforceable and so the subject of negotiations.

In the most interesting case, the shadow of the future is long enough that both cooperative agreements are enforceable. Here there is something to bargain over, namely the "prize" represented by the present value of the difference between the better and the worse deals, $(x - y)/r$. When both agreements are enforceable, the game proves to have multiple subgame perfect equilibria.[35] Even so, all equilibria that involve some chance of delay in the bargaining phase have a common feature, described in the following proposition.

PROPOSITION: Consider any subgame perfect equilibrium of the game in which (1) the agreement reached in the first phase (either x or y) will be successfully enforced in the second phase; and (2) there is positive probability that the bargaining phase will last longer than time $t = 0$. In any such equilibrium, the probability that a state will concede in an instant of time dt conditional on having "stood firm" until time $t > 0$ is constant and approximately equal to

$$\frac{r(1 - x + c_2)}{x - y} dt$$

for state 1, and

$$\frac{r(y + c_1)}{x - y} dt$$

for state 2. Moreover, for small enough r, subgame perfect equilibria of this form exist.

Proof: See the appendix.

As in other complete information wars of attrition, this game has a family of equilibria involving a chance of delay before one side concedes the prize. These are "mixed strategy" equilibria, which may be interpreted as follows. Neither side knows exactly when the other side will quit, but in equilibrium each knows the probability distribution that describes the other side's likely behavior. Holding out poses a trade-off. The longer one holds out, the greater the chance of receiving the prize; but at the same time the costs will be greater if the other side does not back down. In a mixed strategy equilibrium this trade-off is perfectly balanced—the states are always indifferent between conceding at time t and waiting any further length of time. This proves to imply equilibrium probability distributions in which the conditional probability that a state will quit in the next instant is constant.

Using some probability theory, the expressions in the proposition imply that in any equilibrium, if the dispute is not resolved immediately (at $t = 0$), then the expected time until agreement is always

$$\bar{t} = \frac{x - y}{r[1 + c_1 + c_2 - (x - y)]}.$$

Notice that as r approaches 0, $\bar{t}$ approaches infinity. Thus, *as the shadow of the future lengthens, both states choose tougher and tougher bargaining strategies on average, implying longer and longer delay till cooperation begins.*

The rationale behind this result is straightforward. When states care a lot about future payoffs, the expected long-run benefits of getting the better deal are very large [$(x - y)/r$ approaches infinity as r approaches 0]. Thus the potential benefits of holding out increase. At the same time, when a state values future payoffs almost the same as current payoffs, conceding today is little better than conceding tomorrow—thus the costs of holding out are lower as well. With the benefits of holding out rising and the costs falling as the shadow of the future lengthens, equilibrium is maintained only if *both* states adopt tougher bargaining strategies, yielding more delay before agreement.[36]

This logic generalizes easily to another set of empirically relevant cases where the states expect to cooperate not indefinitely but rather for a finite amount of time. For example, arms control treaties, trade agreements, and agreements establishing international regimes are frequently expected to bind for the foreseeable future. By contrast, an agreement among central bankers to coordinate intervention to stabilize a currency has a clear object that will or will not be achieved within a certain length of time. Discount rates do not adequately capture the difference between these sorts of cases. With respect to the model, it is more like saying that there is a time $T > 0$ at which point the gains from cooperating on this issue will disappear, and that this T can vary from small (the exchange-rate case) to very large (regimes rules, and so on). The preceding result generalizes to this case as follows: The smaller T, the more quickly will states reach agreement in the bargaining phase (on average).[37] Thus, if less time is available for states to take advantage of the gains from cooperation, it makes less sense to waste time holding out for a better deal. Likewise, the longer states expect today's agreement to be relevant in the future, the more reason they have to delay agreement by bargaining hard over distributional advantage.

An Incomplete-Information Version

In the complete-information version of the game, the states know exactly how the other side values cooperative versus noncooperative outcomes. This is an implausibly strong assumption. In addition, many economic theorists have argued that uncertainty about another party's value for an agreement can cause inefficient delay in bargaining.[38] For example, in bargaining on agricultural policy, a state may "hold out" in an effort to convince the other side that it has high costs for cooperation and so must be offered favorable terms if a deal is to be struck.

To consider the impact of incomplete information, suppose that the states know their own values for noncooperation (c_1 and c_2), but that they know only the distribution of their opponent's value. To keep things manageably simple, I consider a symmetric case where the feasible agreements are $x = 1$ and $y = 0$, and both states' cost terms, c_1 and c_2, are initially drawn from uniform distributions on the interval $[1, 2]$. Each state is informed of its own cost for noncooperation at the start of the game but not of its opponent's.

A strategy in the bargaining phase now says how long a state will hold out as a function of its privately known cost c_i for noncooperation. In the appendix, I show that the following strategy forms a symmetric Bayesian equilibrium in the bargaining phase: If the state's cost for noncooperation is $c \in [1, 2]$, the state holds out in the bargaining phase until time

$$t(c) = \frac{1}{r}\ln\frac{c}{2(c-1)}. \tag{2}$$

This expression implies that the lower a state's cost for noncooperation, the longer it will hold out for the better deal. Thus "more powerful" types adopt tougher bargaining strategies and are more likely to prevail in the bargaining phase.[39] The catch is that ex ante, the states are uncertain about who is more powerful, in the sense of having lower opportunity costs for no agreement. Indeed, it is precisely this uncertainty that leads them to engage in a costly war of attrition. Willingness to hold out, bearing the costs of noncooperation, acts as a costly signal in the bargaining phase that credibly reveals a state's "power" on the issue in question.

Expression (2) also shows that the main result for the complete-information model holds up in the incomplete-information case, namely that the expected delay before agreement increases as the shadow of the future lengthens. When states care more about future payoffs (that is, the discount rate r is smaller), all types choose tougher bargaining strategies. The ex ante expected time till agreement in this equilibrium is $[(\ln 8) - 1]/r$, or approximately $1/r$. Thus as the discount rate approaches zero, the expected time till agreement approaches infinity.

Bargaining with Many Possible Agreements

Probably the most restrictive assumption made in these models is that there are only two feasible agreements. Although international bargaining about how to cooperate often takes the appearance of a war of attrition—two sides waiting for the other to back down—in principle states can usually offer compromise deals, attempts to "split the difference," and so on. Would the main result in the preceding models hold up if such offers could be made? In particular, if the bargaining phase allowed for continuous offers, would a longer shadow of the future be associated with greater delay before agreement?

In its present condition, bargaining theory does not allow an unambiguous answer. In complete-information bargaining models that allow for continuous offers, agreement typically occurs immediately, independent of the discount rate.[40] With incomplete information, however, multiple equilibria usually exist that may or may not have the property observed in the attrition games. Recently, much interest in the theoretical literature on bargaining has been in the validity of the "Coase conjecture"—the proposition that as the costs of delay go to zero, trade will occur immediately between rational, though incompletely informed, bargainers.[41] (Note that this is the exact opposite of the result given earlier, based on an attrition game.) The Coase conjecture holds under some fairly restrictive conditions; namely, bargaining in which one side makes all the offers, only the receiver of the offers has private information, and it is common knowledge that there are gains from exchange. However, it may or may not hold in different equilibria of alternating offer games in which one or both sides has private information. In fact, in some equilibria the *opposite* of the Coase conjecture holds: As the discount rate approaches zero, the expected time till agreement approaches infinity.[42] Even when bargainers can "divide the pie" in an infinite number of ways, equilibria with attrition dynamics may exist. Tough types hold out longer than weak types, using delay to signal that they must be given a good deal. When the costs of delay are low, more delay is necessary to send the same signal. So although the option of dividing the "pie" in many ways may reduce the likelihood of costly standoffs with attrition dynamics, this possibility remains even with such "continuous offer" bargaining.[43]

EMPIRICAL IMPLICATIONS

Received cooperation theory suggests that in domains where states have long shadows of the future and adequate monitoring capabilities, they should have little trouble arranging mutually beneficial international cooperation. Following the repeated Prisoners' Dilemma analogy, they need only agree to move to the "cooperate-cooperate" option and then enforce this with implicit threats of retaliation for defection. The theory predicts that we should observe new cooperation when something happens to reduce states' discount rates, increase monitoring abilities and information flows, or open up new benefits for coordination in an area where states' shadow of the future is long and monitoring is feasible.

When we distinguish between bargaining and enforcement phases and analyze them together, we obtain a more nuanced and rather different set of predictions.

First, in cases where effective monitoring is thought infeasible or the shadow of the future too short, state leaders will expect that no bargained agreement will be enforceable due to incentives to renege in the enforcement phase. Thus we should observe either (1) discussions about how to make monitoring and enforcement feasible; (2) nonserious bargaining, where states "commit" to vague agreements for various political purposes (in some instances they might make "framework agreements" to structure further discussions); or (3) no bargaining at all. Especially in the last case, a selection effect results. If we observe states bargaining seriously over the terms of cooperation in some issue area, they probably expect that monitoring and enforcement problems are not insuperable. And because the empirical literature on international cooperation typically samples cases by looking for serious bargaining, it may be biased against finding that concerns about reneging and enforcement are important. George Downs, David Rocke, and Peter Barsoom make this point in a different way. They argue that in constructing international agreements states can choose the "depth" of cooperation, and that they will choose to go only as deep as they expect they can successfully enforce.[44]

To some extent we might avoid the selection-effect problem if we sample cases by issue area rather than by looking at serious efforts to construct agreements or the functioning of completed agreements. For example, if we examined the problem of arms control over a span of time rather than specific negotiations and agreements, we could ask, first, whether monitoring and enforcement concerns precluded serious negotiations and mutually beneficial "deeper" cooperation, and, second, how monitoring concerns compared to the bargaining problem as an obstacle over the whole period. Later I briefly sketch such an analysis for U.S.-Soviet arms control in the 1950s and 1960s.

The second prediction is that we should sometimes observe costly, noncooperative standoffs in precisely those circumstances where received cooperation theory would predict cooperation (that is, when the shadow of the future is long and there are potential mutual gains from agreement). Note that the theoretical results given earlier do not predict a long stalemate in every such case. Even in the war-of-attrition model, agreement will often be reached fairly quickly. For example, if success in the distributional struggle is 20 percent better than getting the worse deal ($x = 1$, $y = 0$, $c_1 = c_2 = 5$) and the states' leaders discount future payoffs by 10 percent each year, agreement will be reached within one year about 63 percent of the time in the most inefficient equilibrium of the game. In other, more efficient equilibria the average delay will be less.[45] Allowing for "continuous offer" bargaining, or for the fact that for some issues there may be salient "focal points," might make for quicker agreements still.[46] The prediction is not that a long shadow of the future will make for a costly standoff in every case, but only in some.

The results can be pushed further on this point—they yield comparative-statics predictions about the circumstances under which costly standoffs are more or less likely. First, and most intuitively, the greater the day-to-day opportunity cost of going without agreement, relative to size of the distributional stake at issue, the less the incentive to engage in a costly stalemate. Second, if the gains from cooperation will be available for a fixed amount of time (as in, say, coordinated intervention to stabilize exchange rates), the bargaining problem should be less problematic the shorter the time horizon for cooperation. Third, and most surprisingly from the perspective of existing theory, the bargaining problem should pose a greater obstacle the longer states' "shadow of the future."[47]

Lacking the space for an extensive empirical test, I will use this section to sharpen these general hypotheses and to give a preliminary assessment where possible. I consider each set of general predictions in turn, concentrating most on the first set.

Before beginning, I should stress that the mechanism identified here is clearly not the only reason that international bargaining over how to cooperate is sometimes protracted, contentious, and prone to failure. Other obstacles to agreement include the sheer complexity of many international issues (for example, in the Law of the Sea and the GATT negotiations), scientific and technical disagreements about the likely effects of different cooperative policies, and the time necessary to piece together domestic political coalitions in favor of a particular offer.[48] I focus here on the effects of the shadow of the future because of the interesting way in which it is predicted to effect both the enforcement and the bargaining problem, and because of its importance in the literature.

Bargaining Versus Enforcement Problems

As argued, if we observe states attempting to craft an international agreement, the states' shadow of the future is probably not so short as to make cooperation infeasible due to fears of reneging. Thus the model predicts that bargaining problems will often *appear* to be more salient obstacles to international cooperation than will monitoring and enforcement problems in observed cases of international negotiations.

This hypothesis seems supported by the extensive literature examining the run-ups to international agreements. In the first place, a number of authors note a relative absence of concerns about reneging. Abram Chayes and Antonia Handler Chayes suggest that the "cooperation under anarchy" literature greatly overemphasizes the fear of deliberate cheating as an obstacle to existing international agreements. They state that "It is not conceivable that foreign ministries and government leaders could devote time and energy on the scale they do to preparing, drafting, negotiating, and monitoring treaty obligations unless there is an assumption that entering into a treaty commitment ought to and does constrain the state's own freedom of action and an expectation that the other parties to the agreement will feel similarly constrained."[49] In their analysis of macroeconomic coordination at the 1978 Bonn summit, Robert D. Putnam and Nicholas Bayne "find little evidence that the negotiations were hampered by mutual fear of reneging," and argue more generally that "As a practical matter, it seems unlikely that the fear of intentional defection can explain all, or even most, of the unconsummated opportunities for mutually beneficial cooperation, particularly among Western nations."[50] Michael C. Webb argues that "The record of international macroeconomic adjustment policy coordination . . . suggests that the key issue in international negotiations has been determining how burdens of adjustment . . . will be distributed among countries, not overcoming obstacles to cooperation posed by the fear of cheating in an anarchic world."[51] Downs, Rocke, and Barsoom describe "the bedrock of the managerial school" as "the finding that state compliance with international agreements is generally quite good and that enforcement has played little or no role in achieving and maintaining that record."[52]

Second, numerous case studies find not only that major concerns about enforcement do not predominate in observed cases, but also that the question of "who backs down?" is often at least as or more difficult for states than "will the other side renege on the deal?" Studies of missed cooperation over arms, trade, and finance frequently find states failing to cooperate not because of problems arranging credible commitments but rather due to apparent "deadlock" in bargaining—the failure to find terms acceptable to both sides.[53]

Analysts have responded to such results in two ways, saying either that there must not have been any mutual benefits at issue ("Deadlock") or that "relative-gains problems" explain the missed opportunities. The former explanation may be valid in some cases, but the possibility of bargaining delay—states rejecting current offers in hopes of getting a better deal in the future—needs to be considered. The case evidence given in these studies suggests both that nonagreement entailed costs for the states involved (implying a likelihood of some mutual interest), and that bargaining hard for relative advantage played a major role in making cooperation more difficult.[54]

This is equally true of case studies that explain noncooperation by reference to the "relative-gains problem." A relative-gains problem exists if, for all divisions of a flow of benefits from mutual cooperation, at least one state prefers not to cooperate for the following reason: the state fears that its short-run gains will be outweighed by long-run losses due to future economic or military actions by the other state, which is anticipated to grow stronger due to "relative gains" from the original agreement. Demonstrating that negotiations stalemate due to relative-gains fears rather than a bargaining problem entails showing that at least one state's leaders feared that a specific distributional disadvantage would translate in the future into military danger or state-led economic extortion. Correctly understood, the "relative-gains problem" is a problem of credible commitment rather than a bargaining problem—the inefficiency arises from states' inability to commit not to take advantage of greater relative power in the future.[55]

While Joseph Grieco and Michael Mastanduno have shown the United States, the EC, and Japan all bargaining hard for relative advantage in trade deals, the evidence that this was motivated primarily by fears that the other side might use its "relative gains" for military threats or economic extortion is slim, particularly in Grieco's case of U.S.-EC nontariff barrier negotiations and implementation.[56] Grieco seems to accept that military considerations were not at issue in his cases, and for his evidence Mastanduno says explicitly that "The immediate concern was not military security, but economic well-being."[57] Concerning economic well-being, both authors effectively count any evidence of worries about differential economic growth as confirming the relative-gains hypothesis. But such worries should count only if leaders fear future economic coercion and extortion by the partner-adversary, rather than if they are simply worried about the long-run (absolute) welfare of their countries' high-technology firms in industries marked by increasing returns to scale. If cooperation fails on the latter account, this is not a case of a relative-gains problem, but rather a more simple matter of bargaining for relative advantage within a deal.

Finally, case studies of international negotiations that ultimately *did* yield successful agreement frequently find state agents concentrating far more on bargaining problems than on enforcement and monitoring issues. To give some examples from trade,[58] the major obstacles to the conclusion of each of the last three GATT rounds were not intractable problems of monitoring, commitment, enforcement, or information flows to make enforcement possible. Instead, negotiations have regularly stalemated on questions of who would make the concessions necessary to conclude an agreement. Deadlines declared by the negotiators have been largely useless for eliciting "bottom-line" offers. The key concessions yielding agreement in the Kennedy Round were made only on the eve of a more credible deadline—the expiration of the U.S. executive's negotiating authority granted by Congress. John W. Evans observes that

> It was . . . no coincidence that the apparent settlement in May [1967] came at so nearly the last possible minute. . . . [T]he American negotiators had reason to put off a final compromise until they were certain that no further concessions could be extracted from others, especially the EEC [European Economic Community]. As for other negotiators, the conviction that the United States could not afford to let the Kennedy Round fail must have encouraged the belief that the American negotiators would finally be forced . . . to increase their own concessions. . . . In the days just before May 15, however, any hope that the Community or others may have had of exploiting the American need for a successful Kennedy Round must have faded. The failure of the U.S. administration to ask for an extension of the Trade Expansion Act authority may have provided the most convincing evidence.[59]

Evans concludes that the effect of delay in multilateral trade negotiations is to increase the political costs to any one state for appearing to be the cause of failure, and that such delay is necessary to gain agreements.[60]

In the Uruguay Round, even this U.S. Congress–imposed deadline was (thrice) let pass, as the United States and the EC waited and pushed for the other to back down or back off on the issue of agricultural subsidies. The Omnibus Trade and Competitiveness Act of 1988 expired in December 1990, just after talks on agriculture failed "spectacularly" in Brussels.[61] The Bush administration won an extension of negotiating authority in May 1991 to June 1993; this deadline again passed without agreement.[62] Consistent with the theoretical argument made earlier, it is the very fact that states expect to be bound by a GATT agreement (that is, that it will be largely enforceable) that gives them an incentive to bargain so hard over the precise terms.

Which is the more significant obstacle to beneficial international agreements, bargaining problems or concerns about enforcement and reneging? The selection effect implies that case evidence like that just considered cannot provide an answer (though it can provide evidence about the salience of bargaining problems). As the equilibrium results given earlier suggest, by sampling on negotiations we may be missing cases where no serious bargaining occurs because both sides expect that all mutually beneficial deals would be unenforceable. Further, as Downs, Rocke, and Barsoom argue, the selection effect can operate even in the set of *observed* international agreements, since if states can choose the depth of cooperation on an issue, they will choose to go only as deep as they expect they can enforce.

To some degree, these problems can be addressed by (1) sampling on issue areas rather than negotiations or agreements, and (2) asking whether the state leaders in question believe that they are forgoing substantial benefits because of the enforcement problem and are seeking ways to improve monitoring and enforcement in order to gain greater cooperation (and thus welfare). On the latter point, note that if Downs, Rocke, and Barsoom are correct in their claim that "deep" cooperation—which, by hypothesis, would make all parties *much* better off—is rare due to the enforcement problem, we would expect state leaders to be very unhappy about this. They should recognize the (prisoners') dilemma they face and be actively engaged in seeking ways to resolve or ameliorate the enforcement problem that traps them in a bad collective outcome relative to what is ideally possible. In making their empirical case, Downs, Rocke, and Barsoom argue that U.S.-Soviet arms control agreements did not dramatically alter the course of either side's arms policies, which is consistent with the claim that the superpowers achieved at best "shallow" cooperation. However, they do not argue or establish that U.S. and Soviet leaders saw themselves as forced to forgo highly beneficial "deep" cooperation due to the enforcement problem. I next consider the arms control issue area in the 1950s and 1960s, suggesting that although some evidence supports the view that monitoring and enforcement problems precluded deeper cooperation, the more significant obstacle in this instance was a bargaining problem that rendered moot the issue of gaining "deep" cooperation by better enforcement.

If an enforcement problem plagued arms control in the early Cold War, this probably had to do with monitoring difficulties rather than a short shadow of the future. For most of the Cold War, the shadow of the future was arguably long for both sides' leaderships. Until the later Mikhail Gorbachev years, neither U.S. nor Soviet leaders showed any great concern that the other side was too impatient or politically volatile to be trusted to stick to deals, and both sides surely expected a high probability of continued interactions. Monitoring, by contrast, would at first glance appear to have posed significant barriers to cooperation, especially in the 1950s. The Soviets rejected the idea of on-site inspections, and without this both the Harry Truman and Dwight Eisenhower administrations argued that disarmament and arms control proposals were unenforceable and thus dangerous.[63] It is worth noting that Soviet objections to on-site inspections themselves stemmed from a political commitment (or enforcement) problem—the Soviets did not trust U.S. assurances that inspections would not be used for spying. Nikita Khrushchev put it nicely to Averell Harriman, when Harriman denied that the United States would use inspections for espionage: "You're trying to tell me that if there's a piece of cheese in the room and a mouse comes into the room that the mouse won't go and take the cheese. You can't stop the mouse from going for the cheese."[64]

As the model suggests when monitoring is thought infeasible, what arms control bargaining took place in the 1950s was not serious, especially on the U.S. side. John Foster Dulles in particular was more interested in using arms control bargaining to win the public opinion or propaganda battle than in gaining agreements on arms.[65] Consistent with the argument about selection effects, when serious bargaining finally did occur in the early 1960s, it focused on an issue for which the monitoring issues were resolvable given the technology of the time. One element of the appeal of the 1963 Limited Test Ban Treaty was that it was straightforwardly self-enforcing. Each state could easily determine if the other had resumed atmospheric testing and then reply in kind if necessary.[66]

Similarly, the development of satellite reconnaissance technology in the early 1960s solved monitoring problems that made it possible to bargain in SALT I over limiting antiballistic missile (ABM) systems and new offensive missile deployments. Still unwilling to grant U.S. inspectors ground access, the Soviets were willing to allow verification by "national technical means," as the euphemism used in the 1972 treaty put it.[67] Although questions of whether compliance could be adequately monitored did arise (particularly in the U.S. Senate and Joint Chiefs of Staff[68]), it would be hard to argue that enforcement issues posed the major obstacle to getting a SALT I agreement. Instead, as the model would predict for a case of high discount factors and adequate monitoring capabilities, questions of who would back down on specific demands concerning the number and placement of ABM systems, and more importantly over which missiles would be counted and to what relative levels, were the principal obstacles to concluding the agreement.[69]

Thus, for the period before satellite reconnaissance, there is some evidence that perceived monitoring difficulties did prevent serious bargaining over cooperation and may have also limited the "depth" of what cooperation occurred. But this short account overstates the importance of monitoring issues as obstacles to U.S.-Soviet arms control agreements, especially for the 1950s. Several authors have argued that for important figures in the Eisenhower administration concerns about monitoring were significant but not crucial. Matthew Evangelista concludes that although in the 1950s most U.S. officials were skeptical about the prospects for verification, "they believed, in any case, that U.S. security would be better served by an arms buildup."[70] Dulles, for example, supported the "Open Skies" proposal made at the 1955 Geneva summit not because its acceptance would make "deeper" arms agreements possible by improving monitoring capabilities. Instead, Dulles saw it as a way to divert public and ally pressures for arms control while the U.S. pursued an arms race in which it was doing well.[71]

Evangelista concludes that U.S. officials in the 1950s had "Deadlock" preferences concerning the arms race: "Most American officials evidently preferred the risk of an unconstrained arms race to any conceivable agreement that could be reached with the USSR."[72] If attention is restricted to these specific arms negotiations it may be reasonable to characterize them as "Deadlock." The theory sketched earlier suggests what may be a more fruitful interpretation, however, which embeds the arms negotiations in a larger context of Cold War bargaining. In this larger context, Eisenhower and Dulles did not think of the Cold War in terms of "Deadlock" but rather as a costly standoff or war of attrition. They certainly perceived the arms race as costly, but they also believed that the United States could hold out in the broader Cold War bargaining game longer than the Soviets could, and that this would yield a future outcome worth waiting for. As Dulles put it in a remarkable memo written in June 1955, "The Soviet Bloc economy cannot indefinitely sustain the effort to match our military output. . . . The greater military potential of the United States . . . gives the United States its maximum bargaining power and this is a power which should not be cheaply relinquished."[73] This is a clear statement of war-of-attrition reasoning—Dulles argues in favor of "holding out" despite the costs of arms racing because he thinks the Soviets will have to "back down" first, and the diplomatic and strategic benefits will be worth the costs in the end.[74]

The U.S.-Soviet arms race was a long-lived, costly standoff that is anomalous for received cooperation theory but not for the theory advanced here. As Evangelista suggests, the shadow of the future extended a long way for these two superpowers; so if the race were appropriately conceived as a repeated Prisoners' Dilemma, we would predict that "Both sides would have had an incentive to strengthen measures of verification and move toward cooperation rather than continue to compete indefinitely in a series of mutual defections."[75] Instead, cooperation was rejected. This may not have been because there was no mutual interest in ending the costly arms race but rather because of a bargaining problem—*on what terms* would the race be ended?

Costly Stalemates and Comparative Statics

The preceding section argued that at least one important case of international non-cooperation—the early Cold War arms competition—might be usefully understood in terms of the model developed here. Though often described this way, the competition was not simply "like" a repeated Prisoners' Dilemma where the problem is to achieve cooperation despite incentives to renege. Rather, its dynamics turned crucially on the distributional problem of how or on what terms any mutually beneficial cooperation (an end to the arms race) might take place, a problem that must be resolved before enforcement and monitoring of a deal can begin. Consistent with the model's results, we observe a costly standoff in a case where both sides saw much at stake in the distributional conflict and (arguably) had a long shadow of the future.

Finding other cases of costly standoffs that have a war-of-attrition aspect is not difficult; for example border disputes in which two states incur the costs of arming or poor relations as they "stand firm" on the question of precisely where the border lies or who has sovereignty over which small island. The long-standing Russian-Japanese dispute over ownership of the Kuriles is a case in point, where the mutual costs have been investment, trade, and aid opportunities forgone, along with generally poor diplomatic relations.[76] Similarly, protracted civil wars, which are tragically common, can pose a puzzle for received cooperation theory.[77] There are clearly mutual gains to be had if the warring factions can agree on a constitution to regulate the political and economic life of the country they inhabit. Given that the shadow of the future is likely to be long due to the frequency and expected duration of interaction among the inhabitants of the territory, why do they not move straight away to the "cooperate-cooperate" option of common government and constitution? Although the problem of arranging credible commitments to observe a constitutional settlement's terms is indeed crucial,[78] the mechanism described here may sometimes be relevant as well. Warring factions invariably have conflicting preferences over the terms of a settlement and may hold out for better terms for a long time in a (literal) war of attrition.

Insofar as such cases can be anomalous for received cooperation theory but explicable when we bring the bargaining problem in, this is a success for the theory. Nonetheless, we would like to go beyond this to test for the specific and perhaps counterintuitive dynamic predicted by the war-of-attrition model—that costly standoffs are more likely to occur in cases where state leaderships discount future payoffs relatively little.

To do so, we need to be able to interpret and measure leaders' discount rates empirically, a difficult task since the number of factors that might influence a leadership's value for present versus future benefits is large. Although the personal time preferences of leaders (that is, their impatience) probably explain little variation across states, discounting due to government instability, elections, random domestic political pressures for reneging, and random fluctuations in matters affecting the value of a particular agreement can all vary, whether across states, issue areas, or even specific issues subject to international bargaining.[79] Since all or several of these factors can operate in any specific case, comparing discount rates across cases is problematic. Further, since other things besides discount rates influence the probability of a costly standoff (even in the simple model considered earlier), any systematic effect of discount rates is unlikely to be observed in a small-N study.

Given these problems, the best I can do here is to make broad comparisons using a rough measure—states' expectations about the likely *duration* of an agreement, should an agreement be reached. If the parties expect that an agreement would be likely to govern relations for a long time to come, the parties must not expect exogenous random shocks of various sorts to lead to the termination of the arrangement—thus discounting is probably low. By contrast, if the parties expect that an agreement will probably be short-term because circumstances are likely to change so as to render the agreement irrelevant or unprofitable, their shadow of the future is probably relatively short.

For example, territorial settlements negotiated outside of war are typically expected to be obligatory and observed for a very long time. As noted earlier, for such cases we often observe long, costly stalemates with no agreement. The case of civil wars is similar. The factions involved in civil war know that the premise of a constitutional settlement is that it will govern relations for a long, possibly indefinite period. The model's prediction, then, is that conditional on civil war occurring, protracted, costly standoffs should often be observed, which is consistent with empirical work on the subject.[80]

At the other end of the spectrum, states negotiate short-term international agreements regarding specific "issues of the day" all the time—agreements to intervene collectively in exchange markets, to intervene with military forces in peace-keeping missions, to coordinate public declarations regarding a hostage crisis, and so on. Such agreements, as in the monetary example, frequently oblige the continuous or repeated choices of cooperative actions by the states involved, even if the total duration of cooperation is not expected to be long. Further, states almost invariably face distributional conflicts in bargaining to such agreements. When agreement duration is expected to be short because of likely exogenous shocks, discount rates are low and the prediction is for quick settlement in the bargaining phase. When duration is expected to be short because some specific task is being accomplished (such as exchange-rate stabilization), incentives to stand firm in the bargaining phase are low also. In both cases, the theoretical prediction accords with what is typically observed—a relatively brief bargaining phase so that cooperation can begin while there are still expected benefits to be had.

The international agreements most studied by international political economy scholars—trade, arms, and environmental treaties or regimes—generally fall in between these extremes in terms of state expectations about likely duration. I will not hazard strong generalizations about typical discount rates in these cases, except to say that one might expect the bargaining problem to be worse when states are negotiating over the construction of a *regime* with significant distributional implications (like European monetary union, for instance) as opposed to specific agreements within a regime. Insofar as a regime is expected to govern relations for a long time, the states' distributional stakes are raised at the outset. If this is correct, then, paradoxically, the "stronger" states expect a regime to be, the more difficult it may be for them to reach agreement on its construction.

Counteracting this effect, however, is the fact that negotiations over regime construction typically involve more than two parties. So far I have said nothing about how the theoretical argument extends to problems of international cooperation negotiated and enforced in a multilateral setting. In multilateral bargaining (over, say, regime rules), there can be a new cost associated with holding out for a better deal—the risk that the other parties will cut their own deal, excluding the recalcitrant state. This risk acts very much like a discount rate, since a state's expected future benefits for delay have to be discounted by the probability of exclusion.[81] The theoretical argument made earlier would then suggest that, other things equal, the risk of exclusion in multilateral bargaining will constrain states' ability to engage in costly standoffs, or at least for states not essential to any agreement. For example, Geoffrey Garrett observes that in the bargaining over the Single European Act, "Threats by France and Germany to create some sort of free trade area between themselves were highly credible, and Mitterand and Helmut Kohl consistently raised this prospect when negotiations with Britain became bogged down."[82] This factor works in the opposite direction from the effect of the relative permanence of regime rules; so here I can only note the existence of these two potentially off-setting mechanisms.

CONCLUSION

Problems of international cooperation have a common strategic structure. Before states can implement, monitor, and enforce an international agreement, they must bargain to decide which of many possible agreements to implement. This simple point is obscured or misunderstood by the theoretical apparatus of cooperation theory and its critics. Received theory suggests that some problems of international cooperation are about coordination, whereas others are about monitoring and enforcement, or that in general one of these two options dominates.[83] The model proposed here more accurately and simply depicts the problem of international cooperation as states face it and yields some interesting theoretical implications as well. For example, posing the problem as "bargaining first, then enforcement" leads us to see that bargaining and enforcement problems may interact in a way that cuts against the standard argument about cooperation and the shadow of the future. The more states value future benefits, the greater the incentive to bargain hard for a good deal, possibly fostering costly standoffs that impede cooperation.

I conclude with a clarifying comment on the relationship between bargaining and relative-gains problems and a brief statement of implications for understanding international regimes.

Bargaining Versus Relative Gains

Since Grieco's influential framing of the problem in "Anarchy and the Limits of Co-operation," scholars have distinguished and argued the relative importance of two obstacles to international agreements—problems of monitoring, enforcement, and credible commitment to uphold a deal, and the "relative-gains problem."[84] This article has suggested that the bargaining problem represents a third important obstacle, distinct from the other two. Because relative-gains and bargaining problems are sometimes conflated, I should clarify how they differ.

A relative-gains problem blocks mutually advantageous international cooperation if two conditions are met. First, the states involved are unable to commit not to use relative gains accruing from an agreement to extort or extract further gains in the future. Properly understood, then, the relative-gains problem is a Prisoners' Dilemma–like problem of credible commitment, of the same family as those stressed by the cooperation theorists. It belongs, however, to a species of Prisoners' Dilemma–like problems that are not resolvable by the "Tit-for-Tat" mechanisms of conditional retaliation. In situations where today's interaction changes relative-bargaining power tomorrow, Tit-for-Tat strategies can be insufficient to gain cooperation, because retaliatory actions may be rendered ineffective in the future due to today's shift in bargaining power.[85]

Second, for a relative-gains problem to block cooperation, the states must be unable to divide the gains so that current relative-bargaining power will be preserved in the future. Although this condition is crucial, advocates of the relative-gains argument have not explained why or under what conditions it should be expected to hold.[86] If the answer is that the bargaining problem—distributional conflict over the terms of agreement—may prevent this, it seems that relative-gains problems *require* a bargaining problem to operate at all. An alternative possibility is that if the states are quite risk averse and are also uncertain about future relative gains resulting from any agreement, in principle states might prefer the noncooperative status quo to all divisions of expected relative gains.[87]

The bargaining and relative-gains problems are thus distinct. The latter should be understood as a problem of credible commitment (or anarchy) that may require, in addition, a bargaining problem to operate at all.

Bargaining Problems and International Regimes

Conceiving of problems of international cooperation primarily as analogous to repeated Prisoners' Dilemma games, cooperation theory understands international regimes primarily as institutional solutions to problems of monitoring and enforcement. Thus, in *After Hegemony,* Robert O. Keohane argued that states may create and maintain regimes because they increase information flows about state behavior and so facilitate monitoring and establishing valuable reputations.[88] Likewise, the explicit norms, principles, and rules that mark international regimes are argued to foster a common understanding about what actions constitute "defection," thus making the recognition of defection easier and possibly aiding the coordination of punishment strategies.[89] Finally, Keohane argued that by bundling issues together and regularizing interstate interactions over them, regimes may increase the shadow of the future and so raise the costs of being punished in the repeated Prisoners' Dilemma.[90]

To be fair, Keohane also suggested that states may construct and maintain regimes because these can lower "transaction costs," a large category that includes some costs related to bargaining. He argues that regimes "cluster" issues together, which facilitates side payments and issue linkages, in turn aiding in "the construction of mutually beneficial bargains."[91] Thus regimes might lower the likelihood of costly stalemates by increasing the ease of splitting the difference.

In line with the arguments presented earlier, I would suggest that regimes deserve greater attention as *forums for bargaining* rather than primarily as institutions that aid monitoring and enforcement.[92] Interstate bargaining increasingly takes place in the context of international regimes created by states. How do these regimes ease (or exacerbate) the problem of distributional conflict over the terms of interstate agreements?

Beyond Keohane's idea about side payments and issue linkage, the preceding analysis suggests three mechanisms. First, focal points and bargaining precedents are undoubtedly created by the experience of repeatedly negotiating certain sets of issues within the context of a regime. This is probably true of any repeated bargaining situation, but compare bargaining within a regime with ad hoc, possibly bilateral bargaining that takes place in no larger framework. Almost surely, both the propensity to create focal principles and the force of such principles will be greater in the case of explicit regimes. Regimes establish connections and parallels between different rounds of bargaining and may legitimize focal principles because regimes bear legitimacy as the concrete products of visions of world order. And, as Schelling argued, focal points and principles can be decisive in the resolution of distributional conflict in bargaining.[93]

Second, regimes put explicit structure on interstate bargaining processes; they may specify who can make what sort of offers, when, in what sequence, to whom, and so on. Keohane and others have already observed that such rules might facilitate complex bargaining in multilateral contexts. But bargaining theory suggests other influences as well. The institutions that structure bargaining can affect distributional outcomes and the probability of stalemate or "no agreement."[94]

Third, regimes may lessen the bargaining problem by raising the political costs of failure to agree, since a failure to agree can now have adverse implications for the regime. The examples from GATT rounds, discussed earlier, are emblematic here. As Evans argued, the effect of delay in GATT negotiations was to increase the political costs to any one state for appearing to cause a breakdown.[95] Beyond the Kennedy Round that Evans analyzed, impasse in GATT rounds has regularly been accompanied by dire warnings in the business press about the possibility of a "collapse" of the whole trade regime. Although these warnings were no doubt exaggerations, they are indicative of how the existence of a formal, named, and highly articulated trade regime raised the costs of bargaining failure within the regime. Similar pressures for settlement were associated with the SALT talks, which were likewise played as drama for domestic political audiences.

APPENDIX

DERIVATION OF CONDITION (1). Suppose the enforcement phase begins at time T, with $(z, 1 - z)$ as the per-unit-time payoffs for mutual cooperation. Consider the following strategies for the subgame beginning at T: Each state cooperates for times $t \in [T, T + \Delta)$, and at all $t \geq T + \Delta$ provided that both states cooperated at all $t' \in [T, t - \Delta)$. If either state is ever observed to have deviated (say, at time $t' \geq t$), then both states defect at all times $t \geq t' + \Delta$ regardless of play after t'.

These trigger strategies will form a subgame perfect equilibrium in the subgame beginning at T if neither state has an incentive to deviate after any history following T. Abiding by these strategies yields a payoff of z/r for state 1 and $(1 - z)/r$ for state 2 (as assessed from time $t \geq T$). By deviating at time $t \geq T$, state 1 receives at most

$$\int_0^\Delta ae^{-rs}\, ds - \int_\Delta^x c_1 e^{-rs}\, ds = \frac{1}{r}\big[a(1 - e^{-r\Delta}) - c_1 e^{-r\Delta}\big],$$

assessed from time t on. Thus the condition for state 1 to be willing to abide by the equilibrium strategy is

$$\frac{z}{r} \geq \frac{1}{r}\big[a(1 - e^{-r\Delta}) - c_1 e^{-r\Delta}\big]$$

or

$$r\Delta \leq \ln \frac{a + c_1}{a - z}.$$

A symmetric calculation establishes the relevant minimum $r\Delta$ for state 2 to be willing to stick with the equilibrium strategy.

PROOF OF THE PROPOSITION. The bargaining phase of the game can be re-described as a standard complete-information war of attrition studied by John Maynard Smith, John Riley, and others.[96] In the present case, the prize V is the discounted value of the difference between the better and worse deals, $(x - y)/r$, while the per-unit-time cost of delay is the difference between the worse deal and the state's value for non-cooperation—that is, $y - (-c_1) = y + c_1$ for state 1, and $1 - x - (-c_2) = 1 - x + c_2$ for state 2. As Hirshleifer and Riley show, any equilibrium in which delay may occur involves both sides choosing mixed strategies such that each is indifferent between quitting at every time t and delaying for another instant of time dt.[97] This implies that the marginal benefit of delaying for the instant dt must equal the marginal cost. Let $F_2(t)$ be the cumulative distribution describing a mixed strategy for state 2. The marginal benefit of delay for state 1 is

$$\frac{F_2(t + dt) - F_2(t)}{1 - F_2(t)} \frac{x - y}{r},$$

where the first term is the conditional probability that state 2 will quit in the next instant, and the second term is the value of the prize. The marginal cost of delay for state 1 is $(y + c_1)\, dt$. Thus in any mixed equilibrium we have

$$\frac{F_2(t + dt) - F_2(t)}{1 - F_2(t)} \frac{x - y}{r} = (y + c_1)\, dt.$$

Rearranging and taking limits yields

$$\frac{f_2(t)}{1 - F_2(t)} = \frac{r(y + c_1)}{x - y},$$

where $f_2(t)$ is the density function for $F_2(t)$. This is the condition given in the proposition. Similar logic applies for the hazard rate of quitting for state 1. Q.E.D.

EQUILIBRIUM WITH INCOMPLETE INFORMATION. I will first show that the strategy $t(c)$ given in the text forms a symmetric Bayesian Nash equilibrium in the bargaining phase treated as a game by itself. I will next discuss the extension to the whole (two-phase) game.

The strategy

$$t(c) = \frac{1}{r}\ln\frac{c}{2(c-1)}$$

is strictly decreasing for $c \in [1, 2]$, and so has an inverse $c(t)$, which gives the type c of a player that chooses to quit at time t in the proposed equilibrium. By time t, all types of each player with $c \in [c(t), 2]$ will have quit, if both states are following the strategy $t(c)$. Since, for each state, c is drawn from a uniform distribution on $[1, 2]$, the probability that one's opponent will quit by time t, $F(t)$, is thus $2 - c(t)$. Algebra indicates that $c(t) = 2/(2 - e^{-rt})$ and differentiation that the implied hazard rate for each state is

$$\frac{f(t)}{1 - F(t)} = \frac{-c'(t)}{c(t) - 1} = \frac{2r}{2 - e^{-rt}}. \tag{3}$$

A necessary condition for type c to wish to quit in equilibrium is that the marginal gain from holding out for another instant equals the marginal cost, or, for type c,

$$\frac{f(t)}{1 - F(t)}\frac{1}{r} = c. \tag{4}$$

In other words, the t that solves equation (4) is the best reply for type c, given $F(t)$. (Since the hazard rate given by equation (3) strictly decreases in t, the second-order condition for a maximum that corresponds to equation (4) is satisfied.) Substituting equation (3) into equation (4) yields

$$\frac{2r}{2 - e^{-rt}}\frac{1}{r} = c$$

or

$$\frac{2}{2 - e^{-rt}} = c.$$

But this is just the expression for $c(t)$ derived from the proposed equilibrium strategy $t(c)$ given in the text. Thus if each player expects the opponent to choose according to $c(t)$, then each player maximizes its expected utility by choosing according to $t(c)$, and we have a Bayesian Nash equilibrium for the bargaining phase of the game.[98]

The bargaining phase, however, is not the whole game, and we need to check whether there are profitable deviations for any type when both phases are considered together (and under the assumption that trigger strategies are employed in enforcement phase). In particular, we must consider the possibility that a state might wish to choose a delay time different from $t(c)$, and then defect in the enforcement phase. But it is immediately clear that if r is small enough, no such strategy could be sequentially rational for any type c: If this different delay time were reached, no type would have an incentive to defect in the enforcement phase since the payoff for complying ($y/r = 0$) will surely be larger than the payoff for defecting,

$$\frac{1}{r}\left[a(1 - e^{-r\Delta}) - ce^{-r\Delta}\right]$$

for small enough r.

NOTES

1. See in particular Axelrod 1984; Keohane 1984; Lipson 1984; Oye 1986a; Snidal 1985; and Stein 1982.

2. See Oye 1986a for a description of these games in an international relations context.

3. See in particular Jervis 1978 and Waltz 1979 (for example, 107–11). Specific issue domains that have been characterized as having a Prisoners' Dilemma–like structure are arms levels and force structures (for example, Downs, Rocke, and Siverson 1986; and Waltz 1979, 110); competitive alliance formation (Snyder 1984); arms levels within alliances (Olson and Zeckhauser 1966); imperialism and territorial aggrandizement (for example, Jervis 1976, 66; Howard 1972 is consistent with this interpretation as well); tariff and nontariff barrier policies in trade (for example, Brander and Spencer 1984; and Conybeare 1987); competitive exchange-rate manipulation (Caves, Frankel, and Jones 1993, 549–50); intervention and efforts to dominate peripheral and buffer states (Larson 1987); first-strike incentives and "the security dilemma" (Jervis 1978; and Van Evera 1984); and global commons problems (Hardin 1968).

4. Discussing the possible effects of iteration on play in a simultaneous-move coordination game, Duncan Snidal (1985, 36) suggested that a longer shadow of the future could give states "incentives to be more concerned with the exact distributional consequences of particular coordination outcomes," although he argued that "these considerations will still typically be dominated by the overall stability of the coordination situation." Oye (1986a, 14) makes a related conjecture about the effect of repetition on play in Chicken games.

5. The 1985 *World Politics* issue was reprinted as Oye 1986a.

6. See Jervis 1988, however, for a broader range of criticisms that generally equate both game theory and cooperation theory with the study of repeated Prisoners' Dilemmas. See also Gowa 1986 and Milner 1992. For the relative-gains debate, see Grieco 1988 and Baldwin 1993. Glaser (1994–95) argues that, rightly understood, neorealism predicts the international cooperation under some circumstances.

7. For a few examples, see Downs and Rocke 1990, 1995; Evangelista 1990; Keohane 1984, 1986; Larson 1987; Rhodes 1989; and Weber 1991.

8. Important exceptions include Krasner 1991; Garrett 1992; Sebenius 1992; and Morrow 1994.

9. See Stein 1982; and Snidal 1985.

10. See Martin 1992 and 1993b for more recent applications of this approach to explaining cooperation in economic sanctioning and variation in the design of multilateral institutions.

11. An influential earlier example of this approach was Snyder and Diesing 1977, who had argued that variation in bargaining behavior in international crises could be understood in terms of different strategic structures in 2×2 games.

12. Oye 1986a, 6–11; see also Snidal 1991, 707.

13. Snidal (1991, 704) notes that "Choosing among such different [strategic structures] . . . poses a tough problem at the foundations of IR theory."

14. See, in particular, Putnam 1988; Evans, Jacobson, and Putnam 1993; and Keohane and Milner 1996. For recent work drawing on the 2×2 game approach, see Aggarwal 1996; Conybeare 1987; Martin 1992, 1993b; and Weber 1991. Evangelista (1990, 526) explicitly argues that his study "reinforces criticisms of game theoretic approaches that posit the state as a unitary actor."

15. Krasner 1991.

16. See Krasner 1991, 362, 365; and Grieco 1993, 320.

17. For example, Krasner groups Chicken with Prisoners' Dilemma as an example of a "market failure problem" rather than one of coordination with conflicting interests, as most game theorists see it. He also observes, more justifiably, that in the international relations literature "Battle of the Sexes is hardly noted at all as a possible payoff matrix" (1991, 361).

18. See Nash 1950; and Schelling 1960, chap. 2. Chicken and Battle of the Sexes are thus minimal models of such a problem. Technically, folk theorems (for example, Fudenberg and Tirole 1991, chap. 5) imply that practically all infinitely repeated "mixed motive" games can be bargaining problems in this most basic sense, although the extensive forms of games such as repeated Prisoners' Dilemma are difficult to interpret as models of a bargaining process.

19. The first successful formalization of the dynamic aspect of bargaining is Rubinstein 1982.

For applications in international relations, see Powell 1996; Fearon 1995; and Wagner 1996.

20. See, for examples, Morrow 1989; Powell 1990; and Fearon 1992, 1994a, 1995.

21. Governance structures may also be desired as means for handling unforeseen contingencies, which are often problematic because they render unclear what constitutes reneging. See Hart 1995; and Williamson 1975.

22. The effort parallels that of Morrow (1994), who showed how distributional conflicts might interfere with mutually advantageous pooling of information in regimes. Garrett (1992) and Garrett and Weingast (1993) have also stressed that questions of distribution and enforcement both appear in typical problems of international cooperation.

23. See E. Haas 1980; and P. Haas 1990, 1992.

24. See Paarlberg 1997, 419–20, for an interesting example concerning farm policies and the Uruguay Round.

25. For analyses of cases of this sort, see Bhagwati and Patrick 1990; Conybeare 1986; Odell 1993; Noland 1997; and Rhodes 1989.

26. For theoretical work that understands crisis bargaining in these terms, see Fearon 1992, 1994a; Morrow 1989; Nalebuff 1986; and Powell 1990. On a related problem concerning economic sanctions, see Martin 1993a.

27. Koremenos (1996) gives examples along with an analysis of state motivations for renegotiation and how its anticipation affects regime design.

28. See, for example, Roger Cohen, "Culture Dispute with Paris Now Snags World Accord," *New York Times,* 8 December 1993, A1.

29. On crises as attrition contests, see Nalebuff 1986; and Fearon 1994a. On arms control and trade bargaining, see the examples discussed later. Interestingly, in the econometric literature on labor strikes, war-of-attrition models tend to do better empirically than other, more "continuous" bargaining models. See Kennan and Wilson 1989.

30. I would prefer to use a discrete-time repeated Prisoners' Dilemma, as does the international relations literature, but unfortunately the war-of-attrition bargaining phase is more conveniently modeled in continuous time.

31. Further, assume that $a - b < 0$ so that mutual cooperation is Pareto efficient for all $z \in X$.

32. Assume that if both states "quit" at the same time, the deal implemented is chosen by a fair lottery.

33. Downs, Rocke, and Barsoom (1996) make a closely related point; see later discussion. For analyses of selection effects in international disputes, see Fearon 1994c, 1995.

34. More precisely, the statement is true if we assume that players do not condition the nature of the punishment regime on what happens in the negotiating phase. I make this assumption for the rest of the article.

35. This is true even given the restriction to trigger strategies in the second phase. For a full description of the set of equilibria in the classic (complete information) war of attrition, see Hendricks, Weiss, and Wilson 1988.

36. Another implication of the mixed-strategy equilibrium given in the proposition is that the greater the difference in the two deals, x and y, the lesser the likelihood that states will concede at any given instant. When the two deals are close to identical ($x \approx y$), the players place close to zero weight on holding out. Thus greater distributional conflict implies greater delay and more difficulty in reaching a mutually advantageous deal, as intuition suggests.

37. Of course, fixing a horizon in the present model would raise the issue of the "last-period effect" undermining cooperation altogether in the enforcement phase. Little substantive importance should be attached to this problem, however, since last-period effects in repeated Prisoners' Dilemmas are not robust against small changes in the specification of the game, such as assuming that the date of the last period is not common knowledge (see, for example, Kreps, Milgrom, Wilson, and Roberts 1982).

38. See Kennan and Wilson 1993.

39. The derivative of $t(c)$ is negative for costs $c > 1$, so that types with larger costs for delay quit sooner. This property holds in any Bayesian equilibrium of the game—incentive compatibility conditions imply that if $c' < c,$ then type c' chooses a quit time at least as large as that chosen by type c. See Fudenberg and Tirole 1991, 216–17, for a proof in a standard war of attrition.

40. This is the result for the classic alternating-offer model of Rubinstein 1982. Motty Perry and Philip Reny (1993) have shown that if players are allowed to choose when and whether to make an offer, nontrivial delay may occur in subgame perfect equilibria if it takes time to react to offers.

41. Named for arguments in Coase 1972, the Coase conjecture should not be confused with the better known "Coase theorem."

42. See Fudenberg and Tirole 1991, 422–23, especially note 34. For the result supporting the Coase conjecture, see Gul, Sonnenschein, and Wilson 1986. For contrary equilibria, see Bikhchandani 1992; and Cramton 1992.

43. The strongest results here are given by Abreu and Gul (1994), who show that if players are uncertain about each other's bargaining strategies rather than about their valuations for the good or time, then, almost regardless of the specific bargaining protocol, all equilibria converge to one with attrition dynamics as the time between offers gets small.

44. Downs, Rocke, and Barsoom 1996.

45. More efficient equilibria in the war of attrition involve one side conceding with positive probability at $t = 0$. See Hirshleifer and Riley 1992, 381ff.

46. See Garrett and Weingast 1993, who argue that policy "ideas" can make particular agreements focal; and Weber 1991, who analyzes three cases of U.S.-Soviet arms policy as repeated Prisoners' Dilemmas (antiballistic missile systems, MIRV warheads, and antisatellite weapons). I would argue that in each case Weber takes "focal point" resolutions of issues that might be resolved in many ways as the mutual cooperation outcomes in his Prisoners' Dilemmas.

47. The incomplete-information model also yields predictions about the influence of relative power. In brief, the more powerful state (the one with lower costs for noncooperation) gets its preferred outcome in bargaining, because it holds out longer. This supports Krasner's (1991) argument.

48. On complexity as a source of delay, see Winham 1977. On scientific and technical obstacles (which can interact in interesting ways with the bargaining problem; see Morrow 1994), see E. Haas 1990, P. Haas 1992. Domestic political obstacles to agreement are the subject of a large literature; for some examples, see Evans, Jacobson, and Putnam 1993.

49. Chayes and Chayes 1993, 186–87.

50. Putnam and Bayne 1989, 101, 102. See also Kenen 1989, 31.

51. Webb 1995, 46–47.

52. Downs, Rocke, and Barsoom 1996, 380, who also provide references to the "managerial school."

53. On arms control, see Evangelista 1990; and Downs, Rocke, and Siverson 1986. On trade, see Conybeare 1986; Grieco 1990; and Mastanduno 1991. On finance, see Oye 1986b; and Webb 1995. Citing Harrison Wagner, Oye (1986a, 7) offers the general caution, "When you observe conflict, think Deadlock—the absence of mutual interest—before puzzling over why a mutual interest was not realized." (It is worth noting that if there really is no mutual interest in "cooperation," then "conflict" is actually a good thing from a normative standpoint.)

54. I reconsider Evangelista's case along these lines later.

55. This point is further developed in the conclusion.

56. See Grieco 1990; and Mastanduno 1991. For this criticism, see also Keohane 1993, 280–83; Snidal 1991, 723n1; and especially Liberman 1996, 155–58.

57. See Grieco 1993, 316, 325; and Mastanduno 1991, 109.

58. For examples concerning telecommunications, see Krasner 1991.

59. Evans 1971, 276–77.

60. See also Preeg 1970, 74–76, 139–43, 146–50, chap. 11, esp. 189ff., 260–62; and Paarlberg 1997, 423, who observes that "serious bargaining in GATT does not begin to replace posturing until several years into the round." The "audience cost" mechanism described by Evans operates in other international bargaining contexts as well, such as international crises; see Fearon 1994a.

61. See Winham 1992, 73–74 (who termed the failure spectacular); and Destler 1992, 134–35.

62. *The Economist,* "Better Barter," 23 May 1993, 76. The 1990 deadline was perhaps less credible than that for the Kennedy Round; the 1988 act allowed for a two-year extension of fast-track authority, provided that no disapproval motion passed in Congress.

63. See, for example, Bundy 1988, 164, 297–98; and Evangelista 1990, 514–15.

64. Cited in Seaborg 1981, 241.

65. See Bundy 1988, 296–302; and Evangelista 1990, 520–21.

66. By July 1963, when serious work on the limited test ban began, the United States and the Soviet Union had been bargaining over a comprehensive test ban treaty for six years. The major sticking points were the number of on-site inspections the Soviets would allow and the way these inspections would be conducted. Although

the limited test ban treaty was perceived as "half a loaf" by Kennedy and probably by Khrushchev, what made it feasible was that it did not require the on-site monitoring that the Soviets rejected and U.S. senators demanded for a comprehensive ban. See Seaborg 1981, 240–42; and Bunn 1992, chap. 2.

67. Gaddis concludes that "virtually none of the limited progress the two countries have made in the field of arms control would have been possible had Americans and Russians not tacitly agreed to the use of reconnaissance satellites and other surveillance techniques to monitor compliance" (1987, 233). James A. Schear (1989, 275) suggests that technological advances in the monitoring capabilities "played a crucial role" in laying the groundwork for the SALT I negotiations. See also Bunn 1992, 107; Garthoff 1977, 16; and Newhouse 1973, 70–71, 174.

68. See Newhouse 1973, 162. As in the 1950s, U.S. military objections to SALT I on the grounds of monitoring problems were often just acceptable cover for not liking the terms of the deal.

69. For good treatments of the bargaining, see Newhouse 1973; and Garthoff 1985.

70. Evangelista 1990, 514.

71. Bundy 1988, 298–301.

72. Evangelista 1990, 514.

73. Cited in Bundy 1988, 299.

74. Evangelista agrees that Eisenhower and Dulles viewed arms racing as costly but argues that the Joint Chiefs of Staff did not due to their institutional interests; Evangelista 1990, 524. Further, he maintains that they had "veto power" and could block concessionary policies by Eisenhower; ibid., 527. Although the Joint Chiefs' preferences certainly influenced Eisenhower, they are not formally empowered to veto presidential initiatives. They can, however, testify before Congress, which in particular circumstances may give them an effective veto. If, in this instance, Eisenhower could not have prevailed over them, had he wanted to, then war-of-attrition bargaining was arguably a sufficient but not necessary cause of the policy.

75. Evangelista 1990, 523. Note that this point applies equally to Downs, Rocke, and Barsoom's analysis.

76. See Goodby, Ivanov, and Shimotamai 1995.

77. For data, see Licklider 1995; and Walter 1997.

78. See Fearon 1994b; and Walter 1997. Cooperation theory's Tit-for-Tat mechanism

may be inapplicable in this context because a single "defection" by the faction that gains power can eliminate or permanently weaken opponents, rendering conditional retaliation ineffective for the policing of power-sharing agreements. Thus a commitment problem can make the object of contention (state power) effectively indivisible and so a prime candidate for war-of-attrition bargaining.

79. Simmons successfully uses measures of government instability to proxy for state discount rates in her study of interwar monetary cooperation, though she "recognize[s] that domestic time horizon is only likely to account for a small part of the overall variance in a cooperative outcome, since a large proportion of cases will surely be stable ones, and stable governments will nevertheless vary greatly in their willingness and ability to cooperate" (1994, 286n9).

80. Empirical evidence on the intractability of civil conflicts is summarized in Walter 1997; see also Licklider 1995. As noted earlier, commitment problems can contribute to the problem by making political power hard to divide.

81. See, for example, Baron and Ferejohn's (1989) model of multilateral bargaining in a legislature, where the risk of being excluded from the winning coalition in the next period acts much like a discount factor in leading legislators to accept current proposals.

82. Garrett 1992, 547, who is citing Moravcsik 1991, 38. For more general theoretical arguments that turn on closely related mechanisms, see Gruber 1996; and Snidal 1996.

83. Some influential examples include Keohane 1984; Krasner 1991; Snidal 1985; and Stein 1982.

84. Grieco 1988. For studies of both problems and the debate, see Baldwin 1993.

85. For formal analyses of several settings where this sort of commitment problem appears, see Fearon 1994b, 1995, 1997; and Powell 1991.

86. Snidal 1991, 703, makes this point; see also Liberman 1996. In response, Grieco (1993, 321) simply asserts that "In the real world states can and sometimes do receive unequal gains," and that it is "implausible" to suppose that states might "as a matter of course" resolve relative-gains concerns by bargaining.

87. Snidal (1991, 723n3) seems to allude to this possibility and notes that it is not systematically developed in the relative-gains literature.

88. See Keohane 1984, chap. 6; and Keohane and Axelrod 1985.

89. Keohane 1984, 94, 106.

90. Keohane 1984, 89–90, 103–107.

91. Keohane 1984, 91.

92. See also Morrow 1994, 408–11, for this view.

93. Schelling 1960.

94. See, for example, concerning the European Union, Garrett 1992; and Tsebelis 1994.

95. Evans 1971, 276–77.

96. See, for examples, Maynard Smith 1982; Fudenberg and Tirole 1991; and Hendricks, Weiss, and Wilson 1988.

97. Hirshleifer and Riley 1992, chap. 10. For a more general analysis, see Hendricks, Weiss, and Wilson 1988.

98. As is typical in wars of attrition, the Bayesian Nash equilibrium strategies are also perfect, that is, they imply equilibrium behavior in all subgames. A demonstration is omitted, but see, for example, Fearon 1994a; and Fudenberg and Tirole 1991, 219n11.

REFERENCES

Abreu, Dilip, and Faruk Gul. 1994. Bargaining and Reputation. Mimeo, Princeton University, Princeton, N.J., and Stanford University, Stanford, Calif.

Aggarwal, Vinod. 1996. *Debt Games*. Cambridge: Cambridge University Press.

Axelrod, Robert. 1984. *The Evolution of Cooperation*. New York: Basic Books.

Baldwin, David A., ed. 1993. *Neorealism and Neoliberalism*. New York: Columbia University Press.

Baron, David P., and John A. Ferejohn. 1989. Bargaining in Legislatures. *American Political Science Review* 83:1181–1206.

Bhagwati, Jagdish, and Hugh T. Patrick. 1990. *Aggressive Unilateralism*. Ann Arbor: University of Michigan Press.

Bikhchandani, Sushil. 1992. A Bargaining Model with Incomplete Information. *Review of Economic Studies* 59 (January): 187–203.

Brander, James A., and Barbara J. Spencer. 1984. Trade Warfare: Tariffs and Cartels. *Journal of International Economics* 16:227–42.

Bundy, McGeorge. 1988. *Danger and Survival*. New York: Vintage.

Bunn, George. 1992. *Arms Control by Committee*. Stanford, Calif.: Stanford University Press.

Caves, Richard, Jeffrey Frankel, and Ronald Jones. 1993. *World Trade and Payments: An Introduction*. New York: Harper Collins.

Chayes, Abram, and Antonia Handler Chayes. 1993. On Compliance. *International Organization* 47:147–64.

Coase, Ronald. 1972. Durability and Monopoly. *Journal of Labor and Economics* 15:143–49.

Conybeare, John. 1986. Trade Wars. In *Cooperation Under Anarchy*, edited by Kenneth Oye, 147–72. Princeton, N.J.: Princeton University Press.

———. 1987. *Trade Wars*. New York: Columbia University Press.

Cramton, Peter. 1992. Strategic Delay in Bargaining with Two-Sided Uncertainty. *Review of Economic Studies* 59 (January): 205–25.

Destler, I. M. 1992. *American Trade Politics*. Washington, DC.: IIE.

Downs, George, and David Rocke. 1990. *Tacit Bargaining, Arms Races, and Arms Control*. Ann Arbor: University of Michigan Press.

———. 1995. *Optimal Imperfection?* Princeton, N.J.: Princeton University Press.

Downs, George, and David Rocke, and Peter Barsoom. 1996. Is the Good News about Compliance Good News about Cooperation? *International Organization* 50 (Summer):379–407.

Downs, George, David Rocke, and Randolph Siverson. 1986. Arms Races and Cooperation. In *Cooperation Under Anarchy*, edited by Kenneth Oye, 118–46. Princeton, N.J.: Princeton University Press.

Evangelista, Matthew. 1990. Cooperation Theory and Disarmament Negotiations in the 1950s. *World Politics* 42 (July):502–28.

Evans, John W. 1971. *The Kennedy Round in American Trade Policy*. Cambridge, Mass.: Harvard University Press.

Evans, Peter B., Harold K. Jacobson, and Robert D. Putnam. 1993. *Double-Edged Diplomacy.* Berkeley: University of California Press.

Fearon, James D. 1992. Threats to Use Force: Costly Signals and Bargaining in International Crises. Ph.D. diss., University of California, Berkeley.

———. 1994a. Domestic Political Audiences and the Escalation of International Disputes. *American Political Science Review* 90:715–35.

———. 1994b. Ethnic War as a Commitment Problem. Paper presented at the 90th Annual Meeting of the American Political Science Association, 2–5 September, New York.

———. 1994c. Signaling Versus the Balance of Power and Interests: An Empirical Test of a Crisis Bargaining Model. *Journal of Conflict Resolution* 38:236–69.

———. 1995. Rationalist Explanations for War. *International Organization* 49:379–414.

———. 1997. Bargaining over Objects That Influence Future Bargaining Power. Paper presented at the 93d Annual Meeting of the American Political Science Association, 28–31 August, Washington, D.C.

———. Forthcoming. Selection Effects and Deterrence. In Ken Oye, ed., *Deterrence Debates.*

Fudenberg, Drew, and Jean Tirole. 1991. *Game Theory.* Cambridge, Mass.: MIT Press.

Gaddis, John Lewis. 1987. *The Long Peace.* Oxford: Oxford University Press.

Garrett, Geoffrey. 1992. International Cooperation and Institutional Choice: The European Community's Internal Market. *International Organization* 46: 533–60.

Garrett, Geoffrey, and Barry R. Weingast. 1993. Ideas, Interests, and Institutions: Constructing the European Community's Internal Market. In *Ideas and Foreign Policy,* edited by Judith Goldstein and Robert O. Keohane, 173–206. Ithaca, N.Y.: Cornell University Press.

Garthoff, Raymond. 1977. Salt I: An Evaluation. *World Politics* 31:1–25.

———. 1985. *Detente and Confrontation.* Washington, D.C.: Brookings Institution.

Glaser, Charles. 1994–95. Realists as Optimists: Cooperation as Self-Help. *International Security* 19:50–90.

Goodby, James E., Vladimir I. Ivanov, and Nobuo Shimotamai, eds. 1995. *"Northern Territories" and Beyond: Russian, Japanese, and American Perspectives.* Westport, Conn.: Praeger.

Gowa, Joanne. 1986. Anarchy, Egoism, and Third Images: The Evolution of Cooperation and International Relations. *International Organization* 40 (Winter): 167–86.

Grieco, Joseph. 1988. Anarchy and the Limits of Cooperation: A Realist Critique of the Newest Liberal Institutionalism. *International Organization* 42:485–507.

———. 1990. *Cooperation among Nations.* Ithaca, N.Y.: Cornell University Press.

———. 1993. Understanding the Problem of International Cooperation. In *Neorealism and Neoliberalism,* edited by David A. Baldwin, 301–38. New York: Columbia University Press.

Gruber, Lloyd. 1996. *Ruling the World: Power Politics and the Rise of Supranational Institutions.* Unpublished manuscript. University of Chicago.

Gul, Faruk, Hugo Sonnenschein, and Robert Wilson. 1986. Foundations of Dynamic Monopoly and the Coase Conjecture. *Journal of Economic Theory* 39 (June):155–90.

Haas, Ernst. 1980. Why Collaborate? Issue Linkage and International Regimes. *World Politics* 32 (April):357–405.

———. 1990. *When Knowledge Is Power.* Berkeley: University of California Press.

Haas, Peter. 1990. *Saving the Mediterranean: The Politics of International Environmental Cooperation.* New York: Columbia University Press.

Haas, Peter, ed. 1992. Knowledge, Power, and International Policy Coordination. *International Organization* 46 (Winter). Special issue.

Hardin, Garret. 1968. The Tragedy of the Commons. *Science,* 13 December, 1243–48.

Hart, Oliver. 1996. *Firms, Contracts, and Financial Structure*. Oxford: Oxford University Press.

Hendricks, K., A. Weiss, and C. Wilson. 1988. The War of Attrition in Continuous Time with Complete Information. *International Economic Review* 29:663–80.

Hirshleifer, Jack, and John G. Riley. 1992. *The Analytics of Uncertainty*. Cambridge: Cambridge University Press.

Howard, Michael. 1972. *The Continental Commitment*. London: Temple Smith.

Jervis, Robert. 1976. *Perception and Misperception in International Politics*. Princeton, N.J.: Princeton University Press.

———. 1988. Realism, Game Theory, and Cooperation. *World Politics* 40: 317–49.

Kenen, Peter B. 1989. *Exchange Rates and Policy Coordination*. Ann Arbor: University of Michigan Press.

Kennan, John, and Robert Wilson. 1989. Strategic Bargaining Models and the Interpretation of Strike Data. *Journal of Applied Econometrics* 4 (December): S87–130.

———. 1993. Bargaining with Private Information. *Journal of Economic Literature* 31 (March): 45–104.

Keohane, Robert. 1984. *After Hegemony*. Princeton, N.J.: Princeton University Press.

———. 1986. Reciprocity in International Relations. *International Organization* 40 (Winter): 1–27.

———. 1993. Institutionalist Theory and the Realist Challenge. In *Neorealism and Neoliberalism,* edited by David A. Baldwin, 301–38. New York: Columbia University Press.

Keohane, Robert, and Robert Axelrod. 1985. Achieving Cooperation Under Anarchy. In *Cooperation Under Anarchy,* edited by Kenneth Oye, 226–45. Princeton, N.J.: Princeton University Press.

Keohane, Robert, and Helen Milner, eds. 1996. *Internationalization and Domestic Politics*. Cambridge: Cambridge University Press.

Koremenos, Barbara. 1996. The Duration of International Agreements. Paper presented at the 36th Annual Meeting of the International Studies Association, San Diego, California.

Krasner, Stephen D. 1991. Global Communications and National Power: Life on the Pareto Frontier. *World Politics* 43: 336–66.

Kreps, David, Robert Wilson, Paul Milgrom, and John Roberts. 1982. Rational Cooperation in a Finitely Repeated Prisoner's Dilemma. *Journal of Economic Theory* 245–52.

Larson, Deborah. 1987. Crisis Prevention and the Austrian State Treaty. *International Organization* 41: 27–60.

Liberman, Peter. 1996. Trading with the Enemy: Security and Relative Economic Gains. *International Security* 21: 147–75.

Licklider, Roy. 1995. The Consequences of Negotiated Settlements in Civil Wars, 1945–1993. *American Political Science Review* 89: 681–90.

Lipson, Charles. 1984. International Cooperation in Economic and Security Affairs. *World Politics* 37: 1–23.

Martin, Lisa. 1992. *Coercive Cooperation*. Princeton, N.J.: Princeton University Press.

———. 1993a. Credibility, Costs, Institutions: Cooperation on Economic Sanctions. *World Politics* 45: 406–32.

———. 1993b. Interests, Power, and Multilateralism. *International Organization* 46: 765–92.

Mastanduno, Michael. 1991. Do Relative Gains Matter? America's Response to Japanese Industrial Policy. *International Security* 16 (Summer): 73–113.

Maynard Smith, John. 1982. *Evolution and the Theory of Games*. Cambridge: Cambridge University Press.

Milner, Helen. 1992. International Theories of Cooperation among Nations: Strengths and Weaknesses. *World Politics* 44: 466–96.

Moravscik, Andrew. 1991. Negotiating the Single European Act: National Interests and Conventional Statecraft in the European Community. *International Organization* 45: 19–56.

Morrow, James D. 1989. Capabilities, Uncertainty, and Resolve: A Limited Information Model of Crisis Bargaining.

American Journal of Political Science 33:941–72.

———, 1994. Modeling the Forms of International Cooperation. *International Organization* 48:387–423.

Nalebuff, Barry. 1986. Brinkmanship and Nuclear Deterrence: The Neutrality of Escalation. *Conflict Management and Peace Science* 9 (Spring):19–30.

Nash, John F. 1950. The Bargaining Problem. *Econometrica* 18:155–62.

Newhouse, John. 1973. *Cold Dawn.* New York: Holt, Rinehart and Winston.

Noland, Marcus. 1997. Chasing Phantoms: The Political Economy of the USTR. *International Organization* 51:365–88.

Odell, John S. 1993. International Threats and Internal Politics: Brazil, the European Community, and the United States, 1985–87. In *Double-Edged Diplomacy,* edited by Peter B. Evans, Harold K. Jacobson, and Robert D. Putnam, 233–64. Berkeley: University of California Press.

Olson, Mancur, and Richard Zeckhauser. 1966. An Economic Theory of Alliance. *Review of Economics and Statistics* 48 (August):266–79.

Oye, Kenneth. ed. 1986a. *Cooperation Under Anarchy.* Princeton, N.J.: Princeton University Press.

———. 1986b. The Sterling-Dollar-Franc Triangle: Monetary Diplomacy 1929–1937. In *Cooperation Under Anarchy,* edited by Kenneth Oye, 173–99. Princeton, N.J.: Princeton University Press.

Paarlberg, Robert. 1997. Agricultural Policy Reform and the Uruguay Round: Synergistic Linkage in a Two-Level Game? *International Organization* 51:413–44.

Perry, Motty, and Phillip Reny. 1993. A Non-Cooperative Bargaining Model with Strategically Timed Offers. *Journal of Economic Theory* 59:50–77.

Powell, Robert. 1990. *Nuclear Deterrence Theory: The Problem of Credibility.* Cambridge: Cambridge University Press.

———. 1991. The Problem of Absolute and Relative Gains in International Relations Theory. *American Political Science Review* 85 (December):1303–20.

———. 1996. Bargaining in the Shadow

of Power. *Games and Economic Behavior* 15:255–89.

Preeg, Ernest H. 1970. *Traders and Diplomats.* Washington, D.C.: Brookings Institution.

Putnam, Robert D. 1988. Diplomacy and Domestic Politics: The Logic of Two-Level Games. *International Organization* 42:427–60.

Putnam, Robert D., and Nicholas Bayne. 1989. The Bonn Summit of 1978: A Case Study in Coordination. In *Can Nations Agree? Issues in International Economic Cooperation,* edited by Richard Cooper. Washington, D.C.: Brookings Institution.

Rhodes, Carolyn. 1989. Reciprocity in Trade: The Utility of a Bargaining Strategy. *International Organization* 43:273–300.

Rubinstein, Ariel. 1982. Perfect Equilibrium in a Bargaining Model. *Econometrica* 50:97–109.

Schear, James A. 1989. Verification, Compliance, and Arms Control: The Dynamics of Domestic Debate. In *Nuclear Arguments,* edited by Lynn Eden and Steven E. Miller, 264–321. Ithaca, N.Y.: Cornell University Press.

Schelling, Thomas. 1960. *The Strategy of Conflict.* Cambridge, Mass.: Harvard University Press.

Seaborg, Glenn T. 1981. *Kennedy, Khrushchev, and the Test Ban.* Berkeley: University of California Press.

Sebenius, James K. 1992. Challenging Conventional Explanations of International Cooperation: Negotiation Analysis and the Case of Epistemic Communities. *International Organization* 46:323–66.

Simmons, Beth A. 1994. *Who Adjusts?* Princeton, N.J.: Princeton University Press.

Snidal, Duncan. 1985. Coordination Versus Prisoner's Dilemma: Implications for International Cooperation and Regimes. *American Political Science Review* 79:23–42.

———. 1991. Relative Gains and the Pattern of International Cooperation. *American Political Science Review* 85:701–26.

———. 1996. Membership Has Its Privileges. Mimeo, University of Chicago.

Snyder, Glenn. 1984. The Security Dilemma in Alliance Politics. *World Politics* 36:461–95.

Snyder, Glenn, and Paul Diesing. 1977. *Conflict Among Nations*. Princeton, N.J.: Princeton University Press.

Stein, Arthur. 1982. Coordination and Collaboration: Regimes in an Anarchic World. *International Organization* 36:299–324.

Tsebelis, George. 1994. The Power of the European Parliament as a Conditional Agenda Setter. *American Political Science Review* 88:128–42.

Van Evera, Stephen. 1984. Causes of War. Ph.D. diss., University of California, Berkeley.

Wagner, R. Harrison. 1996. Bargaining and War. Mimeo, University of Texas, Austin.

Walter, Barbara. 1997. The Critical Barrier to Civil War Settlement. *International Organization* 51:335–64.

Waltz, Kenneth N. 1979. *Theory of International Politics*. Reading, Mass.: Addison-Wesley.

Webb, Michael C. 1995. *The Political Economy of Policy Coordination*. Ithaca, N.Y.: Cornell University Press.

Weber, Steve. 1991. *Cooperation and Discord in U.S.-Soviet Arms Control*. Princeton, N.J.: Princeton University Press.

Williamson, Oliver. 1975. *Markets and Hierarchies*. New York: Free Press.

Winham, Gilbert R. 1977. Negotiation as a Management Process. *World Politics* 30:87–114.

———. 1992. *The Evolution of International Trade Agreements*. Toronto: University of Toronto Press.

Reading 3-2

The Morality of the Market
Martin Wolf

A sophisticated market economy works better than any other economic arrangement that has ever existed. After two centuries of unprecedented economic advance, and especially since the collapse of the Soviet Union and China's transition to capitalism, it is hard to argue anything else.

Yet the victory of the market model is detested almost everywhere. Critics grudgingly concede that capitalism may work better than any plausible alternative, but they insist it remains a wicked system, one that rewards immoral behavior—greed, ruthlessness, and indifference to the fate of others—and produces immoral outcomes, namely widening inequality.

This view is most stridently expressed by the anti-globalization left. But a similar, if more subtle, critique has emerged among economists themselves, some of whom even decry capitalism as inherently inhumane and in need of a "human face." It is easy to agree that a market economy requires a supporting system of laws and regulations. It is also easy to accept the desirability of government-sponsored programs of social welfare, provided these are kept within manageable bounds. But the claim that the market economy is immoral is nonsense.

The market economy rests on and encourages valuable moral qualities; provides unprecedented opportunities for people to engage in altruistic activities; underpins individual freedom and democracy; and has created societies that are, in all significant re-

SOURCE: From "The Morality of the Market" by Martin Wolf, *Foreign Policy* (September/October 2001): 47–50 (www.foreignpolicy.com). Copyright © 2001. Reprinted by permission.

spects, less unequal than the traditional hierarchies that preceded them. In short, capitalism is the most inherently just economic system that humankind has ever devised.

It is true that market economies neither create, nor reward, saints. But consider the virtuous behavior that capitalism fosters: trustworthiness, reliability, individual initiative, civility, self-reliance, and self-restraint. These qualities are, critics correctly note, placed in the service of self-interest. Since people are, with few exceptions, self-interested, that should be neither surprising nor shocking.

Yet people are also not completely self-interested. Prosperous market economies generate a vast number of attractive opportunities for those who are not motivated by wealth alone. People can seek employment with non-governmental organizations or charities. They can work in the public sector, as doctors, teachers, or police officers. They can teach the iniquities of capitalism in schools and universities. Those who make a great deal of money can use it for any purpose they wish. They can give it away, for example. Quite a few have.

In the advanced market economies, people care deeply about eliminating pain and injustice and ensuring the welfare of fellow humans and, more recently, animals. This concern exists because a rich, liberal society places enormous emphasis on the health and well-being of the individual. Life is no longer nasty, brutish, and short; rather, it is gentle, kind, and long, and more precious than before.

The savage punishments and casual indignities of two centuries ago are no longer acceptable to civilized people. Nor are slavery and serfdom, both of which were rendered obsolete and immoral under the capitalist system. Militarists, extreme nationalists, communists, and fascists—the anti-liberals—brought these horrors back, if only temporarily. And it is no accident that the creeds that brought them back were fiercely anti-individualistic and anti-market.

Yet another example of changed sensibilities is environmentalism. The environmental catastrophes caused by supposedly benevolent state socialist economies are well documented. The market economy has largely avoided such disasters. That is because prosperous people tend to care more about the environment in which they live than those who are condemned to squalor.

Moreover, only liberal democracy makes it possible for concerns about the environment to be routinely aired and addressed. It affords environmentalists the right to pursue their agendas and to raise money in support of their goals. It segregates the public and private sectors, which enables government to regulate business. And because information is widely disseminated in a free society, companies must adhere to environmental standards if they hope to maintain their reputations.

BRANDING DISSENT

One of the more insidious charges now leveled against the market economy is that it undermines individual liberty and subverts democracy. In her book *No Logo: Taking Aim at the Brand Bullies,* acclaimed anti-globalization campaigner Naomi Klein lapses into paranoia and delusion when she writes of "corporate space as a fascist state where we all salute the logo and have little opportunity for criticism because our newspapers, television stations, Internet servers, streets and retail spaces are all controlled by multinational corporate interests."

In reality, a competitive market economy is a necessary condition for democracy. The bedrock of a market economy is, as the 17th-century philosopher John Locke argued, the right of individuals to own and use property freely, subject to reasonable legal constraints. In turn, the right to own and use property freely gave rise to ideas about political liberty and the rule of law.

Secure property rights require stable, durable governments interested in the long-term health of their countries. As the late economist Mancur Olson observed, "The only societies where individual rights to property and contract are confidently expected to last across generations are the securely democratic societies." But sustained democracy requires the rule of law: The system can only endure if those in power accept free speech and political competition and abide by the results of elections. The rule of law came about as a means of facilitating commerce; in this sense, capitalism provides the basis for democracy, not vice versa.

A planned economy, by contrast, will always go hand-in-hand with tyranny. Vaclav Havel, erstwhile dissident and later president of the Czech Republic, has pointed out that a government that controls the economy will inevitably also control the civic life of a nation. True, some countries have proved the reverse: They have market economies but not democracy nor civil and human rights. But even if all nations with market economies are not (yet) democratic, all democracies have market economies. As the distinguished Hungarian economist Janos Kornai notes, "There has been no country with a democratic political sphere, past or present, whose economy has not been dominated by private ownership and market coordination."

The market supports democracy in another way—through growth. When per capita output rises, a society's condition can be described as "positive sum"—every person in that society can become better off. This outcome makes politics relatively easy to manage. In a static society, however, a "zero-sum" condition prevails: If anyone is to receive more, someone else must receive less. It is a safe bet that if environmentalists imposed a zero-economic growth agenda on a country, that country would swiftly become authoritarian.

And far from stifling democracy, as Klein and her cohorts contend, the market economy manufactures political dissent with unparalleled efficiency. As the Austrian economist Joseph Schumpeter argued in *Capitalism, Socialism, and Democracy,* liberal democracies are the only societies that create their own opposition. Only in a market economy would the wealthy give large sums of money to universities, despite the contempt that many professors and students express for capitalism and the affluent. Only in a market economy could books and newspaper articles condemning the rich and powerful be published and promoted with such success.

Indeed, for all her jeremiads against capitalism, multinationals, and global brands, Klein appears to have done quite well by the market economy. Under no other system could her book have become such an international sensation. Her complaints about media conglomeration ring somewhat hollow considering what a media darling she has become. It could even be said that *No Logo* is now a brand of its own. The market economy does not merely support its critics; it embraces them.

THE GREAT LEVELER

Inequality is considered the scourge of capitalism. Yes, the rewards in market economies are far from equally distributed. However, all complex societies with elaborate divisions of labor are unequal. Those countries with market economies are not only the least unequal, but the inequality they generate is the least harmful. In agrarian kingdoms and feudal societies, kings and lords could seize at will the labor, possessions, and even the lives of subjects, serfs, and slaves. Perhaps the most unequal societies of all were the state-socialist and national-socialist regimes of the 20th century. When, on a whim, Chinese leader Mao Zedong initiated the Great Leap Forward in the late 1950s, some 20 million people died. The irony is that such tyranny was justified by the alleged depredations of capitalism. To eliminate market-driven inequality, all power was concentrated in the hands of the state; the result was an infinitely more unjust distribution of wealth that benefited those who controlled the economy.

It is fashionable now to claim that the market economy has produced staggering global inequality. Disparity in the global distribution of household incomes did increase progressively from the early 19th century to around 1965. But this trend must be properly understood. The proportion of the world's population living on the margins of subsistence—that is, on an income of $1 per day—has actually decreased from more than 80 percent in 1820 to around 20 percent today, despite a roughly six-fold increase in world population.

Moreover, the rise in global inequality was not caused by increased inequality within countries but increased inequality among them. This gap reflects the success of those countries that embraced capitalism and the failure of those that did not. Likewise, the reduction in global inequality that has apparently occurred in the past two decades reflects the successful introduction of dynamic market economies in China and, to a lesser extent, in India.

In all that matters—the ability to define one's aspirations and to enjoy the full rights and protections of citizenship—modern liberal democracies are uniquely equal. Wealthy people have more influence in a democracy than the working class. But compared to the power wielded by the affluent in traditional, hierarchical societies, the influence of today's wealthy is tightly circumscribed.

No millionaire or corporation can flout the law, as a number of scoundrels discovered in 2002. Even Microsoft's Bill Gates, the world's wealthiest person according to *Forbes,* discovered he could not ignore the low-paid lawyers of the Department of Justice when they went after Microsoft's monopolistic abuses. In a competitive market economy subject to the rule of law, Gates can support politicians but not coerce them; cajole customers but not compel them; and control the destiny of his company but not the lives of the people he employs. Gates is neither a tyrant nor an overlord. He is simply a citizen, entrepreneur, investor, and philanthropist.

The liberal market economy is morally imperfect, not least because it reflects the tastes, desires, and motivations of imperfect human beings. A market economy satisfies the desires of the majority more than the tastes of a refined minority. It rewards the hustler more than the sage. It rests on the power of self-interest more than universal benevolence. The relentless tirades against capitalism come from dreamers who compare it with an ideal system that has never existed and from intellectuals who resent their modest status in a society where wealth and prestige are gained by satisfying the wants of ordinary people. It is not the market that is immoral but the sloppy and self-indulgent arguments and attitudes of its critics.

4

✳

Origins of the Modern International System

Reading 4-1

War and the Birth of the Nation State
Richard Bean

INTRODUCTION

The rise of the nation-state is assigned by most historians a central role in the economic growth of Europe. Most recently Douglass North and Robert Thomas have argued that sustained economic growth was made possible only by institutional changes which, themselves, were a consequence of the rise of the nation-state.[1] Thus it is clear that a complete model of the economic growth of Europe will have to account for the rise of the nation-state. That is the humble task of this paper.

The phrase "rise of the nation-state" is quite vague. For the purposes of this paper we shall focus on power. The phenomenon we shall try to explain is the consolidation of political and military power that occurred in Europe in the early modern period. A political map of Europe for the year 1400 A.D. shows a plethora of independent and semi-independent states—kingdoms, principalities, and duchies abounded. By 1600 A.D. the number had been sharply reduced, and within each of the remaining states the power of the central authority had been greatly enhanced. In 1400 A.D. no

SOURCE: From "War and the Birth of the Nation State" by Richard Bean, *The Journal of Economic History*, vol. 33, no. 1 (March 1973): 203–221. Copyright © 1973 Economic History Association. Reprinted by permission of The Cambridge University Press.

prince could prevail against any substantive portion of his feudal barons unless he enjoyed the active support of a similar number of the barons. In 1600 A.D. most princes could be confident that their standing army would suppress all but the most widespread rebellions. This is ground already well trod by military, social, and political historians.[2] From their work it seems apparent that the drastic alteration of the political environment of Europe—the creation of nation-states—was a complex event with manifold origins. Doubtless religion, nationalism, transportation innovations, the rise of cities, population growth, and many other factors were involved, but this paper focuses only on two interrelated phenomena—changes in the art of war and in the power to tax. In this paper I will demonstrate a correlation between some fundamental changes in the art of war and increases in the power of central governments in Western Europe. I will present a model which provides a causal link between these events.

The model of international relations that is the foundation of the explanation for the rise of the nation-state presented by this paper is essentially the theory of the firm of modern economics. At any point in time there are both centripetal and centrifugal forces acting upon a firm and upon a political unit. The existence of indivisibilities and the gains of specialization can give rise to economies of scale for firms in an industry. Analogously, there are advantages of large size among states. The larger state can allow the realization of more gains from trade by providing a larger free trade area, and per capita defense costs should tend to fall because of simple geometry—doubling the area of a state usually less than doubles the border needing defense and so more resources are available per linear mile. If there were no check, no contrary force, the largest firm would have the lowest average costs, would undersell the smaller firms while growing ever larger, and eventually would monopolize the industry. The same process would be expected to occur in the political realm. A state would absorb its smaller neighbors by merger or conquest, waxing ever more irresistible with each addition until the most effective state became the only state.

Few industries are monopolies, and we have never had a world government; clearly economies of scale are checked at some point by decreasing returns. The larger the organization, whether a business firm or a government, the larger are the problems of command and control. As the size and complexity of the organization rise, so does the amount of information that must be handled by the organization, but distance and volume increase the time-lag between stimulus, decision, and reaction. In the case of the state, language, religious, and racial barriers and regional particularism increase the costs of administration and control.

The combination of initial economies of scale and eventually decreasing returns create a "U-shaped" long run average cost curve with, perhaps, a range of constant costs. Competition will tend to eliminate firms whose size is outside the optimal range. Similarly, the interaction of centripetal and centrifugal forces will determine the optimal range of size of the state. States larger than the optimal range tend to disintegrate, and those smaller tend to be absorbed.

The central argument of this paper is that changes in military technology or in administrative technique can alter this range of optimum sizes of the state. It is possible that such a shift in the optimum size range caused the breakup of the Western Roman and Carolingian Empires and very probable that it was responsible for the reamalgamation of states in Western Europe about 1500 A.D. The task of the remainder of this paper is to pinpoint the changes in the arts of war or administration that were responsible for the rise of the nation-state.

THE ARTS OF WAR

Some details of the military history of Europe between 1 A.D. and 1600 A.D. are necessary for an understanding of the fundamental political changes of the era.[3] The dominant fighting force in classical times was the professional infantry of the Roman Legion. Cavalry and light infantry with missile weapons (bow or sling) were purely auxiliary and were relatively few in numbers. The old system of the Roman Legion ended with the fourth century when most of the legions were destroyed in battle by the Goths. The legions were not replaced and we are now uncertain as to what did happen in the art of war during the next four centuries.[4] Probably by 800 A.D., and certainly before 900 A.D., cavalry had become the dominant fighting force of the Turks, Saracens, Byzantines, and of all but the Saxon and Scandinavian fringes of Western Europe.

In general, the system dominating Europe from the eighth until the fourteenth century was based on the man-at-arms. This armored heavy cavalry dominated open field engagements, but the rising strength and numbers of castles made those battles less and less decisive. The typical medieval European army had many more infantry than cavalry, but these foot soldiers were of relatively little military importance. Untrained and ill-armed, the peasant levies usually did most of the dying and little of the killing. Their principal use was in sieges and the decisive importance of the infantry bowmen at Hastings (1066 A.D.) was exceptional. Exceptional too was the rapidity of the Norman conquest. Such speed was possible only because of the general absence of castles in Saxon England.

The undisputed reign of the horsemen in Europe ended in the fourteenth century. The burghers of Flanders at Courtrai (1302 A.D.) and the Scots at Bannockburn (1314 A.D.) showed that under favorable circumstances the pike-phalanx could be invulnerable to the cavalry charge. The Swiss at Morgarten (1315 A.D.) and Laupen (1339 A.D.) re-emphasized the lesson. The English combined dismounted men-at-arms with masses of archers armed with the longbow to destroy the Scot infantry at Dupplin Moor (1332 A.D.) and Halidon Hill (1333 A.D.). The same system beat the feudal cavalry of France at Crécy (1346 A.D.) and consistently thereafter until finally the cannon allowed the French to force the English to move out of their essentially defensive formation at Formigny in 1450 A.D. Until the seventeenth century, cannons were usually of little importance in the field because of their slow rate of fire and their immobility. The cannon was important only where the army weak in artillery chose to stand on the defensive, as at Formigny or Ravenna (1512 A.D.), or where other arms could bring a pike-phalanx to a halt so that it could be shot to pieces at leisure, as at Marignano (1515 A.D.).

The levies of infantry in the medieval period were generally not professional soldiers, a fact that goes far toward explaining their ineffectiveness when opposed by the feudal knight or the man-at-arms who was a professional, well practiced with his weapons and experienced in war. Professional infantry almost completely disappeared from feudal Europe during the Middle Ages. One reason was that the mobility of cavalry made it much better suited to counter raiding parties. A much more important reason is that infantry, whether armed with bow, pike, crossbow, or handgun, are practically helpless in small parties. In the field they are only useful when *en masse* and trained to act *en masse,* as were the professional soldiers of England or Switzerland in their prime in the fourteenth and fifteenth centuries.[5] This is not nearly so true of cavalry. It was, therefore, quite natural that the principal weapon system in a decentralized and non-market society tended to be cavalry.

The feudal castle is as much a part of the modern image of the Middle Ages as is the armored knight. By about 1200 A.D., almost all of Western Europe was dotted with stone castles that were nearly immune from force; their inhabitants were vulnerable only to starvation, a process that could sometimes take years.

The existence of numerous castles made it possible for quite small regions successfully to resist much larger opponents. Nominal feudal superiors and foreign invaders faced the same handicaps: Very often it simply cost more to conquer a region than the region was worth. Castles had to be starved out one by one, and the besieging army had to be fairly large. If not, it could be overwhelmed at an unexpected moment by a relieving force suddenly gathered from the uncovered castles of the region. But a large besieging army was difficult to sustain for months at a time in one place because foragers from the invading army quickly stripped bare the area around the besieged castle. The result was that the attackers often starved faster than the besieged and the siege failed. The consequence of this relative strength of the defense was that, in spite of the many wars in Western Europe between 1100 A.D. and 1450 A.D., war accounted for very few of the changes in the political map of the area. Conquests that did occur were usually very drawn-out affairs. For example, it took Henry V of England nearly ten years to conquer Normandy after his overwhelming victory at Agincourt (1415 A.D.).

In the middle of the fifteenth century, the cannon drastically altered the balance between offense and defense. In 1449—50 A.D., Charles VII of France regained Normandy in a small portion of the time it had taken the English to take it earlier in that century. His new siege train knocked down the old high masonry walls with dispatch, 60 fortified places being reduced in 369 days.[6] The breaching of the walls of Constantinople in 1453 by Turkish siege guns further emphasized the decline in the effectiveness of fortification. Constantinople was considered the strongest place in the world and had stood inviolable for over a millennium. More than fifty years passed before the art of fortification caught up with the new techniques of siege-craft, but by the second decade of the sixteenth century, the balance was again in favor of the defense. From then until the end of the eighteenth century, war was again generally an interminable sequence of sieges punctuated by occasional bloody but indecisive battles in the open field. The main difference in the defense-offense equation between the periods 1100—1440 A.D. and 1525—1790 A.D. was that in the latter period, the minimum effective scale of fortification was considerably larger. This was true of both construction costs and garrison size. As a consequence, there were many fewer places in Europe after 1525 A.D. with effective fortification than had been the case before 1450 A.D.

In summary, until 378 A.D., professional well-drilled infantry was dominant in war in the Western World. Since standardization and a long period of training to act *en masse* are very important with such forces, substantial economies of scale existed in the military realm. Cavalry began to replace infantry as the arbiter of battle after 378 A.D., and by about 750 A.D. this dominance was complete in all of Europe except the Saxon and Scandinavian fringe. Since there was much less military advantage to the centralized training of cavalry than of infantry, there was a greater chance for a decentralized state to survive in a world containing centralized states. The changes that came about in the quality and quantity of castles after 900 A.D. further reduced the military disadvantage of the decentralized state.

In the first half of the fourteenth century, it was demonstrated that, under some circumstances, well-drilled masses of infantry could stand up to cavalry. Further, it was shown that an army combining a well-trained pike-phalanx and missile-armed infantry trained to act *en masse,* or combining either type of infantry with cavalry, could almost always defeat an army made up of cavalry or of cavalry plus almost any number of ill-armed and untrained peasants. The revival of professional infantry as an important military force strengthened the centralized state relative to the decentralized state, and strengthened the monarch relative to his feudal barons. The sudden maturation in 1450 A.D. of the cannon, after a long infancy, as the destroyer of castles made a further and larger change in the art of war in favor of the centralized state, in favor of the aggressor state, in favor of the monarch over the feudal barons. By the 1520's, the art of fortification had advanced until it could cope with the cannon, but the new forts were much larger and more expensive than the medieval castles. For the rest of the century, war was largely a series of sieges carried out by professional soldiers. Infantry weapons and tactics in the sixteenth century gradually evolved to put more emphasis on firearms, but the pike remained important for defense against cavalry until about 1700 A.D., when the bayonet was adopted.

THE SIZE OF ARMIES

One possible yardstick to measure the impact of war upon society is the amount of resources devoted to war-like purposes. In the modern period we might simply compute the defense budgets as percentages of national incomes, but there are no such data for medieval, renaissance, or even early modern Europe. The best that we can accomplish are rough estimates, but even so, there is a clear pattern of national differences and of change over time. Approximate figures exist for the strength of armies and for population from Roman times through the modern era. The ratios of armed forces to the supporting population are limited by the size of the surplus above subsistence generated by the society and by the power of government to appropriate this surplus. Thus, large changes in this ratio over time provide a clue to other social changes.

The figures for military manpower presented in Table 1 are only a sampling from the available secondary literature. Much more complete series could be built up, but it is improbable that the effort would change in any important way the outline sketched here. The medieval figures are particularly weak because they are merely the "best guess" deflation by modern experts of the round numbers given by medieval chronicles. Further, the numbers given here lump mounted and armored knights together with spear-carrying peasants, even though their costs per capita (and their military effectiveness) differed by at least one order of magnitude. Most medieval data pertain to the strength of armies at particular battles. Since these armies usually consisted of short-term feudal levies mobilized for a maximum of 40 days each year, they are deflated in Table 2 by a factor of six to represent full-time equivalents. The resulting overestimate should partly balance the omission of the many castle garrisons left behind by the lords responding to the mobilization order of the king. The sixteenth-century figures generally understate total strength by omitting troops in garrisons at home or those serving in subsidiary war zones.

Although the ratios in Table 2 are only approximations of the actual fractions of the population that could be mobilized by the central authorities, several facts do stand out enough to be accepted with confidence. First, the feudal system of Europe was not able to maintain continuously in the field nearly so large an army in relation to population as were the Roman and early Byzantine Empires.[7] Second, after about 1500, the size of armies maintained in the field relative to the supporting population were several times as great as had been the case during the previous ten centuries. Third, the English,

Table 1. The Strength of Armies
(armies in thousands, populations in millions)

Date	ROMAN		BYZANTINE		ENGLISH		FRENCH		TURKISH		SPANISH-HAPSBURG		SCOTTISH	
	army	pop.	army	pop.	army	pop.	army	pop.	army	pop.	army	pop.	army	pop.
AD 1–350	300–500	50.0												
550			150	20.0										
1071			60	30.0										
1200					25[a]	1.9								
1214							50[a]	7.0						
1300					6	3.3								
1346							30[a]	13.5						
1347					32[a]	3.7								
1410–1450					4.5	2.1								
1460–1470					20[a]	2.3								
1480							12	13						
1500									100[a]	11.0				
1503											15	7.2		
1503–1525							20–45	15.0						
1513													35[a]	.6
1536											67	17.0		

Year				
1544	30	3.2		
1547			23[a]	.7
1557			50	17.0
1560's	30–40	17.0		
1563	9	3.7		
1566			50	22
1585	9	4.5		
1591			57	12.0
1592	10	4.6		
1599	22	4.8		

[a]Indicates a short-term feudal army.

SOURCES: Most of the figures for army strength are from Charles Oman, *A History of the Art of War in the Middle Ages* (2nd ed., London: Methuen, 1924), 2 vols; and *A History of the Art of War in the Sixteenth Century* (London: Methuen, 1937). See also J. F. C. Fuller, *Armament and History* (New York: Scribner's, 1945), p. 45; Trever, *History of Ancient Civilization* (New York: Harcourt, Brace, 1939), II, p. 331; F. C. Dietz, *English Public Finance, 1558–1641* (New York: Century, 1932), pp. 83, 93, 445; and *The New Cambridge Modern History of Europe*, VI, pp. 197, 229, 741, 821; VII, 182, 184. The population data are from J. C. Russell, *British Medieval Population* (Albuquerque: University of New Mexico, 1948), pp. 270, 280, 360–62; and "Ancient and Medieval Population," *Transactions of the American Philosophical Society*, XLVIII, part 3 (1958), pp. 7, 68, 100, 102, 116–18, 148, and *The Cambridge Economic History of Europe*, IV, p. 52. The population figures as used here are quite crude and are often interpolations between uncertain benchmarks.

Table 2. Full-time Soldiers/1000 Population

Date	Roman	Byzan-tine	English	French	Turkish	Spanish-Hapsburg	Scottish
AD 1–350	6. to 10.						
550		7.5					
1071		2.[a]					
1200			[2.][a][b]				
1214				[1.][a]			
1300			2.[a]				
1346				[0.5][a]			
1347			[1.5][a]				
1410–1450			2.[a]				
1460–1470			[1.5][a]				
1480				0.9[a]			
1500					[1.5][a]		
1503						2.[a]	
1503–1525				2.–3.[a]			
1513			10.0[a]				[8.][a]
1536						4.[a]	
1544			10.0[a]				
1547			[0.6][a]				[6.][a]
1557						3.[a]	
1560's				2. or 3.[a]			
1563			0.3[a]				
1566					2. or 3.		
1585			0.3[a]				
1591						4. or 5.[a]	
1592			2.[a]				
1599			4.6				

[a]Less than true ratios because they omit some fortress garrisons or some subsidiary field armies.

[b]Ratios enclosed in brackets [ ] are based on an assumed army strength one sixth of the actual strength of a particular short-term feudal army.

SOURCES: See Table 1.

French, Hapsburgs, and Turks all show similar levels at any given time in their abilities to mobilize their populations—the English governments appearing consistently somewhat more effective, although the high English ratios of the early 1500's are misleadingly high due to the relatively temporary nature of those particular armies.[8] The interesting discontinuities in the series are the fall in the soldier/population ratio at the end of the classical period and the rise in the ratio at the beginning of the sixteenth century. These discontinuities approximately correspond with the beginning and the end of the feudal period and, indeed, may offer one means of dating the period. The question of interest is the causal connection between the altered institutional system and the new ratios of military strength to population.

The ratios in Table 2 may be converted into figures of more modern meaning by assuming that one third of the population was in the labor force and that one full-time member of the labor force was required to support each full-time soldier. Under these assumptions, an approximation of the percentage of the labor force diverted into military affairs is yielded by taking double the known army strength as a percentage of one third of the population. If we further assume that military affairs consumed a proportionate amount of the other factors of production, up to six percent of national income was spent on defense by the Roman Empire, less than one percent in Medieval Europe,[9] over two percent in the sixteenth century, and six to twelve percent in the eighteenth century. The actual figure has been about ten percent in the United States since World War II.

GOVERNMENT REVENUE

The dramatic rise in the size of armies fielded after about 1500 A.D. would be expected to be reflected in the treasury records of the warring governments. The data available before late in the seventeenth century are crude; guesswork and interpolation are unavoidable. Nevertheless, even after adjustment for increasing prices and populations, the evidence indicates that there was a large increase in the ability to raise revenue enjoyed by the governments of Spain, France, and England late in the fifteenth century. In real per capita terms the multiple seems to have been nearly two for England, two for France, and as high as ten or twenty for Spain.[10] There is a slowly rising trend thereafter in the series for France and England, but nothing so dramatic as the leap late in the fifteenth century.

Tables 3 and 4 are summaries of government revenues and the adjustment used to make them comparable over time. It must be emphasized that these data are quite crude. The revenue series are not complete. The population figures are the best guesses of the experts and interpolations between those best guesses. The price deflators used were money wages of building craftsmen because our main interest here is the command over manpower by the central authorities.

The sources of government revenue changed considerably during this period. Medieval kings were expected to meet the normal expenses of government from their "own" revenue—that is, from rents on the crown lands, feudal dues, and other customary sources. In wartime the king could call upon those liable for military service but increasingly preferred to accept "scutage" instead, a cash payment substituting for personal military service. All of these sources of income were strictly limited by feudal custom. In addition, the English crown drew substantial revenue from wool customs, the Spanish from the "mesta" (a sheep-herder's guild), and the French from the "gabelle" or salt monopoly. These two were not easy to increase in time of need, for there was the real danger of killing the goose while grasping for the egg. In the medieval period, kings periodically reaped considerable revenue from coinage debasement, but this ploy was largely abandoned in the Renaissance as being too disruptive to trade.

The final important source of revenue was the form of taxes most like the modern mainstays of government—"tithes," which were wealth or income taxes and sales taxes. These were generally not available except for short periods and then only when voted by the Parliament, Cortez, or Estates General. These taxes were normally granted only in real military emergencies and were usually only one-time levies. In France in the 1440's and in Spain in the 1480's the rulers were able to seize these taxes as a right and thus dispense with the legislative bodies. These fundamental alterations in the implicit "constitutions" made "absolute" monarchy a possibility in those countries. In England the Tudors and then the Stuarts failed to establish a royal right to levy taxes directly, and the attempt of Charles I to bypass Parliament in raising revenue was the direct cause of the English Civil War. The conflict between the governed and the governors over the

Table 3. Annual English Government Revenues

Date	Revenue £ Sterling	Index of Building Craftsmen's Money Wages (1500 = 100)	"Real" Revenue (£)	Population (Millions)	Real Revenue Per Capita (£)	Index of Real Revenue Per Capita (1505– 1509 = 100)
1272–1307	67,000	50	134,000	3.3	.041	93
1307–1327	91,000	63	144,000	(3.5)[b]	.041	93
1327–1377	140,000	80	175,000	3.7	.047	107
1377–1399	139,500	83	168,000	2.2	.076	172
1400	66,000	83	79,500	2.2	.036	82
1413–1422	115,000	100	115,000	2.1	.055	125
1422–1438	57,000	100	57,000	(2.1)	.026	59
1438–1454	70,000	100	70,000	2.2	.032	73
1454–1461	44,000	100	44,000	(2.3)	.019	43
1461–1469	59,000	100	59,000	(2.4)	.025	57
1472–1482	79,000	100	79,000	(2.4)	.033	75
1482–1485	54,000	100	54,000	(2.4)	.023	52
1505–1509	142,000	100	142,000	2.6	.044	100
1552	168,000	125	134,400	3.2	.042	95
1598–1603	520,000[a]	200	260,000	4.81	.054	123
1603–1608	420,000[a]	200	210,000	(5.0)	.042	95
1619	486,000	200	243,000	(5.3)	.043	98
1628	700,000	200	350,000	5.6	.063	143
1631–1635	618,000	233	265,000	(5.6)	.047	107
1640	858,000	233	368,000	(5.7)	.065	148

[a]expenditures.

[b]( ) interpolations.

SOURCES: Revenue 1272–1485 from Sir J. H. Ramsay, *A History of the Revenues of the Kings of England, 1066–1399* (Oxford: Clarendon, 1925), Vol. I, pp. 1, 7, 191, 227, 261, 363, and Vol. II, pp. 86, 146, 292, 427; and *Lancaster and York: A Century of English History, 1399–1455 AD* (Oxford: Clarendon, 1892), Vol. I, pp. 321, 328, 453, and Vol. II, pp. 266–7, 471–2, 560. Revenue 1505–1640 from F. C. Dietz, "English Government Finance, 1485–1558," *University of Illinois Studies in the Social Sciences,* IX (September, 1920), p. 190; and *English Public Finance, 1558–1641* (New York: Century, 1932), pp. 86, 111–12, 185, 269. The wage index was calculated from E. H. Phelps-Brown and S. V. Hopkins, "Seven Centuries of Building Wages," *Economica,* XXII (1955), p. 205. See Table 1 for the sources of the population data.

control of taxes was widespread in Europe at this time—in Sweden, for example, Karl Knutsson was deposed in 1457 A.D. for trying to introduce new taxes.

GOVERNMENT EXPENDITURE

Medieval government expenditures generally moved fairly closely with government revenues. After 1500 A.D. government revenues (especially on the Continent) were much more stable as taxes became permanent instead of episodic, but government ex-

Table 4. Annual French Government Revenues

Date	Revenue Livres Tournois (millions)	Index of Building Craftsmen's Money Wages (1491–1500 = 100)	"Real" Revenue L. t. (millions)	Population (millions)	Real Revenue Per Capita (L. t.)	Index of Real Revenue Per Capita (1500 = 100, wages)	Alternate Index of Real Revenue Per Capita (1500 = 100 wheat)[a]
1222	.23			7.4			24
1228–1238	.2			7.6			18
1335	.46			13.5			15
1420–1435	1.0 to 2.0	119	.8 to 1.7	10.6	.08 to .16	30–60	9–18
1450	3.0	132	2.3	10.6	.22	81	102
1460–1480	to 5.0 or 6.0	103	4.9 or 5.8	12.0	.41 or .48	152–178	150–181
1484–1490	3.0 or 4.0	101	3.0 or 4.0	13.0	.23 or .31	85–115	48–63
1500	4.0	99	4.0	15.0	.27	100	100
1514	4.9	109	4.5	15.5	.29	107	61
1523	5.2	132	3.9	16.0	.24	89	23
1546	9.0	127	7.1	16.5	.43	159	46
1560	12.3	217	5.7	17.0	.34	126	30
1576	15.8	358	4.4	17.0	.26	96	24
1588	18.0	477	3.8	17.0	.22	81	12
1597	30.0	398	7.5	17.0	.44	163	24
1607	31.4	398	7.9	18.0	.44	163	49

[a] Usher's French wheat prices used as the deflator instead of craftsmen wages. Over ranges the median price of wheat was used. Base was median of 1491–1500.

SOURCES: Revenue from F. B. Fryde and M. M. Fryde, in M. M. Postan, E. E. Rich, Edward Miller, eds., *Cambridge Economic History of Europe* (2nd ed.; Cambridge: Cambridge University Press, 1963), III, 479; Ferdinand Lot and Robert Fawtier, *Histoire des institutions Francaises au moyen age* (Paris: Presses Universitaires de France, 1958), II, 159, 270–72; and J.-J. Clamagerar, *Histoire de l'impot en France* (Paris, 1867–1868), I, 324, II 26, 66, 67, 81, 86, 98, 111, 112, 129, 197–202, 230, 338, 339, 381. The wage index was calculated from M. Baulant "Le salaire de ouvriers du batiment a Paris de 1400 a 1726," *Annales: Economies, Societes, Civilisations*, Vol. XXVI (March/April 1971), pp. 482–3. See Table 1 for the population data. Index of French wheat prices used in calculating the Alternate Index of Real Revenue Per Capita was estimated from A. P. Usher, "The General Course of Wheat Prices in France: 1350–1788," *Review of Economics and Statistics*, XII (1930), pp. 162, 167.

penditure still varied considerably over time as periods of peace and war alternated. The costs of war were increasingly met by deficit finance. As a consequence, debt service charges came to bulk large in peace-time budgets.

War, preparation for war, and the payments to debts from previous wars were more important than the sum of all other types of expenditure combined. Reasonably complete expenditure records are rare, but the spadework of historians has yielded us enough cases to make it clear that the importance of war in state budgets was nothing new. The disbursements of Edward III of England for the years 1369–70 A.D. have been summarized and published. When military and naval costs, debt service and re-payment, and sundry foreign policy costs such as bribes and ransoms are summed, they constitute some seventy percent of all expenditures.[11] Henry V, 1413–1422 A.D., spent about two thirds of his budget plus nearly all of the revenues from his French posses-sions in the same way.[12] Henry VII, 1485–1509 A.D., may have been able to keep such costs below half of his budget in some peacetime years, but it seems certain that no other English ruler in that century managed so well. Three quarters of the expenditures in the last five years of Elizabeth I (1598–1603 A.D.) were for war or war-related causes. In the first five years of James I (1603–1608 A.D.) the proportion was cut to one third, but it rose later in his reign.[13]

The same pattern existed on the continent. In France after 1445 A.D., when the *Compagnies d'Ordonnance* were established as a standing army of heavy cavalry some 12,000 strong, their payroll alone stood at 720,000 Livres tournois, "L(t)," out of a budget of perhaps 3 million L(t). Clearly, when other incidental military costs, debt ser-vice, and sundry costs of international relations are added, the sum would considerably exceed the "civilian" share of the budget.[14] Under Louis XI (1461–1483 A.D.) the French army payroll rose from 907,000 L(t) to 2.7 million L(t), while the total rev-enue rose toward 9 million L(t); with other foreign policy costs added, the propor-tion remains over half.[15] The recurrent military crises of the sixteenth century made such expenditures bulk even larger. Single campaigns such as those in 1536 A.D. and 1537 A.D. often consumed more money than the total government revenue for the year. The Hapsburgs had the same problems. In the five years of 1572 to 1576 A.D., more than three quarters of the Spanish budget went to defense and debt service; ex-penditures were half again as large as revenues.[16]

In general it can be said that the revenues of the central governments of Western Europe rose sharply in the second half of the fifteenth century and continued to rise, though more slowly, thereafter. The original increase represented at least a doubling of the real per capita burden upon the citizens. Most of this new revenue was spent on war, with the lesser portion being divided between a more luxuriant court and the support of the expanded bureaucracy that made possible the collection of the new revenues.

PROFESSIONAL ARMIES

In war, as in most trades, the specialist has the advantage. The systems used to support specialists in defense have varied considerably over time in Europe. The Roman Empire levied general taxes to support a professional standing army. A legionnaire enlisted in a unit as a youth and remained in that unit until he retired in his middle age. The system that came to dominate Europe by 900 A.D. was quite different. The feudal system was one of personal obligations that avoided the necessity of a central taxing authority. In theory the king granted large blocks of land to a group of lords in return for their obligation to supply a specified number of soldiers for a specified length of time when the king called for their services. These great lords, in turn, sub-infeudated most of the lands to lesser lords in return for military services. (This process of the "granting of livings" is very similar to what seems to be the modern practice of the Mafia.) The obvious disadvantage of the system is that once the "livings" become hereditary the vassal has a tendency to ignore his obligations to higher authority.

The feudal method of providing defense is likely to produce weak kings and a highly decentralized system of authority. However, in an era when castles were nearly invulnerable to anything but hunger, and heavy cavalry dominated the open battle field, the feudal system proved to be a highly effective defense against foreign aggressors. An aggressor found his way blocked by castles manned by people with strong personal reasons to resist strenuously. Supply considerations made it impossible to bypass them unless the goal was merely to make a quick raid.[17] If the aggressor did stop to besiege the frontier castles he would soon be threatened by the feudal chivalry of the whole realm plus a large body of locally raised peasant infantry.

The feudal levy was not nearly so effective on the offensive as it was on the defensive because it could not be kept in the field for a long enough period of time. Only when the victim was weak enough and close enough at hand was it possible to act as Edward I did in his conquest of Wales—calling up a fraction of the levy at a time in order to have an army in the field continuously all year. The kings of England found that this system was not practical for their wars in the more distant France because such a large part of the 40-day obligation was consumed in just getting to the scene of the action. In the Hundred Years War, the kings of England maintained a year-round army of four to six thousand men paid by the crown, supplemented occasionally with feudal levies. Only thus could sieges be pursued and places such as Calais and Fronsac be defended. England also found it necessary to place garrisons on the Scot border and in Ireland.

The spectacular conquests of the Middle Ages—Saxon England, Sicily, and the Levant—were not carried out by feudal armies. Instead, the conquerors were bands of adventurers who expected to be paid by their share of the loot, and most of that loot was land and serfs. These adventurers were part of a drifting European population of professional soldiers who made up the bulk of the paid retinues maintained by every great lord and king. Since the kings were the greatest of the feudal lords they had the largest retinues, but these could hardly be called standing armies. After deducting the necessary garrisons for the royal castles the residual constituted little more than a bodyguard.

Bodies of mercenary troops were up for hire in Western Europe from at least the twelfth century. Brabancon pikemen, men-at-arms from Flanders, and Genoese crossbowmen all appeared at various times in England during times of civil strife. Such troops frequently appeared in the array of Continental armies and by the fifteenth century composed the bulk of the armies of the Italian city-states. In the rest of Europe, however, such troops were merely supplements to the usual feudal armies, and (except for English long-bowmen and Swiss pikemen) there is no reason to suppose that they were much superior to the feudal troops raised in the usual manner.

In general, mercenaries were hired for an immediate need and were discharged when that need had passed. At the end of major wars unemployed bands of mercenaries frequently became brigands and this problem was the probable cause for the creation of the first standing army in Europe since before the Middle Ages. The *Compagnies d'Ordonnance* were raised in France beginning in 1445 A.D. There were originally twenty companies of 600 men each, posted at various points throughout the country to preserve order. These troops were organized in the modern style in that the officers were royal appointees and served at the pleasure of the king. This contrasts with the previous system of mercenaries, where an individual leader leased his band as his personal property or raised the band under contract. A few years later Louis XI instituted another innovation in the French military system when he established *Francs Archers,* a 16,000 man militia intended to be a national infantry. This experiment was unsuccessful and was abandoned after 1479 A.D. and Swiss mercenary pikemen were ultimately substituted.

The obvious advantages of a standing army over either foreign or domestic enemies who were relying on feudal levies did not go unnoticed by sovereigns outside of France. In 1486 A.D., the Holy Roman Emperor Maximilian raised the *landknechts,* pikemen on the Swiss model, as a permanent force. He made some effort to conceal the fact from the Diet, which had the normal feudal aversion to standing armies.[18] The Spanish also followed suit, and the *tercios* of Spanish infantry ultimately became the best in the world.

CONCLUSIONS

Through the bulk of this paper I have labored to establish the following propositions: changes in the art of war in the fourteenth century greatly increased the importance of infantry and correspondingly reduced the importance of heavy calvary; the maturation of the siege cannon in the mid-fifteenth century practically eliminated the castle as an important factor in war; in the later fifteenth century standing armies began to appear in Europe; at the end of the fifteenth century the size of armies increased sharply, as did the revenues of central governments and their expenditures on military affairs; and finally, in the 1450–1550 A.D. period the first generation of European nation-states coalesced under the control of central authority. My argument is that these events were causally connected. The increased effectiveness of infantry resulted in a shift in the production function of defense so that the minimum efficient size of state was increased and the centralized state was given a greater advantage over the decentralized state. The siege train of cannon, like units of infantry, showed considerable economies of scale, and the flowering of the cannon in the mid-fifteenth century further increased the minimum effective size of states and drastically reduced the ability of the feudal nobility to resist the authority of the central government. All over Western Europe the feudal nobility became subordinate to the central governments—the process being largely complete by 1500 A.D. Once the power to tax had been successfully appropriated by any one sovereign, once he had used that power to bribe or coerce his nobility into acquiescence, that state could face all neighboring states with the choice of being conquered or of centralizing authority and raising taxes. The increases in the size of armies, of government revenues, and of government expenditures on military affairs that occurred in the early sixteenth century are manifestations of this phenomenon. A new equilibrium was established between the states of Europe before the end of the century, and, despite expensive and bloody wars, little change in borders occurred again until the French Revolution.

Economic historians need to be concerned with this concentration of power, because the way in which it occurred probably determined the pattern of economic growth in Europe. The changes in the art of war practically guaranteed the weakening of the feudal nobility, the concentration of power within each state, and the reduction of the number of states. However, there was no certainty as to which faction within the nation would control the new centralized state. In France and Spain the crown managed to gain control of power to tax. In Holland and England these powers were retained by elective bodies in which merchants were heavily represented. In Eastern Europe the great landowners retained substantial control. In Holland and England the domestic policies pursued by the new centralized states were less inimical to economic growth than were the catastrophic policies in Spain and France. In the latter two cases, the crown bought off the nobility by granting tax exemptions and, because the merchants lacked the power to resist, pursued economic policies that ultimately led to economic stagnation. This paper has presented an explanation for the concentration of political power in Europe from 1450 to 1550 A.D. It has not explained why different groups gained control of this power in different states. That task remains a challenge to further research.

NOTES

1. D. C. North and R. P. Thomas, *The Rise of the Western World: A New Economic History* (Cambridge: forthcoming 1973).

2. The reader will doubtless note that many of the notions presented in this paper without attribution are not original to this author, but the explaining of the rise of the nation-state in Europe is a task quite large enough without attempting to trace to its ultimate origin every previous idea on the subject.

3. The details of the military history of Europe are based on Sir Charles Oman, *A History of the Art of War in the Middle Ages,* 2 vols (2nd ed., London: Methuen, 1924), and *A History of the Art of War in the Sixteenth Century* (London: Methuen, 1937).

4. Lynn White, *Medieval Technology and Social Change* (Oxford: Oxford University Press, 1967), pp. 1–38.

5. Oman, *Middle Ages,* II, p. 303.

6. Ibid., p. 226.

7. This is not the same thing as saying that the proportion of total resources devoted to military affairs was larger in the Classical era than in the Middle Ages. We can ascertain, within some limits of uncertainty, the size of field armies. However, the military obligations of the feudal lords were specific and limited. We simply do not know how large were the garrisons left behind by the various lords—ranging from the petty barons to the king himself.

8. The real per capita revenues of the English crown seem to have been only about one third higher than those of the French crown at the beginning of the sixteenth century, but they were perhaps three or four times greater in the High Middle Ages. See Tables 3 and 4. In 1500 there were about ten Livres tournois per pound sterling. See F. C. Dietz, "English Government Finance, 1485–1558," *University of Illinois Studies in the Social Sciences,* IX (September, 1920), p. 215.

9. But see footnote 7.

10. See Tables 3 and 4 for England and France. J. V. Vives, *An Economic History of Spain* (3rd ed. trans., Princeton: Princeton University Press, 1969), p. 312, says the revenue of that royal treasury rose from 800,000 maravedis in 1470 to 22,000,000 maravedis in 1504.

11. Sir J. H. Ramsay, *A History of the Revenues of the Kings of England, 1066–1399* (Oxford: Clarendon, 1925), Vol. II, p. 293.

12. Sir J. H. Ramsay, *Lancaster and York: A Century of English History, 1399–1485 AD* (Oxford: Clarendon, 1925), Vol. I, pp. 317 ff.

13. Dietz, *English Public Finance, 1558–1641* (New York: Century, 1932), pp. 111–12, 216.

14. Oman, *Middle Ages,* II, 432.

15. Charles Petit-Dutaillis, in Ernest Lavisse, ed., *Histoire de France depuis les origines jusqu'à la révolution* (Paris: Hachette, 1911), IV, pt. 2, p. 405n.

16. G. Parker, "Spain, Her Enemies and the Revolt of the Netherlands, 1559–1648," *Past and Present,* IL (1970), p. 85.

17. This is about all that Edward II accomplished during the first half of the Hundred Years War in spite of the great victories of Crécy and Poitiers.

18. Oman, *Sixteenth Century,* p. 75.

Reading 4-2

The Concert of Europe
A Fresh Look at an International System
Richard B. Elrod

R elations between states differ from all other forms of social interaction. As Raymond Aron reminds us, interstate relations "involve, in essence, the alternatives of peace and war."[1] Moreover, the sources of international dissension and discord generally seem to overbalance the forces for harmony. The study of international politics must proceed from certain inescapable assumptions: the inevitable clash of national interests and prestige; the perceptions and misperceptions of statesmen and would-be statesmen; the operation of impersonal technological and social forces that imprison both leaders and led; the irrepressible friction between change and inertia. All these factors—and others—constitute the dynamics of interstate relations that make peace a precious, precarious matter.

History reveals, however, that statesmen were more successful in some periods in the past than during others in managing and controlling these unavoidable tensions. Certain constraining and moderating forces operated that compelled or induced sovereign states to refrain from adventurous and aggressive foreign policies. From 1815 to 1854 European interstate relations clearly conformed to that pattern. No wars occurred between the great powers; a large measure of security and stability characterized the international system. Statesmen exercised self-restraint and cooperated in regulating several diplomatic crises that could easily have degenerated into catastrophe. The explanation for this uncommon willingness on the part of great powers to act with patience and self-abnegation is not simple. Some scholars credit the diplomats of that era with extraordinary skill and perception. In the aftermath of the long and costly wars against revolutionary France, European leaders were understandably appreciative of the need for peace, and they displayed impressive versatility in its preservation. Adherents of the now fashionable premise of the primacy of domestic politics tend to seek the answer in the relative quiescence of internal affairs in the postwar period. Most observers, perhaps, continue to attribute peace to the restoration and operation of the European balance of power.[2]

These explanations are plausible and no doubt partially correct; peace, no less than war, issues from a multiplicity of causes. Yet one important element is often overlooked: the Concert of Europe, the international system within which European governments formulated and conducted policy. The Concert seldom receives much credit for the long period of peace after 1815; some would dispute its peace-keeping function entirely, others would deny its very existence.[3] In this essay, I will consider the Concert of Europe as a conscious and generally effective attempt by European statesmen to maintain peaceful relations between sovereign states. I will also offer some general reflections and tentative conclusions about the meaning, the nature, and the operation of concert diplomacy.[4] For the European Concert—the machinery it developed, the rationale that lay behind it, the rules and procedures it engendered—constituted an essential ingredient of European peace and stability between the Congress of Vienna and

SOURCE: From "The Concert of Europe: A Fresh Look at an International System" by Richard B. Elrod, *World Politics*, vol. 28, no. 2 (1976): 159–174. Copyright © 1976 The Johns Hopkins University Press. Reprinted by permission.

the Crimean War. It was a functioning and promising system of international relations, one that differed quite radically from the balance-of-power politics of the eighteenth century and the total wars of the first half of the twentieth. It is worthy of a brief re-examination.[5]

ORIGINS OF THE CONCERT

The concept of concert diplomacy hardly emerged fully defined or completely thought-out. Certain assumptions and procedures became customary and prescriptive through application. In the first instance, the Concert derived from the common realization of European statesmen of the Napoleonic era that something new and different must be devised to mitigate the increasingly chaotic and warlike balance-of-power system of the previous century. Both critics and defenders of the balance-of-power idea, even during its apogee, recognized that it was unsatisfactory.[6] By the end of the eighteenth century the satirical observation of Alexander Pope, issued as early as 1711, had become ominously prophetic:

> Now Europe's balanc'd, neither Side prevails,
> For Nothing's left in either of the Scales.[7]

Balance-of-power politics—the politics of confrontation—generated intolerable international tensions, produced increasingly serious armed conflicts, and inspired progressively extravagant plans of aggression. It neither maintained peace nor preserved the independence of sovereign states; by the time of the French Revolution, the international system had broken down altogether.[8]

Friedrich von Gentz, writing in 1818, applauded the progress made by European statesmen in transcending the balance-of-power idea, "the principle which has governed, and has also too often troubled and bloodied Europe for three centuries."[9] John Capodistrias, the advisor of Alexander I of Russia, similarly deplored a return to "the terrible empire of anarchy and revolutionary despotism with all the horrors of the *divide et impera* of the old diplomacy."[10] This common determination to surmount the malignant system of the past represented, as one writer remarks, "a revolution in diplomatic history."[11] The Concert of Europe was born, and with it a genuine sense of solidarity and responsibility for Europe, a spirit of "national self-restraint, respect for the public law as defined in treaties, and willingness to enforce its observance by concerted action. . . ."[12]

The Concert connoted, first of all, a new method of diplomacy—diplomacy by congress or conference (or, as Gentz once called it, "the diplomacy of the highway"). In this connection the Concert may be defined as the great powers meeting together at times of international crisis to maintain peace and to develop European solutions to European problems. Statesmen who had finally recognized the necessity of cooperation in the last coalition against Napoleon continued to believe in the advantages of collaboration to maintain the postwar settlement. Lord Castlereagh of Great Britain, who frequently called the congresses "reunions," especially emphasized this function: "I am quite convinced that past habits, common glory and those occasional meetings, displays and repledges are among the best securities Europe now has for a durable peace."[13]

But the Concert of Europe was more than an innovation in diplomatic technique. It cannot be confined simply to the era of the great European congresses between 1815 and 1823.[14] The essential precepts of concert diplomacy survived the congress era and assisted materially in the maintenance of peace until 1854. For the European Concert was also a conceptual norm among the great powers of the proper and permissible aims and methods of international politics. It gradually came to embody a code of conduct for international behavior, one that transcended the ideological division between the three conservative Eastern powers and the more liberal Western states. Each side naturally aspired to use concert diplomacy as an instrument of its own political creed and was sometimes tempted to seek alternative methods to the Concert.[15] Yet for over three decades European statesmen generally shared the assumptions which predicated concert diplomacy, and in most cases were willing to abide by its rules.

RULES OF CONCERT DIPLOMACY

What, then, were the underlying assumptions and the unwritten rules of concert diplomacy? First of all, the Concert of Europe meant great-power tutelage over the rest of Europe. It consisted only of the great powers; lesser states were occasionally consulted when their interests were involved, but they possessed few rights and certainly not that of equality. In the context of the post-Napoleonic period this development was natural and probably necessary. On the surface, moreover, it hardly represented a significant deviation from actual practice in the past. But the idea of the great powers acting in unity was in itself somewhat novel and clearly rested upon a fresh postulate. The recognition of a European community of interests, and commitment to its defense, required of the great European states a new posture and a special accountability. Great-power tutelage was obligatory, for only the great powers possessed the resources, the prestige, and the vision to contend with the transcendent concerns of peace or war, of stability or disorder. As Castlereagh observed in 1818, "the Great Powers feel that they have not only a common interest, but a common duty to attend to."[16] Gentz concluded in the same year that "the five powers at the head of the federation are the only ones who could destroy the general system by changing their policies. Squabbles and changes among the others could never have that effect."[17] Implicit in this judgment was the cynical but accurate assessment that so long as the great powers were in agreement, the lesser states could cause little trouble.

The smaller states were thus shunted aside because the great powers had the responsibility of preserving the peace of Europe and of protecting a European society menaced by revolutionary principles. Equally important was that the emphasis upon great-power unity constituted a barrier against unilateral action by any state; it served to constrain even the great powers. No one power could attempt to settle a European question by an independent and self-regulated initiative. European problems must receive European answers; the policies of each were subject to the scrutiny and sanction of all. Prince Metternich verbalized this concept in 1820 when he remarked that the most essential basis of European repose was "the most absolute solidarity . . . in all questions of a general interest" and the assurance that none of the great powers would ever "proceed alone on such matters."[18] This explains the natural and virtually imperative tendency in concert diplomacy to internationalize diplomatic questions, to replace individual claims and prerogatives by European ones. Aversion to unilateral action or aggrandizement gave birth to the first of the unwritten rules of concert diplomacy: that the proper way of dealing with international crises was through conference diplomacy. Acceptance of this precept was general throughout the first half of the nineteenth century. Admittedly, statesmen sometimes explored other possibilities first and often became exasperated with the cumbersome and time-consuming procedure of diplomacy by conference.[19] Great-power conferences, furthermore, could not resolve all the problems that they considered. Even so, realistic diplomats had to acknowledge the basic efficacy of joint consultation and action. The conference method clearly tended to moderate more extreme positions and to reinforce the conception of the European great powers as a special group, with special responsibilities as well as special privileges.

A second and closely related rule followed logically: that territorial changes in Europe were subject to the sanction of the great powers. Though sometimes an imperfect and unharmonious method of acknowledging necessary alterations, this procedure was the only means of legitimizing new arrangements. The great powers acting in concert determined the acceptable and appropriate limits of change. They revised settlements considered too drastic, and substituted European action and guarantees for unilateral claims. The insistence of the great powers upon reviewing modifications in the international order represented another significant deterrence against immoderate international conduct. By the simple process of submitting questions to "collective deliberation" the actions of revisionist powers were circumscribed.[20]

The two rules of diplomacy by conference and of great-power sanction of change enjoyed a remarkable longevity in European diplomatic practice. They were appealed to, and many times utilized, throughout the nineteenth century. These first two canons, however, pertained only to the general objectives and machinery of concert diplomacy. Among the other ingredients that accounted for the willingness of the great powers to participate in the Concert and to accept its decisions there are two additional prescriptions which were crucial to the successful operation of concert diplomacy. The third dictum was that essential members of the states system must be protected and defended. Obviously this pertained first to the five great powers. But certain areas in which the great powers were in contention could be just as important to the system as the great powers themselves. Excessive weakness as well as superabundant strength of an essential member posed a serious menace to the system. The Ottoman Empire, for example, was necessary to the European system simply because its demise would raise problems so dangerous that general European war and upheaval could not be avoided. European cabinets thus relied upon concert diplomacy to sustain the Turkish Sultan— to replace unilateral pretensions by a European guardianship, to avoid as long as possible the inevitable scramble over the spoils, and to insure that no one power acquired exclusive preponderance in an area affecting the interests of all.

The final rule of concert diplomacy was that great powers must not be humiliated. They must not be challenged either in their vital interests or in their prestige and honor. Concert diplomacy assigned itself the delicate task of restraining revisionist or aggressive states as well as of regulating European difficulties by peaceful means—replacing the confrontation and inherent brinkmanship of balance-of-power politics. Perhaps the oldest and thorniest problem of international systems again challenged diplomatists: how to reach decisions, and how to enforce them, when the disputants were great powers. Inevitably, concert diplomacy proved most vulnerable to the criticism that the Concert functioned well in handling trivial matters concerning the small and weak states, but performed miserably when really important questions were at stake. This charge is both untrue and unfair. Responsible statesmen must approach international affairs, in the apt phrase of George Kennan, as "gardeners and not mechanics."[21] The purpose of concert diplomacy was to maintain peace among the great powers, to prevent unavoidable conflicts of interest from degenerating into actual hostilities. Concert diplomatists realized that no surer method of provoking conflicts existed than openly to confront a great power—to menace its vital concerns or to impugn its honor and prestige.[22] So long as the European Concert functioned, the five great powers had the assurance that both their legitimate rights and their self-esteem would be respected.

That consideration accounts for the evolution of a rather elaborate cumulation of semi-formal procedural safeguards against offending the sensitivities of the great powers. Inattention even to the slightest detail in such matters could seriously debilitate or preclude the operation of the Concert entirely.[23] Consequently, concert diplomacy actively cultivated the conception of the great powers as a unique and special peer group. While lesser states might possibly attend an international gathering, they did not break the magic circle of the elite and powerful. The great powers retained the exclusive prerogative of decision making. Under no circumstances did one invite, in any capacity, a state of the second or third rank which was an enemy of a great power.[24] Furthermore, since decisions had to be voluntary, unanimity rather than majority rule prevailed in European meetings.[25] A legitimate settlement of any question was impossible if even one of the great powers declined to accept it. Such considerations predetermined the agenda of conferences. Questions that entailed a possible challenge to the interests or an affront to the prestige of a great power could not be feasibly discussed or resolved; issues that were embarrassing to any participant had to be excluded. As a result, many important and urgent problems did not receive treatment—simply because concert statesmen preferred to avoid questions that might produce confrontation and possibly war. Concert diplomacy manifestly sought not the best, but the least objectionable, solutions.

THE CONCERT IN OPERATION

The protections against great-power humiliation were necessary and they help greatly to explain the success of conference diplomacy in this period. For one thing, while the conferences met on an *ad hoc* basis, they were definitely not meetings summoned on the spur of the moment, or in which anyone expected mere personal contact between responsible statesmen to surmount all disputes and conflicts of interest. Diplomacy by conference required elaborate and often lengthy preparations.[26] Some delay was necessary to allow passions to cool, to give diplomats time to consult their colleagues and to work out their positions, and above all, to discover what would and what would not be palatable to the other powers in conference. The requisite order included extensive *pourparlers,* perhaps a conference, and then a congress.[27] This procedure insured that only those issues that were amenable to diplomatic treatment were introduced, and constituted a necessary precondition for successful summit diplomacy.

The procedure of concert diplomacy reveals also its primary technique of restraining and moderating intemperate policies on the part of the great powers. In the language of the time, the purpose was "to group" the offending state.[28] Instead of direct military confrontation, the principal means was moral suasion—an appeal to the collective responsibility of the great powers for European peace and stability, to the norm of what the other powers considered appropriate and legitimate behavior. In a sense, the Concert idea became the collective conscience of the European great powers, reminding each of its responsibilities and obligations in international politics. As Metternich observed in 1837 during a conversation on the Eastern Question with the British Ambassador, "Europe is now advanced to the rank of a spectator and a judge and that is what precludes a continuation of the system under which the encroachments of Russia were heretofore conducted."[29] The Tsar, aware that he was now under the observation of his peers, would modify his policy according to their standards. On the whole, concert diplomacy proved remarkably efficacious in rekindling and reinforcing the spirit of self-restraint among the great European powers. Nineteenth-century diplomatic history furnishes several examples of states foregoing gains which they could probably have gotten, mainly because they would otherwise have placed themselves outside the European community and damaged their moral position.[30] Few similar instances can be cited either in the eighteenth or the twentieth centuries. The Concert perhaps never achieved its potential, but neither were its accomplishments insignificant or purely transitory.

Assuredly, nostalgia should not blind us to the obvious imperfections of concert diplomacy. The European Concert was always an unwieldy and often an ineffectual instrument. It depended perhaps too much upon the "good will" of its members, upon the personal dispositions of individual leaders. It did nothing, in short, to challenge directly the doctrine of the ultimate sovereignty of states. Invariably the Concert dealt with the symptoms rather than the causes of international conflict; it was always a negative concept, called into operation by events. Even so, to admit these shortcomings does not vitiate the achievements or refute the promise of concert diplomacy. It was, after all, primarily a vehicle (and a fairly successful one) for the peaceful management of great-power rivalries. Above all, the Concert idea was realistic in the best sense of the word—attuned to, but not narrowly bound by reality.[31] At its worst, the Concert was an impotent assembly, merely adhering to the formalities, unable to resolve important and pressing issues. At its best, it represented a reasonably satisfactory solution to the most difficult problem of international systems: how to accommodate the forces of change and yet preserve peace and stability. Concert diplomacy allowed the great powers to sanction necessary alterations of the existing order; it provided the means of legitimizing change without endangering the general system.

One more thing is clear. European relations during the era of concert diplomacy were characterized by a sense of security, a respect for the public law of Europe, a recognition of a commonly accepted standard of conduct, and a willingness to keep one's own conduct within those limits, that was unknown both to earlier and to later periods.[32] An effective system of restraints existed against unilateral action in concerns that affected the interests of more than one power; so too did a method and a rationale for averting or moderating conflicts between the great powers. Through concert diplomacy the great powers were reminded of what constituted responsible international conduct. The Concert possessed a surprising capability to persuade sovereign states to observe those limits.

THE CONCERT AS AN INTERNATIONAL SYSTEM

A number of provisional conclusions about concert diplomacy may be advanced. One is that certain practices, procedures, and beliefs can, with time and usage, become fairly well-established rules of international behavior. Perhaps the central emphasis placed upon international organizations is misdirected. Concert diplomacy suggests that something practicable is possible between the extremes of an absolute consensus upon right and wrong in international relations (which makes institutional structures for adjudication and enforcement unnecessary), and of elaborate international governmental and judicial organs (which are rendered sterile by the lack of an agreed-upon charter for interpretation and administration).[33] To repeat, the Concert was realistic in trying to manage rather than to eradicate international dissension. Yet it simultaneously advanced a standard for responsible statesmanship and developed an instrumentality that periodically reminded even the most powerful nations of their obligation to conform to that standard.

A second point implied by concert diplomacy, and an important one for operative international systems in general, is that some distribution and equalization of both responsibilities and opportunities is essential among the states considered necessary to the system. No state should be asked to take the lead in maintaining the system, and to bear all the necessary burdens, while another reaps all the benefits. The recognition of some collective responsibility for order demands more than lip service, though historically some states have enjoyed the luxury of being able sporadically to ignore the general international system of which they are a part. States are thus separate, individual, and identifiably different actors; they cannot merely be labeled *A, B,* and *C,* and their posture and probable behavior within a system mathematically calculated. Because of disparities in resources, geographic position, composition, history, and a plethora of other factors, the European states of the nineteenth century had different domestic and foreign situations with which to contend, and different roles to play in the European community. Furthermore, the nature and structure of the international system itself affected each state differently. As long as member states accepted the existing system, they had to recognize these differences and structure their policy accordingly. Nineteenth-century diplomatic history indicates that when a power, or a group of powers, is demonstrably bearing the essential burden of maintaining the order, it should be supported and not be taken advantage of by other states simply because the special position and circumstances of the latter allow them to do so.[34]

Finally, the history of concert diplomacy implies something about the role of ideology in international systems. In the years immediately after the defeat of Napoleon, there was a conservative, antirevolutionary consensus among the great powers (Alexander of Russia was for a time the most liberal member). Moreover, the subsequent division of Europe into two competing ideological camps has been exaggerated. The controversies over both the Holy Alliance and the principle of nonintervention were, at bottom, false issues. Neither had much impact upon actual diplomatic practice.[35] Undeniably, an ideological rift did develop between East and West from the 1820's onward, and the Holy Alliance and nonintervention became convenient symbols and slogans in the resulting debate. Yet concert diplomacy continued to function. It did so because a great-power consensus persisted that transcended political ideology. Efforts to base the Concert upon ideology served only to enfeeble it and to limit its functions. Despite ideological divergences, the European powers still agreed upon the necessity of peace among themselves and accepted concert diplomacy as the means to manage crises that might jeopardize that peace.

But the temptation to play fast and loose with the rules of the game became more and more irresistible.[36] The revolutions of 1848 further eroded the presuppositions of concert diplomacy and produced new leaders and new expectations. The culmination came in the Crimean War, another international crisis over the Eastern Question and one that was, in fact, no more serious than others previously managed successfully by the Concert. It was, moreover, the type of crisis in which concert diplomacy had always been at its best: the avoidance of great-power confrontations over matters of prestige. This time, however, statesmen in key positions failed to exercise self-restraint and refused to honor the rules of the Concert. The sea powers, in particular, were determined to inflict a humiliating defeat upon Russia and to conduct the war as a liberal crusade against autocracy.[37] The Concert of Europe was the victim. To be sure, remnants of the techniques and assumptions of concert diplomacy endured, but the Concert system itself had been destroyed. Nothing emerged to replace it until the 1870's; and then stability was achieved on another, less cooperative and conciliatory basis. To this degree, then, the destruction of the European Concert was willful, if rather lighthearted and frivolous. The other side of the argument is that the forces of change and progress simply bypassed the concept of concert diplomacy. Perhaps so; no one would deny that the European Concert was the product of a specific political, social, and intellectual milieu. Industrialization with all its social and political ramifications surely helped to undermine the essential foundations of concert diplomacy. A variety of developments increased the enticement to use foreign policy to divert domestic disharmony.[38] Perhaps the Concert could not accommodate the age of national states. Most simply, however, concert diplomacy broke down because statesmen refused to abide by its rules—and did not give much thought to what rules of international politics they would prefer as a substitute. They knew only that they had grown weary of its restrictions. The destruction of the European Concert was thus at least in part a generational problem. The remark of Theodore Fontaine, in reference to the 1848 revolutions, applies equally well to the demise of the Concert: "One was tired of the old approach to things. Not that one had suffered particularly under it; no, it was not that. It was rather, that one was ashamed of it."[39]

European statesmen, however, had made more progress than they realized. The Concert of Europe was certainly not the only factor making for peace in the first half of the century; nor could it contend successfully with all the political, social, and economic developments that these decades produced. It could only abate and not remove the causes of interstate rivalry. But in the real world of international relations it performed amazingly well. In a certain sense the evolution of concert diplomacy displays some rather striking parallels to "the growth of political stability" in domestic politics.[40] The European system in the era of the Concert approached the fulfillment of the three conditions posited by Stanley Hoffmann—of "security, satisfaction, and flexibility"—to which all political orders must aspire.[41] The subject merits fresh examination and more interdisciplinary analysis.[42]

NOTES

1. *Peace and War: A Theory of International Relations,* trans. by Richard Howard and Annette Baker Fox (Garden City, N.Y.: Anchor Books 1973), 6.

2. See, for example, A. J. P. Taylor, *The Struggle for Mastery in Europe, 1848–1918* (Oxford: Oxford University Press 1954), xix–xx.

3. W. N. Medlicott concludes that "it was the peace which maintained the Concert and not the Concert that maintained peace." *Bismark, Gladstone, and the Concert of Europe* (London: Athlone Press 1956), 18. Another common view is that the Concert was just the old balance-of-power system perpetuated in another guise: Edward V. Gulick, *Europe's Classical Balance of Power* (New York: Norton 1955), 88n., 156–59. Concert diplomacy admittedly accepted and incorporated the principle of the balance of power. But I believe that a distinction must be drawn (and in fact was drawn) between the balance of power, seen simply as a distribution of power among essential members of the states system,

and balance-of-power politics, which featured confrontation as the first premise, and which had a natural tendency to seek preponderance rather than balance. See Richard Rosecrance, *Action and Reaction in World Politics* (Boston: Little, Brown 1963), for some perceptive comments on this subject.

4. I make no pretense here of presenting an essay based on original research; nor do I wish to quarrel with those scholars who subscribe to alternative interpretations. In justification of the approach I am taking, I wish to offer one additional comment, however. The current emphasis among historians upon the primacy of domestic politics and among international relations theorists upon methodological experimentation and general systems analysis has produced in many cases a disdainful view of "traditional" diplomatic history and of mere "praxeology" (the term is Aron's). While admitting the justice of these critiques to a point, I feel that theory could often be more concretely grounded in actual his-

torical situations and developments, and that such international systems as the Concert of Europe may yet retain instructional value. Moreover, the proponents of the *Primat der Innenpolitik,* while they broaden our understanding of the motivations and formulation of foreign policy, are much less satisfactory in explaining the multifaceted interaction, and the results, of foreign policies once they are introduced into the international arena. Here, it seems to me, the nature and structure of the existing international system becomes crucially important. The Concert of Europe is a good example.

The literature incorporating the approach of the primacy of domestic politics is generally familiar. I refer only to the works of Fritz Fischer, Hans-Ulrich Wehler, Helmut Böhme, and Wolfgang Mommsen in Germany, and Arno J. Mayer in the United States. For some recent trends in international relations research, see Richard B. Finnegan, "International Relations: The Disputed Search for Methods," *Review of Politics,* xxxiv (January 1972), 40–66; and Warren R. Phillips, "Where Have All the Theories Gone?" *World Politics,* xxvi (January 1974), 155–88.

5. I am particularly indebted to the recent work of Paul W. Schroeder, *Austria, Great Britain, and the Crimean War: The Destruction of the European Concert* (Ithaca: Cornell University Press 1972), which contains a trenchant analysis of concert diplomacy in the concluding chapter. The following studies were also of special assistance: Charles K. Webster, *The Art and Practice of Diplomacy* (New York: Barnes and Noble 1962), esp. 55–69; Carsten Holbraad, *The Concert of Europe: A Study in German and British International Theory, 1815–1914* (London: Longmans, Green 1970); Rene Albrecht-Carrie, ed., *The Concert of Europe, 1815–1914* (New York: Harper 1968); F. H. Hinsley, *Power and the Pursuit of Peace: Theory and Practice in the History of Relations between States* (Cambridge: Cambridge University Press 1957); Hinsley, "Reflections on the History of International Relations," in Martin Gilbert, ed., *A Century of Conflict, 1850–1950: Essays for A. J. P. Taylor* (New York: Atheneum 1967), 19–34; Stanley Hoffmann, *The State of War: Essays on the Theory and Practice of International Relations* (New York: Praeger 1965); Aron (fn. 1); and Rosecrance (fn. 3).

6. The critiques by the Abbé de Saint-Pierre at the beginning of the eighteenth century and by Kant at the end are familiar. Yet even Edmund Burke, a defender of equilibrium

politics, conceded during the Seven Years' War that "The balance of power, the pride of modern policy, and originally invented to preserve the general peace as well as the freedom of Europe, has only preserved its liberty. It has been the origin of innumerable and fruitless wars." Quoted in Herbert Butterfield, "The Balance of Power," in H. Butterfield and Martin Wright, eds., *Diplomatic Investigations: Essays in the Theory of International Politics* (Cambridge: Harvard University Press 1966), 144.

7. *Minor Poems,* Norman Ault and John Butt, eds., Twickenham edn., VI (London: Methuen 1954), 82.

8. These judgments contradict the conclusion of many theorists that balance-of-power politics in the eighteenth century permitted only limited wars (the "stylized wars of position that only rarely affected the civilian populations") and was a system of basic moderation. Hoffmann (fn. 5), 101; Hinsley, *Power . . .* (fn. 5), 179. For ample evidence to the contrary, one need only turn to Albert Sorel, *Europe and the French Revolution,* trans. by Alfred Cobban and J. W. Hunt (New York: Anchor Books 1971), esp. 64–85. In comparison to the present century, the warfare of the era of Louis XIV and Frederick the Great may indeed appear mild. Even so, it is most difficult to conceive of the wars of the Sun King as conflicts which did not involve civilian populations; or of the Seven Years' War as a limited war of position; or of the partitions of Poland as an example of the preservation of independent states; or, finally, of the various plans for the destruction of Prussia, Austria, Spain, Sweden, and Turkey as evidences of moderation. Yet all characterized balance-of-power politics in the period. Cf. also Schroeder (fn. 5), 403.

9. *Dépêches inédites du Chevalier de Gentz aux Hospodars de Valachie,* ed. Anton von Prokesch-Osten (Paris: Plon 1876–1877), I, 344–45. An English translation of this essay ("Considerations on the Political System Now Existing in Europe") is available in Mack Walker, ed., *Metternich's Europe, 1813–1848* (New York: Harper 1968), 71–83.

10. Patricia K. Grimsted, *The Foreign Ministers of Alexander I* (Berkeley: University of California Press 1970), 239.

11. H. G. Schenk, *The Aftermath of the Napoleonic Wars: The Concert of Europe—An Experiment* (New York: Oxford University Press 1947), 27.

12. Gordon A. Craig, "The System of Alliances and the Balance of Power," in the *New*

Cambridge Modern History, X (Cambridge: Cambridge University Press 1960), 267.

13. Charles K. Webster, *The Foreign Policy of Castlereagh: Britain and the European Alliance, 1815–1822* (2d ed., London: G. Bell 1934), 144.

14. Several scholars distinguish between the "era of the congresses" and "the Concert of Europe" after 1823. See Irby C. Nichols Jr., *The European Pentarchy and the Congress of Verona, 1822* (The Hague: Martinus Nijhoff 1971), 325.

15. Metternich's efforts to convert the Paris ambassadorial conference into a headquarters for antirevolutionary surveillance and action, and Palmerston's ambitions to create a league of liberal states are well known. For the former, see Guillaume Bertier de Sauvigny, *Metternich et la France après le congres de Vienne, I: De Napoleon à Decazes* (Paris: Hachette 1968), 116; and Webster (fn. 13), 73. Palmerston's desire for a "western confederacy of free states" is discussed in Charles K. Webster, *The Foreign Policy of Palmerston, 1830–1841* (2 vols., London: G. Bell 1951); quote from I, 347.

16. Webster (fn. 13), 160.

17. Gentz (fn. 9), 477; Walker (fn. 9), 73. Castlereagh wrote in September 1815 that "There is not a Power, however feeble, that borders France from the Channel to the Mediterranean that is not pushing some acquisition under the plea of security and rectification of frontier. They . . . are foolish enough to suppose that the Great Powers of Europe are to be in readiness to protect them in the enjoyment of these petty spoils. In truth, their whole conception is so unstatesmanlike that they look not beyond their own sop; compared with this, the keeping together of a European force has little importance in their eyes." W. Alison Phillips, *The Confederation of Europe* (2d ed., London: Longmans, Green 1920), 138.

18. G. Bertier de Sauvigny, "Sainte-Alliance et Alliance dans les conceptions de Metternich," *Revue Historique,* Vol. 223 (April–June 1960), 263.

19. The hassle between Metternich and Palmerston over a conference on the Eastern Question in 1833 (and the resulting delay) is a typical example. See Webster (fn. 15); and M. S. Anderson, *The Eastern Question, 1774–1923* (New York: St. Martin's 1966), 79–87.

20. Phillip E. Mosely, *Russian Diplomacy and the Opening of the Straits Question in 1830 and 1839* (Cambridge: Harvard University Press 1934), 73.

21. *Realities of American Foreign Policy* (Princeton: Princeton University Press 1954), 92.

22. This function of concert diplomacy was recognized even by twentieth-century diplomats. Friedrich von Holstein, in defending the call for a European conference on the first Moroccan crisis, advised the German foreign minister that "this idea has the advantage that while it affects French interests, it does not affect French pride." Holstein to Bülow, April 5, 1995, in Norman Rich and M. H. Fisher, eds., *The Holstein Papers* (Cambridge: Cambridge University Press 1961), IV, 328–29. Cf. Rich, *Friedrich von Holstein* (Cambridge: Cambridge University Press 1965), II, 700, 708.

23. The Congress of Aix-la-Chapelle in 1818 provides several examples of the special care taken not to slight the standing and reputation of great powers. See Bertier de Sauvigny (fn. 15), 189–209; and Webster (fn. 13), 123, 153.

24. The French and British invitation of Cavour to the Paris Congress of 1856 and their repeated efforts in the following decade to include Italy in great-power consultations was a direct violation of this rule and an open insult to the Austrian Empire.

25. Cf. the dispatch of Metternich quoted in Bertier de Sauvigny (fn. 18), 263.

26. Abundant evidence of this facet of concert diplomacy is furnished in the memoranda prepared by Castlereagh and by Baron Humboldt of Prussia prior to the opening of the Congresses of Vienna and Aix-la-Chapelle; they are printed as appendices in Charles K. Webster, *The Congress of Vienna, 1814–1815* (New York: Barnes and Noble 1966), 168–93.

27. As Metternich wrote Gentz in 1823: "Before talking about congresses, it is necessary to come to an accord on many matters, and the way to do this is through simple conferences." Paul R. Sweet, *Friedrich von Gentz* (Madison: University of Wisconsin Press 1941), 239.

28. Castlereagh frequently used the term in regard to Alexander I. His meaning did not differ substantially from Metternich's in the latter's emphasis upon a "point of moral contact" and "une pentarchie morale."

29. Webster (fn. 15), I, 505.

30. This was Metternich's meaning in attributing the Russian retreat in Turkey in 1834 (withdrawal from the Danubian Principalities and reduction of the Turkish war indemnity) to the Tsar's "good will." Ibid., I, 341. Austria herself abjured possible additional gains in Italy for much the same reason: ibid., I, 210. See also

Paul W. Schroeder, *Metternich's Diplomacy at Its Zenith, 1820–1823* (Austin: University of Texas Press 1962); and Alan Reinerman, "Metternich, Italy, and the Congress of Verona, 1821–1822," *The Historical Journal,* XIV (June 1971), 263–87.

31. Something that neither Napoleon III nor Gladstone ever understood was that the Concert could not be used to impose their version of reform upon Europe; that it could not simultaneously seek to avoid armed conflicts between the great powers and promote changes which would probably occasion them. The French Emperor's proclivity for conferences and congresses cannot, I think, be taken very seriously, despite his frequent calls for them (but cf. William Eckhard, "Conference Diplomacy in the German Policy of Napoleon III, 1868–1869," *French Historical Studies,* IV [Spring 1966], 239–64). W. H. C. Smith's conclusion is accurate: "The pattern of Napoleon III's diplomacy rarely varied: when bilateral or unilateral action became too risky, the danger could be lifted by multilateral action." *Napoleon III* (London: Wayland Publications 1972), 159. It is incredible that Napoleon actually believed his various schemes for the reconstruction of Europe could be achieved through congresses or by peaceful means. His proposals included the cession of Venetia to Italy by Austria; the creation of an independent Poland; the destruction of Turkey; and the partition of Austria. See Victor Tapie, "Le traité secret de 1859 entre la France et la Russie," *Études d'histoire moderne et contemporaine,* V (December 1953), 116–47; and Elrod, "Austria and the Venetian Question, 1860–1866," *Central European History,* IV (June 1971), 149–70.

In a similar vein, Gladstone's efforts in the 1880's to resurrect the European Concert so that the great powers could cooperate in imposing British-type reforms upon the Ottoman Empire manifested an alarming misconception of what concert diplomacy was about. The only effect of his attempts was to frighten the continental powers and to solidify their opposition to his overtures. Gladstone then had to choose between the Concert and his ideology (he chose the latter). Medlicott (fn. 3).

32. Certainly the rights of neutral states were less secure after the breakdown of the Concert. See Horst Lademacher, *Die belgische Neutralität als Problem der europäischen Politik, 1830–1914* (Bonn: Ludwig Röhrscheid Verlag 1971), esp. 196–200, 477; and Ann G. Imlah, *Britain and Switzerland, 1845–1860* (Hamden, Conn.: Archon 1966).

33. Austen Chamberlain's comment on the League of Nations seems to fit here: "I am firmly convinced that the true line of progress is to proceed from the particular to the general, and not, as has hitherto been embodied in Covenant and Protocol, to reverse the process and attempt to eliminate the particular by the general." G. P. Gooch, *Studies in Diplomacy and Statecraft* (London: Longmans, Green 1942), 180.

34. A case in point was Britain's treatment of the Austrian Empire in the second half of the century. The British expected Austria to restrain Russia in the east and insisted that a strong Austria was a European necessity. Yet simultaneously they advised reforms and concessions that would have made Austria incapable of performing the requested tasks—or, later in the century, simply ignored her. The retort of the Austrian Ambassador to England in the 1860's was fully justified: "You pretend always to be interested in our prosperity and power; and, in spite of that, you advise us first to cede Venetia, then Galicia. By dint of your interest and friendship, you will finish by reducing us by half." Apponyi to Rechberg, May 18, 1863: *Haus-, Hof-, und Staatsarchiv* (Vienna) (*Politisches Archiv VIII: England*), carton 60.

35. As Metternich noted in 1824, "The Holy Alliance has never played a role in any issue . . . for the simple reason that what is in reality nothing can only produce nothing." Bertier de Sauvigny (fn. 18), 256. Similarly, the definition of nonintervention (attributed to Talleyrand) as a metaphysical and political phrase meaning almost the same thing as intervention was fundamentally accurate. It did not prevent repeated unilateral British interventions (in Spain, Portugal, Greece, and elsewhere) whenever London deemed it necessary. (A recent reassertion that the ideological gulf between East and West was "unbridgeable," however, is Ivan Scott, "Counter-Revolutionary Diplomacy and the Demise of Anglo-Austrian Cooperation, 1820–1823," *The Historian,* XXXIV [May 1972], 465–84.)

36. The change in British policy, which began even before Castlereagh's suicide, was greatly accelerated by his successors, Canning and Palmerston. See Webster (fn. 13), 488–89; and Harold W. V. Temperley, *The Foreign Policy of Canning: England, the Neo-Holy Alliance, and the New World* (2d ed., London: Thomas Nelson 1925), 449, 470–71. Palmerston, though he often participated effectively in concert diplomacy, was increasingly disposed to adopt the promotion

of liberalism and a policy of confrontation with Russia, to prefer British to European diplomatic victories, and to enjoy the "salutary moral humiliation" of other great powers: Webster (fn. 15), I, 406; II, 532, 736. The emergence of Russophobia in Britain was another ominous development: "Great Britain's policy was, in the main, more provocative than Russia's." John H. Gleason, *The Genesis of Russophobia in Great Britain* (Cambridge: Harvard University Press 1950), 2–3.

37. Conclusive arguments are presented in Schroeder (fn. 5); and Winfried Baumgart, *Der Friede von Paris, 1856* (Munich: Oldenburg Verlag 1972).

38. Perhaps the classic example of a foreign venture undertaken to distract domestic unrest in this period was the French expedition to Algiers in 1830. "Only in patriotism and in activity could the French forget their internal disagreements and act as one nation." Douglas Johnson, *Guizot* (Toronto: University of Toronto Press 1963), 265.

39. Joachim Remak, *The Gentle Critic: Theodore Fontaine and German Politics* (Syracuse: Syracuse University Press 1964), 13.

40. J. H. Plumb, *The Growth of Political Stability in England, 1625–1725* (London: Macmillan 1967).

41. Hoffmann (fn. 5), 20.

42. There are some encouraging efforts in this direction on other subjects. Brian Healey and Arthur Stein, applying quantitative methods to a catalogue of events identified by diplomatic historians, examine a number of well-worn clichés about the balance-of-power system and conclude that many of the interpretations are simply invalid: "The Balance of Power in International History: Theory and Reality," *Journal of Conflict Resolution,* XVII (March 1973), 33–61. Paul W. Schroeder's seminal article, "World War I as Galloping Gertie," written from the viewpoint of an historian, emphasizes the systemic dynamics that led to the breakdown of the European system prior to the First World War, *Journal of Modern History,* XLIV (September 1972), 319–45. Gabriel Almond and Scott C. Flanagan, though dealing with political modernization rather than international relations, offer some suggestive insights in discussing "system functionalism" and "political systems and systemic crisis" that could be applied to international systems as well: Almond, Flanagan, and Mundt, *Crisis, Choice, and Change: Historical Studies of Political Development* (Boston: Little, Brown 1973), 5–8, 46–57.

Reading 4-3

Metternich's Theory of European Order
A Political Agenda for "Perpetual Peace"
James R. Sofka

In his magisterial analysis of late-eighteenth- and early-nineteenth-century European politics, Paul Schroeder argues that the Vienna Settlement of 1815 marked a fundamental change in the "governing rules, norms, and practices of international politics." If this "transformation" did indeed occur—and evidence of it is plentiful—then much of the credit for effecting it must be attributed to Prince Clemens Metternich of Austria, the chief architect of the postwar settlement. Metternich conceived of his task at Vienna as far greater than redrawing frontiers and restoring nearly forgotten princes to their thrones. More critically, he articulated a profoundly normative program for the restructuring of the European state system, and sought actively to transcend the predatory milieu of eighteenth-century international relations and replace it with a political order that would insure what most philosophers of the Enlightenment could only visualize: perpetual peace.[1]

SOURCE: From "Metternich's Theory of European Order: A Political Agenda for 'Perpetual Peace'" by James R. Sofka, *The Review of Politics,* vol. 60, no. 1 (Winter 1998): 115–149. Copyright © 1998. Reprinted by permission of the Review of Politics.

METTERNICH'S EXPOSURE TO ENLIGHTENMENT THOUGHT

Metternich remarked near the end of his life that historians would judge him more fairly than his contemporaries, and his prophecy has proven uncannily accurate. In the not so distant past even a casual association of Metternich with Enlightenment liberalism would have been dismissed as ludicrous. However, the commonly received image of Metternich as a benighted reactionary is largely a product of late-nineteenth-century German nationalist historiography, which could barely conceal its disgust toward his attachment to European federalism rather than the cause of national self-determination.[2] This view has gradually been discredited in recent years by Metternich scholars and has been supplanted by a general (if at times uneasy) respect and even admiration of his ability to shape a constructive settlement out of the chaotic variables of the states–system that emerged from the Napoleonic Wars.

Although he was prone to frequent indulgence in self-congratulation, Metternich's political philosophy was more than the accumulated wisdom of elegant *soirée* conversation and idle reflection. The career of the man who considered himself "a kind of titular professor of fundamental truths" bridged the intellectual evolution of Europe from rationalism to romanticism without significant change in orientation. "The most outstanding moral element in me is immutability," he proudly observed in 1818. Most aspects of Metternich's personality and opinions, as well as the parameters of his political thought and diplomatic conduct, were shaped by the philosophical and cultural milieu of the late Enlightenment.[3] Born in 1773 in the Rhineland city of Coblenz, the young Metternich was raised in an atmosphere of considerable wealth and political and intellectual sophistication. His father, Franz Georg Metternich, was an influential Rhineland politician who frequently represented the Habsburg Monarchy at electoral conferences.[4] Metternich's tutor, Friedrich Simon, was a deist fond of quoting Condorcet and d'Alembert who returned to Paris to take up the revolutionary cause in 1794. Though he did not agree with Simon's endorsement of the more radical dimensions of the French Revolution, Metternich admitted that he was influenced by some of his teacher's views and stressed the importance of French rationalism and materialism on his early philosophical and theological education. In 1788 Franz Georg Metternich enrolled his son in the University of Strasbourg, where he resolved to follow an academic career in medicine or chemistry. "My particular vocation," he observed later with a noticeable tinge of remorse, "seemed to me to be the cultivation of knowledge, especially of the exact and physical sciences, which suited my taste particularly." By his own admission he was attracted to the predictable and arithmetic universe of the physical sciences and viewed it as a model for political and social analysis.[5]

Consequently the emphasis Metternich would later place on "immutable truths" was a genuine reflection of his system of reasoning and not merely justificatory posturing. Like his predecessor Kaunitz, he used the scientific method to focus clearly on the forces motivating physical and social systems.[6] He unceasingly argued that rational principles guided his action, just as they governed chemical reactions in a laboratory. "Our calculations are never confined to the passing day or the needs of the moment," he wrote Paul Esterhazy in 1825. "Placed face to face with the future, and giving to temporary embarrassments no other value than that of transient and variable symptoms, our point of view is extended but unchangeable, and our line of action never varies in its direction." Indeed, Metternich often drew comparisons between principles of government and chemistry and pathology. "It has certainly never been questioned," he wrote in 1819, "that society and the advance of society are subject to fundamental laws just definitely as physical forces are subject to other laws differing in many respects from those that function in society and the sphere of morality but less in conflict with them than is generally supposed."[7]

Metternich's rationalism further matured through his legal training at the University of Mainz, which began in 1790. His mentor, Niklas Vogt, was a respected legal scholar whose study of *Das System des Gleichgewichts* (1785) was one of the eighteenth century's most sophisticated studies of international politics. This work postulated the creation of a continental "equilibrium," as well as the necessity for some legal and rational regulation of the European state system, as the highest ethical goal of politics. Vogt, who believed that the "greatest goal of a truly enlightened society is the education of all men as to the importance of the maintenance of [the] balance among both nations and individuals," had a formative and lasting effect on the young Metternich.[8] Under Vogt's tutelage, the international system effectively became a laboratory for implementing the principles of natural philosophy and physical reactions that Metternich had studied at Strasbourg. Politics was understood by the young Metternich, as it was by Kant, in a clinical and rational fashion.

Metternich initially paid scant attention to the French Revolution, which was unquestionably the greatest political event of the age of his youth. In his student years he deplored the Revolution's violent and often arbitrary excesses, but he did not categorically condemn its aims. Significantly, at no time during the 1790s or later did he endorse the intellectual and political program of the British and German counter-revolutionaries. Indeed, Metternich went to great lengths to distance himself from what he viewed as this "romantic" conservatism which he never ceased to condemn as retrograde. "It may be," he noted, "that someone in the year 2240 will discover my name, and tell the world that in this distant past there was at least one man less limited than the mass of his contemporaries who had pushed fatuity to the point of believing that they had reached the apogee of civilization."[9] With such a progressive outlook, it is not surprising that Metternich should seek to reform the workings of the European state system.

Metternich left Mainz in 1792 and began a series of diplomatic apprenticeships in the German states under his father's tutelage. In 1795 he married Eleonore von Kaunitz, granddaughter of the architect of the "diplomatic revolution" of 1756 and member of one of the most influential political families in Vienna, a move which further propelled his meteoric rise to power. He received his own diplomatic appointment to the court of Saxony at Dresden in 1801 and, with his father's intervention, was appointed Austrian ambassador to Prussia in early 1803. In 1805 he helped negotiate the alliance that would be soundly defeated at Austerlitz. Following Austria's defeat, he watched from Vienna as Napoleon reorganized the German states into the Confederation of the Rhine, an organization that would serve as a model for Metternich's own efforts to "federalize" Germany in 1815.

In 1806 Metternich was named Austrian ambassador to Russia, but at the request of Napoleon, who assumed he was Francophilic, he was given the post at Paris instead. Following Austria's decisive defeat at Wagram in 1809, he was appointed minister of foreign affairs. At the age of 36, Metternich had reached the pinnacle of ministerial power in the Habsburg monarchy. In this augmented capacity, he sought to structure a system of world order that would preserve the peace of Europe after the defeat of Napoleon. As he wrote in a circular dispatch to his ambassadors in the spring of 1813, his aim was to create "not a precarious state of affairs, but a general arrangement which will put back the geographical and political relations of the powers on a just and lasting basis."[10] The legal and political theory of the late Enlightenment was his guide in this process.

METTERNICH, KANT, AND THE IDEA
OF "POLITICAL EQUILIBRIUM"

In his 1784 essay "Idea for a Universal History from a Cosmopolitan Viewpoint," which Metternich read at Mainz, Kant argued that the incessant conflict that had plagued eighteenth-century statecraft would hopefully—and counterintuitively—work to create the "perpetual peace" visualized by the Abbé St. Pierre in 1713. "Wars, tense and unremitting military preparations," he noted:

> and the resultant distress which every state must feel within itself, even in the midst of peace—these are the means by which nature drives nations to make initially imperfect attempts, but finally, after many devastations, upheavals and even complete inner exhaustion of their powers, to take the step which reason could have suggested to them without so many sad experiences—that of abandoning a lawless state of savagery and entering a federation of peoples in which every state, even the smallest, could expect to derive its security and rights not from its own power or its own legal judgment, but solely from this great federation, from a united power and the law-governed decisions of a united will.[11]

To Kant, the international "equilibrium"—a federation of states regulated by law and treaty—would logically result from a desire for peace that in turn arose from the horrors of war. Statesmen, observing the miseries of war, would use reason to construct a legal foundation for political interaction between states—as they had long done within them—to limit this tendency to violence. In such an arrangement the destructive forces that had animated world politics in the modern age could be reconciled through a rational analytical process, and the interests of all states could be secured and promoted by an equilibrium based on international law. The result would inevitably be stringent limitations on the ability of states to commit acts of aggression, just as the corresponding ability of individuals within states was restricted by judicial authority. If the competing state interests which divided world society could be mitigated by reason and law and if the autonomy of individual states could be limited, Kant maintained, then general peace could follow. In Kant's analysis, and in the view of earlier writers such as St. Pierre, Jeremy Bentham, and William Penn, the more destructive wars became, the more receptive statesmen would be to finding new ways to eradicate them.

Metternich endorsed the argument of "Idea for a Universal History" and it can be seen as providing the foundation for his approach to world politics.[12] Like Kant he abhorred violence and was repelled by the excesses of the revolutionary mobs he witnessed while in Strasbourg and Mainz, as well as by the battlefields of Germany he observed in the Napoleonic Wars.[13] This escalation of international and internal violence convinced Metternich that drastic and immediate measures had to be taken to arrest what he perceived as a drift toward anarchy. As late as the summer of 1813, when the representatives of the three Allied Powers were formulating a new offensive against Napoleon, Metternich frantically arranged a peace conference in Prague and only reluctantly agreed to participate in the war upon the failure of this mediation attempt.[14]

Metternich's rationalism and aversion to disorder conditioned his profoundly anti-militaristic worldview. "One characteristic of war," he observed, "is that once it has begun laws are no longer imposed by the will of man but by force of circumstance, and another is that circumstances of pure chance become reasons, and that although one may know one's starting point, the same is not true of one's destination." Yet as a practical matter he ruefully admitted to Princess Lieven in 1818, "One is less concerned with those who prevent the cannon going off than with those who fire it. The one is more necessary than the other, but the world runs after the noise." Consequently, as Enno Kraehe notes, Metternich's goal was to structure a system "within which a balance would exist without permanently mobilized armies and interminably marching troops." Rather than ensure Austria's, and Europe's, security in a temporary and precarious "balance of power," Metternich "envisaged a system that would finally come to rest."[15] In championing this idea, Metternich made the attainment and preservation of an "equilibrium" his ultimate objective.

What, then, did the concept of "equilibrium" mean to Metternich at the time of the Congress of Vienna, the first test of this new system of politics? It certainly did not, as we shall see, mean a "balance of power." Although several attempts have been made to analyze these concepts at a systemic level, few examine Metternich's own theory of world order and its application in the post–Vienna period.[16] Despite his early attachment to Newtonian physics, Metternich did not approach international relations entirely mechanistically, and he attempted to outline a higher stage of social existence than one analogous to reactions found in a chemical laboratory.[17] Indeed, the "rediscovery of the old international law," as Hans Rieben asserts, was the predicate of Metternich's thinking on the idea of "equilibrium." His approach to politics, like Kant's, was highly normative, and he was trained to analyze political relationships in a systemic fashion. His devotion to "immutable" principles of order led him to seek to implement and institutionalize a pan–European settlement in 1815 rather than focus solely on regional problems. The latter tendency was scorned by Metternich as "a selfish policy, a policy of fantasy . . . of miserable greed . . . which seeks profit apart from the simplest rules of right . . . and the [pursuit] of which constitutes political wisdom in the eyes of a restless and shortsighted policy."[18]

As conceived by Metternich, the European "equilibrium" was a stable arrangement of powers regulated by international law and operating according to universally recognized ethical principles and treaty obligations.[19] Equilibrium could be achieved if statesmen worked to limit the autonomy of individual states and ordered these actors in a federal system operating according to the principle of collective security. In this arrangement, all of the Great Powers would be united in upholding the general European peace and the legal norms upon which it rested, and would be restrained from pursuing "egotistical" policies by the sanction of international law. The resulting system would integrate states in a legally constituted alliance system that would eliminate the need to resort to force against an external threat. Instead, the system would be regulated by frequent consultations between governments and the resolution of disputes by diplomatic means. Metternich's equilibrium was to be an institutionalized body of cosmopolitan interests which would insure peace by reducing the friction between sovereign states through the means of political integration. Metternich argued that the duty—and in his vocabulary "duty" carried all of the prescriptive weight of Kant's categorical imperative—of all states was "to submit to the common law." This principle, Metternich continued, "exists everywhere, and loses nothing of its correctness, or of the necessity of its application, under whatever form a Government may be placed."

In Metternich's theory, this "law," or institutionalized framework of reciprocal duties, would be negotiated among the European states through diplomatic exchanges and appeals to cosmopolitan interests. These consultations would establish the parameters and obligations of individual state action, and the resulting treaties would assume the force of contract and provide a basis for political interaction. In a succinct summary offered in 1831, Metternich argued that the formula for a European "equilibrium" he had devoted his career to building consisted of three basic principles:

1. The political independence of any legally recognized government, that is to say the liberty it must enjoy to adopt, in its internal affairs as well as in its relations with other states, whatever system it judges most suitable in the interests of its own preservation, security, and tranquility, without damaging the rights of others;

2. The maintenance of all existing treaties, as long as they are not abolished or modified by common agreement between the contracting parties;

3. The pronounced resolution of the powers to assure, by the respect they show for these principles, the peaceful and enlightened relations existing between all of them and under the protection of which the internal peace of states and all the interests which they alone can guarantee, can flourish.[20]

This theoretical construct led to mixed results when it was implemented in the period 1815–1822.[21] However, Metternich never ceased to argue that a political equilibrium based on respect for law and the common interest of the powers in preserving peace was the best practicable means of insuring continental harmony.[22] "The great axioms of political science proceed from the knowledge of the true political interests of all states," he noted. "In these general interest lies the guarantee of their existence, while individual interests to which the transitory movements of the day assign a great importance . . . possess only a relative and secondary value."[23] The paramount general interest that Metternich—a student of late Enlightenment philosophy—could visualize was that of a lasting peace that would benefit all of the powers.

Equilibrium, then, was a description of a goal. Metternich hoped that a European state system structured along the lines Kant had proposed, one which provided for legal stability and political adaptability at the same time, could help lay the foundation for a "durable international relationship" that would suit the interests of all European states.[24] Thus Metternich shared Kant's vision of "perpetual peace"; but his method of attaining it was considerably more pragmatic.[25]

Metternich's theoretical outline of European politics was based upon what Robert Kann termed "supposedly self-evident reason."[26] Significantly, he did not base his policy on the ideology of "legitimacy" popular among conservative contemporaries and which is frequently—and erroneously—assumed to have informed his policy in the postwar period.[27] His theory of international relations was predicated on his conviction that "all states exist as a supra-individual community of interests resting on their commonality as members of [international] society." What Gentz called "the great political family" of Europe was to Metternich a real entity that could function smoothly if statesmen used reason and a cosmopolitan outlook to overwhelm the ambitious parochialism that had characterized European politics for centuries. "By separating carefully the concerns of self-preservation from ordinary politics, and by subordinating all individual interests to the common and general interest," Metternich wrote in 1823, Europe could demonstrate "examples of union and solidarity" unseen in history.[28] Metternich's attraction to an institutionalized structure of international politics that would operate, as Kant had hoped, "automatically" led him to formulate ideas of world order beyond the calculations of day-to-day politics or local struggles for influence.

Metternich was convinced that Austria, like all states, could guarantee its security in only one of two ways: either by entering a federation of states regulated by treaties, or by a direct alliance with another power or coalition to overwhelm a potential threat. Kaunitz, of course, had followed the latter course since he became foreign minister in 1753. Metternich flatly rejected this policy because in his view it only perpetuated a culture of hostility and insecurity in the international system, as alliances invariably produced counter-alliances. His ultimate aim was to undo Kaunitz's system and transcend the predatory universe of eighteenth-century politics and anchor a European security system on a more stable, and predictable, foundation. As a result, Metternich wanted to replace force with law as a sanction on state behavior. His promotion of the idea of "political equilibrium," and his argument that Austria could only find security in a federal Europe was a clear departure from the popular mantra of eighteenth-century international relations theory, the balance of power.

Ironically, however, Metternich is commonly named among the greatest practitioners of balance-of-power diplomacy. Edward Vose Gulick, in his classic but thinly researched study of the concept, argues that Metternich's statecraft was "beautifully illustrative of the thought process of a balance-of-power statesman."[29] Territory and military potential, according to Gulick, were in Metternich's mind the determinants of international relations. Although he notes Gulick's refusal to distinguish between the ideas of "balance of power" and "equilibrium," and faults his lack of documentation, Enno Kraehe also advances the thesis that Metternich focused primarily on the interests of Austria and was indeed conscious of the deterrent principle inherent in balance-of-power theory.[30]

Paul Schroeder is more receptive to a theoretical interpretation of European politics in the post-1815 period.[31] However, while he makes a vigorous effort to distinguish between "equilibrium," "balance of power," and "hegemony," his definitions of these terms are at times difficult to discern. In the process, he loses Metternich's own theory of international politics in his extended treatment of the Anglo-Russian rivalry which in Schroeder's view conditioned nineteenth-century European politics. Focusing on broad systemic dynamics, Schroeder does not fully explain how Metternich, the virtuoso of the Vienna settlement, personally interpreted these ideas or how they informed his political initiatives. Most significantly, he makes no attempt to relate Metternich's ideas to the larger corpus of writings on international politics produced in the eighteenth century, especially those of Kant, Vattel, and Montesquieu. The balance-of-power model understood by Schroeder is essentially Newtonian in theory and mechanistic in operation, while Metternich's theory of equilibrium was rooted in Kantian political philosophy and was legalistic in its structure. The differing conceptual and political implications of these competing approaches to world politics cannot be underscored too boldly.

While the divide between the "balance of power" and "equilibrium" schools appears to be widening, careful reflection on the hypotheses of these arguments suggests that they may, to a great extent, be reconcilable. Metternich assiduously studied regional politics—specifically in Germany and Italy—and an investigation of his approach to these issues is instructive. However, it is important to remember that these were of secondary importance to his larger end: that of maintaining a general European peace.[32] The bedrock assumption of Metternich's theory of the equilibrium was that territorial settlements could not endure unless the broader political relations among the powers were guaranteed by legal means, as only through such a contractual arrangement could the rights of each state be protected. This type of settlement, one that would indeed "transform" the workings of the European state system, was precisely what had been lacking in the eighteenth century, with violent results. For a more accurate understanding of the relationship of local and general interests on the political level, as well as of the balance of power and equilibrium on the theoretical, it is necessary to examine Metternich's repudiation of balance-of-power theory as an adequate model for international relations.

METTERNICH'S ATTACK ON BALANCE-OF-POWER THEORY

Metternich's concentration on systemic and legalistic principles of world order prevented him from joining in the acclamation of militaristic parochialism so common in the eighteenth century, and led him to conclude, though without the grace of Kant's phrase, that to obtain "a permanent and universal peace by means of a so-called *European balance of power* is a pure illusion." Metternich's attack on the concept of the balance of power was based on his own definition of the term, which did not differ substantially from those provided by contemporary or modern interpreters.[33] To Metternich, the balance of power was an essentially Newtonian construct that assumed that the international system evolved through cycles of peace and war, much as a swinging pendulum moved between fixed poles without ceasing its motion, and was predicated on the idea that international politics operated according to quantifiable principles. By measuring and/or manipulating these variables, such as the size of armies, navies, or financial reserves, a state's "power," or capabilities, could be calculated. "Parity" could be obtained by matching these standards and competing with each other for economic and strategic assets, much as Britain and France did in North America throughout the eighteenth century.

Metternich, like Kant, looked upon this model of international relations with contempt.[34] In this model, each state aggressively pursued its own interests with little regard for others beyond simple prudence. No systemic principles of order existed in this Hobbesian universe of state relations, and in Metternich's view it was conductive to international anarchy. Concerned above all with limiting the role of force in international politics, Metternich could never endorse a model in which the potential for war was the only sanction on state behavior. This point introduces Metternich's two principal objections to the balance-of-power system.

First, Metternich condemned the absence of any legal regulatory mechanism in balance-of-power theory. He believed that pursuing such a mechanistic policy would only provide, at best, for "intermediate" political settlements. The systems created by supposedly "balanced" power from 1648–1783 had all quickly deteriorated into renewed violence. Metternich traced these conflicts to systemic weaknesses inherent in the balance-of-power arrangement. Under this theory, the only significant "check" that a state could impose on others was the application of force. Yet the frequent outbreaks of violence that characterized eighteenth-century statecraft seemingly negated the entire rationale for the "balance," and provided concrete illustrations of its limitations. In short, Metternich believed that the balance of power understood as the evaluation and maintenance of a "correlation of forces" was an inadequate basis for a stable European order. In his view, this approach could at best produce brief armistices and treaties devoid of prescriptive value or long-term durability, but could never yield the "perpetual peace" that was his ultimate goal in statecraft. For this reason Metternich in 1815 refused to follow Kaunitz's policy of securing Austria through exclusive alliances, as this would only create a polarized climate in which war was more, rather than less, likely to occur.[35] Metternich observed that the balance-of-power model was, by its premise, a temporary condition,[36] whereas his conception of the equilibrium could be institutionalized. This was a conceptual breakthrough in practical statecraft and required a fresh look at the intricacies of the European system and a command of the theoretical literature of the eighteenth century.[37]

Second, Metternich's idea of the role of the state in international relations differed from that customarily found in balance-of-power theory. The latter was predicated on the assumption that the state was a completely independent, autonomous actor, able (in the ideal) to enter into and abrogate treaties with perfect fluidity. In the eighteenth century, Kaunitz's "reversal of alliances" in 1756 and Frederick II's gambit for Silesia in 1740 were outstanding examples of this approach to world politics. In this model, states have no permanent legal ties to each other but only relationships of convenience to increase their deterrent value to the others. For this reason states frequently—and frantically—shopped for allies upon the death of a sovereign or the eruption of a minor territorial dispute, as balance-of-power thinking held that the outcome of a war could be determined as much by alliance pairings than by actual battlefield engagements.

Metternich, as a true cosmopolitan, flatly rejected this view of state behavior. To him the notion of the state as an end in itself, maximizing its particular objectives in the constant threat of war, was a misguided, if not inherently dangerous, conception of world politics.[38] Deploying a frequent organic metaphor, Metternich considered it symptomatic of an "illness" when a state pursued its ambitions without concern for the general peace of Europe, and went so far as to denounce "individual" state interests as meaningless "abstractions." He condemned this approach by observing that

> In the ancient world, policy isolated itself entirely and exercised the most absolute selfishness, without any other curb than that of prudence. The law of retaliation set up eternal barriers and founded eternal enmities between the societies of men, and upon every page of ancient history is found the principle of mutual evil for evil.[39]

Having observed the effects of two decades of war, including the occupation of Austria after its defeat at Austerlitz in 1805, Metternich insisted on limiting the autonomy of states rather than promoting it, as was the case in balance-of-power theory. Only a political arrangement in Europe that had the ability to "regulate the social field over a broader area than that contained within the borders of a state," could effectively insure a lasting peace.[40]

As a practical statesman, Metternich realized that a mild dosage of "balance of power" thinking was instrumental in diplomatic exchanges, and it would have been foolhardy for him to have ignored the material interests and capabilities of the Great Powers. At times he manipulated these traditional levers of power to help construct the European order he envisaged, as in the case of the alliance of 3 January 1815 among Austria, Britain, and France in the midst of the Saxony crisis at the Congress of Vienna.[41] Yet he never attempted to base the foundation of the entire postwar settlement upon this logic. It is important to remember—as Gulick does not—that these analyses and exploitations of temporary power relationships were a means, and never an end in themselves, in Metternich's statecraft.

As a result, it is most accurate to speak of the "balance of power" as an aspect of Metternich's diplomacy but never its governing principle. His fundamental objective was the realization of a political equilibrium based on treaty and codified in international law. This system would rest on law rather than military power, and operate by diplomacy and compromise rather than force. Metternich anticipated that the balance of power, because of its "self-evident" weaknesses, would become such a demonstrable failure as an organizing principle of international relations that statesmen would be compelled to reject it as a model. It could never support the equilibrium Metternich considered so instrumental in constructing and maintaining a European federation.

METTERNICH'S THEORY OF A EUROPEAN "CONFEDERATION"

In his frequently neglected but important study of *The Confederation of Europe*, Walter Alison Phillips argues that Metternich's plan for European order was "an experiment in international government, an attempt to solve the problem of reconciling central and general control by a 'European Confederation' with the maintenance of the liberties of its constituent states, and thus to establish a juridical system" of international relations.[42] Phillips's thesis, when understood in the context of Metternich's identification with late Enlightenment philosophy, is persuasive and congruent with the facts. Metternich resurrected the idea of a federation of states, first proposed by Erasmus and later echoed by St. Pierre and Kant, to provide a framework for the reconciliation of political disputes among the Great Powers. His plan was legalistic, based on the assumption that political affairs were best directed by the rule of cosmopolitan reason rather than selfish "national interests" and *raison d'état*.

In a letter to Tsar Alexander, written in January 1823, Metternich argued that his formula for a European Confederation had always contained two basic ideas. "In the first place," he noted, governments "must make common cause and unite in one the interest of each in [their] own preservation; in the second place they must establish a central focus for information and direction." His formula for a "transformed" state system rested on the idea that the powers that had defeated Napoleon should retain and broaden their wartime cooperation into a lasting Alliance, or Union, that would ensure peace through a collective security system. Metternich anticipated that France itself would be incorporated into the system, and he sought moderate peace terms with Paris in 1814 and 1815 in order to provide for this contingency. Whereas a traditional coalition, in Gentz's phrase, was a partnership based on a temporary "congruence of interests," Metternich's proposed postwar Alliance—the practical collective security system that was the expression of the idea of "equilibrium"—was based on "the permanent underlying interests of [all] states within a given system." Metternich hoped to create a unity among the five Great Powers that was rooted in cooperation rather than competition.[43]

Under the familiar coalition system, which had characterized international relations from 1648 to 1815, alliances were based upon immediate threats and perceived security requirements. Coalition diplomacy was the operational mechanism of the balance-of-power model that Metternich found so misguided and dangerous. This formula provided no permanent guarantees to any of the contracting powers; a change in government, or the fortunes of war, could quickly shatter a coalition, as had happened in the Seven Years' War with the death of Empress Elisabeth of Russia in 1762. The advantage of his collective security proposal, Metternich reasoned, was that no power was the catalyst for the alliance, and thus there was no defensive animosity built into the system. For this reason, Metternich's alliance system could be institutionalized and operate—as Kant had suggested—"automatically."[44]

Since his first study of legal and political theory at Mainz, Metternich viewed the concept of federalism as a logical basis for European order and an efficient and flexible means of conflict resolution. Metternich's assumption that states operated in a societal, and not anarchical, milieu and that the general interest of a durable peace must take precedence over individual interests and goals formed the core of his formula for a confederation of European states and was consonant with his training in late Enlightenment philosophy and its idealistic aspirations. Indeed, this type of union had never been attempted before, but Metternich saw it as the most ambitious means of preserving peace without the constant threat of war that was inherent in—indeed, vital to—the balance-of-power or coalition model. Metternich exulted in 1817 that this "revolutionary" idea would, if it remained the governing principle of European diplomacy, "insure for a considerable time what the good Abbé de St. Pierre wished to establish forever."[45]

Frederick II had quipped to Voltaire in 1742 that all St. Pierre's plan lacked was the "consent of Europe" along with "a few similar trifles." Metternich hoped to build this shared consent following the Napoleonic Wars, and invoked the horrific physical, human, and financial costs of this long conflict to underscore the "self-evident" rationalism of his proposals. The time to fashion a plan of European order, Metternich sensed, had never been more opportune. Building this confederation, as Metternich indicated to the tsar, was a two-stage process. First, the powers had to agree to enter into it and second it had to be maintained, or "enforced," by diplomatic means. The first task, ironically, would prove to be easier to accomplish than the second. In 1815 four of the five Great Powers had been allied with each other for two years, and some had been acting in concert since 1793. France, although defeated in war, was under the control of a nominally friendly government and represented by agents receptive to some of Metternich's ideas. Each of the five states had a common interest in a comprehensive settlement which would establish a basic, and predictable, pattern for individual foreign policies. Each, of course, had its own ambitions, but the fact that these competing interests had been accommodated through cooperation in the wartime league was of dramatic importance in establishing the political and territorial settlement at the Congress of Vienna.

Metternich clearly realized, however, that this political "transformation" would not be accomplished immediately. The European federation he envisaged required careful and deliberate construction, and he believed that this process could best be served if the powers cooperated on points of fundamental common interests and reserved more controversial subjects for future discussion. In this manner he hoped that the Confederation would begin to settle differences that would, under the old balance-of-power model, likely have proven insurmountable. Cognizant that competitive ambitions and animosities would continue to erupt unless each power realized that it had a stake in preserving a general peace which none wanted to risk, Metternich planned to avoid confrontation by "concentrating on living in peace and harmony. The best way to achieve that desired end," he maintained, "is to avoid subjects of discussion on which agreement is unlikely and to attempt, equally carefully, to meet on grounds of common interests." Metternich's conviction that such a durable peace would serve the "common interests" of all states consequently became the theoretical bedrock of the Confederation, and he was not alone in this opinion. British Foreign Secretary Robert Stewart, Viscount Castlereagh, for his part, bluntly informed Liverpool in November 1814 that he was approaching the peace negotiations in such a manner "as to make the establishment of a *just Equilibrium* in Europe the first Object of my Attention, and to Consider the assertion of minor Points of Interest as subordinate to this great End."[46]

Despite Castlereagh's optimism, the political interests of the Great Powers in 1815 were diverse and in some instances conflictual. In Metternich's view, these differences could be reconciled through a federal system, in which each state could pursue its interests within a system regulated by treaties and diplomatic exchanges. With each power restrained by these provisions as well as by its own interest in preserving peace, the Confederation could effectively preserve the "equilibrium" by guaranteeing that each state would be deterred from an offensive foreign policy for fear of automatically bringing the other four into league against it. Unlike the coalition model, the force of international law would trigger a response "automatically," as Kant had suggested, regardless of which power exceeded its limits. Yet Metternich hoped that such a state of affairs would never come to pass if the Confederation was properly managed by prudent and preventative diplomacy, and if rational statesmen understood that peace outweighed whatever benefits they might obtain through aggression.[47]

Like Montesquieu, Metternich recognized that "states have, like individuals, different temperaments." These differences in internal institutions and political cultures indicated, as he put it in 1821, that "a particular interest or situation will predominate in a state just as a particular passion or weakness influences individuals. These different attitudes are not slow to make themselves known, heard, and felt." This did not mean, however, that European politics would necessarily remain anarchical and ruthlessly competitive. If the individual governments were truly parts of a cosmopolitan society—and Metternich never doubted that they were—then "the same results that would be found in a family consultation should, by the same right, be found in a meeting of powers."[48] In short, competing interests could, and for the sake of reducing international tensions, should be permitted to express themselves, but only under the controlling aegis of the European Confederation.

Castlereagh, whose own ideas on the efficacy of such a system had been refined through conversations with Metternich, expressed this federalist logic succinctly in his important State Paper of 5 May 1820, in which he argued that

> We cannot in all matters reason or feel alike; we should lose the Confidence of our respective Nations if we did, and the very affectation of such an Impossibility would soon render the Alliance an Object of Odium, and Distrust, whereas if we keep it within its *common sense* limits, the Representative Governments, and those which are more purely Monarchical, may well find each a common Interest, and a common Facility for discharging their Duties under the Alliance, without creating an Impression that they have made a surrender of the first principles upon which their respective Governments are founded. Each Government will then retain its due faculty of Independent Action, always recollecting, that they have all a common Refuge in the Alliance, as well as a common Duty to perform, whenever such a danger shall really exist, as against that which the Alliance was specially intended to provide.[49]

Beyond the legal and normative force of treaties, the principles upon which the Alliance would operate, therefore, were a shared interest in peace and cosmopolitanism. Although each state, with its unique form of government and political culture, would define and pursue its interests differently, the "law of nations" would provide a basic outline for the conduct of international relations.[50]

Metternich never lost sight of the security needs of Austria, but he realized that these requirements, as well as those of the other powers, ultimately depended on the respect for treaties and international law he had been trained to uphold. In short, the interests of individual states were best secured, in Metternich's logic, if they stopped "going it alone" and cooperated in securing a peace that would be injurious to none. This idealistic approach was completely alien to the balance-of-power tradition, which sought to maximize the diplomatic options of the individual state, and was ridiculed by its practitioners, such as British Foreign Secretary George Canning in his famous aphorism of "Every nation for itself and God for them all."[51] Metternich, who ceaselessly argued that the smooth operation of the European federation was dependent upon restraint, dismissed the idea that any one state could or should manipulate the Alliance for its own ends. He noted in 1822 that the power of the European Alliance can neither be replaced nor supplemented by another. Imagine one monarchy controlling the combined resources of the Alliance—not only would such tremendous power not take the place of the Alliance, but it would gain nothing by attempting to do so, because it would be contrary to the *moral* power of the Alliance. It would be contrary for the very reason that the Alliance is clearly composed of heterogeneous parts and because, although it works towards a single, positive end [European Union], it embodies guarantees for the most widely varying interests.[52]

Although Bertier de Sauvigny notes that Metternich's thinking on the nature of the postwar union underwent "at least four consecutive and at times even simultaneous forms," each embodied the idea of guaranteeing the interests of each of the Great Powers through a federal arrangement. "If such is the spirit of the Alliance," Metternich argued, "then in its active application to special cases it should submit to the common law. . . . To attack the principle of the Alliance is to attack society."[53]

Metternich first conceived of the European federation as an extension of the cooperation that had underscored the wartime Quadruple Alliance of 1813–1815 in a legally institutionalized form. In 1818 he managed to thwart Alexander's efforts to establish a Franco-Russian alliance and, with Castlereagh's backing, ensured that France did not reenter the state system under exclusively Russian auspices.[54] On paper at least, the five Great Powers, despite their divergent interests, were united by treaties and regulated by international law, and ceased to manipulate combinations against a specified "outside" actor. In this model foreign policy would ideally become, as Ferrero observes, "the projection of reciprocal confidence." Throughout his career Metternich argued that all states could participate in this union and share in its benefits and responsibilities regardless of their form of government or geographical position. As late as 1847 he still held out hope that "a community of interests" could be found to protect the European peace.[55]

IMPLEMENTING THE CONFEDERATION:
THE ORIGINS OF THE "CONFERENCE SYSTEM"

Metternich's idealism was not devoid of a pragmatic appreciation of the political system of Europe. Unlike St. Pierre, Rousseau, or Kant, Metternich was a minister with political responsibility for the interests of a state. He recognized that a simple appeal for harmony would, as a general rule, be a useless deterrent unless it was supported by a concrete political agenda, and fully realized that the theoretical programs of the eighteenth-century philosophers all lacked enforcement mechanisms beyond fanciful descriptions of "ought to be." To prescribe a political equilibrium and European federation was one thing; to preserve it in a universe of competing state interests was another. It was the latter problem, that of translating "ought" into "is," that Metternich sought to resolve in the period 1815–1822 with his "conference system." This policy, a completely novel approach to international politics, reflected Metternich's faith in reason as well as his observation of the dynamics of continental politics.

Shortly after the Congress of Vienna, Friedrich von Gentz suggested that Metternich work toward the creation of a permanent European "Assembly" in a neutral capital as a means of preserving continental peace. Gentz proposed that this body could be structured along the lines of the German Confederation, with representatives of the powers deciding on "European" foreign policy collectively through a deliberative process. Metternich was sympathetic to the legal premises of Gentz's reasoning, but he nevertheless rejected his colleague's suggestions on the basis of his concern that a permanent Congress of European states would become inefficient and hobbled by bureaucracy.[56] Moreover, there was always the risk that one or two states might dominate such an assembly given unequal financial or military resources. Metternich's preferred solution to the enforcement question was not a permanent "league of nations," but the "conference system," which he developed in conjunction with Castlereagh.

The conference system, outlined in Article VI of the Vienna Treaty, was intended to be a diplomatic framework designed for the efficient and peaceful resolution of international disputes. It operated on a provisional basis and was therefore, according to Metternich, more responsive to immediate political needs than a formal international tribunal or court. Article VI provided for a means of conflict resolution by mandating that each power, before taking action which might be injurious to the interests of others—such as pressing a territorial claim or authorizing a military intervention—would agree to discuss its grievances, concerns, and objectives at a meeting convened specifically for this purpose. Conference diplomacy was predicated upon Metternich's avowed assumption that "the establishment of international relations upon the basis of reciprocity, under the guarantee of respect for acquired rights, and the conscientious observance of [pledged] faith constitutes, at the present day, the essence of politics, of which diplomacy is only the daily application."[57] In practical terms, the Conference System was the instrumentality through which the Confederation was sustained and functioned on a regular basis.

Metternich anticipated that this formula would best enable the powers to assess the case at hand and reach a satisfactory agreement by rational diplomacy and shared interests in upholding the principles and aims of the European Confederation. Through the mechanism of the Conference System, each state retained its autonomy—more so than under Gentz's proposed league—but it was bound to the others by an intricate series of multilateral diplomatic exchanges. To be effective, the system required close cooperation among the European governments, as well as a willingness to debate problems rather than attempt to resolve them by an immediate recourse to force. In short, the conference system upheld the Confederation by requiring that each state receive permission from the others before embarking on a course of action which might destabilize the peace. By dealing with specific issues as they arose, Metternich hoped that each conference could cover the matter at hand in considerable detail and from a variety of perspectives.[58]

To Metternich, the greatest advantage of this program of frequent meetings between the powers was its ability to resolve conflicts in a preventative, rather than *post-facto,* manner. The Vienna conference was an example of the latter: it sought to restructure European politics in the aftermath of a catastrophic war. Metternich's progressive political outlook led him to regard the necessity of such "reconstructive" meetings as epitaphs on shortsighted statesmanship: with proper management, the wars they resolved should never have started. In Metternich's view it was more rational—and politically advisable—to deal with potential threats to the peace before they became overwhelming. For this reason, preventative diplomacy was the form, as well as the objective, of the conference system. Supremely confident in his own diplomatic abilities, Metternich placed almost unlimited faith in the capacity of rational statesmen to resolve virtually any obstacle to continental peace. As he euphorically remarked at the Congress of Laibach in 1821, "Is there anything in the world which today can take the place of ink, pens, a conference table with its green cover, and a few greater or smaller bunglers?"[59]

Following this logic, Metternich argued that frequent consultations among the powers would reinforce the bonds of treaties that united them, and would therefore not only "enforce" or "guarantee" the peace by efficient resolution of disputes, but would strengthen the Confederation by reducing competition among individual states for primacy. According to Kant and Metternich, the threat of a general war destructive to all powers acted as "Nature's guarantee" that rational statesmen would find their interests best secured through cooperation and compromise rather than the unpredictable fortunes of war.[60] The delicate machinery of the Confederation of Europe, the first practical attempt at "European" government, was designed to integrate all states into a system based on law, reciprocity, and respect for each other's interests. This zealous adherence to the formula of the conference system informed Metternich's approach to international relations after 1815, and was the source of his early impressive success and later overwhelming failure to establish and preserve a "European" foreign policy in the competitive universe of the postwar state system.[61]

A REVIEW OF METTERNICH'S THEORY OF EUROPEAN ORDER

Metternich's theory of international relations was anchored on the idea of "political equilibrium." This concept, which was an extension of eighteenth-century federalist theory, led Metternich to conclude that the states of Europe should be structured in a legally regulated system in which each would possess sovereignty but would be regulated at the supranational level by mutual respect for interests as well as the restraint inherent in any legally constituted political system. This vision was completely distinct from the competitive, militaristic, and anarchical milieu of eighteenth-century statecraft. Metternich's theory of international relations was heavily indebted to Kantian ideas of universality and cosmopolitanism and shared assumptions about the utility and practicality of a general European peace. It was, without question, a highly normative interpretation of world politics. Metternich promoted Wilhelm von Humboldt's idea of "the limits of state action" rather than the vigorous pursuit of selfish objectives in which the autonomy of the state was considered sacred. This idea informed his diplomacy throughout his career and was the source of both his stunning successes up to 1820 and his eventual disillusionment later. As Srbik concludes, in Metternich's statecraft "theory and action were in balance," and the latter was consistently directed towards achieving the goals set by the former.[62]

Few statesmen of the eighteenth century were more faithfully wedded to the philosophical program of the late Enlightenment than Metternich. Castlereagh, impressed with his broad view of the international system, called him an "Inveterate Theorist" of politics, a view shared by most of Metternich's contemporaries yet surprisingly by few modern observers.[63] Metternich approached international relations from a strictly legalist perspective. He condemned the old "Cabinet diplomacy" and the idea of the balance of power as insufficient guarantors of political stability, and supplanted them with an idea of a general and perpetual continental peace achieved and maintained through the rule of law and the pragmatic recognition that it served the interests of all states. It was not without justification that Metternich could inform Wellington in 1824 that "Europe," and not his adoptive Austria, was his true "fatherland."

Metternich's lasting contribution to the study of theories of international relations was his reliance on the principle of a confederal and cooperative states-system regulated by the principle of collective security. This permanent alliance could, in Metternich's view, accomplish what the traditional coalition system could not: successfully insure a lasting and enlightened peace in Europe.[64] Metternich believed that states could be united without reference to a common enemy, but rather on the conviction that all were pledged to uphold a peace that was injurious to none. The Confederation would be supported and enforced by the "conference system," which would resolve disputes proactively through diplomacy rather than war. If this logic became the institutional basis for European politics, he doubted that a serious external threat would ever arise within the European system. Metternich, in short, worked to restructure completely the methodology of eighteenth-century diplomacy. He rejected militarism, distrusted the balance of power, condemned standing armies, and never tired of pointing out the dangers of narrowly "particularist" statesmanship. This was a restatement, and practical refinement, of the earlier logic of Erasmus, St. Pierre, and Kant; but Metternich's diplomacy marked the first time that it had ever been tried in practice.

It is indeed appropriate, therefore, to speak of Metternich's statecraft as emblematic of a conceptual and practical "transformation" in the methodology and objectives of European diplomacy. The idealism of the late Enlightenment, inculcated in Metternich since his adolescence, as well as his recognition that the endless cycles of war that characterized eighteenth-century politics needed to be conclusively—and irrevocably—arrested informed his approach to the issue of postwar order at Vienna in 1815.[65] Metternich's goal was no less ambitious than that repeated in the endless stream of "peace projects" of the eighteenth century, but his means of attaining it were considerably more pragmatic. It is impossible to separate this "transformation" from the philosophy of the Enlightenment, as the peace of 1815, although long vilified by nationalists hostile to Metternich's cosmopolitanism, represented an attempt to translate these norms into practice. With current attempts at cementing a "European Union" sparking tremendous scholarly and political interest, Metternich's formula pays revisiting.

NOTES

1. Paul Schroeder, *The Transformation of European Politics, 1763–1848* (Oxford: Clarendon Press, 1994), p. vii.

2. Quite naturally the main focus of these nationalist criticisms was Metternich's refusal to endorse German unification and his insistence that the German states should be incorporated in a federal, decentralized political system. This line of attack, which assumed a high profile in the early twentieth century, was followed most vocally and venomously by Heinrich von Treitschke in his magisterial—and widely read—*History of Germany in the Nineteenth Century,* 7 vols. (New York: McBride, Nest and Co., 1915–1919); and the later work of Viktor Bibl, *Metternich: Der Dämon Österreichs* (Vienna: J. Gunther, 1936). For an overview of this dimension of Metternich historiography, see Paul Schroeder, "Metternich Studies Since 1925," *Journal of Modern History* 33 (1961): 237–60; and James R. Sofka, "Metternich, Jefferson, and the Enlightenment: Statecraft and Political Theory in Early Nineteenth Century Europe and America"

(Ph.D. diss. University of Virginia, 1995), conclusion.

3. Metternich to Joseph Hübner, January 26, 1850, cited in Guillaume de Bertier de Sauvingy, *Metternich and His Times* (London: Longman and Todd, 1962), p. 31. Metternich to Princess Dorothea Lieven, 22 December 1818. Emil Mika, ed., *Geist und Herz Verbündet: Metternich's Briefe an die Gräfin Lieven* (Vienna: W. Andermann, 1942), p. 87. Hans Rieben, *Prinzipiengrundlage und Diplomatie in Metternich's Europapolitik, 1814–1848* (Aarau: H. R. Sauerlander and Co., 1942), p. 9.

4. For an overview of Metternich's intellectual tastes and erudite salon conversation, the memoirs of George Ticknor, a Harvard law professor who visited Metternich in July 1836, are instructive. George Ticknor, ed., *The Life, Letters, and Journals of George Ticknor,* vol. II (Boston: J. R. Osgood and Co., 1876), chap. 1. The best surveys of Metternich's early life and family background are found in Heinrich Ritter von Srbik, *Metternich: Der Staatsmann und der*

Mensch, 3 vols. (Munich and Vienna: 1925–
1954) I: 53–96; Enno E. Kraehe, *Metternich's
German Policy, volume I: The Contest with Napoleon, 1799–1814* (Princeton: Princeton University Press, 1963), chap. 1; and Dorothy Gies
McGuigan, *Metternich and the Duchess* (Garden
City, NY: Doubleday, 1975), chap. 2.

5. Metternich reviewed his early education
in a letter to the Russian Foreign Minister Karl
Robert Nesselrode in 1817. He noted that "at
the age of twenty a deep and long-continued research in the Holy Books made me an atheist after the fashion of d'Alembert and Lalande, or a
Christian after that of Chateaubriand." Metternich to Karl Robert Nesselrode, 20 August 1817.
Prince Richard Metternich ed., *Aus Metternich's
nachgelassenen Papieren,* 8 vols. (Vienna: W. Brau-
muller, 1880–1884). First five volumes translated in English as *The Memoirs of Prince Metternich* (New York: C. Scribner's Sons, 1881–
1882). Hereafter I will use NP to refer to the
German edition and MM for the English text.
This quote from MM, 3: 67–68. Metternich
later observed that throughout the 1790s he
"diligently attended lectures on Geology, Chemistry, and Physics. Man and his life seemed to
me to be objects worthy of study" (MM, 1: 23).
He assiduously studied Newton, Kepler, and
LaPlace, and the latter's works so impressed him
that he carried copies of them in his diplomatic
bag throughout his tenure as foreign minister
(McGuigan, *Metternich and the Duchess,* p. 496).
Srbik maintains that Metternich's scientific training was responsible for his demonstrated "strong
impulse to search in the psychological and physical world for universal laws and then test them
empirically and experimentally in the factual
realm and prove them correct" (Srbik, "Der
Ideengehalt des 'Metternichischen Systems,'"
Historische Zeitschrift 131 [1925]: 243–45).

6. For a comparison of Metternich's and
Kaunitz's political views and Newtonian method
of reasoning, see Peter Richard Rohden, *Die
klassische Diplomatie von Kaunitz bis Metternich*
(Leipzig: Koehler and Ameland, 1939), chaps. 1
and 2. On Kaunitz's legendary "political algebra"
and its debt to the Enlightenment, see Walter
Dorn, *Competition for Empire 1740–1763* (New
York: Harper and Brothers, 1940), pp. 296–300;
Franz A.J. Szabo, "Prince Kaunitz and the Balance of Power," *International History Review* 1
(1979): 399–408, as well as Szabo's full-length
study of *Kaunitz and Enlightened Absolutism,
1753–1780* (Cambridge: Cambridge University
Press, 1994).

7. Metternich to Paul Esterhazy, 7 August
1825 (MM, 4: 222); Srbik, "Ideengehalt,"
p. 245; Metternich to Count Ludwig Lebzeltern,
15 December 1819, cited in Bertier, *Metternich
and His Times,* p. 33.

8. Cited in Steven Stargardter, *Niklas Vogt
1756–1836: A Personality of the Late German Enlightenment and Early Romantic Movement* (New
York: Garland Publishers, 1991), p. 137. I am indebted to this excellent and original study of
Metternich's teacher. In his autobiography Metternich referred to Vogt as "one of my most
zealous friends," even though the two later had
serious disagreements over the structure of the
German Confederation (MM, 1: 11). Indeed, in
1836 the professor would be buried on the estate
of his most famous student.

9. Metternich noted later that he was all
but oblivious of the French Revolution in the
early 1790s, as the bulk of his time was consumed in the laboratory. "I was happy in this scientific circle," he wrote, "and allowed the Revolution to rage and rave without feeling any call
to contend with it" (MM, 1: 23). His only political act in this period was the publication of a
short anonymous pamphlet—under the revealing pseudonym "A Friend of Universal Peace"
—in 1794 urging the electors of the western
German states to defend their lands in the event
of a French attack (MM, 1: 340–47). On the
revolution, see Srbik, *Metternich,* 1: 65–96;
Kraehe, *German Policy,* 1: 10–18; MM, 1: 4–17.
For his opinion of and disagreements with Burke
and his adherents, see Henry A. Kissinger, *A
World Restored: Metternich, Castlereagh, and the
Problems of Peace, 1815–1822* (Boston: Houghton Mifflin, 1957), pp. 193–4; NP, 3: 451.

10. On the period 1806–1809, see Srbik,
Metternich, 1: 99–122 and Kraehe, *German Policy,*
vol. I, chaps. 2–4. Metternich's own account of
his life in this period is in his Autobiography, but
it was written late in life and should be read with
a careful eye for details that began to escape his
memory. MM, 1: 45–121; Kraehe, *German Policy,* 1: 51; cited in McGuigan, *Metternich and the
Duchess,* p. 39.

11. Kant, "Idea for a Universal History,"
Kant's Political Writings, ed. Hans Reiss (Cambridge: Cambridge University Press, 1991),
p. 47. For an analysis of Kant's idea of universal
federalism, see Charles Dupuis, *Le Droit des Gens
et les Rapports des Grandes Puissances avec les autrés
etats avant le pacta de la Societé des Nations* (Paris,
1921); Kurt von Raumer, *Ewiger Friede: Frieden-
srufe und Friedenspläne seit der Renaissance* (Mu-

nich: K. Alber, 1953); Patrick Riley, *Kant's Political Philosophy* (Totowa, NJ: Rowman and Littlefield, 1983), chap. 6; Andrew Hurrell, "Kant and the Kantian Paradigm in International Relations," *Review of International Studies* 16 (1989): 183–205. For a broader view of eighteenth-century ideas on international federalism, see Mario Einaudi, *The Early Rousseau* (Ithaca: Cornell University Press, 1967), chap. 7; C. E. Vaughan, ed., *The Political Writings of Jean-Jacques Rousseau,* vol. 1 (New York: John Wiley and Sons, Inc., 1962), pp. 399–435; Stanley Hoffmann, "Rousseau on War and Peace," *Janus and Minerva: Essays in the Theory and Practice of International Politics* (Boulder and London: Westview Press, 1987), pp. 25–51; M. S. Anderson, *The Rise of Modern Diplomacy, 1450–1919* (London: Longman, 1993), pp. 204–38; Francis Ruddy, *International Law in the Enlightenment* (New York: Oceana Publications, 1975); E. V. Souleyman, *The Vision of World Peace in Seventeenth and Eighteenth Century France* (New York: G. P. Putnam's Sons, 1941); D. Heater, *The Idea of European Unity* (New York: St. Martin's Press, 1992).

12. Srbik, "Ideengehalt," p. 248.

13. "Peace," Metternich observed in 1808, "does not exist within a revolutionary situation, and whether Robespierre declares eternal war against the châteaux or Napoleon makes it against the Powers, the tyranny is the same, and the danger is only more general" (Metternich to Stadion, 27 April 1808, MM, 2: 205).

14. On the abortive Prague Conference of July–August 1813, see McGuigan, *Metternich and the Duchess,* chap. 8 and Kraehe, *German Policy,* 1: 181–86. Metternich glosses over this effort in his "Autobiographical Memoir." No doubt he was unwilling to appear to posterity as an initial opponent of the ultimately successful coalition of 1813 (MM, 1: 196–99).

15. Metternich to Paul Esterhazy, 24 August 1821, cited in Bertier, *Metternich and His Times,* p. 69. Metternich to Princess Lieven, 6 December 1818 (Mika, *Geist und Herz Verbündet,* p. 69; Kraehe, *German Policy,* 1: 302).

16. A representative sample of these arguments can be found in Harold Nicholson, *The Congress of Vienna* (New York: Harcourt, Brace and Co., 1946), pp. 38–41; Henry A. Kissinger, *A World Restored,* chap. 4; and Edward Vose Gulick, *Europe's Classical Balance of Power* (Ithaca: Cornell University Press, 1955). The problem of world order in the post-Vienna era has been subject to close examination in a series of articles in the *American Historical Review* 97 (1992): 683–

735. These attempt to trace the roots of the balance of power–versus–equilibrium debate and offer new insights into Allied diplomacy in the Congress period. Paul Schroeder's essay, "Did the Vienna System Rest on a Balance of Power?" concludes that it did not, and this idea is echoed in his recent *Transformation of European Politics.* Enno Kraehe's rejoinder, "A Bipolar Balance of Power," contends that both Britain and Russia attempted to manipulate combinations in central Europe and that Metternich's diplomacy was centered on securing a pivotal role for Austria against a perceived Russian threat. Robert Jervis, in his essay on "A Political Science Perspective on the Balance of Power and the Concert," uses quantitative modelling to outline the theoretical basis of the Congress system. Wolf Gruner asks "Was There a Reformed Balance of Power System or Cooperative Great Power Hegemony?" and concludes that the system did indeed rest on a multipolar, or pentarchical, balance of power.

17. In taking this position Metternich followed the example set by other leading eighteenth-century political philosophers. Many Enlightenment theorists, including Montesquieu, Diderot, Kant, and Holbach, wrote extensively on natural science before turning to political questions. See William Piper, "Kant's Contact with British Empiricism," *Eighteenth Century Studies* 12 (1978/79): 174–89; Ira Wade, *The Structure and Form of the French Enlightenment,* 2 vols. (Princeton: Princeton University Press, 1977); Alan Charles Kors, *d'Holbach's Coterie: An Enlightenment in Paris* (Princeton: Princeton University Press, 1976), Part I; Nannerl O. Keohane, *Philosophy and the State in France: The Renaissance to the Enlightenment* (Princeton: Princeton University Press, 1980), chap. 14; Georges Gusdorf, *l'avènement des Sciences humaines au siècle des Lumières* (Paris, 1973); and Souleyman, *Vision of World Peace.*

18. Rieben, *Metternich's Europapolitik,* p. 14. On this point see the important article by Srbik, "Metternich's Plan der Neuordnung Europas, 1814–1815," *Mitteilungen des Instituts für österreichischen Geschichtsforshung* 50 (1936): 109–26. MM, 1: 36–38.

19. It is important to clear up some confusing terminology on the subject of "equilibrium." The "equilibrium" described by Metternich would in today's literature be referred to as a collective security structure or legal federation. Authors during and after the Congress of Vienna frequently used different terms to describe this order. Castlereagh commonly used "The Al-

liance" or "Union" to refer to it, whereas the more theoretically minded Friedrich von Gentz preferred "Gleichgewichts"—equilibrium—or "European Union." All of these are referring to the same architecture of a supranational federation of states regulated by treaty and operating according to the principle of reciprocity rather than the competitive and militaristic system of the balance of power. See below.

20. Metternich to Esterhazy, 7 August 1825 (MM, 4: 225). Metternich to Count Anton Apponyi, 2 June 1831 (NP, 5: 161).

21. On this point, see Sofka, "Metternich, Jefferson, and the Enlightenment," Part I, chaps. 3–6.

22. As Friedrich von Gentz, one of Metternich's closest advisers, put it in 1818, "This scheme of things has its inconveniences. But it is certain that, could it be made durable, it would offer the best possible combination to assure the prosperity of peoples, and the maintenance of the peace, which is one of its first prerequisites." "Considerations on the Political System Now Existing in Europe," 1818. Full text printed in Mack Walker, ed., *Metternich's Europe* (New York: Walker, 1968), p. 72.

23. MM, 1: 36. He added that "since an isolated state no longer exists, and is found only in the annals of the heathen world, or in the abstractions of so-called philosophers, we must always view the *society of nations* as the essential condition of the modern world." Metternich's emphasis. The reference to "philosophers" is, no doubt, directed against Hobbes's state of nature.

24. Rieben, *Metternich's Europapolitik,* p. 14. Naturally this state of affairs worked to Austria's advantage. However, it was equally beneficial to the other powers. This appeal to self-interest through cosmopolitan principles was one of the chief arguments Metternich used to persuade the other states to endorse this formula. As Kraehe notes, Metternich was convinced that "Austria's welfare was linked far more clearly to the European equilibrium than to any local advantages she might salvage in the form of territorial aggrandizement" (*German Policy,* 1: 29). If Austria's interests alone motivated Metternich's policies, it is arguable that he would not have pursued as ambitious or idealistic a design as this to provide for general peace. Rather, he could have employed the more expedient and direct tactic of forming a special alliance with Britain, France, or Russia in order to create an external guarantee of Austria's security, as Kaunitz did throughout the late eighteenth century. This idea, however,

was rejected by Metternich on the grounds that it marked a continuation, rather than a departure, of the eighteenth-century system of coalition diplomacy which in his view was responsible for much of the disarray and militarism of the past six decades. See below.

25. Kant's vision of international federalism was predicated upon the idea that the domestic institutions of the constituent states should be modelled along similar federalist theory. On the domestic side of Kant's theory of "perpetual peace," see Riley, *Kant's Political Philosophy,* chaps. 4–5; Hans Saner, *Kant's Political Thought: Its Origins and Development* (Chicago: University of Chicago Press, 1973), chaps. 8–11; and Dieter Henrich, "Kant on the Meaning of Rational Action in the State," in *Kant's Political Philosophy: The Contemporary Legacy,* ed. Ronald Beiner and William James Booth (New Haven: Yale University Press, 1993). I argue that Metternich shared this view, although space here does not permit an extended evaluation of this theory. On Metternich's attempt to create a federal constitution for Italy, Germany, and the Habsburg Monarchy as a whole, see Sofka, "Metternich, Jefferson, and the Enlightenment," Part I, chap. 5; and Arthur G. Haas, *Metternich, Reorganization, and Nationality, 1813–1818: A Study of Foresight and Frustration in the Rebuilding of the Austrian Empire* (Wiesbaden: F. Skiner, 1963).

26. Robert A. Kann, "Metternich: A Reappraisal of His Impact on International Relations," *Journal of Modern History* 32 (1960): 333–39. He argued that in adopting this position Metternich presaged Woodrow Wilson's formula for the collective security structure of the League of Nations by over a century.

27. "I have struck out from my customary diplomatic vocabulary the use of the words *legitimacy* and *divine right,*" Metternich wrote in 1837. "The words *legitimate* and *legitimacy* express an idea which is in my opinion more easily grasped by minds unaccustomed to serious discussion if it is represented by the word *right. Legitimacy* as a noun is used to qualify the right of succession to the throne; the same word, used as an adjective, can be applied to *anything.* One is the legitimate owner of a house or whatever it may be, and in the same way it expresses the idea of legal right. . . . The idea and the word *right* fulfills its duty much better in this respect than do those of *legitimacy* and *divine right"* (Metternich to Apponyi, 22 January 1837, cited in Bertier, *Metternich and His Times,* p. 37). Emphasis Metternich's. His mockery of the conservatives—

"minds unaccustomed to serious discussion"—
is obvious. Compare this with Henry Kissinger's discussion of the term "legitimacy" in
A World Restored, chap. 11. Kissinger argues
that Metternich did indeed understand this
concept in universal and normative terms, but
provides little evidence to support this case and
does not compare it to Kant's idea of "legitimate" right, the sense in which Metternich
interpreted it.

28. Srbik, "Ideengehalt," p. 250. Hans
Schmalz, *Versuche einer gesamteuropäische Organisation, 1815–1820* (Aarau, 1940), p. 13; Metternich to Tsar Alexander, January [undated] 1823
(MM, 3: 672).

29. Gulick, *Europe's Classical Balance of
Power,* p. 112. Unfortunately he bases this view
entirely on the contentious Saxony issue at the
Congress of Vienna in December 1814. Metternich's proposed alliance with Britain and France
against Russia and Prussia on this issue has frequently been invoked as evocative of balance of
power thinking (see Gulick, *Europe's Classical
Balance of Power,* chap. 9). Yet it is doubtful
whether Metternich would have followed
through with this idea. Modern research by
Kraehe and Schroeder places this question in a
more appropriate setting: that Metternich was
perhaps using the mechanisms of the old balance-of-power model in order to achieve a
higher end: creating and preserving a general
peace not just in Germany but also in Europe as
a whole. Kraehe, *Metternich's German Policy, vol.
2: The Congress of Vienna, 1814–1815* (Princeton: Princeton University Press, 1983), chap. 10;
Schroeder, *Transformation of European Politics,*
pp. 523–38. Gulick, *Europe's Classical Balance of
Power,* fails to take heed of these overarching ambitions and treats the Saxony affair as a purely
dynastic dispute. The interests involved at the
Congress were, however, indisputably greater.

30. See Kraehe, "A Bipolar Balance of
Power," for this argument. This thesis also animates his two volumes on Metternich's German
policy. As he notes in volume I, "The balance of
power, Metternich sensed, is not primarily a
doctrine but a condition, which exists when the
various states, each pursuing its selfish interests,
reach mutually recognized points of diminishing
returns" (p. 255).

31. See Schroeder, "Did the Vienna System
Rest on a Balance of Power?" for this argument.
His earlier work, "The Nineteenth Century System: Balance of Power or Political Equilibrium?"
Review of International Studies 15 (1989): 135–53,

makes a similar case but with greater theoretical
vigor. It is important to note that Schroeder's
view of Metternich has evolved with further research. In an earlier study, he dismissed Metternich's post-Vienna diplomacy as devoid of any
theoretical program or practical goal "other than
to prevent change" (*Metternich's Diplomacy at Its
Zenith, 1820–1823* [Austin: University of Texas
Press, 1962], p. 243).

32. Rieben, *Metternich's Europapolitik,*
pp. 37–55.

33. Kant, "On the Common Saying: "That
May Be True in Theory but It Does Not Apply
in Practice'" (1792), Reiss, *Kant's Political Writings,* p. 92. On the theory of the balance of
power from the eighteenth century to the present, see M. S. Anderson, "Eighteenth Century
Theories of the Balance of Power," in *Studies in
Diplomatic History,* ed. R. M. Hatton and M. S.
Anderson (London: Archon Books, 1970); Franz
A. J. Szabo, "Prince Kaunitz and the Balance of
Power"; Frank Manuel, *The Age of Reason*
(Ithaca: Cornell University Press, 1951), chap. 9;
Raymond Aron, *Peace and War: A Theory of International Relations* (New York: Doubleday; 1966),
part 1, chap.5; Hedley Bull, *The Anarchical Society: A Study of Order in World Politics* (New York:
Columbia University Press, 1977), part 2, chap.
5; Inis Claude, *Power in International Relations*
(New York: Random House, 1962); F. H. Hinsley, *Power and the Pursuit of Peace: Theory and
Practice in the History of Relations Between States*
(Cambridge: Cambridge University Press, 1966),
part 2; Kenneth Waltz, *Theory of International Politics* (New York: Random House, 1979), chap. 6;
Hans J. Morgenthau, *Politics Among Nations,* 3rd
ed. (New York: Knopf, 1961), part 4; Arnold
Wolfers, *Discord and Collaboration* (Baltimore:
Johns Hopkins University Press, 1962), chap. 8;
Richard Little, "Deconstructing the Balance of
Power: Two Traditions of Thought," *Review of
International Studies* 15 (1989): 87–100; Morton
Kaplan, *System and Process in International Politics*
(New York: John Wiley and Sons, 1957); William B. Moul, "Measuring the 'Balances of
Power': A Look at Some Numbers," *Review of
International Studies* 15 (1989): 101–21; Jeremy
Black, "The Theory of the Balance of Power in
the First Half of the Eighteenth Century: A
Note on Sources," *Review of International Studies*
9 (1983): 55–61; M. Wright, ed., *The Theory
and Practice of the Balance of Power, 1486–1914*
(New York, 1975).

34. See Metternich's explicit—and vigorous—condemnation of it in MM, 1: 37–9.

35. See Rohden, *Klassische Diplomatie,* chaps. 1–2, conclusion.

36. Kraehe, *German Policy,* 1: 255.

37. For this reason Metternich, upon taking over the Foreign Ministry in 1809, leaned heavily for advice on younger theoreticians such as Friedrich von Gentz, who were educated in the same tradition as he and shared his new approach to the international system. Significantly, Gentz was a student of Kant's at Königsberg and proofread his *Critique of Judgment.* Although he later became influenced by the romantic and historicist conservatism of Burke, Gentz began his career as a Kantian federalist who applauded Metternich's early efforts to make the conference system operational. See Murray Forsyth, "The Old European States-System: Gentz versus Hauterive," *The Historical Journal* 23 (1980): 521–38, and "Friedrich von Gentz: An Assessment," *Studies in History and Politics* 2 (1981–82): 127–55; Paul Sweet, *Friedrich von Gentz* (Madison, WI: University of Wisconsin Press, 1941); Golo Mann, *Secretary of Europe: The Life of Friedrich von Gentz* (New Haven: Yale University Press, 1946).

38. As Srbik argues, to Metternich "the state was not an end in itself like the pure *Machtstaat,* but is bound to the others through the eternal moral order and the idea of justice" ("Ideengehalt," p. 250).

39. Rieben, *Metternich's Europapolitik,* pp. 13–4; Metternich to Kaiser Franz, 17 August 1819. Haus-, Hof-, und Staatsarchiv, Vienna: Staatskanzlei: Vorträge, 1819. Carton 219, fol. 31–4. These documents were used with the gracious permission of Professor Enno E. Kraehe of the University of Virginia. MM, 1: 37.

40. Cited in Srbik, "Ideengehalt," p. 247.

41. This incident is best discussed by Kraehe in *German Policy,* 2: 284–98.

42. Walter Alison Phillips, *The Confederation of Europe: A Study of the European Alliance, 1813–1823 as an Experiment in the International Organization of Peace* (London: Longmans, Green and Co., 1914), p. 9. This highly original work was unfortunately eclipsed by the First World War. Phillips's articles in the influential *Cambridge Modern History,* ed. Lord Acton, made the same argument. See volume X, *The Restoration* (Cambridge: Cambridge University Press, 1907), chap. 1. These essays were influential on the succeeding generation of Metternich scholars such as Srbik, and were the first serious attempts to remove Metternich from the "reactionary" camp where he was unceremoniously placed by

Treitschke. Schmalz's *Versuche einer gesamteuropäische Organisation* makes a similar case and is heavily indebted to Phillips's work.

43. Metternich to Tsar Alexander, January [undated] 1823. MM, 3: 672; Forsyth, "Old European States-System," p. 525.

44. Kant, "Idea for a Universal History," Reiss, *Kant's Political Writings,* p. 48. On the concept of collective security as a model for international politics, see Aron, *Peace and War,* part 4, chap. 23; Bull, *Anarchical Society,* part 2, chap. 6; Wolfers, *Discord and Collaboration,* chap. 12; Hoffmann, "International Systems and International Law," *Janus and Minerva,* pp. 149–77.

45. Metternich to Nesselrode, 20 August 1817. MM, 3: 70.

46. Metternich to Philip von Neumann, 31 October 1832. NP, 5: 384. Castlereagh to Liverpool, 11 November 1814, PRO: F.O. 92, v. 141. This excellent series of papers is in the microfilm set of "Correspondence of Viscount Castlereagh From the Continent, 1814–1822," published by the Public Record Office, London. Castlereagh's emphasis. Note that Castlereagh did not use the more common—and misunderstood—eighteenth-century phrase of a "balance" of forces or power. On Talleyrand's view of the equilibrium, see Guglielmo Ferrero, *The Reconstruction of Europe: Talleyrand and the Congress of Vienna, 1814–1815* (New York: G. P. Putnam's Sons, 1941).

47. Srbik, "Ideengehalt," p. 258.

48. Metternich to Prince Paul Esterhazy, 5 March 1821 (cited in Bertier, *Metternich and His Times* p. 68).

49. Castlereagh's State Paper of 5 May 1820 (cited in Thomas G. Barnes, ed., *Nationalism, Industrialization, and Democracy 1815–1914: A Documentary History of Modern Europe,* 3 vols. [New York: Little, Brown; 1980], 3: 12. Castlereagh's emphasis).

50. That is why Talleyrand was so insistent that the phrase "law of nations" be inserted into the declaration announcing the opening of the Congress of Vienna on 1 November 1814. Ferrero, *Talleyrand,* pp. 164–65.

51. Metternich, upon reading this part of Canning's speech of 12 December 1826, which was intended as a blatant repudiation of his idea of a European League, stated that "it comes close to delirium." Metternich to Count Heinrich Bombelles, 8 January 1827 (cited in Bertier, *Metternich and His Times,* p. 219).

52. Metternich to Lebzeltern, 10 January 1822, cited in Bertier, *Metternich and His Times,* p. 144. Metternich's emphasis.

53. On Metternich's four conceptions of the Alliance, see Bertier, *Metternich and His Times;* "Sainte-Alliance et Alliance dans les conceptions de Metternich," *Revue Historique* 233 (1960): pp. 249–75; Metternich to Esterhazy, 7 August 1825. MM, 4: 225–26.

54. In reviewing the nature of these deliberations, Metternich used mathematical notation to illustrate the difference between his view of French integration and that proposed by Alexander. The formula he outlined succinctly captures the basis of his thinking on a European collective security system:

Present state of the Alliance: 4
Future state of the Meetings: 5
(1) Prince Metternich's Proposal:
$$5 = 1 + 4$$
(2) Russian Proposal:
$$1 + 1 + 1 + 1 + 1 = 5$$
Positive results of these proposals:
Given (1): 5: 4 + 1
Given (2): 5: 2 + 3

(cited in Bertier, *Metternich and His Times,* p. 138).

55. Ferrero, *Talleyrand,* p. 167; Metternich to Apponyi, 12 April 1847 (cited in Bertier, *Metternich and His Times,* p. 152).

56. On this idea and its origins, see Dupuis, *Droit des Gens,* chap. 3; Schmalz, *Versuche einer gesamteuropäische Organisation;* Forsyth, "Old European States-System"; and Mann, *Secretary of Europe.* Metternich put the question bluntly in 1823: "Must European politics be subjected to a representative diplomatic system? Would the most delicate problems be settled by meetings of 40 or 50 Minister-Delegates, independent of each other, voting by a show of hands, reaching, by means of a majority that would often be problematical or inadmissible, decisions on matters which an intimate meeting of 3 or 4 governments, experienced in prudence, barely manage to settle satisfactorily?" Metternich's Comments on the Circular Despatch of the Württemberg Cabinet, 2 January 1823 (NP, 4: 30–31).

57. MM, 1: 37. On Castlereagh's role, see C. K. Webster, *The Foreign Policy of Castlereagh, 1812–1822,* 2 vols. (London: G. Bell and Sons, 1925–1931), 2: 29–73; Hinsley, *Power and the Pursuit of Peace,* pp. 220–12.

58. As he noted later in life, "For a conference of Powers to be of use, it is in the first place necessary that *the object of the meeting should be precisely defined.* . . . Next, it needs to be well organized, for without this, meetings quickly turn into real anarchy." Metternich to Apponyi, 25 January 1832 (cited in Bertier, *Metternich and His Times,* p. 121. Metternich's emphasis).

59. Metternich to (addressee unknown), 10 January 1821 (MM, 3: 480–81).

60. Kant made this point in "Perpetual Peace" (1795). Reiss, *Kant's Political Writings,* pp. 108–14.

61. On the collapse of this system, see Sofka, "Metternich, Jefferson, and the Enlightenment," Part I, chap. 3.

62. Srbik, *Metternich,* 2: 559.

63. Castlereagh to Charles Stewart, 19 January 1821. Text of letter in Webster, *Castlereagh,* 2: 600.

64. It should also be noted that Metternich conceived of international politics in truly global terms, and frequently commented on the rise of the United States and its effect on Europe. He noted to Kaiser Franz during the Latin American revolts in 1819 that "for Europe there remains nothing more to do than to watch the fire [in Latin America] burn, the results of which must necessarily strengthen the power of the United North American States to an incalculable extent. As things stand now and in the foreseeable future, America can in five years get to where it otherwise would have taken two centuries." He was, with the promulgation of the Monroe Doctrine four years later, proven quite right. Metternich to Kaiser Franz, 24 August 1819 (HHSA: St. V., Carton 219, folio 153–4).

65. See Schroeder, *Transformation of European Politics,* pp. 579–81.

5

✺

World Wars I and II

Reading 5-1

Perceptions and Alliances
in Europe, 1865–1940
Thomas J. Christensen

While some structural realists and their liberal and institutionalist critics continue to fight a high-profile battle about the fundamental nature of international politics, a quieter discussion is progressing about how to integrate various aspects of realist thinking into a more coherent approach to security politics.[1] The goal of this discussion is to marry the two major strands of contemporary realist thought: balance-of-power theory and security dilemma theory. Recent works advocate combining structural variables, such as the number of great actors in the system and the distribution of capabilities among them, with security dilemma variables, such as the comparative efficacy of offensive versus defensive doctrines given available weaponry and military training.[2]

These writings are persuasive when reminding us that it is not enough to know how many great powers there are or how materially strong they are in comparison to one another. Even if we accept realist notions about international anarchy and its implications, we must also know how military power can be used in order to know if any given distribution of capabilities will prove destabilizing. Leaders will judge these two factors

SOURCE: From "Perceptions and Alliances in Europe, 1865–1940" by Thomas J. Christensen, *International Organization*, vol. 51, no. 1 (Winter 1997): 65–97. Copyright © 1997 IO Foundation and the Massachusetts Institute of Technology. Reprinted by permission of the MIT Press Journals.

together when analyzing their security environment and designing appropriate responses to it.

Though sympathetic to these recent efforts, I argue that in order to shed light on the alliance policies of the great powers in the multipolar systems of the nineteenth and twentieth centuries, at a minimum we must include in our analysis the perceptions and misperceptions of both the realist variables: the balance of power and the relative efficacy of offense and defense. Even if leaders think in terms consistent with realist assumptions, in complex multipolar environments they will often misread either the distribution of capabilities in the system and/or the efficacy of military offensives and defensives. This will lead to policies that may be driven by concerns about power and security but that may still seem at odds with the predictions of both balance-of-power and security dilemma theories. Specifically, when leaders perceive the frontline state in a potential alliance to be more powerful than its immediate rivals, they will tend to avoid a prewar alliance. If leaders believe that the frontline potential ally is weaker than immediate rivals but that defense has the military advantage, they will tend to form only a weak prewar alliance. If, however, they perceive their frontline potential ally as relatively weak and believe that offensives are feasible, they will tend to form a tight prewar alliance.

Below I will analyze how perceptions and misperceptions of the balance-of-power and security dilemma variables combined to affect the alliance politics of the great powers before the cold war. I build on my previous work with Jack Snyder, which focused on how perceptions of security dilemma variables—the efficacy of offensive and defensive doctrines—affected the alliance behavior of the great powers before the two world wars. I argue that by adding the variable of the perception of the balance of power, we can more fully explain cases from the nineteenth century while shedding additional light on the twentieth-century cases we had originally addressed.[3] In the empirical sections of the article, I compare my approach to alternative explanations for these states' security policies, including explanations that emphasize the roles of domestic politics, ideology, and the objective strategic environment.

The first empirical section addresses the security strategies of the great powers before the wars of German unification (the Austro-Prussian war of 1866 and the Franco-Prussian war of 1870). In this section, I argue that the approach advocated here explains the cases in question better than either our original thesis or James Morrow's alternative approach, which emphasizes the alleged domestic political trade-offs that leaders face when choosing between arms and alliances.[4] The following section briefly addresses great power relations before World War I. It integrates William Wohlforth's findings on perceptions of the balance of power with arguments that emphasize the importance of European leaders' false belief in offensive military advantage.[5] I then offer a more extensive critical discussion of recent work by Randall Schweller and others on British, French, and Soviet strategy before World War II.[6] I argue that, for British and Soviet leaders, analyses of the power balance and the offense-defense balance in land warfare were integrally connected and strongly affected their policies toward France in 1939–40. The article concludes by briefly discussing the potential implications of the approach here for the post–cold war world.

PERCEPTIONS AND THE TIGHTNESS OF ALLIANCES

Critiquing the indeterminacy of structural realism in explaining the foreign policies of states in a multipolar world, Snyder and I noted that in this century very different, if not opposite, paths led from structural multipolarity to systemwide war. Before World

War I, great powers tied themselves tightly to allies so that a small conflict quickly spread, involving all of the major powers. In contrast, before World War II the wartime allies passed the cost of opposing Adolf Hitler early onto one another, leaving him a free hand in Central Europe, time to build a more dangerous military machine, and the opportunity to deliver a knockout blow to France. Though structure mattered in both cases, a structural approach alone cannot explain such differing outcomes. In the spirit of Robert Jervis's work on the security dilemma, we grafted a nonstructural variable—leaders' perceptions about the relative efficacy of offensive or defensive doctrines—onto Kenneth Waltz's structural theory. By doing so we sought to predict when multipolar balancing coalitions would tend to overreact or underreact in the face of security challenges.[7] Our central argument was that under multipolar conditions, if leaders believe offensive military doctrines to be efficacious, the likelihood of tight alliances ("chain gangs") and quick escalation is high, while if they believe that defenses are hardy, they will try to pass the costs of opposing challengers early onto other actors.[8]

In multipolar worlds, what connects perceived offensive efficacy with the formation of tight alliances is the fear that initial enemy offensives will be successful and that initial successes will snowball. In other words, since they believe victory will be decided early, leaders in frontline states without immediate allies believe they run a high risk of being eliminated quickly in the first round of fighting; hence, they look for close allies. They are able to find close allies when leaders in second-line states share their strategic assessments and therefore fear that, if their allies are destroyed in the first round, they will be isolated and could be more easily eliminated in the second round by an aggressor nourished by first-round spoils. So, in 1914, when Austria mobilized for war, so did Germany. When Russia mobilized for war, so did France.

What connects defensive hardiness with buck-passing is a belief in relative security abundance: long attritional wars mean that, while opposing the attacker first may be very costly, it will likely be even more costly to the attacker. Even if a more powerful attacking country can eventually win a one-on-one confrontation by outlasting its weaker victim, it cannot do so quickly. So to the degree that they enter into alliances at all, leaders in second-line states believe that they should hold off giving assistance until it is absolutely necessary. By doing so, they believe that in the second round of fighting they will face a weaker foe, ground down by the earlier sacrifices of their frontline ally. Frontline states, of course, will always benefit from tight alliances and early assistance from second-line allies, regardless of the perceptions about offensive or defensive efficacy. When defenses are perceived to be hardy, leaders in frontline states will ask for prompt outside assistance in countering threats, but with little effect. In fact, this strategy will appear to leaders in second-line states as an attempt to pass the early cost of arming and fighting onto them. While encouraging the frontline state to develop hardy defenses, leaders in second-line states will do as little as possible to assist in that process, believing generally that the more assistance they lend, the less the frontline state might do for itself.

A more easily testable thesis about alliance behavior might include only the actual distribution of capabilities and the actual relative efficacy of offensive versus defensive military strategies. However, before the two world wars, leaders were almost entirely wrong in their predictions about the early course of military conflict. Thus, when examining the offense/defense variable, Snyder and I incorporated a perceptual element. This article takes that logic one step further and also adds a perceptual element to the balance-of-power variable. Misperceptions of either of the bedrock realist factors—the distribution of capabilities or the relative efficacy of offensive or defensive doctrines—should lead to behavior radically different from what we would expect from actors with more accurate perceptions.

Perceived efficacy of offensive versus
defensive military doctrines

		Offensives effective: wars decided quickly	Defenses robust: attritional wars
Perceived power of frontline potential ally in comparison with immediate rivals	Inferior/equal capabilities	Tight prewar alliance (chain ganging)	Weak prewar alliance (buck-passing)
	Superior capabilities	Avoidance of prewar alliance commitments	Avoidance of prewar alliance commitments

FIGURE 1. Perceptions of security and alliance strategy in multipolar worlds.

If leaders misperceive the distribution of capabilities, they may stand aside at crucial junctures in a conflict, overreact to insignificant threats, or even assist the wrong side in a war. If leaders mistake stronger states for weaker ones, they may even join the side of the mighty, thereby behaving more like bandwagoners than balancers.[9] However, when observing any given bilateral conflict, leaders in second-line states may prefer victory for the frontline state perceived to be the stronger of the two. In multipolar worlds, such a preference might exist when the second-line state shares with that apparently stronger state a rivalry with an uninvolved fourth power. Even in these instances, though, the perceptions of the balance of power should dissuade the second-line state from committing to assist the apparently stronger actor early in the bilateral conflict in question.

In Figure 1, the variable on the left side is the apparent power of a frontline potential ally in comparison with its immediate rivals as perceived by leaders of the frontline state and of its second-line potential allies. If leaders in frontline states believe their own nation is powerful enough to win the early battles of a war alone then those leaders are unlikely to pay the necessary costs and take the necessary risks to convince second-line states to join with them in tight prewar alliances. Since second-line states will almost certainly demand reciprocal benefits, confident leaders in frontline states are likely to view tight alliances as a pleasant but unnecessary luxury and settle for an independent security policy, regardless of their perceptions of the relative efficacy of offensive and defensive doctrines. If they view offensives as effective, they will try to overrun their enemies. If they view the defense as robust they will simply try to grind attackers down against their defensive positions.

If leaders in second-line states believe their potential frontline ally to be more powerful than its immediate enemy or enemies, they will be more confident that the frontline ally will survive the early stages of war alone. They will therefore find it unnecessary to tie themselves tightly to that potential ally. If leaders in second-line states perceive offensive doctrines to be efficacious given current technologies, they may believe that their frontline potential ally will be able to destroy its enemies by taking the offensive alone. They may, however, fear that weaker enemies may be able to mobilize faster than the potential frontline ally and reduce the initial power gaps by launching damaging early offensives. If so, second-line state leaders may decide to lend support early, so prewar alliances are not out of the question. However, even under such circumstances, leaders in second-line states may believe that the greater overall capabilities of the frontline state will offset the value for the weaker enemies of striking first. For these reasons, second-line states are less likely to make significant prewar commitments to frontline states perceived as superior, even in worlds where offensives seem feasible. In worlds where leaders perceive defenses to be quite hardy and frontline potential allies to be stronger than immediate rivals, prewar alliances are even less likely. Not only will leaders in second-line states expect war to be attritional and slow, with the result that their potential ally will survive the early rounds of fighting alone, but also they will expect the stronger state to emerge victorious from any attritional war in both the short and the long term.

If leaders in second-line states view their potential ally as weaker than its immediate frontline adversary, then the perceptions of the offense-defense balance that Snyder and I discussed become very important. In such instances, if offensives are considered efficacious by leaders in the second-line state, those leaders are likely to ally early and tightly with their apparently vulnerable frontline ally in order to prevent enemy offensives from destroying the ally in the short term. This alliance pattern may not hold, however, when the apparently weaker state is perceived to have some special advantage in mobilizing offensives against the apparently stronger one. For example, if leaders in second-line states believe that the materially weaker ally can mobilize larger offensive forces more quickly than the stronger state, even though the latter has more equipment and troops overall, those leaders might predict that the weaker state's offensive may serve to diminish the overall power differences between the two frontline states. In such instances, by planning to intervene, but only after the first round of fighting, the second-line state can minimize costs to itself while ensuring that its frontline ally does not suffer reversals when its stronger but slower enemy is able to mobilize counteroffensives.

If leaders in second-line states view their potential frontline ally as relatively weak but also view defensive advantage as quite hardy, then they may believe that attacks on the frontline potential ally, even by stronger states, will be unsuccessful and will serve only to weaken the stronger attacker by attrition. In such cases, the temptation will be to pass the early costs of war to the weaker frontline ally and to prepare to assist it later if it requires such assistance to survive the drawn-out attritional war.

Perceptions of the power balance and the offense-defense balance can often be interrelated. Leaders may condition their beliefs regarding offensive and defensive efficacy on the ratio of capabilities across combatants. For example, they may believe that a minimum ratio of power must be met before a nation can carry out an effective attritional defense against a stronger attacker. Therefore, the balance of power estimation may directly affect calculation of the strategic importance of offensive or defensive advantage. Leaders are also more likely to prefer offensive doctrines if they believe that their distant allies are too weak to fight a stronger enemy alone.[10]

In many cases, distinguishing whether strategic assessments are based on beliefs about the distribution of capabilities, offensive or defensive advantage, or both is difficult. For example, if offensives are efficacious only when states have highly trained armies with skillful and innovative officers, how does one separate the military's skill level (a national capability) from the more general technical and material conditions that favor mobility and attack?[11] Because I am interested here most in perceptions and not objective conditions and because I will consider perceptions of both power and security dilemma variables, this problem is not nearly as knotty as it would be if I were arguing that objective conditions were driving policies or that perceptions of one security factor and not the other was all-important in any case. For the purposes of this article, I wish to demonstrate only that some combination of perceptions about power and security dilemma variables led to the alliance decisions in question.

THE SOURCES OF ALLIANCE STRATEGY IN THE NINETEENTH CENTURY: SECURITY PERCEPTIONS OR DOMESTIC POLITICAL TRADE-OFFS?

The Austro-Prussian War

In a 1993 article, Morrow criticized my earlier article with Snyder by analyzing events on the Continent from 1866 to 1870.[12] In the first of his two cases from the period, Morrow focuses on events leading to the 1866 Austro-Prussian war, in which the Prussian army quickly crushed Austrian and other German confederation forces at Königgrätz (Sadowa). In the process, Prussia took a giant leap toward unifying Germany under Berlin's leadership.

As Morrow points out, Napoleon III of France did not want any single power to dominate within the German confederation. Of course, the Hapsburg monarchy did not want to see Germany unified under Prussian leadership either. Adopting our own theoretical viewpoint, Morrow first asks why, given their common interest in preventing Prussian dominance of Germany, Austria and France failed to ally at all, especially when the offensive advantages provided by new rifles and railroads should have led to a tight Franco-Austrian alliance.[13]

Morrow's alternative approach argues that leaders do not consider only the international environment when choosing grand strategies. When facing challenges abroad, they must also calculate domestic resistance to arms increases or additional alliance commitments. As his title suggests, Morrow views arming and alliances as contending alternatives for security policy (internal or external balancing in neorealist terminology). Morrow argues that, given a certain level of threat, we can predict a state's preferred mix of arms and alliance commitments by comparing the relative marginal political cost of each option in the domestic arena. Though he argues that one must weigh the costs of each strategy against the security benefits gained, Morrow generally concentrates on the domestic cost, not the international benefits, side of the equation. In his nineteenth-century cases, Morrow argues that, for both Austria and France, the domestic costs of an alliance overrode any consideration of security benefits to be gained by forging such an alliance. What prevented an otherwise logical alliance against the ascendant Prussia in 1866 was the Franco-Austrian dispute over Italian issues and, in particular, Venetia, which Austria held and France wanted Austria to cede to Italy.

Morrow's analysis of the Austro-Prussian war suffers from three shortcomings. First, when applying our original model to the alliance policies of the great powers before the war, he fails to consider leadership perception of offensive or defensive efficacy, focusing instead on weapons and logistics. Second, in a related fashion, he fails to offer evidence that, even before the battle at Königgrätz, leaders outside of Berlin believed offensives had the advantage and the attacker could win quickly. Finally, Morrow fails to recognize that while Napoleon III saw German unification as a threat, like most European leaders (including the Austrians) he believed that the intra-German balance of power strongly favored Austria over Prussia.

Napoleon's Belief in Austrian Superiority Napoleon III misperceived the strategic environment in 1866, but he was not blinded by lust for Venetia or by Bismarck's clever promise to compel Austria to cede Venetia to Italy if France remained neutral in the war. More than anything, he was fooled by the apparent strength of the Austrian military. Like most strategic analysts in Europe at the time, Napoleon's error centered on a poor estimation of the intra-German balance of power. Addressing the myth of Napoleon as Bismarck's dupe, Alfred Cobban writes, "Louis Napoleon, of course, was not foolish enough to count on Bismarck's gratitude for the reward of his neutrality. *He believed that Austria was the stronger of the two Germanic powers,* and with his old pro-Italian and anti-Austrian obsession, *gladly saw Italy join in on the side of Prussia to redress the balance* and wrench Venetia from the Austrian empire."[14] Napoleon did not fail to assist Austria because of the domestic politics of the Italian issue. He failed to do so because he believed that Austria was the stronger of the two German powers.[15] After speaking with Napoleon, the British ambassador in Paris reported in June 1866: "The conversation continued for some time as to the chances of Austria's success, the Emperor, I think, inclining to the opinion that she would lick the Prussians."[16] Even after Italy joined on the Prussian side, Napoleon's military analysts advised him that Austria would likely prevail in the war.[17] Though Napoleon III apparently recognized the superiority of Prussian needle guns before the outbreak of fighting, he believed that these were at best factors that would mitigate the continuing overall military superiority of Austria. In a conversation with the British ambassador just before the battle at Königgrätz, he judged "the Austrian army the better of the two—the Prussian the better appointed."[18]

The Austro-Prussian war was waged between a previously dominant power in the German confederation, Austria, and a rising challenger, Prussia.[19] During such power shifts, determining which side has the upper hand is very difficult. Napoleon III was mistaken in estimating the balance of power in Europe, but in his defense, he was hardly alone. The Austrian defeat at Königgrätz was a shock to the world and thus routinely has been associated with terms like "thunderclap." As Dennis Showalter states, "Statesmen and soldiers throughout Europe were stunned by Königgrätz and its aftermath . . . (in most capitals) the question dominating newspapers, cabinets, and officers' messes alike was 'how did this happen?'"[20]

Austria, too, was overconfident in its ability to defeat Prussia. While not desiring war, brash Austrian officials believed that if Bismarck insisted on war, Austria alone could defeat Prussia, whose forces it outmanned by 50 percent.[21] In fact, as H. M. Hozier wrote, in March 1866 the Austrian council of war "decided that Austria was strong enough to take the field against Prussia and Italy at the same time. . . . Too high an estimate appears to have been formed of the strength of Austria, and far too low a calculation made of the powers of Prussia; for the opinion . . . seems to have been that Austria could only emerge from such a war as a decisive victor."[22]

We have established that both Austrian and French leaders believed Austria was the dominant power in the intra-German struggle, so the puzzle about why France did not ally with Austria is fully solved. Given the prevailing consensus in Europe about Austrian dominance, by allying with Austria, Paris would have been bandwagoning, not balancing. But as far as the thesis here is concerned, one question remains: since Napoleon III believed Prussia to be the weaker party, why did he not ally with Prussia to deter Austrian aggression or assist Prussian troops once war started? In other words, although the question of why France failed to chain gang with a potential ally is valid, the potential ally at the question's center is Prussia, not Austria. The real puzzle thus lies not in Napoleon's allowing a free hand to Bismarck but rather in his concurrent promise of nonintervention to Vienna.

Napoleon's Belief in Attritional War Snyder and I both argue that one cannot look at the actual balance of offensive versus defensive advantage when determining whether multipolarity will tend toward either buck-passing or chain ganging. Since the predictions of leaders before World Wars I and II were almost entirely wrong, we recognized the necessity of adopting an additional perceptual variable, leadership beliefs about the efficacy of various strategies.

A similar perceptual approach must be applied to the Austro-Prussian war. Prussian field marshal Moltke's offensive strategies were effective at Königgrätz, but neither French nor Austrian leaders had been able to predict such an outcome. Showalter writes, "Expert opinion in most capitals had predicted either an Austrian victory or a campaign of mutual exhaustion."[23] Louis Napoleon's analysis was the same.[24] René Arnaud writes, "The whole of Europe was expecting an Austrian victory, or at all events a long war . . . and it was for this reason that Napoleon III had dreamed of intervening as mediator and as the sovereign arbiter between two exhausted combatants."[25]

Of the two potential outcomes he anticipated—Austrian victory or a war of attrition—Napoleon III greatly preferred the latter, so to the degree that he took action at all during the crisis preceding war, he did so with the purpose of guaranteeing a lengthy war. Believing the combined forces of Italy and Prussia to be roughly equal to those of Austria alone, Napoleon fostered an Italian-Prussian alliance.[26] By encouraging Italy to attack the Austrian flank and tie down Prussian forces in the event of an Austro-Prussian war, Napoleon III believed he was guaranteeing an attritional outcome by reducing the likelihood of the only imaginable short-war scenario: a quick Austrian victory. For just such a reason, Napoleon intervened in order to end a paralyzing standoff between Italy and Prussia, each of whom wanted to secure concessions from Austria without war by involving the other in a conflict with Austria.[27]

According to the Italian minister to Paris at the time, Count Nigra, misperception of the balance of power and his belief that the war would be lengthy drove Napoleon's desire for war and a Prussian-Italian alliance. In 1893 he recalled:

> Napoleon said: "It is advisable for Italy to conclude the treaty with Prussia, for only then will Prussia dare to attack Austria. Only then will the forces be equalised and a balance established, which will give Prussia a prospect for victory. In this way Italy will get Venice and France will enjoy the advantage of a conflict between the two powers [Austria and Prussia], by whose alliance she is held in check." . . . He imagined that the forces of the conflicting states were now [after the Prussian-Italian pact] roughly equal, but there he made a great mistake. The battle of Königgrätz took him completely by surprise; he had assumed that battles would be won and lost, and that he would in the meantime be free to arrange matters as he liked.[28]

Count Nigra's recollection is consistent with the accounts of other contemporaries of Napoleon. William Edward Johnston, an American close to powerful members of the French elite at the time, wrote that Napoleon was profoundly astonished by the outcome at Königgrätz because he had expected a war in which "both parties were going to exhaust themselves."[29] In fact, according to various sources Napoleon was so confident that war would be attritional, he much preferred an Austro-Prussian struggle to peace.[30]

While we have no direct statement by Napoleon III about the advantage of defense, his well-documented belief that war would be attritional seems a fine proxy for the offense-defense variable employed in the model above. Given his belief in defensive hardiness, Napoleon III passed the buck to the local powers opposing Austria, the state Napoleon perceived to be the strongest. By adding perceptions of the distribution of capabilities to our earlier thesis about perceptions of defensive efficacy, we capture almost all of the important dynamics of the case. We can understand both why Napoleon III passed the buck and why he passed it to Prussia and Italy, not Austria.

As for Austria, the assurance in its own safety, based primarily on the relative size of its army in comparison to Prussia's, was amplified by its belief that defensive strategies had the advantage. Though new railroad and rifle technology allowed for effective Prussian offensive methods, those new methods were unknown outside of Prussia and were largely unavailable to other states, including Austria, which had less developed rail networks.[31] Showalter writes, "The Prussians' success in utilizing the railroads to their own advantage is thrown into even sharper relief by the performance of their enemies. *Feldzeugmeister* Benedek, despite his reputation as one of the most aggressive and hard-driving Hapsburg generals, was unable or unwilling to overrule his Chief of Staff, *Generalmajor* Gideon von Krismanic. Krismanic's operations plan stressed the importance of concentrating the Austrian army at a suitable 'position' against which the Prussian offensive might shatter itself."[32] Though tactically the Austrians often rushed the well-armed Prussian troops once the latter had invaded an Austrian-controlled sector, the overall Austrian strategy was classically defensive, emphasizing the concentration of defensive forces against presumably overextended attackers and eschewing the mobile flanking maneuvers of the better-trained and better-equipped Prussian forces.[33]

Austrian policy toward the controversy over Venetia demonstrates that domestic political pressures related to Italy were of only secondary importance in Austrian strategy. Initially, Austrian Emperor Francis Joseph did not think he needed French assistance to defeat Italy and Prussia, so he would not cede Venetia as payment for an alliance with France (as we have already seen, this cession would have failed to secure such an alliance anyway). For similar reasons of overconfidence, in March he refused to cede Venetia to gain Italian neutrality in the war.[34] But later, when France bluffed by threatening to enter on the side of Prussia if Austria did not cede Venetia, Francis Joseph perceived the threat to Austrian security to be real.[35] He therefore discounted any domestic political costs and agreed to cession of Venetia as the price of French neutrality.[36] If we wished to argue that the domestic politics of the Venetia issue, not security perceptions, were driving Austria's policy toward France, we would have to explain why Austria had not been willing to give up Venetia for an alliance with France yet was willing to give it up for French neutrality.

By June 1866 France had guaranteed Austrian cession of Venetia regardless of the outcome of the fighting to come. Napoleon had forced both Prussia and Austria to promise Venetia to Italy as the price of French neutrality. Therefore, in no way can one argue that tacit French support for Prussia and Italy was driven primarily by concerns over the future of Venetia. The secondary nature of the Venetia issue is most clearly driven home by Napoleon's prompt about-face after he learned of the swift and dramatic Prussian victories against Austria. He not only reportedly regretted having weakened Austria by forcing it to cede Venetia but also began coercing Italy and Prussia to settle for an early peace and thereby helped prevent further advances at Austria's expense.[37]

Bismarck in 1866: The Benefits of Justified and Conditional Confidence

While by 1866 Bismarck was confident that Prussia could defeat Austria alone in war, he did not ignore the inherent dangers of multipolarity. He did seek foreign assistance, in Italy, to increase the likelihood of victory over Austria. More important, he sought and secured a guarantee of French neutrality by agreeing to the cession of Venetia if Prussia won the war. As long as France did not ally with Vienna, Prussia was confident that it could overrun Austria.

Until the October 1865 meeting with Napoleon III at Biarritz, Bismarck had always sought a tight alliance with France before planning an attack on Austria. But at Biarritz, Bismarck became convinced by Moltke that Prussia could defeat Austria without French assistance. As a result, Bismarck's strategy changed to one of merely guaranteeing French neutrality.[38] The case fits the approach here perfectly. As Prussian leaders came to view Prussia as stronger than Austria, they pursued alliance with France less vigorously.

Bismarck was both fortunate and unfortunate that French leaders believed in defensive advantage in 1865–66. He was initially unfortunate in that Napoleon III's belief in attritional war meant that France would not ally tightly with Prussia before the war, even though France thought Prussia was weaker than Austria. So Bismarck's pre-Biarritz hope of building a strong alliance against Austria before risking war was eliminated by French buck-passing, as Snyder and I would predict. Once Bismarck decided Prussia could fight alone, however, France's belief in the likelihood of attritional war carried great benefits for Berlin. Because French leaders did not fear war as much as they might have if they had perceived offensives as highly effective, Paris did nothing to prevent war in Central Europe. This meant Bismarck had a free hand to begin hostilities if he so desired. In fact, Paris encouraged him. Moreover, Napoleon III's skepticism about the efficacy of Prussian offensives led him to believe that Austria's initial numerical advantage was likely to hold up against a Prussian offensive. He worried then that the combination of defensive advantage and Austrian numerical superiority would lead to a crushing defeat for Prussia if the latter attacked alone. To hedge against the possibility of postwar Austrian dominance of Germany and to foster Prussian belligerence, Napoleon III encouraged Italy to join on Prussia's side against Austria. French belief in both attritional war and Prussian weakness not only allowed Prussia to fight but also helped Berlin obtain an ally in that fight.

The Franco-Prussian War

If the myths of Austrian superiority and attritional war drove alliance behavior before Königgrätz, they certainly did not do so after that decisive battle. So a puzzle remains about why Austria and France did not form a tight alliance before the next major European war. While the answer to this question is complicated, the approach offered here captures many more of the important dynamics of the case than does Morrow's trade-off thesis.

The war was sparked by France's contentious diplomacy toward Prussia, which was driven largely by a governmental legitimacy crisis and popular hypernationalism. The approach here does not address the domestic politics of French belligerence, but it helps explain why France found itself fighting alone. Four major factors prevented a Franco-Austrian alliance: (1) France's confidence in its ability to defeat Prussia quickly and alone in at least the early stages of war, particularly if France mobilized first and launched the early offensives; (2) Austria's fundamental agreement that France was likely to win the early battles of the war even without Austrian assistance; (3) the continuing inability of Austria to mobilize quickly in the event of war, which had helped seal its fate in 1866; (4) and the Russian threat to Austria's flank, a problem directly related to Russian overestimation of French power and one that a less confident France may have tried to eliminate through diplomacy before fighting erupted.

The Impact of Domestic Politics in France The Franco-Prussian war, if not caused by, was at least hastened by France's attempt to humiliate Prussia after Berlin agreed to remove the controversial Hohenzollern candidacy (Prince Leopold) for the Spanish throne. Though Bismarck's infamous response, the Ems dispatch, was indeed provocative, it followed a vindictive French attempt to secure not only Prussian reversal on Spanish policy but also a statement by Kaiser William suggesting his culpability for ever having supported Prince Leopold. Confident and still bitter over France's about-face after Königgrätz, Bismarck dragged his reluctant Kaiser into war via the Ems dispatch. It was French diplomatic clumsiness, however, that angered William and provided Bismarck a clear opportunity to do this.[39]

France's high-stakes strategy was driven by two factors: the desire for a great diplomatic victory to bolster state legitimacy at home and arrogance about the prospect of war with Prussia, driven partially by the first factor above but more so by the mistaken, but historically rooted, beliefs that French forces were more effective than their Prussian counterparts and that France would gain great military advantages by mobilizing first for war.[40] In psychological terms, the French leadership suffered simultaneously from both motivated and cognitive biases.[41]

French Weakness and Overconfidence French diplomatic aggressiveness meant that war came before the military had completed the more important phases of its reform program, and this was partially to blame for the army's pathetic performance against the Prussians. Moreover, French leaders' overconfidence together with their belief in offensive advantage meant that Paris believed allies, especially those with slow mobilization rates, would be unnecessary to France in the early going. As Morrow himself writes, "The Austrians and Italians informed the French that their forces could not be ready for combat for at least six weeks after the start of mobilization. The French believed they would gain victories over the Prussians in that period that would draw Austria and Italy into the war [on France's side] without a formal alliance. The French also saw little advantage in sacrificing their interests in Rome as the price for an alliance that offered little immediate support."[42]

Morrow's historical account is accurate, but he draws the wrong lesson from it. After the passage above, he concludes, "An alliance by the two [Austria and France] against Prussia was difficult to form because of the Italian issue that had dramatic implications for both states' domestic politics."[43] This may be true enough, but it misses the main point. If France wanted an alliance guarantee from Austria, it would have to offer something in return—if not Italian interests, then something else. One possibility would have been a public guarantee to assist Austria if it were attacked by Russia. But France did not want to pay anything to Vienna because Austrian assistance against Prussia was seen as unnecessary to winning the crucial early battles of the war, after which Napoleon III correctly believed that Austria planned to enter the war against Prussia anyway.

A more cautious France may have stalled for time, allowing further French military reforms, Austrian preparation for war, and an alliance agreement with Austria and Italy. Because his military and civilian advisers predicted the early course of the war very poorly, Napoleon III did not make the necessary effort to secure early support from Italy and Austria before declaring war on Prussia.[44] French overconfidence spilled into the streets. As Cobban describes it, "'*À Berlin*' was the war-cry on the boulevards and the password of the army. There was a run on maps of Germany in the shops; it would have been unpatriotic, defeatist, and absurd to suggest that maps of France might be more useful."[45] The French army leaders were so confident that they distributed only German maps to their own troops.[46] Battle forecasts by military advisers were beset with hyperbole, and members of the French Senate were supremely confident of French victory.[47]

Most French leaders in 1870 may have believed that offense had the advantage, but since they falsely believed that France could mobilize an effective offensive force before Prussia could respond they applied this assessment only to their own offensives—at least in the opening stages of the war. Napoleon said to the Austrian ambassador just before the war, "the winner will be the one who can be ready first."[48] French leaders also believed that when French offensives were shown to be effective, the southern German states over which Prussia had gained dominance in 1866 would defect, thus damaging Prussia's numerical power and allowing France to "cut Germany in two," as Empress Eugenie put it.[49]

But this was all fantasy. The French would learn not only that their own military was extremely weak and poorly organized but also that the Prussian military was more effective than the French military on both offense and defense. Moreover, the theory, created in Vienna, that the southern German states would defect from Prussia and join France rested on specific assumptions and preconditions not met by the overconfident French leaders. Such a defection would occur only if southern Germans viewed the war as having been provoked by Prussia purely over Hohenzollern interests in Spain. After Prussia removed Leopold's candidacy, many (including Austrian leaders) saw France's obnoxious insistence on humiliating the Kaiser as the real cause of war. Southern Germans then viewed France as the aggressor, and they rallied behind Prussia.[50]

Before the battle at Königgrätz, European analysts believed France had the strongest military by far, with Austria as its closest rival.[51] From Königgrätz France seemed to have learned only two lessons: a real one about Austria's weakness and a more questionable one about offensive advantage. But most French military leaders failed to learn the most important lesson, namely, that the rising Prussia could not be defeated with certainty by any single European army, including their own. After 1866, Napoleon III instituted military reforms so that France could mobilize more soldiers in case of war. Though Napoleon himself was consistently nervous about French preparations during 1866–70, in July 1870 General Lebouef convinced the French leadership that France was ready for war. Moreover, Napoleon subscribed to the Austrian theory that when war started, initial French victories would lead to the defection of the southern German states from Berlin's federation, thus diminishing Prussia's overall power and providing a pretense for Austrian entrance into the war on France's side.[52] A. J. P. Taylor writes: "The Second Empire had always lived on illusion; and it now committed suicide in the illusion that it could somehow destroy Prussia without serious effort."[53]

In 1870 most leaders outside of Prussia also agreed that French forces were superior and would win at least the opening rounds of the war.[54] Though Prussia had more men under arms than France in 1870, France had been the greatest land power on the Continent since long before the rise of Napoleon Bonaparte. In 1870 France also spent significantly more on defense than any Continental European power except Russia.[55] Many, including the French, comforted their nationalist egos after Königgrätz by attributing the Prussian victory over Austria to new technologies, namely, new rifles, not to the superior skill and discipline of Prussian officers and soldiers.[56] If one accepted this self-serving myth, then it would follow that once the French army had obtained new rifles (which it had by 1870), there was no reason to believe that France could not maintain its position as the premier ground force in Europe. As Michael Howard states, "the completeness of the Prussian success in 1870 thus astounded the world."[57]

Austria and the Russia Problem　The widely held belief in the superiority of French troops helps explain Austrian behavior in 1870, as well. Austrian leaders believed that France would likely win at least the early phases of the war without significant Austrian assistance.[58] Austrian leaders still hoped France would win because Austria needed to worry about both Prussia and Russia, Prussia's supporter and Austria's eastern threat.[59] Given Austrian leaders' beliefs about the likelihood of early French dominance in the war and France's failure to reassure Austria publicly that, if Austria entered the war early, France would assist it in defending against Russia, France was unsuccessful in gaining an early alliance with Austria. Still, the Austrians were prepared to enter into the conflict on the French side after the first round of French victories. This would not only ensure against potential Prussian counteroffensives in the next round of fighting but, by moving Austrian troops north, would also hedge against French domination of the south German states if Prussia totally collapsed.[60] So whether French offensives were to be successful only in the first rounds of the war or whether France's anticipated early victories were to cripple Prussia more permanently and more fully offset the Prussian military's numerical advantages, Austria had a national interest in joining the fight against Prussia, but not at the onset of hostilities.

Of course, once Vienna realized that France was losing, it had a clearer incentive to assist France against Austria's intra-German rival, Prussia. But after the war started, it quickly became too late for Austria to take effective action to save France. Austrian mobilization would take six weeks. Within a few weeks of the initial fighting, French defeat seemed inevitable: Vienna thus rejected any eleventh-hour action to save France. As Taylor describes the problem for Vienna, "The Austrians kept out of the war solely from a well-founded reluctance not to tie themselves to a country that was already defeated."[61]

Though Napoleon did offer secret prewar assurances to Vienna regarding Russia, the mistakenly confident French were unwilling to take the real risks necessary to guarantee allies overtly and warn their adversaries before declaring war.[62] Had the French been less confident, they may very well have allied tightly with Austria before war broke out.

This perceptual approach explains Russian behavior as well. Russian leaders believed that France was likely stronger than Prussia and, therefore, warned Austria early that if it entered the war on the side of France, Russia would attack it from the east. The Russians believed that the short-term threat was to Prussia (not France) and so they chained themselves to Prussia by threatening to enter the war if Austria mobilized.[63] As the actors at the time seemed to realize, a tighter Austro-French alliance may have created two opposing chain gangs (France, Austria, and Italy versus Prussia and Russia) that might have dragged all of continental Europe into war, as tight alliances would in 1914.[64]

In his treatment of the Austrian case, Morrow offers domestic political reasons for why Vienna could not ally with France against Prussia. In addition to continuing disputes over Italy, these included Hungarian ambivalence toward any increase of Austrian power within Austria-Hungary and the resistance of the Austrian public to helping France gain control over German populations near the Rhine. However, the evidence strongly suggests that Vienna's policies were not driven primarily by domestic political concerns but rather by Austrian leaders' perceptions and misperceptions of standard security considerations. If domestic politics were really the deciding factor in keeping Austria from fighting with France against Prussia, then why was Austria preparing to join France in feeding off of a wounded Prussia after the first rounds of the war?

THE TWO WORLD WARS

Before the two world wars, states engaged in very little trade-off between arms and allies. Instead, security policy seemed largely driven by the degree of threat perceived by political and military leaders. Before World War I, when leaders felt they or their allies were relatively vulnerable to offensives, most European nations built weapons and tightened formal or informal alliances at a rather frantic pace.[65] Alternatively, before 1939, when defense was believed to have the advantage in Continental warfare, tight alliances did not form, and where loose ones existed, they were quickly abandoned, as in the case of France and the Little Entente in Eastern Europe.

But interwar alliances were not weak because the future allies were arming at an extremely fast pace. Between 1931 and 1935 France cut its defense expenditures by nearly 30 percent, with the bulk of the cuts coming from arms procurement funds. In 1930 France implemented a 1928 decision to reduce conscription service to one year, thus reducing the quality and quantity of potential combatants at a time when the demographic catastrophes of World War I were soon to cut deeply into the potential pool of French soldiers.[66] Between 1934 and 1938 neither Britain nor France increased weapons procurement at anywhere near the rate of their rival Germany.[67] While the Socialist Premier Leon Blum committed much more toward French defense after the 1936 Rhineland crisis than his conservative critics would later recognize, even measured as a share of gross national product, Germany's defense budgets were still more than double those of France in the late 1930s.[68]

When Britain and France did accelerate their weapons procurement most impressively—after Hitler secured control over the Sudetenland at the Munich conference (September 1938) and then seized the Czech rump state (March 1939)—they also simultaneously increased their strategic cooperation. Arms and alliances were complementary, not rival, goods, and leaders determined their proper mix more by strategic analysis of the international environment than by measuring the relative costs of each in the domestic arena.

World War I

In 1914, both beliefs about the offense-defense balance and the balance of power affected the security policies of the major powers. Most of the important dynamics are captured by the standard thesis in the literature, which emphasizes the importance of offensive biases in creating tight alliances and quick escalation in the early phases of the war. Because it is persuasive and widely accepted, I will only review that thesis briefly here. I will focus instead on how adding the variable of perceptions about the distribution of capabilities sheds light on other interesting aspects of this case.

Before World War I great powers tied themselves tightly to allies, so a small conflict quickly spread, involving all of the major powers. They did so largely because they believed that offensives had the strategic advantage, that the war would be short, and that early victories could easily snowball into major advantages.[69] As Raymond Aron argued, one need only observe the lack of financial and military preparedness for the long war that ensued to be certain that European leaders were shocked by the hardiness of defenses and the attritional nature of land warfare.[70]

Though not challenging the widespread consensus on the importance of perceptions of the offense-defense balance before World War I, Wohlforth's work helps us understand how estimations of the balance of power also contributed to the conflict. French and Russian beliefs that they were each individually weaker than Germany helped convince Russia to adopt an active offensive strategy against the Central Powers. If Germany were allowed to attack France while Russia remained on the defensive, then Russia would lose an opportunity to attack a weakened German flank abandoned by forces attacking westward. Moreover, if France were knocked out of the war Russia might later have had to face the Central Powers alone.[71] If the Russians had believed that either Russia or France was individually more powerful than Germany, then Russian attitudes about the desirability of offensives and early entrance into the war might have been different.

Britain was a bit of an outlier in 1914, limiting its initial commitment to France and Russia. This strategy was partially based on Britain's natural defensive advantages as an island, and British analysts' prescient predictions that conflict in Europe might bog down in attritional warfare.[72] As Wohlforth points out, British analysts also valued more highly than others the overall capabilities of the French and Russian militaries, particularly the latter.[73] So, the combined perceptions of the offense-defense balance and the balance of power made the British leaders relatively sanguine about the chances of French and Russian containment of the Central Powers on land. Therefore, at least in comparison to France and Russia, Britain was relatively uninvolved in prewar military and diplomatic developments on the Continent. Even so, this was not because Britain had chosen arms over allies; British military expenditures increased more slowly in the years 1909–13 than those of any of the major powers on the Continent.[74] As in the case of Russia, British beliefs about the balance of power reinforced the tendencies created by beliefs about the offense-defense balance.

World War II

British Strategy toward France One of the standard conclusions of neorealist treatments of World War II is that Britain, France, and the Soviet Union passed the buck to one another, leaving Hitler a free hand in Central Europe and a greater opportunity to eliminate the great powers through piecemeal aggression. One of the classic examples of the buck-passing phenomenon is the lack of stronger strategic cooperation between Britain and France in the years leading to General Guderian's blitz. Whereas authors have differed over whether, given multipolar conditions, defensive doctrines led to buck-passing or whether the desire to pass the buck led to defensive doctrines, many accounts agree that beliefs about defensive efficacy and the desire to pass the buck combined to lead to suboptimal alliance formation in the face of Nazi aggression.[75]

Implicit in the standard accounts is an important argument about the distribution of power within the multipolar set. Particularly in the case of British and French relations with Germany, the assumption is that Germany was stronger than either of the allies individually and that leaders in both Paris and London knew that alliance with the other would therefore be necessary if Germany were to attack. If this were not the case, defensive biases might not have had anything to do with British and French alliance behavior. Instead, the weak alliance might have been better explained by British and French overestimation of their national capabilities. As I will demonstrate below, British and French leaders understood that Germany was stronger than either France or Britain alone, but British leaders in particular believed that defensive advantages would strongly reduce the importance of those power gaps. Therefore, as the approach here would predict, Britain allied with France but not very vigorously.

In a 1993 article, Schweller argued against the standard account from two perspectives. First, citing London's concern about German knockout blows against Britain, he calls into question the notion that British leaders believed that defense had the advantage in 1939–40. Schweller points out that as May 1940 approached, the British became increasingly concerned that Britain, not France, would become the first target of German aggression in the west; thus Britain was even less likely to send forces to France.

Second, Schweller argues that the security of Britain and France did not constitute a collective good. In a nutshell, Schweller contends that, as "middle powers" or "second-ranking powers," Britain and France were so outclassed by the powerful Germany that even if they had tightly coordinated their efforts they would have been unable to take on Germany effectively. They had little choice but to wait for the assistance of one of the other true poles in the system (the Soviet Union and the United States) to enter the fray. In the meantime they rationally "distanced" themselves from each other in the hopes that they could avoid being targeted next by the third pole, Germany. For Britain, then, any significant effort to assist France would serve only to drain British resources and annoy Hitler, thus making an attack on Britain more likely in the short term.[76] Finally, Schweller contends that, as an island, Britain's defense requirements were incompatible with those of France, a land power. Schweller writes, "Britain was threatened by an air and sea assault; France by a land invasion. Thus, if one of the allies was able to secure its borders against a German attack, it does not follow that the other's frontiers were thereby defended"[77] Robert Kaufman offers a thesis that dovetails with Schweller's on this score, arguing that British alliance behavior toward France was too weak to qualify as balancing behavior at all.[78]

Both in the period before the Munich conference, when Neville Chamberlain and other civilian leaders were attempting to prevent war through appeasement, and after Munich and the fall of the Czech rump state, when leaders abandoned appeasement, British strategists considered carefully what course a war with Germany would take if either accommodation or deterrence failed to keep the peace. Schweller's account misses important aspects of British strategic analysis in both periods. First, British strategists' focus on the danger of a knockout blow from Germany against the home islands was integrally related to the belief that such a blow would be impossible on the Continent. As early as September 1936, British strategist Colonel Ismay linked the inability to win quick victories on land with the possibility that Germany might try to level a knockout blow against Britain.[79] In September 1938, Ismay justified the accelerated home air defense program by "bearing in mind the advantage which the defensive has over the offensive in land warfare, and in particular the strength of the Maginot Line." He believed this meant that Germany "could hardly hope for a rapid decision on land."[80] Despite these beliefs, the British understood that the French would need assistance on land over the long run. They accordingly planned to create an expeditionary force and a territorial army to send to the Continent. The main issue was one of timing: was a large ground force to be created and equipped in advance of hostilities or should current resources be devoted to air defense? Largely because of belief in the efficacy of French defenses, the answer was generally to emphasize air and naval defenses.[81] There would be plenty of time to send reinforcements later, British analysts believed, because the next war on the Continent would likely resemble the last one.[82]

Though the fear that Britain might be struck first persisted and grew in 1939–40, especially after the German attack on Poland, it did so not because German seizure of France did not matter in British calculations nor because Britain felt it could do nothing to help France. Rather, it persisted because British leaders believed France's defensive advantage in ground warfare made France too tough a nut to crack in the short term, even without a massive early infusion of British assistance. As a February 1939 Chiefs of Staff report clearly states, Britain feared it might be the first target of attack because, "France could not resist alone after the defeat of Great Britain; (and) a full-scale attack on France would involve heavy losses which might have a serious effect on German morale."[83] Britain had such faith in short-term French defense that it often placed less value in the protection provided to Britain by the English Channel than that provided to France by the Maginot Line.

British leaders indeed feared attack from the air and sea, but this did not mean that France was unimportant. They realized correctly that such attacks would be made much easier if Germany controlled air strips and ports across the channel from England. German access to the French coast meant shorter flights for German bombers and fighters, allowing the Luftwaffe more time over British targets. British access to French air strips would similarly ease British air assaults on Germany. Moreover, German control of French ports would make a German sea landing in Britain much easier in the same way that access to British ports would be critical to the Allied landing at Normandy in June 1944. While Schweller correctly points out that German seizure of Belgium alone would have significantly closed the gap for Germany, even in such circumstances France would have been important for Britain. French bases would allow for easier attacks on German positions in Belgium as well as easier counterattacks on Germany's industrial heartland, the Ruhr, positioned dangerously close to France's eastern borders.[84]

This strategic analysis is not just twenty-twenty hindsight; it was shared by British analysts at the time. British documents from 1938 and 1939 clearly demonstrate that Britain viewed French security as important to its own; Britain understood that France would eventually need its assistance against the larger Germany; Britain expected French defenses to hold for a considerable period of time with only limited assistance from Britain; and Britain planned to offer France more significant help after that initial period.

As early as spring 1938, British analysts made one thing very clear in their strategic assessments: French defense mattered to Britain, even if Belgium fell. Britain wanted France to extend its defenses from northeastern France, where the formal Maginot Line ended, to the sea. While heavy Maginot-type defenses would sink in the lowlands along the Franco-Belgian border, various lighter antitank barricades were considered possible. British discussion of this shortcoming in France's strategy demonstrates not only the importance of France but also the early problem of buck-passing in the budding alliance. Lord Hankey wrote to Chamberlain on 28 April 1938, "All our co-operation with France, whether by air or sea and eventually by land, will be very much less effective if the Germans get the [French] channel ports. It is therefore a strong *French* interest to cover them by an extension of the Maginot Line [to the sea]. . . . Incidentally it is a strong British interest, but it would be advisable *not* to say so or else the French might ask us to pay!"[85] Whereas Chamberlain expressed concerns about losing the Belgian ports and argued that a Maginot Line to the sea would abandon Belgium, the overwhelming British concern was with the French ports. As Hankey put it, "It would be a nuisance to have the Germans in Belgium again, but better in Belgian ports than in French ports."[86] Even before Munich French defense was "vital" to British security, but Ismay and others suspected that French leaders might be trying to pass the costs of defending northern France onto Britain.[87]

As for Britain, it too intended largely to ride free on France's defensive efforts but only to the degree that French defenses were deemed to be sufficiently strong to hold out. As Hankey communicated to the earl of Halifax, the level of faith in French defenses would determine the size and readiness of the British Expeditionary Force.[88] Some British analysts, such as Orme Sargent, did not bemoan the possible dissolution of the British-French alignment on the Continent, adopting a position consistent with Schweller's distancing strategy.[89] Sargent's views on this matter, however, were not widely held and were explicitly criticized by his peers. One colleague wrote to Sargent, "If we and the French are really to fall apart into some sort of isolation or bisolation, we shall not long be even second-class powers. And if we aren't going to try to hold even that rank, any 'extent' of armament will have been wasted."[90] In case of war, Britain clearly needed both arms and allies, and most British leaders correctly saw that there was no trade-off between the two. But even if one accepted this general prescription, two important questions remained: how much of a commitment should Britain make to France for the first round of hostilities, and how much should it build up home forces? Here we see a trade-off between arms and allies but one that has nothing to do with the domestic political costs of rearmament. Both strategies would require strengthening of the British military and sacrifice from British taxpayers.

After Munich, British concerns for French security only increased. In February 1939, the chiefs of staff argued that "It is difficult . . . to say how the security of the United Kingdom could be maintained if France were forced to capitulate."[91] In a similar tone, the Committee for Imperial Defense reported, "We are indeed assuming a mutual commitment which is even more close and binding than those existing with some of our Dominions."[92] Despite this commitment in principle, the British strategy toward French defense in 1939 was based strongly on Britain's general faith in defensive advantage and in particular on the effectiveness of the Maginot Line. With the initial upgrading of the German threat after Munich, Britain planned on sending only two advance divisions before a declaration of war. Approximately ten additional divisions were to be sent in two shifts, one sixty days after the outbreak of war and one six months after its outbreak. In order to reassure France and prevent it from accommodating Hitler, in March 1939 Leslie Hore-Belisha discussed a larger potential expeditionary force of nineteen divisions in the House of Commons.[93] Britain's goal was to reassure Paris that Britain was committed to French defense for the longer term. London feared that, otherwise, France might panic and seek a separate peace with Hitler.

In the first nine months of 1939, just prior to the British and French declarations of war, Britain upgraded its assessment of the importance of France to its own security and began planning a large and more promptly deployed British Expeditionary Force (BEF) for the Continent. Although the British made grandiose plans in September 1939 for a thirty-two division BEF by the second year of war and for an eventual commitment of fifty-five divisions, London never managed to assemble more than ten divisions for the BEF by the time of Germany's invasion of the Low Countries and France in May 1940. That force was only about half the size of what Britain had sent to Europe by the first half of 1915, and it constituted only 10 percent of joint Anglo-French forces on the Continent. Two reasons underlay London's anemic effort: first, Britain's goal was to save its strategic resources until its forces were absolutely necessary on the Continent, and, second, Britain simply lacked the large number of sufficiently trained forces to fulfill its longer-term plans more promptly. Both the general lack of preparedness in the British army and the conservative deployment of available troops were rooted in the long-held belief that the French army would hold on the defensive. The British strategists held this belief even more strongly than their French counterparts, though the latter were also often supremely overconfident on this score.[94]

As a British strategic memorandum for the Anglo-French Staff Conversations in March 1939 confirms, the British knew that their strategy meant that when Germany attacked France, combined French and British land forces on the Continent would be outnumbered, even if relative parity could be obtained on the northern French border in the earliest rounds of fighting. But they believed that "from a defensive point of view France's numerical inferiority . . . is, to a great extent, mitigated by her foresight in creating a strong system of fortifications along the Eastern frontiers."[95] In fact, Britain was so confident in the ability of defensive strategies to offset the effects of power differentials that London held real hope that even Belgian defenses might be able to hold out for a significant period of time against Germany.[96] While British analysts worried about the possibility of Germany going around the Maginot Line, as it eventually did in 1940,

Britain seemed reassured that the French troops freed up by the Maginot Line would allow for sufficiently high troop concentrations both in northern France and in the south, facing Italy.[97] While British leaders recognized France's material weakness compared with Germany, they were falsely reassured by their faith in defensive advantage.

When British leaders pointed to the relative weakness of combined British and French forces in comparison to German forces at the onset of hostilities, they were referring not to forces in a single theater but to forces on the Continent as a whole. There can be little doubt that it was underestimation of the potential for effective offensives by British and French leaders, not the overall material weakness of the British and French nations, that most directly led to the quick collapse of France in spring 1940. Even though the BEF and British air contingents in France almost certainly would have been larger had British leaders realized earlier the danger of German offensives, even with the smaller BEF the German and the Anglo-French forces in the northern French theater were roughly equal in spring 1940. John Mearsheimer and others have argued that, for this reason, numbers of troops and weapons were not the main problem for France and Britain on land; strategy was.[98] But there was one important way in which defensive biases did make Anglo-French forces weaker than their German enemies. As Mearsheimer points out in a later work, the long-held faith in French defenses led Britain to devote relatively few resources to training its land army in the 1930s, so British soldiers were no match for their German counterparts in May 1940.[99]

Even after General Guderian's blitz, rather than simply distancing itself from the French crisis, London underwent torturous deliberations about whether or not to send more British air power to France. Although Britain never devoted more than 25 percent of its home-based fighters to France, after the initial assault on France Britain rushed additional air force units to the Continent. Subsequent to receiving extremely negative reports from the front, however, the cabinet decided in mid-May against any further increase of Britain's commitment on the Continent. The pace of French collapse, not British apathy, drove Britain's decision.[100] Even after the fall of Paris, Britain did not distance itself from France. To preserve some hope of future resistance to Hitler in France, London offered to merge with the remaining Free French troops, thus removing any lingering doubt about who would be attacked next by Hitler.

In discussing the problem of British and French alliance, the approach here merely makes explicit the argument that already has been made by scholars who emphasize the importance of British defensive biases in the late 1930s. If British and French leaders had believed that each of their nations was individually stronger than Germany, they would not have perceived a need for joint British and French action, and, therefore, no tragedy of the common would have occurred.[101] The real difference between Schweller's account and the standard accounts is not his argument that Germany was more powerful than Britain or France individually but his contention that Germany was more powerful than Britain and France combined. However well-supported by data on steel ingots and shipping tonnage, Schweller's argument that Britain was not a pole but a middle power in Europe does not hold much weight when one observes British staying power in a once-on-one conflict with Germany.[102] Britain's repelling of German air assaults, many of which were launched from French soil, and the slim margin of victory in that painful battle demonstrate both that Britain was a very significant actor in the war and that the fall of France was strategically important to London.

France as a Frontline Seeker of Allies As a frontline state, France was naturally seeking a tight alliance with Britain. Unsurprisingly, France was clearly unhappy about Britain's level of commitment to continental defense. British ambassador Phipps reported to London in late 1938 that the small size of the British army signaled to some French observers that "France can only rely on Great Britain 'to fight to the last French-man.'"[103] French statistics suggested that the British government mobilized its citizenry for war at only one-fifth the rate of France, a contention the British rejected bitterly in bilateral discussions.[104]

As war approached, France predictably remained very concerned about the short-term implications of Britain's long-war strategy. French general Dentz complained in November 1938 that "France does not intend to allow England to fight her battles with French soldiers."[105] A November 1939 British memorandum reported that the French were hoping for more help in 1940 than the British were offering. The British had attempted to convince the French that if they offered less in 1940, they would be able to offer substantially more in what Britain believed to be the crucial year of 1941. However, the report stated that Paris "would rather have more immediate help at the risk of less eventual help, than more help in 1941 at the expense of 1940."[106]

French leaders' demand for a tighter alliance with Britain was related more to France's position as a frontline state than it was to any fundamental disagreement with British predictions about the long-term and attritional nature of land warfare.[107] As Martin Alexander argues, during the so-called Phony War (September 1939–April 1940) Paris's efforts to limit the costs of opposing Germany early had as much to do with French civilians' desire to emerge economically competitive from the expected Allied victory as it did from French military leaders' concern that France might be knocked out of the war if it did not secure massive British assistance in the earliest stages of war.[108]

In 1939–40 France was upset both by the size of British army deployments in France and by Britain's cautious attitude toward the use of airpower on the Continent. Not only did Britain keep the bulk of its air force in Britain for home defense but it proposed air strategies on the Continent that reflected Britain's defensive biases and beliefs in long attritional wars. As one might expect from a frontline state. France urged Britain to use its airpower to provide support for French ground troops. Britain believed that the Allied air forces should instead be used to attack German industrial centers to injure German morale and slow German production for the long haul. France worried that this would increase French costs on the battlefield while putting at risk French cities, which seemed to French leaders to be the easiest civilian targets for German retaliation. While France eventually did convince British leaders to use some airpower against German forces in the early rounds of war, many of the British forces were not well-equipped or trained for such missions. As with the BEF ground forces, this lack of preparation is partially traceable to British strategists' long-held faith in the staying power of French land defenses.[109]

The Soviet Union as Buck-Passer Both Schweller and Morrow make valid points about the domestic political differences that led to the rocky relationship between Joseph Stalin and the Western Allies, particularly France. Coding the Soviet Union as a revisionist state, Schweller argues convincingly that because of their different goals, revisionist states will find it difficult to ally with status quo states. These differences were important, but the ability of all the nonfascist powers to overcome them by 1942 suggests that something in addition to domestic politics was also at work. Domestic political differences made earlier improved relations difficult at least partially because leaders perceived themselves as less threatened than they actually were. In other words, while friendlier countries may indeed have allied more quickly, once all the powers in

Europe realized that their security was scarce, they overcame their domestic inhibitions and allied with one another against Germany.

Schweller agrees with the basic thesis that Soviet leaders hoped for a prolonged war of attrition between France and Germany, during which the Soviet Union would build its strength while its rivals sapped each other's. In Schweller's account Stalin was surprised that France fell quickly because the Soviet leader misperceived the balance of power in the system as multipolar (when, Schweller contends, it was tripolar). Whereas Snyder and I emphasize that Stalin overestimated the hardiness of French defenses, Schweller argues that Stalin overestimated the power of France more generally. Both arguments fit the approach offered in this article.

Cynthia Roberts offers an explanation of Stalin's behavior that bridges the gap between the perception of offensive or defensive efficacy and the perception of the relative power of various nations. Roberts argues that with the exception of his belief in the potential for successful Soviet offensives, Stalin subscribed to the World War I lesson that war among the great powers would likely be attritional. However, his belief in defensive advantage and attritional war was limited only to countries he believed were of sufficient size. Roberts writes:

> [A factor] that qualified Soviet perceptions of defensive advantage was Stalin's assumption that many states on the European continent could not hold their own against an aggressor for a prolonged period. He distinguished between strong states such as France and weak, unreliable ones, particularly those that occupied the Western border of the Soviet Union. Fearing that the neutral states along the Soviet frontier were falling dominoes that would either succumb to the German hegemon or willingly engage in bandwagoning, Stalin sought security through expansion and domination, exhibiting a pattern of behavior more common when offense has the advantage.[110]

Thus, Stalin believed in the likelihood of attritional war only if the defender was of sufficient size not simply to be overrun by the larger attacker. While France was deemed by Stalin to be of sufficient size, the nations of Central Europe were not.

Like Napoleon III after the Austrian defeat at Königgrätz, Stalin was shocked that the war in France ended so quickly, complaining to the politburo, "Couldn't they [the French] put up any resistance at all?"[111] Either Stalin was wrong because he failed to realize that France was just another weak, falling domino, as Schweller suggests, or because he did not realize the full implications of the new armored blitz strategies employed by Germany, as Snyder and I suggest. Actually, Stalin apparently misperceived the European security environment on both counts. Not only did he (falsely) believe that defense had the advantage in the western theater but also he believed that Britain and France combined were much more powerful than Germany.[112] Though this latter belief was indeed incorrect, I believe that Schweller exaggerates Stalin's mistakes by arguing that France and Britain combined were weaker than Germany. I take the position that the relative numerical parity of German and Franco-British forces on the northern French frontier in May 1940, and the later survival of Great Britain alone in circumstances less favorable to blitz offensives together suggest that Stalin's most important error was his failure to recognize the effectiveness of German land offensives, rather than his misreading of British, French, and German national endowments. In any case, as D. C. Watt argues, Stalin's misreading of Franco-British staying power in ground warfare and his general fear of Western buck-passing contributed to his failure in 1939 to pursue more vigorously a security arrangement with Great Britain.[113]

CONCLUSION: POTENTIAL IMPLICATIONS
FOR THE POST–COLD WAR WORLD

Misperceptions of the balance of power are most likely during radical shifts in the distribution of power, when traditionally powerful states are overtaken by formerly weaker ones. Lessons of history and habit may cause leaders to deem the traditionally more powerful state to be the stronger, but this is not always the case. Most European analysts made this mistake in 1866 and 1870, underestimating Prussia's power as it quickly overtook Europe's second-ranking land power, Austria, and then the longtime leader on the Continent, France.

Given the major power shifts occurring in the region, sensitivity to perceptions and misperceptions of basic security conditions may be especially important in analyzing the stability of a rapidly changing post–cold war East Asia. Post–cold war East Asian multipolarity could prove especially dangerous because miscalculations of the balance of military power seem almost inevitable given the complex factors at work in the region: the collapse of Russian influence, the rise of China, the uncertain level of future U.S. deployments, the possibility of a unified and nuclear Korea, the uncertainties about the degree and timing of Japanese militarization, and the lack of institutional frameworks to improve transparency. For example, analysts already have difficulty in determining how continued economic growth in China will convert into power that Beijing can harness and project abroad. It is similarly difficult to know whether unification under Seoul's leadership will quickly make Korea a major actor in the region or whether that outcome will be slowed greatly by the costs of absorbing and integrating the North. Also, as Stephen Walt argues, the kind of revolutionary political changes that seem possible in China and likely in Korea may lead potential adversaries to misread those nations' overall strength in potentially destabilizing ways.[114]

Some might argue that the era of nineteenth- and early-twentieth-century power politics is over and that because of technological and normative changes, very few, if any, lessons might be drawn about the future world from European balance-of-power politics before World War II. Hence, even if East Asian governments cannot accurately assess one another's power, this failure will have few real-world consequences because leaders will no longer be thinking in terms of relative military power, security threats, and alliance problems. This argument is dubious for a variety of reasons. First, leaders in East Asia continue to view one another with the type of mistrust that was endemic to traditional European balance-of-power politics. Regional actors view with concern the rise of Chinese power and would likely view with even more concern the development of Japanese force projection capability. Even if we believe that a normative and institutional revolution in Western Europe has rendered that region peaceful and thus traditional balance-of-power theories obsolete, such a revolution is at best in its larval stages in East Asia.[115] As Aaron Friedberg points out, because it lacks the institutions, domestic political structures, and dense economic interdependence of contemporary Western Europe, traditional realist concerns may prevail in East Asia for the foreseeable future.[116]

Aside from norms and institutions, the existence of nuclear weapons provides another reason to believe the post–cold war world will be fundamentally different from the pre–cold war era. Scholars have argued that, along with cold war bipolarity, the condition of mutually assured destruction (MAD), which nuclear weapons made possible, made alliances in the cold war less critical to the great powers than in the earlier period. The tendency of superpowers to "balance internally" enabled them to avoid becoming dragged into crisis and war by obstreperous allies.[117]

Even if we accept such an argument about the pacifying effects of MAD during the cold war, it may not apply to post–cold war East Asia for two reasons. First, whether all of the significant powers in the region will indeed develop nuclear arsenals is not clear. While Japan and a future unified Korea certainly will have the capability to develop them if they so choose, domestic political forces and international pressures may prevent them from traveling the nuclear road. As post–cold war Germany so clearly demonstrates, the realist argument that advanced states will mimic the capabilities of the greatest powers in the system is hardly a lawlike rule of international politics.

Additionally, even if all the states in the region should acquire nuclear weaponry, the condition of MAD would be very difficult to achieve among all of the potential rivals. Many scholars believe the cold war peace to have been caused by the dual factors of MAD and bipolarity, but they have not carefully considered that the former condition may have depended almost entirely on the latter.[118] Because each superpower was certain of which targets it needed to retaliate against and which first strikes it needed to survive, bipolarity may have made possible the bedrock precondition of MAD—secure second-strike capability against all possible foes. The likelihood that each state in a multipolar East Asia could design nuclear arsenals to provide secure second-strike capability against all potential foes, including regional alliances of nuclear states, is extremely small.

The best argument against the relevance of pre–cold war lessons for post–cold war East Asia is that the United States is now playing the role of honest broker and guarantor of regional security. American deterrence prevents states from exploiting perceived advantages, and American reassurance comforts nervous elites about the potential threats posed by their neighbors. For example, leaders in all capitals of the region seem reassured by the U.S. presence in Japan, which they generally view as a welcome alternative to Japanese remilitarization. If the United States were to withdraw its forces from the region, not only would this likely spark security dilemmas, arms races, and spirals of tension, but, given the difficulties discussed above, it would likely lead to gross and potentially dangerous miscalculations of the balance of power in the region by local actors. For this reason a careful study of the causes of multipolar instability prior to the cold war may still be relevant for the future of international politics. If both American leaders and the American public understand these problems, they may more readily accept the role of outside arbiter in regions like East Asia where there are few homegrown forces for long-term stability.

Whether studying historical or future cases of security politics, the most recent realist scholarship is correct to focus on both the distribution of capabilities and the relative efficacy of offensive and defensive doctrines. As the historical cases above have shown, however, to analyze actual policy decisions we must understand how leaders at the time perceived both the power balance and the offense-defense balance. Unless we have reason to believe that leaders in the next century will face a simpler world than their counterparts from the nineteenth and early twentieth centuries, we must allow for the possibility that future leaders might misread in dangerous ways either or both of these important determinants of national security.

NOTES

1. See Mearsheimer 1994–95 and 1995; Keohane and Martin 1995; Kupchan and Kupchan 1995; Ruggie 1995; and Wendt 1995.

2. See Glaser 1994–95; and Lynn-Jones 1995. For a related argument, see Powell 1994.

3. Christensen and Snyder 1990. For a more recent work on psychology and alliances, see Reiter 1994.

4. Morrow 1993.

5. Wohlforth 1987.

6. See Schweller 1993; Kaufman 1992; and Walt 1992a.

7. See Waltz 1979; and Jervis 1978.

8. For the original buck-passing arguments, see Waltz 1979, chap. 8; and Posen 1984.

9. For the distinction between balancing and bandwagoning, see Waltz 1979, 126.

10. Sagan 1986; Van Evera 1987; and Mueller 1995, 52.

11. Addressing this problem by introducing to realism the concept of "missions capability" and "military-capabilities theory" is Glaser 1994–95.

12. Morrow 1993.

13. Morrow 1993, 206–23 and especially 211.

14. Cobban 1965, 181.

15. See Lord Cowley to Lord Stanley, 26 July 1866, in Wellesley and Sencourt 1934, 300; Sencourt 1933, 286; Gall 1986, 285 and 346; Friedjung 1935, 212; and Taylor 1971, 165.

16. Lord Cowley to Lord Clarendon, 4 June 1866, in Wellesley and Sencourt 1934, 273–74.

17. Pottinger 1966, 106 and 155.

18. Napoleon is quoted by the British ambassador, Lord Cowley, in Corley 1961, 275.

19. Taylor 1967, 84.

20. Showalter 1975, 213.

21. Morrow 1993, 218.

22. Hozier 1908, 20.

23. See Showalter 1975, 213; and Pflanze 1963, 291.

24. See Duff 1978, 164; and Eyck 1958, 128.

25. Arnaud 1967, 298.

26. See Gall 1986, 285–86; and Friedjung 1935, 150–57.

27. See Pflanze 1963, 291; Taylor 1967, 83; and Friedjung 1935, 150–51.

28. Friedjung 1935, appendix 3, 321.

29. Johnston 1907, 497.

30. See Friedjung 1935, 92; Aubry 1940, 380; and Wellesly 1929, 298.

31. See Showalter 1975, 112; and Bueno de Mesquita and Lalman 1992, 230.

32. Showalter 1975, 67, italics original.

33. For the distinction between tactical defensives and strategic offensives, see Howard 1961, 1–8. On the lack of Austrian mobility at the front and the disastrous decisions for bayonet charges by local commanders, see Whitton 1923, 90; and Friedjung, 1935, 220–21.

34. Pflanze 1963, 292.

35. For documentation of the French

threat, see Prince Metternich to Count Mensdorff, 6 June 1866, in Wellesley and Sencourt 1934, 274–78.

36. See Pflanze 1963, 288; Taylor 1971, 166; Sked 1989, 179; Mosse 1958, 213–14; and Kann 1974, 272–73. See also Lord Cowley to Lord Clarendon, 11 May 1866, and Prince Metternich to Count Mensdorff, 21 May 1866, in Wellesley and Sencourt 1934, 266–67 and 269–71, respectively.

37. Wellesley 1929, 310–11. See also Lord Cowley to Lord Stanley, 10 July 1866, in Wellesley and Sencourt 1934, 292–94.

38. Taylor 1967, 80–81.

39. Aubry 1940, chap. 33.

40. See Cobban 1965, 193–206; and Prince Metternich to Baron Beust, 8 July 1870, in Wellesley and Sencourt 1934, 363.

41. Jervis, Lebow, and Stein 1985, especially chaps. 1 and 2.

42. Morrow 1993, 223.

43. Ibid.

44. Pflanze 1963, 449.

45. Cobban 1965, 202.

46. Brodsky 1978, 279.

47. See Bierman 1988, 335; and Carr 1991, 200–201.

48. Prince Metternich to Baron Beust, 8 July 1870, in Wellesley and Sencourt 1934, 363.

49. See Howard 1961, chap. 2; and Bierman 1988, 335.

50. For documentation, see Baron Vitzthum to Count Andrassy, 16 January 1873 (reporting events of 11 July 1870), and Lord Lyons to Lord Granville, 12 July 1870, in Wellesley and Sencourt 1934, 365–69.

51. See Showalter 1975, 121; and Cobban 1971, 202.

52. Howard 1961, chap. 1.

53. Taylor 1971, 204.

54. Ibid., 208.

55. Taylor 1971, xxvii.

56. Showalter 1975, 213.

57. Howard 1961, 1.

58. See Taylor 1971, 208–9.

59. Howard 1961, 46.

60. Taylor 1971, 208.

61. Taylor 1967, 127. See also Sked 1989, 242.

62. For evidence that Austria would have entertained an alliance with France if the latter had made guarantees concerning Russia, see Gall 1986, 338.

63. Jelavich 1974, 154–57.

64. Pflanze 1963, 429.

65. On European defense spending in the late nineteenth and early twentieth centuries, see Taylor 1971, xxviii. For a careful analysis demonstrating that alliances were not used to substitute for domestic defense spending in Europe from 1870 to 1914, see Siverson and Most 1987, 131–60.

66. See Kirshner 1995, 93; and Lee 1985, 56 and 64.

67. Schweller 1993, 88.

68. Doughty 1985, 164.

69. See Van Evera 1984; Snyder 1984; and Christensen and Snyder 1990.

70. Aron 1954, chap. 1.

71. Wohlforth 1987, 358–60 and 376.

72. Christensen and Snyder 1990, 155–56.

73. Wohlforth 1987, 355–58.

74. Hobson 1993, 465.

75. For the argument that multipolarity led to buck-passing and in turn to defensive doctrines, see Posen 1984. For the argument that multipolarity and defensive biases combined to lead to buck-passing, see Christensen and Snyder 1990. For a domestic political culture explanation of great power doctrines, see Kier forthcoming.

76. Schweller 1993.

77. Ibid., 88.

78. Kaufman 1992.

79. Peden 1979, 126.

80. Ismay is quoted in Howard 1972, 123.

81. Peden 1979, 136–38.

82. Mearsheimer 1988, 117 and 170.

83. Cited in Schweller 1993, 89.

84. On the importance of French air bases to Britain, see Young 1978, 222–23.

85. Hankey to Prime Minister, 28 April 1938, in CAB 21, 554 14/4/13, PRO. Emphases and exclamation original.

86. Hankey to Chamberlain, 28 April 1938, CAB 21, 554 14/4/13, PRO.

87. Ismay to Hankey, 26 April 1938, CAB 21, 554 14/4/13, PRO.

88. Hankey to Halifax, 26 January 1938, CAB 21, C 8452/580/18, PRO.

89. Minutes of Discussion about Letter Dated October 13, 1938, 17 October 1938, FO 371 21612 C 12161/1050/17, PRO, 137–38.

90. A letter signed "RB" (apparently Robert Barclay) in response to a strategic analysis by Orme Sargent, 18 October 1938, FO 371 21612 C 12161/1050/17, PRO, 137–38.

91. Howard 1972, 127.

92. Committee for Imperial Defense to Strang, 14 February 1939, FO 371 22923 C2751/281/17, PRO, 323, par. 4.

93. "Committee for Imperial Defense Strategical Appreciation Sub-committee Procedure for Meeting to be held on the 1st March, 1939," section 6, FO 371 22923 C2751/281/17, PRO. For the Hore-Belisha statement, see Adamthwaite 1977, 253.

94. Gates 1981, 26–36.

95. "Anglo-French Staff Conversations: 1939 British Strategical Memorandum," 18 March 1939, FO 371 22923 C 3893/281/17, PRO, 11, par. 17.

96. Ibid., 30.

97. "Conversation with General Gamelin: Meeting Presided Over by Sir Thomas Inskip," 26 September 1938, FO 371 21782 10722/18, PRO.

98. For an analysis that stresses the importance of Germany's strategy over its capabilities, see Mearsheimer 1983, chaps. 3 and 4. Also see Walt 1992a, 455–56.

99. Mearsheimer 1988, 172–73.

100. See Willmott 1989, 93–95; and Gates 1981, 79 and 378–79.

101. Schweller 1993, 87–91. For the original collective goods theory, see Olson 1965. For Olson's application of his ideas to alliance theory, see Olson and Zeckhauser 1966.

102. For examples of important data sets that disagree with Schweller's finding that Britain and France combined were weaker than Germany prior to World War II, see Kennedy 1987, 202 and 330.

103. Phipps to Halifax, 16 November 1938, FO 371 21600 C 14025/55/17, PRO.

104. Gates 1981, 29.

105. Dentz is quoted in Adamthwaite 1977, 246.

106. Burgin (Minister of Supply) to Halifax, 15 November 1939, FO 371 22918 C 18731/130/17, PRO.

107. Gates 1981, 27–28 and 58.

108. Alexander 1990, 21–22.

109. Gates 1981, 58, 78–79, and 378–79.

110. Roberts 1992, 107.

111. Stalin is quoted in Christensen and Snyder 1990, 157.

112. Ibid., 157.

113. Watt 1989, chaps. 20 and 24.

114. Walt 1992b.

115. See Johnston 1995; and Christensen 1995 and 1996.

116. Friedberg 1993–94.
117. Jervis 1989, 24–25 and 121.

118. See Waltz, 1986, 327–28; and Jervis 1989, 24–25 and 121.

REFERENCES

Adamthwaite, Anthony. 1977. *France and the coming of the Second World War, 1936–39*. London: Frank Cass.

Alexander, Martin S. 1990. The fall of France, 1940. *Journal of Strategic Studies* 13:10–44.

Amaud, René. 1967. *The second republic and Napoleon III*. Translated by E. F. Buckley. New York: AMS Press.

Aron, Raymond. 1954. *The century of total war*. Garden City, N.Y.: Doubleday.

Aubry, Octave. 1940. *The second empire*. Translated by Arthur Livingston. New York: J. B. Lippincott.

Bierman, John, 1988. *Napoleon III and his carnival empire*. New York: St. Martin's.

Bridge, F. R. 1990. *The Habsburg monarchy among the Great Powers. 1815–1918*. New York: Berg.

Brodsky, Alyn. 1978. *Imperial charade: A biography of Emperor Napoleon III and Empress Eugenie, 19th-century Europe's most successful adventurers*. Indianapolis, Ind.: Bobbs-Merrill.

Bueno de Mesquita, Bruce, and David Lalman. 1992. *War and reason: Domestic and international imperatives*. New Haven, Conn.: Yale University Press.

Carr, William, 1991. *The origins of the wars of German unification*. London: Longman.

Christensen, Thomas J. 1995. Structure, perceptions, and aspirations in Chinese security policy. Paper presented to the conference on international relations theory and Chinese foreign policy, Harvard University, 21–22 April.

———. 1996. Chinese realpolitik. *Foreign Affairs* 75(5):37–52.

Christensen, Thomas, J., and Jack Snyder. 1990. Chain gangs and passed bucks: Predicting alliance patterns in multipolarity. *International Organization* 44:137–68.

Cobban, Alfred. 1965. *A history of modern France*. Vol. 2, *1799–1871*. New York: Penguin Books.

Corley, T. A. B. 1961. *Democratic despot: A life of Napoleon III*. London: Barrie and Rockliff.

Doughty, Robert Allan. 1985. *The seeds of disaster: The development of French army doctrine*. Hamden, Conn.: Archon Books.

Duff, David. 1978. *Eugenie and Napoleon III*. New York: William Morrow.

Eyck, Erich. 1958. *Bismarck and the German empire*. London: George Allen and Unwin.

Friedberg, Aaron. 1993–94. Ripe for rivalry: Prospects for peace in a multipolar Asia. *International Security* 18(3): 5–34.

Friedjung, Heinrich. 1935. *The struggle for supremacy in Germany, 1859–1866*. Translated by A. J. P. Taylor and W. L. McElwee. London: Macmillan.

Gall, Lothar. 1986. *Bismarck: The white revolutionary*. Vol. 1, *1851–1871*. Translated by J. A. Underwood. London: Allen and Unwin.

Gates, Eleanor M. 1981. *The end of the affair: The collapse of the Anglo-French alliance, 1939– 40*. London: George Allen and Unwin.

Glaser, Charles. 1994–95. Realists as optimists: Cooperation as self-help. *International Security* 19(3):50–90.

Hobson, John M. 1993. The military-extraction gap and the wary titan: The fiscal-sociology of British defence policy 1870–1913. *Journal of European Economic History* 22:461–506.

Howard, Michael. 1961. *The Franco-Prussian War: The German invasion of France, 1870–71*. New York: Macmillan.

———. 1972. *The Continental commitment: The dilemma of British defense policy in the era of two world wars*. London: Temple Smith.

Hozier, H. M. 1908. *The Seven Weeks' War: Its antecedents and its incidents*. London: Macmillan.

Jelavich, Barbara. 1974. *St. Petersburg and Moscow: Tsarist and Soviet foreign policy.*

1814–1974. Bloomington: Indiana University Press.

Jervis, Robert. 1978. Cooperation under the security dilemma. *World Politics* 30(2):167–214.

———. 1989. *The meaning of the nuclear revolution: Statecraft and the prospect of armageddon.* Ithaca, N.Y.: Cornell University Press.

Jervis, Robert, Richard Ned Lebow, and Janice Gross Stein. 1985. *Psychology and deterrence.* Baltimore, Md.: Johns Hopkins University Press.

Johnston, Alastair Iain. 1995. Realism and Chinese security policy in the post–cold war era. Paper presented at the workshop on realism and international relations after the cold war, Olin Institute, Harvard University, 8–9 December.

Johnston, Robert Matteson, ed. 1907. *Memoirs of "Malakoff."* Vol. 2, London: Hutchinson and Co.

Kann, Robert A. 1974. *A history of the Habsburg empire, 1526–1918.* Berkeley: University of California Press.

Kaufman, Robert G. 1992. To balance or to bandwagon? Alignment decisions in 1930s Europe. *Security Studies* 1: 417.

Kennedy, Paul. 1987. *The rise and fall of the Great Powers: Economic change and military conflict from 1500 to 2000.* New York: Random House.

Keohane, Robert O., and Lisa L. Martin. 1995. The promise of institutionalist theory. *International Security* 20(1): 39–51.

Kier, Elizabeth. Forthcoming. *Imagining war: French and British military doctrines between the wars.* Princeton, N.J.: Princeton University Press.

Kirshner, Jonathan. 1995. *Currency and coercion: The political economy of international monetary power.* Princeton, N.J.: Princeton University Press.

Kupchan, Charles A., and Clifford A. Kupchan. 1995. The promise of collective security. *International Security* 20(1):52–61.

Lee, Bradford A. 1985. Strategy, arms and the collapse of France, 1930–40. In *Diplomacy and intelligence in the Second World War: Essays in honour of F. H.*

Hinsley, edited by Richard Langhorne. Cambridge: Cambridge University Press.

Lynn-Jones, Sean M. 1995. Offense-defense theory and its critics. *Security Studies* 4:660–91.

Mearsheimer, John J. 1983. *Conventional deterrence.* Ithaca, N.Y.: Cornell University Press.

———. 1988. *Liddell Hart and the weight of history.* Ithaca, N.Y.: Cornell University Press.

———. 1994–95. The false promise of international institutions. *International Security* 19(3):5–49.

———. 1995. A realist reply. *International Security* 20(1):82–93.

Morrow, James D. 1993. Arms versus allies: Trade-offs in the search for security. *International Organization* 47:207–33.

Mosse, W. E. 1958. *The European powers and the German question, 1848–71.* Cambridge: Cambridge University Press.

Mueller, Karl. 1995. Patterns of alliance: Alignment balancing and stability in Eastern Europe. *Security Studies* 5: 38–76.

Olson, Mancur, Jr. 1965. *The logic of collective action: Public goods and the theory of groups.* Cambridge, Mass.: Harvard University Press.

Olson, Mancur, and Richard Zeckhauser. 1966. An economic theory of alliances. *Review of Economics and Statistics* 48:266–79.

Peden, G. C. 1979. *British rearmament and the treasury, 1932–39.* Edinburgh: Scottish Academic Press.

Pflanze, Otto. 1963. *Bismarck and the development of Germany: Period of unification, 1815–1871.* Vol. 1. Princeton, N.J.: Princeton University Press.

Posen, Barry. 1984. *The sources of military doctrine: France, Britain, and Germany between the world wars.* Ithaca, N.Y.: Cornell University Press.

Pottingrer, E. Ann. 1966. *Napoleon III and the German crisis: 1865–1866.* Cambridge, Mass.: Harvard University Press.

Powell, Robert. 1994. Anarchy in international relations: The neorealist-neoliberal debate. *International Organization* 45:313–44.

Public Record Office (PRO), Cabinet and all its committees (CAB) and Foreign Office (FO). Kew Gardens, United Kingdom.

Reiter, Dan. 1994. Learning, realism, and alliances: The weight of the shadow of the past. *World Politics* 46:490–526.

Roberts, Cynthia. 1992. Prelude to disaster: Soviet security policy between the world wars. Ph.D. diss., Columbia University.

Ruggie, John Gerard. 1995. The false premise of realism. *International Security* 20:62–70.

Sagan, Scott D. 1986. 1914 revisited. *International Security* 11(2):151–72.

Schweller, Randall. 1993. Tripolarity and the Second World War. *International Studies Quarterly* 37:73–103.

Sencourt, Robert. 1993. *Napoleon III: The modern emperor.* New York: Appleton-Century.

Showalter, Dennis E. 1975. *Railroads and rifles: Soldiers, technology, and the unification of Germany.* Hamden, Conn.: Anchor Books.

Siverson, Randolph M., and Benjamin A. Most. 1987. Substituting arms and alliances, 1870–1914: An exploration in comparative foreign policy. In *New directions in the study of foreign policy,* edited by Charles F. Hermann, Charles W. Kegley, Jr., and James N. Rosenau. Boston: Allen and Unwin.

Sked, Alan. 1989. *The decline and fall of the Habsburg empire, 1815–1918.* London: Longman.

Snyder, Jack L. 1984. *The ideology of the offensive: Military decision making and the disasters of 1914,* Ithaca, N.Y.: Cornell University Press.

Taylor, A. J. P. 1967. *Bismarck: The man and the statesman.* New York: Vintage.

———. 1971. *The struggle for mastery of Europe.* New York: Oxford University Press.

Van Evera, Stephen. 1984. The cult of the offensive and the origins of the First World War. *International Security* 9(1):58–107.

———. 1987. Offense, defense, and strategy: When is offense best. Paper presented at the annual meeting of the American Political Science Association, 1987.

Walt, Stephen M. 1992a. Alliance, threats, and U.S. grand strategy: A reply to Kaufman and Labs. *Security Studies* 1:448–82.

———. 1992b. Revolution and war. *World Politics* 44:321–68.

Waltz, Kenneth. 1979. *Theory of international politics.* Reading, Mass.: Addison-Wesley.

———. 1986. A response to my critics. In *Neorealism and its critics,* edited by Robert O. Keohane. New York: Columbia University Press.

Watt, Donald Cameron. 1989. *How war came: The immediate origins of the Second World War, 1938–39.* New York: Pantheon.

Wellesley, F. A., ed. 1929. *Secrets of the second empire: Private letters from the Paris embassy:* London: Harper and Brothers.

Wellesley, Sir Victor, and Robert Sencourt. 1934. *Conversations with Napoleon III.* London: Ernest Benn.

Wendt, Alexander. 1995. Constructing international politics. *International Security* 20(1):71–80.

Whitton, F. E. 1923. *The decisive battles of modern times.* London: Constable and Company.

Willmott, H. P. 1989. *The great crusade: A new complete history of the Second World War.* New York: Free Press.

Wohlforth, William C. 1987. The perception of power: Russia in the pre-1914 balance. *World Politics* 39(3):353–81.

Young, Robert. 1978. *In command of France: French foreign policy and military planning 1933–1940.* Cambridge, Mass.: Harvard University Press.

Reading 5-2

The Coming of the Second World War
John Lukacs

The two world wars are the mountain ranges that dominate the historical landscape of the twentieth century. We still live in their shadows, in America as well as in Europe. Only with these wars did European and American history begin to coincide. The revolutions of 1820, 1830, 1848 and the wars leading to the unification of Italy and Germany marked the nineteenth century in European history, while the major events in American history were the westward movement, the Civil War and mass immigration. These events had certain transatlantic connections, yet not decisive ones. But in the twentieth century the two world wars have been the main events in the history of Europe and America as well.

For Europe World War I may have been more decisive than World War II, which was a radical continuation in many ways of the first war. For the United States World War II was more significant, both in its extent and in its consequences. American participation in World War I was short, and soon after the war American involvement in European affairs was repudiated for at least 20 years by the majority of American people. When Germany attacked Poland on September 1, 1939, many Americans believed that somehow, or in some way, the United States would become involved. President Franklin D. Roosevelt expressed this when he declared U.S. neutrality at the start of the war, but added that he could not ask his fellow countrymen to be neutral in their sentiments.

This was very different from 1914, when the expressions of President Woodrow Wilson and the American people reflected a sometimes smug satisfaction toward the European war: that kind of war was something America had long left behind in its progressive, democratic evolution. It was typical of the Old World, not of the New. During World War I American neutrality was not abandoned until 1917; in World War II the United States was a de facto belligerent many months before Pearl Harbor.

In 1918 President Wilson announced, and tried to put into practice, the idea that this would be the war to end all wars. The history of the next 20 years was to prove him woefully wrong. It is one of the ironies of history that while for Americans the consequences of World War II were much more worrisome than those of World War I, it may well have been World War II—with all of its unsatisfactory consequences—that brought about the end of the period of world wars.

In general terms, from about 1770 to 1848 the American and the French revolutions characterized a time of great democratic revolutions. Many wars of that period, including the Napoleonic and even the Mexican wars, were merely consequences of those turbulent times. But the broadest wave of European revolutions in 1848–49 turned out to be in reality the end of the era of revolutions. Instead, a series of wars followed in which, for various reasons, Germany played an increasingly important role. (The German people turned out to be better at waging wars than making revolutions.) This period of wars ended in 1945 with the final defeat and division of the German

SOURCE: From "The Coming of the Second World War" by John Lukacs, *Foreign Affairs*, vol. 68, no. 4 (Fall 1989): 165–174. Copyright © 1989 by the Council on Foreign Relations. Reprinted by permission.

Reich, the division of Europe and the end of the European Age. It also marked the first (and perhaps the last) use of atomic weapons.

II

The start of both world wars involved miscalculations. In 1914 these miscalculations— and the responsibility for declaring the war—were shared by all the European governments and their general staffs, with the possible exception of Belgium. In 1939 the miscalculations that began the war were those of a single leader, Adolf Hitler. As in 1914, these miscalculations involved an incorrect estimate of what a potential adversary would or would not do. Hitler had hoped in 1939 that Britain would not, at the last moment, honor its guarantee to Poland. Remembering 1914, when there had been no clear commitment of British intentions, Prime Minister Neville Chamberlain offered a guarantee in 1939 to Poland (the first, and presumably the last, such obligation by the British to an east European state), hoping that such a definite commitment would deter Hitler. It did not. Instead, during the last days of August, Hitler tried to drive a wedge in the alliance between Britain and Poland by offering an ostensibly, but not truthfully, reasonable settlement to his eastern neighbor. He did not succeed. After obvious hesitation Britain declared war on Germany—56 hours after Germany began the bombing and invasion of Poland.

Yet Hitler was not altogether wrong. Although Britain and France declared war, they stopped short of waging war—with the exception of a few tentative incursions over German airspace and a substantial war at sea. They did nothing to aid their Polish ally while the western frontier of Germany was held by only a few German divisions. This reluctant effort, which American journalists dubbed the "phony war," lasted throughout the fall, winter and early spring. It sapped the morale of the French and, to some extent, of the British, and it helped Hitler come close to winning in the early summer of 1940.

A deeper and greater miscalculation, however, eventually cost Hitler the war. In 1939 he had come to believe that time was working against him and in favor of the west European democracies, whose rearmament had begun. He believed that the superiority of the German armed forces would lessen and erode at the latest by 1942 or 1943. His Italian ally, Benito Mussolini, disagreed, arguing that although Britain and France had begun to rearm and resist Germany and Italy, their opposition would not last long. Without actual war, Mussolini wrote, the costly resolve of the west European democracies would not sustain itself. Their resistance would not stiffen and increase, it would weaken and diminish. In sum, time was not on the side of Paris and London. Mussolini, who repeated this argument once more to Hitler in January 1940, was probably right.

But Hitler would not listen, for deeper reasons welling up from within. His view of his life and destiny had changed. Sometime in the winter of 1937–38 Hitler became convinced that he would not live much longer and that therefore the time had come to translate the prospect of a greater German Reich into action, before it was too late. Thus he moved in 1938 to incorporate Austria into Germany and to subdue Czechoslovakia, and in 1939 he pushed to reduce Poland to a satellite or, at most, to a junior ally of Germany—even at the risk of war.

This last statement requires further explanation. A. J. P. Taylor was the first noteworthy historian in the early 1960s who tried to refute the accepted idea that Hitler had a definite timetable of conquest.[1] Hitler, according to Taylor, was a German national leader profiting from situations as they arose. This argument is not altogether untrue, except that there was nothing particularly German about that. Napoleon did not have a timetable of conquest either, a point that Taylor chose to ignore. In any event, Taylor was wrong about Hitler's purposes regarding Poland and about the actual outbreak of the war. Since Hitler's territorial demands in August 1939 were not excessive, Taylor wrote that Danzig was the key problem: "Only Danzig prevented cooperation between Germany and Poland." But this misses the more essential point. Hitler wanted the Polish state to come within Germany's sphere of influence. Concessions on Danzig were to be but the first step along a path that would end with Poland becoming not only Germany's ally and junior partner, but its satellite. He wanted to put an end to a Poland independent enough to have a foreign policy of its own.

Hitler's primary foreign policy requirement was to ensure the vassalage of neighboring countries, rather than the actual annexation of their territories. This was what he gained from both the Austrians and Czechs. But the Poles were different. Their refusal to surrender launched the Second World War. For this Hitler never forgave them. This was probably the main reason—even beyond his racist antagonisms—for his cruel and oppressive treatment of the Polish people, a brutal treatment that would be visited on no other people except the Jews of Europe and Russia.

III

This leads to the larger and unresolved problem of Hitler's policy toward the Soviet Union in 1939. Nine days before Germany's invasion of Poland, his foreign minister, Joachim Ribbentrop, signed in Moscow the German–Soviet nonaggression pact, which included a secret protocol that provided for the division of much of eastern Europe. Hitler thought that this pact, which amounted to a stunning diplomatic defeat for the British and the French, would further deter them from fulfilling their recently assumed obligations to Poland. Instead, on August 25, the British government extended its guarantee to Poland into a formal alliance. Together with Mussolini's decision of Italian nonbelligerence communicated to Berlin that same day, the British decision persuaded Hitler to postpone the commencement of military operations by five days (during which time he tried to drive a wedge between Poland and Britain). Yet nothing indicates that his pact with Stalin was a sine qua non for starting war. Had Hitler made no pact with Stalin, he still would have attacked Poland.

What would have happened without the German-Soviet pact? Most historians opine that the dominant, if not the consuming, factor in Hitler's worldview was his anticommunism and his vision of *Lebensraum,* which included portions of European Russia. They argue that the wars against Poland and the western powers were simply a preliminary stage to the ultimate invasion of the Soviet Union. Yet there are some reasons to question this view. There is absolutely no evidence in German military papers or in Hitler's own words to suggest that, after the conquest of Poland, Germany would have continued eastward against the Soviet Union. On the Soviet side, there are many reasons to believe that in September 1939, even without a German-Soviet pact, Stalin would have acted essentially as he did: i.e., seeking some kind of accommodation with the Germans over the crushed body of a Polish state.

This was the essence of Stalin's conduct in September 1938 during the Munich crisis. For a long time people believed (and some historians still believe) that one main reason why the Munich "settlement" was a disaster was because it made Stalin skeptical of the value of an alliance with France and Britain, and that Stalin's doubts eventually led him to seek the accommodation with Hitler. Since the Soviet Union had been allied with France and Czechoslovakia at the time of the Munich conference, many historians maintain that in 1938, unlike 1939, the Soviet Union would have been a military ally of the western democracies. (As the first volume of his wartime memoirs shows, Winston Churchill believed this as late as 1948.) Yet all of the evidence from the diplomatic, military and intelligence documents accumulated since the end of World War II suggests that, the Soviet alliance with Czechoslovakia notwithstanding, Stalin would not have gone to war in 1938 to help the Czechs.

Hitler must have known that. In any event, the strongest evidence against the prevailing notion of Hitler following a timetable is the absence of any mention of Russia in the famous Hossbach memorandum of the conference on November 5, 1937. During this meeting, Hitler told his generals to prepare for war, if need be. Yet he hardly mentioned Russia in his war plans before, or during, the Munich crisis. What he thought about Stalin at that time we do not know. (We do know that during the war Hitler often spoke of Stalin with considerable respect, if not admiration.)

In March and April 1939 it was Moscow that approached Berlin. What happened thereafter was a triangle of negotiations and intrigues. The British and French were trying to bring Russia into their alliance system. Chamberlain would occasionally suggest to the Germans that if they were only more reasonable about Poland, a proper and honest relationship between Britain and Germany could be ensured. Hitler, on the other hand, allowed hints to be dropped to London and Paris about a possible German arrangement with the Soviet Union, which they failed to take seriously until it was too late. Stalin, secretive and cunning by nature, dropped no hints to the British about his approaches to the Germans and few hints to the Germans about his negotiations with the British, which were not going well.

For this failure the dilatory and overly cautious policies of the British and French have often been blamed. They were slow and reluctant to send their missions to Moscow. When they finally did, they consisted of second-rank personages. The British, even more than the French, were unwilling and unable to produce serious military and political commitments. Yet there is not the slightest evidence that Stalin was willing to enter into any alliance with the western democracies if he could make a deal with Germany instead—which is what happened in the end.

The pact did not start World War II, but it put an end to the political geography of Europe that had been established after World War I. On a larger scale, something else happened. The year 1939 marked the return of Russia and the United States to the European scene after a virtual absence of 20 years.

IV

The English revolutions of the seventeenth century, the American and the French revolutions of the eighteenth century, the Meiji Restoration in Japan in the nineteenth century, to say nothing of Hitler's "national revolution" in 1933, were significant events that enhanced the power of these nations, often through war.

The Russian Bolshevik Revolution of 1917 was an exception. It was the consequence of a war and not the source of one; it led to a diminution, not an accretion, of national power. It meant a Russian withdrawal from Europe—geographically, militarily, economically, politically and ideologically. Geographically, the frontier of the "new" Russia retreated eastward (as its capital, too, moved back from Petersburg to

Moscow)—in some places it moved back to the Russian frontiers established by Peter the Great and Catherine II nearly two centuries before. Militarily, the dissolution of the Russian army preceded the Bolshevik Revolution—indeed, it was a condition for it; consequently the armed power of Russia was not much of a factor in the European balance of power for about 20 years. Economically, Soviet trade with its European neighbors was minimal, a fragment of what it had been before 1914. Politically, the Soviet Union became a near outcast, separated from the rest of Europe by its own volition. (The term "iron curtain" was not invented by Churchill in 1946. It had been current 25 years earlier, when Lenin's regime chose to close Russia's frontiers as hermetically as possible.) Ideologically, too, the impact of the Soviet Union upon Europe was less than many people then believed (and some people even now believe). It was unlike the American and the French revolutions, which found successful emulators in many places, especially among neighboring peoples. Contrary to Lenin's original predictions, from World War I to World War II communism failed to establish itself anywhere outside the Soviet Union (except Outer Mongolia). It was especially repellent to its east European neighbors.

The change came in 1939. At the threshold of a new European war, Moscow found that it was being solicited. Stalin, who was the opposite of Lenin, that is, a statesman rather than a revolutionary, understood this very well. Russia would reenter eastern Europe and recover some of those territories that Lenin and his cohorts had given up 20 years before. That was Stalin's main goal, not the propagation of international communism—as shown not only by his subsequent actions but also by the language of Soviet declarations of the period.

In this sense the imperial tendency of the Soviet Union, assumed at the end of World War II (and greatly enhanced by its military victories), was already discernible at the beginning of 1939. The western democracies would not be able to defeat, let alone contain, the German Third Reich. By 1940—well before the United States entered the war—the British recognized that the only alternative to German domination over most of Europe was a hardly avoidable acquiescence to Soviet rule in much of eastern Europe.

In the summer of 1939, however, another factor contributed to the British and French resolution to declare war on Germany. This was the presence—or, rather, the growing shadow—of the United States on the European scene. After the First World War both the Soviet Union and the United States chose to withdraw from Europe. Yet unlike the Soviets', America's withdrawal was only military and political, not economic and cultural. By 1939 a considerable and influential minority of the American people, unlike those in Moscow, evinced a new, anxious and concerned interest in the ominous events in Europe. Even more important was President Roosevelt's conclusion that it was in the American interest to encourage resistance to Hitler in some European capitals, especially in Paris and London. This conclusion had matured in the president's mind during the winter of 1938–39. Mindful of the widespread isolationist currents that still prevailed in the United States, he did not proclaim it openly to the American people. It was nonetheless discernible from his tone in a few presidential statements and in his suggestions to personal envoys in Paris and elsewhere.

Hitler's statements, beginning in January 1939, showed that he was well aware of President Roosevelt's inclinations. From that time on he began to consider Roosevelt as his principal enemy—a conviction that Hitler held to the end. All of this preceded the outbreak of war. In September 1939, unlike in August 1914, American neutrality was not a fixed and seemingly immovable factor. In 1939 and 1940 every European government was aware of the increasing American presence in the constellation of forces and the growing attention and respect paid to the United States as a result. This developed more than two years before the actual American entry into the war.[2]

V

The reappearance of both Russia and America on the European scene in 1939 foreshadowed the coming of a new world after the war when these two superpowers would govern the destinies of much of Europe and the globe. But in important ways the worlds of 1939 and 1945 were very different. Because of the global rise and the eventual conflict of the two superpowers, it has been customary to consider the conflict between communism and capitalism, incarnated principally by the Soviet Union and the United States, as if that were the spine, the main feature, of the twentieth century since 1917. This perspective has been occasionally presented by Marxist, anti-Marxist, leftist, rightist, Soviet, American, French and German historians. Yet this perspective is false. The outbreak (and also the course) of World War II had nothing to do with communism or with capitalism. In 1939 Soviet and American relations with each other were relatively unimportant.

Erupting in war in September 1939, the world's previous quarter-century was marked by the existence of a triangular conflict among the great powers, but which also tended to be reflected within each country. There was democratic capitalism, incarnated by the United States, Britain, the English-speaking nations and the west and north European democracies. There was communism, incarnated solely by the Soviet Union and represented, indirectly and ineffectively, by the scattering of communist parties and their sympathizers around the world. And there was a new kind of nationalism, elevated to the level of an official state philosophy, a new kind of faith that substituted for religion, of which the most extreme incarnation was the German Third Reich but which had other incarnations elsewhere. In 1939 this third force was the most powerful one in Europe. Eventually it took the alliance of the other two powers to defeat it. Just as within Germany, Japan, Italy and other countries, neither communism nor democratic capitalism was able to withstand the power of the extreme nationalists, so during the war neither the western democracies nor the Soviet Union was able to defeat Germany alone. It took their strange alliance to accomplish that.

In September 1939 much of this lay in the future. Few people saw it as we see it—or, more precisely, should see it—now. But there was another, related element in the history of that period. The texture of political history had changed. The ideas and the practices that states such as the German Third Reich, the Soviet Union or the liberal democracies represented had active sympathizers abroad. During World War I there were very few people who, because of their ideological preferences, wished for the defeat of their own state and for the triumph of its adversaries. (Even Lenin does not constitute an exception: true, he wished for the collapse of the Tsarist Russian state but then he also wished for the collapse of every other government; while he accepted German help and funds, he was not a German sympathizer.)

By 1939, however, there were people in every European country (and also elsewhere) whose hatred of their governments and of the political system was so intense that they were willing to work for their defeat. Thus not only were communists across the globe committed to helping the Soviet Union; there were nationalists of different stripes who admired the new Germany. Within Germany there were men and women who were willing to risk their lives in order to thwart the triumph of Hitler. The latter were true patriots, rather than nationalists—as indeed the emerging incarnations of resistance to Hitler's Germany in 1940 involved traditionalist patriots such as Churchill or Charles de Gaulle, motivated as they were by their old-fashioned principles of patriotism, liberty and honor.

There was, finally, yet another difference between 1914 and 1939. The peoples of Europe swept into the First World War with frenzied enthusiasm. In September 1939 they went to war in a serious, disciplined way. The British entered the conflict with a silent determination. The Germans, who were supposed to have been whipped into fanaticism by Hitler's propaganda, took up arms with a fatalism that was toneless rather than serene. It stood in grave contrast to their relief when Kaiser Wilhelm II had called them to war in 1914. In 1939 those Europeans who sought relief in the coming of the war were a small minority, the exception. In 1914 it was the majority that had found relief in it, almost everywhere.

In 1914 most governments, and people, expected a short European war. In 1939 no one expected a short war, perhaps with the solitary exception of Hitler. In 1914 the peoples of Europe thought of another European war; only later did popular terminology make it a "World War." In 1939 everyone knew that this was the start of the Second World War. No one knew that it was also to be the last European war.

NOTES

1. A. J. P. Taylor, *The Origins of the Second World War,* New York: Atheneum Press, 1962.

2. More than a year before Pearl Harbor an American presidential election, for the first time in history, became an important element in the calculations of the statesmen of the world. That this was obvious in Churchill's case needs no illustration. But Hitler berated Mussolini in October 1940 for attacking Greece before the American presidential election; around the same time Stalin instructed Molotov to visit Berlin only after that election.

Reading 5-3

The Cult of the Offensive and the Origins of the First World War
Stephen Van Evera

During the decades before the First World War a phenomenon which may be called a "cult of the offensive" swept through Europe. Militaries glorified the offensive and adopted offensive military doctrines, while civilian elites and publics assumed that the offense had the advantage in warfare, and that offensive solutions to security problems were the most effective.

This article will argue that the cult of the offensive was a principal cause of the First World War, creating or magnifying many of the dangers which historians blame for causing the July crisis and rendering it uncontrollable. The following section will first outline the growth of the cult of the offensive in Europe in the years before the war, and then sketch the consequences which international relations theory suggests should

SOURCE: From "The Cult of the Offensive and the Origins of the First World War" by Stephen Van Evera, *International Security,* vol. 9, no. 1 (Summer 1984): 58–107. Copyright © 1984. Reprinted by permission of the MIT Press Journals.

follow from it. The second section will outline consequences which the cult produced in 1914, and the final section will suggest conclusions and implications for current American policy.

THE CULT OF THE OFFENSIVE AND INTERNATIONAL RELATIONS THEORY

The Growth of the Cult

The gulf between myth and the realities of warfare has never been greater than in the years before World War I. Despite the large and growing advantage which defenders gained against attackers as a result of the invention of rifled and repeating small arms, the machine gun, barbed wire, and the development of railroads, Europeans increasingly believed that attackers would hold the advantage on the battlefield, and that wars would be short and "decisive"—a "brief storm," in the words of the German Chancellor, Bethmann Hollwerg.[1] They largely overlooked the lessons of the American Civil War, the Russo-Turkish War of 1877–78, the Boer War, and the Russo-Japanese War, which had demonstrated the power of the new defensive technologies. Instead, Europeans embraced a set of political and military myths which obscured both the defender's advantages and the obstacles an aggressor would confront. This mindset helped to mold the offensive military doctrines which every European power adopted during the period 1892–1913.[2]

In Germany, the military glorified the offense in strident terms, and inculcated German society with similar views. General Alfred von Schlieffen, author of the 1914 German war plan, declared that "Attack is the best defense," while the popular publicist Friedrich von Bernhardi proclaimed that "the offensive mode of action is by far superior to the defensive mode," and that "the superiority of offensive warfare under modern conditions is greater than formerly."[3] German Chief of Staff General Helmuth von Moltke also endorsed "the principle that the offensive is the best defense," while General August von Keim, founder of the Army League, argued that "Germany ought to be armed for attack," since "the offensive is the only way of insuring victory."[4] These assumptions guided the Schlieffen Plan, which envisaged rapid and decisive attacks on Belgium, France, and Russia.

In France, the army became "Obsessed with the virtues of the offensive," in the words of B. H. Liddell Hart, an obsession which also spread to French civilians.[5] The French army, declared Chief of Staff Joffre, "no longer knows any other law than the offensive. . . . Any other conception ought to be rejected as contrary to the very nature of war,"[6] while the President of the French Republic, Clément Fallières, announced that "The offensive alone is suited to the temperament of French soldiers. . . . We are determined to march straight against the enemy without hesitation."[7] Emile Driant, a member of the French chamber of deputies, summarized the common view: "The first great battle will decide the whole war, and wars will be short. The idea of the offense must penetrate the spirit of our nation."[8] French military doctrine reflected these offensive biases.[9] In Marshall Foch's words, the French army adopted "a single formula for success, a single combat doctrine, namely, the decisive power of offensive action undertaken with the resolute determination to march on the enemy, reach and destroy him."[10]

Other European states displayed milder symptoms of the same virus. The British military resolutely rejected defensive strategies despite their experience in the Boer War which demonstrated the power of entrenched defenders against exposed attackers. General W. G. Knox wrote, "The defensive is never an acceptable role to the Briton, and he makes little or no study of it," and General R. C. B. Haking argued that the offensive "will win as sure as there is a sun in the heavens."[11] The Russian Minister of War, General V. A. Sukhomlinov, observed that Russia's enemies were directing their armies "towards guaranteeing the possibility of dealing rapid and decisive blows. . . . We also must follow this example."[12] Even in Belgium the offensive found proponents: under the influence of French ideas, some Belgian officers favored an offensive strategy, proposing the remarkable argument that "To ensure against our being ignored it was essential that we should attack," and declaring that "We must hit them where it hurts."[13]

Mythical or mystical arguments obscured the technical dominion of the defense, giving this faith in the offense aspects of a cult, or a mystique, as Marshall Joffre remarked in his memoirs.[14] For instance, Foch mistakenly argued that the machine gun actually strengthened the offense: "Any improvement of firearms is ultimately bound to add strength to the offensive. . . . Nothing is easier than to give a mathematical demonstration of that truth." If two thousand men attacked one thousand, each man in both groups firing his rifle once a minute, he explained, the "balance in favor of the attack" was one thousand bullets per minute. But if both sides could fire ten times per minute, the "balance in favor of the attacker" would increase to ten thousand, giving the attack the overall advantage.[15] With equally forced logic, Bernhardi wrote that the larger the army the longer defensive measures would take to execute, owing to "the difficulty of moving masses"; hence, he argued, as armies grew, so would the relative power of the offense.[16]

British and French officers suggested that superior morale on the attacking side could overcome superior defensive firepower, and that this superiority in morale could be achieved simply by assuming the role of attacker, since offense was a morale-building activity. One French officer contended that "the offensive doubles the energy of the troops" and "concentrates the thoughts of the commander on a single objective,"[17] while British officers declared that "Modern [war] conditions have enormously increased the value of moral quality," and "the moral attributes [are] the primary causes of all great success."[18] In short, mind would prevail over matter; morale would triumph over machine guns.

Europeans also tended to discount the power of political factors which would favor defenders. Many Germans believed that "bandwagoning" with a powerful state rather than "balancing" against it was the guiding principle in international alliance-formation.[19] Aggressors would gather momentum as they gained power, because opponents would be intimidated into acquiescence and neutrals would rally to the stronger side. Such thinking led German Chancellor Bethmann Hollweg to hope that "Germany's growing strength . . . might force England to realize that [the balance of power] principle had become untenable and impracticable and to opt for a peaceful settlement with Germany,"[20] and German Secretary of State Gottlieb von Jagow to forecast British neutrality in a future European war: "We have not built our fleet in vain," and "people in England will seriously ask themselves whether it will be just that simple and without danger to play the role of France's guardian angel against us."[21] German leaders also thought they might frighten Belgium into surrender: during the July crisis Moltke was "counting on the possibility of being able to come to an understanding [with Belgium] when the Belgian Government realizes the seriousness of the situation."[22] This ill-founded belief in bandwagoning reinforced the general belief that conquest was relatively easy.

The belief in easy conquest eventually pervaded public images of international politics, manifesting itself most prominently in the widespread application of Darwinist notions to international affairs. In this image, states competed in a decisive struggle for survival which weeded out the weak and ended in the triumph of stronger states and races—an image which assumed a powerful offense. "In the struggle between nationalities," wrote former German Chancellor Bernhard von Bülow, "one nation is the hammer and the other the anvil; one is the victor and the other the vanquished. . . . it is a law of life and development in history that where two national civilisations meet they fight for ascendancy."[23] A writer in the London *Saturday Review* portrayed the Anglo-German competition as "the first great racial struggle of the future: here are two growing nations pressing against each other . . . all over the world. One or the other has to go; one or the other will go."[24] This Darwinist foreign policy thought reflected and rested upon the implicit assumption that the offense was strong, since "grow or die" dynamics would be impeded in a defense-dominant world where growth could be stopped and death prevented by self-defense.

Consequences of Offense-Dominance

Recent theoretical writing in international relations emphasizes the dangers that arise when the offense is strong relative to the defense.[25] If the theory outlined in these writings is valid, it follows that the cult of the offensive was a reason for the outbreak of the war.

Five major dangers relevant to the 1914 case may develop when the offense is strong, according to this recent writing. First, states adopt more aggressive foreign policies, both to exploit new opportunities and to avert new dangers which appear when the offense is strong. Expansion is more tempting, because the cost of aggression declines when the offense has the advantage. States are also driven to expand by the need to control assets and create the conditions they require to secure themselves against aggressors, because security becomes a scarcer asset. Alliances widen and tighten as states grow more dependent on one another for security, a circumstance which fosters the spreading of local conflicts. Moreover, each state is more likely to be menaced by aggressive neighbors who are governed by the same logic, creating an even more competitive atmosphere and giving states further reason to seek security in alliances and expansion.

Second, the size of the advantage accruing to the side mobilizing or striking first increases, raising the risk of preemptive war.[26] When the offense is strong, smaller shifts in ratios of forces between states create greater shifts in their relative capacity to conquer territory. As a result states have greater incentive to mobilize first or strike first, if they can change the force ratio in their favor by doing so. This incentive leads states to mobilize or attack to seize the initiative or deny it to adversaries, and to conceal plans, demands, and grievances to avoid setting off such a strike by their enemies, with deleterious effects on diplomacy.

Third, "windows" of opportunity and vulnerability open wider, forcing faster diplomacy and raising the risk of preventive war. Since smaller shifts in force ratios have larger effects on relative capacity to conquer territory, smaller prospective shifts in force ratios cause greater hope and alarm, open bigger windows of opportunity and vulnerability, and enhance the attractiveness of exploiting a window by launching a preventive attack.

Fourth, states adopt more competitive styles of diplomacy—brinkmanship and presenting opponents with *faits accomplis,* for instance—since the gains promised by such tactics can more easily justify the risks they entail. At the same time, however, the risks of adopting such strategies also increase, because they tend to threaten the vital interests of other states more directly. Because the security of states is more precarious and more tightly interdependent, threatening actions force stronger and faster reactions, and the political ripple effects of *faits accomplis* are larger and harder to control.

Fifth, states enforce tighter political and military secrecy, since national security is threatened more directly if enemies win the contest for information. As with all security assets, the marginal utility of information is magnified when the offense is strong; hence states compete harder to gain the advantage and avoid the disadvantage of disclosure, leading states to conceal their political and military planning and decision-making more carefully.

The following section suggests that many of the proximate causes of the war of 1914 represent various guises of these consequences of offense-dominance: either they were generated or exacerbated by the assumption that the offense was strong, or their effects were rendered more dangerous by this assumption. These causes include: German and Austrian expansionism; the belief that the side which mobilized or struck first would have the advantage; the German and Austrian belief that they faced "windows of vulnerability"; the nature and inflexibility of the Russian and German war plans and the tight nature of the European alliance system, both of which spread the war from the Balkans to the rest of Europe; the imperative that "mobilization meant war" for Germany; the failure of Britain to take effective measures to deter Germany; the uncommon number of blunders and mistakes committed by statesmen during the July crisis; and the ability of the Central Powers to evade blame for the war. Without the cult of the offensive these problems probably would have been less acute, and their effects would have posed smaller risks. Thus the cult of the offensive was a mainspring driving many of the mechanisms which brought about the First World War.

THE CULT OF THE OFFENSIVE AND THE CAUSES OF THE WAR

German Expansion and Entente Resistance

Before 1914 Germany sought a wider sphere of influence of empire, and the war grew largely from the political collision between expansionist Germany and a resistant Europe. Germans differed on whether their empire should be formal or informal, whether they should seek it in Europe or overseas, and whether they should try to acquire it peacefully or by violence, but a broad consensus favored expansion of some kind. The logic behind this expansionism, in turn, rested on two widespread beliefs which reflected the cult of the offensive: first, that German security required a wider empire; and second, that such an empire was readily attainable, either by coercion or conquest. Thus German expansionism reflected the assumption that conquest would be easy both for Germany and for its enemies.

Prewar statements by German leaders and intellectuals reflected a pervasive belief that German independence was threatened unless Germany won changes in the status quo. Kaiser Wilhelm foresaw a "battle of Germans against the Russo-Gauls for their very existence," which would decide "the existence or non-existence of the Germanic race in Europe,"[27] declaring: "The question for Germany is to be or not to be."[28] His Chancellor, Bethmann Hollweg, wondered aloud if there were any purpose in planting new trees at his estate at Hohenfinow, near Berlin, since "in a few years the Russians would be here anyway."[29] The historian Heinrich von Treitschke forecast that "in the long run the small states of central Europe can not maintain themselves,"[30] while other Germans warned, "If Germany does not rule the world . . . it will disappear from the map; it is a question of either or," and "Germany will be a world power or nothing."[31] Similarly, German military officers predicted that "without colonial possessions [Germany] will suffocate in her small territory or else will be crushed by the great world powers" and foresaw a "supreme struggle, in which the existence of Germany will be at stake. . . ."[32]

Germans also widely believed that expansion could solve their insecurity: "Room; they must make room. The western and southern Slavs—or we! . . . Only by growth can a people save itself."[33] German expansionists complained that German borders were constricted and indefensible, picturing a Germany "badly protected by its unfavorable geographic frontiers. . . ."[34] Expansion was the suggested remedy: "Our frontiers are too narrow. We must become land-hungry, must acquire new regions for settlement. . . ."[35] Expanded borders would provide more defensible frontiers and new areas for settlement and economic growth, which in turn would strengthen the German race against its competitors: "the continental expansion of German territory [and] the multiplication on the continent of the German peasantry . . . would form a sure barrier against the advance of our enemies. . . ."[36] Such utterances came chiefly from the hawkish end of the German political spectrum, but they reflected widely held assumptions.

Many Germans also failed to see the military and political obstacles to expansion. The Kaiser told departing troops in early August, "You will be home before the leaves have fallen from the trees,"[37] and one of his generals predicted that the German army would sweep through Europe like a bus full of tourists: "In two weeks we shall defeat France, then we shall turn round, defeat Russia and then we shall march to the Balkans and establish order there."[38] During the July crisis a British observer noted the mood of "supreme confidence" in Berlin military circles, and a German observer reported that the German General Staff "looks ahead to war with France with great confidence, expects to defeat France within four weeks. . . ."[39] While some German military planners recognized the tactical advantage which defenders would hold on the battlefield, most German officers and civilians believed they could win a spectacular, decisive victory if they struck at the right moment.

Bandwagon logic fed hopes that British and Belgian opposition to German expansion could be overcome. General Moltke believed that "Britain is peace loving" because in an Anglo-German war "Britain will lose its domination at sea which will pass forever to America"[40]; hence Britain would be intimidated into neutrality. Furthermore, he warned the Belgians, "Small countries, such as Belgium, would be well advised to rally to the side of the strong if they wished to retain their independence," expecting Belgium to follow this advice if Germany applied enough pressure.[41]

Victory, moreover, would be decisive and final. In Bülow's words, a defeat could render Russia "incapable of attacking us for at least a generation" and "unable to stand up for twenty-five years," leaving it "lastingly weakened,"[42] while Bernhardi proposed that France "must be annihilated once and for all as a great power."[43]

Thus, as Robert Jervis notes: "Because of the perceived advantage of the offense, war was seen as the best route both to gaining expansion and to avoiding drastic loss of influence. There seemed to be no way for Germany merely to retain and safeguard her existing position."[44] The presumed power of the offense made empire appear both feasible and necessary. Had Germans recognized the real power of the defense, the notion of gaining wider empire would have lost both its urgency and its plausibility.

Security was not Germany's only concern, nor was it always a genuine one. In Germany, as elsewhere, security sometimes served as a pretext for expansion undertaken for other reasons. Thus proponents of the "social imperialism" theory of German expansion note that German elites endorsed imperialism, often using security arguments, partly to strengthen their domestic political and social position.[45] Likewise, spokesmen for the German military establishment exaggerated the threat to Germany and the benefits of empire for organizationally self-serving reasons. Indeed, members of the German elite sometimes privately acknowledged that Germany was under less threat than the public was being told. For example, the Secretary of State in the Foreign Office, Kiderlen-Wächter, admitted, "If we do not conjure up a war into being, no one else certainly will do so," since "The Republican government of France is certainly peace-minded. The British do not want war. They will never give cause for it. . . ."[46]

Nevertheless, the German public believed that German security was precarious, and security arguments formed the core of the public case for expansion. Moreover, these arguments proved persuasive, and the chauvinist public climate which they created enabled the elite to pursue expansion, whatever elite motivation might actually have been. Indeed, some members of the German government eventually felt pushed into reckless action by an extreme chauvinist public opinion which they felt powerless to resist. Admiral von Müller later explained that Germany pursued a bellicose policy during the July crisis because "The government, already weakened by domestic disunity, found itself inevitably under pressure from a great part of the German people which had been whipped into a high-grade chauvinism by Navalists and Pan-Germans."[47] Bethmann Hollweg felt his hands tied by an expansionist public climate: "With these idiots [the Pan-Germans] one cannot conduct a foreign policy—on the contrary. Together with other factors they will eventually make any reasonable course impossible for us."[48] Thus the search for security was a fundamental cause of German conduct, whether or not the elite was motivated by security concerns, because the elite was allowed or even compelled to adopt expansionist policies by a German public which found security arguments persuasive.

The same mixture of insecurity and perceived opportunity stiffened resistance to German expansion and fuelled a milder expansionism elsewhere in Europe, intensifying the conflict between Germany and its neighbors. In France the nationalist revival and French endorsement of a firm Russian policy in the Balkans were inspired partly by a growing fear of the German threat after 1911,[49] partly by an associated concern that Austrian expansion in the Balkans could shift the European balance of power in favor of the Central Powers and thereby threaten French security, and partly by belief that a war could create opportunities for French expansion. The stiffer French "new attitude" on Balkan questions in 1912 was ascribed to the French belief that "a territorial acquisition on the part of Austria would affect the general balance of power in Europe and as a result touch the particular interests of France"—a belief which assumed that the power balance was relatively precarious, which in turn assumed a world of relatively strong offense.[50] At the same time some Frenchmen looked forward to "a beautiful war which will deliver all the captives of Germanism,"[51] inspired by a faith in the power of the offensive that was typified by the enthusiasm of Joffre's deputy, General de Castelnau: "Give me 700,000 men and I will conquer Europe!"[52]

Russian policy in the Balkans was driven both by fear that Austrian expansion could threaten Russian security and by hopes that Russia could destroy its enemies if war developed under the right conditions. Sazonov saw a German-Austrian Balkan program to "deliver the Slavonic East, bound hand and foot, into the power of Austria-Hungary," followed by the German seizure of Constantinople, which would gravely threaten Russian security by placing all of Southern Russia at the mercy of German power.[53] Eventually a "German Khalifate" would be established, "extending from the banks of the Rhine to the mouth of the Tigris and Euphrates," which would reduce "Russia to a pitiful dependence upon the arbitrary will of the Central Powers."[54] At the same time some Russians believed these threats could be addressed by offensive action:

Russian leaders spoke of the day when "the moment for the downfall of Austria-Hungary arrives,"[55] and the occasion when "The Austro-Hungarian ulcer, which to-day is not yet so ripe as the Turkish, may be cut up."[56] Russian military officers contended that "the Austrian army represents a serious force. . . . But on the occasion of the first great defeats all of this multi-national and artificially united mass ought to disintegrate."[57]

In short, the belief that conquest was easy and security scarce was an important source of German-Entente conflict. Without it, both sides could have adopted less aggressive and more accommodative policies.

The Incentive to Preempt

American strategists have long assumed that World War I was a preemptive war, but they have not clarified whether or how this was true.[58] Hence two questions should be resolved to assess the consequences of the cult of the offensive: did the states of Europe perceive an incentive to move first in 1914, which helped spur them to mobilize or attack? If so, did the cult of the offensive help to give rise to this perception?

The question of whether the war was preemptive reduces to the question of why five principal actions in the July crisis were taken. These actions are: the Russian preliminary mobilization ordered on July 25–26; the partial Russian mobilization against Austria-Hungary ordered on July 29; the Russian full mobilization ordered on July 30; French preliminary mobilization measures ordered during July 25–30; and the German attack on the Belgian fortress at Liège at the beginning of the war. The war was preemptive if Russia and France mobilized preemptively, since these mobilizations spurred German and Austrian mobilization, opening windows which helped cause war. Thus while the mobilizations were not acts of war, they caused effects which caused war. The war was also preemptive if Germany struck Liège preemptively, since the imperative to strike Liège was one reason why "mobilization meant war" to Germany.

The motives for these acts cannot be determined with finality; testimony by the actors is spotty and other direct evidence is scarce. Instead, motives must be surmised from preexisting beliefs, deduced from circumstances, and inferred from clues which may by themselves be inconclusive. However, three pieces of evidence suggest that important preemptive incentives existed, and helped to shape conduct. First, most European leaders apparently believed that mobilization by either side which was not answered within a very few days, or even hours, could affect the outcome of the war. This judgment is reflected both in the length of time which officials assumed would constitute a militarily significant delay between mobilization and offsetting counter-mobilization, and in the severity of the consequences which they assumed would follow if they mobilized later than their opponents.

Second, many officials apparently assumed that significant mobilization measures and preparations to attack could be kept secret for a brief but significant period. Since most officials also believed that a brief unanswered mobilization could be decisive, they concluded that the side which mobilized first would have the upper hand.

Third, governments carried out some of their mobilization measures in secrecy, suggesting that they believed secret measures were feasible and worthwhile.

The Perceived Significance of Short Delays Before and during the July crisis European leaders used language suggesting that they believed a lead in ordering mobilization of roughly one to three days would be significant. In Austria, General Conrad believed that "every day was of far-reaching importance," since "any delay might leave the [Austrian] forces now assembling in Galicia open to being struck by the full weight of

a Russian offensive in the midst of their deployment."[59] In France, Marshall Joffre warned the French cabinet that "any delay of twenty-four hours in calling up our reservists" once German preparations began would cost France "ten to twelve miles for each day of delay; in other words, the initial abandonment of much of our territory."[60] In Britain, one official believed that France "cannot possibly delay her own mobilization for even the fraction of a day" once Germany began to mobilize.[61]

In Germany, one analyst wrote that "A delay of a single day . . . can scarcely ever be rectified."[62] Likewise Moltke, on receiving reports of preparations in France and Russia during the July crisis, warned that "the military situation is becoming from day to day more unfavorable for us," and would "lead to fateful consequences for us" if Germany did not respond.[63] On July 30 he encouraged Austria to mobilize, warning that "every hour of delay makes the situation worse, for Russia gains a start."[64] On August 1, the Prussian ministry of war was reportedly "very indignant over the day lost for the mobilization" by the German failure to mobilize on July 30.[65] The German press drove home the point that if mobilization by the adversary went unanswered even briefly, the result could be fatal, one German newspaper warning that "Every delay [in mobilizing] would cost us an endless amount of blood" if Germany's enemies gained the initiative; hence "it would be disastrous if we let ourselves be moved by words not to carry on our preparations so quickly. . . ."[66]

Thus time was measured in small units: "three days," "day to day," "a single day," "the fraction of a day," or even "every hour." Moreover, the consequences of conceding the initiative to the adversary were thought to be extreme. The Russian Minister of Agriculture, Alexander Krivoshein, warned that if Russia delayed its mobilization "we should be marching toward a certain catastrophe,"[67] and General Janushkevich warned the Russian foreign minister that "we were in danger of losing [the war] before we had time to unsheath our sword" by failing to mobilize promptly against Germany.[68] General Joffre feared that France would find itself "in an irreparable state of inferiority" if it were outstripped by German mobilization.[69] And in Germany, officials foresaw dire consequences if Germany conceded the initiative either in the East or the West. Bethmann Hollweg explained to one of his ambassadors that if German mobilization failed to keep pace with the Russian, Germany would suffer large territorial losses: "East Prussia, West Prussia, and perhaps also Posen and Silesia [would be] at the mercy of the Russians."[70] Such inaction would be "a crime against the safety of our fatherland."[71]

Germans also placed a high value on gaining the initiative at Liège, since Liège controlled a vital Belgian railroad junction, and German forces could not seize Liège with its tunnels and bridges intact unless they surprised the Belgians. As Moltke wrote before the war, the advance through Belgium "will hardly be possible unless Liège is in our hands . . . the possession of Liège is the *sine qua non* of our advance." But seizing Liège would require "meticulous preparation and surprise" and "is only possible if the attack is made at once, before the areas between the forts are fortified," "immediately" after the declaration of war.[72] In short, the entire German war plan would be ruined if Germany allowed Belgium to prepare the defense of Liège.

This belief that brief unanswered preparations and actions could be decisive reflected the implicit assumption that the offense had the advantage. Late mobilization would cost Germany control of East and West Prussia only if Russian offensive power were strong, and German defensive power were weak; mobilizing late could only be a "crime against the safety" of Germany if numerically superior enemies could destroy it; lateness could only confront Russia with "certain catastrophe" or leave it in danger of "losing before we have time to unsheath our sword" if Germany could develop a powerful offensive with the material advantage it would gain by preparing first; and lateness could only condemn France to "irreparable inferiority" if small material inferiority translated into large territorial losses. Had statesmen understood that in reality the defense had the advantage, they also would have known that the possession of the initiative could not be decisive, and could have conceded it more easily.

Was Secret Preparation Believed Feasible? The belief that delay could be fatal would have created no impulse to go first had European leaders believed that they could detect and offset their opponents' preparations immediately. However, many officials believed that secret action for a short time was possible. Russian officials apparently lacked confidence in their own ability to detect German or Austrian mobilization, and their decisions to mobilize seem to have been motivated partly by the desire to forestall surprise preparation by their adversaries. Sazonov reportedly requested full mobilization on July 30 partly from fear that otherwise Germany would "gain time to complete her preparations in secret."[73] Sazonov offers confirmation in his memoirs, explaining that he had advised mobilization believing that "The perfection of the German military organization made it possible by means of personal notices to the reservists to accomplish a great part of the work quietly." Germany could then "complete the mobilization in a very short time. This circumstance gave a tremendous advantage to Germany, but we could counteract it to a certain extent by taking measures for our own mobilization in good time."[74]

Similar reasoning contributed to the Russian decision to mobilize against Austria on July 29. Sazonov explains that the mobilization was undertaken in part "so as to avoid the danger of being taken unawares by the Austrian preparations."[75] Moreover, recent experience had fuelled Russian fears of an Austrian surprise: during the Balkan crisis of 1912, the Russian army had been horrified to discover that Austria had secretly mobilized in Galicia, without detection by Russian intelligence; and this experience resolved the Russian command not to be caught napping again. In one observer's opinion, "the experience of 1912 . . . was not without influence as regards Russia's unwillingness to put off her mobilization in the July days of 1914."[76]

Top Russian officials also apparently believed that Russia could itself mobilize secretly, and some historians ascribe the Russian decision to mobilize partly to this erroneous belief. Luigi Albertini writes that Sazonov did not realize that the mobilization order would be posted publicly and that, accordingly, he "thought Russia could mobilize without Germany's knowing of it immediately."[77] Albertini reports that the German ambassador caused "real stupefaction" by appearing at the Russian ministry for foreign affairs with a red mobilization poster on the morning of mobilization,[78] and concludes that the "belief that it was possible to proceed to general mobilization without making it public may well have made Sazonov more inclined to order it."[79]

Contemporary accounts confirm that the Russian leadership believed in their own ability to mobilize in secret. The memorandum of the Russian Ministry for Foreign Affairs records that Sazonov sought to "proceed to the general mobilization as far as possible secretly and without making any public announcement concerning it," in order "To avoid rendering more acute our relations with Germany."[80] And in informing his government of Russian preliminary mobilization measures which began on July 26, the French ambassador indicated Russian hopes that they could maintain secrecy: "Secret preparations will, however, commence already today,"[81] and "the military districts of Warsaw, Vilna and St. Petersburg are secretly making preparations."[82] His telegram informing Paris of Russian general mobilization explained that "the Russian government has decided to proceed secretly to the first measures of general mobilization."[83]

Like their Russian counterparts, top French officials also apparently feared that Germany might mobilize in secret, which spurred the French to their own measures. Thus during the July crisis General Joffre spoke of "the concealments [of mobilization] which are possible in Germany,"[84] and referred to "information from excellent sources [which] led us to fear that on the Russian front a sort of secret mobilization was taking place [in Germany]."[85] In his memoirs, Joffre quotes a German military planning document acquired by the French government before the July crisis, which he apparently took to indicate German capabilities, and which suggested that Germany could take "quiet measures . . . in preparation for mobilization," including "a discreet assembly of complementary personnel and materiel" which would "assure us advantages very difficult for other armies to realize in the same degree."[86] The French ambassador to Berlin, Jules Cambon, also apparently believed that Germany could conduct preliminary mobilization measures in secret, became persuaded during the July crisis that it had in fact done this, and so informed Paris: "In view of German habits, [preliminary measures] can be taken without exciting the population or causing indiscretions to be committed. . . ."[87] For their part the Germans apparently did not believe that they or their enemies could mobilize secretly, but they did speak in terms suggesting that Germany could surprise the Belgians: German planners referred to the *"coup de main"* at Liège and the need for "meticulous preparation and surprise."[88]

To sum up, then, French policymakers feared that Germany could mobilize secretly; Russians feared secret mobilization by Germany or Austria, and hoped Russian mobilization could be secret; while Central Powers planners saw less possibility for preemptive mobilization by either side, but hoped to mount a surprise attack on Belgium.[89]

Did Statesmen Act Secretly? During the July crisis European statesmen sometimes informed their opponents before they took military measures, but on other occasions they acted secretly, suggesting that they believed the initiative was both attainable and worth attaining, and indicating that the desire to seize the initiative may have entered into their decisions to mobilize. German leaders warned the French of their preliminary measures taken on July 29,[90] and their pre-mobilization and mobilization measures taken on July 31;[91] and they openly warned the Russians on July 29 that they would mobilize if Russia conducted a partial mobilization.[92] Russia openly warned Austria on July 27 that it would mobilize if Austria crossed the Serbian frontier,[93] and then on July 28 and July 29 openly announced to Germany and Austria its partial mobilization of July 29,[94] and France delayed full mobilization until after Germany had taken the onus on itself by issuing ultimata to Russia and France. However, Russia, France, and Germany tried to conceal four of the five major preemptive actions of the crisis: the Russians hid both their preliminary measures of July 25–26 and their general mobilization of July 30, the French attempted to conceal their preliminary mobilization measures of July 25–29, and the Germans took great care to conceal their planned *coup de main* against Liège. Thus states sometimes conceded the initiative, but sought it at critical junctures.

Overall, evidence suggests that European leaders saw some advantage to moving first in 1914: the lags which they believed significant lay in the same range as the lags they believed they could gain or forestall by mobilizing first. These perceptions probably helped spur French and Russian decisions to mobilize, which in turn helped set in train the German mobilization, which in turn meant war partly because the Germans were determined to preempt Liège. Hence the war was in some modest measure preemptive.

If so, the cult of the offensive bears some responsibility. Without it, statesmen would not have thought that secret mobilization or preemptive attack could be decisive. The cult was not the sole cause of the perceived incentive to preempt; rather, three causes acted together, the others being the belief that mobilization could briefly be conducted secretly, and the systems of reserve manpower mobilization which enabled armies to multiply their strength in two weeks. The cult had its effect by magnifying the importance of these other factors in the minds of statesmen, which magnified the incentive to preempt which these factors caused them to perceive. The danger that Germany might gain time to complete preparations in secret could only alarm France and Russia if Germany could follow up these preparations with an effective offensive; otherwise, early secret mobilization could *not* give "a tremendous advantage" to Germany, and such a prospect would not require a forestalling response. Sazonov could have been tempted to mobilize secretly only if early Russian mobilization would forestall important German gains, or could provide important gains for Russia, as could only have happened if the offense were powerful.

"Windows" and Preventive War

Germany and Austria pursued bellicose policies in 1914 partly to shut the looming "windows" of vulnerability which they envisioned lying ahead, and partly to exploit the brief window of opportunity which they thought the summer crisis opened. This window logic, in turn, grew partly from the cult of the offensive, since it depended upon the implicit assumption that the offense was strong. The shifts in the relative sizes of armies, economies, and alliances which fascinated and frightened statesmen in 1914 could have cast such a long shadow only in a world where material advantage promised decisive results in warfare, as it could only in an offense-dominant world.

   The official communications of German leaders are filled with warnings that German power was in relative decline, and that Germany was doomed unless it took drastic action—such as provoking and winning a great crisis which would shatter the Entente, or directly instigating a "great liquidation" (as one general put it).[95] German officials repeatedly warned that Russian military power would expand rapidly between 1914 and 1917, as Russian carried out its 1913–1914 Great Program, and that in the long run Russian power would further outstrip German power because Russian resources were greater.[96] In German eyes this threat forced Germany to act. Secretary of State Jagow summarized a view common in Germany in a telegram to one of his ambassadors just before the July crisis broke:

> Russia will be ready to fight in a few years. Then she will crush us by the number of her soldiers; then she will have built her Baltic fleet and her strategic railways. Our group in the meantime will have become steadily weaker. . . . I do not desire a preventive war, but if the conflict should offer itself, we ought not to shirk it.[97]

Similarly, shortly before Sarajevo the Kaiser reportedly believed that "the big Russian railway constructions were . . . preparations for a great war which could start in 1916" and wondered "whether it might not be better to attack than to wait."[98] At about the same time Chancellor Bethmann Hollweg declared bleakly, "The future belongs to Russia which grows and grows and becomes an even greater nightmare to us,"[99] warning that "After the completion of their strategic railroads in Poland our position [will be] untenable."[100] During the war, Bethmann confessed that the "window" argument had driven German policy in 1914: "Lord yes, in a certain sense it was a preventive war," motivated by "the constant threat of attack, the greater likelihood of its inevitability in the future, and by the military's claim: today war is still possible without defeat, but not in two years!"[101]

   Window logic was especially prevalent among the German military officers, many of whom openly argued for preventive war during the years before the July crisis. General Moltke declared, "I believe a war to be unavoidable and: the sooner the better" at the infamous "war council" of December 8, 1912,[102] and he expressed similar views to his Austrian counterpart, General Conrad, in May 1914: "to wait any longer meant a diminishing of our chances; as far as manpower is concerned, one cannot enter into a competition with Russia,"[103] and "We [the German Army] are ready, the sooner the better for us."[104] During the July crisis Moltke remarked that "we shall never hit it again so well as we do now with France's and Russia's expansion of their armies incomplete," and argued that "the singularly favorable situation be exploited for military action."[105] After the war Jagow recalled a conversation with Moltke in May 1914, in which Moltke had spelled out his reasoning:

> In two–three years Russia would have completed her armaments. The military superiority of our enemies would then be so great that he did not know how we could overcome them. Today we would still be a match for them. In his opinion there was no alternative to making preventive war in order to defeat the enemy while we still had a chance of victory. The Chief of General Staff therefore proposed that I should conduct a policy with the aim of provoking a war in the near future.[106]

Other members of the German military shared Moltke's views, pressing for preventive war because "conditions and prospects would never become better."[107] General Gebstattel recorded the mood of the German leadership on the eve of the war: "Chances better than in two or three years hence and the General Staff is reported to be confidently awaiting events."[108] The Berlin *Post,* a newspaper which often reflected the views of the General Staff, saw a window in 1914: "at the moment the state of things is favorable for us. France is not yet ready for war. England has internal and colonial difficulties, and Russia recoils from the conflict because she fears revolution at home. Ought we to wait until our adversaries are ready?" It concluded that Germany should "prepare for the inevitable war with energy and foresight" and "begin it under the most favorable conditions."[109]

German leaders also saw a tactical window of opportunity in the political constellation of July 1914, encouraging them to shut their strategic window of vulnerability. In German eyes, the Sarajevo assassination created favorable conditions for a confrontation, since it guaranteed that Austria would join Germany against Russia and France (as it might not if war broke out over a colonial conflict or a dispute in Western Europe), and it provided the Central Powers with a plausible excuse, which raised hopes that Britain might remain neutral. On July 8, Bethmann Hollweg reportedly remarked, "If war comes from the east so that we have to fight for Austria-Hungary and not Austria-Hungary for us, we have a chance of winning."[110] Likewise, the German ambassador to Rome reportedly believed on July 27 that "the present moment is extraordinarily favorable to Germany,"[111] and the German ambassador to London even warned the British Prime Minister that "there was some feeling in Germany . . . that trouble was bound to come and therefore it would be better not to restrain Austria and let trouble come now, rather than later."[112]

The window logic reflected in these statements is a key to German conduct in 1914: whether the Germans were aggressive or restrained depended on whether at a given moment they thought windows were open or closed. Germany courted war on the Balkan question after Sarajevo because window logic led German leaders to conclude that war could not be much worse than peace, and might even be better, if Germany could provoke the right war under the right conditions against the right opponents. German leaders probably preferred the status quo to a world war against the entire Entente, but evidence suggests that they also preferred a continental war against France and Russia to the status quo—as long as Austria joined the war, and as long as they could also find a suitable pretext which they could use to persuade the German public that Germany fought for a just cause. This, in turn, required that Germany engineer a war which engaged Austrian interests, and in which Germany could cast itself as the attacked, in order to involve the Austrian army, to persuade Britain to remain neutral, and to win German public support. These window considerations help explain both the German decision to force the Balkan crisis to a head and German efforts to defuse the crisis after it realized that it had failed to gain British neutrality. The German peace efforts after July 29 probably represent a belated effort to reverse course after it became clear that the July crisis was not such an opportune war window after all.

Window logic also helped to persuade Austria to play the provocateur for Germany. Like their German counterparts, many Austrian officials believed that the relative strength of the Central Powers was declining, and saw in Sarajevo a rare opportunity to halt this decline by force. Thus the Austrian War Minister, General Krobatin, argued in early July that "it would be better to go to war immediately, rather than at some later period, because the balance of power must in the course of time change to our disadvantage," while the Austrian Foreign Minister, Count Berchtold, favored action because "our situation must become more precarious as time goes on,"[113] warning that unless Austria destroyed the Serbian army in 1914, it would face "another attack [by] Serbia in much more unfavorable conditions" in two or three years.[114] Likewise, the Austrian foreign ministry reportedly believed that, "if Russia would not permit the localization of the conflict with Serbia, the present moment was more favorable for a reckoning than a later one would be"[115]; General Conrad believed, "If it comes to war with Russia—as it must some day—today is as good as any other day"[116]; and the Austrian ambassador to Italy believed an Austro-Serbian war would be "a piece of real good fortune," since "for the Triple Alliance the present moment is more favorable than another later."[117]

Thus the First World War was in part a "preventive" war, launched by the Central Powers in the belief that they were saving themselves from a worse fate in later years. The cult of the offensive bears some responsibility for that belief, for in a defense-dominated world the windows which underlie the logic of preventive war are shrunken in size, as the balance of power grows less elastic to the relative sizes of armies and economies; and windows cannot be shut as easily by military action. Only in a world taken by the cult of the offensive could the window logic which governed German and Austrian conduct have proved so persuasive: Germans could only have feared that an unchecked Russia could eventually "crush us by the numbers of her soldiers," or have seen a "singularly favorable situation" in 1914 which could be "exploited by military action" if material superiority would endow the German and Russian armies with the ability to conduct decisive offensive operations against one another. Moltke claimed he saw "no alternative to making preventive war," but had he believed that the defense dominated, better alternatives would have been obvious.

The cult of the offensive also helped cause the arms race before 1914 which engendered the uneven rates of military growth that gave rise to visions of windows. The German army buildup after 1912 was justified by security arguments: Bethmann Hollweg proclaimed, "For Germany, in the heart of Europe, with open boundaries on all sides, a strong army is the most secure guarantee of peace," while the Kaiser wrote that Germany needed "More ships and soldiers . . . because our existence is at stake."[118] This buildup provoked an even larger Russian and French buildup, which created the windows which alarmed Germany in 1914.[119] Thus the cult both magnified the importance of fluctuations in ratios of forces and helped to fuel the arms race which fostered them.

The Scope and Inflexibility of Mobilization Plans

The spreading of World War I outward from the Balkans is often ascribed to the scope and rigidity of the Russian and German plans for mobilization, which required that Russia must also mobilize armies against Germany when it mobilized against Austria-Hungary, and that Germany also attack France and Belgium if it fought Russia. Barbara Tuchman writes that Europe was swept into war by "the pull of military schedules," and recalls Moltke's famous answer when the Kaiser asked if the German armies could be mobilized to the East: "Your Majesty, it cannot be done. The deployment of millions cannot be improvised. If Your Majesty insists on leading the whole army to the East it will not be an army ready for battle but a disorganized mob of armed men with no arrangements for supply."[120] Likewise, Herman Kahn notes the "rigid war plan[s]" of 1914, which "were literally cast in concrete,"[121] and David Ziegler notes the influence of military "planning in advance," which left "no time to improvise."[122]

The scope and character of these plans in turn reflected the assumption that the offense was strong. In an offense-dominant world Russia would have been prudent to mobilize against Germany if it mobilized against Austria-Hungary; and Germany probably would have been prudent to attack Belgium and France at the start of any Russo-German war. Thus the troublesome railroad schedules of 1914 reflected the offense-dominant world in which the schedulers believed they lived. Had they known that the defense was powerful, they would have been drawn towards flexible plans for limited deployment on single frontiers; and had such planning prevailed, the war might have been confined to Eastern Europe or the Balkans.

Moreover, the "inflexibility" of the war plans may have reflected the same offensive assumptions which determined their shape. Russian and German soldiers understandably developed only options which they believed prudent to exercise, while omitting plans which they believed would be dangerous to implement. These judgments in turn reflected their own and their adversaries' offensive ideas. Options were few because these offensive ideas seemed to narrow the range of prudent choice.

Lastly, the assumption of offense-dominance gave preset plans greater influence over the conduct of the July crisis, by raising the cost of improvisation if statesmen insisted on adjusting plans at the last minute. Russian statesmen were told that an improvised partial mobilization would place Russia in an "extremely dangerous situation,"[123] and German civilians were warned against improvisation in similar terms. This in turn reflected the size of the "windows" which improvised partial mobilizations would open for the adversary on the frontier which the partial mobilization left unguarded, which in turn reflected the assumption that the offense was strong (since if defenses were strong a bungled mobilization would create less opportunity for others to exploit). Thus the cult of the offensive gave planners greater power to bind statesmen to the plans they had prepared.

Russian Mobilization Plans On July 28, 1914, Russian leaders announced that partial Russian mobilization against Austria would be ordered on July 29. They took this step to address threats emanating from Austria, acting partly to lend emphasis to their warnings to Austria that Russia would fight if Serbia were invaded, partly to offset Austrian mobilization against Serbia, and partly to offset or forestall Austrian mobilization measures which they believed were taking place or which they feared might eventually take place against Russia in Galicia.[124] However, after this announcement was made,

Russian military officers advised their civilian superiors that no plans for partial mobilization existed, that such a mobilization would be a "pure improvisation," as General Denikin later wrote, and that sowing confusion in the Russian railway timetables would impede Russia's ability to mobilize later on its northern frontier. General Sukhomlinov warned the Czar that "much time would be necessary in which to re-establish the normal conditions for any further mobilization" following a partial mobilization, and General Yanushkevich flatly told Sazonov that general mobilization "could not be put into operation" once partial mobilization began.[125] Thus Russian leaders were forced to choose between full mobilization or complete retreat, choosing full mobilization on July 30.

The cult of the offensive set the stage for this decision by buttressing Russian military calculations that full mobilization was safer than partial. We have little direct evidence explaining why Russian officers had prepared no plan for partial mobilization, but we can deduce their reasoning from their opinions on related subjects. These suggest that Russian officers believed that Germany would attack Russia if Russia fought Austria, and that the side mobilizing first would have the upper hand in a Russo-German war (as I have outlined above). Accordingly, it followed logically that Russia should launch any war with Austria by preempting Germany.

Russian leaders had three principal reasons to fear that Germany would not stand aside in an Austro-Russian conflict. First, the Russians were aware of the international Social Darwinism then sweeping Germany, and the expansionist attitude toward Russia which this worldview engendered. One Russian diplomat wrote that Germany was "beating all records of militarism" and "The Germans are not . . . wholly without the thought of removing from Russia at least part of the Baltic coastline in order to place us in the position of a second Serbia" in the course of a campaign for "German hegemony on the continent."[126] Russian military officers monitored the bellicose talk across the border with alarm, one intelligence report warning: "In Germany at present, the task of gradually accustoming the army and the population to the thought of the inevitability of conflict with Russia has begun," noting the regular public lectures which were then being delivered in Germany to foster war sentiment.[127]

Second, the Russians were aware of German alarm about windows and the talk of preventive war which this alarm engendered in Germany. Accordingly, Russian leaders expected that Germany might seize the excuse offered by a Balkan war to mount a preventive strike against Russia, especially since a war arising from the Balkans was a "best case" scenario for Germany, involving Austria on the side of Germany as it did. Thus General Yanushkevich explained Russia's decision to mobilize against Germany in 1914: "We knew well that Germany was ready for war, that she was longing for it at that moment, because our big armaments program was not yet completed . . . and because our war potential was not as great as it might be." Accordingly, Russia had to expect war with Germany: "We knew that war was inevitable, not only against Austria, but also against Germany. For this reason partial mobilization against Austria alone, which would have left our front towards Germany open . . . might have brought about a disaster, a terrible disaster."[128] In short, Russia had to strike to preempt a German preventive strike against Russia.

Third, the Russians knew that the Germans believed that German and Austrian security were closely linked. Germany would therefore feel compelled to intervene in any Austro-Russian war, because a Russian victory against Austria would threaten German safety. German leaders had widely advertised this intention: for instance, Bethmann Hollweg had warned the Reichstag in 1912 that if the Austrians "while asserting their interests should against all expectations be attacked by a third party, then we would have to come resolutely to their aid. And then we would fight for the maintenance of our own position in Europe and in defense of our future and security." [129] And in fact this was precisely what happened in 1914: Germany apparently decided to attack on learning of Russian *partial* mobilization, before Russian full mobilization was known in Germany.[130] This suggests that the role of "inflexible" Russian plans in causing the war is overblown—Russian full mobilization was sufficient but not necessary to cause the war; but it also helps explain why these plans were drawn as they were, and supports the view that some of the logic behind them was correct, given the German state of mind with which Russia had to contend.

In sum, Russians had to fear that expansionist, preventive, and alliance concerns might induce Germany to attack, which in turn reflected the German assumption that the offense was strong. The Russian belief that it paid to mobilize first reflected the effects of the same assumption in Russia. Had Europe known that the defense dominated, Russians would have had less reason to fear that an Austro-Russian war would spark a German attack, since the logic of expansionism and preventive war would presumably have been weaker in Germany, and Germany could more easily have tolerated some reduction in Austrian power without feeling that German safety was also threatened. At the same time, Russian soldiers would presumably have been slower to assume that they could improve their position in a Russo-German war by mobilizing preemptively. In short, the logic of general mobilization in Russia largely reflected and depended upon conclusions deduced from the cult of the offensive, or from its various manifestations. Without the cult of the offensive, a partial southern mobilization would have been the better option for Russia.

It also seems probable that the same logic helped persuade the Russian General Staff to eschew planning for a partial mobilization. If circumstances argued against a partial mobilization, they also argued against planning for one, since this would raise the risk that Russian civilians might actually implement the plan. This interpretation fits with suggestions that Russian officers exaggerated the difficulties of partial mobilization in their representations to Russian civilians.[131] If Russian soldiers left a partial mobilization option undeveloped because they believed that it would be dangerous to exercise, it follows that they also would emphasize the difficulty of improvising a southern option, since they also opposed it on other grounds.

German Mobilization Plans   The Schlieffen Plan was a disastrous scheme which only approached success because the French war plan was equally foolish: had the French army stood on the defensive instead of lunging into Alsace-Lorraine, it would have smashed the German army at the French frontier. Yet General Schlieffen's plan was a sensible response to the offense-dominant world imagined by many Germans. The plan was flawed because it grew from a fundamentally flawed image of warfare.

In retrospect, Germany should have retained the later war plan of the elder Moltke (Chief of Staff from 1857 to 1888), who would have conducted a limited offensive in the east against Russia while standing on the defensive in the west.[132] However, several considerations pushed German planners instead toward Schlieffen's grandiose scheme, which envisioned a quick victory against Belgium and France, followed by an offensive against Russia.

First, German planners assumed that France would attack Germany if Germany fought Russia, leaving Germany no option for a one-front war. By tying down German troops in Poland, an eastern war would create a yawning window of opportunity for France to recover its lost territories, and a decisive German victory over Russia would threaten French security by leaving France to face Germany alone. For these reasons they believed that France would be both too tempted and too threatened to stand aside. Bernhardi, among others, pointed out "the standing danger that France will attack us on a favorable occasion, as soon as we find ourselves involved in complications elsewhere." [133] The German declaration of war against France explained that France might suddenly attack from behind if Germany fought Russia; hence, "Germany cannot leave to France the choice of the moment" at which to attack. [134]

Second, German planners assumed that "window" considerations required a German offensive against either France or Russia at the outset of any war against the Entente. German armies could mobilize faster than the combined Entente armies; hence, the ratio of forces would most favor Germany at the beginning of the war. Therefore, Germany would do best to force an early decision, which in turn required that it assume the offensive, since otherwise its enemies would play a waiting game. As one observer explained, Germany "has the speed and Russia has the numbers, and the safety of the German Empire forbade that Germany should allow Russia time to bring up masses of troops from all parts of her wide dominions." [135] Germans believed that the window created by these differential mobilization rates was big, in turn, because they believed that both Germany and its enemies could mount a decisive offensive against the other with a small margin of superiority. If Germany struck at the right time, it could win easily—Germans hoped for victory in several weeks, as noted above—while if it waited it was doomed by Entente numerical superiority, which German defenses would be too weak to resist.

Third, German planners believed that an offensive against France would net them more than an offensive against Russia, which explains the western bias of the Schlieffen Plan. France could be attacked more easily than Russia, because French forces and resources lay within closer reach of German power; hence, as Moltke wrote before the war, "A speedy decision may be hoped for [against France], while an offensive against Russia would be an interminable affair." [136] Moreover, France was the more dangerous opponent not to attack, because it could take the offensive against Germany more quickly than Russia, and could threaten more important German territories if Germany left its frontier unguarded. Thus Moltke explained that they struck westward because "Germany could not afford to expose herself to the danger of attack by strong French forces in the direction of the Lower Rhine," and Wegerer wrote later that the German strike was compelled by the need to protect the German industrial region from French attack. [137] In German eyes these considerations made it too dangerous to stand on the defensive in the West in hopes that war with France could be avoided.

Finally, German planners believed that Britain would not have time to bring decisive power to bear on the continent before the German army overran France. Accordingly, they discounted the British opposition which their attack on France and Belgium would elicit: Schlieffen declared that if the British army landed, it would be "securely billeted" at Antwerp or "arrested" by the German armies, [138] while Moltke said he hoped that it would land so that the German army "could take care of it." [139] In accordance with their "bandwagon" worldview, German leaders also hoped that German power might cow Britain into neutrality; or that Britain might hesitate before entering the war, and then might quit in discouragement once the French were beaten—Schlieffen expected that, "If the battle [in France] goes in favor of the Germans, the English are likely to abandon their enterprise as hopeless"—which led them to further discount the extra political costs of attacking westward. [140]

Given these four assumptions, an attack westward, even one through Belgium which provoked British intervention, was the most sensible thing for Germany to do. Each assumption, in turn, was a manifestation of the belief that the offense was strong.

Thus while the Schlieffen Plan has been widely criticized for its political and military naiveté, it would have been a prudent plan had Germans actually lived in the offense-dominant world they imagined. Under these circumstances quick mobilization would have in fact given them a chance to win a decisive victory during their window of opportunity, and if they had failed to exploit this window by attacking, they would eventually have lost; the risk of standing on the defense in the West in hopes that France would not fight would have been too great; and the invasion of France and Belgium would have been worth the price, because British power probably could not have affected the outcome of the war.

Thus the belief in the power of the offense was the linchpin which held Schlieffen's logic together, and the main criticisms which can be levelled at the German war plan flow from the falsehood of this belief. German interests would have been better served by a limited, flexible, east-only plan which conformed to the defensive realities of 1914. Moreover, had Germany adopted such a plan, the First World War might well have been confined to Eastern Europe, never becoming a world war.

"Mobilization Means War"

"Mobilization meant war" in 1914 because mobilization meant war to Germany: the German war plan mandated that special units of the German standing army would attack Belgium and Luxemburg immediately after mobilization was ordered, and long before it was completed. (In fact Germany invaded Luxemburg on August 1, the same day on which it ordered full mobilization.) Thus Germany had no pure "mobilization" plan, but rather had a "mobilization and attack" plan under which mobilizing and attacking would be undertaken simultaneously. As a result, Europe would cascade into war if any European state mobilized in a manner which eventually forced German mobilization.

This melding of mobilization and attack in Germany reflected two decisions to which I have already alluded. First, Germans believed that they would lose their chance for victory and create a grave danger for themselves if they gave the Entente time to mobilize its superior numbers. In German eyes, German defenses would be too weak to defeat this superiority. As one German apologist later argued, "Germany could never with success have warded off numerically far superior opponents by means of a defensive war against a mobilized Europe" had it mobilized and stood in place. Hence it was "essential for the Central Powers to begin hostilities as soon as possible" following mobilization.[141] Likewise, during the July crisis, Jagow explained that Germany must attack in response to Russian mobilization because "we are obliged to act as fast as possible before Russia has the time to mobilize her army."[142]

Second, the German war plan depended on the quick seizure of Liège Germany could only secure Liège quickly if German troops arrived before Belgium prepared its defense, and this in turn depended on achieving surprise against Belgium. Accordingly, German military planners enshrouded the planned Liège attack in such dark secrecy that Bethmann Hollweg, Admiral Tirpitz, and possibly even the Kaiser were unaware of it.[143] They also felt compelled to strike as soon as mobilization was authorized, both because Belgium would strengthen the defenses of Liège as a normal part of the Belgian mobilization which German mobilization would engender, and because otherwise Belgium eventually might divine German intentions towards Liège and focus upon preparing its defense and destroying the critical bridges and tunnels which it controlled.

Both of these decisions in turn reflected German faith in the power of the offense, and were not appropriate to a defense-dominant world. Had Germans recognized the actual power of the defense, they might have recognized that neither Germany nor its

enemies could win decisively even by exploiting a fleeting material advantage, and decided instead to mobilize without attacking. The tactical windows that drove Germany
to strike in 1914 were a mirage, as events demonstrated during 1914–1918, and Germans would have known this in advance had they understood the power of the defense.
Likewise, the Liège *coup de main* was an artifact of Schlieffen's offensive plan; if the Germans had stuck with the elder Moltke's plan, they could have abandoned both the Liège
attack and the compulsion to strike quickly which it helped to engender.

Brinkmanship and *Faits Accomplis*

Two *faits accomplis* by the Central Powers set the stage for the outbreak of the war: the
Austrian ultimatum to Serbia on July 23, and the Austrian declaration of war against
Serbia on July 28. The Central Powers also planned to follow these with a third *fait accompli,* by quickly smashing Serbia on the battlefield before the Entente could intervene. These plans and actions reflected the German strategy for the crisis: "*fait accompli*
and then friendly towards the Entente, the shock can be endured," as Kurt Riezler had
summarized.[144]

This *fait accompli* strategy deprived German leaders of warning that their actions
would plunge Germany into a world war, by depriving the Entente of the chance to
warn Germany that it would respond if Austria attacked Serbia. It also deprived diplomats of the chance to resolve the Austro-Serbian dispute in a manner acceptable to Russia. Whether this affected the outcome of the crisis depends on German intentions—if
Germany sought a pretext for a world war, then this missed opportunity had no importance, but if it preferred the status quo to world war, as I believe it narrowly did,
then the decision to adopt *fait accompli* tactics was a crucial step on the road to war. Had
Germany not done so, it might have recognized where its policies led before it took irrevocable steps, and have drawn back.

The influence of the cult of the offensive is seen both in the German adoption of
this *fait accompli* strategy and in the disastrous scope of the results which followed in its
train. Some Germans, such as Kurt Riezler, apparently favored brinkmanship and *fait
accompli* diplomacy as a means of peaceful expansion.[145] Others probably saw it as a
means to provoke a continental war. In either case it reflected a German willingness to
trade peace for territory, which reflected German expansionism—which in turn
reflected security concerns fuelled by the cult of the offensive. Even those who saw *faits
accomplis* as tools of peaceful imperialism recognized their risks, believing that necessity
justified the risk. Thus Riezler saw the world in Darwinistic terms: "each people wants
to grow, expand, dominate and subjugate others without end . . . until the world has
become an organic unity under [single] domination."[146] *Faits accomplis* were dangerous
tools whose adoption reflected the dangerous circumstances which Germans believed
they faced.

The cult of the offensive also stiffened the resistance of the Entente to the Austro-
German *fait accompli,* by magnifying the dangers they believed it posed to their own security.[147] Thus Russian leaders believed that Russian security would be directly jeop-
ardized if Austria crushed Serbia, because they valued the power which Serbia added to
their alliance, and because they feared a domino effect, running to Constantinople and
beyond, if Serbia were overrun. Sazonov believed that Serbian and Bulgarian military
power was a vital Russian resource, "five hundred thousand bayonets to guard the Balkans" which "would bar the road forever to German penetration, Austrian invasion."[148] If this asset were lost, Russia's defense of its own territories would be jeopard-
ized by the German approach to Constantinople: Sazonov warned the Czar, "First

Serbia would be gobbled up; then will come Bulgaria's turn, and then we shall have her on the Black Sea." This would be "the death-warrant of Russia" since in such an event "the whole of southern Russia would be subject to [Germany]."[149]

Similar views could be found in France. During the July crisis one French observer warned that French and Serbian security were closely intertwined, and the demise of Serbia would directly threaten French security:

> To do away with Serbia means to double the strength which Austria can send against Russia: to double Austro-Hungarian resistance to the Russian Army means to enable Germany to send some more army corps against France. For every Serbian soldier killed by a bullet on the Morava one more Prussian soldier can be sent to the Mosselle. . . . It is for us to grasp this truth and draw the consequences from it before disaster overtakes Serbia.[150]

These considerations helped spur the Russian and French decisions to begin military preparations on July 25, which set in train a further sequence of events: German preliminary preparations, which were detected and exaggerated by French and Russian officials, spurring them on to further measures, which helped spur the Germans to their decision to mobilize on July 30. The effects of the original *fait accompli* rippled outward in ever-wider circles, because the reactions of each state perturbed the safety of others—forcing them to react or preempt, and ultimately forcing Germany to launch a world war which even it preferred to avoid.

Had Europe known that, in reality, the defense dominated, these dynamics might have been dampened: the compulsion to resort to *faits accomplis,* the scope of the dangers they raised for others, and the rippling effects engendered by others' reactions all would have been lessened. States still might have acted as they did, but they would have been less pressured in this direction.

Problems of Alliances: Unconditionality and Ambiguity

Two aspects of the European alliance system fostered the outbreak of World War I and helped spread the war. First, both alliances had an unconditional, offensive character—allies supported one another unreservedly, regardless of whether their behavior was defensive or provocative. As a result a local war would tend to spread throughout Europe. And second, German leaders were not convinced that Britain would fight as an Entente member, which encouraged Germany to confront the Entente. In both cases the cult of the offensive contributed to the problem.

Unconditional ("Tight") Alliances Many scholars contend that the mere existence of the Triple Alliance and the Triple Entente caused and spread the war. Sidney Fay concluded, "The greatest single underlying cause of the War was the system of secret alliance," and Raymond Aron argued that the division of Europe into two camps "made it inevitable that any conflict involving two great powers would bring general war."[151] But the problem with the alliances of 1914 lay less with their existence than with their nature. A network of defensive alliances, such as Bismarck's alliances of the 1880s, would have lowered the risk of war by facing aggressors with many enemies, and by making status quo powers secure in the knowledge that they had many allies. Wars also would have tended to remain localized, because the allies of an aggressor would have stood aside from any war that aggressor had provoked. Thus the unconditional nature of alliances rather than their mere existence was the true source of their danger in 1914.

The Austro-German alliance was offensive chiefly and simply because its members had compatible aggressive aims. Moreover, German and Russian mobilization plans left their neighbors no choice but to behave as allies by putting them all under threat of attack. But the Entente also operated more unconditionally, or "tightly," because Britain and France failed to restrain Russia from undertaking mobilization measures during the July crisis. This was a failure in alliance diplomacy, which in turn reflected constraints imposed upon the Western allies by the offensive assumptions and preparations with which they had to work.

First, they were hamstrung by the offensive nature of Russian military doctrine, which left them unable to demand that Russia confine itself to defensive preparations. All Russian preparations were inherently offensive, because Russian war plans were offensive. This put Russia's allies in an "all or nothing" situation—either they could demand that Russia stand unprepared, or they could consent to provocative preparations. Thus the British ambassador to St. Petersburg warned that Britain faced a painful decision, to "choose between giving Russia our active support or renouncing her friendship."[152] Had Russia confined itself to preparing its own defense, it would have sacrificed its Balkan interests by leaving Austria free to attack Serbia, and this it would have been very reluctant to do. However, the British government was probably willing to sacrifice Russia's Balkan interests to preserve peace;[153] what Britain was unable to do was to frame a request to Russia which would achieve this, because there was no obvious class of defensive activity that it could demand. Edward Grey, the British Foreign Secretary, wrote later:

> I felt impatient at the suggestion that it was for me to influence or restrain Russia. I could do nothing but express pious hopes in general terms to Sazonov. If I were to address a direct request to him that Russia should not mobilize, I knew his reply: Germany was much more ready for war than Russia; it was a tremendous risk for Russia to delay her mobilization. . . . I did most honestly feel that neither Russian nor French mobilization was an unreasonable or unnecessary precaution.[154]

One sees in this statement a losing struggle to cope with the absence of defensive options. Russia was threatened, and must mobilize. How could Britain object?

Britain and France were also constrained by their dependence upon the strength and unity of the Entente for their own security, which limited their ability to make demands on Russia. Because they feared they might fracture the Entente if they pressed Russia too hard, they tempered their demands to preserve the alliance. Thus Poincaré wrote later that France had been forced to reconcile its efforts to restrain Russia with the need to preserve the Franco-Russian alliance, "the break up of which would leave us in isolation at the mercy of our rivals."[155] Likewise Winston Churchill recalled that "the one thing [the Entente states] would not do was repudiate each other. To do this might avert the war for the time being. It would leave each of them to face the next crisis alone. They did not dare to separate."[156] These fears were probably overdrawn, since Russia had no other option than alliance with the other Entente states, but apparently they affected French and British behavior.[157] This in turn reflected the assumption in France and Britain that the security of the Entente members was closely interdependent.

French leaders also felt forced in their own interests to aid Russia if Russia embroiled itself with Germany, because French security depended on the maintenance of Russian power. This in turn undermined the French ability to credibly threaten to discipline a provocative Russia. Thus the British ambassador to Paris reflected French views when he cabled that he could not imagine that France would remain quiescent during a

Russo–German war, because "If [the] French undertook to remain so, the Germans would first attack [the] Russians and, if they defeated them, they would then turn round on the French."[158] This prospect delimited French power to restrain Russian conduct.

Third, British leaders were unaware that German mobilization meant war, hence that peace required Britain to restrain Russia from mobilizing first, as well as attacking. As a result, they took a more relaxed view of Russian mobilization than they otherwise might, while frittering away their energies on schemes to preserve peace which assumed that war could be averted even after the mobilizations began.[159] This British ignorance reflected German failure to explain clearly to the Entente that mobilization did indeed mean war—German leaders had many opportunities during the July crisis to make this plain, but did not do so.[160] We can only guess why Germany was silent, but German desire to avoid throwing a spotlight on the Liège operation probably played a part, leading German soldiers to conceal the plan from German civilians, which led German civilians to conceal the political implications of the plan from the rest of Europe.[161] Thus preemptive planning threw a shroud of secrecy over military matters, which obscured the mechanism that would unleash the war and rendered British statesmen less able to wield British power effectively for peace by obscuring what it was that Britain had to do.

Lastly, the nature of German war plans empowered Russia to involve France, and probably Britain also, in war, since Germany would be likely to start any eastern war by attacking westward, as Russian planners were aware. Hence France and Britain would probably have to fight for Russia even if they preferred to stand aside, because German planners assumed that France would fight eventually and planned accordingly, and the plans they drew would threaten vital British interests. We have no direct evidence that Russian policies were emboldened by these considerations, but it would be surprising if they never occurred to Russian leaders.

These dynamics reflected the general tendency of alliances toward tightness and offensiveness in an offense-dominant world. Had Europe known that the defense had the advantage, the British and French could have more easily afforded to discipline Russia in the interest of peace, and this might have affected Russian calculations. Had Russia had a defensive military strategy, its allies could more easily and legitimately have asked it to confine itself to defensive preparations. Had British leaders better understood German war plans, they might have known to focus their efforts on preventing Russian mobilization. And had German plans been different, Russian leaders would have been more uncertain that Germany would entangle the Western powers in eastern wars, and perhaps proceeded more cautiously.

The importance of the failure of the Western powers to restrain Russia can be exaggerated, since Russia was not the chief provocateur in the July crisis. Moreover, too much can be made of factors which hamstrung French restraint of Russia, since French desire to prevent war was tepid at best, so French inaction probably owed as much to indifference as inability. Nevertheless, Russian mobilization was an important step toward a war which Britain, if not France, urgently wanted to prevent; hence, to that extent, the alliance dynamics which allowed it helped bring on the war.

The Ambiguity of British Policy   The British government is often accused of causing the war by failing to warn Germany that Britain would fight. Thus Albertini concludes that "to act as Grey did was to allow the catastrophe to happen,"[162] and Germans themselves later argued that the British had led them on, the Kaiser complaining of "the grossest deception" by the British.[163]

The British government indeed failed to convey a clear threat to the Germans until after the crisis was out of control, and the Germans apparently were misled by this. Jagow declared on July 26 that "we are sure of England's neutrality," while during the war the Kaiser wailed, "If only someone had told me beforehand that England would take up arms against us!"[164] However, this failure was not entirely the fault of British leaders; it also reflected their circumstances. First, they apparently felt hamstrung by the lack of a defensive policy option. Grey voiced fear that if he stood too firmly with France and Russia, they would grow too demanding, while Germany would feel threatened, and "Such a menace would but stiffen her attitude."[165]

Second, British leaders were unaware of the nature of the German policy to which they were forced to react until very late, which left them little time in which to choose and explain their response. Lulled by the Austro-German *fait accompli* strategy, they were unaware until July 23 that a crisis was upon them. On July 6, Arthur Nicolson, undersecretary of the British foreign office, cheerfully declared, "We have no very urgent and pressing question to preoccupy us in the rest of Europe."[166] They also were apparently unaware that a continental war would begin with a complete German conquest of Belgium, thanks to the dark secrecy surrounding the Liège operation. Britain doubtless would have joined the war even if Germany had not invaded Belgium, but the Belgian invasion provoked a powerful emotional response in Britain which spurred a quick decision on August 4. This reaction suggests that the British decision would have been clearer to the British, hence to the Germans, had the nature of the German operation been known in advance.

Thus the British failure to warn Germany was due as much to German secrecy as to British indecision. Albertini's condemnation of Grey seems unfair: governments cannot easily take national decisions for war in less than a week in response to an uncertain provocation. The ambiguity of British policy should be recognized as an artifact of the secret styles of the Central Powers, which reflected the competitive politics and preemptive military doctrines of the times.

Why So Many "Blunders"?

Historians often ascribe the outbreak of the war to the blunders of a mediocre European leadership. Barbara Tuchman describes the Russian Czar as having "a mind so shallow as to be all surface," and Albertini refers to the "untrained, incapable, dull-witted Bethmann-Hollweg," the "mediocrity of all the personages" in the German government, and the "short-sighted and unenlightened" Austrians. Ludwig Reiners devotes a chapter to "Berchtold's Blunders"; Michael Howard notes the "bland ignorance among national leaders" of defense matters; and Oron Hale claims that "the men who directed international affairs in 1914 were at the lowest level of competence and ability in several decades."[167]

Statesmen often did act on false premises or fail to anticipate the consequences of their actions during the July crisis. For instance, Russian leaders were initially unaware that a partial mobilization would impede a later general mobilization;[168] they probably exaggerated the military importance of mobilizing against Austria quickly;[169] they falsely believed Germany would acquiesce to their partial mobilization; they probably exaggerated the significance of the Austrian bombardment of Belgrade;[170] they falsely believed a general Russian mobilization could be concealed from Germany; and they mobilized without fully realizing that for Germany "mobilization meant war."[171]

German leaders encouraged Russia to believe that Germany would tolerate a partial Russian mobilization, and failed to explain to Entente statesmen that mobilization meant war, leading British and Russian leaders to assume that it did not.[172] They also badly misread European political sentiment, hoping that Italy, Sweden, Rumania, and even Japan would fight with the Central Powers, and that Britain and Belgium would stand aside.[173] For their part, Britain and Italy failed to warn Germany of their policies; and Britain acquiesced to Russian mobilization, apparently without realizing that Russian mobilization meant German mobilization, which meant war. Finally, intelligence mistakes on both sides made matters worse. Russian leaders exaggerated German and Austrian mobilization measures, some German reports exaggerated Russian mobilizations, and French officials exaggerated German measures, which helped spur both sides to take further measures.[174]

What explains this plethora of blunders and accidents? Perhaps Europe was unlucky in the leaders it drew, but conditions in 1914 also made mistakes easy to make and hard to undo. Because secrecy was tight and *faits accomplis* were the fashion, facts were hard to acquire. Because windows were large and preemption was tempting, mistakes provoked rapid, dramatic reactions that quickly made the mistake irreversible. Statesmen seem like blunderers in retrospect partly because the international situation in 1914 was especially demanding and unforgiving of error. Historians castigate Grey for failing to rapidly take drastic national decisions under confusing and unexpected circumstances in the absence of domestic political consensus, and criticize Sazonov for his shaky grasp of military details on July 28 which no Russian civilian had had in mind five days earlier. The standard implicit in these criticisms is too stiff—statecraft seldom achieves such speed and precision. The blame for 1914 lies less with the statesmen of the times than with the conditions of the times and the severe demands these placed on statesmen.

Blamecasting

The explosive conditions created by the cult of the offensive made it easier for Germany to spark war without being blamed, by enabling that country to provoke its enemies to take defensive or preemptive steps which confused the question of responsibility for the war. German advocates of preventive war believed that Germany had to avoid blame for its outbreak, to preserve British neutrality and German public support for the war. Moreover, they seemed confident that the onus for war *could* be substantially shifted onto their opponents. Thus Moltke counselled war but warned that "the attack must be started by the Slavs,"[175] Bethmann Hollweg decreed that "we must give the impression of being forced into war,"[176] and Admiral von Müller summarized German policy during the July crisis as being to "keep quiet, letting Russia put herself in the wrong, but then not shying away from war."[177] "It is very important that we should appear to have been provoked" in a war arising from the Balkans, wrote Jagow, for "then—but probably only then—Britain can remain neutral."[178] And as the war broke out, von Müller wrote, "The mood is brilliant. The government has succeeded very well in making us appear as the attacked."[179]

These and other statements suggest an official German hope that German responsibility could be concealed. Moreover, whatever the source of this confidence, it had a sound basis in prevailing military conditions, which blurred the distinction between offensive and defensive conduct, and forced such quick reactions to provocation that the question of "who started it?" could later be obscured. Indeed, the German "innocence campaign" during and after the war succeeded for many years partly because the war developed from a rapid and complex chemistry of provocation and response which could easily be misconstrued by a willful propagandist or a gullible historian.[180] Defenders seemed like aggressors to the untrained eye, because all defended quickly and aggressively. Jack Snyder rightly points out . . . that German war plans were poorly adapted for the strategy of brinkmanship and peaceful expansion which many Germans pursued until 1914, but prevailing European military arrangements and beliefs also facilitated the deceptions in which advocates of preventive war believed Germany had to engage.

CONCLUSION

The cult of the offensive was a major underlying cause of the war of 1914, feeding or magnifying a wide range of secondary dangers which helped pull the world to war. The causes of the war are often catalogued as an unrelated grab-bag of misfortunes which unluckily arose at the same time; but many shared a common source in the cult of the offensive, and should be recognized as its symptoms and artifacts rather than as isolated phenomena.

The consequences of the cult of the offensive are illuminated by imagining the politics of 1914 had European leaders recognized the actual power of the defense. German expansionists then would have met stronger arguments that empire was needless and impossible, and Germany could have more easily let the Russian military buildup run its course, knowing that German defenses could still withstand Russian attack. All European states would have been less tempted to mobilize first, and each could have tolerated more preparations by adversaries before mobilizing themselves, so the spiral of mobilization and counter-mobilization would have operated more slowly, if at all. If armies mobilized, they might have rushed to defend their own trenches and fortifications, instead of crossing frontiers, divorcing mobilization from war. Mobilizations could more easily have been confined to single frontiers, localizing the crisis. Britain could more easily have warned the Germans and restrained the Russians, and all statesmen could more easily have recovered and reversed mistakes made in haste or on false information. Thus the logic that led Germany to provoke the 1914 crisis would have been undermined, and the chain reaction by which the war spread outward from the Balkans would have been very improbable. In all likelihood, the Austro-Serbian conflict would have been a minor and soon-forgotten disturbance on the periphery of European politics.

This conclusion does not depend upon how one resolves the "Fischer controversy" over German prewar aims; while the outcome of the Fischer debate affects the *way* in which the cult caused the war, it does not affect the importance which the cult should be assigned. If one accepts the Fischer-Geiss-Röhl view that German aims were very aggressive, then one emphasizes the role of the cult in feeding German expansionism, German window thinking, and the German ability to catalyze a war while concealing responsibility for its by provoking a preemption by Germany's adversaries. If one believes that Germany was less aggressive, then one focuses on the role of the incentive to preempt in spurring the Russian and French decisions to mobilize, the nature of Russian and German mobilization plans, the British failure to restrain Russia and warn Germany, the scope and irreversibility of the effects of the Austro-German *fait accompli,* and the various other blunders of statesmen.[181] The cult of the offensive would play a different role in the history as taught by these two schools, but a central role in both.

The 1914 case thus supports Robert Jervis and other theorists who propose that an offense-dominant world is more dangerous, and warns both superpowers against the offensive ideas which many military planners in both countries favor. Offensive doctrines have long been dogma in the Soviet military establishment, and they are gaining adherents in the United States as well. This is seen in the declining popularity of the nuclear strategy of "assured destruction" and the growing fashionability of "counterforce" nuclear strategies,[182] which are essentially offensive in nature.[183]

The 1914 case bears directly on the debate about these counterforce strategies, warning that the dangers of counterforce include but also extend far beyond the well-known problems of "crisis instability" and preemptive war. If the superpowers achieved disarming counterforce capabilities, or if they believed they had done so, the entire political universe would be disturbed. The logic of self-protection in a counterforce world would compel much of the same behavior and produce the same phenomena that drove the world to war in 1914—dark political and military secrecy, intense competition for resources and allies, yawning windows of opportunity and vulnerability, intense arms-racing, and offensive and preemptive war plans of great scope and violence. Smaller political and military mistakes would have larger and less reversible consequences. Crises would be harder to control, since military alerts would open and close larger windows, defensive military preparations would carry larger offensive implications, and smaller provocations could spur preemptive attack. Arms control would be harder to achieve, since secrecy would impede verification and treaties which met the security requirements of both sides would be harder to frame, which would circumscribe the ability of statesmen to escape this frightful world by agreement.

"Assured destruction" leaves much to be desired as a nuclear strategy, and the world of "mutual assured destruction" ("MAD") which it fosters leaves much to be desired as well. But 1914 warns that we tamper with MAD at our peril: any exit from MAD to a counterforce world would create a much more dangerous arrangement, whose outlines we glimpsed in the First World War.

NOTES

1. Quoted in L. L. Farrar, Jr., "The Short War Illusion: The Syndrome of German Strategy, August–December 1914," *Militaergeschictliche Mitteilungen*, No. 2 (1972), p. 40.

2. On the origins of the cult of the offensive, see Jack Lewis Snyder, "Defending the Offensive: Biases in French, German, and Russian War Planning, 1870–1914" (Ph.D. dissertation, Columbia University, 1981), forthcoming as a book from Cornell University Press in 1984; . . . and my "Causes of War" (Ph.D. dissertation, University of California, Berkeley, 1984), chapter 7. On the failure of Europeans to learn defensive lessons from the wars of 1860–1914, see Jay Luvaas, *The Military Legacy of the Civil War: The European Inheritance* (Chicago: University of Chicago Press, 1959); and T. H. E. Travers, "Technology, Tactics, and Morale: Jean de Bloch, the Boer War, and British Military Theory, 1900–1914," *Journal of Modern History*, Vol. 51 (June 1979), pp. 264–286. Also relevant is Bernard Brodie, *Strategy in the Missile Age* (Princeton: Princeton University Press, 1965), pp. 42–52.

A related work which explores the sources of offensive and defensive doctrines before World War II is Barry R. Posen, *The Sources of Military Doctrine: France, Britain, and Germany Between the World Wars* (Ithaca: Cornell University Press, 1984), pp. 47–51, 67–74, and passim.

3. Gerhard Ritter, *The Schlieffen Plan: Critique of a Myth*, trans. Andrew and Eva Wilson, with a Foreword by B. H. Liddell Hart (London: Oswald Wolff, 1958, reprint ed., Westport, Conn.: Greenwood Press, 1979), p. 100; and Friedrich von Bernhardi, *How Germany Makes War* (New York: George H. Doran Co., 1914), pp. 153, 155.

4. Imanuel Geiss, ed., *July 1914: The Outbreak of the First World War: Selected Documents* (New York: W. W. Norton, 1967), p. 357; and Wallace Notestein and Elmer E. Stoll, eds., *Conquest and Kultur: Aims of the Germans in Their Own Words* (Washington, D.C.: U.S. Government Printing Office, 1917), p. 43. Similar ideas developed in the German navy; see Holger H. Herwig, *Politics of Frustration: The United States in German Naval Planning, 1889–1941* (Boston: Little, Brown & Co., 1976), pp. 42–66.

5. B. H. Liddell Hart, *Through the Fog of War* (New York: Random House, 1938), p. 57.

6. In 1912, quoted in John Ellis, *The Social History of the Machine Gun* (New York: Pantheon, 1975), pp. 53–54.

7. Barbara Tuchman, *The Guns of August* (New York: Dell, 1962), p. 51.

8. In 1912, quoted in John M. Cairns, "International Politics and the Military Mind: The Case of the French Republic, 1911–1914," *The Journal of Modern History,* Vol. 25, No. 3 (September 1953), p. 282.

9. On the offensive in French prewar thought, see B. H. Liddell Hart, "French Military Ideas before the First World War," in Martin Gilbert, ed., *A Century of Conflict, 1850–1950* (London: Hamilton Hamish, 1966), pp. 135–148.

10. Richard D. Challener, *The French Theory of the Nation in Arms, 1866–1939* (New York: Columbia University Press, 1955), p. 81. Likewise, Joffre later explained that Plan XVII, his battle plan for 1914, was less a plan for battle than merely a plan of "concentration. . . . I adopted no preconceived idea, other than a full determination to take the offensive with all my forces assembled." Theodore Ropp, *War in the Modern World,* rev. ed. (New York: Collier, 1962), p. 229.

11. In 1913 and 1914, quoted in Travers, "Technology, Tactics, and Morale," p. 275.

12. In 1909, quoted in D. C. B. Lieven, *Russia and the Origins of the First World War* (New York: St. Martin's Press, 1983), p. 113.

13. See Tuchman, *Guns of August,* pp. 127–131.

14. Marshall Joffre, *Mémories du Maréchel Joffre* (Paris: Librarie Plon, 1932), p. 33. Joffre speaks of "le culte de l'offensive" and "d'une 'mystique de l'offensive'" of "le caractère un peu irraisonné."

15. Ropp, *War in the Modern World,* p. 218.

16. Ibid., p. 203. See also Bernhardi, *How Germany Makes War,* p. 154.

17. Captain Georges Gilbert, quoted in Snyder, "Defending the Offensive," pp. 80–81.

18. The *Field Service Regulations* of 1909 and Colonel Kiggell, quoted in Travers, "Technology, Tactics, and Morale," pp. 273, 276–277.
Even when European officers recognized the new tactical power of the defense, they often resisted the conclusion that the defender would also hold the strategic advantage. Thus Bernhardi wrote that while "the defense as a form of fighting is stronger than the attack," it remained true that "in the conduct of war as a whole the offensive mode of action is by far superior to the defensive mode, especially under modern conditions." Bernhardi, *How Germany Makes War,* p. 155. See also Snyder, "Defending the Offensive," pp. 152–154, 253–254; and Travers, "Technology, Tactics, and Morale," passim.

19. On these concepts, see Kenneth N. Waltz, *Theory of International Politics* (Reading, Mass.: Addison-Wesley, 1979), pp. 125–127; and Stephen M. Walt, "The Origins of Alliances" (Ph.D. dissertation, University of California, Berkeley, 1983).

20. December 2, 1914, quoted in Fritz Fischer, *War of Illusions: German Policies from 1911 to 1914,* trans. Marian Jackson, with a Foreword by Alan Bullock (New York: W. W. Norton, 1975), p. 69.

21. February 1914, quoted in Geiss, *July 1914,* p. 25. For more examples, see Fischer, *War of Illusions,* pp. 133, 227; and Wayne C. Thompson, *In the Eye of the Storm: Kurt Riezler and the Crises of Modern Germany* (Iowa City: University of Iowa Press, 1980), p. 120.

22. August 3, quoted in Bernadotte E. Schmitt, *The Coming of the War: 1914,* 2 vols. (New York: Charles Scribner's Sons, 1930), Vol. 2, p. 390n.

23. Prince Bernhard von Bülow, *Imperial Germany,* trans. Marie A. Lewenz (New York: Dodd, Mead & Co., 1915), p. 291. On international social Darwinism, see also H. W. Koch, "Social Imperialism as a Factor in the 'New Imperialism,'" in H. W. Koch, ed., *The Origins of the First World War* (London: Macmillan, 1972), pp. 329–354.

24. Joachim Remak, *The Origins of World War I, 1871–1914* (Hinsdale, Ill.: Dryden Press, 1967), p. 85. Likewise the British Colonial Secretary, Joseph Chamberlain, declared that "the tendency of the time is to throw all power into the hands of the greater empires," while the "minor kingdoms" seemed "destined to fall into a secondary and subordinate place. . . ." In 1897, quoted in Fischer, *War of Illusions,* p. 35.

25. See Robert Jervis's pathbreaking article, "Cooperation under the Security Dilemma," *World Politics,* Vol. 30, No. 2 (January 1978), pp. 167–214; and Chapter 3 of my "Causes of War." Also relevant are George H. Quester, *Offense and Defense in the International System* (New York: John Wiley & Sons, 1977); John Herz, "Idealist Internationalism and the Security Dilemma," *World Politics,* Vol. 2, No. 2 (January 1950), pp. 157, 163; and Herbert Butterfield, *History and Human Relations* (London: Collins, 1950), pp. 19–20. Applications and elaborations include: Shai Feldman, *Israeli Nuclear Deterrence* (New York: Columbia University Press, 1982); idem, "Superpower Security Guarantees in the

1980's," in *Third World Conflict and International Security, Part II,* Adelphi Paper No. 167 (London: International Institute for Strategic Studies, 1981), pp. 34–44; Barry R. Posen, "Inadvertent Nuclear War? Escalation and NATO's Northern Flank," *International Security,* Vol. 7, No. 2 (Fall 1982), pp. 28–54; Jack Lewis Snyder, "Perceptions of the Security Dilemma in 1914," in Robert Jervis and Richard Ned Lebow, eds., *Perceptions and Deterrence,* forthcoming in 1985; and Kenneth N. Waltz, *The Spread of Nuclear Weapons: More May Be Better,* Adelphi Paper No. 171 (London: International Institute for Strategic Studies, 1981). Of related interest is John J. Mearsheimer, *Conventional Deterrence* (Ithaca: Cornell University Press, 1983).

26. In a "preemptive" war, either side gains by moving first; hence, one side moves to exploit the advantage of moving first, or to prevent the other side from doing so. By contrast, in a "preventive" war, one side foresees an adverse shift in the balance of power, and attacks to avoid a more difficult fight later.

"Moving first" in a preemptive war can consist of striking first *or mobilizing* first, if mobilization sets in train events which cause war, as in 1914. Thus a war is preemptive if statesmen attack because they believe that it pays to strike first; or if they mobilize because they believe that it pays to mobilize first, even if they do not also believe that it pays to strike first, if mobilizations open "windows" which spur attacks for "preventive" reasons, or if they produce other effects which cause war. Under such circumstances war is caused by preemptive actions which are not acts of war, but which are their equivalent since they produce conditions which cause war.

A preemptive war could also involve an attack by one side and mobilization by the other —for instance, one side might mobilize to forestall an attack, or might attack to forestall a mobilization, as the Germans apparently attacked Liège to forestall Belgian preparations to defend it (see below). Thus four classes of preemption are possible: an attack to forestall an attack, an attack to forestall a mobilization, a mobilization to forestall an attack, or a mobilization to forestall a mobilization (such as the Russian mobilizations in 1914).

The size of the incentive to preempt is a function of three factors: the degree of secrecy with which each side could mobilize its forces or mount an attack; the change in the ratio of forces which a secret mobilization or attack would produce; and the size and value of the additional territory which this changed ratio would allow the attacker to conquer or defend. If secret action is impossible, or if it would not change force ratios in favor of the side moving first, or if changes in force ratios would not change relative ability to conquer territory, then there is no first-strike or first-mobilization advantage. Otherwise, states have some inducement to move first.

On preemption, see Thomas C. Schelling, *Arms and Influence* (New Haven: Yale University Press, 1966), pp. 221–259; and idem, *Strategy of Conflict* (New York: Oxford University Press, 1963), pp. 207–254.

27. In 1912, quoted in Thompson, *Eye of the Storm,* p. 42.

28. In 1912, quoted in Fischer, *War of Illusions,* p. 161.

29. V. R. Berghahn, *Germany and the Approach of War in 1914* (London: Macmillan, 1973), p. 186.

30. In 1897, quoted in Notestein and Stoll, *Conquest and Kultur,* p. 21.

31. Houston Chamberlain and Ernest Hasse, quoted in Fischer, *War of Illusions,* pp. 30, 36.

32. *Nauticus,* in 1900, quoted in Berghahn, *Germany and the Approach of War in 1914,* p. 29; and Colmar von der Goltz, quoted in Notestein and Stoll, *Conquest and Kultur,* p. 119.

33. Otto Richard Tannenberg, in 1911, quoted in Notestein and Stoll, *Conquest and Kultur,* p. 53.

34. Crown Prince Wilhelm, in 1913, quoted in ibid., p. 44. Likewise Walter Rathenau complained of German "frontiers which are too long and devoid of natural protection, surrounded and hemmed in by rivals, with a short coastline. . . ." In July 1914, quoted in Fischer, *War of Illusions,* p. 450.

35. Hermann Vietinghoff-Scheel, in 1912, quoted in William Archer, ed., *501 Gems of German Thought* (London: T. Fisher Unwin, 1916), p. 46.

36. Albrecht Wirth, in 1901, quoted in Notestein and Stoll, *Conquest and Kultur,* p. 52.

37. Quoted in Tuchman, *Guns of August,* p. 142.

38. Von Loebell, quoted in Fischer, *War of Illusions,* p. 543.

39. The English Military Attaché, quoted in Luigi Albertini, *The Origins of the War of 1914,* 3 vols., trans. and ed. Isabella M. Massey (London: Oxford University Press, 1952–57; reprint ed., Westport, Conn.: Greenwood Press,

1980), Vol. 3, p. 171; and Lerchenfeld, the Bavarian ambassador in Berlin, quoted in Fischer, *War of Illusions*, p. 503.

40. In 1913, quoted in Fischer, *War of Illusions*, p. 227.

41. In 1913, quoted in Albertini, *Origins of the War*, Vol. 3, p. 441. See also Bernhardi's dismissal of the balance of power, in Friedrich von Bernhardi, *Germany and the Next War*, trans. Allen H. Powles (New York: Longmans, Green & Co., 1914), p. 21.

42. In 1887, quoted in Fischer, *War of Illusions*, p. 45.

43. In 1911, quoted in Tuchman, *Guns of August*, p. 26.

44. Jervis, "Cooperation under the Security Dilemma," p. 191.

45. Examples are: Arno Mayer, "Domestic Causes of the First World War," in Leonard Krieger and Fritz Stern, eds., *The Responsibility of Power* (New York: Macmillan, 1968), pp. 286–300; Berghahn, *Germany and the Approach of War*; Fischer, *War of Illusions*, pp. 257–258; and Imanuel Geiss, *German Foreign Policy, 1871–1914* (Boston: Routledge & Kegan Paul, 1976). A criticism is Marc Trachtenberg, "The Social Interpretation of Foreign Policy," *Review of Politics*, Vol. 40, No. 3 (July 1978), pp. 341–350.

46. In 1910, quoted in Geiss, *German Foreign Policy*, p. 126.

47. Admiral von Müller, quoted in Fritz Stern, *The Failure of Illiberalism* (London: Allen & Unwin, 1972), p. 94.

48. In 1909, quoted in Konrad H. Jarausch, *The Enigmatic Chancellor: Bethmann Hollweg and the Hubris of Imperial Germany* (New Haven: Yale University Press, 1973), p. 119. See also ibid., p. 152; and Geiss, *German Foreign Policy*, pp. 135–137. As Jules Cambon, French ambassador to Germany, perceptively remarked: "It is false that in Germany the nation is peaceful and the government bellicose—the exact opposite is true." In 1911, quoted in Jarausch, *Enigmatic Chancellor*, p. 125.

49. See Eugen Weber, *The Nationalist Revival in France, 1905–1914* (Berkeley and Los Angeles: University of California Press, 1968), passim; and Snyder, "Defending the Offensive," pp. 32–33.

50. By the Russian ambassador to Paris, A. P. Izvolsky, quoted in Schmitt, *Coming of the War*, Vol. 1, p. 21.

51. *La France Militaire*, in 1913, quoted in Weber, *Nationalist Revival in France*, p. 127.

52. In 1913, quoted in L. C. F. Turner, *Origins of the First World War* (London: Edward Arnold, 1970), p. 53.

53. Serge Sazonov, *Fateful Years, 1909–1916* (London: Jonathan Cape, 1928), p. 179. See also Schmitt, *Coming of the War*, Vol. 1, p. 87.

54. Sazonov, *Fateful Years*, pp. 191, 204.

55. Izvolsky, in 1909, quoted in Schmitt, *Coming of the War*, Vol. 1, p. 129.

56. Sazonov, in 1913, quoted in ibid., p. 135.

57. *Sbornik glavnogo upravleniia general' nogo shtaba*, the secret magazine of the Russian general staff, in 1913, quoted in William C. Fuller, "The Russian Empire and Its Potential Enemies" (manuscript, 1980), p. 21. British resistance was also driven by security concerns: during the July crisis the London *Times* warned that "the ruin of France or the Low Countries would be the prelude to our own," while other interventionists warned that Antwerp in German hands would be a "pistol pointed at the heart of England," and that the German threat to France and the Low Countries created "a deadly peril for ourselves." The *Times* on August 4, quoted in Geoffrey Marcus, *Before the Lamps Went Out* (Boston: Little, Brown, 1965), p. 305; and the *Pall Mall Gazette* and James Gavin, on July 29 and August 2, quoted in ibid., pp. 243, 268.

58. Suggesting that World War I was preemptive are: Herman Kahn, *On Thermonuclear War* 2nd ed. (New York: The Free Press, 1969), pp. 359–362; Schelling, *Arms and Influence*, pp. 223–224; Jervis, "Cooperation under the Security Dilemma," pp. 191–192; Quester, *Offense and Defense*, pp. 110–111; Richard Ned Lebow, *Between Peace and War: The Nature of International Crisis* (Baltimore, Md.: The Johns Hopkins University Press, 1981), pp. 238–242.

59. July 29, quoted in Albertini, *Origins*, Vol. 2, p. 670.

60. July 29, from Marshall Joffre, *The Personal Memoirs of Marshall Joffre*, 2 vols., trans. T. Bentley Mott (New York: Harper & Brothers, 1932), Vol. 1, p. 125.

61. Eyre Crowe, on July 27, quoted in Geiss, *July 1914*, p. 251.

62. Kraft zu Hohenlohe-Ingelfingen, in 1898, quoted in Ropp, *War in the Modern World*, p. 203.

63. To Bethmann Hollweg, on July 29, quoted in Geiss, *July 1914*, p. 284.

64. Quoted in Schmitt, *Coming of the War,* Vol. 2, p. 196.

65. Ibid., p. 265n.

66. The *Reinisch-Westfälische Zeitung,* July 31, quoted in Jonathan French Scott, *The Five Weeks* (New York: John Day Co., 1927), p. 146.

Likewise after the war General von Kluck, who commanded the right wing of the German army in the march on Paris, claimed that if the German army had been mobilized and deployed "three days earlier, a more sweeping victory and decisive result would probably have been gained" against France, and Admiral Tirpitz complained that German diplomats had given Britain and Belgium several crucial days warning of the German attack on July 29, which "had an extraordinarily unfavorable influence on the whole course of the war." A delay of "only a few days" in the preparation of the British expeditionary force "might have been of the greatest importance to us." Schmitt, *Coming of the War,* Vol. 2, p. 148n.; and Albertini, *Origins,* Vol. 3, p. 242n.

A more relaxed opinion was expressed by the Prussian war minister, General Falkenhayn, who seemed to feel that it would be acceptable if German mobilization "follows two or three days later than the Russian and Austrian," since it "will still be completed more quickly than theirs." Schmitt, *Coming of the War,* Vol. 2, p. 147. However, he also expressed himself in favor of preemption at other junctures. See ibid., p. 297; and Berghahn, *Germany and the Approach of War,* p. 203.

67. To Sazonov, July 30, quoted in Geiss, *July 1914,* p. 311.

68. To Sazonov, July 30, quoted in Albertini, *Origins,* Vol. 2, p. 566.

69. August 1, Poincaré reporting Joffre's view, quoted in Albertini, *Origins,* Vol. 3, p. 100.

70. August 1, quoted in Schmitt, *Coming of the War,* Vol. 2, p. 264.

71. August 1, quoted in Albertini, *Origins,* Vol. 3, p. 167.

72. Ritter, *The Schlieffen Plan,* p. 166. On the Liège attack, see also Snyder, "Defending the Offensive," pp. 203, 285–287.

73. Paleologue's diary, quoted in Albertini, *Origins,* Vol. 2, p. 619.

74. Sazonov, *Fateful Years,* pp. 202–203. The memorandum of the day of the Russian foreign ministry for July 29 records that Russian officials had considered whether Germany seri-ously sought peace, or whether its diplomacy "was only intended to lull us to sleep and so to postpone the Russian mobilization and thus gain time wherein to make corresponding preparations." Quoted in Geiss, *July 1914,* pp. 296–297.

75. Sazonov, *Fateful Years,* p. 188.

76. A. M. Zayonchovsky, quoted in Lieven, *Russia and the Origins of the First World War,* p. 149.

77. Albertini, *Origins,* Vol. 2, p. 624.

78. Ibid., quoting Taube who quoted Nolde.

79. Ibid., p. 573. See also p. 584, suggesting that "Sazonov was such a greenhorn in military matters as to imagine the thing could be done, and was only convinced of the contrary when on 31 July he saw the red notices, calling up reservists, posted up in the streets of St. Petersburg." This point "provides the key to many mysteries" (p. 624).

80. For July 31, in Geiss, *July 1914,* p. 326.

81. Paleologue, July 25, in Albertini, *Origins,* Vol. 2, p. 591.

82. Paleologue, July 26, in ibid., p. 592.

83. Ibid., p. 620.

84. August 1, quoted in Joffre, *Personal Memoirs,* p. 128.

85. July 29, quoted in ibid., p. 120.

86. Ibid., p. 127.

87. Cambon dispatch to Paris, July 21, quoted in ibid., p. 119. Joffre records that Cambon's telegram, which mysteriously did not arrive in Paris until July 28, convinced him that "for seven days at least the Germans had been putting into effect the plan devised for periods of political tension and that our normal methods of investigation had not revealed this fact to us. Our adversaries could thus reach a condition of mobilization that was almost complete," reflecting Joffre's assumption that secret German measures were possible.

88. Moltke, quoted in Ritter, *The Schlieffen Plan,* p. 166.

89. During the July crisis, adversaries actually detected signs of most major secret mobilization activity in roughly 6–18 hours, and took responsive decisions in 1–2 days. Accordingly, the maximum "first mobilization advantage" which a state could gain by forestalling an adversary who otherwise would have begun mobilizing first was roughly 2–4 days. Orders for Russian preliminary mobilization measures were issued in sequential telegrams transmitted be-

tween 4:00 p.m. on July 25 and 3:26 a.m. on July 26; Berlin received its first reports of these measures early on July 26; and at 4:00 p.m. on July 27 the German intelligence board concluded that Russian premobilization had in fact begun, for a lag of roughly one and one-half to two days between the issuance of orders and their definite detection. Sidney B. Fay, *The Origins of the World War,* 2 vols., 2nd ed. rev. (New York: Free Press, 1966), Vol. 2, pp. 310–315; and Ulrich Trumpener, "War Premeditated? German Intelligence Operations in July 1914," *Central European History,* Vol. 9 (1976), pp. 67–70. Full Russian mobilization was ordered at 6:00 p.m. on July 30, first rumors reached Berlin very late on July 30, more definite but inconclusive information was received around 7:00 a.m. July 31, reliable confirmation was received at 11:45 a.m., and German preliminary mobilization was ordered at 1:00 p.m., for a lag of roughly 20 hours. Fay, *Origins of the World War,* Vol. 2, p. 473; Schmitt, *Coming of the War,* Vol. 2, pp. 211–212, 262–265; and Trumpener, "War Premeditated?," pp. 80–83. French preliminary measures were begun on July 25, expanded on July 26, further expanded on July 27, and remained substantially undetected on July 28. Secondary sources do not clarify when Germany detected French preliminary measures, but it seems that German discovery lagged roughly two days behind French actions. Schmitt, *Coming of the War,* Vol. 2, pp. 17–19; Joffre, *Personal Memoirs,* pp. 115–118; and Trumpener, "War Premeditated?," pp. 71–73. As for Liège, it was not captured as quickly as German planners had hoped, but was not properly defended when the Germans arrived, and was taken in time to allow the advance into France.

90. Albertini, *Origins,* Vol. 2, p. 491.

91. Schmitt, *Coming of the War,* Vol. 2, pp. 267–268.

92. Ibid., p. 105.

93. Albertini, *Origins,* Vol. 2, p. 529.

94. Ibid., pp. 549, 551; and Geiss, *July 1914,* pp. 262, 278, 299.

95. Von Plessen, quoted in Isabell V. Hull, *The Entourage of Kaiser Wilhelm II, 1888–1918* (New York: Cambridge University Press, 1982), p. 261. Thus Bethmann summarized German thinking when he suggested on July 8 that the Sarajevo assassination provided an opportunity either for a war which "we have the prospect of winning" or a crisis in which "we still certainly have the prospect of maneuvering the Entente

apart. . . ." Thompson, *In the Eye of the Storm,* p. 75.

96. The Russian program planned a 40 percent increase in the size of the peacetime Russian army and a 29 percent increase in the number of officers over four years. Lieven, *Russia & the Origins of the First World War,* p. 111.

97. July 18, quoted in Schmitt, *Coming of the War,* Vol. 1, p. 321.

98. June 21, quoted in Fischer, *War of Illusions,* p. 471, quoting Max Warburg.

99. July 7, quoted in ibid., p. 224, quoting Riezler.

100. July 7, quoted in Jarausch, "The Illusion of Limited War," p. 57. Likewise on July 20, he expressed terror at Russia's "growing demands and colossal explosive power. In a few years she would be supreme—and Germany her first lonely victim." Quoted in Lebow, *Between Peace and War,* p. 258n.

101. Jarausch, "The Illusion of Limited War," p. 48. Likewise Friedrich Thimme quoted Bethmann during the war: "He also admits that our military are quite convinced that they could still be victorious in the war, but that in a few years time, say in 1916 after the completion of Russia's railway network, they could not. This, of course, also affected the way in which the Serbian question was dealt with." Quoted in Volker R. Berghahn and Martin Kitchen, eds., *Germany in the Age of Total War* (Totowa, N.J.: Barnes and Noble, 1981), p. 45.

102. Fischer, *War of Illusions,* p. 162.

103. Berghahn, *Germany and the Approach of War,* p. 171.

104. Geiss, *German Foreign Policy,* p. 149.

105. Berghahn, *Germany and the Approach of War,* p. 203.

106. Quoted in J. C. G. Röhl, ed., *From Bismarck to Hitler: The Problem of Continuity in German History* (London: Longman, 1970), p. 70.

107. Leuckart's summary of the views of the General Staff, quoted in Geiss, *July 1914,* p. 69. For more on advocacy of preventive war by the German army, see Martin Kitchen, *The German Officer Corps, 1890–1914* (Oxford: Clarendon Press, 1968), pp. 96–114; and Hull, *Entourage of Kaiser Wilhelm II,* pp. 236–265.

108. August 2, quoted in Fischer, *War of Illusions,* p. 403.

109. February 24, 1914, in Schmitt, *Coming of the War,* Vol. 1, p. 100n.; and Fischer, *War of Illusions,* pp. 371–272.

110. Jarausch, "Illusion of Limited War," p. 58. Earlier Bülow had explained why the Agadir crisis was an unsuitable occasion for war in similar terms: "In 1911 the situation was much worse. The complication would have begun with Britain; France would have remained passive, it would have forced us to attack and then there would have been no *causus foederis* for Austria . . . whereas Russia was obliged to join in." In 1912, quoted in Fischer, *War of Illusions,* p. 85.

111. Schmitt, *Coming of the War,* Vol. 2, p. 66n.

112. Ibid., Vol. 1, p. 324, quoting Lichnowsky, on July 6.

113. July 7, quoted in Geiss, *July 1914,* pp. 81, 84.

114. July 31, quoted in Schmitt, *Coming of the War,* Vol. 2, p. 218.

115. Ibid., Vol. 1, p. 372, quoting Baron von Tucher on July 18.

116. In October 1913, quoted in Gerhard Ritter, *The Sword and the Scepter: The Problem of Militarism in Germany,* 4 vols., trans. Heinz Norden (Coral Gables, Fla.: University of Miami Press, 1969–73), Vol. 2, p. 234. Likewise the *Militärisch Rundschau* argued for provoking war: "Since we shall have to accept the contest some day, let us provoke it at once." On July 15, 1914, quoted in Schmitt, *Coming of the War,* Vol. 1, p. 367. For more on preventive war and the Austrian army, see Ritter, *Sword and the Scepter,* Vol. 2, pp. 227–239.

117. Count Merey, July 29, quoted in Albertini, *Origins,* Vol. 2, p. 383.

118. Both in 1912, quoted in Jarausch, *Enigmatic Chancellor,* p. 95; and Fischer, *War of Illusions,* p. 165.

119. On the motives for the Russian buildup, see P. A. Zhilin, "Bol'shaia programma po usileniiu russkoi armii," *Voenno-istoricheskii zhurnal,* No. 7 (July 1974), pp. 90–97.

120. Tuchman, *Guns of August,* pp. 92, 99.

121. Kahn, *On Thermonuclear War,* pp. 359, 362.

122. David W. Ziegler, *War, Peace and International Politics* (Boston: Little, Brown, 1977), p. 25.

123. By Generals Yanushkevich and Sukhomlinov, according to Sazonov, quoted in Albertini, *Origins,* Vol. 2, p. 566. See also M. F. Schilling, "Introduction," in *How the War Began,* trans. W. Cyprian Bridge, with a Foreword by S. D. Sazonov (London: Allen & Unwin, 1925), pp. 16, 63.

124. On the Russian decision, see Schmitt, *Coming of the War,* Vol. 2, pp. 85–87, 94–101; and Albertini, *Origins,* Vol. 2, pp. 539–561.

125. Anton I. Denikin, *The Career of a Tsarist Officer: Memoirs, 1872–1916,* trans. Margaret Patoski (Minneapolis: University of Minnesota Press, 1975), p. 222; Albertini, *Origins,* Vol. 2, p. 559; Schilling, *How the War Began,* p. 16.

126. G. N. Trubetskoy, in 1909, quoted in Lieven, *Russia and the Origins of the First World War,* p. 96.

127. The Kiev District Staff, February 23, 1914, quoted in Fuller, "The Russian Empire and Its Potential Enemies," p. 17.

128. Albertini, *Origins,* Vol. 2, p. 559. See also Fuller, "The Russian Empire and Its Potential Enemies," p. 16.

129. In 1912, quoted in Stern, *Failure of Illiberalism,* p. 84. Likewise the Kaiser explained that security requirements compelled Germany to defend Austria: "If we are forced to take up arms it will be to help *Austria,* not only to defend ourselves against Russia but against the Slavs in general and to remain *German. . . .*" In 1912, quoted in Fischer, *War of Illusions,* pp. 190–191, emphasis in original. The German White Book also reflected this thinking, declaring that the "subjugation of all the Slavs under Russian sceptre" would render the "position of the Teutonic race in Central Europe untenable." August 3, 1914, quoted in Geiss, *German Foreign Policy,* p. 172.

130. See Schmitt, *Coming of the War,* Vol. 2, pp. 198–199; and Albertini, *Origins,* Vol. 3, pp. 7, 17–27; also Vol. 2, p. 485n. As Jagow plainly told the Russians on July 29: "If once you mobilize against Austria, then you will also take serious measures against us. . . . We are compelled to proclaim mobilization against Russia. . . ." Schmitt, *Coming of the War,* Vol. 2, p. 140.

131. See L. C. F. Turner, "The Russian Mobilization in 1914," *Journal of Contemporary History,* Vol. 3, No. 1 (January 1968), pp. 72–74. But see also Lieven, *Russia and the Origins of the First World War,* pp. 148–150.

Likewise German soldiers exaggerated the difficulties of adapting to eastward mobilization, as many observers note, e.g., Tuchman, *Guns of August,* p. 100, and Lebow, *Between Peace and War,* p. 236.

132. Assessing the Schlieffen Plan are Ritter, *The Schlieffen Plan,* and Snyder, "Defending the Offensive," pp. 189–294.

133. Bernhardi, quoted in Anon., *Germany's War Mania* (London: A. W. Shaw, 1914), p 161

134. Albertini, *Origins,* Vol. 3, p. 194. Moreover, these fears reflected views found in France. When Poincaré was asked on July 29 if he believed war could be avoided, he reportedly replied: "It would be a great pity. We should never again find conditions better." Albertini, *Origins,* Vol. 3, p. 82n. Likewise in 1912 the French General Staff concluded that a general war arising from the Balkans would leave Germany "at the mercy of the Entente" because Austrian forces would be diverted against Serbia, and "the Triple Entente would have the best chances of success and might gain a victory which would enable the map of Europe to be redrawn." Turner, *Origins* p. 36. See also the opinions of Izvolsky and Bertie in Schmitt, *Coming of the War,* Vol. 1, pp. 20–21, and Vol. 2, p. 349n.

135. Goschen, in Schmitt, *Coming of the War,* Vol. 2, p. 321.

136. Moltke, in General Ludendorff, *The General Staff and Its Problems,* trans. F. A. Holt (New York: E. P. Dutton, n.d.), Vol. 1, p. 61.

137. Geiss, *July 1914,* p. 357; and Alfred von Wegerer, *A Refutation of the Versailles War Guilt Thesis,* trans. Edwin H. Zeydel (New York: Alfred A. Knopf, 1930), p. 310.

138. Ritter, *Schlieffen Plan,* pp. 71, 161–162; and Geiss, *German Foreign Policy,* p. 101. See also Ritter, *Schlieffen Plan,* p. 161. But see also Moltke quoted in Turner, *Origins of the World War,* p. 64.

139. Ritter, *Sword and the Scepter,* Vol. 2, p. 157.

140. Ritter, *The Schlieffen Plan,* p. 163. See also Bethmann Hollweg, quoted in Fischer, *War of Illusions,* pp. 169, 186–187.

141. Von Wegerer, *Refutation,* pp. 307–309.

142. August 4, quoted in Alfred Vagts, *Defense and Diplomacy* (New York: Kings Crown Press, 1956), p. 306. Likewise Bethmann Hollweg explained that, if Russia mobilized, "we could hardly sit and talk any longer because we have to strike immediately in order to have any chance of winning at all." Fischer, *War of Illusions,* p. 484.

143. Albertini, *Origins,* Vol. 2, p. 581; Vol. 3, pp. 195, 250, 391; Ritter, *Sword and the Scepter,* Vol. 2, p. 266; and Fay, *Origins,* Vol. 1, pp. 41–42.

144. July 8, quoted in John A. Moses, *The Politics of Illusion: The Fischer Controversy in German Historiography* (London: George Prior, 1975), p. 39. Austria declared war on Serbia, as one German diplomat explained, "in order to forestall any attempt at mediation" by the Entente; and the rapid occupation of Serbia was intended to "confront the world with a '*fait accompli.*'" Tschirschky, in Schmitt, *Coming of the War,* Vol. 2, p. 5; and Jagow, in Albertini, *Origins,* Vol. 2, p. 344; see also pp. 453–460.

145. On Riezler's thought, see Moses, *Politics of Illusion,* pp. 27–44; and Thompson, *In the Eye of the Storm.*

146. Quoted in Moses, *Politics of Illusion,* pp. 28, 31. Likewise during the war Riezler wrote that unless Germany gained a wider sphere of influence in Europe "we will in the long run be crushed between the great world empires . . . Russia and England." Thompson, *In the Eye of the Storm,* p. 107.

147. I am grateful to Jack Snyder for this and related observations.

148. Schmitt, *Coming of the War,* Vol. 1, p. 131n. See also Lieven, *Russia and the Origins of the First World War,* pp. 40–41, 99–100, 147.

149. Fay, *Origins,* Vol. 2, p. 300; Sazonov, *Fateful Years,* p. 179; Schmitt, *Coming of the War,* Vol. 1, p. 87.

150. J. Herbette, July 29, in Albertini, *Origins,* Vol. 2, p. 596.

151. Fay, *Origins,* Vol. 1, p. 34; and Raymond Aron, *The Century of Total War* (Boston: Beacon Press, 1955), p. 15.

152. Buchanan, in Fay, *Origins,* Vol. 2, p. 379.

153. See Geiss, *July 1914,* p. 176; and Albertini, *Origins,* Vol. 2, p. 295.

154. Albertini, *Origins,* Vol. 2, p. 518.

155. Ibid., p. 605.

156. Winston Churchill, *The Unknown War* (New York: Charles Scribner's Sons, 1931), p. 103.

157. Thus Grey later wrote that he had feared a "diplomatic triumph on the German side and humiliation on the other as would smash the Entente, and if it did not break the Franco-Russian alliance, would leave it without spirit, a spineless and helpless thing." Likewise during July 1914 Harold Nicolson wrote: "Our attitude during the crisis will be regarded by Russia as a test and we must be careful not to alienate her." Schmitt, *Coming of the War,* Vol. 2, pp. 38, 258.

158. Bertie, on August 1, in Schmitt, *Coming of the War,* Vol. 2, p. 349n.

159. Geiss, *July 1914,* pp. 198, 212–213, 250–251; Albertini, *Origins,* Vol. 2, pp. 330–336.

160. See Albertini, *Origins,* Vol. 2, pp. 479–481; Vol. 3, pp. 41–43, 61–65. Albertini writes that European leaders "had no knowledge of what mobilization actually was . . . what consequences it brought with it, to what risks it exposed the peace of Europe. They looked on it as a measure costly, it is true, but to which recourse might be had without necessarily implying that war would follow." This reflected German policy: Bethmann's ultimatum to Russia "entirely omitted to explain that for Germany to mobilize meant to begin war," and Sazonov gathered "the distinct impression that German mobilization was not equivalent to war" from his exchanges with German officials. Vol. 2, p. 479; Vol. 3, pp. 41–43.

161. Kautsky and Albertini suggest that the German deception was intended to lull the Russians into military inaction, but it seems more likely that they sought to lull the Belgians. Albertini, *Origins,* Vol. 3, p. 43.

162. Ibid., Vol. 2, p. 644.

163. Ibid., p. 517. See also Tirpitz, quoted in ibid., Vol. 3, p. 189.

164. Ibid., Vol. 2, p. 429; and Tuchman, *Guns of August,* p. 143. See also Albertini, *Origins,* Vol. 2, pp. 514–527, 643–650; and Jarausch, "Illusion of Limited War."

165. Albertini, *Origins,* Vol. 2, p. 631; and Schmitt, *Coming of the War,* Vol. 2, p. 90.

166. Schmitt, *Coming of the War,* Vol. 1, pp. 417–418.

167. Tuchman, *Guns of August,* p. 78; Albertini, *Origins,* Vol. 2, pp. 389, 436; Vol. 3, p. 253; Ludwig Reiners, *The Lamps Went Out in Europe* (New York: Pantheon, 1955), pp. 112–122; Howard quoted in Schelling, *Arms and Influence,* p. 243; and Oron J. Hale, *The Great Illusion: 1900–1914* (New York: Harper & Row, 1971), p. 285.

168. Albertini, *Origins,* Vol. 2, pp. 295–296.

169. See Turner, *Origins of the First World War,* pp. 92–93; Albertini, *Origins,* Vol. 2, p. 409; Vol. 3, pp. 230–231; but see also Lieven, *Russia and the Origins of the First World War,* pp. 148–149.

170. Reiners, *Lamps Went Out in Europe,* p. 135; and Albertini, *Origins,* Vol. 2, p. 553.

171. Albertini, *Origins,* Vol. 2, p. 574, 579–581; Vol. 3, pp. 56, 60–65.

172. Ibid., Vol. 2, pp. 332, 479–482, 485, 499–500, 550; Vol. 3, pp. 41–43, 61–65; Geiss, *July 1914,* pp. 245, 253, 266.

173. See Albertini, *Origins,* Vol. 2, pp. 334, 673, 678; Vol. 3, p. 233; Geiss, *July 1914,* pp. 226, 255, 302, 350–353; Schmitt, *Coming of the War,* Vol. 1, pp. 72–74, 322; Vol. 2, pp. 52–55, 149, 390n. Also relevant is Albertini, *Origins,* Vol. 2, pp. 308–309, 480, 541.

174. See generally Lebow, *Between Peace and War,* pp. 238–242; and Albertini, *Origins,* Vol. 3, pp. 67–68. For details on Russia see Albertini, *Origins,* Vol. 2, pp. 499, 545–546, 549, 566–567, 570–571, 576; Schmitt, *Coming of the War,* Vol. 2, pp. 97–98, 238, 244n.; Schilling, *How the War Began,* pp. 61–62; and Sazonov, *Fateful Years,* pp. 193, 199–200, 202–203. For details on France, see Joffre, *Personal Memoirs,* Vol. 1, pp. 117–128; and Albertini, *Origins,* Vol. 2, p. 647; Vol. 3, p. 67. On Germany see Trumpener, "War Premediated?" pp. 73–74; Albertini, *Origins,* Vol. 2, pp. 529, 560, 637; Vol. 3, pp. 2–3, 6–9; and Geiss, *July 1914,* pp. 291–294.

175. In 1913, in Albertini, *Origins,* Vol. 2, p. 486.

176. On July 27, 1914 in Fischer, *War of Illusions,* p. 486.

177. On July 27, in J. C. G. Röhl, "Admiral von Müller and the Approach of War, 1911–1914," *Historical Journal,* Vol. 12, No. 4 (1969), p. 669. In the same spirit, Bernhardi (who hoped for Russian rather than British neutrality) wrote before the war that the task of German diplomacy was to spur a French attack, continuing: "[W]e must not hope to bring about this attack by waiting passively. Neither France nor Russia nor England need to attack in order to further their interests. . . . [Rather] we must initiate an active policy which, without attacking France, will so prejudice her interests or those of England that both these States would feel themselves compelled to attack us. Opportunities for such procedures are offered both in Africa and in Europe. . . ." Bernhardi, *Germany and the Next War,* p. 280.

178. In 1913, in Fischer, *War of Illusions,* p. 212.

179. Röhl, "Admiral von Müller," p. 670.

180. On this innocence campaign, see Imanuel Geiss, "The Outbreak of the First World War and German War Aims," in Walter

Laqueur and George L. Mosse, eds., *1914: The Coming of the First World War* (New York: Harper and Row, 1966), pp. 71–78.

181. A useful review of the debate about German aims is Moses, *Politics of Illusion*.

182. On the growth of offensive ideas under the Reagan Administration, see Barry R. Posen and Stephen Van Evera, "Defense Policy and the Reagan Administration: Departure from Containment," *International Security,* Vol. 8, No. 1 (Summer 1983), pp. 24–30. On counterforce strategies, a recent critical essay is Robert Jervis, *The Illogic of American Nuclear Strategy* (Ithaca: Cornell University Press, 1984).

183. "Counterforce" forces include forces which could preemptively destroy opposing nuclear forces before they are launched, forces which could destroy retaliating warheads in flight towards the attacker's cities, and forces which could limit the damage which retaliating warheads could inflict on the attacker's society if they arrived. Hence, "counterforce" weapons and programs include highly accurate ICBMs and SLBMs (which could destroy opposing ICBMs) *and air* defense against bombers, ballistic missile defense for cities, and civil defense. Seemingly "defensive" programs such as the Reagan Administration's ballistic missile defense ("Star Wars") program and parallel Soviet ballistic missile defense programs are in fact *offensive* under the inverted logic of a MAD world. See Posen and Van Evera, "Defense Policy and the Reagan Administration," pp. 24–25.

6

❇

Cold War and Beyond

Reading 6-1

Who Won the Cold War— and Why It Matters
Bruce D. Berkowitz

S cholars, analysts, and politicians care deeply about how and why the cold war ended—not because of its innate historical interest, but because of its profound implications for current American policy. Did the Soviet empire collapse in part because of the Reagan administration's policies, thereby validating a "tough" conservative approach to foreign policy? Or did it collapse in spite of Ronald Reagan's policies, for reasons that justify the dovish cold war posture defined by negotiation, coexistence, and détente?

As one might expect, the interpreters tend to divide into two camps depending on their own prior status as hawk or dove. What is more surprising, however, is that six years after the fall of the Berlin Wall, the cold war doves have been doing the more credible job of presenting their case—surprising because, according to most estimates, the West *won* the cold war. After all, the Soviet Union collapsed, Germany reunited within NATO, and NATO and the European Union are now free to debate whether to allow

SOURCE: From "Who Won the Cold War—and Why It Matters" by Bruce D. Berkowitz, *Orbis*, vol. 40, no. 1 (Winter 1996): 164–171. Copyright © 1996. Reprinted with permission from the Foreign Policy Research Institute.

Poland, Hungary, and the Czech Republic to become members. Weren't those the goals that cold war hawks had pursued for forty years?

Well, yes. But other things have happened as well, and the cold war doves' success in presenting their version of history owes much to the new problems that have followed the breakup of the Soviet Union: ethnic conflict in Central Europe, political instability in the Third World, and the threat that Soviet nuclear weapons might fall into the wrong hands. All this has given cold war doves an opening to argue that the hawks' policies resulted in a messy ending that more enlightened policies might have averted.

Currently, the cold war doves are best represented by Raymond Garthoff's book, *The Great Transition: American-Soviet Relations and the End of the Cold War.* Garthoff, a former State Department official and CIA analyst, is currently a senior fellow at the Brookings Institution. His tome articulating the dove position is weighty, solidly researched, heavily footnoted, and just plain big.

Garthoff's argument can be summarized as follows: Mikhail Gorbachev was a true reformer who realized the Soviet Union needed to democratize, reduce military spending, and introduce market structures in order to survive. Alas, the United States failed to appreciate Gorbachev's motives, good intentions, and daring. Consequently, U.S. leaders continued to pressure the Soviets in international affairs, refusing especially to make concessions in arms control (read: "give up Star Wars"). As a result, Gorbachev had to placate his own right wing and was unable to carry out the needed reforms. That in turn accelerated Soviet economic decline and stoked internal unrest, the attempted coup of August 1991, and, ultimately, the breakup of the Soviet Union.

Garthoff's argument rests heavily on "what could have been." If only we had been more enlightened, he suggests, we would today have a stable Soviet Union that was more or less democratic, and certainly one that exercised greater control over all of those nuclear weapons. Garthoff's argument also attempts to vindicate many of the Democratic Party's positions of the 1980s, such as the Nuclear Freeze and Walter Mondale's promise to "draw the line in the skies" by terminating the Strategic Defense Initiative.

Unfortunately, there are at least two problems with Garthoff's argument. First, we cannot replay history, so there is simply no way to prove that a more conciliatory policy by the United States would have preserved Gorbachev or otherwise produced a tidier ending for the cold war. Just because we are dissatisfied with the hand that we were dealt does not mean there is a logical rule ensuring the liberals' policies would have dealt us a better one. One could imagine, for example, that if the United States had been more conciliatory in resisting Soviet adventures in the developing world, provided various forms of economic relief, and eased up on the military front, then Soviet leaders would have simply eased up on reform because the pressure had subsided.

Secondly, Garthoff tends to neglect what the Soviets were doing in the 1970s and 1980s, as though they were just biding time, waiting for an economic crisis that would force them to adopt reforms that would in turn topple their entrenched elites (and, incidentally, contradict one hundred years of Marxist theory). In fact, the Soviet Union was an aggressive and opportunistic competitor in the international scene. Remember the crushing of Solidarity in Poland? The support of revolutionary movements throughout the developing world? The Soviet-instigated coup in, and later invasion of, Afghanistan? The Soviets' own space-weapons programs, preparations for protracted nuclear combat, and massive conventional force buildups in Europe and Asia? Garthoff is too willing to ignore all this, and when he does acknowledge Soviet provocations, he paints them in a sympathetic light.

Garthoff also carries a heavy load of historical baggage. Today, he says that the economic decline of the Soviet Union would inevitably have brought reform, no matter what the United States did. Yet at the time, most of the Left did not believe the Soviet Union was destined to collapse. The liberal argument held that, if anything, the Soviet Union was so strong it could not be coerced by U.S. pressure. Thus, the Left argued, the United States needed to reach an accommodation with Moscow, especially when the risk of thermonuclear Armageddon was added to the calculus.

According to Peter Schweizer, it was on this point that the Reagan administration differed from all of its cold war–era predecessors. Schweizer is a journalist, so his contribution to the debate is significantly more svelte and readable than Garthoff's, and much more direct in making its point. In *Victory: The Reagan Administration's Secret Strategy That Hastened the Collapse of the Soviet Union,* Schweizer writes that, unlike previous administrations and contrary to the common wisdom of the time, the Reagan administration did not take for granted the permanence of the Soviet regime and believed that its economic inefficiency, bloated bureaucracy, overbuilt military, and ethnic divisions were not just weaknesses, but potentially fatal fault lines. Thus, according to Schweizer, the Reaganauts arrived in office with an explicit strategy designed to push the Soviet Union over the economic precipice. This strategy consisted of several interlocking components.

The first component was economic warfare. The Reagan administration wanted to prevent the Soviet Union from earning hard currency from the sale of natural resources, and to deny the Soviets access to Western technology. These were lifelines that would enable the inherently doomed Soviet economy to survive longer than it otherwise might. Thus, writes Schweizer, in 1982, the Reagan administration opposed the proposed pipeline that would have permitted the Soviets to sell Siberian natural gas to Europe. Economic warfare also explained why the Reaganauts were so determined to enforce export controls on computers, advanced machine tools, and other items that the Soviets were unable to manufacture for themselves.

A second component of the strategy was the Reagan administration's military buildup. As David Stockman recalled in his infamous *Atlantic Monthly* interview and later memoirs, the Reagan administration (and Secretary of Defense Caspar Weinberger in particular) had a simple criterion for determining how much to spend on defense: more is better than less.[1] At a minimum, Weinberger was determined to raise U.S. defense spending higher than levels planned under the Carter administration. The objective was to keep the pressure on the Soviets to maintain their own outsized levels of military spending; the underlying assumption was that the Soviets would break before we would.

Strategic missile defense—after a while, even proponents called the program "Star Wars"—was a cornerstone of this second component. The Soviets had invested heavily in large, land-based ICBMs, and a successful missile defense program might have rendered that investment obsolete. More likely, the Soviets would have been forced to pour more money into their strategic nuclear forces to maintain their effectiveness, and more money into their own defense programs in order to maintain parity with the United States.

The third component was political action aimed at supporting dissident movements in Eastern Europe and guerrilla armies opposed to Soviet-backed regimes in countries such as Nicaragua, Afghanistan, and Angola. By the early 1980s, a school of thought focusing on the "costs of empire" had developed in the United States, led by Henry Rowen, Herb Meyer, and others.

Previously, most analysts had focused on the threat presented by the expanding network of satellite countries and client states that the Soviet Union had built up after

World War II. Much of the debate revolved around such fears as communist South Yemen undermining the Saudi regime, the Soviets using bases in Angola to interdict oil shipping routes, or the Sandanistas exporting revolution throughout Latin America. The new Reagan school of thought spied in those Soviet client states another massive drain on the Soviet economy and the domestic legitimacy of the Soviet regime, particularly once Afghanistan looked like it was becoming the Soviet Union's Vietnam.

Much of the effort aimed at deepening the costs of empire to the Soviet Union was covert. Indeed, the Iran/*contra* affair was a direct by-product of this program, however much a zealous CIA director (William Casey) and a loose cannon in the National Security Council (Oliver North) may have struck out on their own. And the administration was perfectly clear about its intentions. President Reagan himself explained them explicitly in his State of the Union address to Congress in 1986, and many operations—such as U.S. support to the National Endowment for Democracy—were entirely overt.

Ergo, the hawk interpretation of the cold war: the Reaganauts' strategy worked. After all, they proposed a military buildup and hard-line policy, followed through with them, and—just as they predicted—saw the Soviet Union consigned to "the ash heap of history," to use the phrase that President Reagan borrowed from none other than Lenin.

There is much to be said for this interpretation—not least, the apparent logic between cause and effect—but there are also a few glitches that need to be addressed.

Schweizer probably overstates the degree to which previous American leaders accepted the permanence of the Soviet Union. To be sure, Schweizer is at his best when he quotes liberals such as Seweryn Bialer, who wrote in 1982 that "the Soviet Union is not now nor will it be during the next decade in the throes of a true systemic crisis, for it boasts enormous unused reserves of political and social stability" (p. xiv), and Lester Thurow, who wrote in the late 1980s, "Can economic command significantly compress and accelerate the growth process? The remarkable performance of the Soviet Union suggests that it can" (p. xv). But even Henry Kissinger was writing in 1979 that "the imposing monolith of totalitarian states often obscures their latent weakness. The Soviet system is unstable politically; it has no mechanism for succession . . . nor is their economic system impressive."[2]

More significant is the empirical problem. Schweizer argues that a well-defined, resolutely executed program of toppling the Soviet Union was in place from 1981 until 1987 when, according to Schweizer, the Iran/*contra* scandal derailed all other national security initiatives, and the Reagan administration began simply to ride out its time in office.

It is easy to forget that there was, in fact, quite a range of views within the Reagan administration on national security issues. The competition between Weinberger and Secretary of State George Shultz remains legendary. Casey kept some, if not many, aspects of his covert action campaign to himself. Also, the Reagan National Security Council staff was relatively weak compared to the cabinet departments. Indeed, the Reagan administration managed to go through national security advisors at the rate of one every 1.5 years, and there never was a top gun at the NSC with the vision and stature of a Kissinger or Brzezinski. So, if there was a comprehensive, coherent strategy, where did it reside?

It is also easy to mistake the passing of paper and political debates for real substance. Despite liberal claims that Ronald Reagan embarked on a reckless arms race, the Reagan-era buildup was modest in real terms. Although the increase in defense spending from the depths of the 1970s to the height of the mid-1980s was significant, one needs to maintain overall perspective. The fact is that between 1950 and 1991, the U.S. defense budget, adjusted for inflation, hovered steadily around $300 billion a year in 1995 dollars, rising no more than 15 percent above this level in peak years (the Korean War, the Vietnam War, and the first term of the Reagan administration), and never dropping more than 15 percent below this level (the late 1950s and mid-1970s). Moreover, as a percentage of GNP, defense spending drifted steadily downward during this period, with only slight rises during Vietnam and the Reagan buildup. For the record, the projection for 1999 is 2.8 percent, the lowest since 1940.

The visible effects on U.S. military force structure were also more modest than doves feared or hawks boasted. The number of carrier battle groups rose from twelve to fifteen; the air force added one hundred new bombers; the number of active army divisions rose from sixteen to eighteen; and so on. True, the readiness of U.S. forces improved (as did morale and the quality of the forces), but the signs of U.S. military power that the Soviets would most likely detect did not change that much. Even the much vaunted Star Wars threat remained an R&D program throughout the 1980s.

Still, Schweizer has the broad outline right. Certainly he is closer to the mark than Richard Ned Lebow and Janice Gross Stein, who argue the opposite extreme in *We All Lost the Cold War*. Lebow and Stein come from the nihilistic school that maintains nations can have no sense of direction, the cold war was the creation of leaders pressured by domestic politics and stumbling in the dark with nuclear weapons, and it was only through sheer luck we did not blow ourselves up. Lebow and Stein also promote the "we were wrong, you were wrong" school of thought that allows leaders who wind up on the losing side to rationalize their shortcomings. (Mikhail Gorbachev provides a promotional blurb for the jacket.)

Aside from the fundamental error of suggesting the moral equivalence of a largely free, democratic state and a largely unfree, totalitarian state, the problem with Lebow and Stein is that, if their argument is true, one is left wondering whether policy matters at all. Lebow and Stein make much of the confusion, disagreement, and misconception that occur at high levels whenever policy is debated, most especially during crises, suggesting that officials are just along for the ride and that their influence is limited in any case. But promoting a broad vision and engineering the politics to realize national objectives in the midst of such apparent chaos is precisely what leadership is all about.

Even so, Schweizer's story needs to be tempered with the reality of how politics work. The Reagan administration's national policy was, like any other modern government's, the product of politics. In the real world, government policies are like outcomes in the free market—the aggregate result of efforts and initiatives of individuals, rarely the perfect representation of a single plan.

In the case of the Reagan administration, the government leadership consisted of a confederation of hardliners who saw the opportunity to topple the Soviets and had the determination to do so (William Casey and possibly U.N. ambassador Jeane Kirkpatrick); moderates who thought that toppling would be desirable if possible, but was not highly likely (George Shultz); middleweight officials outside the inner circle, with no real vision or strategic agenda (national security advisors Robert McFarlane and John Poindexter come to mind); and Reagan loyalists who viewed themselves as lieutenants whose duties were simply to carry out in detail whatever Reagan adopted as general policy (Weinberger, especially on defense spending). At lower levels, combat continued on a routine basis between what the British would have considered "wet" softliners (e.g., Richard Burt, U.S. assistant secretary of state for European affairs) and "dry" hardliners (e.g., Richard Perle, assistant secretary of defense for international security policy). What emerged from the competing bureaucracies was a set of policies that probably did hasten the collapse of the Soviet empire (whether it could have been managed more tidily is another matter) but fell short of being a carefully calculated plan.

This is also one reason why the collection of documents edited by Christopher Simpson, *National Security Directives of the Reagan and Bush Administrations,* is so useful. Simpson includes the policy documents that Schweizer cites as the basis of his thesis. (Indeed, Simpson uses Schweizer as the reference, since the documents themselves remain classified.) Simpson also includes additional documents that support Schweizer's thesis, such as the September 1982 National Security Decision Directive 54, "United States Policy Toward Eastern Europe" (pp. 195–98), which was aimed at putting a wedge between the Soviets and their satellite allies. However, in reading the collection, one also sees that there was a range of viewpoints among the officials and agencies that constituted the administration, and not all of them had the long-range objective of bringing down the Soviet Empire.

Ronald Reagan's most important contribution was that his administration managed to shift fundamentally the national security debate and provide a vision for U.S. objectives that had disappeared under his predecessors. In retrospect, it was probably the president's dramatic rhetoric—referring to the Soviet Union as "the evil empire" and the "focus of evil in the world today"—that jerked the discussion of U.S.-Soviet policy away from a position of tolerating long-term coexistence with the Soviets and toward a belief that the cold war could indeed be resolved in the foreseeable future on terms favorable to the United States.

That idea—unbelievably radical when it was introduced—was, in fact, consistent with the long-term objective of containment theory, the goal that had *nominally* served as the basis of U.S. policy but had lost its support under the hammering of Vietnam, the malaise of the 1970s, and Soviet political-military gains. Reagan's rhetoric enraged Western liberals almost as much as it enraged the Soviet leadership. Yet one has to wonder whether the cold war would have ended as neatly as Garthoff and other liberals suggest had there been no Reagan administration.

But if Ronald Reagan can take at least that much credit for the end of the cold war, why is the left wing doing so demonstrably well in the "spin control" contest? The first, most obvious explanation is that the media and the public have already forgotten the terror of the cold war's nuclear threat and are obsessed instead with the frustrating problems of the new era, such as proliferation in North Korea and Iran; ethnic conflict in Rwanda and Bosnia; religious fundamentalism in Iran, Algeria, and elsewhere; and the general chaos of refugee flows, narcotics trafficking, trade wars, and the prospect of a new cold war with a belligerent, unstable China.

But a second, more specific answer is to be found in the success of the left wing (calling the Clinton administration "left" is a simplification but not an oversimplification) in not only providing a possible alternative story about how the cold war ended, but pinning the problems of the *post*–cold war era on the messy breakup of the Soviet Union occasioned by the Reagan offensive. The Right has provided a plausible story for how the cold war ended but has not dealt with the messy breakup, so they are falling behind in the debate.

The "new world disorder" has been acknowledged by Clinton administration thinkers. Their answer is a national strategy of "engagement and enlargement," according to which the United States and its allies need to promote market democracy in the rest of the world in order to eliminate the new threats listed above. This translates into a diplomacy of "aggressive multilateralism," based on the hope that the United Nations can act as a responsible mediator and decisive actor. On the military side, it translates into peacekeeping, nation-building operations, and other "operations other than war."

There is lots of room to criticize this policy—it may not be necessary to alleviate these new threats by attacking them at their roots, for example. And expecting the United Nations to act responsibly in any sense may be heroic. Also, nation-building sounds suspiciously like the liberals' policy of government-assisted economic development and social engineering exported to foreign lands just when most Americans have become convinced that it does not work at home.

Alas, you cannot beat something with nothing, and so far that is all the right wing has delivered. To date, conservatives have criticized the Clinton administration for intervening in Haiti and Bosnia, but they have not offered their own criteria for when intervention is necessary. They argue for larger defense budgets but provide no rationale of their own for spending the funds. And since they generally oppose intervention, they make everyone wonder what their larger defense budget is for. Finally, to complete the confusion, conservatives divide among themselves on the issue of trade, with free traders on one side and the supporters of Ross Perot and Patrick Buchanan on the other.

Unanimity is not necessary for effective policy making—the Reagan administration proved that—but a coherent vision is. Until such a vision is provided, conservatives will find themselves in the odd position of having won the cold war, only to be robbed of the credit—and influence—they think they have earned. In the era of "spin control," history is not necessarily written by the victors.

NOTES

1. See David A. Stockman, *The Triumph of Politics: Why the Reagan Revolution Failed* (New York: Harper and Row, 1986), pp. 286–99.

2. Henry Kissinger, *The White House Years* (Boston, Mass.: Little, Brown and Co., 1979),

p. 119. Many Kissinger critics, however, claim that he was much less convinced of the Soviets' weakness when in office, and that his policies were essentially accommodationist.

Reading 6-2

Is the Cold War Really Over?
Sergei Kortunov

Hardly any serious—be it western or domestic—political analysts will say that the Cold War is just an episode of the 20th century. Having produced a defining impact on the state of international relations for at least 40 years, this phenomenon has left an indelible mark not only on its external side but has also deeply reflected on the very substance of world and national development in those years, affecting the political, socio-economic, and even psychological aspects of the life of many (maybe even all) nations and continents in the world.

SOURCE: From "Is the Cold War Really Over?" by Sergei Kortunov, *International Affairs* (Moscow), vol. 44, no. 5 (1998): 141–154.

One most important factor of the Cold War, which inflicted a serious and hard-to-cure trauma on the man of the 20th century, was the threat of mutual nuclear annihilation—that is to say, the threat of mankind's self-destruction—in a nuclear war. It called into question many values that were hitherto considered unshakable, even axiomatic. It brought the world to the verge of an Apocalypse, shaking to its very foundations human consciousness which was forced to doubt the very possibility of further existence and evolution of world civilization. After all, since mankind entered the nuclear age, it has lived in a situation when the mechanism of destruction was fully operational and the trigger was on the verge of being pulled suddenly and unexpectedly. Reason refused to believe that so much hinged on so little, that the entire natural world surrounding mankind as well as human civilization itself, which added to the miracles of evolution the miracles of art, science, social organization, and spiritual enlightenment, could disappear at one fell swoop—just like that.

Owing to the extremely great importance of the Cold War in the history not only of the 20th century but of world history as a whole, it is essential to analyze a number of important questions. Many of them remain moot or lend themselves to different interpretations. They include the following:

- When did the Cold War begin and who initiated it? What tasks did the initiator put forward?

- Has the Cold War ended? Have its results been summed up, and who has become the winner and the loser in it?

- What implications did the Cold War have for Russia and for the entire world?

Without answering these questions, it is hardly possible for Russia to build an effective partnership with the leading states of the world or a just and equitable and therefore stable international security system for the 21st century.

SOURCES

First of all, it needs to be noted that the Cold War per se is a generally recognized fact. Neither does anyone in principle question the year when it began—1945. But from then on—in particular, on the issue of sources and the initiators of the Cold War—both Western and domestic historians and political scientists begin to differ, oftentimes fundamentally.

As is known, Soviet historiography laid the blame for the beginning of the Cold War entirely on the Western countries, primarily the United States and Great Britain, citing W. Churchill's Fulton speech as the historical date marking its outbreak.

Despite the historical incontestability of the Fulton demarche, Western political science has always sought to lay the blame at someone else's door, linking the onset of the Cold War with the "imperial ambitions" of the USSR and the personal ambitions of J. Stalin.

None of these viewpoints, I believe, are absolutely correct or even exhaustive. Thus, for instance, the Soviet theory does not fully answer the question of what causes underlay the collapse of the anti-Nazi coalition precisely in 1945. Furthermore, with the benefit of hindsight, it would be more appropriate to date the beginning of the Cold War not as the fall but the summer of 1945, in particular following H. Truman's decision to drop a nuclear bomb on two Japanese cities. The bombing of Hiroshima and Nagasaki was psychologically targeted not so much against Japan as against the USSR.

Moreover, the "intimidation" of the Soviet Union per se was already part of the new Cold War technology. As for W. Churchill's Fulton speech, it only officially recorded what was already happening de facto.

Neither is the Western interpretation of events convincing enough. By 1945, the division of Europe had already been completed and formalized in the Yalta and Potsdam Agreements. The USSR had no intention or capability to move further—be it in Europe or in Asia. So it is historically incorrect to talk about any "ambitions" of the Soviet Union or J. Stalin.

The Soviet and the Western theories are right in one respect: The Cold War is the result of a "hot" war—WWII. For this reason alone it could not have been a confrontation between the "free world" and "totalitarian Communism" (the liberal theory) or a class struggle between world imperialism and the "buttress of peace and socialism" (a mirror-like Soviet version). None of these over simplified interpretations can account for the depth of international confrontation after Yalta and Potsdam. And this is only natural: Liberal and Communist ideologies are not antipodes but just two branches of rationalist Western philosophy.

As N. Narochnitskaia justly points out in her article, Russia and the Russians in World History, had Great Russia, after the end of the Great Patriotic War (WWII), been able to shed its Communist pseudo-religion and emerge as a Russian empire, the Cold War would have started all the same. Because the USSR won the Great Patriotic War as Great Russia, not as a Red Empire. As a result of the war, the continuity of Russian history, which seemed to be broken forever, was restored while the West began to perceive the Soviet Union [as] a geopolitical successor to the Russian empire. The USSR's de-facto succession with respect to the Russian empire became the most important, although never publicly declared, outcome of Yalta and Potsdam.[1]

In this context it is characteristic that the West began especially to hate the USSR exactly in 1945, which manifested itself the most conspicuously in Allen Dulles' doctrine (which he had formulated well before 1945, i.e., long before the Fulton speech and even before the end of WWII). Under this doctrine, the ultimate aim of the struggle against the USSR was the elimination of the Soviet people as the most unruly and rebellious people on Earth as well as the final and irreversible extinguishing of its consciousness. Later on the Russian people was not included among the "oppressed nations" (presumably oppressed by Communism) whose week is marked every year. A corresponding law, adopted by the U.S. Congress in 1959 under No. 86-90 on the initiative of the U.S. Ukrainian Congress, enumerated among the victims of the "imperialist policy of Communist Russia," not only the peoples of Eastern Europe and of the USSR Union republics but also those of "mainland China and Tibet" and on the other hand, the peoples of mythical "Idel-Ural, Kazakia, and the historical-geographic region of Turkestan."[2]

Russian émigrés, under the guidance of such prominent figures as A. L. Tolstaya, the younger daughter of the well known Russian author and aircraft designer I. I. Sikorsky, were unsuccessful in protesting against such overt discrimination. Moreover, the West, using a mean trick ("Russia is the prison of nations"), declared the Russians the "oppressors" of the aforementioned nations. When, in the fall of 1991 (that is to say, after the "victory of democracy in Russia"), one congressman proposed repealing this law, his initiative was not supported. The same happened with the proposal by Petr Budzilovich, chairman of the Congress of Russian Americans, to use the Week of the Oppressed Nations to pay tribute to the people of Russia for renouncing Communism in democratic elections.[3]

This makes it crystal clear that the Cold War was not just a physical or ideological containment of the Red Empire in the spirit of G. Kennan but a concept of total rejection of the Soviet state as a historical and geopolitical phenomenon and, above all, as a successor to Russian history. To call things by their proper names, the aforementioned Law No. 86-90 proclaimed the division of the Soviet state as an aim of U.S. foreign policy. So the main aspect of the Cold War was not "the struggle against Communism" but the struggle against "Russian imperialism"—moreover, on Russia's historical territory per se.[4]

Such plans, in effect, did not in any way differ from the plans of the German Nazis. Thus, in his speech on "Eastern problems," on 20 July 1941, A. Rosenberg said: "Our foreign policy tasks should be aimed to support—in an ingenious and effective way—the aspiration of all these (living in Russia—S.K.) peoples for freedom and to give them definite forms of statehood; that is to say, to separate out, in a natural way, state formations from the huge territory of the Soviet Union and to direct them against Moscow, thus saving the German empire from the Eastern threat for centuries to come." Moreover, it was proposed to divide the territory of the USSR (Great Russia) into four "commissariats" of Great Germany: the Baltics (which was also planned to include Belarus), "free" Ukraine, the Caucasus, and Russia per se (the territory of the present-day Russian Federation minus the Caucasus).[5]

Here is an excerpt from another noteworthy document, a secret memorandum of the German Imperial Ministry for Occupied Eastern Territories, No. P77a/44d, dated 12 April 1944: "The struggle against Bolshevism is only a struggle against an alien ideology; yet standing behind it is the exponent of this way of thought—the Great Russian but ultimately Great Slavic state power. . . . Europe has no ways of eliminating the danger that has threatened it for over centuries other than by dividing Russia. In this conflict, the form of state organization of our Eastern neighbor has practically no importance whatsoever. If the division does not succeed, it will only be a matter of time when the European Slavs unite under Moscow's leadership and stifle the rest of Europe. So it is not enough to separate the Caucasus and Turkestan from Russia; it is also necessary that Slavic nationalities also evolve separately, as different states, and this guideline by the Ministry for Eastern Occupied Territories should be conveyed to all agencies and departments concerned as guidance for action in the future. It is not easy to strictly separate Russians from Belorussians and Cossacks. In practice it can be difficult to decide to which clan or tribe particular people belong. It is not important how such situations will be resolved; what is important is that the general line be maintained. We must go down this path so far that the identity of a Ukrainian or a Cossack be as distinct as that of a Dutchman or a Bulgarian."[6] Even before that, Goebbels formulated the aims of the war in the East as follows: "Russia will be divided into components. Every republic should be discreetly given freedom. The idea is not to allow the existence of a giant empire in the East ever again. Bolshevism will be a thing of the past. Thus we will fulfill our true historic mission."[7]

It is noteworthy that the legitimacy and legality of historical Russia before the 1917 Revolution has never been called into question even by its most avowed rivals on the international arena. This was first done by Nazi Germany and then, after it was routed, by the U.S. Congress. In this context we can say that in 1945 the world anti-Russian center moved from Berlin to Washington. It is also highly indicative that anti-Soviet (but in effect anti-Russian) euphoria did not allow the West to stop the Cold War in the 50s–60s, when there was every possibility for doing this. Thus, for instance, at the conference of foreign ministers of the USSR, the United States, Britain, and France in Berlin, on 25 January through 18 February 1954, the Soviet Union raised the question of signing an all-European collective security treaty, which would help overcome the division of Europe. The Western countries categorically refused to do that, arguing that such a treaty was allegedly designed to supersede NATO, which had apparently evolved in response to the Soviet threat. When the Soviet Union expressed its readiness, together with the governments concerned, to consider its participation in NATO, which would have resulted in a situation whereby the North Atlantic bloc would cease to be a closed military organization, it was also rejected. This idea, as the subsequent identical U.S., British, and French notes said, was at variance with the principles underlying the defense and security efforts of the Western nations, interconnected by the bonds of mutual trust. . . . Should the Soviet Union become a member of the Organization, it would be able to use its power of veto in the decision-making process.[8]

Thus, despite the repeated efforts by the USSR to stop the confrontation, the Western powers did not wish to do this. Likewise, they categorically refused to incorporate Russia into their political, military, and economic institutions (unlike Germany, Japan, Italy and other countries that were defeated in the war). Later, during the period of détente (60s–70s), itself no longer fearing Communism, the West worked hard to debunk it on the territory of historical Russia. Because it understood that the Red idea united and consolidated the superpower, holding it firmly together. In the 80s—that is to say, the time when the Soviet state, while remaining ideologically rather tough, could no longer be described as totalitarian, let alone "terrorist"—the West suddenly declared the USSR "an evil empire." At the same time it supported those destructive forces within the USSR that were trying to discredit the legitimacy of the Soviet state per se. The "late" Soviet Communists, above all M. Gorbachev, A. Yakovlev, and E. Shevardnadze, bear their share of responsibility for this. As T. Graham, counselor of the U.S. Embassy in Moscow, pointed out, glasnost and especially the process of filling in the blanks of Soviet history finally de-legitimized the Soviet state. Official attempts to rehabilitate the victims of the Stalin period soon brought about some unsettling questions about the Lenin legacy and the importance of the Great October Revolution, the system's core myth. Likewise, revelations concerning Stalin diplomacy in the 30s raised the question about the Soviet Union's responsibility for the outbreak of WWII as well as the idea that the heroic sacrifice on the part of the Soviet Union in that war could have been avoided had Stalin followed a different policy toward Germany. Briefly, Gorbachev's policy irreparably discredited the legitimate principle of the Soviet system and cast a serious shadow on the two fundamental myths: the October Revolution and the victory of the Soviet Union in WWII.[9]

THE WAR GOES ON

Has the Cold War ended? In the broad political sense, probably yes. But when did this happen?

I believe that this did not happen in 1991, i.e., not at the moment of the breakup of the USSR. This model of terminating the Cold War did not exist in any of the CIA scenarios. This, incidentally, is recognized by S. Talbott. Just 10 years ago, he wrote in 1996, many of us could not even imagine that we or at least our children would live to see a time when the Soviet Union would renounce Marxism-Leninism and peacefully break up into 12 independent countries.[10]

The beginning of the end of the Cold War can probably be dated 1985, when a new Soviet leadership, led by M. Gorbachev, came to power. By that time the need for ending the confrontation was clearly understood by the whole society. The major landmarks on this road were as follows: the Soviet-U.S. meeting in Reykjavik, negotiations on nuclear and space weapons, the signing of the 1987 Treaty on Intermediate-Range and Shorter-Range Missiles, the Vienna negotiations on the CFE Treaty, and unilateral tactical nuclear arms cuts in Europe. However, after WWII, the main watershed between the confrontation and the post-confrontation period in the history of international relations was evidently the withdrawal of Soviet troops from the East European countries. The subsequent fall of the Berlin Wall only symbolized this unprecedented unilateral move, which, incidentally, was made absolutely voluntarily, without any outside pressure.

At the same time there is good reason to say that the Cold War is not quite over. One of the most compelling arguments in favor of this conclusion is the preservation of the nuclear deterrence doctrine, an organic element of the international security system that has evolved after WWII. Major U.S. documents show that the doctrine of nuclear containment of Russia is still an organic and inalienable part of U.S. military-political thinking which therefore has not undergone any substantial changes even after the officially declared end of the Cold War. This, among other things, is evidenced by a secret directive signed by U.S. President B. Clinton in November 1997, which, most likely with the knowledge of the White House, was made public.[11]

The new directive only confirmed the conclusions of those Russian and U.S. experts who had all along talked about an exclusively political character of the Russian-U.S. agreement on the non-targeting of missiles against each other. Technically, however, zero targeting does not require any conversion of modern strategic nuclear arms command and control systems or any additional time. Moreover, it is impossible to verify or control this measure. According to B. Blair, a well known U.S. expert in the field, it will take no more than 10 seconds to restore missile flight programs from "zero-target" status.[12] This, of course, does not diminish the political importance of the zero-targeting declaration. Simply, we should not think that they once and for all take the sides beyond the framework of nuclear deterrence (that is to say, the strategic doctrine of the Cold War) and create a stable foundation for partnership.

Other evidence in favor of the fact that the Cold War is not quite over is the unprecedented geopolitical offensive by the U.S. after the Cold War was declared history. It should in all fairness be admitted that this offensive was provoked by the grossest miscalculations on the part of the Soviet leadership which failed to ensure the continuity of Russia's geopolitical interests in the late 80s–early 90s. Hardly anyone would disagree with the fact that by the time the withdrawal of Soviet troops from Central and East European countries was inevitable and responded to the country's national interests. The collapse of the Warsaw Pact and the reunification of Germany were just as inevitable. It is another matter that all this time there still were prerequisites and possibilities for resolving these problems with due consideration for the interests of the USSR, in particular, by legally formalizing the Western obligations not to undermine the geopolitical status quo in Europe, including by NATO eastward expansion. And the West —this has to be admitted in all fairness—was ready for this at the time. After all, in the late 80s, no one could envision, not even in a nightmare, the possibility of the Czech Republic, Poland, and Hungary, let alone the Baltic states, joining the alliance.

However, subsequently, as it watched the geopolitical retreat by new Russia in 1991–1995, in the spirit of the "late USSR," fantastic in its scale, the West came to adopt a strategy of a "new containment of Russia," including by NATO eastward expansion. And it hastened to consolidate Russia's concessions as its geopolitical acquisitions. Instead of the promised admission to the "civilized community of democratic countries," Russia began to be unceremoniously pushed out from the seas and other vital geopolitical areas. In 1996–1997, the Berlin Wall, apparently destroyed forever, suddenly moved toward the borders of the Moscow kingdom. Meanwhile, the belated statements by the Russian Foreign Ministry in 1993–1994 to the effect that Russia considered the entire CIS territory a zone of its vital interests were perceived as "imperial ambitions."

Moreover, in a bid to consolidate the division of Russia's historical statehood, a well tested method was applied—playing up the right of nations to self-determination—which was used already in the early 20s against those states which the West was interested to see weaken. Whereas with respect to Western states the right to self-determination contradicts "the very idea of the state as a territorial and political entity" as well as the right of the rest of the people and the state to unity—moreover, "violates the sovereignty of an already evolved state"—with respect to Russia, and only with respect to Russia, according to a conclusion by two League of Nations commissions of international experts, the right of nations to self-determination was to apply as an unshakable international norm.[13] Such an interpretation of this principle was ingeniously inculcated into the minds of latter-day "national" leaders with the help of the proven technology of the Cold War—after it was supposedly over.

Thus, whereas by the late 80s Russia had indeed ended the Cold War with the West (it will be recalled once again that the withdrawal of troops from Eastern Europe, the abolition of the Warsaw Pact, the unification of Germany, the unilateral reductions of nuclear weapons, and the termination of a number of military programs let alone the "dissolution" of the USSR, were all undertaken by Russia of its own free will—rather, under internal domestic pressure than pressure from the outside), the West nonetheless, rather, continued this war. And while Russia was indulging in "new thinking," the West managed to interpret the outcome of the Cold War as its geopolitical capitulation, as the renunciation of its historical succession and therefore of the historical and post-war fundamentals of foreign policy and its traditional zones of influence.

By early 1998, the ring of geopolitical encirclement, based on pragmatic, utilitarian interests, very far removed from the postulates of "new thinking," tightened around Russia. Meanwhile, the proponents of these interests started talking about their "global leadership" after their "victory" in the Cold War. In the 1990s, they have reaffirmed that old geopolitical truths are still in. And if this is the case, the Cold War cannot be considered to be fully over.

"WINNERS" AND "LOSERS"

The idea of the West's full and unconditional "victory" in the Cold War is among the underlying myths of contemporary Western consciousness. This postulate is recorded in fundamental U.S. documents, including the National Security Strategy. It is also used for domestic consumption—with a view to mobilizing the Americans to exercise their "leadership" in the world. H. Kissinger and Z. Brzezinski keep talking about the U.S. "victory." B. Clinton widely used the thesis about the "victory" in the Cold War as part of his election campaign rhetoric in 1995. The American Heritage Foundation, in its memorandum, America in a Secure World, formulated it in the most glaring and crude form: The crash of the Soviet empire and of world Communism is a victory of the United States that has little parallel in world history.[14]

However, something else is amazing: This myth, which has substantially damaged Russian-U.S. relations, has also become a myth in the minds not only of well known "proponents of the conspiracy theory," inclined to see all our failures as resulting from insidious interference by external forces, but also in the consciousness of the most radical part of domestic democrats who do not at all deny Russia's "defeat" nor conceal their joy over it, or their contribution to it. Even some political analysts, who refer to themselves as the "political center," are ready to accept the "defeat." For instance, M. Deliagin writes categorically: "It is high time for Russia to admit what the whole world has already understood: The Cold War has ended in victory for the United States. The victory of the democratic forces in Russia in their internal civil confrontation with totalitarianism on the external political arena meant a nationwide defeat, which resulted in the destruction of the defeated state—the USSR." [15]

At the same time the Russian political elite—both democratic and Communist leaning—developed a trend toward a complete denial of the mistakes in the foreign policy sphere that were made by the Russian leadership in the late 80s–early 90s. I believe that E. Kozhokin summed up the nature of this phenomenon the most aptly: "It is much more convenient for the 'democrats' to pretend that the West has never carried on an unrelenting struggle against our former motherland, Russia-USSR, and that it was only by our own efforts that we destroyed the 'evil empire.' The 'Communists' do not want to admit the responsibility of the CPSU for such an ineffectual and irrational running of the country, which at the end of the day predetermined its defeat in the global confrontation." [16]

It is high time to make a well-balanced assessment of the outcome of the Cold War. Because the various misperceptions and myths on this score demoralize our people, develop a sense of wounded pride, and aggravate the national inferiority complex on one hand, and on the other, owing to this, can lead to aggressive "discharges" of national protest energy. Either of this is extremely dangerous both for Russia and for the world community.

Let us start off with the fact that even if someone has "lost" the Cold War, this was certainly not the Russian Federation which emerged as a sovereign state, independent of the USSR, in 1991. Strictly speaking, the Russian Federation was "fighting" against the USSR on the side of the West. It was only after the breakup of the USSR (when "Russia seceded from Russia") that the national elite (which "aimed at Communism but hit Russia"), seeing the unceremonious behavior of the West, began to doubt the "anti-Soviet" line (which proved to be anti-Russian). In the late 80s–early 90s, this elite was frenziedly trampling on the USSR without understanding that it was trampling on Russia as a national formation.

Of course, there is no way we can deny the involvement of the West, above all of the United States, in the disintegration of the USSR. However, the most complex and truly tectonic processes that the USSR was undergoing in the 80s and that Russia is going through in the 90s were, without a doubt, triggered mainly by internal, not external, factors. It is the height of folly and conceit to attribute all these processes to U.S. "victory."

The historical truth is that, having built up internal contradictions, the Soviet Communist system disintegrated—imploded from within. It could, of course, be assumed that the West has been more successful in its ideological struggle ("psychological warfare" if you will). It should probably also be recognized that the KGB was "outplayed" by the CIA (in any event, the devastating defeat of Soviet special services is admitted even by their own representatives). And still the breakup of the Soviet system and the Communist regime (but not of Great Russia) is above all an internal process—natural and inevitable—because both the system and the regime were based on a shaky foundation. And if anyone has won out over us, this was, as a matter of fact, Russia itself, which found enough strength to abandon the Communist pseudo-religion.

It is another matter that the country's historical transformation from totalitarianism to a free and democratic model of evolution, from an administration and command system to a market economy and a state based on the rule of law, from a closed to an open society (a transformation, it needs to be pointed out, which is still far from complete) could have occurred without the disintegration of the USSR was it not for a large number of gross strategic miscalculations by the ruling elite of the late Soviet Union. A great share of the blame also falls on the national elite as a whole. It [is] in this sense—and only in this sense—that we can, and should, talk about the country's nationwide defeat. Especially if we act on the assumption that Russia is not a state that has appeared out of thin air but is a historical successor to the Russian empire and the USSR. In this respect we could probably also talk about the defeat of Great Russia: As a result of internal transformation, its national elite ended up totally demoralized and divided, unable to carry through a constructive renewal and revision of national values and ideals, to create a viable strategy for the country's development or to work out such neutralizing ideological mechanisms that would offset the negative, destructive fallout from the inevitable collapse of the Communist regime.

Even so none of this gives cause to talk about a total "defeat" of Russia in the Cold War or the unconditional "victory" of the United States. The end of the Cold War cannot in principle be seen in terms of "victory" or "loss" because it was a war of positions, a war of ideologies, and, as a matter of fact, it was not waged for geopolitical acquisitions. It was a contest of two ideologies, two lifestyles which had the semblance of a historical contest of economic systems or of the arms race. Yet it was not the Western lifestyle—although its influence cannot be understated—and certainly not the NATO military machine that won out in this war.

It should also be added here that none of the documents of the early 90s talk about Russia's "defeat" or "capitulation"—be it the CFE Treaty or the "2 + 4" formula on the reunification of Germany or the 1990 Paris Charter. Quite the contrary, these documents record the obligation of all OSCE member countries to build a single Great Europe without dividing lines, based on an absolutely equal partnership. The West, however, interpreted the collapse of the USSR precisely as an utter "defeat" of Russia. This interpretation became necessary in order to revise in its favor the Yalta-Potsdam world order, i.e., the outcome of WWII which Russia definitely won. It is noteworthy that even after the "victory of democracy" in Russia, it came to be dubbed as "the core of the evil empire"—on the assumption that it perfidiously changed only its facade but not its essence. In other words, the hatred toward Communism and the Soviet system (since they are nonexistent today) is now quite openly being shifted toward Russia itself. The ideology of "Sovietophobia" was verbally transformed into the ideology of "Russophobia."

This ingenuous ideological operation only strengthens the confidence that the West's "lofty" struggle against Soviet Communism was just a fig leaf which in fact covered the real war against historical Russia. And if the collapse of "totalitarianism" is interpreted as "capitulation" of the millennium-old Russian civilization to Western liberal values, then the entire history of relations between the West and Russia in the 20th century has been nothing but an imitation of the struggle with Bolshevism. The main substance and the main objective of the West's policy was in fact to divide the territory of historical Russia. In working to achieve this goal, it unscrupulously and cynically took advantage of the country's periods of weakness as well as of Russia's antinational elite. This was done first in 1917, with the help of the Bolsheviks. Then, when Russia recovered the status of a great power, an attempt was made to do it in 1941, with the help of Hitler. In 1991, it was done with the help of Cold War technology.

Assuming the utter "defeat" of Great Russia, its entire historical existence is called

into question. Moreover, not only the future but also the past, which is becoming uncertain, questionable, and dubious. By accepting the "triumph of the winner," Russia
challenges the historical destiny of the Russian people, negates its past, depriving it of
any sense of purpose, and calls into question the meaning and objectives of Russia's history and its national identity. Russian history is thus being "unwound," as it were, until the Russian historical time is completely destroyed because this—not only the division of the Russian historical space—will, strictly speaking, be the final ideological
victory of the West. However, it is impossible to destroy something that has existed on
Earth without destroying the memory of it. This is why the farcical debunking of Russian history, its ritual ridiculing, occupied such an important place in the Cold War
technology. (This is a step forward compared to Marquis de Custin, who in his book
Russia in 1839 was mainly out to frighten.) The West itself is also a master of this
weapon but the real virtuosity in this respect was achieved by the Soviet (and post-
Soviet) liberal intelligentsia with its habits of double moral standards, "giving the regime the finger behind their back," cynical innuendoes, and the overt rejection of
everything that could be sacred to "this" country.

Thus, recognition of the West's "rightness" in the Cold War means not at all the
renunciation of Communism but the recognition of the fallacy of the entire Russian
historical idea—*of the entire Russian Orthodox idea in history as a whole*. The Russian
people, who throughout centuries have worked for the benefit of Russian statehood,
resisting the onslaught by the West, comes across in this light as merely an exponent of
"imperial arrogance" and its resistance, as just the consequence of natural depravity and
groundless "ambitions." It so happens that, having withstood the onslaught of Catholi-
cism; having defended—at the cost of a sea of blood—the Russian borders in the north,
south, west, and east; having defeated the Teutonic Order, the Osman Empire, and
Napoleon, and having finally smashed Nazi Germany, the Russian people in the end
humbly—and even joyfully—bowed to America! And for the sake of what?

The flip side of the recognition of total "defeat" in the Cold War is Russia's recognition of itself as an "evil empire" or—in a milder but more humiliating form—as a
freakish deviation from the "mainstream world path." And therefore as a failure of
world history. This in its turn leads to submission to the West whose values acquire the
status of "global human" values. It is just one step from here to Russia's self-recognition
as "a redundant country" (Z. Brzezinski's expression), and its self-annihilation.

True, there is one positive side to the myth of "defeat." It helps the growth of national consciousness and therefore the recovery of Russia's own identity which has
apparently been lost forever and dissolved in the Soviet period of history. (The well pronounced and sharply growing Americanophobia is a negative byproduct of this undoubtedly healthy nation-wide reaction to the overt triumph of the "winner." Moreover, as it is generally typical of traditional Russian consciousness, it is not aimed against
the people and not even against the country but against the concrete form of conduct
by that country.) And the stronger the offensive by the "winner," the more rapidly this
process is evolving. From this point of view, the Americans greatly benefit Russia because they thus recognize that present-day Russia is not some new country but a successor to the Russian empire and to the Soviet Union. It bears the historical responsibility for the crimes of czarism and the Communist leaders. This is its karma. But at the
same time it also bears responsibility for its future as Great Russia and with it the responsibility for the future of the whole world.

Nevertheless, it needs to be stressed that this trend is potentially dangerous because
it can provoke extreme forms of Russian nationalism. Overt attempts to fix the outcome
of the destruction of Russian statehood no matter what under the pretext of the "legit-

imate" collapse of the "totalitarian USSR" could ultimately lead to the conclusion that without a direct and unambiguous restoration of the historical legal succession of the Russian Federation—not of 1991 or 1922 but of 1917—it will be impossible to eliminate the very basis of the present condition of the Russians as a divided nation.

So the United States is hardly well advised to play up the thesis about its "victory" in the Cold War. This is not in its own interests. In the Cold War—in any event, long term—there are no, and there can be no, "winners" or "losers." We could probably say that thus far it is Russia that is paying the highest price for the end of the Cold War although it should in theory have benefited from it the most. This is not to say, however, that the other side in the not very distant future will not pay its own price for it. At any rate, judging by the latest article by S. Huntington, The Erosion of U.S. National Interests,[17] this future, indeed, is not too far away. Such is the ill-starred lot of the "victor." N. Berdia'ev once said: "Woe not unto the losers—woe unto the winners." Because they miss the moment when they should stop and say to themselves: "Enough." They miss the moment when they should restrain themselves; it is difficult for them to mobilize their reaction of self-control; they are overwhelmed by euphoria over their "victories," the feeling of strength and muscle flexing. Aestheticism of force is a great temptation for the "winner." And the more the Americans today assert the unicentrical model and the more they insist on it and the more excited they are by their "victory" in the Cold War, the more serious the challenges that America will face in the 21st century. Reaction not only from Russia but also from other countries will not be slow in coming, and it will be all the more acute and all the less predictable, the more arrogantly and dogmatically the present "winner" behaves.

In concluding this discussion about the "winners" and "losers," it needs to be said that the collapse of the USSR is, without a doubt, a national catastrophe. Yet, as S. Kurginian rightly points out, there are three types of catastrophes. First, catastrophes of exhaustion, when the potential of a civilized community has been exhausted, leading to the death of civilization. Second, catastrophes of shift (upheaval), when the mechanisms whereby society impacts on the elite and actuates its leading minority become ineffectual. And third, catastrophes of inversion, or inverted catastrophes, whereby governing systems degenerate and are converted to new codes with the national identity intact.[18]

The catastrophe of the disintegration of the USSR is a catastrophe of shift and to a certain extent a catastrophe of inversion, but in no way is it a catastrophe of exhaustion. Therefore it is a rectifiable catastrophe. A new model of national evolution should take into account the entire experience of catastrophes that have accompanied Russian history, and provide effective mechanisms for averting them in the future. This, however, is a separate subject.

The Cold War specific is that it is a creeping catastrophe. Whereas its beginning can be determined, its end is almost impossible to define. Its ultimate spatial/temporal context is essentially blurred. Some very fine, subtle technologies, oftentimes appearing imperceptible, have been used in the Cold War.

But then the following question arises: Maybe even now we fail to appreciate that these technologies are being used against us? After all, there is no bombing, there are no tanks rolling on, and there are no airborne assault operations—there is none of this. This, however, does not mean that a new Munich has not as yet occurred.

In any event, certain circles in the West are harboring plans of Russia's further dismemberment. These plans are reflected in Z. Brzezinski's latest book, *Geostrategy for Eurasia*. In it, he writes about a "free confederative Russia comprised of European Russia, the Siberian Republic, and the Far East Republic." With this configuration,

Brzezinski stresses, it will be easier for Russia to maintain close economic relations with its neighbors. Each of such confederative entities will be able to successfully develop its creative potential on the local level, which has throughout centuries been suppressed by the heavy bureaucratic hand of Moscow. For its part, a decentralized Russia will be less inclined to display imperial ambitions.[19] This goes even further than the aforementioned plans of Nazi Germany, which at least did not plan to divide Russia's heartland. Incidentally, 80 years ago, the United States also tended to support Russia's integrity. In 1918, W. Wilson, in one of the famous 14 points of the Versailles Peace Treaty, declared the unacceptability of Russia's disintegration. And he was right because he knew that once Russia began to be divided up, the United States would end up with nothing— everything would be seized by the Japanese, the British, and the French. Yet by the end of the century the situation has changed: Transnational financial capital has evolved which basically could not care less about state borders. It is only important that all key positions are held by representatives of this capital. It is vital to control raw materials and energy resources. If, to this end, Russia has to be divided into three republics united by a weak confederation, or into 40 belligerent monarchies at war with each other, it will agree to this without a second's hesitation. And if this is the case, the Cold War will continue.

NOTES

1. See: *International Affairs,* 1993, No. 7.
2. See: K. Mialo. *Mezhdu Zapadom i Vostokom (Between West and East).* M., 1996, p. 110.
3. *Nezavisimaia Gazeta,* 24 July 1996.
4. See: *International Affairs,* 1993, No. 7.
5. See: *Russia-XXI,* 1994, pp. 158–174.
6. *Iuridicheskaia Gazeta,* 1992, No. 5, p. 29.
7. Ibid.
8. *Nezavisimaia Gazeta,* 7 April 1997.
9. T. Graham. *Russian Foreign Policy and the Crisis of Russian Statehood. 20 April 1995. Report to a seminar at the Carnegie Endowment Moscow Branch.*
10. *Nezavisimaia Gazeta,* 27 November 1996.
11. *International Affairs,* 1998, No. 1.
12. *The Washington Post,* 15 October 1996.
13. Zarevand. *Turkey and Panturkism.* Paris, 1930, pp. 27–28.
14. *Newsweek,* 27 March 1991.
15. *Finansovye Izvestia,* 15 January 1998.
16. *Argumenty i Fakty,* 1997, No. 20.
17. *Foreign Affairs,* 1997, No. 5.
18. *Russia-XXI,* 1993, No. 2, p. 25.
19. *Nezavisimaia Gazeta,* 24 October 1997.

7

❇

Evolution of the
World Economy

Reading 7-1

The Legends of Bretton Woods
Francis J. Gavin

Did the Bretton Woods monetary system really provide for economic stability and international cooperation over the quarter century following World War II? That is certainly the conventional wisdom among statesmen, foreign-policy analysts, and academics. The institutions and rules established by the 1944 agreements have been hailed as some of the most important economic and even political accomplishments of the cold war era. As a noted historian recently wrote, "Bretton Woods is the most revered name in international monetary history, perhaps in economic history." [1]

Assessing the performance of Bretton Woods is especially important now because of the widespread dissatisfaction with current monetary arrangements. Recent events, most notably the collapse of the Mexican peso and the steep decline of the dollar against the yen, have increased the concern for the fate of the dollar and the rules of the world monetary regime. Each unanticipated shift in exchange rates is talked about in grave tones, as if greater disaster will follow if the dollar is not stabilized and the system is not reformed. A failure to act, it is warned, could recreate the destructive conditions of the 1930s, a time marked by competitive devaluations, capital controls, and protec-

SOURCE: From "The Legends of Bretton Woods" by Francis J. Gavin, *Orbis,* vol. 40, no. 2 (Spring 1996): 183–198. Copyright © 1996. Reprinted with permission from the Foreign Policy Research Institute.

tionism that in turn produced isolationism, autarky, and eventually war. W. L. Givens has likened the post–Bretton Woods record of dollar devaluation to a cocaine addiction and argued that "a massive deterioration of the dollar's value, particularly relative to the yen, has masked the problem of declining competitiveness and functioned as a habitual surrogate for both industrial policy and productivity improvement."[2] Diane Kunz predicted that "without a pronounced shift in Washington's policy, the decline of the dollar could resurrect the ghosts of the 1930s."[3] And a conference of internationally renowned monetary economists faulted the world's governments for failing to emulate the leadership and cooperation demonstrated by the United States and Great Britain in 1944:

> In the last two decades international monetary relations have been characterized by latent instability, and more recently by severe tensions. Yet the issue of reforming the international monetary system does not appear on the agenda of the policymakers of the major countries involved.[4]

International monetary reform seems especially critical now because of the supposed primacy of economic factors over military considerations in the post–cold war world. This point is hardly debated any more. As a Clinton administration official was quoted as saying, "Everyone acknowledges that economics now plays a central role in foreign policy—that battle is over."[5] There is a widely held belief that peace can be assured only by building up international institutions and creating rules that promote global stability, cooperation, and interdependence. By this standard, current monetary arrangements seem grossly inadequate, a veritable "non-system" dominated by speculators and national authorities who pursue profit or narrow national interest at the cost of international stability. It is argued that current monetary relations are plagued by an exchange-rate volatility that wastes resources, creates acrimony, and promotes protectionism.

Many of these monetary reformers are nostalgic for the good old days of Bretton Woods. Kunz described Bretton Woods as the cornerstone of U.S. foreign economic policy, a crucial part of America's postwar domestic prosperity and ultimate success in the cold war: "Bretton Woods would have a significant bottom-line impact on the American economy."[6] The rules and institutions established at Bretton Woods, it is assumed, subordinated market speculation and national self-interest to the higher goal of international cooperation through a stable exchange-rate regime monitored and enforced by the rules of the International Monetary Fund (IMF). The authors of the plan wanted a system that would "avoid competitive devaluations among currencies; the fund would stabilize foreign-exchange rates, encourage the flow of productive capital among participating nations, help stabilize price levels, promote sound credit practices and reduce barriers to foreign trade."[7] That they succeeded—and thus laid a foundation for international growth, interdependence, and cooperation in the years following World War II—was a view oft repeated during the summer of 1994, in celebration of the fiftieth anniversary of the Bretton Woods conference.

That is why so many analysts want to re-establish a similar system. Judy Shelton, a senior research associate at the Hoover Institution, argues that international monetary reform is necessary to avoid a "global meltdown," and that reforms should be based on the successful elements of the Bretton Woods system:

> The next effort to build a new world monetary order should reflect an appreciation for what has worked well in the past. It should start with the same basic framework laid out in the old Bretton Woods approach: fixed exchange rates

among national currencies anchored by a government commitment to redeem in gold.[8]

Last July, the Bretton Woods Commission, led by the former chairman of the Federal Reserve, Paul Volcker, announced an effort to encourage an economic supergovernment to coordinate exchange rates. According to the *New York Times:*

> A half century after the about to be victorious Allies of World War II put in place bold plans for a global financial system and two decades after that system was formally abandoned, a high profile group of economists, bankers, and diplomats is trying to put it back together again.[9]

Should the Bretton Woods monetary system be held in such high esteem, or are many of the standard beliefs about it simply incorrect? The answer, alas, is the latter. First, the Bretton Woods system was not driven by some grand idealistic purpose on the part of its founders, but by considerations of national interest. The British especially saw in the agreements a chance to immunize their planned social programs from international balance-of-payments pressures and to acquire generous amounts of American aid without political concessions. Secondly, the Bretton Woods agreements did not create financial stability, economic interdependence, and international cooperation. In fact, the plan to abolish exchange controls while at the same time establishing fixed exchange rates, full convertibility, free trade, and domestic autonomy was unworkable from the start. What emerged after the war was an ad hoc system plagued by non-convertibility, trade restrictions, and capital controls. These flaws were largely hidden through generous allotments of American aid. When the major European currencies were made convertible in late 1958, the system promptly began to break down. For the next ten years, monetary relations were marked by a chaos and instability that strained relations among the Western allies. Indeed, the internal contradictions of the Bretton Woods system virtually guaranteed contentious balance-of-payments issues that, absent an effective adjustment mechanism, could only be resolved politically. Whether or not monetary relations and dollar policy should be reformed today is certainly debatable, but the history of postwar monetary relations does not provide a helpful vision of what any new system should look like.

THE BRETTON WOODS AGREEMENTS

The Bretton Woods agreements of 1944 were the most ambitious and far-reaching monetary agreements among sovereign states in history. American and British financial officials, led by Harry Dexter White and John Maynard Keynes, hoped to set up a system that would maintain stable exchange rates, allow nations' currencies to be converted into an asset over which they had no issuing control, and provide an effective mechanism to adjust exchange rates in the event that a fundamental balance-of-payments disequilibrium did emerge. In the case of non-fundamental deficits that normally arose in international transactions, the deficit country would pay with a reserve asset (gold or a key currency convertible into gold) or seek short-term financing from the International Monetary Fund.[10]

This system differed greatly from a traditional gold standard, in which the domestic money supply, hence the domestic price level, was directly determined by the national gold stock. Under the gold standard, a balance-of-payments deficit would be paid for through the export of gold, resulting in a decrease in the domestic money base and a deflation of prices. The decreased purchasing power would lower that country's imports, and the increased international demand for that country's lower-priced goods would increase exports, naturally correcting the balance-of-payments deficit. Conversely, an influx of gold, by increasing the domestic monetary base and domestic prices, had the opposite effect of boosting imports and discouraging exports, thereby eliminating a payments surplus. According to standard market theory, any disequilibrium would be adjusted more or less automatically, eliminating the need for government interference. In reality, the gold standard worked as well as it did before World War I because capital flows from London, and to a lesser extent Paris, kept the system functioning smoothly.

White, and especially Keynes, believed that an adjustment process based on deflating the economy of a deficit country was draconian at a time when governments were promising full employment and generous social spending after the war. Decreasing the monetary base in a deficit country would lead to a fall in national income, unleashing unemployment and necessitating cuts in government spending. To avoid such a politically unacceptable system, the Bretton Woods regime allowed nations to import and export gold without penalty. Deficits were to be corrected through IMF assistance and small, discrete changes in the exchange rate. Although the Bretton Woods agreements were hailed as the hallmark of international cooperation, in reality they provided national economic and political authorities an unprecedented amount of immunity from the pressures of the market. Macroeconomic decisions were the sole province of domestic governments, who were often quick to sacrifice measures that would bring about a payments equilibrium in order to achieve domestic goals.

Because it was generally believed that the existing gold stock was too small to sustain the growing demand for international liquidity, the Bretton Woods regime would be a two-tiered system whereby certain key currencies that were convertible into gold, such as the dollar and eventually sterling, could be used in lieu of gold to settle international transactions. It was believed that such a measure would conserve the use of gold and dramatically increase the amount of liquidity available to finance international transactions. International liquidity required that the economies of the key currency countries run payments deficits. But how large a deficit? Too little, and it was feared that liquidity would dry up and international transactions disappear; too large, and the resulting inflation would test the value of the key currency and set off a large-scale conversion into gold.

What were the larger motives of the founders of the plan? It has often been noted how remarkable it was that Keynes and White, despite the vastly different economic priorities of the countries they represented, were able to come up with such an extraordinary compromise.[11] Indeed, Keynes's original plan envisioned a "currency union" in which countries would have to pay a penalty on their *surplus* payments balances. Additionally, debtor nations would have unrestricted and virtually unlimited access to the resources of the clearing fund without having to seek international approval or make domestic adjustments to correct payments disequilibrium.[12] That plan had an enormous inflationary bias and would have allowed Britain to tap the immense resources of the United States without having to go through the arduous and embarrassing process of asking for direct aid.

Were White and Keynes driven, as Shelton has argued, "by a humanitarian desire to prevent the kind of financial stresses and economic dislocations that might lead to future wars"? Shelton nicely sums up the conventional wisdom:

> In short, Keynes and White were convinced that international economic cooperation would provide a new foundation of hope for a world all too prone to vio-

lence. "If we can continue," Keynes observed, "this nightmare will be over. The brotherhood of man will have become more than a phrase."[13]

Keynes's own writing calls this interpretation into doubt. Not only would his plan protect Britain's intended full-employment policies from balance-of-payments pressures, but it would also present a convenient and politically painless way to get money out of the United States in the guise of international reform:

> It would also be a mistake to invite of our own motion, direct financial assistance after the war from the United States to ourselves. Whether as a gift or a loan without interest or a gratuitous redistribution of gold reserves. The U.S. will consider that we have had our whack in the shape of lend-lease and a generous settlement of consideration. . . . We in particular, in a distressed and ruined continent, will not bear the guise of the most suitable claimant for a dole. . . . On the contrary. If we are to attract the interest and enthusiasm of the Americans, *we must come with an ambitious plan of an international complexion, suitable to serve the interests of others sides ourselves.* . . . It is not with our problems of ways and means that idealistic and internationally minded Americans will be particularly concerned.[14]

The Americans rejected the currency union plan as too radical, but the British came up with a substitute in the so-called scarce-currency clause, which permitted extensive capital controls and trade discrimination against major surplus countries. Both Keynes and R. F. Harrod, a Treasury official, suggested that the scarce-currency clause not be discussed in public for fear that the U.S. Congress might figure out its true implications. Harrod wrote, "In view of the need for 'good handling' the less public lucidity there is on this matter the better." And Keynes stated, "The monetary fund, in particular, has the great advantage that to the average Congressman it is extremely boring."[15]

The clause was included in the agreements, but the Americans interpreted it very narrowly, a fact that created much bitterness in Britain. In later years, the British government blamed many of its economic woes on the narrow interpretation of Article VII by the Americans:

> In particular, United States policy in the Fund has been directed . . . to making the "scarce currency" clause a dead letter. We thought originally that this clause might give some real protection against a dollar shortage; indeed, Lord Keynes' conviction that this was so was one of the main factors which led His Majesty's Government and Parliament to accept the Loan Agreement. Once the clause comes into operation, it gives wide freedom for discriminatory exchange and trade controls against the scarce currency; and then there is real pressure on the country concerned to play its full part in putting the scarcity right, e.g. by drastic action such as we want the United States to take to stimulate imports.[16]

The British had little to complain about, however, because the larger political goal of promoting European reconstruction and eventual union led the United States to permit extensive dollar discrimination while furnishing billions of dollars of aid.

THE FLAWS OF THE BRETTON WOODS PLAN

In its final form, Bretton Woods was unworkable because it lacked an adequate adjustment mechanism. That guaranteed persistent payments imbalances, which threatened exchange-rate stability. Exchange-rate stability could be maintained only by providing ever increasing amounts of "liquidity," a process that created enormous political difficulties and ultimately undermined confidence in the system.

Why were the fixed exchange rates unstable? The plan, unlike a pure gold standard, affirmed the primacy of domestic economic goals, including the maintenance of full-employment economies, over strict balance-of-payments concerns. But exchange-rate stability can be sustained only when there is comparable price stability between countries. If prices change markedly because of inflation or deflation in a given domestic economy, then currency exchange rates must change accordingly or else their initial par rates will quickly be rendered meaningless. When exchange rates are not changed to reflect price changes, balance-of-payments disequilibriums emerge. Such a situation would be especially problematic if the initial par values were already out of line, which was often the case because nations had a large say in setting their own rates.

This payments disequilibrium was a constant source of financial instability in the postwar era. For example, if Britain's domestic economic goals produced a yearly inflation rate of 10 percent, and the United States pursued policies that resulted in 4 percent inflation, then the pound-to-dollar exchange rate would have to be adjusted to avoid a balance-of-payments disequilibrium. But that obviously contradicted the goal of exchange-rate stability, and there was no easy mechanism to adjust the exchange rate without creating havoc. The Bretton Woods system, despite its advertising, gave an unusual advantage to currency traders, who could easily discern what currencies were in need of revaluation and could simply put pressure on a vulnerable currency until its government exhausted its reserves and lost its will to defend the old exchange rate. Speculators made fortunes when sterling was devalued in 1949 and 1967. The only way to avoid such devaluations was to impose capital controls, which every major country, including the United States, had to install at some point during the Bretton Woods era in order to maintain its exchange rate.

A second flaw, less well recognized but equally serious, was the method of providing liquidity in the Bretton Woods system. Liquidity is simply another word used to describe reserve assets that are transferred from debtor countries to cover their payments gap. In order to offset a negative balance of payments and maintain a fixed exchange rate, nations have to supply some universally accepted asset over which they have no issuing control. Until 1914, that asset was gold. Because planners believed that there was not enough gold to supply world liquidity needs, key currencies, such as the dollar and sterling, would be used to supplement or replace gold to settle international transactions.

That brought up a larger question: how stable and cooperative would a system be that required the world's largest economy to run persistent balance-of-payments deficits? The dollar, fixed against gold at $35/ounce, had to do double duty under the Bretton Woods system: first, as a national currency; secondly, as an international reserve asset. But sooner or later, the amount of dollar liabilities held for this reserve purpose was bound to become larger than the value of the gold stock backing its value. At that point, holders of the reserve asset, in this case dollars, might question the ability of the reserve country to maintain the convertibility of its currency; they might start exchanging their dollars for gold until the American supply was exhausted. That would naturally worry the reserve country, which would take steps to limit the deficit and the loss of gold. But that, it was feared, would decrease the amount of liquidity in the whole global system, which could lead to deflation and a seizing up of international transactions.

In sum, Bretton Woods guaranteed failure. More and more liquidity was needed to maintain fixed exchange rates in the growing international economy. But because the worldwide gold stock was limited, most of the liquidity was supplied by the American payments deficit. As this deficit increased, doubts arose everywhere as to the ratio of dollars to the gold backing them up. This confidence problem was known as the "Triffin dilemma" after the economist, Robert Triffin, who first pointed it out in 1960.

Nevertheless, the dilemma remained largely misunderstood during the 1960s. Instead of improving the adjustment mechanism to correct the payments imbalances, economists and policymakers focused on finding ways to provide more liquidity. But that only masked and exacerbated the original problem—the differential inflation rates that produced large imbalances among countries in a fixed-rate regime. Since it was difficult to adjust exchange rates, and most governments refused to alter domestic priorities for balance-of-payments purposes, leaders clamored for liquidity to finance balance-of-payments deficits. But it was rarely pointed out that such liquidity would be unnecessary if there were an efficient, effective, and automatic process for adjusting imbalances, as provided for by a gold standard or—the opposite extreme—a flexible exchange rate system.

Instead, all manner of stopgaps were invented to fudge the structural contradiction in the currency system: swap agreements, a gold pool, Roosa bonds, increased authority for the IMF, and the Special Drawing Rights (SDR). These innovative institutions, regimes, and rules fostered an illusion of international cooperation but in fact allowed a dysfunctional system to limp along through ever more elaborate suppression of the workings of the market.

MANAGING DISEQUILIBRIUM:
MONETARY RELATIONS, 1946–1968

The Bretton Woods blueprint for exchange-rate stability, hard convertibility, and international cooperation through the International Monetary Fund soon proved untenable. In 1947, buoyed by an enormous stabilization loan given by the United States after the cessation of Lend-Lease, the British attempted to make sterling convertible into gold and dollars, as stipulated by the Bretton Woods agreements. That first real test of the agreements proved a dismal failure. There was an immediate run on the pound, and within months Britain ran down the loan. Convertibility was suspended, and no other major currency would attempt anything approaching hard convertibility until the end of 1958. That failure convinced the United States to provide direct aid to Britain and Western Europe through the Marshall Plan. It also persuaded the Americans to accept widespread trade discrimination and monetary controls aimed at the dollar and dollar goods, in clear violation of the terms of Bretton Woods. Some of the monetary restrictions were lifted in 1958, but much of the trade discrimination against U.S. goods continues to this day.

The pretense of exchange-rate stability was abandoned shortly thereafter when Britain undertook a massive devaluation of sterling in order to make its exports more competitive and to write down wartime debts. The British did not seek the approval of the IMF or any of their major non-Commonwealth trading partners except for the United States. The 1949 devaluation outraged the nations of Western Europe and threatened to undo the tentative movement toward European trade and monetary integration. The lesson learned by other nations was that there was no punishment for a unilateral devaluation. If one of the countries that helped design the Bretton Woods system flouted its rules, how could other nations be expected to go along? Other devaluations soon followed.

Where was the International Monetary Fund, which was supposed to be the source of liquidity for temporary payments imbalances and the enforcer of international monetary rules? In actuality, the IMF was emasculated in the 1940s and 1950s, with little authority or voice in international economics. Liquidity was supplied to the world by direct U.S. aid, through programs like the Marshall Plan, Harry S. Truman's "Point Four" program, and the Military Assistance Program. In fact, signatories of the Marshall Plan were strictly *forbidden* from using the IMF to correct payments imbalances. The Marshall Plan actually created a monetary system for Western Europe—the European Payments Union—that provided for extremely limited intra-European convertibility and allowed significant discrimination against dollar transactions (discrimination that had been forbidden except under extreme circumstance in Bretton Woods). It was only much later, and for largely political reasons, that the IMF became a player in world monetary relations.

Only in December 1958 did the major Western European economies establish current-account convertibility. Some argue that this marked the true beginning of the Bretton Woods system. It was also the beginning of the massive U.S. payments imbalances that were to plague the system until its collapse. The American deficit was first identified as a cause for concern towards the end of 1958, when U.S. secretary of the treasury Robert Anderson became alarmed at its growing size. An American deficit was not news; deficits had been run throughout the 1950s. It was the size of the deficit, and the fact that excess dollars were being turned in for gold instead of being held as reserves, that concerned Anderson. He worried that the amount of dollars held abroad would soon be larger than the value of the gold stock promised to back those dollars. That would make the dollar vulnerable to a speculative attack in the event of a political or economic crisis, and a run on the dollar would surely undermine confidence in the whole monetary system at a critical moment in the cold war.

The Eisenhower administration debated various policies to reduce the deficit until the matter came to a head during the summer and fall of 1960. The price of gold on the London free market increased to over $40 an ounce, providing an enormous incentive for anyone abroad holding dollars to buy gold from the U.S. Treasury at $35 an ounce, then sell it in London for a substantial profit. But by 1960 there was not enough U.S. gold to cover these overseas dollars. America's promise to sell gold at a fixed price, a promise that was the foundation of all international monetary rules, thus became a magic money machine for overseas holders of dollar liabilities. The reasons that gold had been bid up included the tensions over Berlin, the burgeoning American payments deficit, and the fear of loose monetary and fiscal policies under a Kennedy presidency. But instead of recognizing the flaws in the system, American policymakers wrongly blamed the market. After 1960, the United States introduced measures to protect the dollar, and the system it upheld, from future attack. Capital controls, at first mild and "voluntary" but eventually quite obtrusive, were introduced. Restrictions on tourism were initiated. As noted, various stopgaps were instituted in Western countries to restrict and control currency and gold markets. That the world's largest and apparently healthiest economy had to take such steps seemed strange, but the gold guarantee and fixed exchange rates could be maintained only by increasingly complex controls. What was perhaps most alarming was the impact that these monetary matters had on U.S. foreign policy and relations with NATO.

By any measure, the United States during the 1960s possessed overwhelming economic strength, commanding a larger share of the world's wealth than any modern nation in history. That wealth was convincingly exhibited by the American ability to dispense billions of dollars in aid to its allies and station hundreds of thousands of troops in foreign countries. Yet the United States's whole foreign policy—including the global containment of communism—was absurdly endangered by movements in the price of gold in London. After the gold crisis of 1960, it seemed logical to policymakers to blame the U.S. payments imbalance and shortage of gold on two factors: speculators operating in a free market and American overseas commitments. After all, the United States still consistently maintained a sizable current-account surplus (positive balance of trade) throughout this period.

So a fierce debate raged within the Eisenhower, Kennedy, and Johnson administrations over the impact that vital U.S. foreign-policy commitments were having on the balance of payments and price of gold. Dwight D. Eisenhower and his top aides feared that unless U.S. commitments were reduced, the payments balance would deteriorate, the gold outflow would worsen, and the international monetary system would be destroyed. The resulting economic collapse might well fracture the NATO alliance and hand the Soviet Union a victory in the cold war without a shot being fired. Of course, that never happened, and it is arguable whether it could have happened. But the important point is the fact that concerns over the dollar and the international monetary system had a major impact on foreign-policy decisions.

All three administrations met the crisis with policies that antagonized alliance relations. Although American troop reductions in Europe were never fully carried out, mere discussion of the issue damaged confidence in the U.S. commitment to defend Western Europe. Ultimately, West Germany, Japan, and others "agreed" to offset the full balance-of-payments cost of the American troops. The president of the Bundesbank also promised to hold American dollars and not turn them in for gold. Both the offset agreement and the gold guarantee created great tensions in the American-German relationship. Attempts to get Charles de Gaulle's France to cooperate on monetary matters failed miserably, worsening an already strained alliance.

Neither these nor any other measures could repair the fundamental problems of the Bretton Woods system. Throughout the 1960s, policymakers and outside observers produced dozens of plans to reform the international monetary system but reached no consensus. The task became urgent when Britain, in the face of massive speculation on the currency markets, was forced to devalue sterling again in November 1967. Johnson administration officials feared that speculators would attack the dollar next. The payments deficit, which had been brought under control in 1965, ballooned during the next two years, primarily because of the cost of the Vietnam War.

The Johnson administration announced a program on January 1, 1968, that included border taxes and export subsidies, steep travel taxes, increased offset payments from allies, limits on overseas lending by American banks, and mandatory controls on capital investment abroad. The program had enormous political costs, especially in an election year. Overseas, especially in continental Europe, the plan provoked an outcry. The Atlantic Alliance, strained to the breaking point in 1966 and 1967 by internal crises, was pressured further by the administration's plan. Worse still, the plan reversed a cardinal tenet of postwar American foreign economic policy: to promote open markets and free trade around the world.

The American public found it hard to understand how U.S. policymakers had gotten the nation into such a mess. Milton Friedman, in a widely read *Newsweek* column, condemned Johnson's program:

How low we have fallen! The United States, the land of the free, prohibits its businessmen from investing abroad and requests its citizens not to show their faces or open their pocketbooks in foreign ports. The United States, the wealthiest nation in the world, announces that its foreign policy will no longer be determined by its national interest and its international commitments but by the need to reduce government spending abroad by $500 million.[17]

To compound matters, the harsh balance-of-payments program was completely ineffective. By March 1968, the Johnson administration was forced to call an emergency meeting of the world's finance ministers, and finally to ask the British government to close its gold market. Under enormous political pressure from the United States, it was agreed that a two-tiered gold market would be established: a private market in which the price of gold would be determined by supply and demand, and an intergovernmental market where the price would remain $35 an ounce. Of course, the finance ministers had also to agree not to buy or sell gold on the open market. That meant the United States could exert enormous political pressure on world bankers to hold their dollars without fear of being overwhelmed by the private market. When the Nixon administration subsequently ended convertibility altogether in 1971, then abandoned fixed exchange rates in 1973, it was almost an anti-climax. The Bretton Woods system was already dead—a victim of its own contradictions. What replaced it—the term is illustrative—was the current system of sometimes free, sometimes managed exchange rates called the "dirty float."

GOLD, DOLLARS, AND POWER

Imagine the public reaction if the global leaders of a particular industry colluded to suppress the workings of the free market and arbitrarily fix the price of their goods. People would be outraged, and the corporate heads would be charged with conspiracy and restraint of trade. Why then should an international monetary system that arbitrarily fixed prices and repressed its market mechanism be hailed as a highpoint of international cooperation? While there are important differences, it seems odd to honor a system that was so inherently unstable. It seems even odder that so many people look to this system as a model for future monetary reform.

Although the Bretton Woods system has been subject to a certain amount of criticism within the highly technical world of international monetary economics, most historians and political scientists (and many economists) hold an idealized view of the system.[18] Even those economists who have criticized the system have failed to understand that economic issues were inextricably linked with political considerations. And few have questioned the idea that the controversial authors of the Bretton Woods plan were driven by anything but the most idealistic purposes.

That brings up an important question: why did American policymakers go to such great lengths to preserve a deeply flawed monetary system? Did the political benefits outweigh the costs of the Bretton Woods system? And why was there such a fear of abandoning fixed exchange rates for a more flexible exchange-rate system that had a market-driven adjustment mechanism?

There were certainly disadvantages for the United States in the system. As the reserve currency country, the United States was to a certain extent trapped by the system in ways other countries were not. From 1958 on, there was a constant fear that the ratio of dollar liabilities to American gold would increase to a level that might cause a loss of foreign confidence in the dollar and a run to the Treasury Department's gold window. A mass conversion to gold would force the United States to suspend convertibility, which would wipe out the dollar's value as a reserve and transaction currency. The ensuing competition among central banks for scarce gold could subject the international economy to paralyzing deflation. The resulting collapse of liquidity could freeze world trade and investment, but ending the American payments deficit could have an equally disastrous impact on the international economy. While in hindsight this fear derived from a misunderstanding of the liquidity issue, it was real in the minds of American statesman.[19]

U.S. policymakers had to worry constantly about the payments deficit and felt they had to sacrifice important domestic-policy goals and even foreign-policy imperatives in order to maintain the dollar's value. It angered them that much of the deficit was caused by expenditures made to defend Europe and Asia from the Soviet Union. And what seemed particularly outrageous was the fact that the United States could be pressured for political reasons by the countries in the system, the most obvious example being Charles de Gaulle's policy of converting dollars into gold, even when it made little economic sense to do so.

So why did the United States not abandon the system sooner? One important factor was the intellectual influence of the conventional wisdom about the history of monetary relations between the wars. It was a widely held belief that the economic collapse of the 1930s was due to a failure of international monetary cooperation. Most postwar economists and policymakers believed that speculation-driven capital flight had ruined the gold standard and destroyed international liquidity. The collapse of the rules of the game unleashed a vicious competition, whereby countries pursued beggar-thy-neighbor policies of competitive devaluations and trade restrictions. To most, the enemy was a free market "out of control." What these policymakers failed to realize is that competitive devaluations and beggar-thy-neighbor actions were caused by *government* policy, not the workings of the market. The free market was made the scapegoat for disastrous political decisions. In the postwar world, by contrast, the market would be tamed and national interest replaced with international cooperation based on enlightened rules and institutions. And few economists seemed to understand how chaotic and inefficient the Bretton Woods system actually was, since massive American aid and intervention tended to obscure its failings. The only voice calling for free exchange rates during the 1950s was Milton Friedman's, but his ideas were completely ignored until the 1960s, when other economists finally started to doubt the wisdom of the Bretton Woods system.[20] Hence, a deeply flawed intellectual framework guided postwar planners in most Western countries, especially the United States, and still commands disciples even today.

Another and perhaps more important reason why the United States stuck so long with a bad system was the fact that international disequilibrium *benefited* the United States in many ways. Because the dollar was an international currency held for reserve and intervention purposes, the United States received the benefits of seigniorage. That is, the fact that foreign central banks held dollars in reserve enabled American consumers to purchase foreign goods and services without having to give anything other than a promise to pay in return. It was like automatic credit. That arrangement could be maintained as long as the dollar was "as good as gold," when holding dollars in the form of short-term, interest-bearing securities was probably preferable to buying gold, which earned no interest income and had high transaction costs.

Most important, the Bretton Woods system also served a larger purpose in terms of American political and strategic goals: it fostered an image of Western unity and cooperation during the cold war. One of the foremost goals of American foreign policy in the postwar world was the rebuilding and eventual unification of Western Europe. The Bretton Woods monetary system could not function without massive government intervention and transnational collaboration. Between 1958 and 1968, when the Bretton Woods system was supposedly at its height, a whole series of agreements, regimes, rules, and institutions had to be invented—a revivified IMF, swap agreements, the gold pool, the group of ten, the Organization for Economic Cooperation and Development, the General Arrangements to Borrow, SDR, the Kennedy Round of GATT negotiations, the Working Party Three, and the Basle club—without which the whole system would have collapsed. The appearance of such unity and cooperation within the West was an important part of cold war strategy. And in fact, the system guaranteed that Western Europe (and Japan) had a stake in what the United States did, and vice-versa, because the reserve currency at the heart of the system was the dollar, a dollar whose convertibility into gold at a fixed price was considered fundamental to the prosperity of the Western economies.

WHERE DO WE GO FROM HERE?

To be sure, monetary relations have been turbulent since 1968, when the private and public gold markets were separated and the fiction of Bretton Woods came to an end. The bright hopes that floating exchange rates would create perfect equilibrium and stability have been to some extent disappointed. Many have claimed that there have been "overshoots" and wide fluctuations, which have misallocated resources. But constant intervention by these same central bankers has been responsible for many of the problems of the post–Bretton Woods period. It has been this intervention, this "managed" or "dirty" floating, that has prevented a truly flexible exchange-rate regime from coming into existence. Still, disappointment with the results of the managed float has made many misty-eyed for the days of Bretton Woods, or even the traditional gold standard. But regardless of the virtues of the nineteenth-century system, it is quite impossible today to imagine that national governments would relinquish their autonomy and accept the risk of severe deflation that comes with a "hard" gold standard.[21] So that leaves 1) a return to Bretton Woods, or 2) an even freer market that discourages central-bank intervention altogether.

The latter is unquestionably the way to go. For all the criticism, the post–Bretton Woods period has witnessed an unparalleled explosion of international trade and financial transactions. Indeed, real per capita growth in the United States was higher during the floating exchange-rate period of 1974–1989 (2.1 percent per year) than it was during the Bretton Woods period of 1946–1970 (2.0 percent per year) or even the gold-standard period of 1881–1913 (1.8 percent per year).[22] Moreover, the recent growth has spread broadly to regions like the Pacific Rim and South America. Growth during the Bretton Woods period was concentrated in Western Europe and Japan, areas that were the largest beneficiaries of American aid and trade favoritism. The more recent growth may have much to do with the drastic reduction in exchange and capital controls that has come about during the post–Bretton Woods era. Emerging economies can now tap a vast reservoir of private capital, and they have a much greater incentive to remain credit worthy than in the past. Today, private investment dwarfs international aid programs, which were, in any case, often driven more by politics than economic logic.

Is exchange-rate volatility really the fault of the post–Bretton Woods non-system? As a recent publication pointed out, that is the equivalent of a drunk driver blaming unsafe roads for his accident.[23] Since 1973, the economic policies of the United States and other developed nations have often been contradictory. In the 1980s, a mixture of loose fiscal policy and tight monetary policy created massive swings in capital flows, which produced substantial exchange-rate volatility. Happily, under the current non-system, the market is free to punish profligate and irresponsible governments. And given the performance of government financiers and central bankers during the twentieth century, is that really such a bad thing?

NOTES

1. Margaret Garritsen de Vries, "Bretton Woods Fifty Years Later: A View from the International Monetary Fund," in *The Bretton Woods–GATT System: Retrospect and Prospect after Fifty Years,* ed. Orin Kirshner (Armonk, N.Y.: M. E. Sharpe, 1996), p. 128.

2. W. L. Givens, "Economic Cocaine: America's Exchange Rate Addiction," *Foreign Affairs,* July/Aug. 1995, p. 17.

3. Diane B. Kunz, "The Fall of the Dollar Order: The World the United States Is Losing," *Foreign Affairs,* July/Aug. 1995, p. 26.

4. Peter B. Kenen, Francesco Papadia, and Fabrizio Saccomanni, eds., *The International Monetary System: Proceedings of a Conference Organized by the Banca d'Italia* (Cambridge: Cambridge University Press, 1994), introductory statement, p. 1.

5. Anonymous source reported as "one of Mr. Clinton's top economic advisors," quoted in David E. Sanger, "Trade's Bottom Line: Business Over Politics," *New York Times,* July 30, 1995.

6. Kunz, "The Fall of the Dollar Order," p. 23.

7. Judy Shelton, "How to Save the Dollar," *Wall Street Journal,* July 15, 1994.

8. Judy Shelton, *Money Meltdown: Restoring Order to the Global Currency System* (New York: Free Press, 1994), p. 289.

9. Peter Passell, "Bretton Woods: A Policy Revisited," *New York Times,* July 21, 1994.

10. Much of this discussion is taken from two sources. See Richard Cooper, *The International Monetary System: Essays in World Economics* (Cambridge, Mass.: MIT Press, 1987); and Paul de Grauwe, *International Money: Post-War Trends and Theories* (Oxford: Clarendon Press, 1989).

11. See John Ikenberry, "The Political Origins of Bretton Woods," in *A Retrospective on the Bretton Woods System: Lessons for International Monetary Reform,* ed. Michael Bordo and Barry Eichengreen (Chicago, Ill.: University of Chicago Press, 1993), pp. 155–82; and Richard

Gardner, *Sterling-Dollar Diplomacy in Current Perspective: The Origins and Prospects of Our International Economic Order* (New York: Columbia University Press, 1980).

12. For a description of Keynes's original monetary plans, see Donald Moggridge, ed., *The Collected Writings of John Maynard Keynes,* Vol. XXV, *Activities 1940–1944, Shaping the Post-War World: The Clearing Union* (Cambridge: Cambridge University Press, 1980).

13. Shelton, *Money Meltdown,* p. 17.

14. Moggridge, *The Collected Writings of John Maynard Keynes,* Vol. XXV, p. 42.

15. Ibid., pp. 267, 445.

16. Memorandum by the president of the Board of Trade, *The Future of Multilateral International Economic Co-operation,* CP (49) 188, Sept. 12, 1949, Public Record Office, Kew, England, p. 4.

17 Milton Friedman, "The Price of the Dollar," in *Dollars and Deficits: Inflation, Monetary Policy and the Balance of Payments* (Englewood Cliffs, N.J.: Prentice-Hall, Inc., 1968), p. 240. Originally published in *Newsweek,* Jan. 29, 1968.

18. For a non-specialist who was an exception to this rule, see Henry Hazlitt, *From Bretton Woods to World Inflation: A Study of Causes and Consequences* (Chicago, Ill.: Regnery Gateway, 1984).

19. See Brendan Brown, *The Flight of International Capital: A Contemporary History* (London: Biddles, Ltd., 1987), pp. 1–15.

20. See Milton Friedman, "The Case for Flexible Exchange Rates," in *Essays in Positive Economics* (Chicago, Ill.: University of Chicago Press, 1953), pp. 157–203.

21. Barry Eichengreen, *International Monetary Arrangements for the 21st Century* (Washington, D.C.: Brookings Institution, 1994), pp. 41–47, comments by Toyoo Gyohten, p. 146. See also Marcello De Cecco, *The International Gold Standard: Money and Empire* (London: Francis Pinter, 1984).

22. See Bordo and Eichengreen, eds., *A Retrospective on the Bretton Woods System,* p. 8.
23. The analogy is attributed to Rudiger Dombusch, quoted in "Why Currencies Over-

shoot," in *Economics: Ten Modern Classics* (New York: The Economist Newspaper Group, 1991).

Reading 7-2

The Rise of Free Trade in Western Europe, 1820–1875
C. P. Kindleberger

I

The textbook theory of tariffs, and their converse, the movement to freer trade, has more elements than we need for the nineteenth century, but also lacks some. In the usual comparative statics, a tariff may be said to have ten effects: on price, trade, production (the protective effect), consumption, revenue, terms of trade, internal income distribution, monopoly, employment and the balance of payments.

For present purposes we can dispense with the employment effect. The terms-of-trade effect arises only in connection with export taxes; and the monopoly effect must be converted to dynamic form, that increased imports stimulate growth by forcing competition and responsive innovation.

We may illustrate the bulk of the needed effects with the simplest of partial-equilibrium diagrams of a familiar sort. In Figure 1, an import tariff, t, raises the domestic price P_t above the world price P_w (assumed to be unaffected by the tariff), reduces trade from MM to $M'M'$, expands production by MM' and reduces consumption by $M'M$. An increase in rent to producers consists of the quadrilateral a; revenue accruing to the government is represented by b. Removal of the tariff reverses all movements. An export tax in Figure 2 reduces price and trade, cuts down on producers' rent, increases consumption, reduces production and earns governmental revenue. Conversely, removal of an export tax raises price, production and producers' rent, enlarges trade, reduces domestic consumption, loses revenue. In the nineteenth century when direct taxation was limited, the revenue effect could not be disregarded as it is today. Prohibition of exports or imports had in varying degree all other effects on price, trade, production, consumption, redistribution, monopoly, but wiped out revenue (and the terms of trade). This assumed that the prohibition or prohibitive tax was not undermined by smuggling.

Static theory needs two further elements. The first is a theory of incidence. With more than two factors, are rents retained by the initial recipient or are they competed away in bidding for still more scarce resources? The second is another factor, or institutional interest, beyond the normal agriculture and manufacturing, that is, the merchant, with whom may be included shipping. The merchant is interested in maximizing trade not for its impact on production or consumption, but to increase turnover, on

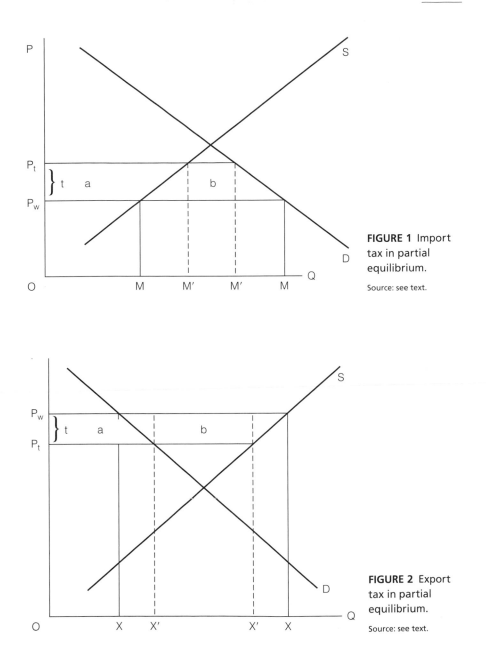

FIGURE 1 Import tax in partial equilibrium.

Source: see text.

FIGURE 2 Export tax in partial equilibrium.

Source: see text.

which, provided national merchants and ships are used, he earns a return. For trade, any goods will do, including those of foreigners which have no impact on domestic production or consumption of the goods in question. (Shipping interests of course insist on the use of national-flag vessels.)

Such is the economic model. Political and sociological elements will be added as required and will include: the view (for example, of Cobden) that free trade leads to peace; trade treaties as foreign treaties in general, desired for reasons of foreign policy, balance of power and the like; ideology, bandwagon effects and the need of most men to be consistent. It is especially necessary to indicate the relationships between economic interest and political power.

In his interesting study of the formation of the United States tariff of 1824, Jonathan Pincus asserts that tariff-making can be explained by the success or failure of various interests in obtaining rents, the quadrilateral *a* in Figure 1. In this view, the tariff is a collective good, passage of which requires limited numbers of concentrated producers: if the interested parties are diffuse, the fallacy of composition takes over as each element seeks to become a "free rider," leaving the transactions costs of engineering the tariff change to others. This is a theory applicable to representative democracies, and leaves little room for executive leadership.[1] Nor does it make allowance for intermediate goods.

That diffuse interests are less well served than concentrated ones in the legislative process is widely accepted in the theory of tariff formation in comparing producers and final consumers. Households count for little in tariff-making since the interest of any one is too small to stir it to the political effort and financial cost necessary to achieve results. With intermediate goods however, the consumption effect cannot be disregarded, as industries which rely on a given import, or on a product exported by another industry, may be as effectively concentrated as producers of final goods.

On the Pincus theory, the movement toward free trade in Western Europe would have to be based on the dominance of the interests of consumers of intermediate imports over those of their producers, and of producers of exports over consumers of exported intermediates. A variety of other general explanations have been offered.

In Bastiat's view, the rise of free trade was the result of the spread of democracy.[2] Free trade has also been regarded as the interest of the bourgeois class in England and the landed aristocracy on the Continent, while protection has been sought by the aristocracy in England and the bourgeois manufacturing classes on the Continent.[3]

Somewhat more dynamically, Johnson asserts that countries whose competitiveness in world markets is improving tend to move in the free-trade direction while countries whose competitiveness is deteriorating tend to move to increasing protection. A footnote states "Outstanding examples are the adoption of free trade by Britain in the 19th century . . . the espousal of freer trade by the United States and Canada in the period after the Second World War."[4]

In what follows we shall find these views insufficiently detailed.

II

The beginnings of free trade internationally go back to the eighteenth century. French Physiocratic theory enunciated the slogan *laisser faire, laisser passer* to reduce export prohibitions on agricultural products. Pride of place in practice, however, goes to Tuscany, which permitted free export of the corn of Sienese Maremma in 1737, after the Grand Duke Francis had read Sallustio Bandini's *Economical Discourse*.[5] Beset by famine in 1764, Tuscany gradually opened its market to imported grain well before the Vergennes Treaty of 1786 between France and Britain put French Physiocratic doctrine into practice. Grain exports in Tuscany had been restricted under the "policy of supply," or "provisioning," or "abundance," under which the city-states of Italy limited exports from the surrounding countryside in order to assure food to the urban populace. Bandini and Pompeo Neri pointed out the ill effects this had on investment and productivity in agriculture.

The policy of supply was not limited to food. In the eighteenth and early nineteenth century exports were restricted in, among others, wool and coal (Britain), ashes, rags, sand for glass and fire wood (Germany), ship timbers (Austria), rose madder (the Netherlands), and silk cocoons (Italy). The restrictions on exports of ashes and timber from Germany had conservation overtones. The industrial revolution in Britain led further to prohibitions on export of machinery and on emigration of artisans, partly to increase the supply for local use, but also to prevent the diffusion of technology on the Continent. We return to this below.

What was left in the policy of supply after the Napoleonic War quickly ran down. Prohibition of export of raw silk was withdrawn in Piedmont, Lombardy and Venetia in the 1830's, freedom to export coal from Britain enacted in the 1840's. Details of the relaxation of restrictions are recorded for Baden[6] as part of the movement to occupational freedom. The guild system gradually collapsed under the weight of increasing complexity of regulations by firms seeking exceptions for themselves and objecting to exceptions for others. A number of prohibitions and export taxes lasted to the 1850's— as industrial consumers held out against producers, or in some cases, like rags, the collectors of waste products. Reduction of the export tax on rags in Piedmont in 1851 produced a long drawn-out struggle between Cavour and the industry which had to close up thirteen plants when the tax was reduced.[7] To Cavour salvation of the industry lay in machinery and the substitution of other materials, not in restricting export through Leghorn and Messina to Britain and North America.

Elimination of export taxes and prohibitions in nineteenth-century Europe raises doubt about the universal validity of the theory of the tariff as a collective good, imposed by a concentrated interest at the expense of the diffuse. The interest of groups producing inputs for other industries are normally more deeply affected than those of the consuming industries, but it is hardly possible that the consuming is always less concentrated than the producing industry.

III

The question of export duties sought by domestic manufacturers on their raw materials, and of import duties on outputs demanded by producers for the domestic market was settled in the Netherlands in the eighteenth century in favor of mercantile interests.[8] These were divided into the First Hand, merchants, shipowners and bankers; the Second Hand, which carried on the work of sorting and packing in staple markets, and wholesaling on the Continent; and the Third Hand, concerned with distribution in the hinterland. Dutch staple trade was based partly on mercantile skills and partly on the pivotal location of Amsterdam, Rotterdam, and other staple towns dedicated to trade in particular commodities, largely perishable, non-standardized and best suited to short voyages. The First Hand dominated Dutch social and political life and opposed all tariffs on export or import goods, above a minimum for revenue, in order to maximize trade and minimize formalities. From 1815 to 1830 when Holland and Belgium were united as the Low Countries, the clash between the Dutch First Hand and Belgian producers in search of import protection from British manufactures was continuous and heated.

The First Hand objected to taxes for revenue on coffee, tea, tobacco, rice, sugar and so on, and urged their replacement by excises on flour, meat, horses and servants.[9] Tariffs for revenue must be held down to prevent smuggling and to sustain turnover. The safe maximum was given variously as three percent,[10] five percent[11] and on transit even as one-half percent. Transit in bond, and transit with duty-cum-drawback were thought too cumbersome. The Dutch made a mistake in failing to emulate London which in 1803 adopted a convenient entrepôt dock with bonding.[12] Loss of colonies and of overseas connections in the Napoleonic Wars made it impossible from early in the period to compete with Britain in trade. Equally threatening was Hamburg which supplied British and colonial goods to Central Europe in transit for one-half percent revenue duty maximum,[13] many products free, and all so after 1839.[14] More serious, however, was the rise of direct selling as transport efficiency increased. Early signs of direct selling can be detected at the end of the seventeenth century when Venice and Genoa lost their role as intermediary in traffic between Italy and the West.[15] By the first half of the nineteenth century, they were abundant. "By the improved intercourse of our time (1840), the seller is brought more immediately into contact with the producer."[16] Twenty years earlier, the Belgian members of a Dutch Belgian fiscal commission argued that "there was no hope of restoring Holland's general trade. Owing to the spread of civilization, all European countries could now provide for themselves in direct trading."[17]

It is a mistake to think of merchants as all alike. As indicated, First, Second and Third Hands of the Netherlands had different functions, status and power. In Germany, republican merchants of Hamburg differed sharply from those of the Imperial city, Frankfurt, and held out fifty years longer against the Zollverein.[18] Within Frankfurt there were two groups, the English-goods party associated with the bankers, and the majority, which triumphed in 1836, interested in transit, forwarding, retail and domestic trade within the Zollverein. In Britain a brilliant picture had been drawn of a pragmatic free trader, John Gladstone, father of William, opposed to timber preferences for Canada, enemy of the East India Company monopoly on trade with China and India, but supportive of imperial preference in cotton and sugar, and approving of the Corn Laws on the ground of support for the aristocracy he hoped his children could enter via politics.[19] The doctrinaire free traders of Britain were the cotton manufacturers like Gladstone's friend, Kirman Finlay, who regarded shipowners and corn growers as the two great monopolists.

The doctrinaire free trade of the Dutch merchants led to economic sclerosis,[20] or economic sickness.[21] Hamburg stayed in trade and finance and did not move into industry. In Britain, merchants were ignorant of industry, but were saved by the coming of the railroad and limited liability which provided an outlet for their surplus as direct trading squeezed profits from stapling. The economic point is simple: free trade may stimulate, but again it may lead to fossilization.

IV

The movement toward freer trade in Britain began gross in the eighteenth century, net only after the Napoleonic Wars. In the initial stages, there was little problem for a man like Wedgewood advocating free trade for exports of manufactures under the Treaty of Vergennes with France, but prohibitions on the export of machinery and emigrations of artisans.[22] Even in the 1820's and 1830's, a number of the political economists—Torrens, Baring, Peel, Nassau Senior—favored repeal of the Corn Laws but opposed export of machinery.[23] The nineteenth century is seen by Brebner not as a steady march to *laisser-faire* but as a counterpoint between Smithian *laisser-faire* in trade matters and, after the Reform Bill, Benthamic intervention of 1832 which produced the Factory, Mines, Ten Hours and similar acts from 1833 to 1847.[24]

First came the revenue aspect, which was critical to the movement to freer trade under Huskisson in the 1820's, Peel in the 1840's, and Gladstone in the 1850's. Huskisson and Gladstone used the argument that the bulk of revenue was produced by taxes on a few items—largely colonial products such as tea, coffee, sugar, tobacco and wine and spirits—and that others produced too little revenue to be worth the trouble. Many were redundant (for example, import duties on products which Britain exported). Others were so high as to be prohibitory or encouraged smuggling and reduced revenue. When Peel was converted to free trade, it was necessary to reintroduce the income tax before he could proceed with repeal of 605 duties between 1841 and 1846, and reductions in 1035 others. The title of Sir Henry Parnell's treatise on freer trade (1830) was *Financial Reform*.

But Huskisson was a free trader, if a cautious one. He spoke of benefits to be derived from the removal of "vexatious restraints and meddling interference in the concerns of internal industry and foreign commerce."[25] Especially he thought that imports stimulated efficiency in import-competing industry. In 1824 the prohibition on silk imports had been converted to a duty of thirty percent regarded as the upper limit of discouragement to smuggling. In a speech on March 24, 1826, said by Canning to be the finest he had heard in the House of Commons, Huskisson observed that Macclesfield and Spitalfield had reorganized the industry under the spur of enlarged imports, and expanded the scale of output.[26] Both Michel Chevalier[27] and Count Cavour[28] referred to this positive and dynamic response to increased imports in England.

Restrictions on export of machinery and emigration of artisans went back, as indicated, to the industrial revolution. Prohibition of export of stocking frames was enacted as early as 1696. Beginning in 1774 there was a succession of restrictions on tools and utensils for the cotton and linen trades and on the emigration of skilled artisans. The basis was partly the policy of supply, partly naked maintenance of monopoly. Freedom had been granted to the emigration of workmen in 1824. After the depression of the late 1830's, pressure for removal of the prohibition came from all machinery manufacturers. Following further investigation by a Select Committee of Parliament, the export prohibition was withdrawn.

The main arguments against prohibition of the export of machinery and emigration of artisans were three: they were ineffective, unnecessary and harmful. Ineffectuality was attested to by much detail in the Select Committee reports on the efficiency of smuggling. Machinery for which licenses could not be obtained could be dispatched illegally in one of a number of ways—by another port, hidden in cotton bales, in baggage or mixed with permitted machinery and in a matter of hours. Guaranteed and insured shipments could be arranged in London or Paris for premia up to thirty percent.

That prohibition was unnecessary was justified first by the inability of foreigners, even with English machinery and English workmen, to rival English manufacturers. Britain has minerals, railways, canals, rivers, better division of labor, "trained workmen habituated to all industrious employments."[29] "Even when the Belgians employed English machines and skilled workers, they failed to import the English spirit of enterprise, and secured only disappointing results."[30] In 1825, the Select Committee concluded it was safe to export machinery, since seven-year-old machinery in Manchester was already obsolete.[31]

In the third place it was dangerous. Restriction on emigration of artisans failed to prevent their departure, but did inhibit their return.[32] Restriction of machinery, moreover, raised the price abroad through the cost of smuggling, and stimulated production on the Continent. Improvement in the terms of trade through restriction of exports (but failure to cut them off altogether) was deleterious for its protective effect abroad.

Greater coherence of the Manchester cotton spinners over the machinery makers spread over Manchester, Birmingham and London may account for the delay from 1825 to 1841 in freeing up machinery, and support Pincus' theory on the need of concentrated interests. But the argument of consistency was telling. In 1800 the Manchester manufacturers of cloth had demanded a law forbidding export of yarn, but did not obtain it.[33] The 1841 Second Report concluded that machinery making should be put on the same footing as other departments of British industry.[34] It is noted that Nottingham manufacturers approved free trade but claim an exception in regard to machinery used in their own manufacture.[35] Babbage observed that machinery makers are more intelligent than their users, to whose imagined benefits their interests are sacrificed, and referred to the "impolicy of interfering between two classes."[36] In the end, the Manchester Chamber of Commerce became troubled by the inconsistency and divided; the issue of prohibition of machinery was subsumed into the general attack on the Corn Laws.[37] In the 1840's, moreover, the sentiment spread that Britain should become the Workshop of the World, which implied the production of heavy goods as well as cotton cloth and yarn.[38]

Rivers of ink have been spilled on the repeal of the Corn Laws, and the present paper can do little but summarize the issues and indicate a position. The questions relate to the Stolper-Samuelson distribution argument, combined with the Reform Bill of 1832 and the shift of political power from the landed aristocracy to the bourgeois; incidence of the Corn Laws and of their repeal, within both farming and manufacturing sectors; the potential for a dynamic response of farming to lower prices from competition; and the relation of repeal to economic development on the Continent, and especially whether industrialization could be halted by expanded and assured outlets for agricultural produce, a point of view characterized by Gallagher and Robinson[39] as "free-trade imperialism." A number of lesser issues may be touched upon incidentally: interaction between the Corn Laws and the Zollverein, and its tariff changes in the 1840's; the question of whether repeal of the Corn Laws, and of the Navigation Acts would have been very long delayed had it not been for potato famine in Ireland and on the Continent; and the question of whether the term "free-trade imperialism" is better reserved for Joseph Chamberlain's Empire preference of fifty years later.

In the normal view, the Reform Bill of 1832 shifted power from the land and country to the factory and city, from the aristocratic class to the bourgeois, and inexorably led to changes in trade policies which had favored farming and hurt manufacturing. One can argue that repeal of the Corn Laws represented something less than that and that the Reform Bill was not critical. The movement to free trade had begun earlier in the Huskisson reforms; speeches in Parliament were broadly the same in 1825 when it was dominated by landed aristocrats as in the 1830's and 1840's. Numbers had changed with continued manufacturing expansion, but nothing much more. Or one can reject the class explanation, as Polanyi does, and see something much more ideological. "Not until the 1830s did economic liberalism burst forth as a crusading passion." The liberal creed involved faith in man's secular salvation through a self-regulating market, held with fanaticism and evangelical fervor.[40] French Physiocrats were trying to correct only one inequity, to break out of the policy of supply and permit export of grain. British political economists of the 1830's and 1840's, who won over Tories like Sir Robert Peel and Lord Russell, and ended up in 1846 with many landlords agreeable to repeal of the

Corn Laws, represented an ideology.[41] "Mere class interests cannot offer a satisfactory explanation for any long-run social process."[42]

Under a two-sector model, free trade comes when the abundant factor acquires political power and moves to eliminate restrictions imposed in the interest of the scarce factor which has lost power. In reality factors of production are not monolithic. Some confusion in the debate attached to the incidence of the tax on imported corn within both farming and manufacturing. The Anti-Corn Law League of Cobden and Bright regarded it as a tax on food, taking as much as twenty percent of the earnings of a hand-loom weaver. Cobden denied the "fallacy" that wages rose and fell with price of bread.[43] Benefits, moreover, went to the landlord and not to the farmer or farm-laborer, as rents on the short leases in practice rose with the price of corn.[44] There are passages in Cobden which suggest that hurt of the Corn Laws fell upon the manufacturing and commercial classes rather than labor[45] but the speeches run mainly in terms of a higher standard of living for the laborer who would spend his "surplus of earnings on meat, vegetables, butter, milk and cheese," rather than on wheaten loaves.[46] The Chartists were interested not in repeal, but in other amenities for the workers. Peel's conversion waited on his conclusion that wages did not vary with the price of provision, and that repeal would benefit the wage earner rather than line the pockets of the manufacturer.[47]

In any event, with Gladstone's reductions in duties on meat, eggs and dairy products, with High Farming, and an end to the movement off the farm and out of hand-work into the factory real wages did rise in the 1850's, but so did profits on manufacturing. As so often in economic debates between two alternatives, history provides the answer which economists abhor, both. Nor did repeal bring a reduction in incomes to landlords—at least not for thirty years—as the farm response to repeal, and to high prices of food produced by the potato famine, was more High Farming.

Cobden may have only been scoring debating points rather than speaking from conviction when on a number of occasions he argued that the repeal would stimulate landlords "to employ their capital and their intelligence as other classes are forced to do in other pursuits" rather than "in sluggish indolence," and to double the quantity of grain, or butter, or cheese, which the land is capable of providing,[48] with "longer leases, draining, extending the length of fields, knocking down hedgerows, clearing away trees which now shield the corn"[49] and to provide more agricultural employment by activity to "grub up hedges, grub up thorns, drain, ditch."[50] Sir James Caird insisted that High Farming was the answer to the repeal of the Corn Laws[51] and many shared his view.[52] The fact is, moreover, that the 1850's were the Golden Age of British farming, with rapid technical progress through the decade though it slowed thereafter. Repeal of the Corn Laws may not have stimulated increased efficiency in agriculture, but they did not set it back immediately, and only after the 1870's did increases in productivity run down.

The political economists in the Board of Trade—Bowring, Jacob, MacGregor—sought free trade as a means of slowing down the development of manufacturing on the Continent. They regarded the Zollverein as a reply to the imposition of the Corn Laws, and thought that with its repeal Europe, but especially the Zollverein under the leadership of Prussia, could be diverted to invest more heavily in agriculture and to retard the march to manufacturing. There were inconsistencies between this position and other facts they adduced: Bowring recognized that Germany had advantages over Great Britain for the development of manufacturing, and that Swiss spinning had made progress without protection.[53] The 1818 Prussian tariff which formed the basis for that of the Zollverein was the lowest in Europe when it was enacted—though the levying of tariffs on cloth and yarn by weight gave high effective rates of protection despite low nominal duties to the cheaper constructions and counts. Jacob noted that the export supply elasticity of Prussian grain must be low, given poor transport.[54] "To export machinery, we must import corn,"[55] but imports of corn were intended to prevent the development of manufacturers abroad, whereas the export of machinery assisted it. The rise and progress of German manufacturing was attributed to restrictions on the admission of German agricultural products and wood, imposed by France and England, but also to "the natural advantages of the several states for manufacturing industry, the genius and laborious character and the necessities of the German people, and . . . especially the unexampled duration of peace, and internal tranquility which all Germany enjoyed."[56]

The clearest statements are those of John Bowring. In a letter of August 28, 1839, to Lord Palmerston he asserted that the manufacturing interest in the Zollverein "is greatly strengthened and will become stronger from year to year unless counteracted by a system of concessions, conditional upon the gradual lowering of tariffs. The present state of things will not be tenable. The tariffs will be elevated under the growing demands and increasing power of the manufacturing states, or they will be lowered by calling into action, and bringing over to an alliance, the agricultural and commercial interests."[57] In his testimony before the Select Committee on Import Duties in 1840 he went further: "I believe we have created an unnecessary rivalry by our vicious legislation; that many of these countries never would have been dreamed of being manufacturers."[58]

On this showing, the repeal of the Corn Laws was motivated by "free trade imperialism," the desire to gain a monopoly of trade with the world in manufactured goods. Zollverein in the 1830's merely indicated the need for haste.[59] Torrens and James Deacon Hume, among others, had been pushing for importing corn to expand exports in the 1820's, before Zollverein was a threat.

Reciprocity had been a part of British commercial policy in the Treaty of Vergennes in 1786, in treaties reducing the impact of the Navigation Laws in the 1820's and 1830's. The French were suspicious, fearing that they had been out-traded in 1786. They evaded Huskisson's negotiations in 1828. But reciprocity was unnecessary, given David Hume's law. Unilateral reduction of import duties increased exports.[60] Restored into the British diplomatic armory in 1860, reciprocity later became heresy in the eyes of political economists, and of the manufacturing interest as well.

The view that ascribes repeal of the Corn Laws to free-trade imperialism, however, fails adequately to take account of the ideology of the political economists, who believed in buying in the cheapest market and selling in the dearest, or of the short-run nature of the interests of the Manchester merchants themselves. It was evident after the 1840's that industrialization on the Continent could not be stopped, and likely that it could not be slowed down. The Navigation Acts were too complex; they had best be eliminated.[61] The Corn Laws were doomed, even before the Irish potato famine, though that hastened the end of both Corn Laws and Navigation Acts, along with its demonstration of the limitation of market solutions under some circumstances.[62]

"A good cause seldom triumphs unless someone's interest is bound up with it."[63] Free trade is the hypocrisy of the export interest, the clever device of the climber who kicks the ladder away when he has attained the summit of greatness.[64] But in the English case it was more a view of the world at peace, with cosmopolitan interests served as well as national.

It is difficult in this to find clearcut support for any of the theories of tariff formation set forth earlier. Free trade as an export-interest collective good, sought in a representative democracy by concentrated interests to escape the free rider would seem to require a simple and direct connection between the removal of the tariff and the increase in rents. In the repeal of the Corn Laws, and the earlier tariff reductions of Huskisson and Peel, the connection was roundabout—through Hume's law, which meant that increased imports would lead to increased prices or quantities (or both) exported on the one hand, and/or through reduced wages, or higher real incomes from lower food prices on the other. Each chain of reasoning had several links.

Johnson's view that free trade is adopted by countries with improving competitiveness is contradictory to the free-trade-imperialism explanation, that free trade is adopted in an effort to undermine foreign gains in manufacturing when competitiveness has begun to decline. The former might better account in timing for Adam Smith's advocacy of free trade seventy years earlier—though that had large elements of French Physiocratic thought—or apply to the 1820's when British productivity was still improving, before the Continent had started to catch up. In turn, free-trade imperialism is a better explanation for the 1830's than for the end of the 1840's, since by 1846 it was already too late to slow, much less to halt, the advance of manufacturing on the Continent.

Vested interests competing for rents in a representative democracy, thrusting manufacturers seeking to expand markets, or faltering innovators, trying as a last resort to force exports on shrinking markets—rather like the stage of foreign direct investment in Vernon's product cycle when diffusion of technology has been accomplished—none of these explanations seems free of difficulties as compared with an ideological explanation based on the intellectual triumph of the political economists, their doctrines modified to incorporate consistency. The argument took many forms: static, dynamic, with implicit reliance on one incidence or another, direct or indirect in its use of Hume's law. But the Manchester School, based on the political economists, represented a rapidly rising ideology of freedom for industry to buy in the cheapest and sell in the dearest market. It overwhelmed the Tories when it did not convert them. Britain in the nineteenth century, and only to a slightly lesser extent the Continent, were characterized by a "strong, widely-shared conviction that the teachings of contemporary orthodox economists, including Free Traders, were scientifically exact, universally applicable, and demanded assent."[65] In the implicit debate between Thurman Arnold who regarded economic theorists (and lawyers) as high priests who rationalize and sprinkle holy water on contemporary practice, and Keynes who thought of practical men as responding unconsciously to the preaching of dead theorists, the British movement to free trade is a vote, aided by the potato famine, for the view of Keynes.

V

France after 1815 was a high-tariff country which conformed to the Pincus model for a representative democracy with tariffs for various interests, except that (a) there were tariffs for all, and (b) it was not a democracy. The Physiocratic doctrine of *laisser-faire* for agricultural exports had been discredited in its reciprocal form by the disaster wreaked by imports up to 1789 under the Treaty of Vergennes. The Continental system, moreover, provided strong protection to hothouse industries which was continued in the tariff of 1816, and elaborated in 1820 and 1822. To the principles of Turgot, that there should be freedom of grain trade inside France but no imports except in period of drought, were added two more: protection of the consumer by regulating the right of export of wheat—a step back from Physiocratic doctrine—and protecting the rights of producers by import tariffs.[66] In introducing the tariff of 1822 for manufactures, Saint-Cricq defended prohibitions, attacked the view that an industry which could not survive with a duty of twenty percent should perish, saying that the government intended to protect all branches together: "agriculture, industry, internal commerce, colonial production, navigation, foreign commerce finally, both of land and of sea."[67]

It was not long, however, before pressures for lower duties manifested themselves. Industries complained of the burden of the tariff on their purchases of inputs, and especially of the excess protection accorded to iron. It was calculated that protection against English iron cost industrial consumers fifty million francs a year and had increased the price of wood—used for charcoal, and owned by the many noble *maîtres de forges*—by thirty percent on the average and in some places fifty percent.[68] Commissions of inquiry in 1828 and 1834 recommended modifications in duties, especially to enlarge supplies which local industry was not in a position to provide, and to convert prohibitions into tariffs. A tumult of conflict broke out in the Chamber among the export interests of the ports, the textile interests of Alsace and Normandy, the *maîtres de forges* and the consumers of iron, with no regard, says the protectionist Gouraud, for the national interest. The Chambers were then dissolved by the cabinet, and tariffs adjusted downward, in coal, iron, copper, nitrates, machinery, horses. Reductions of the 1830's were followed in the peaks of business by similar pressure for reductions in prosperous phases of the cycle of the 1840's and 1850's.[69]

A troubling question that involved conflicting interests in this period was presented by sugar, for which it was impossible to find a solution agreeable at the same time to colonial planters, ship-owners, port refiners, consumers and the treasury. Colonial supply was high cost and a 55 francs per 100 kilograms duty on foreign supplies was needed to keep the sugar ports content. This, however, made it economical to expand beet-sugar production, begun during the Continental blockade, and the sugar ports turned to taxing this domestic production, less heavily at first, but with full equality in 1843. By this time it was too late, and with the freeing of the slaves in 1848, French colonial sugar production no longer counted.

The free-trade movement in France had its support in Bordeaux, the wine-exporting region; Lyon, interested in silk; and Paris, producer of so-called Paris article for sale abroad (cabinet ware, perfumes, imitation jewelry, toys and so on). Later Norman agricultural interests in the export of butter and eggs to London teamed up with Bordeaux in wine to resist the attempts by textile interests to enlist agriculture in favor of higher tariffs.[70]

Intellectual support to free trade led by Bastiat from Bordeaux, and with Michel Chevalier as its most prestigious member, is dismissed by Lévy-Leboyer[71] as unimportant. Nonetheless, Chevalier had an important part in the negotiation of the treaty, and in persuading Napoleon III to impose it on France in the face of the united opposition of the Chamber of Deputies. Some attention to his thought is required.

The prime interest of the *Société d'Economie Politique* and of Chevalier was growth.[72] His two-year visit to the United States in 1833–1835 impressed him with the contribution of transport to economic growth and contributed to his 1838 major work on *The Material Interests of France in Roads, Canals and Railroads.* American protectionist doctrine of Henry Carey seems not to have affected him. Polytechnician, graduate of the *Ecole des Mines,* Chevalier's first interest in freer trade came from a project to establish woolen production in the Midi, and to obtain cheaper wool.[73] Much of his later reasoning was in terms of the penalty to industry from expensive materials: Charging 35 francs for a quintal of iron worth 20 imposes on industry "the labor of Sisyphus and the work of Penelope."[74] His major argument, at the *Collège de France,* and in his *Examen du Système Commercial,* cited the success of Spitalfield and Macclesfield when Huskisson permitted competition of imports; and the experience of the manufacturers of cotton and woolen textiles in Saxony who were worried by the enactment of Zoll-verein but sufficiently stimulated by import competition so that in two or three years their industry was flourishing.[75] The letter of Napoleon III to Fould[76] talks in specifics of the need to abolish all duties on raw materials essential to industry to encourage pro-duction, and to reduce by stages the duties on goods which are consumed on a large scale. In the more general introduction it states that "lack of competition causes indus-try to stagnate," echoing the Chevalier view. Chevalier himself was one of the judges of the Universal Exposition of 1855 in Paris and noted that France received so many prizes that no one dared confess to being a protectionist.[77]

There were economic purposes behind the Anglo-French treaty, as evidenced by the proposal in France in 1851 for tariffs of twenty percent, ten percent and a duty-free on wholly manufactured goods, semi-finished manufactures and raw materials;[78] by ac-tual reductions in duties on coal, iron and steel in 1852 as the railroad boom picked up; and by the legislative proposal designed by Napoleon III in 1855, but not put forward until after the Crimean War, to admit 241 items duty free, reduce tariffs on 19 others, remove all prohibitions and set a top limit of thirty percent. This last was turned down by the Chamber and Napoleon promised not to submit a new tariff proposal be-fore 1861.

Economic interests were involved, and the theories of great men like Cobden and Chevalier. However, there was more: Napoleon III was starting to engage on foreign adventure. He wanted to rid Italy of Austrian rule by use of arms. The British opposed his military measures, despite their recent use of force in Crimea. The treaty was used to hold British neutrality, as much as or more than to stimulate growth in France. Moreover, it did not need to be submitted to the Chamber. Under the Constitution of 1851, the Emperor had the sole power to make treaties, and such treaties encompassed those dealing with trade.

The move was successful both politically and economically. With the help of the French armies, Italy was unified under the leadership of Piedmont, and French growth never faltered under the impetus of increased imports. French industries met competi-tion successfully and checked the growth of imports after two years.[79] While its effects are intermingled with those of the spread of the French railroad network, it "helped to bring about the full development of the industrial revolution in France."[80]

Further, it added impetus to the free-trade movement in Europe. This was under way in the early 1850's, following repeal of the Corn Laws. The Swiss constitution of 1848 had called for a tariff for revenue only and protective duties were reduced pro-gressively from 1851 to 1885. The Netherlands removed a tariff on ship imports and a prohibition against nationalization of foreign ships. Belgium plugged gap after gap in its protective system in the early 1850's, only to turn around at the end of the decade and adopt free trade down the line. Piedmont, as we shall see, and Spain, Portugal, Norway and Sweden (after 1857) undertook to dismantle their protective and prohibitive re-strictions.[81] With the Anglo-French treaty the trickle became a flood. France, Ger-many, Italy and Britain engaged in negotiating reciprocal trade treaties with the most-favored nation clause.[82]

Following French defeat at Sedan in 1870 and the abdication of Louis Napoleon, the Third Republic brought in the protectionist Thiers. The Cobden treaty was de-nounced in 1872. Reversal of policy waited upon the repeal of the Le Chapelier law of 1791, taken in the heat of the French revolution against associations, which forbade economic interests from organizing. Dunham claims that a country with leadership would have accepted a moderate tariff in 1875, but that the free traders had neither or-ganization nor conviction, that is, too many free riders.[83]

The French movement to free trade was taken against the weight of the separate interests,[84] in the absence of strong export interests, with an admixture of economic theory of a dynamic kind, and imposed from above. The motivation of that imposition was partly economic, partly, perhaps even mainly, political. Moreover, it had a bandwagon effect in spreading freer trade.

In the French case, the leadership overwhelmed the concentrated economic interests. That leadership earned its surplus to use Frohlich, Oppenheimer and Young's expression, in a coin different than economic, that is, in freedom to maneuver in foreign policy. It may be possible to subsume increases in leadership surplus in this form into an "economic theory of national decision-making" with costs to vested interests accepted in exchange for political benefits to a national leader, ruling by an imposed constitution, the legitimacy of which is not questioned. The effort seems tortured.

VI

As mentioned earlier, the Prussian tariff of 1818 was regarded when it was enacted as the lowest in Europe.[85] But the duties on coarse yarns and textiles were effectively high, since the tariff was levied by weight. Jacob in 1819 noted that the "system of the Prussian government has always been of manufacturing at home everything consumed within the Kingdom; of buying from others, nothing that can be dispensed with," adding "As scarcely any competition exists, but with their own countrymen, there is little inducement to adopt the inventions of other countries, or to exercise their facilities in perfecting their fabrics; none of these have kept pace. . . ."[86] Baden, on joining the Zollverein which adopted the Prussian tariff for the totality, believed itself to be raising its tariff level when it joined.[87] What Baden did, however, was to acquire enforcement: its long border had previously been effectively open.

The Prussian tariff dominated that of the Zollverein, organized in the years from 1828 to 1833, primarily because Prussia took a very liberal view of tariff revenues. Most goods by sea entered the German states via Prussia, directly or by way of the Netherlands, but the text of the Zollverein treaty of 1833 provided that the revenues from the duties after deduction of expenses would be divided among the contracting states according to population.[88] Prussia thus received 55 percent, Bavaria 17 percent, Saxony 6.36 percent, Wurtemberg 5.5 percent, and so on, and was said in 1848 to have sacrificed about two million talers a year, exclusive of the fiscal loss sustained by smuggling along the Rhine and Lake Constance.[89] This can be regarded as a side-payment made by the beneficiary of income-distribution under Pareto-optimal conditions to gain its policy, or as the disproportionate share of overhead costs of the collective good saddled on the party that most wanted it.[90]

Despite adjustments made in Prussian customs duties between 1819 and 1833, the tariff remained low by British standards. Junker grain growers were hopeful of importing British manufactures in order to sell Britain more grain. Junker bureaucrats, brought up on Adam Smith and free trade by instinct, were fearful that highly protective rates would reduce the revenue yield.[91]

Outside of Prussia plus Hamburg and Frankfurt and the other grain-growing states of Mecklenburg, Pomerania, and so on, there was interest in higher tariffs, but apart from the Rhineland, little in the way of organized interests. Von Delbrück comments that Prussia and Pomerania had free trade interests and shipping interests, but that outside the Rhineland, which had organized Chambers of Commerce under the French occupation, there were few bureaucrats, or organs with views on questions of trade and industry. Nor did the Prussian government see a need to develop them.[92]

Saxony was sufficiently protected by its interior location so as not to feel threatened by low tariffs, which, as mentioned, were not really low on coarse cloths. On joining the Zollverein, Baden was concerned over raising its tariff, and worried lest it be cut off from its traditional trading areas of Switzerland and Alsace. It fought with the Zollverein authorities over exemptions for imported capital equipment, but gradually evolved into a source of pressure, with Bavaria and Wurtemberg, for higher tariffs on cotton yarns and iron. Fischer points out that the request for lifting the duty on cotton yarns from two talers per centner to five was resisted by the weavers of Prussia (the Rhineland) and Silesia.[93]

Cotton yarns and iron were the critical items. Shortly after the formation of Zollverein, a trend toward protection was seen to be under way.[94] The Leipsig consul reported a new duty on iron to the Board of Trade in February 1837 and observed that the switch from imports of cotton cloth to imports of yarn pointed in the direction of ultimate exclusion of both.[95] Bowring's letter of August 1839 noted that the manufacturing interest was growing stronger, that the existing position was untenable, and that tariffs would be raised under the growing demands and increasing power of the manufacturing states, or would be lowered by an alliance between the agricultural and commercial interests.[96]

Open agitation for protection began two and one-half years after the formation of the Zollverein when the South pushed for duties on cotton yarns. Linen yarns and cloth went on the agenda in 1839 and iron, protection for which was sought by Silesian and west German ironwork owners, beginning in 1842.[97] But these groups lacked decisive power. The Prussian landed nobility covered their position by citing the interests of the consumers,[98] and Prince Smith, the expatriate leader of the doctrinaire free traders, in turn tried to identify free trade and low tariffs with the international free-trade movement rather than with the export-interests of the Junkers.[99] The tariff on iron was raised in 1844, those on cotton yarns and linen yarns in 1846. Von Delbrück presents in detail the background of the latter increases, starting with the bureaucratic investigations into linen, cotton, wool and soda, with their negative recommendation, continuing through the negotiations, in which Prussia was ranged against any increase and all the others in favor, and concluding that the Prussian plenipotentiary to the Zollverein conference was right in not vetoing the increases, as he could have done, operating on the theory that a compromise was more important than the rationally correct measure of this or that tariff.[100] The head of the Prussian Handelsamt was not satisfied with the outcome of the conference but had to accept it.

From 1846 on, the direction of Zollverein tariffs was downward, aided first by the repeal of the Corn Laws and secondly by the Cobden-Chevalier treaty. With the increases of the 1840's and English reductions, the Zollverein tariff from one of the lowest in Europe had become relatively high. Von Delbrück was one of the doctrinaire free traders in the Prussian civil service and notes that in 1863 he had been trying for a reduction on the tariff in pig iron for seven years, since the tariff reform of 1856, which reordered but did not lower duty schedules. He also wanted a reduction in the tariff on cotton cloth; duties on woolens were no longer needed. The opportunity came with the announcement of the Anglo-French treaty. He noted that Austria had gone from prohibitions to tariffs, that the Netherlands had reformed its tariffs with a five percent maximum on industrial production, and that the levels of Italian duties were lower than those in Germany. "Could we stay away from this movement? We could not."[101]

Bismarck was no barrier to the Junker bureaucracy. His view about tariff negotiations was expressed in 1879 in the question: "Who got the better of the bargain?" Trade treaties, he believed, were nothing in themselves but an expression of friendship. His economic conscience at this time, he said later, was in the hands of others.[102] Moreover, he had two political ends which a trade treaty with France might serve: to gain her friendship in the Danish question, and to isolate Austria which was bidding for a role in the German Confederation.[103] Austrian tariffs were high. The lower the levels of the Zollverein the more difficulty she would have in joining it and bidding against Prussia for influence. The Zollverein followed the 1863 treaty with France with a series of others.

Exports of grain from Prussia, Pomerania, and Mecklenberg to London as a percentage of total English imports hit a peak in 1862 at the time of the Civil War[104] and proceeded down thereafter as American supplies took over. The free-trade movement nonetheless continued. Only hesitation prevented a move to complete free trade at the peak of the boom in 1873.[105] There is debate whether the crash later in the year triggered off the return to protection in 1879 or not. Victory in 1871 had enlarged competition in iron and cotton textiles by including Alsace and Lorraine in the new German Empire. Radical free traders and large farmers achieved the reduction in duties on raw iron in 1873 and passed legislative provision for their complete removal in 1877.[106] But Lambi notes that *Gewerbefreiheit* (freedom of occupation) had caused dissatisfaction and in some versions subsumed free trade.[107] By 1875 the iron interests are organizing to resist the scheduled elimination of iron duties in 1877.

The difference between the 1873 depression which led to tariffs, and the 1857 crisis which did not, lay in (a) the fact that the interests were not cohesive in the earlier period, and (b) that Britain did not keep on lowering duties in the later period as it had in the first.[108] On the first score the Verein Deutscher Eisen- und Stahl Industrielle was formed in 1873 after vertical integration of steel back to iron mining had removed the opposition between the producers and consumers of iron. This much supports the view of the effectiveness of concentrated interests achieving their tariff goals when scattered interests will not—though again it has nothing to do with representative democracy. On the other hand, the free traders also organized; in 1868 the Kongress Nord-Deutscher Landwirte was organized, and in 1871 it was broadened to cover all Germany. In 1872, a Deutsche Landwirtschaftsrat was formed.[109] Many of these organizations and the once free-trade Congress of German Economists were subverted and converted to protection after 1875, but a new Union for the Promotion of Free Trade was formed in September 1876.[110] German economic interests as a whole became organized, and the struggle was among interests concentrated on both sides.

Abandonment of the opposition of the landed interests is perhaps critical. Consumers of iron in machinery, they opposed tariffs on iron up to 1875, but with the decline in the price of grain and the threat of imports, their opposition collapsed. It might have been possible to support tariffs for grain and free trade for iron, but inconsistency is open to attack. After von Delbrück's resignation or discharge in April 1876, Bismarck forged the alliance of bread and iron. As widely recounted, he had strong domestic political motives for higher tariffs on this occasion, as contrasted with his international political gains from lower tariffs up to 1875.

In general, however, the German case conforms to the Stolper-Samuelson explanation: the abundant factor wants free trade; when it becomes relatively scarce, through a gain in manufacturing at home and an expansion of agriculture abroad, it shifts to wanting tariffs. Doctrine was largely on the side of free trade. List's advocacy of national economy had little or no political force. His ultimate goal was always free trade, and his early proposal of ten percent duties on colonial goods, fifteen percent on Continental and fifty percent on British was more anti-British than national.[111] In the 1840's he was regarded in Germany, or at least by the Prussians, as a polemicist whose views were offered for sale.[112] Bismarck is often regarded as the arch-villain of the 1879 reversal of Zollverein low tariffs, but it is hard to see that his role was a major one.

VII

Italian moves in the direction of free trade prior to 1850 were tentative and scattered. The abandonment of the policy of supply in Tuscany in the eighteenth century has been mentioned earlier, as well as the removal of prohibitions on the export of raw silk in Piedmont, Lombardy and Veneto. Lombard and Venetian tariff policies were largely imposed by Austria, which was perhaps not wholly indifferent to local interests and to the promotion of industry.[113] Piedmont concluded a series of trade treaties with the larger states, especially France and Britain, and in 1847–48, explored a tariff union with Tuscany and the Papal states.[114] But the major initiatives were taken after Cavour became Minister of Agriculture, Industry and Commerce, when Minister of Finance (1851) and then Prime Minister (1852). The low tariffs which Cavour achieved for the Kingdom of Sardinia were subsequently extended to Italy as a whole after its unification in 1860 under Cavour's leadership, and followed by a series of trade agreements lowering import duties still further.

As a young man Cavour had visited France and Britain, once in 1833–1835 and again in 1842–1843. Like Chevalier, whose lectures he attended in the second visit, he was interested in growth, through banks, public works, and especially market forces encouraged by freedom of trade. He knew Babbage, Nassau Senior, Cobden, de Tocqueville, Sismondi, Cherbuliez, Michalet, Pellegrino Rossi (an Italian free-trader, resident in Paris), Chevalier, and Faucher, wrote long papers on English Poor Laws, the Irish question and the Corn Laws.

Cavour was attacked as a doctrinaire who deserted a tried and effective system to follow an abstract theory,[115] but has been defended by biographers as having "a genius for the opportune."[116] His fifty-two speeches on the tariff question as Finance Minister had high educational quality, says Thayer, and achieved an economic revolution. There are views that Cavour's successful pressure for free trade represented economic interests. He was a large landowner and the low tariff has been said to "reflect clearly the interests of the large landowners."[117] Piedmont agriculture was related to western European markets for rice, silks, wine and hides.[118] The application of Piedmont's low tariff to all of Italy has been said to assure the interests of the ruling classes of Britain and France.[119]

For the most part, however, it seems evident that in following low tariff policies in the Kingdom of Sardinia in the early 1850's and in Italy after unification in 1860, Cavour was operating on the basis of a theory. His views were widely shared. Prodi notes that the liberal faith in freedom through the market in 1860 not only triumphed but remained sure and irrefutable. There were some like Cappellarsi who wanted to reduce tariffs slowly as industry was getting ready to export, as in England, and Martullo who was conscious of the differences between Italy and England, and elastic in his application of Adam Smith to Italy.[120] For the most part, however, the tariff problem was ignored in Italy until the inquiry of 1870. Industrialists, led by the wool manufacturer

Rossi, disliked the Piedmont low tariff and especially the twenty or more trade treaties which followed. Limited transport over land meant, however, that there was no unified domestic market for local manufacturers to exploit.

Clough[121] observes that the advantages which were supposed to devolve automatically from the free movement of goods in international commerce did not seem to accrue to Italy. For one thing, loss of custom revenues upset the finances of first Sardinia and then Italy, despite a vigorous expansion of trade.[122] Customs duties had provided 14.7 million lire out of a total revenue of 69.4 million.[123] Secondly, the balance of payments turned adverse, partly, perhaps mainly, as a result of Cavour's and his successors' programs of public works. Piedmont ran up a large debt which later developed on the Kingdom of Italy. In 1866 it became necessary to halt redemption of the lira in gold and the depreciation of the currency during the *corso forzoso* (forced circulation) alleviated some of the effects of competitive imports. But the spread of the railroad in the 1860's and the low tariff policies proved ruinous to industry, especially in the South. The Sardinian tariff schedule was by and large at the same level as those of Modena, Parma and Tuscany, well below that of Lombardy in most goods, though higher in others, but far below the levels of the Papal States and especially of the Kingdom of the Two Sicilies (Naples).[124] After a long period when the country was "strangely deaf" to the troubles caused by the low tariff,[125] the Commission of Inquiry was launched in 1870, the tariff was raised in 1878, and a new system of high tariffs on industry, modified by trade agreements favoring agriculture, was instituted in its place.[126]

IX

My first conclusion reached from this survey was that free trade in Europe in the period from 1820 to 1875 had many different causes. Whereas after 1879, various countries reacted quite differently to the single stimulus of the fall in the price of wheat— England liquidating its agriculture, France and Germany imposing tariffs, though for different political and sociological reasons, Italy emigrating (in violation of the assumptions of classical economics), and Denmark transforming from producing grain for export to importing it as an input in the production of dairy products, bacon and eggs[127]—before that the countries of Europe all responded to different stimuli in the same way. Free trade was part of a general response to the breakdown of the manor and guild system. This was especially true of the removal of restrictions on exports and export taxes, which limited freedom of producers. As more and conflicting interests came into contention, the task of sorting them out became too complex for government (as shown in *Gewerbeförderung* in Baden, and the refinement of the Navigation Laws in England), and it became desirable to sweep them all away.

Part of the stimulus came from the direct self-interest of particular dominant groups, illustrated particularly by the First Hand in the Netherlands. In Britain, free trade emerged as a doctrine from the political economists, with a variety of rationalizations to sustain it in particular applications: anti-monopoly, increases to real wages, higher profits, increased allocative efficiency, increased productivity through innovation required by import competition. In France, the lead in the direction of free trade came less from the export interests than from industrial interests using imported materials and equipment as inputs, though the drive to free trade after 1846 required the overcoming of the weight of the vested interests by strong governmental leadership, motivated by political gain in international politics. The German case was more straightforward: free trade was in the interest of the exporting grain and timber-producing classes, who were politically dominant in Prussia and who partly bought off and partly overwhelmed the rest of the country. The Italian case seems to be one in which doctrines developed abroad which were dominant in England and in a minority position in France, were imported by strong political leadership and imposed on a relatively disorganized political body.

Second thoughts raise questions. The movement to free trade in the 1850's in the Netherlands, Belgium, Spain, Portugal, Denmark, Norway and Sweden, along with the countries discussed in detail, suggests the possibility that Europe as a whole was motivated by ideological considerations rather than economic interests. That Louis Napoleon and Bismarck would use trade treaties to gain ends in foreign policy suggests that free trade was valued for itself, and that moves toward it would earn approval. Viewed in one perspective, the countries of Europe in this period should not be considered as independent economies whose reactions to various phenomena can properly be compared, but rather as a single entity which moved to free trade for ideological or perhaps better doctrinal reasons. Manchester and the English political economists persuaded Britain which persuaded Europe, by precept and example. Economic theories of representative democracy, or constitutional monarchy, or even absolute monarchy may explain some cases of tariff changes. They are little help in Western Europe between the Napoleonic Wars and the Great Depression.

NOTES

1. See Jonathan Pincus, "A Positive Theory of Tariff Formation Applied to Nineteenth-Century United States," Ph.D. dissertation, Stanford University, 1972. For the theory of collective goods, see M. Olson, Jr., *The Logic of Collective Action: Public Goods and the Theory of Groups* (Cambridge, Mass.: Harvard University Press, 1965; rev. ed., 1971); Albert Breton, *The Economic Theory of Representative Democracy* (Chicago: Aldine, 1974); and, introducing leadership, N. Frohlich, J. A. Oppenheimer and O. R. Young, *Political Leadership and Collective Goods* (Princeton: Princeton University Press, 1971). Frohlich, Oppenheimer and Young view leaders as political entrepreneurs, interested in maximizing their "surplus" or profit in providing collective goods against taxes, extortions, donations or purchases.

2. Cited by Alexander Gerschenkron, *Bread and Democracy in Germany* (Berkeley: University of California Press, 1943), p. 65.

3. Karl F. Helleiner, *Free Trade and Frustration, Anglo-Austrian Negotiations, 1860–70* (Toronto: Toronto University Press, 1973), p. 63.

4. Harry G. Johnson, "Economic Theory of Protectionism, Tariff Bargaining and the Formation of Customs Unions," *Journal of Political Economy*, LXXIII (1965), 256–83.

5. James Montgomery Stuart, *The History of Free Trade in Tuscany* (London: Cassell, Potter & Galpin, 1876), p. 24.

6. Wolfram Fischer, *Der Staat und die Anfänge der Industrialisierung in Baden, 1800–1850* (Berlin: Duncker u. Humblot, 1962).

7. Luigi Bulferetti and Claudio Costanti, *Industria e Commercio in Liguria nell' età del Risorgimento (1700–1861)* (Milan: Banca Commerciale Italiana, 1966), pp. 495–501.

8. H. R. C. Wright, *Free Trade and Protection in the Netherlands, 1816–30: A Study of the First Benelux* (Cambridge: Cambridge University Press, 1955), pp. 58–59.

9. Ibid., p. 112.

10. Ibid., p. 139.

11. Ibid., p. 113.

12. G. R. Porter, *The Progress of the Nation* (New ed., London: John Murray, 1847), Chapter 16.

13. Joachim F. E. Bläsing, *Das goldene Delta und sein eisernes Hinterland, 1815–1841, von niederländisch-preußischen zu deutschniederländischen Wirtschaftsbeziehungen* (Leiden: H. E. Stenfert Kroese, 1973), p. 85.

14. John MacGregor, *Germany, Her Resources, Government, Union of Customs and Power under Frederick William IV* (London: Whittaker and Co., 1948), p. 246.

15. Luigi Bulferetti and Claudio Costanti, *Industria e Commercio in Liguria,* Chapter 2.

16. John Bowring, "Report on the Prussian Commercial Union, 1840," *Parliamentary Papers,* 1840, Volume XXI, p. 38.

17. H. R. C. Wright, *Free Trade and Protection,* p. 124.

18. Helmut Böhme, *Frankfurt und Hamburg: Des Deutsches Reiches Silber- und Goldloch und die Allerenglishte Stadt des Kontinents* (Frankfurt-am-Main: Europäische Verlagsanstalt, 1968), Chapter 1.

19. S. G. Checkland, *The Gladstones, A Family Biography, 1764–1851.* (Cambridge: Cambridge University Press, 1971), pp. 139, 333.

20. Francois Crouzet, "Western Europe and Great Britain: 'Catching Up' in the First Half of the Nineteenth Century," in A. J. Youngson, ed., *Economic Development in the Long Run* (London: Allen & Unwin, 1972), p. 120.

21. Joachim F. E. Bläsing, *Das goldene Delta,* p. 83.

22. Herbert Heaton, *Economic History of Europe* (New York: Harper & Bros., 1936), pp. 398–99.

23. Bernard Semmel, *The Rise of Free Trade Imperialism: Classical Political Economy, The Empire of Free Trade and Imperialism, 1750–1850* (Cambridge: Cambridge University Press, 1970), pp. 181 ff.

24. J. Bartlett Brebner, "Laissez-Faire and State Intervention in Nineteenth Century Britain," in E. M. Carus-Wilson, ed., *Essays in Economic History,* Vol. 3 (London: Edward Arnold, 1962), pp. 254–256.

25. *William Huskisson (The Speeches of the Right Honorable)* (London: John Murray, 1832), II, p. 328.

26. Ibid., pp. 503–05.

27. Pierre Labracherie, *Michel Chevalier et ses idées économiques* (Paris: Picart, 1929), p. 131.

28. A. J. White, *Early Life and Letters of Cavour, 1810–1848* (London: Oxford University Press, 1925), p. 131 (*sic*).

29. Report of the Select Committee on the Laws Relating to the Export of Tools and Machinery, 30 June 1825, in *Parliamentary Papers, Reports of Committee* (1825), Vol. V, p. 12.

30. H. R. C. Wright, *Free Trade and Protection,* p. 130.

31. *Report of the Select Committee,* p. 44.

32. Charles Babbage, *The Economy of Machinery and Manufactures* (London: Charles Knight, 4th ed., 1835), p. 363.

33. Karl Polanyi, *The Great Transformation* (New York: Farrar & Rinehart, 1944), p. 136.

34. Second Report of the Select Committee on Exportation of Machinery, 1841, in *Parliamentary Papers* (1841), Vol. VII, p. xx.

35. Ibid., p. xiv.

36. Charles Babbage, *The Economy of Machinery,* p. 364.

37. A. E. Musson, "The 'Manchester School' and Exportation of Machinery," *Business History,* XIV (January 1972), 49.

38. J. D. Chambers, *The Workshop of the World British Economic History, 1820–1880* (London: Oxford University Press, 2nd ed., 1968), Chapter I.

39. J. Gallagher and R. Robinson, "The Imperialism of Free Trade," *Economic History Review,* 2nd ser., VI (1953), 1–15.

40. Karl Polanyi, *The Great Transformation,* pp. 133–37.

41. D. C. Moore, "The Corn Laws and High Farming," *Economic History Review,* 2nd ser., XVIII (December 1965).

42. Karl Polanyi, *The Great Transformation,* pp. 152–53.

43. Richard Cobden, *Speeches on Questions of Public Policy,* John Bright and James E. Thorold Rogers, ed., Vol. I (London: Macmillan, 1870), pp. 4, 18.

44. Ibid., p. 57.

45. The Corn Laws "inflict the greatest amount of evil on the manufacturing and commercial community . . ." (Ibid., p. 57). "Silversmiths and jewellers get orders not from the Duke of Buckingham but from Manchester, from Glasgow or Liverpool or some other emporium of manufactures" (Ibid., p. 90).

46. Ibid., p. 106.

47. J. D. Chambers, *The Workshop,* p. 71.

48. Richard Cobden, *Speeches,* p. 70.

49. Ibid., p. 100.

50. Ibid., p. 103.

51. Sir James Caird, *High Farming . . . The Best Substitute for Protection,* pamphlet, 1848, in Lord Ernle, *English Farming Past and Present* (London: Longmans Green, 4th ed., 1937), p. 374.

52. D. C. Moore, "The Corn Laws and High Farming."

53. John Bowring, *Report on the Prussian Commercial Union,* p. 55.

54. Lucy Brown, *The Board of Trade and the Free-Trade Movement, 1830–1842* (Oxford: Clarendon Press, 1958), pp. 135, 171 ff.

55. Testimony of Thomas Ashton, in *First Report of the Select Committee,* para. 235.

56. John MacGregor, *Germany, Her Resources,* p. 68.

57. John Bowring, *Report on the Prussian Commercial Union*, p. 287.

58. *Minutes Evidence*, p. 59, para. 782.

59. Bernard Semmel, *The Rise of Free Trade Imperialism*, p. 149.

60. D. C. M. Platt, *Finance, Trade and Politics in British Foreign Policy, 1815–1914* (Oxford: Clarendon Press, 1968), p. 87.

61. J. H. Clapham, "The Last Years of the Navigation Acts," in E. M. Carus-Wilson, ed., *Essays in Economic History*, p. 161.

62. Cecil Woodham-Smith, *The Great Hunger: Ireland, 1845–1849* (New York: Harper & Row, 1962).

63. Mill, cited by Bernard Semmel, *The Rise of Free Trade Imperialism*, p. 207.

64. List, cited by Kenneth Fielden, "The Rise and Fall of Free Trade," in C. J. Bartlett, ed., *Britain Pre-eminent: Studies in British World Influence in the Nineteenth Century* (London: Macmillan, 1969), p. 85.

65. Ibid., p. 78.

66. Charles Gouraud, *Histoire de la politique commerciale de la France et son influence sur le progrès de la richesse publique depuis le moyen age jusqu'à nos jours*, I, II (Paris: Auguste Durand, 1854), p. 198.

67. Ibid., p. 208.

68. Léon Amé, *Etudes sur les tariffs de douanes et sur les traités de commerce*, I, II (Paris: Imprimerie Nationale, 1876), pp. 170–74.

69. Maurice Lévy-Leboyer, *Histoire économique et sociale de la France depuis 1848* (Paris: Cours de Droit, Institut d'études politiques, 1951–52), p. 96.

70. Michel Augé-Laribé, *La politique agricole de la France de 1880 à 1940* (Paris: Presses Universitaires de France, 1950), p. 66.

71. Maurice Lévy-Leboyer, *Histoire économique et sociale*, p. 92.

72. Michel Lutfalla, "Aux origines du libéralisme économique de la France," *Revue d'histoire économique et sociale*, L (1972), 500, 515, 517.

73. Maurice Lévy-Leboyer, *Histoire économique et sociale*, p. 95.

74. Michel Chevalier, *Cours d'economie politique, Fait au Collège de France*, I, II, III (2nd ed., Paris: no publisher stated, 1855), p. 538.

75. Pierre Labracherie, *Michel Chevalier*, pp. 130–31.

76. S. Pollard and C. Holmes, *Documents of European Economic History. Vol. I: The Process of Industrialization, 1750–1870* (New York: St. Martin's Press, 1968), pp. 384–86.

77. Michel Chevalier, *Cours d'economie politique*, p. 521.

78. A. A. Illasu, "The Cobden Chevalier Commercial Treaty of 1860," *The Historical Journal*, XIV (March 1971), 80.

79. Marcel Rist, "Une experience française de liberation des échanges au dixneuvième siècle: le traité de 1860," *Revue d'Economie Politique*, 66 année (novembre–decembre 1956), p. 937.

80. Arthur L. Dunham, *The Anglo-French Treaty of Commerce of 1850 and the Progress of the Industrial Revolution in France* (Ann Arbor: University of Michigan Press, 1930), p. 179.

81. Hans Rosenberg, *Die Weltwirtschaftskrise von 1857–1859* (Stuttgart-Berlin: Verlag von W. Kohlhammer, 1934), pp. 24–26.

82. Most lists are given separately by country. For an overview, see Sidney Pollard, *European Economic Integration, 1815–1870* (New York: Harcourt, Brace and Jovanovich, Inc., 1974), p. 117. The impact of repeal of the timber duties and the Navigation Acts in stimulating export-led growth in Scandinavia is treated by Victor D. Norman, "Trade Liberalization and Industrial Growth: The Impact of British Trade Liberalization in the 1840s on Industrialization in the Scandinavian Countries" (MIT, unpublished, December 1970), p. 82. The stimulus to shipping in Norway and to timber exports in Sweden led via linkages to industrialization which the free trade imperialists were seeking to avoid.

83. Arthur L. Durham, *The Anglo-French Treaty of Commerce*, p. 333.

84. Apart from consumers of imported materials and machinery. But see the view of Lhomme that the State adopted free trade because it loved the *grande bourgeoisie* and knew their interests better than they did; that the *grande bourgeoisie* recognized this fact and agreed with the tariff reductions except for a few intransigent protectionists like Pouyer-Quartier. See Jean Lhomme, *La Grande Bourgeoisie au Pouvoir, 1830–1880* (Paris: Presses Universitaires de France, 1960), p. 179. It is, however, impossible to accept this rationalization.

85. S. Pollard, *European Economic Integration*, p. 112; William Huskisson, *The Speeches of —*, III, p. 131.

86. William Jacob, *A View of the Agriculture, Manufactures, Statistics and Society in the State of Germany and Parts of Holland and France* (London: John Murray, 1820), pp. 201–02.

87. Wolfram Fischer, *Der Staat und die Anfänge der Industrialisierung*, pp. 128, 134.

88. S. Pollard and C. Holmes, *Documents of Economic History*, I, p. 374.

89. John MacGregor, *Germany, Her Resources*, p. 6.

90. Mancur Olson, Jr., and Richard Zeckhauser, "An Economic Theory of Alliances," *Review of Economics and Statistics,* XLVIII (August 1966). For a view emphasizing the revenue aspects of the Zollverein, and especially saving in the costs of collection and the reduction in smuggling, see Rolf H. Dumke, "The Political Economy of Economic Integration, The Case of the Zollverein of 1834" (Queen's University *Discussion Paper,* 153, presented to the Canadian Economics Association, June 5, 1974). Revenues available from the Zollverein permitted the petty princes to maintain their rule without democratic concessions to bourgeois interests.

91. *European Economic Integration,* p. 112.

92. Rudolph von Delbrück, *Lebenserinnerungen,* I (Leipsig: Duncker u. Humblot, 1905), pp. 142–44.

93. Wolfram Fischer, *Der Staat und die Anfänge der Industrialisierung,* p. 136.

94. William H. Dawson, *Protection in Germany: A History of German Fiscal Policy during the Nineteenth Century* (London: P. S. King and Son, 1904), p. 20.

95. Lucy Brown, *The Board of Trade,* p. 113.

96. John Bowring, *Report on the Prussian Commercial Union,* p. 287.

97. Rudolph von Delbrück, *Lebenserinnerungen,* p. 147.

98. Hans Rosenberg, *Die Weltwirtschaftskrise,* p. 207.

99. W. O. Henderson, "Prince Smith and Free Trade in Germany," Chapter 7 in W. O. Henderson, *Britain and Industrial Europe, 1750–1870: Studies in British Influence on the Industrial Revolution in Western Europe* (Liverpool: Liverpool University Press, 1954), p. 171.

100. Rudolph von Delbrück, *Lebenserinnerungen,* pp. 162–64.

101. Ibid., p. 200.

102. William H. Dawson, *Protection in Germany,* p. 21.

103. Ivo Nikolai Lambi, *Free Trade and Protection in Germany, 1868–1879* (Wiesbaden: Franz Steiner Verlag, 1963), p. 5.

104. Wolfgang Zorn, "Wirtschafts- und socialgeschichtliche Zusammenhänge der deutschen Reichsgründungszeit, 1859–1879," in Helmut Böhme, ed., *Probleme der Reichsgründungszeit, 1848–1879* (Cologne-Berlin: Kipenheur & Witsch, 1968), p. 296.

105. Kenneth D. Barkin, *The Controversy over German Industrialization, 1890–1902* (Chicago: University of Chicago Press, 1970), p. 33.

106. Ibid.

107. Ivo Nikolai Lambi, *Free Trade and Protection,* pp. 83, 113.

108. Hans Rosenberg, *Die Weltwirtschaftskrise,* p. 195.

109. Ivo Nikolai Lambi, *Free Trade and Protection,* p. 57.

110. Ibid., p. 191.

111. Judith Blow Williams, *British Commercial Policy and Trade Expansion, 1750–1850* (London: Oxford University Press, 1973), p. 199.

112. Werner Thiedig, *Englands Uebergang zum Freihandel und die deutsche Handelspolitik, 1840–1856* (Giessen: no publisher stated, 1927; 40-page summary of a thesis), pp. 31–32.

113. Kent Roberts Greenfield, *Economics and Liberalism in the Risorgimento, A Study of Nationalism in Lombardy, 1814–1848* (Baltimore: Johns Hopkins University Press, rev ed., 1965), p. 113.

114. Shepherd B. Clough, *The Economic History of Modern Italy* (New York: Columbia University Press, 1964), p. 27.

115. A. J. Whyte, *The Political Life and Letters of Cavour, 1848–1861* (London: Oxford University Press, 1930), p. 73.

116. William Roscoe Thayer, *The Life and Times of Cavour* (Boston: Houghton Mifflin, 1921), p. 133.

117. Antonino Pedone, "La Politica del Commercio Estere," in Giorgio Fua, ed., *Le Sviluppo Economico in Italia,* Vol. II, Gli Aspetti generali (Milan: Franco Agnelli Editore, 1969), p. 242.

118. Valerio Castronovo, *Economia e societa in Piemonte dell' unitá al 1914,* (Milan: Banca Commerciale Italiana, 1969), p. 16.

119. Mori, quoted by Gino Luzzato, *L'economia italiana dal 1861 al 1914,* Vol. I (1861–1894) (Milan: Banca Commerciale Italiana, 1963), p. 28n.

120. Romano Prodi, "Il protezionismo nella politica e nell' industria italiana dall' unificazione al 1886," *Nuova Rivista Storica,* L fasc. I–II, 1966, pp. 1–10.

121. Shepherd B. Clough, *The Economic History of Modern Italy,* p. 114.

122. Isidore Sachs, *L'Italie, ses finances et son développement économique depuis l'unification du royaume, 1859–1884, d'après des documents officiels* (Paris: Librairie Guillaumin, 1885), p. 748.

123. Paolo Norsa and Mario Pozzo, *Imposte e tasse in Piemonte durante il periodo cavouriano* (Turin: Museo Nazionale del Risorgimento, 1961), pp. 16, 17.

124. Giannino Parravicina, *La politica fiscale e le entrate effective del Regno d'Italia* (Archivo Economico dell'Unificazione Italiana, Turin: ILTE, 1958), p. 326.

125. Gino Luzzato, *L'economia italiana,* p. 28.

126. Frank J. Coppa, "The Italian Tariff and the Conflict Between Agriculture and Industry: The Commercial Policy of Liberal Italy, 1860–1922," *The Journal of Economic History,* XXX (December 1970), 742–69.

127. C. P. Kindleberger, "Group Behavior and International Trade," *Journal of Political Economy,* LIX (February 1951), 30–47.

REFERENCES

Amé, Leon. *Etudes sur les tariffs de douanes et sur les traités de commerce,* I, II. Paris: Imprimerie nationale, 1876.

Augé-Laribé, Michel. *La Politique agricole de la France de 1880 a 1940.* Paris: Presses Universitaires de la France, 1950.

Babbage, Charles. *The Economy of Machinery and Manufactures.* London, 4th ed.: Charles Knight, 1835.

Barkin, Kenneth D. *The Controversy over German Industrialization, 1890–1902.* Chicago: University of Chicago Press, 1970.

Benaerts, Pierre. *Les origines de la grande industrie allemande.* Paris: Turot, 1933.

Bläsing, Joachim F. E. *Das goldene Delta und sein eisernes Hinterland, 1815–1841. von niederländisch-preuschischen zu deutschniederländischen Wirtschaftsbeziehungen.* Leiden: H. E. Stenfert Kroese, 1973.

Böhme, Helmut. *Frankfurt und Hamburg: Des Deutsches Reiches Silber- und Goldloch und die Allerenglishte Stadt des Kontinents.* Frankfurt-am-Main: Europäische Verlagsanstalt, 1968.

Bowring, John. "Report on the Prussian Commercial Union, 1840," *Parliamentary Papers,* 1840, Volume XXI, p. 200.

Brebner, J. Bartlett. "Laissez-faire and State Intervention in Nineteenth-Century Britain," in E. M. Carus-Wilson, ed., *Essays in Economic History,* Vol. 3. London: Edward Arnold, 1962, pp. 252–262.

Breton, Albert. *The Economic Theory of Representative Democracy.* Chicago: Aldine, 1974.

Brown, Lucy. *The Board of Trade and the Free-Trade Movement, 1830–1842.* Oxford: Clarendon Press, 1958.

Bulferetti, Luigi, and Claudio Costanti. *Industria e Commercio in Liguria nell'età del Risorgimento (1700–1861).* Milan: Banca Commerciale Italiana, 1966.

Caird, Sir James. *High Farming . . . The Best Substitute for Protection,* pamphlet, 1848, cited in Lord Ernle, *English Farming Past and Present.* London: Longmans Green, 4th ed., 1937, p. 374.

Castronovo, Valerio. *Economia e societa in Piemonte dell' unità al 1914.* Milan: Banca Commerciale Italiana, 1969.

Chambers, J. D. *The Workshop of the World British Economic History, 1820–1880.* London: Oxford University Press, 2nd ed., 1968.

Checkland, S. G. *The Gladstones, A Family Biography, 1764–1851.* Cambridge: Cambridge University Press, 1971.

Chevalier, Michel. *Cours d'économie politique.* Fait au Collège de France, I, II, III, 2nd ed. no publisher stated, 1855.

Clapham, J. H. "The Last Years of the Navigation Acts," in E. M. Carus-Wilson, ed., *Essays in Economic History.* London: Edward Arnold, 1962, pp. 144–78.

Clough, Shepherd B. *The Economic History of Modern Italy.* New York: Columbia University Press, 1964.

Cobden, Richard. *Speeches on Questions of Public Policy.* Edited by John Bright and James E. Thorold Rogers. Vol. I. London: Macmillan, 1870.

Coppa, Frank J. "The Italian Tariff and the Conflict between Agriculture and Industry: The Commercial Policy of Liberal Italy, 1860–1922." *The Journal of Economic History,* XXX (December 1970), 742–69.

Crouzet, François. "Western Europe and Great Britain: 'Catching Up' in the First Half of the Nineteenth Century," in A. J. Youngson, ed., *Economic Development in the Long Run.* London: Allen & Unwin, 1972, pp. 98–125.

Dawson, William H. *Protection in Germany: A History of German Fiscal Policy during* the Nineteenth Century. London: P. S. King and Son, 1904.

von Delbrück, Rudolph. Lebenserinnerungen, I, II. Leipsig: Duncker u. Humblot, 1905.

Dumke, Rolf H. "The Political Economy of Economic Integration: The Case of the Zollverein of 1834." Queens University *Discussion Paper,* No. 153, presented to the Canadian Economics Association, June 5, 1974.

Dunham, Arthur L. *The Anglo-French Treaty of Commerce of 1850 and the Progress of the Industrial Revolution in France.* Ann Arbor: University of Michigan Press, 1930.

Fielden, Kenneth. "The Rise and Fall of Free Trade," in C. J. Bartlett, ed., *Britain Pre-eminent: Studies in British World Influence in the Nineteenth Century.* London: Macmillan, 1969, pp. 76–100.

Fischer, Wolfram. *Der Staat und die Anfänge der Industrialisierung in Baden, 1800–1850.* Berlin: Duncker u. Humblot, 1962.

Frolich, N., J. A. Oppenheimer, and O. R. Young. *Political Leadership and Collective Goods.* Princeton: Princeton University Press, 1971.

Gallagher, J., and R. Robinson. "The Imperialism of Free Trade." *Economic History Review,* 2nd ser., VI (1953), 1–15.

Gerschenkron, Alexander. *Bread and Democracy in Germany.* Berkeley: University of California Press, 1943.

Gouraud, Charles. *Histoire de la politique commerciale de la France et son influence sur le progrès de la richesse publique depuis les moyens ages jusquà nos jours,* I, II. Paris: August Durand, 1854.

Greenfield, Kent Roberts. *Economics and Liberalism in the Risorgimento: A Study of Nationalism in Lombardy, 1814–1848,* rev. ed. Baltimore: Johns Hopkins University Press, 1965.

Heaton, Herbert. *Economic History of Europe.* New York: Harper & Bros., 1936.

Helleiner, Karl F. *Free Trade and Frustration: Anglo-Austrian Negotiations, 1860–70.* Toronto: University of Toronto Press, 1973.

Henderson, W. O. "Prince Smith and Free Trade in Germany." Ch. 7 in W. O. Henderson, *Britain and Industrial Europe, 1750–1870: Studies in British Influence on the Industrial Revolution in*

Western Europe. Liverpool: Liverpool University Press, 1954.

The Speeches of the Right Honourable William Huskisson. London: John Murray, 1832.

Illasu, A. A. "The Cobden Chevalier Commercial Treaty of 1860." *The Historical Journal,* XIV (March 1971), 67–98.

Johnson, Harry G. "Economic Theory of Protectionism, Tariff Bargaining and the Formation of Customs Unions." *Journal of Political Economy,* LXXIII (1965), 256–83, reproduced in P. Robson, ed., *International Economic Integration.* Harmondsworth: Penguin, 1972, pp. 99–142.

Keynes, John Maynard. *The General Theory of Employment, Interest and Money.* New York: Harcourt, Brace and Co., 1936.

Kindleberger, C. P. "Group Behavior and International Trade." *Journal of Political Economy,* LIX (February 1951), 30–47.

Labracherie, Pierre. *Michel Chevalier et ses idées économiques.* Paris: Picart, 1929.

Lambi, Ivo Nikolai. *Free Trade and Protection in Germany, 1868–1879.* Wiesbaden: Franz Steiner Verlag, 1963.

Lévy-Leboyer, Maurice. *Historie économique et sociale de la France depuis 1848.* Paris: Les Cours de Droit, Institut d'études politiques, 1951–52.

Lhomme, Jean. *La Grande Bourgeoisie au Pouvoir, 1830–1880.* Paris: Presses Universitaire de France, 1960.

Lutfalla, Michel. "Aux origines de la libéralisme économique de la France." *Revue d'histoire économique et sociale,* L (1972), 494–517.

Luzzato, Gino. *L'economia italiana dal 1861 al 1914,* Vol. I (1861–1894). Milan: Banca Commerciale Italiana, 1963.

MacGregor, John. *Germany, Her Resources, Government, Union of Customs and Power under Frederick William IV.* London: Whittaker and Co., 1948.

McCord, Norman. *Free Trade: Theory and Practice from Adam Smith to Keynes.* London: Newton Abbot, David & Charles, 1970.

Moore, D. C. "The Corn Laws and High Farming." *Economic History Review,* 2nd series, XVIII (December 1965), 544–61.

Musson, A. E. "The 'Manchester School' and Exportation of Machinery." *Busi-*

ness History, XIV (January 1972), 17–50.

Norman, Victor D. "Trade Liberalization and Industrial Growth: The Impact of British Trade Liberalization in the 1840s on Industrialization in the Scandinavian Countries." Unpublished paper, M.I.T., December 1970.

Norsa, Paolo, and Mario Pozzo. *Imposte e tasse in Piemonte durante il periodo cavouriano.* Turin: Museo nazionale del Risorgimento, 1961.

Olson, M., Jr. *The Logic of Collective Action: Public Goods and the Theory of Groups.* Cambridge, Mass.: Harvard University Press, 1965, rev. ed., 1971.

Olson, Mancur, Jr., and Richard Zeckhauser. "An Economic Theory of Alliances." *Review of Economics and Statistics,* XLVIII (August 1966), 266–79.

Parravicina, Giannino. *La Politia fiscale e le entrate effective del Regno d'Italia.* Archivo Economico dell' Unificazione Italiana. Turin: ILTE, 1958.

Pedone, Antonino. "La Politica del commercio estere," in Giorgio Fua, ed., *Le Sviluppo Economico in Italia,* vol. II, Gli aspetti generali. Milan: Franco Angelli Editore, 1969.

Pincus, Jonathan J. "A Positive Theory of Tariff Formation Applied to Nineteenth Century United States." Dissertation for the Ph.D., Stanford University, 1972.

Platt, D. C. M. *Finance, Trade and Politics in British Foreign Policy, 1815–1914.* Oxford: Clarendon Press, 1968.

Polanyi, Karl. *The Great Transformation.* New York: Farrar & Rinehart, 1944.

Pollard, Sidney. *European Economic Integration, 1815–1870.* New York: Harcourt Brace Jovanovich, Inc., 1974.

Pollard, S., and C. Holmes. *Documents of European Economic History. Vol. 1: The Process of Industrialization, 1750–1870.* New York: St. Martin's Press, 1968.

Porter, G. R. *The Progress of the Nation.* New ed., London: John Murray, 1847.

Prodi, Romano. "Il protezionismo nella politica e nell' industria italiana dall' unificazione al 1886." *Nuova Rivista Storica,* L. Fasc. I–II, 1966, pp. 1–74.

Rist, Marcel. "Une experience française de liberation des échanges au dixneuvième siècle: le traité de 1860." *Revue d'Economie Politique,* 66 annee (novembre–decembre 1956), pp. 908–61.

Robinson, Moncure. *Obituary Notice of Michel Chevalier, 1806–1879.* Read to the American Philosophical Society, May 7, 1880.

Rosenberg, Hans. *Die Weltwirtschaftskrise von 1857–1859.* Stuttgart-Berlin: Verlag von W. Kohlhammer, 1934.

Sachs, Isidore. *L'Italie, ses finances et son developpement économique depuis l'unification du royaume, 1859–1884,* d'après des documents officiels. Paris: Librairie Guillaumin, 1885.

Second Report of the Select Committee on Exportation of Machinery, 1841 (11 June 1841), *Parliamentary Papers,* 1841, Vol. VII.

Semmel, Bernard. *The Rise of Free Trade Imperialism: Classical Political Economy, The Empire of Free Trade and Imperialism, 1750–1850.* Cambridge: Cambridge University Press, 1970.

Stuart, James Montgomery. *The History of Free Trade in Tuscany, with Remarks on Its Progress in the Rest of Italy.* London: Cassell, Potter & Galpin, 1876.

Thayer, William Roscoe. *The Life and Times of Cavour.* Boston: Houghton Mifflin, 1921.

Thiedig, Werner. *Englands Übergang zum Freihandel und die deutsche Handelspolitik, 1840–1856.* Giessen: no publisher stated, 1927 (40-page summary of a thesis).

Whyte, A. J. *Early Life and Letters of Cavour, 1810–1848.* London: Oxford University Press, 1925.

Whyte, A. J. *The Political Life and Letters of Cavour, 1848–1861.* London: Oxford University Press, 1930.

Woodham-Smith, Cecil. *The Great Hunger: Ireland, 1845–1849.* New York: Harper & Row, 1962.

Wright, H. R. C. *Free Trade and Protection in the Netherlands, 1816–30: A Study of the First Benelux.* Cambridge: Cambridge University Press, 1955.

Zorn, Wolfgang. "Wirtschafts- und sozialgeschichtliche Zusammenhänge der deutschen Reichsgründungszeit, 1859–1879," in Helmut Böhme, ed., *Probleme der Reichsgrundungszeit, 1848–1879.* Cologne-Berlin: Kipenheuer & Witsch, 1968.

8

Globalization and Fragmentation

Reading 8-1

World Orders, Old and New
Richard Falk

Throughout this century, there has been a recurrent concern about world order—
that is, about the distribution of power and authority among the political actors on
the global stage. World order is a descriptive term that is neutral as to whether peace is
kept and other goals realized. A given world order can be appraised from several stand-
points. Among these are whether it upholds stability, avoiding large-scale war and discouraging the use of force in international relations. Others evaluate world order by reference to certain widely shared values, such as peace, equity, rule of law, human rights,
degrees of democratization, and environmental protection. From this point of view, a
given world order can improve or deteriorate over time, depending on how it is assessed.

George Bush struck a resonant note during the Persian Gulf crisis of 1990–1991
when he repeatedly called for a "new world order." At the time, President Bush meant
making effective use of the United Nations to show that aggression does not succeed.
In the specific instance, this meant using the UN to reverse Iraq's conquest of Kuwait,
thereby supplanting the "old world order" that relied on alliances among states and the
balance of power mechanism. The collective effort worked—Iraq withdrew from
Kuwait—but not much more has been heard since about the new world order. Was it

SOURCE: From "World Orders, Old and New" by Richard Falk, *Current History,* vol. 98, no. 624 (January 1999): 29–34. Copyright
© 1999 Current History, Inc. Reprinted by permission.

just a mobilizing phrase in the midst of a global crisis, or was there a major cumulative change under way with respect to global security, and the manner in which power and authority are distributed in the world of the 1990s? As we approach the millennial threshold of the year 2000, can we discern the contours of a new world order being shaped by an interplay among states, market forces, and transnational popular movements?

WILSON'S WORLD ORDER

Until World War I, there reigned a complacent consensus that world order depended on maintaining a balance of power among leading states, the "great powers." These countries were all European, and prevailing ideas about world order were decidedly Eurocentric. The rest of the world was treated as a periphery, and most other societies were under direct or indirect colonial rule. But with the entry of the United States into World War I, which proved decisive in shaping the outcome of the war, the traditional European control of world order arrangements was strongly challenged.

Woodrow Wilson, the American president, posed this challenge provocatively by his insistence on replacing a balance of power approach to world order with one based on collective security under the auspices of the organized international community. To this end, the League of Nations was established in Geneva as part of the World War I peace settlement reached at Versailles in 1919. And two years later a Permanent Court of International Justice came into existence at The Hague. Wilson's ideas about world order seemed visionary when expressed in words—World War I was "a war to end all wars"—but timid in execution. The League of Nations preserved the sovereignty of states by giving every member country a veto; as a result, important decisions depended on a unanimous vote. And there was no intention of transferring peacekeeping capabilities or authority to this new organization.

In retrospect, it seems easy to understand why Wilson's proposals were such a failure. First, participating in a world organization situated in Europe seemed to repudiate America's adherence to isolationism, which had served the United States well during its first century and a half of independence. Isolationism as a policy meant staying aloof from European political life, and thereby staying clear of the continent's tendencies toward alliance diplomacy, arms races, and warfare. The League concept was thus bound to be sharply criticized in the United States, and the attack eventually prevailed. The League was established, but the United States never joined the organization that it was instrumental in founding.

Second, Europe's statesmen remained oriented around power politics at the level of states, and they were exceedingly skeptical about the League's capacity to protect their national interests or prevent future wars. Their endorsement of the League idea was decidedly half-hearted, and appeared to be mainly an expression of diplomatic deference to Woodrow Wilson, a gesture of gratitude for the American role in the war. It was also a discreet way to deal with what the foreign offices of Europe regarded as a naïve demand by large sections of the public for a new type of world order that would abolish the danger of war.

Third, from the outset the League proposals were careful to preserve sovereign rights in order to make the League politically acceptable to European and American leaders. But this made it clear that the promise of collective security was a pipe dream.

For the League to be in a position to act effectively in response to aggression would have required both a unified political will and a credible commitment to make available the necessary manpower and military capabilities. The rise of fascism and Japanese militarism in the next decade confirmed the League's impotence as a political actor.

The 1930s represented a kind of double failure with respect to the choice of world order strategies. The first failure involved an abandonment of any serious effort to apply the balance of power mechanism to contain further German expansion. The response by the major European governments to Hitler's expansionist ambitions was one of "appeasement," a policy of accommodating Germany's territorial and political demands in the vain hope that a series of concessions would bring satisfaction to Germany, ending the threat to the established order without the ordeal of another war. At the same time, a second failure occurred as these appeasing moves also demonstrated the feebleness of the League's commitment to use the collective capabilities of international society on behalf of states that were the victims of international aggression. The weakness exhibited in Europe was also displayed in response to Japanese military expansion in Asia first tested by the failure to respond to the Japanese conquest of Manchuria in 1931.

Despite the disappointing League reaction to aggression, there was something about the idea of "an organized international community" that seemed useful and necessary for any future world order. Indeed, the presence of an institutional center for world politics has not been allowed to disappear from the international scene. Yet despite its persistence, and even an expansion of its role, the global institutional buildup has not had the transformative impact on international life that animated Wilson's crusade for a transcendence of traditional balance of power, realist statecraft.

A NEW QUEST FOR SECURITY

The magnitude of World War II confirmed for world opinion that the efforts of the 1930s were insufficient to discourage aggression and prevent the onset of major war. It also convinced many policymakers that the punitive approach to Germany the victors adopted after World War I had had a perverse impact. Punishment seemingly inclined Germany to embrace an extremist form of nationalism that had posed a more severe threat to the established order in Europe and beyond than would have resulted from treating Germany as a "normal" state. And because of Hitler's invasion of the Soviet Union, the war also showed that a temporary alliance against fascism between the communist and capitalist worlds was possible, and in the end, successful.

The shaping of future world order after World War II was even further removed from European control than after World War I. Unlike the earlier war, the Second World War seemed to have been a "just war" that, although extremely costly in lives and treasure, achieved a worthwhile result by ridding the world of the menace of fascist rule, especially given the atrocities committed by the Nazi Germans and Imperial Japanese. In this sense, the world order message was clear: in relation to core concerns of geopolitics neither war nor aggression could be tolerated in the future. But what, then?

At the end of World War II, the official response was initially based on the idea that the cooperation between East and West that had produced victory in war could lead to stability in peacetime, provided only that the defeated powers were kept in permanent check. But from the outset of peace in 1945 there were many doubters behind the scenes. In Moscow and the capitals of Europe, as well as in the inner recesses of the Washington bureaucracy, there emerged the view that a resumed ideological rivalry between East and West was all but inevitable. This rivalry would be dominated by the two countries that had emerged from the last war as "superpowers," the United States and the Soviet Union.

These two contradictory perspectives on how to conceive of post-1945 world order had their ardent adherents, causing much public confusion at the time. On the one side were the neo-Wilsonian proponents of collective security who looked to a "United Nations" to keep the peace, and who believed that in view of the atomic bomb, war had become a suicidal option with apocalyptic potential. The most urgent task was to achieve complete disarmament with respect to this new weaponry of mass destruction, a task that emphasized the need for a strong organization like the United Nations with independent peacekeeping capabilities.

The United Nations was deliberately designed to avoid the fatal flaws, or at least some of them, that had incapacitated the League. The main international organization would have its headquarters in New York City. This would accomplish the dual objective of acknowledging United States preeminence in world affairs and ensuring that America's isolationist tradition did not lead the most important country in the world to remain outside the organization. Furthermore, in the interest of strengthening the United Nations, a careful crafting of its powers departed from the League myth that all sovereign states were equal.

This time around the power of decision was located in the United Nations Security Council, where five leading states would participate as permanent members enjoying a right of veto over the council's decisions. In essence, the United Nations was founded on the premise that it could be effective only if the geopolitical realities were acknowledged in its structure and operations. And it was conceded that the United Nations could only hope to be effective in relation to war and peace issues if a geopolitical consensus existed. This consensus was defined as the five permanent members: the United States, Soviet Union, France, China, and the United Kingdom, the main members of the victorious alliance in World War II. If the pattern of conflict that preceded the formation of the United Nations continued after 1945, then the organization would agree on joint action. But if emergent patterns of conflict were to split the permanent members of the Security Council, then the United Nations would likely find itself paralyzed in the face of world crises. Of course, with the advent of the cold war, this is what happened: the peace and security role of the United Nations was marginalized. States, using their military capabilities and alliance arrangements, fell back on more traditional means of achieving stability.

In the background, also, was the world order imperative of finding a way to inhibit aggression without provoking World War III, a goal reinforced by the Soviet acquisition of a nuclear weapons capability in the early 1950s. Both superpowers proceeded to rely on military capabilities and ideologically oriented alliances to impart order at the core of world politics; violent conflict was limited by tacit agreement to Asia, Africa, and Latin America. Almost all the fighting and dying in the course of more than 125 wars in the period between 1945 and 1989 occurred in non-Western countries, with the struggles often intensified by interventions that reflected the East-West struggle for global ascendancy. Despite close calls in Berlin and Cuba, both Moscow and Washington were prudent in crisis situations and became increasingly sensitive to their solemn shared interest in avoiding the outbreak of a major war.

WORLD ORDER'S ECONOMIC DIMENSION

Almost as prominent in the anxieties of statesmen at the time was the fear that only the war concluded in 1945 had ended the global economic crisis of the 1930s, and that the restoration of peace might well lead quickly back to economic depression. The searing experience of the Great Depression had hit hard the richest and most powerful countries, bringing them to the brink of revolution. Many observers at the time believed that it was only World War II that lifted countries out of their doldrums, generating jobs and encouraging unprecedented international cooperation.

From 1945 onward, economic policy became an important aspect of world order. One side of the effort was to provide institutional mechanisms to promote stability in the economic relations among Western states, which took the primary form of the so-called Bretton Woods institutions: the International Monetary Fund and the World Bank. Another side was the vigorous attempt to facilitate the economic reconstruction of Europe through massive aid transfers from the United States in the form of the Marshall Plan, moves justified at the time as a way to provide markets for United States exports and to offset the drift of several key European countries toward communism.

Still another economic adjustment was what has been usefully called "military Keynesianism": continued government spending in the military sector during peacetime, providing jobs and contributing to consumer spending and investment opportunities. Instead of demobilizing if the security threat diminishes, the level of military spending is maintained at a high level to sustain consumer demand and soften the impact of cyclical behavior.

The economic approach to world order was generally successful, giving Europe and North America long periods of sustained economic growth, with much shorter and less severe intervals of cyclical adjustment (identified as "recessions"). In the end, the relative economic success of the West—contrasted with the failures of the Soviet bloc, especially in relation to the bloc's own consumer markets—was more important in bringing the cold war to a one-sided finish than the relative weight of Western military superiority. Of course, because the West was far richer, it could afford to finance a huge military buildup while still bringing prosperity to its citizens.

But the West also saw a fundamental shift in economic policy start to take place in the 1980s. As the world became more economically interconnected, and as the threat of a socialist alternative diminished, the United States and Britain moved toward a more market-oriented approach to economic policy that emphasized the control of inflation and fiscal discipline (especially balanced budgets). These shifts were partly ideological interpretations of the capitalist ethos, and partly justified as necessary responses to the challenges economic globalization posed. In effect, the state moved toward a reduced responsibility for the social and collective well-being of society, and left these problems to be addressed by the private sector. To varying degrees, the social democratic version of the compassionate state has been replaced by the neoliberal cruel state.

GLOBALIZATION AND FRAGMENTATION

These globalizing economic tendencies are changing the way we think about world order as the century draws to a close. Contradictory forces are challenging the supremacy of the state from above and from below. Especially at the regional level, new frameworks, regimes, and worldviews are taking hold and partially superseding the organizing role of the state. Such developments weaken traditional loyalties and raise important questions about the nature of citizenship. At the same time, there is also dynamism at local levels as well, a fragmenting dynamic that intensifies ethnic and subnational identities. These trends undermine the state's claim to provide national identity and to preempt the powerful energies that make nationalism such a formidable force in modern history.

It is evident that growing economic interconnectedness, combined with the influence of the Internet and a global media (especially television) that glamorizes consumerism and creates a common awareness of breaking news in real time, is reshaping our sense of world order in fundamental respects. The state is no longer as dominant on the global stage. Global market forces, in the form of multinational corporations and banks, exert a strong independent influence and operate internationally with only minimal regulation. Also significant is the emergence of local and transnational initiatives that are organized by voluntary groupings of people concerned about issues that may range from of the construction of a dam or government oppression. World order is being shaped by these various social forces, producing a transition from a world of sovereign, territorial states to an emergent global village.

We do not know where these tendencies will lead except to take note of the degree to which globalization is generating contradictory reactions of consolidation and fragmentation. On the one side there are important moves toward regionalizing the organization of economic and political life, a process that has gone furthest in Europe. On the other there are a variety of intense moves to affirm particular ethnic and religious identities, and to challenge the authority of larger frameworks. Even in Europe, the expansion of the European Union has been accompanied by the revival of local nationalisms that had been previously contained within the modern secular state. This dynamic has been pathologically evident in the former Yugoslavia, but it has been more moderately expressed in countries such as Spain and Britain, where minority peoples have become more protective of their national languages and traditions and less deferential to the territorial state.

TOWARD HUMANE GOVERNANCE?

As we approach a new century, indeed a new millennium, it is quite natural to speculate about the future, and to wonder whether the extraordinary technological breakthroughs of the recent past will be translated into social and political arrangements that are beneficial for the peoples of the world. The logic of the market, along with population growth and rising levels of consumption, seems to be pushing humanity in the direction of nonsustainability. It has been difficult to induce political leaders to introduce policies that constrain consumption so as to slow down the processes of environmental deterioration and climate change. The longer term challenges of sustainability do not seem easily addressed by the time horizons that govern market forces or the accountability of politicians.

There has been an encouraging trend toward democratization and human rights. There has also been a more questionable ideological effort to associate the adoption of democracy with respect for the autonomy of the private sector. There is an effort under way as well to extend some dimensions of democratic governance beyond state-society relations, such as the current project, strongly backed by global civil society, to establish an international court with the authority to prosecute those accused of crimes against humanity and genocide; and the idea of holding even political and military leaders accountable is a development bringing a democratic dimension to world order. Another movement in this direction is the call for greater transparency and less secrecy on the part of international financial institutions, including the IMF, the World Bank, and the United Nations, especially the Security Council.

The goals of humane governance are not yet fully clear, and involve a process of discovery, especially through the action of global civil society. Several aspects of global humane governance enjoy widespread support as necessary normative ideas. These include concerns about sustainability, broadened human rights enforcement, and increased democratization of state-society relations. They also encompass:

- the abolition of all weapons of mass destruction by verified stages and global monitoring, with moves toward the demilitarization of relations among states;

- the encouragement of regional frameworks for economic, political, and cultural coordination, and for the establishment of zones of peace;

- the facilitation of intercivilization contact and dialogue with the objective of reconciling secular ideas of a strict separation of religion and politics with many non-Western calls for a governing process more directly infused by spirituality and religious practices.

Such an enumeration is intended to depict moral and legal trends as well as to set forth a policy agenda. It ignores countervailing ideas and trends so as to clarify the contours of a potentially emergent form of world order that would deserve to be considered as a type of global humane governance. This is not a prediction that such a result is likely to occur. It is an assertion of the possibility, which becomes more probable to the extent that social forces throughout the world act to make it happen. As never before, the peoples of the world hold their destiny, and that of future generations, in their own hands. We can only hope that their political imagination is attuned to these brighter possibilities.

Reading 8-2

States of Discord
Thomas Friedman and Robert Kaplan

TECHNO LOGIC (FRIEDMAN)

What is globalization? The short answer is that globalization is the integration of everything with everything else. A more complete definition is that globalization is the integration of markets, finance, and technology in a way that shrinks the world from a size medium to a size small. Globalization enables each of us, wherever we live, to reach around the world farther, faster, deeper, and cheaper than ever before and at the same time allows the world to reach into each of us farther, faster, deeper, and cheaper than ever before.

SOURCE: From "States of Discord" by Thomas Friedman and Robert Kaplan, *Foreign Policy* (March/April 2002): 64–70 (www.foreignpolicy.com). Copyright © 2002 by the Carnegie Endowment for International Peace. Reprinted by permission.

I believe this process is almost entirely driven by technology. There's a concept in strategic theory—the sort of things Bob Kaplan has written about—stating that capabilities create intentions. In other words, if you give people B-52s, they will find ways to use them. This concept is quite useful when thinking about globalization, too. If I have a cell phone that can call around the world at zero marginal cost to 180 different countries, I will indeed call around the world to 180 different countries. If I have Internet access and can do business online, a business in which my suppliers, customers, and competitors are all global, then I will be global, too. And I will be global whether there is a World Trade Organization agreement or not.

Since September 11, 2001, many people have asked me if terrorism will stop the process of globalization. I had often wondered about this sort of situation: What would happen if we did reach a crisis moment, a crisis like terrorism, or a major financial crisis, and things started to go in reverse? People would say, "Bring back the walls!" But I knew that was going to be a particularly defining moment for us, because that's when we were all going to wake up and finally realize that technology had destroyed the walls already—that the September 11 terrorists made their reservations on Travelocity.com.

BAD NEWS IS NEXT (KAPLAN)

Let me try to give a slightly richer definition of globalization. The best historical metaphor I can come up with is China in the third century B.C., when the Han overlordship replaced the period of the warring states (following the short interlude of the Qin dynasty). Think of it: You had this massive mainland China, thousands of miles across, with little states constantly coalescing into bigger states over the centuries. And then, for a long period, you had six or so major states fighting each other. Finally, they were unified by a series of balance-of-power agreements, by an embryonic bureaucracy developing in all of them, and by the Chinese language. What the Han dynasty represented was not a single state; it was a serious reduction of conflict among the warring states, so that the highest morality was the morality of order, with everyone giving up a share of their independence for the sake of greater order. I'm not talking about some sort of "world government" over China. It was just a loose form of governance, where everything affected or constrained everything else.

Today, too, everything affects everything else—we're affected by disease pandemics in Africa, by *madrassas* (seminaries) in Pakistan—but there is still nothing like a global leviathan or a centralizing force. The world is coming together, but the international bureaucracy atop it is so infantile and underdeveloped that it cannot cope with growing instability.

And more complexity does lead to more instability. Today, we have several factors driving this relationship. First, we are seeing youth bulges in many of the most unstable countries. Big deal if the world population is aging; that doesn't interest me for the next five or ten years. I care about the many countries or areas like the West Bank, Gaza, Nigeria, Zambia, and Kenya where over the next 20 years the population of young, unemployed males between the ages of 14 and 29 is going to grow. And as we all know from television, one thing that unites political unrest everywhere is that it's carried out by young males. Another factor is resource scarcity—the amount of potable water available throughout the Middle East, for instance, is going to decrease substantially over the next 25 years. When you put them together, these driving forces lead to sideswipes, such as the September 11 attacks. Another sideswipe could be an environmental event like an earthquake in an intensely settled area, like Egypt or China, that could lead to the removal of a strategic regime.

In *The Lexus and the Olive Tree,* Tom wrote that globalization doesn't end geopolitics. That's the key. Globalization is not necessarily *good* news; it's just *the* news. And the news could get scarier and scarier, because more interconnections will lead to complexity before they'll lead to stability.

STATE OF PROGRESS (FRIEDMAN)

Bob brought up the role of the state and of governance; these are absolutely crucial issues. Some people believe that the state will wither away and matter less in an era of globalization. I believe exactly the opposite: The state matters much more in a globalized world.

Why? Well, the first thing we have to understand about globalization is that, oddly enough, it's not global. It affects different regions in different ways, and it links different countries in different ways. Yet every part of the world is directly or indirectly being globalized in some way. In this context, the state matters more, not less. If I could just use one image to describe the state—including political institutions, courts, oversight agencies, the entire system of governance—I would say it's like a plug, and it's the plug that your country uses to connect with globalization.

If that plug is corroded, corrupted, or the wires aren't connected, the flow between you and that global system—what I call the "electronic herd"—is going to be very distorted, and you are going to feel the effects of that distortion. But if the plug works well, the flow between you and the global system will be much more enriching.

The dirty little secret about globalization—and it takes a lot of countries a long time to figure it out—is that the way to succeed in globalization is to focus on the fundamentals. It's not about the wires or about bandwidth or about modems. It's about reading, writing, and arithmetic. It's about churches, synagogues, temples, and mosques. It's about rule of law, good governance, institution building, free press, and a process of democratization. If you get these fundamentals right, then the wires will find you, and the wires will basically work. But if you get them wrong, nothing will save you.

Consider Botswana and Zimbabwe. Both countries have problems, but Botswana was probably in the top 20 percent of countries last year in per capita income growth. Zimbabwe was, I dare say, certainly in the bottom 20 percent. These two countries are right next to each other. Botswana has its problems, to be sure; it's not some ideal paradise. But it has decent democratization, decent institutions left over by the British, decent free press, and decent oversight and regulatory bodies.

And Zimbabwe? Zimbabwe has President Robert Mugabe. Now, if you told me right now that in five years I'll be able to get a fair trial in Zimbabwe, I'd say that Zimbabwe is going to be fine. But if you tell me I won't get a fair trial in Zimbabwe in five years, then it doesn't matter if everyone in Zimbabwe has an Internet address, a personal computer, a Palm Pilot, and a cell phone. If the institutions through which these people have to operate to generate growth and interact with the global system are corrupted and corroded, then all the gadgetry in the world won't make a dime's worth of difference.

Or just compare Egypt and the East Asian countries. They started out with about the same per capita income in 1953, but now there's a huge disparity between them. People who have studied these parts of the world point to two fundamental differences: One is the value placed on education. The other is how leaders justify their rule.

In Asia, which had autocratic regimes for several decades, leaders tended to justify their rule with a simple trade-off: Give me your democracy and I will give you prosperity. And people gave up many democratic rights and they got prosperity. The more prosperous they became, the more the relationship between them and the regime changed, until ultimately, you had a tip-over point, and these became democratic countries in almost every case. But what happened in Egypt? The leader said, don't judge me on whether I brought you a better standard of living; judge me on how I confronted the British, how I confronted the Americans, and how I confronted the Israelis. Give me your rights, and I'll give you the Arab-Israeli conflict. That was a bad trade. As a result, we see a huge gap between the two.

That's why with globalization, leadership matters more, not less. If you have the calcified Brezhnevite management that Egypt has, then it's no wonder that the Cairo skyline has barely changed in 50 years. But if your management "gets it"—as a corporation or a country—then you'll benefit from globalization.

STATE OF WAR (KAPLAN)

I agree that good things are going to happen in a more global world (and humanists will duly celebrate them), but foreign policy crises are about what goes wrong. In the short run, I'm pessimistic. Remember that poverty does not lead to revolutions—development does. The revolutions in Mexico and France were preceded by years of dramatic and dynamic economic development, as well as urbanization and population movements. And what have we seen for the last 10 years, which Tom has described so well in his columns? Incredible dynamism, with middle classes emerging in China, Indonesia, and Brazil. But this development will not automatically lead to West German–style democracies. They may eventually, but for the next 20 or 30 years, they will experience more and more turbulence.

Of course, part of the trouble with some states is that they are states in name only. North Africa exemplifies this problem. In North Africa, you have three age-old civilization clusters: Egypt, Tunisia, and Morocco. They all have their problems, but all three are far healthier as states than, say, Algeria or Libya. Why is that? Why did Algeria and Libya get so radical and suffer through civil wars? Because they were never states to begin with.

Tunisia has been a state since Roman times. There's a state mentality there, even without democracy. Citizens argue about the budget and about education. The leader does not have to be oppressive, because a state community already exists. But Algeria and Libya are geographic expressions that were not cobbled together as states until relatively recently. The only institutionalizing force there is radical ideology.

Certainly, you could argue that Africa is in a class by itself. But consider the European Union. Despite its fits and starts, if you look at the European Union emerging out of a coal and steel consortium in the early 1950s, which included France, Germany, the Benelux countries, and Italy, and then expanded to England, etc., you see a gradual superstructure growing. At the same time, however, localism emerges. You see Catalonia and the German *länder* (states) reasserting themselves. And yet, I must ask, who today would fight for Belgium? Who would fight for Germany? So, on balance, I think the state is weakening in Europe. But if the European community develops into a vapid, insipid bureaucratic despotism that only excites the upper-middle classes and the Brussels Eurocrats, there will be a backlash. That's why you have retrograde nationalist backlashes.

But here's where Tom is right: States make war. And they make war because they have political accountability to people who are stuck in geographic space and because they must defend their citizenry and are therefore willing to take big risks on military strikes. The United Nations would never do that. To have the guts to make war, you have to have your own citizenry on your back; you must be physically responsible for them. I believe that, in the next 10 years or so, major wars will be very state-driven.

LET THEM EAT PIZZA (FRIEDMAN)

Bob mentioned the divides in Europe between local and national and regional identities. That discussion raises a larger question: Will globalization turn out to be simply Americanization? Some people believe globalization will homogenize us only on the surface. Japanese kids may wear jeans and my own kids may eat sushi. But underneath those jeans, those kids may still remain completely Japanese, while my kids are in reality still just hot dog–loving American teenagers. Others argue that globalization is going to homogenize us to our very roots, in which case I would agree that it really will become culturally lethal.

But I think that is an unanswerable question right now. Early 20th-century U.S. novelist Thomas Wolfe wrote that you can't go home again. With globalization, I worry whether we won't be able to leave home again, that everywhere will start to look like everywhere else. There are two ways to make people homeless: One is to take away their home, and the other is to make their home look like everybody else's home. Yet I take some succor from the fact that the most popular food in the world today is not the Big Mac, but pizza. And what is pizza? It's a flat piece of bread that every society has, on which every society and every community throws its own local ingredients and culture. In India, you can get tandoori pizza; in Japan, you can get sushi pizza; and in Mexico, you can get salsa pizza.

In the same way, my hope for the Internet is that it will become an instrument for sharing cultures, not for spreading some kind of American cultural dominance to the world. And while I have great sympathy for people who fear the latter outcome, I think it's really still an open question as to which will prevail. For example, people have proclaimed the death of regionalism in America for a long time. But I tell you, when I go back to my home state of Minnesota, I speak Minnesotan. I slip right back in there. Anyone who thinks that there's no place like home anymore, and there's no Minnesota, has really never come from a region with a strong identity.

SAY YOUR PRAYERS (KAPLAN)

I'd like to take a more specific angle on the question of culture and values. One of the biggest elements of globalization has been urbanization. Fifty years ago, the Middle East was rural; cities like Tunis, Casablanca, and Damascus had 200,000 or 300,000 or 400,000 people. Karachi, for instance, had 400,000 people in 1947. Today, Karachi has 9 million inhabitants. Even Tunis has 2 million.

And there has been a value change as well, with a more stark, more abstract, more ideological form of Islam emerging to cope with urbanization. When people lived in villages, religion was part and parcel of the daily routine of life; it wasn't conscious. In the hill villages of Afghanistan, women did not wear veils, because virtually every man they saw was a relative of some kind. But when they migrated into cities, suddenly they were among strangers, so the veil came on.

When they migrated into pseudo-Western cities such as Cairo, they were suddenly confronted with anonymity. Do you know what is amazing about cities like Cairo, Damascus, and Tunis? Yes, they're poor: Services are horrible, street lights don't work, and the police forces are fairly useless. Yet crime is actually quite low. Except for the odd pickpocket, who's in an area where tourists tend to go, it's perfectly safe to walk around with a lot of cash in your wallet.

How could that be? How can you minimize petty, random crime despite the kind of urbanization that sent crime through the roof in New York City in the mid-19th century, when Walt Whitman was writing about it? The answer: intensification of religion. Indeed, any time in history when there was tremendous economic change—with dynamism, development, and disruption—religion adapted. For a more contemporary example, just look at the megachurches in the midwestern United States. Sure, East Coast sophisticates laugh at them, but that is a classic form of adaptation to economic change. And in the Middle East, what we call fundamentalism was just a Darwinian way of coping with urbanization. Unfortunately, it also provided a fertile petri dish for the emergence of disease germs like terrorists.

BIKINIS IN A NUDIST COLONY (FRIEDMAN)

I'm a bit more optimistic than Bob when thinking about the impact of globalization on personal freedoms and democracy. Consider China. I've been visiting China for the last 15 years. And every time I go, it's a more open place, with more personal freedoms, more rule of law, and more people empowered to challenge the government. And I don't know where it ends or where the tip-over point is. All I know is that this transformation in China is largely due to the forces of globalization.

Of course, we also saw the forces of globalization on September 11, 2001. Again, globalization goes both ways. It can threaten democracies as well as strengthen them. But on net, I do believe that with the right leadership, globalization will be a force for more openness, more rule of law, and more opportunities for people to enjoy personal freedoms and challenge authorities.

My own view is that China is on the verge of experiencing the biggest leveraged buyout in history. The business community has now been invited into the Communist Party—I was there when that happened. Think about that: Capitalists in the Communist Party!

I can deal with a lot of contradictions in my life, but wearing bikinis in a nudist colony or serving steak at a vegetarian restaurant strikes me as no longer manageable. The presence of capitalists in the Communist Party represents a very deep change; it tells us that the system is really moving somewhere else. I believe that over time we will basically see the business community—the capitalist side of China—buying out the Communist Party.

FREEDOM FROM LANGUAGE (KAPLAN)

Well, Tom, I think there are a lot of unnecessary arguments about democracy and globalization, because we have become trapped by language. Unfortunately, we've defined democracy as the holding of parliamentary elections now or in six months. This definition is simply wrong. At the end of World War I, the novelist Joseph Conrad sent a letter to a friend in which he wrote that we don't really fight for elections or "democracy" but for openness and freedom and human rights—in whatever form they may take in any particular country. I think that's the right way to look at it.

Countries that already have sizable middle classes and decent political institutions may be ripe for the icing on the cake: democratic elections. We've seen that in Taiwan and South Korea, and in the southern cone of Latin America, despite Argentina's troubles. But there are other places where holding elections too soon could lead to the opposite result.

For instance, Tunisia has increased the size of its middle class from 6 percent to roughly 50 percent of the population. Tunisia has one of the most open societies in the Arab world, with cybercafes everywhere—yet it has all been done through benign despotism. Had they held elections eight or so years ago, I believe there would be less freedom today. Similarly, Egypt is in a terrible situation, but if you demanded elections there tomorrow, there is a good likelihood that more oppression and a worse human rights situation could result. So what we have to do on this question of democracy is look at each individual country and place as it comes.

Reading 8-3

Globalization and Its Discontents
Duncan Green and Matthew Griffith

On 11 September the *Financial Times* published an article entitled "The mosquitoes begin to swarm," the first of a four-part series on what it described as the counter-capitalist movement. The author, James Harding, vividly captured the chaotic energy of a "movement of movements" based on a pervasive "queasiness about capitalism."

> It is wide in its tactics and ambitions, violent and revolutionary on the edges, peaceful and reformist in the main. It rushes in often contradictory directions, anti-corporate and entrepreneurial, anarchist and nostalgic, technophobe and futuristic, revolutionary and conservative all at the same time.
>
> It does not have one source. Many tributaries have swollen counter-capitalism: the anti-apartheid movement, the campaigns against US intervention in Central America, environmentalism, the emergence of protest movements in the Third World, famine relief in Africa, the Asian financial crisis, human rights protection, Acid House raves in Europe, road rallies organized by Reclaim the Streets and hip-hop music in the US.

Following the attacks on the World Trade Center and the Pentagon, the remaining three articles were hurriedly spiked. The political and social momentum of the movement appeared to have gone into deep freeze. Some groups appeared to be morphing into the nucleus of an anti-war movement; others tried to continue with business as usual, issuing policy documents and calls for supporter actions on the debt burden and the WTO ministerial meeting in Qatar.

Even before the 11 September attacks, the movement was entering a period of uncertainty. Six weeks earlier, violence by both police and protesters in the streets of Genoa during the G8 summit had left a young Italian protester dead, many injured, and a brewing sense of crisis over the movement's direction.

SOURCE: From "Globalization and Its Discontents" by Duncan Green and Matthew Griffith, *International Affairs* (London), vol. 78, no. 1 (January 2002): 49–68. Copyright © 2002 the Royal Institute of International Affairs. Reprinted by permission of Blackwell Publishers, Ltd.

The débâcle in Genoa, when mainstream protesters from the "Drop the Debt" coalition of NGOs decided to pull out of a protest march which had been months in preparation, stood in sharp contrast to the G8 in Birmingham in 1998. Then, a ring of 70,000 people, mainly from church development agencies such as CAFOD and Christian Aid, had formed a human circle around the summit and forced the debt issue onto the G8 agenda, resulting in improved debt relief terms for dozens of developing countries. In Birmingham, the sideshow was the Reclaim the Streets party, an all-night rave organized by a growing coalition which was later involved in "Stop the City," an anti-capitalist protest which sought to close down the City of London in June 1999. By Genoa, the order of importance had been reversed in terms of public profile, if not in numbers. After Genoa, mainstream development NGOs began to question the viability of mass protest, in a rethink that was suddenly interrupted by terror and war.

This article explores the nature of this movement, the challenges that faced it before the events of September 2001 and the subsequent militarization of global politics, and the likely impact on it of those events.

WHAT'S IN A NAME?

The term most commonly used for this phenomenon is the "anti-globalization movement"; but it is neither solidly anti-globalization, nor a single movement.

On core issues such as democracy, the environment, and international trade and investment rules, what parts of the movement *support* is as important as what they oppose: increased grassroots participation and accountability in policy-making; improved environmental protection and the internalization of environmental costs; reform of world trade rules to benefit the weakest countries and communities. However, because the objects of support are heterogeneous and at times contradictory, the "anti" label has stuck, to the frustration of many of the movement's leaders and thinkers. Struggling with this issue, activists organizing the World Social Forum scheduled for Porto Alegre in January 2002 chose for its slogan "Another World is Possible."[1]

Nor is it a single movement, with an agreed common purpose and systems of command and control. Rather it is, as the *FT* put it, "a movement of movements" or even a "mood." There are some overlapping aims, but also several significant cleavages—between reformists and rejectionists, and between parts of the labour, environmental and Southern movements. Bearing these caveats in mind, this essay will follow Naomi Klein and refer to this confluence of political currents, in a somewhat quaint 1960s shorthand, simply as "the movement."

THE WORLD OUTSIDE

Although globalization (understood here as the increasing interconnectedness of individuals, groups, companies and countries) has been going on for centuries if not millennia, the past twenty years have seen a spectacular growth in its intensity, scope and visibility as a public issue. The origins of the movement are rooted in and in large part unified by this period of globalization. It is therefore worth briefly examining the events and processes that shaped this political reaction.

While increasing integration through trade and investment has been a feature of the global economy since the Second World War, several pivotal events in recent decades have led to a sudden acceleration in its social and political prominence. In the North, the oil crisis and the suspension of dollar convertibility in 1972 marked the end of the "long boom" of post-1945 Keynesianism. They also triggered the meteoric rise of the global capital markets which made earning and keeping "market confidence" an increasingly important determinant of government policies.

In the South, the Mexican government's near-default on its foreign debt in 1982 marked the end of the postwar era of import-substituting industrialization and began a long and painful period for developing countries, characterized by the burden of massive foreign indebtedness, and the rise in political influence of the IMF, World Bank and international capital markets, all three of which ushered policy-makers away from development policies focused on the domestic market, and towards a strategy of export-led growth.

Finally, the fall of the Berlin Wall in 1989 and the subsequent collapse of Soviet communism led to the rapid integration of what became known as the "transition economies" of the former Soviet Union into a seemingly triumphant model of market-driven economic change.

At a political level, these events brought in their wake two important developments. The crisis in state-led development in the Third World and the discrediting of the old Soviet-based left was also accompanied by—and a major cause of—the disorientation of the left as a whole. Certain trends within "globalization" in turn compounded this disorientation. The first of these was a shift in power away from the state, driven increasingly by global economic trends (such as global financial markets) that eroded governments' ability to manage their economies. The result was a perceived crisis in social democracy.

The second trend was the rise of the New Right. By the early 1980s the market was seen to have won a definitive triumph over the state, leading to the resurgence of free market ideology. John Kennedy's "twilight time," characterized by American fear of a looming Soviet threat, gave way to a new dawn for liberal democracies and, more importantly, for a global market based on the aggressive economic model of Anglo-Saxon capitalism. The elision of "market democracy" became a staple item in Western leaders' lexicon.

At an economic level, these political developments helped drive the rapid expansion of trade and investment flows, as large parts of Latin America and Asia adopted export-led growth strategies, and the countries of the former Soviet empire were rapidly, if partially, absorbed into an increasingly integrated global economy. "Globalization" quickly became the shorthand for this model of expansion—a heady and complex mix of technological, economic, political and cultural change.

Globalization was accompanied and underpinned by a set of interlocking institutional developments at both international and national levels. First, the existing structures of global economic governance were overhauled. The World Bank and the IMF redefined their roles, moving swiftly away from Keynesian operating principles to become bastions of neo-liberalism. A web of bilateral, regional and global international trade and investment agreements, culminating in the creation of the World Trade Organization in 1995, bound the new system in place. At the national level in the West, the left, driven by the need for both electoral success and reconciliation with new market realities, moved from social democracy towards a much more uncritical acceptance of the market as the organizing principle of the economy.

The early 1990s thus saw a remarkable degree of internal consensus over the model of global economic and political management promoted by global institutions and the most powerful state players—a model variously titled "neoliberalism" or the "Washington consensus," a term first coined by economist John Williamson in 1989 to describe

a core set of ten policy recommendations which formed the core of structural adjustment programmes around the world.

But the "end of history" dominance of the neo-liberal variant of globalization
proved short-lived. Events throughout the 1990s undermined both the ideological and
theoretical foundations of the Washington consensus, and its political base of support.
Globalization and the erosion of national sovereignty drew growing public attention to
the undemocratic and closed nature of increasingly powerful global institutions and the
influence and lack of accountability of global corporations. The movement grew to
protest at, and fill, these lacunae in the system of global economic governance.

The Asian crisis of 1997 (caused in part by excessive liberalization of financial markets which was then misdiagnosed, aggravated and perpetuated by the IMF) was perhaps the most significant event to undermine neo-liberal theory. But the Mexican peso
crisis of 1994 and the catastrophe of free market reform in Russia (where life expectancy
fell sharply in the period after 1990[2]) also created serious doubts in the minds of policy-makers. By the late 1990s, liberalization as a panacea was being called into question
even by free market economists like Krugman and Bhagwati, as well as prominent practitioners like George Soros. Neo-liberal hubris gave way to cautious self-doubt, especially over the problems of liberalized capital markets.

As doubts grew, so did political opposition. The economic consequences of this
phase of globalization unified in opposition a diverse array of actors. Downsizing and
corporate restructuring, privatization, the erosion of workers' rights and the changing
nature of production and supply chains activated opposition from the labour movement
in both the North and the South. Global warming, unsustainable growth and the depletion of resources created hostility from environmentalists, who were further outraged over the perceived threat to environmental legislation from trade rules in the
WTO, for example, when four Asian nations successfully challenged provisions of the
US Endangered Species Act forbidding the sale in the United States of prawns caught
in ways that kill endangered sea turtles. The erosion of the nation-state and of democratic institutions antagonized proponents of state-led development, democrats and
some on the political right. Increasing corporate power and social inequality catalysed
the traditional left and a whole host of other left-of-centre actors. Structural adjustment
programmes and growing Southern marginalization and inequality radicalized civil society and some political parties in the developing world.

For many in the movement, the OECD's abandonment in 1998 of talks to establish a multilateral agreement in investment (MAI) and the collapse a year later of the
third WTO ministerial meeting in Seattle marked a turning point in the "imperial over-
stretch" in neo-liberal globalization. Although this form of globalization was promoted
by the most powerful global actors, the social and political base of support for it was always narrow. With its ideology in question, its programme creating politically damaging side-effects and its main institutions looking increasingly rudderless and bewildered,
a new set of political actors rushed to fill the gaps. In all its chaotic glory, the movement
was born.

THE MOVEMENT: WHO'S WHO?

There is a basic need to recognize that despite the big contributions that a global
economy can undoubtedly make to global prosperity, we also have to confront
. . . the far reaching manifestations of inequality between and within nations. The
real debate associated with globalization is, ultimately, not about the efficiency of

markets, nor about the importance of modern technology. The debate, rather, is about inequality of power.[3]

At first sight the movement looks an incongruous political mix of contradictions, colours and cultures—in parts vocal and aggressive, in others quiet and conciliatory. Although its political and social origins are diverse, they all involve a response to the economic events of the past twenty years, in particular the neo-liberal form of globalization and its most visible symbols, the institutions of global economic governance. The movement's milestones have been the G8, IMF and WTO summits that it has attended and disrupted or influenced to differing degrees—Birmingham 1998, Seattle 1999, Prague 2000, Genoa 2001, each accompanied by a panoply of fringe events and protests.

Although this opposition may be its primary unifying force, it would be grossly simplistic to portray the movement as being solely reactive. Traditionally, a political force may rely on a unified opposing theory, charismatic leaders and revolutionary cadres, but the movement is very far from being a traditional political animal. It is united at heart by a concern for social justice and a refusal to accept the depredations of the powerful and the exclusion of the poor and the powerless from the mainstream political system. In this sense it is not a negative movement, but a positive attempt at inclusion.

Nor is the vast bulk of the movement "anti-globalization"—all are contesting the future direction of globalization, but almost every current within it has a strong internationalist outlook. Indeed, the products of globalization have proved indispensable to the growth of the movement. The internet and email have created a global conversation between grassroots organizations and NGOs around the world, a daily exchange of information, viewpoints and ideas which was previously the exclusive prerogative of the rich and powerful. The spread of global brands, and the global reach of the WTO and the IMF, have provided common rallying points for protest—the founding of the WTO in 1995 in particular put an institutional face on what had previously been an amorphous process, a gift to the protest movement.

While the movement is to some extent a collection of separate fragments, the past ten years have seen significant progress. Serious divisions persist, but there has been a growing consensus (or at least a greater awareness and tolerance of difference) between labour, environmentalists and development NGOs on many issues where there once was hostility—for example on child labour, or the attitudes of environmentalists to poverty. In the UK, one recent example is the creation of the Trade Justice Movement, a coalition of eleven NGOs including the Royal Society for the Protection of Birds, CAFOD and Friends of the Earth.[4] However, after the events of 11 September 2001, that partial unity will be tested by the changed environment of economic recession, militarization and heightened concerns over national security. Moreover, the potential absorption of its more reformist currents, as policy-makers begin to adopt their rhetorical and even policy clothes, is likely to bring divisions between reformists and rejectionists to the surface.

The movement has become an important international player in its own right, helping to redefine public notions of democracy, accountability and collective mobilization. The *Financial Times* sees it as a "fifth estate," a valuable global counterbalance in a world of ageing and often inadequate global institutions.[5] In recent years it has achieved some notable successes:

- *Jubilee 2000:* This largely church-based coalition was credited by the British government with putting debt back on the international agenda. Initially started in the UK, Jubilee groups were set up in dozens of countries, North and South.

Many, especially in the South, rapidly moved on to campaign on wider globalization-related issues such as the impact of transnational corporations and structural adjustment programmes.

- *Attac:* This French-based network of intellectuals and activists has taken the lead in promoting the introduction of the "Tobin tax" (a small tax on currency transactions designed to curb speculative capital flows), and was influential in persuading the French government both to support a study of the tax and to oppose the MAI.

- *Corporate social responsibility:* Public criticism and campaigning on corporate misconduct, for example over pollution or abusive labour practices, backed by increasing pressure from institutional investors, have prompted numerous initiatives to improve corporations' social and environmental performance.[6] In the United States, student-led grassroots anti-sweatshop campaigns have galvanized political life on the campuses to a degree not seen since the Vietnam War.

Although it defies firm categorizations, the movement can be roughly divided into three strands: statists, alternatives and reformists.

The statists believe the current process of globalization has been a disaster, and seek to defend and rebuild the role of the state in economic management after the neoliberal assault of the last twenty years. This group is dominated by the traditional left, some sections of the labour movement and a large proportion of Southern activists. Through this group runs a strong sense of rejectionism and even conservatism. Some, such as a few of the US labour unions protesting in Seattle, want to retain the state's ability to protect domestic industries from cheap imports. Others, such as prominent Filipino activist Walden Bello, reject the terms of globalization outright, feeling that any alternative, including the abolition of the IMF and WTO, could not fail to be an improvement on present realities. Despite its focus on the nation-state, this group retains a strong sense of internationalism.

The alternatives are both highly visible and the hardest to define, though often labelled "anarchist." This element of the movement is strongly driven, and best understood, in cultural terms. Its members reject globalization in passing, but concentrate more on building small-scale alternatives, be they ecologists running organic businesses, followers of the *Small is beautiful* author E. F. Schumacher, activists seeking to "deconstruct" corporate power and global brands, or Zapatistas who wish to gain rights and land and make a statement about globalization's marginalizing effect. These groups oppose the encroachment of the market or the market's power relations into their cultural or political spaces. Most are also small, decentralized and strongly "anti-corporate."

The reformists make up the majority of formally structured groups involved in the movement, or at least dominate the thinking of their leaderships. Their aim is "partial change to try and offset current injustices and inequalities."[7] The reformists act within current political systems and advocate gradualism and peaceful change. Most accept a role for the market, but believe it must be better regulated and managed in order to achieve socially just and sustainable outcomes. This group includes some trade unions, faith groups, charities and development organizations (like CAFOD and Oxfam), and most mainstream environmental groups (including Friends of the Earth), as well as issue-specific campaigns like "Drop the Debt" or the call for the Tobin Tax.

The reformist current has also made strong inroads into global and national politics, going far beyond the usual suspects. The *Financial Times,* James Wolfensohn at the World Bank, Nobel Prize–winning economists such as Amartya Sen or Joseph Stiglitz, Kofi Annan, the corporate social responsibility movement, George Soros and Lionel Jospin could all be called "reformists." Indeed, after their post–11 September speeches, so could Tony Blair and Gordon Brown. As Lord Desai puts it: "The reformists view themselves as the only true defenders of globalization. They believe that both isolationist calls to reverse the process and supporters' insistence on 'ultra-liberal' forms of global capitalism are bound to de-rail globalization, with tragic consequences."[8]

However, several caveats are warranted over this attempt to disaggregate the movement. Many NGOs and even individuals span more than one current: for example, Friends of the Earth is both reformist and alternative. Author Naomi Klein, one of the movement's most prominent figures since the publication of her book *No logo,* may base her critique of globalization primarily in cultural terms and is a source of inspiration to the anti-corporate wing of the movement, but is herself essentially a progressive reformist. Within mainstream NGOs, supporters and Southern partners often espouse more radical options than their full-time staff and leaders.

Nor does this picture do justice to the depth and breadth of the movement in the South. Clare Short routinely dismissed protests as the work of "misguided white middle-class activists" in the North, but the largest protests over the WTO have been in India. Brazil is rapidly becoming a centre of the movement, witnessed by the huge gatherings of activists in Porto Alegre in January 2001 and 2002, held as a "people's response" to the business summits in Davos. The movement in the North draws inspiration and guidance from a number of prominent southern intellectuals such as Vandana Shiva (India), Martin Kohr (Malaysia) and Walden Bello (Philippines, but based in Bangkok) and the work of the NGOs to which they belong.[9] Finally, none of these categories describes the nihilist currents, few in numbers in Seattle, but significant in Genoa, who were there for a "rage against the machine" punch-up, rather than political debate.

One area in which the South undoubtedly needs the North is in raising issues surrounding the gender impact of globalization. NGOs, women's organizations and some trade unions have drawn attention to the growth in the number of women working in the export-processing zones that have sprung up in numerous Third World cities and ports. While such jobs have often brought new levels of economic independence, wages and working conditions are in many cases deplorable. Networks such as DAWN have also highlighted the wider gender impacts of processes such as export agriculture, privatization and structural adjustment.[10]

Finally, anti-capitalism and anti-Americanism are two complex and cross-cutting issues which threaten to divide the movement. Anti-capitalism is strong among the alternatives, and to a lesser extent among the statists, but the reformists have concluded that working with the market can produce results, and are willing to swallow their scepticism and work alongside corporations. Anti-Americanism is a strong current within both the statist and alternative wings of the movement, and has become particularly problematic since 11 September, for example over the attitude the movement should take (if any) to the US-led counter-offensive against the al-Qaida network.

A DEVELOPMENT NGO CRITIQUE OF GLOBALIZATION

As globalization consolidated and expanded its influence, disquiet over its nature and impact grew in many initially disconnected arenas in both the developing and developed worlds.

In the UK, the basic NGO critique of globalization developed over the course of 2000, as aid agencies debated the World Bank's flagship 2000 *World Development Report* and engaged with the Department for International Development over its White Paper on globalization and development.[11] An intensive round of written and oral submissions and debates sharpened arguments and clarified both common ground and areas of difference.[12] A number of underlying concerns about the direction of political and economic globalization crystallized during these discussions.

The debate over the White Paper also helped inform a shift in NGO emphasis from debt to trade, a change already boosted by the growing notoriety of the WTO following the collapse of the 1999 Seattle ministerial meeting. The success of the Jubilee 2000 debt coalition in the late 1990s had confirmed the importance of policy and advocacy work as a core activity of NGOs and a significant source of influence on Northern policy-makers. While debt remains an important issue, of keen interest to NGOs, experience on the ground in the 1980s and 1990s drew their attention to the wider social impact of structural adjustment and trade liberalization.

Kevin Watkins of Oxfam sees the increasing involvement of Northern development NGOs in policy and advocacy as stemming from a recognition of the inadequacies of an exclusive reliance on traditional in-country project work. "We might spend US$20m on a school in rural Kenya, only to find that nobody could afford to send their children to school . . . We discovered that you cannot operate small islands of development success in a sea of macro-economic failure."[13] Over the past ten years, NGOs have given far higher priority to research and lobbying work. UK NGOs seem to have made particular strides in this area, and are usually disproportionately represented in NGO engagement with international institutions.

THE MAIN CONCERNS

In general, NGO and civil society concerns stem from the realization that while globalization has led to benefits for some, it has not led to benefits for all.[14] The benefits appear to have gone to those who already have the most, while many of the poorest have failed to benefit fully and some have even been made poorer. For example, trade liberalization has meant that many small farmers in developing countries have been hit by import surges of heavily subsidized food imports from the United States and EU.[15]

Equity and redistribution are increasingly recognized as the "missing link" between globalization and poverty reduction. Recent research shows that improved equity leads not only to faster poverty reduction for a given amount of growth, but also to faster growth.[16] What is good for poor people is good for the economy as a whole. Yet up to now, globalization has frequently been linked to increasing inequality.[17]

New research also points to the importance of national differences. The same policy reforms have different outcomes in different countries, depending on the structure of the economy, the initial distribution of assets, and the nature of economic and political institutions. Policy responses to globalization should be appropriate to particular cases in terms of the instruments used, the sequencing of reforms and the combination of policies implemented.

However, even though the evidence points to the importance of diversity, developing country governments are pushed by international rule-making, whether under the auspices of the WTO, through the pressures exerted by structural adjustment packages, or by the need to reassure the markets, towards greater homogeneity of policy response. The challenge for policy-makers is to find ways of making national and international rule-making accommodate appropriate diversity of policy rather than reduce diversity to a minimum.

A linked concern of NGOs is that the drive for liberalization is based too much on dogma and ideology rather than on careful examination of the evidence and assessment of likely impact. They are not alone in this. A recent report by the UK House of Commons Select Committee on International Development concluded "We are astonished at the lack of empirical study of the Uruguay Round on developing countries. Adequate resources must be provided to fund such a review."[18] To date, no such review has even begun. For many NGOs, the empirical flimsiness of the intellectual case for liberalization was one of the main revelations of the White Paper process.

One of the lessons of recent years is that liberalization and deregulation have very different costs and benefits when applied to the three areas of financial flows, direct investment and trade. Arguments and evidence for one should not be applied to the others. The increasing frequency and severity of financial crises in recent years demonstrate the need for serious reforms of the global financial architecture. Crises hurt the poor disproportionately, and increase inequality, making the achievement of growth favourable to the poor harder thereafter. For the least developed economies, debt cancellation remains one of the most efficient ways of freeing the resources needed to fight poverty.

One of the most high-profile areas of public concern (demonstrated by the impact and worldwide sales of Naomi Klein's *No logo*) is that the increasing size and dominance of transnational corporations is making them both more influential and more unaccountable.

Public concern over excessive corporate power has led both to calls for increased international regulation and to pressure on companies to regulate themselves through the introduction of "codes of conduct" for themselves and their suppliers. While sometimes derided as PR exercises, self-regulation by the more serious companies appears to be leading to improvements on the ground.[19] In financial circles, this pressure has been accompanied by a greater awareness that successful companies must take into account a range of "non-financial risks" including social, environmental and ethical issues.[20]

There are also fears that competition between countries wishing to attract foreign investment and technology could lead to a "race to the bottom" in terms of tax incentives and labour market suppression, thereby minimizing the potential social benefits offered by the private sector. The impact of foreign direct investment on employment, on export performance and on domestic industry is not guaranteed, and governments must be able to provide a regulatory framework to maximize the benefits and minimize the costs.

Finally, although most mainstream NGOs believe strongly that it is essential to have rules governing international trade, they severely criticize the particular set of rules established in the WTO. A multilateral trading system is necessary to ensure that weaker nations are not discriminated against by the strong in both North-South and South-South relations. However, rule-making must proceed at a pace that is appropriate for the weakest members of the system, and the rules made in the WTO must be the right rules for development and poverty reduction. Current rules open Northern governments to well-founded accusations of double standards on issues such as protection for domestic industries and support for domestic farmers, and provide insufficient flexibility to enable Southern governments to pursue their development goals.

NGOs returned from the WTO's fourth ministerial meeting in Doha in November 2001 evenly divided between those that saw their cup as half full, and those that believed it was half empty. The optimists pointed to a successful defence of developing countries' rights to override patent rules on medicines in the interests of public health, and a newfound commitment to technical assistance and so-called "special and differential treatment" for developing countries. Pessimists pointed to the lack of progress on many issues of critical importance to developing countries and the continued imbalance of power and negotiating capacity within the organization.[21] The round of global trade negotiations launched at Doha will provide the acid test for many NGOs over whether the WTO can become a genuinely pro-development multilateral institution, or whether it is locked irredeemably into a 1980s-era mindset of uncritical support of liberalization.

HEGEMONIC SHIFTS

Neither the advocates or the critics of globalization have been static or monolithic. Over the 20-year period covered by this article, different tendencies have risen and fallen on both sides of the argument, leading to convergence in some areas and continued differences in others. In general terms, comparing today's debate with that of the mid-1980s, perhaps the high-water mark of the "Washington consensus" of neo-liberalism, it is clear that significant changes have occurred in the thinking of policy-makers. In part this has been a response to some of the more catastrophic results of gung-ho liberalization: the débâcle of free market reforms in Russia, the Mexican crisis of 1994 and the Asian financial crisis of 1997–8 led to some serious soul-searching and admissions of mistakes, deflating the excessive self-confidence of the 1980s.

The growth of the movement both fed off and accelerated this rethink. Politicians recognized a need to respond to public disquiet, for example in the G8's decision to put debt on the agenda at its 1998 Birmingham summit, or when Chancellor Schröder and Prime Minister Jospin ordered a study of the Tobin Tax in 2001. In 1999, the IMF committed itself to the 2015 targets for halving world poverty, drawn up by the OECD and agreed at the UN Millennium Summit in Geneva in June 2000. A growing number of prominent economists questioned the impact of unfettered markets on the poor; among them were Joseph Stiglitz and Amartya Sen, both of whom achieved further prominence with the award of the Nobel Prize (in 2001 and 1998 respectively).

The surest sign of this "hegemonic shift" within the system is that when there are genuine doubts in the minds of policy-makers, a comparatively small number of demonstrators can have a disproportionate political impact. One of the present authors estimated the numbers physically blockading the Seattle conference centre at just a few thousand; compare that with the minimal impact of the hundreds of thousands of demonstrators who marched regularly during the Cold War years, protesting against the installation on UK bases of nuclear cruise missiles.

These partial successes have both strengthened the reformists within the movement and endangered its unity by heightening the points of difference between them and the rejectionists. The difficulties posed by partial victories were most clearly demonstrated in the Jubilee 2000 movement, when at the height of its policy successes at the Cologne G8 summit in 1999 the more radical "Jubilee South" wing, based in countries such as South Africa and Nicaragua, condemned the Northern Jubilee organizations for their reformist acceptance of the status quo. Alejandro Bendana, a former Sandinista leader and Jubilee South leader, condemned northern NGOs for "replacing politics with policy."

The more evangelical wing of the free marketeers also suffered some significant political setbacks, notably the disaster in Seattle and the abandonment in 1998 of OECD talks on an MAI which would, critics claimed, have further skewed the imbalance between corporate rights and responsibilities, and greatly reduced states' abilities to channel investment in the interests of development.

The extent and the limitations of this rethink in the corridors of power is demonstrated by the complex and nuanced approach taken by the British government since the Labour Party came to power in 1997. The new government promptly upgraded international development to create a new department with, in Clare Short, a high-profile minister of Cabinet rank at its head. Years of falling aid were reversed, and the department's policies were overhauled to try to give it a clear focus on development and poverty reduction, rather than the mere provision of aid. Two development White Papers appeared in the space of four years, the first a framework for aid, the second on the development impact of globalization. Chancellor of the Exchequer Gordon Brown has shown a keen interest in development issues and led the international debt relief effort.

Throughout this period, relations with NGOs in general, and with the movement in particular, have been difficult. Clare Short has persistently portrayed the protesters as anti-globalization, and therefore, in her view, anti-development. Her department appears convinced (often on the basis of the sketchiest of evidence) that progress lies in further market reforms in the South, and in opening up Northern markets to developing country exports. Issues such as sovereignty and national specificity have received short shrift from civil servants who generally espouse the need to "save Southern governments from themselves" through further market opening. While the debate in the run up to the globalization White Paper in the end secured some moderation in the triumphantly neo-liberal tone of early drafts, at the time it seemed like the kind of frustrating dialogue of the deaf analysed in Ravi Kanbur's paper on the *World Development Report* process.[22]

Underlying the political debate has been a steady shift in public opinion, with messages on several fronts—press exposés of poor working conditions, public protest and the growing availability and prominence of "fair trade" products—combining to make the public increasingly aware of the social impact of globalization. According to MORI, opinion polls show that in 2001, 46 per cent of UK consumers thought that corporate social responsibility was important, up from 28 per cent in 1997.[23]

From inside the movement, as NGO campaigns and policy specialists constantly move on to the next battleground, it is easy to lose sight of how much has changed since the early 1980s. There is now a much more nuanced understanding among decision-makers of the differences between liberalization of finance, direct investment and trade; at the very least, most wings of the private sector pay lip service to notions of corporate social responsibility; some of the most notorious excesses of free market zeal have been curbed. Along the way, NGOs have developed their research and policy capacity, and have earned a good deal of respect. Indeed, "death by consultation" is now a growing problem, as invitations pour in from government departments, international financial institutions, socially responsible investment managers and dozens of private companies seeking to clean up both their act and their image. Even the largest NGOs are having to reject many requests for consultation and focus their engagement activities more tightly according to strategic priorities.

GENOA AND THE PROBLEM OF VIOLENCE

Even before the attack on the World Trade Center, profound soul-searching had broken out within the ranks of the movement. At the G8 meeting in Genoa, the media limelight had been dominated by the actions of a core group of violent protesters, known as the "Black Bloc," and the excessive response of the police, which led to the death of one young protester and numerous injuries.

The rise in violent protest, and its violent suppression, has brought both benefits and costs for the movement. In the short term it has led to increased media coverage, at least in terms of column inches, although the impact on public opinion has probably been less clear. It has also brought a new readiness from policy-makers to talk to the moderate currents of the movement and try to contain the impact of future protests— after Seattle, indeed, the reaction within the World Bank and IMF was almost one of panic, as they raced to engage NGOs over future meetings. However, these short-term benefits are not worth the long-term political price, as the movement risks becoming divided and discredited, and its many middle-class, middle-aged or elderly supporters alienated by the TV images of apparently random violence against police and property.

Genoa marked the latest stage in an apparently unstoppable escalation in violence, as a current of violent anarchism began to feed off the movement's set-piece protests. In the UK, this current had achieved prominence in previous protests such as the Class War and "Bash the Rich" marches in the 1980s, and had infiltrated some of the anti poll-tax demonstrations of the early 1990s and the largely peaceful "Reclaim the Streets" and "Stop the City" protests later in the decade.

The tradition of violent protest seemed stronger in Europe than in the United States. In Seattle, for example, violent protesters numbered scarcely a few dozen, while hundreds of people, if not thousands, risked their safety in non-violent direct action in the face of remarkably incompetent and violent policing. Indeed, the extraordinary shambles of the Seattle Police Department may have made a significant contribution to the escalating violence of summit protests. Not only did they unleash apparently random volleys of tear gas at non-violent protests, but they appeared to have neither plans nor equipment for crowd control. European delegates fighting their way through the crowds to reach the conference commented that the level of trouble was no worse than that at the average Saturday football match at home!

The actions of this violent and growing minority proved an enormous challenge for an amorphous movement with no clear command and control systems. In a hurried conference call after Genoa, Walden Bello expressed frustration at the "parasitical mode" of the violent minority who would "stay at the edges of the march and from there provoke the police by throwing rocks at them." He concluded: "It would be naïve not to expect them to descend in force on the next big mobilization. We can either go into the next one in a state of denial, or we can be prepared." Bello saw the options as a combination of dialogue with the violent fringe, physically distancing peaceful demonstrators from them and, if necessary, applying the movement's non-violent direct action (NVDA) techniques to them. "Unless measures such as these are incorporated, there might be many among us who would find it difficult to wholeheartedly mobilize people for the next mass action."

None of the three options outlined by Bello looked likely to succeed. Instead, what was emerging, even before 11 September 2001, was a view among some of the movement's more strategic thinkers that the tactic of summit protests was rapidly passing its sell-by date. True, in Birmingham, Cologne and Seattle the protests had achieved remarkable results and boosted morale, and the attendant publicity had catalysed new levels of support. But in Genoa there were few gains, and the violence allowed leaders such as Tony Blair to write off the entire protest as a "travelling circus of anarchists."

Barry Coates, director of the World Development Movement, points out that one of the most successful campaigns in recent years, which blocked the agreement of an MAI, barely used street protest, opting instead for a far wider range of tactics. Face-to-face lobbying, alliance-building, the arrival in politicians' mailboxes of thousands of letters, cards and emails from the public, stories placed with sympathetic journalists, working through trade union and political party structures, targeting companies and institutional investors, the production of well-researched critiques and alternative proposals through international coordination via the Internet. According to Coates, the people on the streets in Genoa were "just the tip of the iceberg. Some people want to go to the barricades—it's all very macho and sexy, but it's not always the best tactic. The ultimate battle is not on the streets, but when you persuade opinion formers of the rightness of your ideas, and it becomes impossible for the government to maintain its position. And that is happening, on the MAI, on the regulation of TNCs, on reform of the WTO."

THE MOVEMENT AND WAR: THE IMPACT OF 11 SEPTEMBER 2001

Since 11 September, terrorism and war have dominated international politics, and questions about the nature of globalization have been sidelined. The WTO ministerial meeting in Doha in November, which agreed a new round of global trade talks, barely made the evening news in Europe and America. The movement, once the centre of international attention, has been portrayed as at best an irrelevance, and at worst vaguely culpable and dangerous.[24] According to the *Financial Times,* it "was not just a movement, it was a mood. Its main platform—the street—is not as open as it was. Its message, always complicated, is now much more loaded. Its audience—politicians, the press and the public—are seriously distracted . . . it has been robbed of its momentum."[25] The temptation may be to think that the movement's time has passed, that it will now pass into history as an ante-bellum self-indulgence, tolerated because of the end of the Cold War and the 1990s economic boom. But is this the case?

Things have certainly changed, but we are sceptical of the view that since 11 September everything is different. Understanding what may happen to the movement means exploring deeper questions—about its political and social origins, the economic issues that it addresses and the future of the system to which it is a response.

This article is written in November 2001, while fighting still continues in Afghanistan. At this stage, any predictions are at best educated guesses. Whatever the immediate result of the conflict in Afghanistan, a wider and more drawnout "war against terrorism" could pose challenges to the movement. We may see a move to an international system of more rigid alliances, comparable to the Cold War years. This would be reflected in the workings of interstate relations and in the global governance institutions. There may be greater politicization of aid, lending and trade—witness the IMF's sudden readiness to bail out the Pakistani regime, or the pressure on WTO members to agree a new round of global trade talks as a "response to terrorism." If security issues completely eclipse other concerns in the minds of Western governments, developing country regimes may once again be judged solely according to their allegiances, rather than their democratic credentials or their commitment to better the lives of their citizens. In such a system the voice of civil society could easily be suppressed. Authoritarian anti-terrorist legislation could all too easily end up being used against demonstrators.

The domestic and international political agenda may alter. There may no longer be an appetite for a "movement of self-doubt" in the West. Tolerance for loose coalitions with violent fringes could evaporate. The public, politicians and media would no longer be as receptive to the protesters' message. In the new order, will the rights of protest be sacrificed on the altar of national security?

On the economic front, recession may well alter the domestic and international agendas, the public mood and the availability of finance for campaign groups. Recession could lead to splits within the movement, for example between Northern labour unions intent on protecting US and European jobs, and development agencies that worry about the impact of Northern protectionism on worker welfare in developing countries.

However, while recession and increased security concerns may sap the movement's momentum in the short term, the underlying cause of the movement—the specific nature of the current form of economic globalization and the failings of the current form of global governance—has not been fundamentally affected. As long as these circumstances remain, so will public disquiet and protest.

An international system in which all things are left to the unfettered market will further heighten political, social and economic inequality. The role of politics is to mitigate this tendency by pursuing the goals of social justice and the common good. The present forms of global governance have not been performing this function well. The need for a voice to ensure that these issues are addressed remains urgent. In an increasingly globalized world, the movement has already played an important part in catalysing a move away from the excesses of 1980s "market idolatry"; and it will continue to do so. In all likelihood global institutions, governments and NGOs will continue in much the same way, as they should do, in a useful and fruitful interaction and dialogue.

There are indeed signs that the events of 11 September have added momentum to the need to rethink the current international system. In a speech in New York in mid-November, Gordon Brown forcefully made the case for a global "new deal": "We have a choice. Globalization can be for the people or against the people . . . Badly managed, globalization will lead to wider inequality, deeper division and a dangerous era of distrust and rising tension . . . Instead we will advance social justice on a global scale—and we will do so with more global cooperation, not less, and with stronger, not weaker, international institutions."[26]

It seems that we have entered a period of instability in international relations. The collapse of effective states in many parts of the Third World and the former Soviet Union, the emergence of new (or resurgence of old) forms of non-state conflict and the increasing loss of states' monopoly over the use of force have created a world of new insecurities. The attacks on New York and Washington demonstrated that nowhere in the West is immune.

Since September there has been a greater willingness to address the sources of heightened global insecurity, including rising global economic inequality. Before the attacks, Lord Desai wrote presciently:

> It could be that for the first time in decades the bottom rung seems to have dropped from the global social ladder, that along with overall prosperity there are more and more pockets around the world where people seem to have nothing to lose. Regardless of where they are, people are terrified of widening disparities. Many are all too aware that the Zapatista insurrection and Landless Peasant Movement land occupations are comparatively benign outbursts by those left behind, that unless something is done we can expect more violent eruptions with unpredictable consequences.[27]

In an era where globalization is one of the primary drivers behind global politics and economics, the need to reflect upon the sustainability and future direction of globalization itself is unavoidable. There now seems to be an appetite for this among international decision-makers. One of Washington's first actions after 11 September was to pay its backlog of $621 million in dues to the UN system.[28] At the WTO ministerial meeting in Doha, the United States, and to a lesser extent the EU, showed an unusual readiness to compromise in the interests of securing agreement with developing countries.

There is always the danger that this new tone will fade away, along with memories of 11 September, and that global leaders will return to the cut and thrust of business as usual. In either case, when assessing the possible future of the movement, it is important to recall the trends that were developing before September.

Over the past ten years, the dynamics of the interplay between globalization, the global governance institutions and the movement have been changing. The debate around globalization has shifted away from the entrenched positions of the early 1990s, as global institutions have gradually responded to public and political pressure by becoming more inclusive and democratic. Moreover, new global actors have arisen with new roles and new voices. One of the most striking features of the Doha meeting was the strength, sophistication and unity of the countries of the Africa Group.[29] These trends will continue to evolve and, in the medium to long term, are likely to lead to greater changes in the nature and composition of the movement than even the catastrophic events of September 2001.

To some degree, the future of the movement depends on how it copes with its own success. As with many previous political movements, the hardest periods and greatest strains are caused by the achievement of partial victories. The movement's diversity and sheer breadth of views and positions will make this particularly difficult. In a landscape of partial reform, the old black and white divisions into the "pro" and "anti" globalization camps are no longer credible or accurate (if, indeed, they ever were). Tensions have always existed between the aims of environmentalists, developmentalists and the labour movement, but in recent years these have been managed, as the movement has increasingly proved itself able to cope with difference and diversity. That ability will be tested as differences widen between reformists and the rejectionists throughout the different strands of the movement.

Up to now, a united front has been comparatively easy to maintain when faced with the inflexibility of neo-liberal globalization. Now, however, limited reforms appear to be on offer. For the reformists, partial improvements of the kind now regularly on the agenda at organizations such as the IMF, World Bank and WTO look like welcome victories; for the rejectionists, they merely look like devious attempts to delay radical change.

The different NGO reactions during and after the Doha meeting illustrated some of these tensions. Environmentalists welcomed the introduction of stronger text and negotiations on a limited range of environmental issues; trade unions deplored the lack of strong language on labour rights. Since the main opponents of including both labour and environmental issues in the WTO are developing country governments (which see them as likely sources of back-door protectionism against their exports), development NGOs skirted round both issues, and were themselves divided or whether the final Doha declaration was on balance good or bad for developing countries. The debate between "cup half full" and "cup half empty" interpretations of Doha looked likely to endure for some time.

These debates will test the movement's ability to cope with difference, but the strongest force in shaping its future development will be external, stemming from the pace and depth of change in the institutions of global governance. Profound political change has usually sprung from war and economic collapse, not from the power of argument alone. Even the Asia crisis, with its devastating impact on the lives of millions of citizens, was sufficient to lead only to comparatively minor reform of global capital markets in the short term. Will the new-found sense of global insecurity be sufficient to prompt a more profound reappraisal?

The likelihood of reform will depend on the breadth of political leaders' understanding of the question of security. If they opt for a narrow definition, the chances of reform are slim. If, on the other hand, they accept that security cuts both ways, then the West's search for enhanced stability could lead to a greater recognition of the threats posed by rising inequality and the exclusion of the fifth of humanity (1.2 billion people) who still survive on less than a dollar a day. The very dark cloud of 11 September and its aftermath may still reveal an unexpected silver lining.

Meanwhile, whatever the outcome of the debate over security, the movement will remain an important counterbalance within the international system. Its evolution will be primarily a response to changes in the system itself, and it will continue to prod decision-makers towards addressing issues of exclusion, inequality and injustice. Indeed, if such prodding reinforces the incipient signs of a "new deal" on the management of the world economy, the protesters may yet prove to be the "true defenders of globalization" in leading the efforts on all sides to create a more secure world for all.

NOTES

1. <www.worldsocialforum.org>.

2. According to the UNDP, the collapse in life expectancy in eastern Europe during the 1990s meant that 10 million men died during that decade who would otherwise have survived to see in the millennium. See <www.worldbank.org/html/prddr/trans/julaug99>.

3. Amartya Sen, *Observer,* 25 June 2000.

4. <www.tradejusticemovement.org.uk>.

5. *Financial Times,* 10 October 2001.

6. See e.g. <www.ethicaltrade.org> or <www.justpensions.org>.

7. R. Cohen and S. Raj, *Global social movements* (London: Athlone, 2000).

8. Meghnad Desai and Yahia Said, "The new anti-capitalist movement: money and global civil society," in H. Anheier, M. Glasius and M. Kaldor, eds, *Global civil society 2001* (Oxford: Oxford University Press, 2001).

9. See websites for Third World Network, <www.twnside.org.sg>, and Focus on the Global South, <www.focusweb.org>.

10. Development Alternatives with Women for a New Era, <www.dawn.org.fj>.

11. *World Development Report 2000/01: Attacking Poverty* (New York: Oxford University Press, 2000), <www.worldbank.org/poverty/wdrpoverty/>; *Eliminating world poverty: making globalization work for the poor* (London: Department for International Development, 2001), <www.globalization.gov.uk/>. For an insightful analysis of the origins of the rancorous public debate over the *World Development Report,* see Ravi Kanbur, *Economic policy, distribution and poverty: the nature of disagreements* (New York: Cornell University, December 2000).

12. NGO submissions are listed on <www.globalization.gov.uk/>, and available from individual NGOs.

13. *Financial Times,* 13 July 2001.

14. This section is based on "A human development approach to globalization: a submission by Christian Aid and CAFOD on the government's White Paper on globalization," May 2000, <www.cafod.org.uk/policy/polhumdevglobfull.shtml>.

15. *Agriculture, trade and food security: issues and options in the WTO negotiations from the perspective of developing countries* (Rome: FAO, 1999).

16. L. Hanmer, N. de Jong, R. Kurian and J. Mooij, "Are the DAC targets achievable? Poverty and human development in the year 2015," *Journal of International Development* 11: 4, 1999, pp. 547–63.

17. For a recent discussion on this issue, see Branko Milanovic, *True world income distribution, 1988 and 1993: first calculation based on household surveys alone* (Washington DC: World Bank, Development Research Group, February 2001).

18. *After Seattle,* Report by House of Commons Select Committee on International Development (London: Stationery Office, Dec. 2000).

19. See e.g. <www.ethicaltrade.org>.

20. For more information, see <www.justpensions.org>.

21. For a full analysis, see Duncan Green, "CAFOD analysis of WTO Doha Declarations," on <www.cafod.org.uk/policy>.

22. Kanbur, *Economic policy, distribution and poverty.*

23. Talk by Charlotte Hines, MORI, at IPPR lunch, Labour Party Conference, 3 Oct. 2001.

24. The editor of the *New Republic,* Peter Beinart, wrote that "the anti-globalization movement . . . is, in part, a movement motivated by hatred of the United States" (*New Republic,* 24 Sept. 2001).

25. *Financial Times,* 10 Oct. 2001.

26. Gordon Brown, "Spreading social justice across the world," 16 Nov. 2001.

27. Meghnad Desai and Yahia Said, "The new anti-capitalist movement: money and global civil society," in Anheier et al., eds, *Global civil society 2001.*

28. UN press release, 17 Oct. 2001.

29. For a fuller analysis of the outcome of the Doha meeting, see <www.cafod.org.uk/livefromdoha/doha_analysis.shtml>.

9

Security

Reading 9-1

Guessing the Rules
Conflict Resolution in the Post–Cold War Era
Pamela Aall

W̲hen the Soviet Union shattered into a dozen pieces, many students and practitioners of foreign policy and conflict resolution also lost their bearings. The bipolar international system which had provided an organizing framework for foreign policies and scholarly work was gone, replaced by a new world. To the surprise of many, the decade following the Cold War did not develop into a warm peace. It was tumultuous, bloody, riven by horrifying conflict not across national borders but across towns and roads and neighborhoods. It was also a decade of large scale political and social transformation, largely toward democratic processes, personal freedom, unprecedented individual access to information, and of an astonishing growth in the global economy. Although we could see the new reality, its meaning remained elusive. Was there a new theory to explain this world? Had we arrived at the end of history, as Francis Fukuyama (1989) proposed, an end in which the growing embrace of liberal democracy presaged a more peaceful world? Or were we heading for a clash of civilizations, as Samuel Hunt-

SOURCE: From "Guessing the Rules: Conflict Resolution in the Post–Cold War Era" by Pamela Aall, *Peace and Conflict: Journal of Peace Psychology*, vol. 8, no. 3 (2002): 277–280. Copyright © 2002 by Lawrence Erlbaum Associates, Inc. Reprinted by permission.

ington (1993) thought, that would fuel war based on belief and identity between major cultural blocs?

The operational requirements of the period were also unclear. Were peace and stability more likely if post–Cold War conflicts were allowed to flare and die down without third party interference or were we—the amorphous, unorganized international community—morally obliged to respond to these conflicts to relieve human suffering? If so, did the United States have a special responsibility to guarantee peace, promote democracy, and punish wrongdoers around the world or was this the role of the United Nations? What part should the burgeoning number of nongovernmental organizations (NGOs) and international civil society play in the response to these conflicts?

In these three books, Stanley Hoffmann, Ronnie Lipschutz, and the many authors of the Stern and Druckman volume, attempt to answer the questions discussed earlier, to find meaning in the turbulent 1990s, and to offer guidance for the years to come. Although these books are quite different, they agree on a number of basic points. The first is a recognition of the complexity that characterizes the current international system and lies at the heart of these conflicts. This complexity introduces in all three volumes a reluctance to develop a theory or make predictions on a grand scale. All three, however, attempt to draw lessons from experiences of the Cold War and its aftermath, analyzing these lessons in a way that is accessible and relevant to policymakers as well as to students of international affairs and conflict resolution. The second area of broad agreement is that the conceptual tools that we have used to explain international relations and underpin past policies have either proved inadequate or at least in need of reexamination.

The volumes are also united in their interest in examining the changing nature of state sovereignty over the past decades, the role of individuals and nonofficial institutions in peacemaking and governance, and the normative basis for responding to conflict. All three envision a world governed not solely by sovereign states pursuing their own national interests but by coalitions of political entities—including states, international organizations, and global civil society. These common traits—the search for new answers to old and new problems, the insistence that the individual and civil society structures are important components of international affairs and conflict resolution, the inclusion of ethical issues in their analyses—make these books important reading not only for the dedicated political scientist and policymaker, but for all interested in the causes of and responses to conflict.

Ronnie Lipschutz, associate professor of politics at the University of California at Santa Cruz, comes closest to offering a new framework for understanding the international system. His basic contention is that the nation-state has come to the end of its run. He asserts—as does Stanley Hoffmann—that state sovereignty is being eroded both from above and from below. The increased empowerment of individuals and the growing global economic system challenge states' abilities to carry out traditional functions—providing security, regulating capital flows, and controlling certain information. In this new world, Lipschutz contends, threats to national security are less tangible than the old threats of militaries amassing on borders, but more difficult to manage because they exist as much in the mind as in reality. The fear of the "other" that characterized Rwanda's and Bosnia's ethnic and identity-based conflicts was the result not of ancient hatreds but of the difficulties that people have in coping with great transformations, including the erosion of state authority. Lipschutz, however, does not believe that increased conflict is an inevitable consequence of the weakening of the state but finds hope in the emergence of a global civil society which, with much work and imagination, may unite individuals in voluntary transborder political structures that could compensate for the lost authority of the state.

Stanley Hoffmann's *World Disorders: Troubled Peace in the Post–Cold War Era* does not try to lay out a new vision of the future, but deals with the here and now, with the ethical and practical dilemmas raised by international intervention in internal conflicts. Hoffmann, who is the Buttenwieser University Professor at Harvard University, wrote these 18 elegant essays over a 15-year period. In them he treats a number of different areas, including theory (with a special focus on the strengths and limitations of international liberalism), the role that the United States and United Nations (UN) should play in the new world, and the relation of nationalism, ethnicity, and a new world order. Written in a humanist tradition, each of these wide-ranging essays could be read alone, but altogether they argue persuasively for international intervention for the protection of human rights and international security, and for moral, activist policies on the part of powerful states and the UN.

Paul C. Stern, study director at the National Research Council, and Daniel Druckman, professor of conflict resolution at George Mason University, have edited a substantial volume which is the result of a 5-year study of theory and practice in international conflict resolution in the post–Cold War period. It brings together leading scholars in the field and covers a number of critical, operational issues. A methodologically sophisticated project, its aim was to examine whether the Cold War diplomatic and nonofficial approaches to conflict resolution were still appropriate for the post–Cold War world. The project did not examine all the theories and tools of conflict resolution, but drew lessons about some important, understudied elements: for instance, using force in support of peace, nonofficial methods of conflict resolution, new actors and institutions, strategies to make peace stick, and the challenges of evaluating conflict resolution interventions. The individual chapters are excellent, but as a result of the selective approach to the subject matter, they do not necessarily build a comprehensive picture of post–Cold War international conflict resolution.

Since these books were published, the world saw on September 11th, 2001, another dramatic event which may produce change as profound as the end of the Cold War. How well do these books hold up in this changed situation? Of the three, the Lipschutz book is the most challenged by recent events, as the international terrorist network shows the nasty flip side of a system of global civil society. But in so far as they deal with phenomena that are still with us—desperate conflicts in out-of-the-way corners of the world, debates on the meaning of security and national interest, confusion over the moral imperatives to respond to humanitarian disaster—these books are as relevant today as they were prior to September 11, 2001. We ignore these conflicts and their consequences for us at our own risk.

REFERENCES

Fukuyama, F. (1989). The end of history? *National Interest, 14,* 3–18.

Huntington, S. P. (1993). Clash of civilizations? *Foreign Affairs, 72,* 22–49.

Reading 9-2

Behind the Curve
Globalization and International Terrorism
Audrey Kurth Cronin

The coincidence between the evolving changes of globalization, the inherent weaknesses of the Arab region, and the inadequate American response to both ensures that terrorism will continue to be the most serious threat to U.S. and Western interests in the twenty-first century. There has been little creative thinking, however, about how to confront the growing terrorist backlash that has been unleashed. Terrorism is a complicated, eclectic phenomenon, requiring a sophisticated strategy oriented toward influencing its means and ends over the long term. Few members of the U.S. policy-making and academic communities, however, have the political capital, intellectual background, or inclination to work together to forge an effective, sustained response. Instead, the tendency has been to fall back on established bureaucratic mind-sets and prevailing theoretical paradigms that have little relevance for the changes in international security that became obvious after the terrorist attacks in New York and Washington on September 11, 2001.

The current wave of international terrorism, characterized by unpredictable and unprecedented threats from nonstate actors, not only is a reaction to globalization but is facilitated by it; the U.S. response to this reality has been reactive and anachronistic. The combined focus of the United States on state-centric threats and its attempt to cast twenty-first-century terrorism into familiar strategic terms avoids and often undermines effective responses to this nonstate phenomenon. The increasing threat of globalized terrorism must be met with flexible, multifaceted responses that deliberately and effectively exploit avenues of globalization in return; this, however, is not happening.

As the primary terrorist target, the United States should take the lead in fashioning a forward-looking strategy. As the world's predominant military, economic, and political power, it has been able to pursue its interests throughout the globe with unprecedented freedom since the breakup of the Soviet Union more than a decade ago. Even in the wake of the September 11 terrorist attacks on the World Trade Center and the Pentagon, and especially after the U.S. military action in Afghanistan, the threat of terrorism, mostly consisting of underfunded and ad hoc cells motivated by radical fringe ideas, has seemed unimportant by comparison. U.S. strategic culture has a long tradition of downplaying such atypical concerns in favor of a focus on more conventional state-based military power.[1] On the whole, this has been an effective approach: As was dramatically demonstrated in Afghanistan, the U.S. military knows how to destroy state governments and their armed forces, and the American political leadership and public have a natural bias toward using power to achieve the quickest results. Sometimes it is important to show resolve and respond forcefully.

The United States has been far less impressive, however, in its use of more subtle tools of domestic and international statecraft, such as intelligence, law enforcement, economic sanctions, educational training, financial controls, public diplomacy, coalition building, international law, and foreign aid. In an ironic twist, it is these tools that

SOURCE: From "Behind the Curve: Globalization and International Terrorism" by Audrey Kurth Cronin, *International Security*, vol. 27, no. 3 (Winter 2002/2003): 30 –58. Copyright © 2003 President and Fellows of Harvard College and the Massachusetts Institute of Technology. Reprinted by permission of the MIT Press Journals.

have become central to the security of the United States and its allies since September 11. In an era of globalized terrorism, the familiar state-centric threats have not disappeared; instead they have been joined by new (or newly threatening) competing political, ideological, economic, and cultural concerns that are only superficially understood, particularly in the West. An examination of the recent evolution of terrorism and a projection of future developments suggest that, in the age of globalized terrorism, old attitudes are not just anachronistic; they are dangerous.

Terrorism as a phenomenon is not new, but for reasons explained below, the threat it now poses is greater than ever before. The current terrorist backlash is manifested in the extremely violent asymmetrical response directed at the United States and other leading powers by terrorist groups associated with or inspired by al-Qaeda. This backlash has the potential to fundamentally threaten the international system. Thus it is not just an American problem. Unless the United States and its allies formulate a more comprehensive response to terrorism, better balanced across the range of policy instruments, the results will be increasing international instability and long-term failure.

The article proceeds in five main sections. First, it provides a discussion of the definition, history, causes, and types of terrorism, placing the events of September 11, 2001, in their modern context. Second, it briefly describes key trends in modern terrorism, explaining how the phenomenon appears to be evolving. Third, it analyzes the implications of these trends for the stability and security of the international community generally, and the United States and its allies more specifically. Fourth, the article outlines the prospects of these trends. It concludes with a range of policy recommendations suggested by the analysis.

DEFINITION, ORIGINS, MOTIVATIONS, AND TYPES OF MODERN TERRORISM

The terrorist phenomenon has a long and varied history, punctuated by lively debates over the meaning of the term. By ignoring this history, the United States runs the risk of repeating the plethora of mistakes made by other major powers that faced similar threats in the past. This section begins with an explanation of the definition of terrorism, then proceeds to an examination of terrorism's origins, major motivations, and predominant types.

Definition of Terrorism

Terrorism is notoriously difficult to define, in part because the term has evolved and in part because it is associated with an activity that is designed to be subjective. Generally speaking, the targets of a terrorist episode are not the victims who are killed or maimed in the attack, but rather the governments, publics, or constituents among whom the terrorists hope to engender a reaction—such as fear, repulsion, intimidation, overreaction, or radicalization. Specialists in the area of terrorism studies have devoted hundreds of pages toward trying to develop an unassailable definition of the term, only to realize the fruitlessness of their efforts: Terrorism is intended to be a matter of perception and is thus seen differently by different observers.[2]

Although individuals can disagree over whether particular actions constitute terrorism, there are certain aspects of the concept that are fundamental. First, terrorism always has a political nature. It involves the commission of outrageous acts designed to precipitate political change.[3] At its root, terrorism is about justice, or at least someone's perception of it, whether man-made or divine. Second, although many other uses of violence are inherently political, including conventional war among states, terrorism is distinguished by its nonstate character—even when terrorists receive military, political, economic, and other means of support from state sources. States obviously employ force for political ends: When state force is used internationally, it is considered an act of war; when it is used domestically, it is called various things, including law enforcement, state terror, oppression, or civil war. Although states can terrorize, they cannot by definition be terrorists. Third, terrorism deliberately targets the innocent, which also distinguishes it from state uses of force that inadvertently kill innocent bystanders. In any given example, the latter may or may not be seen as justified; but again, this use of force is different from terrorism. Hence the fact that precision-guided missiles sometimes go astray and kill innocent civilians is a tragic use of force, but it is not terrorism. Finally, state use of force is subject to international norms and conventions that may be invoked or at least consulted; terrorists do not abide by international laws or norms and, to maximize the psychological effect of an attack, their activities have a deliberately unpredictable quality.[4]

Thus, at a minimum, terrorism has the following characteristics: a fundamentally political nature, the surprise use of violence against seemingly random targets, and the targeting of the innocent by nonstate actors.[5] All of these attributes are illustrated by recent examples of terrorism—from the April 2000 kidnapping of tourists by the Abu Sayyaf group of the Philippines to the various incidents allegedly committed by al-Qaeda, including the 1998 bombings of the U.S. embassies in Kenya and Tanzania and the September 11 attacks. For the purposes of this discussion, the shorthand (and admittedly imperfect) definition of terrorism is the threat or use of seemingly random violence against innocents for political ends by a nonstate actor.

Origins of Terrorism

Terrorism is as old as human history. One of the first reliably documented instances of terrorism, however, occurred in the first century B.C.E. The Zealots-Sicarii, Jewish terrorists dedicated to inciting a revolt against Roman rule in Judea, murdered their victims with daggers in broad daylight in the heart of Jerusalem, eventually creating such anxiety among the population that they generated a mass insurrection.[6] Other early terrorists include the Hindu Thugs and the Muslim Assassins. Modern terrorism, however, is generally considered to have originated with the French Revolution.[7]

The term "terror" was first employed in 1795, when it was coined to refer to a policy systemically used to protect the fledgling French republic government against counterrevolutionaries. Robespierre's practice of using revolutionary tribunals as a means of publicizing a prisoner's fate for broader effect within the population (apart from questions of legal guilt or innocence) can be seen as a nascent example of the much more highly developed, blatant manipulation of media attention by terrorist groups in the mid- to late twentieth century.[8] Modern terrorism is a dynamic concept, from the outset dependent to some degree on the political and historical context within which it has been employed.

Decolonization and Antiglobalization: Drivers of Terrorism?

Although individual terrorist groups have unique characteristics and arise in specific local contexts, an examination of broad historical patterns reveals that the international system within which such groups are spawned does influence their nature and motivations. A distinguishing feature of modern terrorism has been the connection between sweeping political or ideological concepts and increasing levels of terrorist activity internationally. The broad political aim has been against (1) empires, (2) colonial powers, and (3) the U.S.-led international system marked by globalization. Thus it is important to understand the general history of modern terrorism and where the current threat fits within an international context.

David Rapoport has described modern terrorism such as that perpetuated by al-Qaeda as part of a religiously inspired "fourth wave." This wave follows three earlier historical phases in which terrorism was tied to the breakup of empires, decolonization, and leftist anti-Westernism.[9] Rapoport argues that terrorism occurs in consecutive if somewhat overlapping waves. The argument here, however, is that modern terrorism has been a power struggle along a continuum: central power versus local power, big power versus small power, modern power versus traditional power. The key variable is a widespread perception of opportunity, combined with a shift in a particular political or ideological paradigm. Thus, even though the newest international terrorist threat, emanating largely from Muslim countries, has more than a modicum of religious inspiration, it is more accurate to see it as part of a larger phenomenon of antiglobalization and tension between the have and have-not nations, as well as between the elite and underprivileged within those nations. In an era where reforms occur at a pace much slower than is desired, terrorists today, like those before them, aim to exploit the frustrations of the common people (especially in the Arab world).

In the nineteenth century, the unleashing of concepts such as universal suffrage and popular empowerment raised the hopes of people throughout the western world, indirectly resulting in the first phase of modern terrorism. Originating in Russia, as Rapoport argues, it was stimulated not by state repression but by the efforts of the czars to placate demands for economic and political reforms, and the inevitable disappointment of popular expectations that were raised as a result. The goal of terrorists was to engage in attacks on symbolic targets to get the attention of the common people and thus provoke a popular response that would ultimately overturn the prevailing political order. This type of modern terrorism was reflected in the activities of groups such as the Russian Narodnaya Volya (People's Will) and later in the development of a series of movements in the United States and Europe, especially in territories of the former Ottoman Empire.

The dissolution of empires and the search for a new distribution of political power provided an opportunity for terrorism in the nineteenth and twentieth centuries. It climaxed in the assassination of Archduke Franz Ferdinand on June 28, 1914, an event that catalyzed the major powers into taking violent action, not because of the significance of the man himself but because of the suspicion of rival state involvement in the sponsorship of the killing. World War I, the convulsive systemic cataclysm that resulted, ended the first era of modern terrorism, according to Rapoport.[10] But terrorism tied to popular movements seeking greater democratic representation and political power from coercive empires has not ceased. Consider, for example, the Balkans after the downfall of the former state of Yugoslavia. The struggle for power among various Balkan ethnic groups can be seen as the final devolution of power from the former Ottoman Empire. This postimperial scramble is also in evidence elsewhere—for example, in Aceh, Chechnya, and Xinjiang, to mention just a few of the trouble spots within vast (former) empires. The presentation of a target of opportunity, such as a liberalizing state or regime, frequently evokes outrageous terrorist acts.

According to Rapoport, a second, related phase of modern terrorism associated with the concept of national self-determination developed its greatest predominance after World War I. It also continues to the present day. These struggles for power are another facet of terrorism against larger political powers and are specifically designed to win political independence or autonomy. The mid-twentieth-century era of rapid decolonization spawned national movements in territories as diverse as Algeria, Israel, South Africa, and Vietnam.[11] An important by-product was ambivalence toward the phenomenon in the international community, with haggling over the definition of terrorism reaching a fever pitch in the United Nations by the 1970s.

The question of political motivation became important in determining international attitudes toward terrorist attacks, as the post—World War II backlash against the colonial powers and the attractiveness of national independence movements led to the creation of a plethora of new states often born from violence. Arguments over the justice of international causes and the designation of terrorist struggles as "wars of national liberation" predominated, with consequentialist philosophies excusing the killing of innocent people if the cause in the long run was "just." Rapoport sees the U.S. intervention in Vietnam, and especially the subsequent American defeat by the Vietcong, as having catalyzed a "third wave" of modern terrorism; however, the relationship between the Vietnam conflict and other decolonization movements might just as easily be considered part of the same phase. In any case, the victory of the Vietcong excited the imaginations of revolutionaries throughout the world and, according to Rapoport, helped lead to a resurgence in terrorist violence. The Soviet Union underwrote the nationalist and leftist terrorist agendas of some groups, depicting the United States as the new colonial power—an easy task following the Vietnam intervention—and furthering an ideological agenda oriented toward achieving a postcapitalist, international communist utopia. Other groups, especially in Western Europe, rejected both the Soviet and capitalist models and looked admiringly toward nationalist revolutionaries in the developing world.[12] Leftist groups no longer predominate, but the enduring search for national self-determination continues, not only in the areas mentioned above but also in other hot spots such as the Basque region, East Timor, Sri Lanka, and Sudan.

Terrorism achieved a firmly international character during the 1970s and 1980s,[13] evolving in part as a result of technological advances and partly in reaction to the dramatic explosion of international media influence. International links were not new, but their centrality was. Individual, scattered national causes began to develop into international organizations with links and activities increasingly across borders and among differing causes. This development was greatly facilitated by the covert sponsorship of states such as Iran, Libya, and North Korea, and of course the Soviet Union, which found the underwriting of terrorist organizations an attractive tool for accomplishing clandestine goals while avoiding potential retaliation for the terrorist attacks.

The 1970s and 1980s represented the height of state-sponsored terrorism. Sometimes the lowest common denominator among the groups was the concept against which they were reacting—for example, "Western imperialism"—rather than the specific goals they sought. The most important innovation, however, was the increasing commonality of international connections among the groups. After the 1972 Munich Olympics massacre of eleven Israeli athletes, for example, the Palestinian Liberation Organization (PLO) and its associated groups captured the imaginations of young radicals around the world. In Lebanon and elsewhere, the PLO also provided training in the preferred techniques of twentieth-century terrorism such as airline hijacking, hostage taking, and bombing.

Since the September 11 attacks, the world has witnessed the maturation of a new phase of terrorist activity, the jihad era, spawned by the Iranian Revolution of 1979 as well as the Soviet defeat in Afghanistan shortly thereafter. The powerful attraction of religious and spiritual movements has overshadowed the nationalist or leftist revolutionary ethos of earlier terrorist phases (though many of those struggles continue), and it has become the central characteristic of a growing international trend. It is perhaps ironic that, as Rapoport observes, the forces of history seem to be driving international terrorism back to a much earlier time, with echoes of the behavior of "sacred" terrorists such as the Zealots-Sicarii clearly apparent in the terrorist activities of organizations such as al-Qaeda and its associated groups. Religious terrorism is not new; rather it is a continuation of an ongoing modern power struggle between those with power and those without it. Internationally, the main targets of these terrorists are the United States and the U.S.-led global system.

Like other eras of modern terrorism, this latest phase has deep roots. And given the historical patterns, it is likely to last at least a generation, if not longer. The jihad era is animated by widespread alienation combined with elements of religious identity and doctrine—a dangerous mix of forces that resonate deep in the human psyche.

What is different about this phase is the urgent requirement for solutions that deal both with the religious fanatics who are the terrorists and the far more politically motivated states, entities, and people who would support them because they feel powerless and left behind in a globalizing world. Thus if there is a trend in terrorism, it is the existence of a two-level challenge: the hyperreligious motivation of small groups of terrorists and the much broader enabling environment of bad governance, nonexistent social services, and poverty that punctuates much of the developing world. Al-Qaeda, a band driven by religious extremism, is able to do so much harm because of the secondary support and sanctuary it receives in vast areas that have not experienced the political and economic benefits of globalization. Therefore, the prescription for dealing with Osama bin Laden and his followers is not just eradicating a relatively small number of terrorists, but also changing the conditions that allow them to acquire so much power. Leaving aside for the moment the enabling environment, it is useful to focus on the chief motivations of the terrorists themselves, especially the contrasting secular and spiritual motivations of terrorism.

Leftist, Rightist, Ethnonationalist/Separatist, and "Sacred" Terrorism

There are four types of terrorist organizations currently operating around the world, categorized mainly by their source of motivation: left-wing terrorists, right-wing terrorists, ethnonationalist/separatist terrorists, and religious or "sacred" terrorists. All four types have enjoyed periods of relative prominence in the modern era, with left-wing terrorism intertwined with the Communist movement,[14] right-wing terrorism drawing its inspiration from Fascism,[15] and the bulk of ethnonationalist/separatist terrorism accompanying the wave of decolonization especially in the immediate post–World War II years. Currently, "sacred" terrorism is becoming more significant.[16] Although groups in all categories continue to exist today, left-wing and right-wing terrorist groups were more numerous in earlier decades. Of course, these categories are not perfect, as many groups have a mix of motivating ideologies—some ethnonationalist groups, for example, have religious characteristics or agendas[17]—but usually one ideology or motivation dominates.

Categories are useful not simply because classifying the groups gives scholars a more orderly field to study (admittedly an advantage), but also because different motivations have sometimes led to differing styles and modes of behavior. Understanding the type of terrorist group involved can provide insight into the likeliest manifestations of its violence and the most typical patterns of its development. At the risk of generalizing, left-wing terrorist organizations, driven by liberal or idealist political concepts, tend to prefer revolutionary, antiauthoritarian, antimaterialistic agendas. (Here it is useful to distinguish between the idealism of individual terrorists and the frequently contradictory motivations of their sponsors.) In line with these preferences, left-wing organizations often engage in brutal criminal-type behavior such as kidnapping, murder, bombing, and arson, often directed at elite targets that symbolize authority. They have difficulty, however, agreeing on their long-term objectives.[18] Most left-wing organizations in twentieth-century Western Europe, for example, were brutal but relatively ephemeral. Of course, right-wing terrorists can be ruthless, but in their most recent manifestations they have tended to be less cohesive and more impetuous in their violence than leftist terrorist groups. Their targets are often chosen according to race but also ethnicity, religion, or immigrant status, and in recent decades at least, have been more opportunistic than calculated.[19] This makes them potentially explosive but difficult to track.[20] Ethnonationalist/separatist terrorists are the most conventional, usually having a clear political or territorial aim that is rational and potentially negotiable, if not always justifiable in any given case. They can be astoundingly violent, over lengthy periods. At the same time, it can be difficult to distinguish between goals based on ethnic identity and those rooted in the control of a piece of land. With their focus on gains to be made in the traditional state-oriented international system, ethnonationalist/separatist terrorists often transition in and out of more traditional paramilitary structures, depending on how the cause is going. In addition, they typically have sources of support among the local populace of the same ethnicity with whom their separatist goals (or appeals to blood links) may resonate. That broader popular support is usually the key to the greater average longevity of ethnonationalist/separatist groups in the modern era.[21]

All four types of terrorist organizations are capable of egregious acts of barbarism. But religious terrorists may be especially dangerous to international security for at least five reasons.

First, religious terrorists often feel engaged in a Manichaean struggle of good against evil, implying an open-ended set of human targets: Anyone who is not a member of their religion or religious sect may be "evil" and thus fair game. Although indiscriminate attacks are not unique to religious terrorists, the exclusivity of their faith may lead them to dehumanize their victims even more than most terrorist groups do, because they consider nonmembers to be infidels or apostates—as perhaps, for instance, al-Qaeda operatives may have viewed Muslims killed in the World Trade Center.

Second, religious terrorists engage in violent behavior directly or indirectly to please the perceived commands of a deity. This has a number of worrisome implications: The whims of the deity may be less than obvious to those who are not members of the religion, so the actions of violent religious organizations can be especially unpredictable. Moreover, religious terrorists may not be as constrained in their behavior by concerns about the reactions of their human constituents. (Their audience lies elsewhere.)

Third, religious terrorists consider themselves to be unconstrained by secular values or laws. Indeed the very target of the attacks may be the law-based secular society that is embodied in most modern states. The driving motivation, therefore, is to overturn the current post-Westphalian state system—a much more fundamental threat than is, say, ethnonationalist terrorism purporting to carve out a new secular state or autonomous territory.

Fourth, and related, religious terrorists often display a complete sense of alienation from the existing social system. They are not trying to correct the system, making it more just, more perfect, and more egalitarian. Rather they are trying to replace it. In some groups, apocalyptic images of destruction are seen as a necessity—even a purifying regimen—and this makes them uniquely dangerous, as was painfully learned on September 11.[22]

Fifth, religious terrorism is especially worrisome because of its dispersed popular support in civil society. On the one hand, for example, groups such as al-Qaeda are able to find support from some Muslim nongovernmental foundations throughout the world,[23] making it truly a global network. On the other hand, in the process of trying to distinguish between the relatively few providers of serious support from the majority of genuinely philanthropic groups, there is the real risk of igniting the very holy war that the terrorists may be seeking in the first instance.

In sum, there are both enduring and new aspects to modern terrorism. The enduring features center on the common political struggles that have characterized major acts of international terrorism. The newest and perhaps most alarming aspect is the increasingly religious nature of modern terrorist groups. Against this historical background, the unique elements in the patterns of terrorist activity surrounding September 11 appear starkly.

KEY TRENDS IN MODERN TERRORISM

By the late 1990s, four trends in modern terrorism were becoming apparent: an increase in the incidence of religiously motivated attacks, a decrease in the overall number of attacks, an increase in the lethality per attack, and the growing targeting of Americans.

Statistics show that, even before the September 11 attacks, religiously motivated terrorist organizations were becoming more common. The acceleration of this trend has been dramatic: According to the RAND–St. Andrews University Chronology of International Terrorism,[24] in 1968 none of the identified international terrorist organizations could be classified as "religious"; in 1980, in the aftermath of the Iranian Revolution, there were 2 (out of 64), and that number had expanded to 25 (out of 58) by 1995.[25]

Careful analysis of terrorism data compiled by the U.S. Department of State reveals other important trends regarding the frequency and lethality of terrorist attacks. The good news was that there were fewer such attacks in the 1990s than in the 1980s: Internationally, the number of terrorist attacks in the 1990s averaged 382 per year, whereas in the 1980s the number per year averaged 543.[26] But even before September 11, the absolute number of casualties of international terrorism had increased, from a low of 344 in 1991 to a high of 6,693 in 1998.[27] The jump in deaths and injuries can be partly explained by a few high-profile incidents, including the bombing of the U.S. embassies in Nairobi and Dar-es-Salaam in 1998;[28] but it is significant that more people became victims of terrorism as the decade proceeded. More worrisome, the number of people killed per incident rose significantly, from 102 killed in 565 incidents in 1991 to 741 killed in 274 incidents in 1998.[29] Thus, even though the number of terrorist attacks declined in the 1990s, the number of people killed in each one increased.

Another important trend relates to terrorist attacks involving U.S. targets. The number of such attacks increased in the 1990s, from a low of 66 in 1994 to a high of 200 in the year 2000.[30] This is a long-established problem: U.S. nationals consistently have been the most targeted since 1968.[31] But the percentage of international attacks against U.S. targets or U.S. citizens rose dramatically over the 1990s, from about 20 percent in 1993–95 to almost 50 percent in 2000.[32] This is perhaps a consequence of the increased role and profile of the United States in the world, but the degree of increase is nonetheless troubling.

The increasing lethality of terrorist attacks was already being noticed in the late 1990s, with many terrorism experts arguing that the tendency toward more casualties per incident had important implications. First it meant that, as had been feared, religious or "sacred" terrorism was apparently more dangerous than the types of terrorism that had predominated earlier in the twentieth century. The world was facing the resurgence of a far more malignant type of terrorism, whose lethality was borne out in the larger death toll from incidents that increasingly involved a religious motivation.[33] Second, with an apparent premium now apparently placed on causing more casualties per incident, the incentives for terrorist organizations to use chemical, biological, nuclear, or radiological (CBNR) weapons would multiply. The breakup of the Soviet Union and the resulting increased availability of Soviet chemical, biological, and nuclear weapons caused experts to argue that terrorist groups, seeking more dramatic and deadly results, would be more drawn to these weapons.[34] The 1995 sarin gas attack by the Japanese cult Aum Shinrikyo in the Tokyo subway system seemed to confirm that worry. More recently, an examination of evidence taken from Afghanistan and Pakistan reveals al-Qaeda's interest in chemical, biological, and nuclear weapons.[35]

In addition to the evolving motivation and character of terrorist attacks, there has been a notable dispersal in the geography of terrorist acts—a trend that is likely to continue. Although the Middle East continues to be the locus of most terrorist activity, Central and South Asia, the Balkans, and the Transcaucasus have been growing in significance over the past decade. International connections themselves are not new: International terrorist organizations inspired by common revolutionary principles date to the early nineteenth century; clandestine state use of foreign terrorist organizations occurred as early as the 1920s (e.g., the Mussolini government in Italy aided the Croat Ustasha); and complex mazes of funding, arms, and other state support for international terrorist organizations were in place especially in the 1970s and 1980s.[36] During the Cold War, terrorism was seen as a form of surrogate warfare and seemed almost palatable to some, at least compared to the potential prospect of major war or nuclear cataclysm.[37] What has changed is the self-generating nature of international terrorism, with its diverse economic means of support allowing terrorists to carry out attacks sometimes far from the organization's base. As a result, there is an important and growing distinction between where a terrorist organization is spawned and where an attack is launched, making the attacks difficult to trace to their source.

Reflecting all of these trends, al-Qaeda and its associated groups[38] (and individuals) are harbingers of a new type of terrorist organization. Even if al-Qaeda ceases to exist (which is unlikely), the dramatic attacks of September 2001, and their political and economic effects, will continue to inspire similarly motivated groups—particularly if the United States and its allies fail to develop broad-based, effective counterterrorist policies over the long term. Moreover, there is significant evidence that the global links and activities that al-Qaeda and its associated groups perpetuated are not short term or anomalous. Indeed they are changing the nature of the terrorist threat as we move further into the twenty-first century. The resulting intersection between the United States, globalization, and international terrorism will define the major challenges to international security.

THE UNITED STATES, GLOBALIZATION, AND INTERNATIONAL TERRORISM

Whether deliberately intending to or not, the United States is projecting uncoordinated economic, social, and political power even more sweepingly than it is in military terms. Globalization,[39] in forms including Westernization, secularization, democratization, consumerism, and the growth of market capitalism, represents an onslaught to less privileged people in conservative cultures repelled by the fundamental changes that these forces are bringing—or angered by the distortions and uneven distributions of benefits that result.[40] This is especially true of the Arab world. Yet the current U.S. approach to this growing repulsion is colored by a kind of cultural naïveté, an unwillingness to recognize—let alone appreciate or take responsibility for—the influence of U.S. power except in its military dimension. Even doing nothing in the economic, social, and political policy realms is still doing something, because the United States is blamed by disadvantaged and alienated populations for the powerful Western-led forces of globalization that are proceeding apace, despite the absence of a focused, coordinated U.S. policy. And those penetrating mechanisms of globalization, such as the internet, the media, and the increasing flows of goods and peoples, are exploited in return. Both the means and ends of terrorism are being reformulated in the current environment.

The Means

Important changes in terrorist methods are apparent in the use of new technologies, the movement of terrorist groups across international boundaries, and changes in sources of support. Like globalization itself, these phenomena are all intertwined and overlapping but, for ease of argument, they are dealt with consecutively here.

First, the use of information technologies such as the internet, mobile phones, and instant messaging has extended the global reach of many terrorist groups. Increased access to these technologies has so far not resulted in their widely feared use in a major cyberterrorist attack: In Dorothy Denning's words, terrorists "still prefer bombs to bytes."[41] Activists and terrorist groups have increasingly turned to "hacktivism"—attacks on internet sites, including web defacements, hijackings of websites, web sit-ins, denial-of-service attacks, and automated email "bombings"—attacks that may not kill anyone but do attract media attention, provide a means of operating anonymously, and are easy to coordinate internationally.[42] So far, however, these types of attacks are more an expense and a nuisance than an existential threat.

Instead the tools of the global information age have led to enhanced efficiency in many terrorist-related activities, including administrative tasks, coordination of operations, recruitment of potential members, communication among adherents, and attraction of sympathizers.[43] Before the September 11 attacks, for example, members of al-Qaeda communicated through Yahoo email; Mohammed Atta, the presumed leader of the attacks, made his reservations online; and cell members went online to do research on subjects such as the chemical-dispersing powers of crop dusters. Although not as dramatic as shutting down a power grid or taking over an air traffic control system, this practical use of technology has significantly contributed to the effectiveness of terrorist groups and the expansion of their range.[44] Consider, for example, the lethal impact of the synchronized attacks on the U.S. embassies in 1998 and on New York and Washington in 2001, neither of which would have been possible without the revolution in information technology. When he was arrested in 1995, Ramzi Yousef, mastermind of the 1993 World Trade Center attack, was planning the simultaneous destruction of eleven airliners.[45]

The internet has become an important tool for perpetuating terrorist groups, both openly and clandestinely. Many of them employ elaborate list serves, collect money from witting or unwitting donors, and distribute savvy political messages to a broad audience online.[46] Groups as diverse as Aum Shinrikyo, Israel's Kahane Chai, the Popular Front for the Liberation of Palestine, the Kurdistan Workers' Party, and Peru's Shining Path maintain user-friendly official or unofficial websites, and almost all are accessible in English.[47] Clandestine methods include passing encrypted messages, embedding invisible graphic codes using steganography,[48] employing the internet to send death threats, and hiring hackers to collect intelligence such as the names and addresses of law enforcement officers from online databases.[49] All of these measures help to expand and perpetuate trends in terrorism that have already been observed: For example, higher casualties are brought about by simultaneous attacks, a diffusion in terrorist locations is made possible by internet communications, and extremist religious ideologies are spread through websites and videotapes accessible throughout the world.

More ominous, globalization makes CBNR weapons increasingly available to terrorist groups.[50] Information needed to build these weapons has become ubiquitous, especially through the internet. Among the groups interested in acquiring CBNR (besides al-Qaeda) are the PLO, the Red Army Faction, Hezbollah, the Kurdistan Workers' Party, German neo-Nazis, and the Chechens.[51]

Second, globalization has enabled terrorist organizations to reach across international borders, in the same way (and often through the same channels) that commerce and business interests are linked. The dropping of barriers through the North American Free Trade Area and the European Union, for instance, has facilitated the smooth flow of many things, good and bad, among countries. This has allowed terrorist organizations as diverse as Hezbollah, al-Qaeda, and the Egyptian al-Gama'at al-Islamiyya to move about freely and establish cells around the world.[52] Movement across borders can obviously enable terrorists to carry out attacks and potentially evade capture, but it also complicates prosecution if they are apprehended, with a complex maze of extradition laws varying greatly from state to state. The increased permeability of the international system has also enhanced the ability of nonstate terrorist organizations to collect intelligence (not to mention evade it); states are not the only actors interested in collecting, disseminating, and/or acting on such information. In a sense, then, terrorism is in many ways becoming like any other international enterprise—an ominous development indeed.

Third, terrorist organizations are broadening their reach in gathering financial resources to fund their operations. This is not just an al-Qaeda phenomenon, although bin Laden's organization—especially its numerous business interests—figures prominently among the most innovative and wealthy pseudocorporations in the international terrorist network. The list of groups with global financing networks is long and includes most of the groups identified by the U.S. government as foreign terrorist organizations, notably Aum Shinrikyo, Hamas, Hezbollah, and the Tamil Tigers. Sources of financing include legal enterprises such as nonprofit organizations and charities (whose illicit activities may be a small or large proportion of overall finances, known or unknown to donors); legitimate companies that divert profits to illegal activities (such as bin Laden's large network of construction companies); and illegal enterprises such as drug smuggling and production (e.g., the Revolutionary Armed Forces of Colombia—FARC), bank robbery, fraud, extortion, and kidnapping (e.g., the Abu Sayyaf group, Colombia's National Liberation Army, and FARC).[53] Websites are also important vehicles for raising funds. Although no comprehensive data are publicly available on how lucrative this avenue is, the proliferation of terrorist websites with links or addresses for contributions is at least circumstantial evidence of their usefulness.

The fluid movement of terrorists' financial resources demonstrates the growing informal connections that are countering the local fragmentation caused elsewhere by globalization. The transit of bars of gold and bundles of dollars across the border between Afghanistan and Pakistan as U.S. and allied forces were closing in on the Taliban's major strongholds is a perfect example. Collected by shopkeepers and small businessmen, the money was moved by operatives across the border to Karachi, where it was transferred in the millions of dollars through the informal *hawala* or *hundi* banking system to the United Arab Emirates.[54] There it was converted into gold bullion and scattered around the world before any government could intervene. In this way, al-Qaeda preserved and dispersed a proportion of its financial resources.[55] In addition to gold, money was transferred into other commodities—such as diamonds in Sierra Leone and the Democratic Republic of Congo, and tanzanite from Tanzania—all while hiding the assets and often making a profit,[56] and all without interference from the sovereign governments that at the time were at war with al-Qaeda and the Taliban.[57]

As this example illustrates, globalization does not necessarily require the use of high technology: It often takes the form of traditional practices used in innovative ways across increasingly permeable physical and commercial borders. Terrorist groups, whose assets comparatively represent only a small fraction of the amount of money that is moved by organized crime groups and are thus much more difficult to track, use everything from direct currency transport (by couriers) to reliance on traditional banks, Islamic banks, money changers (using accounts at legitimate institutions), and informal exchange (the *hawala* or *hundi* system).

This is by no means a comprehensive presentation of global interpenetration of terrorist means, and some of the connections described above have existed for some time and in other contexts. The broad strategic picture, however, is of an increasing ability of terrorist organizations to exploit the same avenues of communication, coordination, and cooperation as other international actors, including states, multinational corporations, nongovernmental organizations, and even individuals. It would be naïve to assume that what is good for international commerce and international communication is not also good for international terrorists[58]—who are increasingly becoming opportunistic entrepreneurs whose "product" (often quite consciously "sold") is violence against innocent targets for a political end.

The Ends

The objectives of international terrorism have also changed as a result of globalization. Foreign intrusions and growing awareness of shrinking global space have created incentives to use the ideal asymmetrical weapon, terrorism, for more ambitious purposes.

The political incentives to attack major targets such as the United States with powerful weapons have greatly increased. The perceived corruption of indigenous customs, religions, languages, economies, and so on are blamed on an international system often unconsciously molded by American behavior. The accompanying distortions in local communities as a result of exposure to the global marketplace of goods and ideas are increasingly blamed on U.S.-sponsored modernization and those who support it. The advancement of technology, however, is not the driving force behind the terrorist threat to the United States and its allies, despite what some have assumed.[59] Instead, at the heart of this threat are frustrated populations and international movements that are increasingly inclined to lash out against U.S.-led globalization.

As Christopher Coker observes, globalization is reducing tendencies toward instrumental violence (i.e., violence between states and even between communities), but it is enhancing incentives for expressive violence (or violence that is ritualistic, symbolic, and communicative).[60] The new international terrorism is increasingly engendered by a need to assert identity or meaning against forces of homogeneity, especially on the part of cultures that are threatened by, or left behind by, the secular future that Western-led globalization brings.

According to a report recently published by the United Nations Development Programme, the region of greatest deficit in measures of human development—the Arab world—is also the heart of the most threatening religiously inspired terrorism.[61] Much more work needs to be done on the significance of this correlation, but increasingly sources of political discontent are arising from disenfranchised areas in the Arab world that feel left behind by the promise of globalization and its assurances of broader freedom, prosperity, and access to knowledge. The results are dashed expectations, heightened resentment of the perceived U.S.-led hegemonic system, and a shift of focus away from more proximate targets within the region.

Of course, the motivations behind this threat should not be oversimplified: Anti-American terrorism is spurred in part by a desire to change U.S. policy in the Middle East and Persian Gulf regions as well as by growing antipathy in the developing world vis-à-vis the forces of globalization. It is also crucial to distinguish between the motivations of leaders such as Osama bin Laden and their followers. The former seem to be more driven by calculated strategic decisions to shift the locus of attack away from repressive indigenous governments to the more attractive and media-rich target of the United States. The latter appear to be more driven by religious concepts cleverly distorted to arouse anger and passion in societies full of pent-up frustration. To some degree, terrorism is directed against the United States because of its engagement and policies in various regions.[62] Anti-Americanism is closely related to antiglobalization, because (intentionally or not) the primary driver of the powerful forces resulting in globalization is the United States.

Analyzing terrorism as something separate from globalization is misleading and potentially dangerous. Indeed globalization and terrorism are intricately intertwined forces characterizing international security in the twenty-first century. The main question is whether terrorism will succeed in disrupting the promise of improved livelihoods for millions of people on Earth. Globalization is not an inevitable, linear development, and it can be disrupted by such unconventional means as international terrorism. Conversely, modern international terrorism is especially dangerous because of the power that it potentially derives from globalization—whether through access to CBNR weapons, global media outreach, or a diverse network of financial and information resources.

PROSPECTS FOR THE FUTURE

Long after the focus on Osama bin Laden has receded and U.S. troops have quit their mission in Afghanistan, terrorism will be a serious threat to the world community and especially to the United States. The relative preponderance of U.S. military power virtually guarantees an impulse to respond asymmetrically. The lagging of the Arab region behind the rest of the world is impelling a violent redirection of antiglobalization and antimodernization forces toward available targets, particularly the United States, whose scope and policies are engendering rage. Al-Qaeda will eventually be replaced or redefined, but its successors' reach may continue to grow via the same globalized channels and to direct their attacks against U.S. and Western targets. The current trajectory is discouraging, because as things currently stand, the wellspring of terrorism's means and ends is likely to be renewed: Arab governments will probably not reform peacefully, and existing Western governments and their supporting academic and professional institutions are disinclined to understand or analyze in depth the sources, patterns, and history of terrorism.

Terrorism is a by-product of broader historical shifts in the international distribution of power in all of its forms—political, economic, military, ideological, and cultural. These are the same forms of power that characterize the forces of Western-led globalization. At times of dramatic international change, human beings (especially those not benefiting from the change—or not benefiting as much or as rapidly from the change) grasp for alternative means to control and understand their environments. If current trends continue, widening global disparities, coupled with burgeoning information and connectivity, are likely to accelerate—unless the terrorist backlash, which is increasingly taking its inspiration from misoneistic religious or pseudoreligious concepts, successfully counters these trends. Because of globalization, terrorists have access to more powerful technologies, more targets, more territory, more means of recruitment, and more exploitable sources of rage than ever before. The West's twentieth-century approach to terrorism is highly unlikely to mitigate any of these long-term trends.

From a Manichaean perspective, the ad hoc and purportedly benign intentions of the preponderant, secular West do not seem benign at all to those ill served by globalization. To frustrated people in the Arab and Muslim world, adherence to radical religious philosophies and practices may seem a rational response to the perceived assault, especially when no feasible alternative for progress is offered by their own governments. This is not to suggest that terrorists should be excused because of environmental factors or conditions. Instead, Western governments must recognize that the tiny proportion of the population that ends up in terrorist cells cannot exist without the availability of broader sources of active or passive sympathy, resources, and support. Those avenues of sustenance are where the center of gravity for an effective response to the terrorist threat must reside. The response to transnational terrorism must deal with the question of whether the broader enabling environment will increase or decrease over time, and the answer will be strongly influenced by the policy choices that the United States and its allies make in the near future.

CONCLUSIONS AND POLICY PRESCRIPTIONS

The characteristics and causes of the current threat can only be analyzed within the context of the deadly collision occurring between U.S. power, globalization, and the evolution of international terrorism. The U.S. government is still thinking in outdated terms, little changed since the end of the Cold War. It continues to look at terrorism as a peripheral threat, with the focus remaining on states that in many cases are not the greatest threat. The means and the ends of terrorism are changing in fundamental, important ways; but the means and the ends of the strategy being crafted in response are not.

Terrorism that threatens international stability, and particularly U.S. global leadership, is centered on power-based political causes that are enduring: the weak against the strong, the disenfranchised against the establishment, and the revolutionary against the status quo. Oversimplified generalizations about poverty and terrorism, or any other single variable, are caricatures of a serious argument.[63] The rise in political and material expectations as a result of the information revolution is not necessarily helpful to stability, in the same way that rising expectations led terrorists to take up arms against the czar in Russia a century ago. Indeed the fact that so many people in so many nations are being left behind has given new ammunition to terrorist groups; produced more sympathy for those willing to take on the United States; and spurred Islamic radical movements to recruit, propagandize, and support terrorism throughout many parts of the Muslim world. The al-Qaeda network is an extremist religious terrorist organization, its Taliban puppet regime was filled with religious zealots, and its suicide recruits were convinced that they were waging a just holy war. But the driving forces of twenty-first-century terrorism are power and frustration, not the pursuit of religious principle. To dismiss the broad enabling environment would be to focus more on the symptoms than the causes of modern terrorism.

The prescriptions for countering and preventing terrorism should be twofold: First, the United States and other members of the international community concerned about this threat need to use a balanced assortment of instruments to address the immediate challenges of the terrorists themselves. Terrorism is a complex phenomenon; it must be met with short-term military action, informed by in-depth, long-term, sophisticated analysis. Thus far, the response has been virtually all the former and little of the latter. Second, the United States and its counterterrorist allies must employ a much broader array of longer-term policy tools to reshape the international environment, which enables terrorist networks to breed and become robust. The mechanisms of globalization need to be exploited to thwart the globalization of terrorism.

In the short term, the United States must continue to rely on capable military forces that can sustain punishing air strikes against terrorists and those who harbor them with an even greater capacity for special operations on the ground. This requires not only improved stealthy, long-range power projection capabilities but also agile, highly trained, and lethal ground forces, backed up with greater intelligence, including human intelligence supported by individuals with language skills and cultural training. The use of military force continues to be important as one means of responding to terrorist violence against the West, and there is no question that it effectively preempts and disrupts some international terrorist activity, especially in the short term.[64]

Over time, however, the more effective instruments of policy are likely to remain the nonmilitary ones. Indeed the United States needs to expand and deepen its nonmilitary instruments of power such as intelligence, public diplomacy, cooperation with allies, international legal instruments, and economic assistance and sanctions. George Kennan, in his 1947 description of containment, put forth the same fundamental argument, albeit against an extremely different enemy.[65] The strongest response that the United States can muster to a serious threat has to include political, economic, and military capabilities—in that order; yet, the U.S. government consistently structures its policies and devotes its resources in the reverse sequence.

The economic and political roots of terrorism are complex, increasingly worrisome, and demanding of as much breadth and subtlety in response as they display in their genesis. The United States must therefore be strategic in its response: An effective grand strategy against terrorism involves planning a global campaign with the most effective means available, not just the most measurable, obvious, or gratifying. It must also include plans for shaping the global environment after the so-called war on terrorism has ended—or after the current political momentum has subsided.

The United States, working with other major donor nations, needs to create an effective incentive structure that rewards "good performers"—those countries with good governance, inclusive education programs, and adequate social programs—and works around "bad performers" and intervenes to assist so-called failed states. Also for the longer term, the United States and its allies need to project a vision of sustainable development—of economic growth, equal access to basic social needs such as education and health, and good governance—for the developing world. This is particularly true in mostly Muslim countries whose populations are angry with the United States over a perceived double standard regarding its long-standing support for Israel at the expense of Palestinians, policies against the regime of Saddam Hussein at the expense of some

Iraqi people, and a general abundance of American power, including the U.S. military presence throughout the Middle East. Whether these policies are right or wrong is irrelevant here; the point is that just as the definition of terrorism can be subjective and value laden, so too can the response to terrorism take into account perceptions of reality. In an attempt to craft an immediate military response, the U.S. government is failing to put into place an effective long-term grand strategy.

This is not just a problem for the U.S. government. The inability to develop a strategy with a deep-rooted, intellectually grounded understanding of the history, patterns, motivations, and types of terrorism is reflective of the paucity of understanding of the terrorist phenomenon in the academic community. Terrorism is considered too policy-oriented an area of research in political science,[66] and it operates in an uncomfortable intersection between disciplines unaccustomed to working together, including psychology, sociology, theology, economics, anthropology, history, law, political science, and international relations. In political science, terrorism does not fit neatly into either the realist or liberal paradigms, so it has been largely ignored.[67] There are a few outstanding, well-established senior scholars in the terrorism studies community—people such as Martha Crenshaw, David Rapoport, and Paul Wilkinson—but in the United States, most of the publicly available work is being done in policy-oriented research institutes or think tanks that are sometimes limited by the narrow interests and short time frames of the government contracts on which they depend. Some of that research is quite good,[68] but it is not widely known within the academy. The situation for graduate students who wish to study terrorism is worse: A principal interest in terrorism virtually guarantees exclusion from consideration for most academic positions. This would not necessarily be a problem if the bureaucracy were more flexible and creative than the academy is, but as we know from the analysis of the behavior of U.S. agencies shortly before September 11, it is not. In the United States, academe is no more strategic in its understanding of terrorism than is the U.S. government.

The globalization of terrorism is perhaps the leading threat to long-term stability in the twenty-first century. But the benefit of globalization is that the international response to terrorist networks has also begun to be increasingly global, with international cooperation on law enforcement, intelligence, and especially financial controls being areas of notable recent innovation.[69] If globalization is to continue—and there is nothing foreordained that it will—then the tools of globalization, including especially international norms, the rule of law, and international economic power, must be fully employed against the terrorist backlash. There must be a deliberate effort to move beyond the current episodic interest in this phenomenon: Superficial arguments and short attention spans will continue to result in event-driven policies and ultimately more attacks. Terrorism is an unprecedented, powerful nonstate threat to the international system that no single state, regardless of how powerful it may be in traditional terms, can defeat alone, especially in the absence of long-term, serious scholarship engaged in by its most creative minds.

NOTES

1. The issue of U.S. strategic culture and its importance in the response to international terrorism is explored in more depth in Audrey Kurth Cronin, "Rethinking Sovereignty: American Strategy in the Age of Terror," *Survival,* Vol. 44, No. 2 (Summer 2002), pp. 119–139.

2. On the difficulty of defining terrorism, see, for example, Omar Malik, *Enough of the Definition of Terrorism!* Royal Institute of International Affairs (London: RIIA, 2001); and Alex P. Schmid, *Political Terrorism: A Research Guide* (New Brunswick, N.J.: Transaction Books,

1984). Schmid spends more than 100 pages grappling with the question of a definition, only to conclude that none is universally accepted.

3. Saying that terrorism is a political act is not the same as arguing that the political ends toward which it is directed are necessarily negotiable. If violent acts do not have a political aim, then they are by definition criminal acts.

4. The diabolical nature of terrorism has given resonance to Robert Kaplan's view that the world is a "grim landscape" littered with "evildoers" and requiring Western leaders to adopt a "pagan ethos." But such conclusions deserve more scrutiny than space allows here. See Steven Mufson, "The Way Bush Sees the World," *Washington Post,* Outlook section, February 17, 2002, p. B1.

5. R. G. Frey and Christopher W. Morris, "Violence, Terrorism, and Justice," in Frey and Morris, eds., *Violence, Terrorism, and Justice* (Cambridge: Cambridge University Press, 1991), p. 3.

6. Walter Laqueur, *Terrorism* (London: Weidenfeld and Nicolson, 1977, reprinted in 1978), pp. 7–8; and David C. Rapoport, "Fear and Trembling: Terrorism in Three Religious Traditions," *American Political Science Review,* Vol. 78, No. 3 (September 1984), pp. 658–677.

7. David C. Rapoport, "The Fourth Wave: September 11 in the History of Terrorism," *Current History,* December 2001, pp. 419–424; and David C. Rapoport, "Terrorism," *Encyclopedia of Violence, Peace, and Conflict* (New York: Academic Press, 1999).

8. Ironically, Robespierre's tactics during the Reign of Terror would not be included in this article's definition of terrorism, because it was state terror.

9. Rapoport, "The Fourth Wave."

10. Ibid., pp. 419–420.

11. Ibid., p. 420.

12. Adrian Gulke, *The Age of Terrorism and the International Political System* (London: I. B. Tauris, 1995), pp. 56–63.

13. This is not to imply that terrorism lacked international links before the 1970s. There were important international ties between anarchist groups of the late nineteenth century, for example. See David C. Rapoport, "The Four Waves of Modern Terrorism," in Audrey Kurth Cronin and James Ludes, eds., *The Campaign against International Terrorism* (Washington, D.C.: Georgetown University Press, forthcoming).

14. Groups such as the Second of June Movement, the Baader-Meinhof Gang, the Red Brigades, the Weathermen, and the Symbionese Liberation Army belong in this category.

15. Among right-wing groups would be other neo-Nazi organizations (in the United States and Europe) and some members of American militia movements such as the Christian Patriots and the Ku Klux Klan.

16. The list here would be extremely long, including groups as different as the Tamil Tigers of Sri Lanka, the Basque separatist party, the PLO, and the Irish Republican Army (IRA) and its various splinter groups.

17. Bruce Hoffman notes that secular terrorist groups that have a strong religious element include the Provisional IRA, Armenian factions, and perhaps the PLO; however, the political/separatist aspect is the predominant characteristic of these groups. Hoffman, "Terrorist Targeting: Tactics, Trends, and Potentialities," *Technology and Terrorism* (London: Frank Cass, 1993), p. 25.

18. An interesting example is France's Action Directe, which revised its raison d'être several times, often altering it to reflect domestic issues in France—anarchism and Maoism, dissatisfaction with NATO and the Americanization of Europe, and general anticapitalism. See Michael Dartnell, "France's Action Directe: Terrorists in Search of a Revolution," *Terrorism and Political Violence,* Vol. 2, No. 4 (Winter 1990), pp. 457–488.

19. For example, in the 1990s Germany and several other European countries experienced a rash of random arson attacks against guest houses and offices that provided services to immigrants, many of whom were Middle Eastern in origin. Other examples include the violence associated with groups such as Europe's "football hooligans." A possible American example of the opportunistic nature of right-wing terrorism may be the anthrax letter campaign conducted in October 2001. See Susan Schmidt, "Anthrax Letter Suspect Profiled: FBI Says Author Likely Is Male Loner; Ties to Bin Laden Are Doubted," *Washington Post,* November 11, 2001, p. A1; and Steve Fainaru, "Officials Continue to Doubt Hijackers' Link to Anthrax: Fla. Doctor Says He Treated One for Skin Form of Disease," *Washington Post,* March 24, 2002, p. A23.

20. It is interesting to note that, according to Christopher C. Harmon, in Germany, 1991 was the first year that the number of indigenous rightist radicals exceeded that of leftists. Harmon, *Terrorism Today* (London: Frank Cass, 2000), p. 3.

21. For example, in discussing the longevity of terrorist groups, Martha Crenshaw notes only three significant terrorist groups with ethnonationalist ideologies that ceased to exist within ten years of their formation (one of these, EOKA, disbanded because its goal—the liberation of Cyprus—was attained). By contrast, a majority of the terrorist groups she lists as having existed for ten years or longer have recognizable ethnonationalist ideologies, including the IRA (in its many forms), Sikh separatist groups, Euskadi Ta Askatasuna, the various Palestinian nationalist groups, and the Corsican National Liberation Front. See Crenshaw, "How Terrorism Declines," *Terrorism and Political Violence,* Vol. 3, No. 1 (Spring 1991), pp. 69–87.

22. On the characteristics of modern religious terrorist groups, see Bruce Hoffman, *Inside Terrorism* (New York: Columbia University Press, 1998), especially pp. 94–95; and Bruce Hoffman, "Terrorism Trends and Prospects," in Ian O. Lesser, Bruce Hoffman, John Arguilla, Michelle Zanini, and David Ronfeldt, eds., *Countering the New Terrorism* (Santa Monica, Calif.: RAND, 1999), especially pp. 19–20. On the peculiar twists of one apocalyptic vision, see Robert Jay Lifton, *Destroying the World to Save It: Aum Shinrikyo, Apocalyptic Violence, and the New Global Terrorism* (New York: Henry Holt, 1999).

23. There is a long list of people and organizations sanctioned under Executive Order 13224, signed on September 23, 2001. Designated charitable organizations include the Benevolence International Foundation and the Global Relief Foundation. The list is available at http://www.treas.gov/offices/enforcement/ofac/sanctions/t11ter.pdf (accessed November 26, 2002).

24. The RAND–St. Andrews University Chronology of International Terrorism is a databank of terrorist incidents that begins in 1968 and has been maintained since 1972 at St. Andrews University, Scotland, and the RAND Corporation, Santa Monica, California.

25. Hoffman, *Inside Terrorism,* pp. 90–91; and Nadine Gurr and Benjamin Cole, *The New Face of Terrorism: Threats from Weapons of Mass Destruction* (London: I. B. Tauris, 2000), pp. 28–29.

26. Statistics compiled from data in U.S. Department of State, *Patterns of Global Terrorism,* published annually by the Office of the Coordinator for Counterterrorism, U.S. Department of State.

27. Ibid. For a graphical depiction of this information, created on the basis of annual data from *Patterns of Global Terrorism,* see Cronin, "Rethinking Sovereignty," p. 126.

28. In the 1998 embassy bombings alone, for example, 224 people were killed (with 12 Americans among them), and 4,574 were injured (including 15 Americans). U.S. Department of State, *Patterns of Global Terrorism, 1998.*

29. Ibid. For a graphical depiction of deaths per incident, created on the basis of annual data from *Patterns of Global Terrorism,* see Cronin, "Rethinking Sovereignty," p. 128.

30. Ibid.

31. Hoffman, "Terrorist Targeting," p. 24.

32. U.S. Department of State, *Patterns of Global Terrorism,* various years.

33. Examples include Bruce Hoffman, *"Holy Terror": The Implications of Terrorism Motivated by a Religious Imperative,* RAND Paper P-7834 (Santa Monica, Calif.: RAND, 1993); and Mark Juergensmeyer, "Terror Mandated by God," *Terrorism and Political Violence,* Vol. 9, No. 2 (Summer 1997), pp. 16–23.

34. See, for example, Steven Simon and Daniel Benjamin, "America and the New Terrorism," *Survival,* Vol. 42, No. 1 (Spring 2000), pp. 59–75, as well as the responses in the subsequent issue "America and the New Terrorism: An Exchange," *Survival,* Vol. 42, No. 2 (Summer 2000), pp. 156–172; and Hoffman, "Terrorism Trends and Prospects," pp. 7–38.

35. See Peter Finn and Sarah Delaney, "Al-Qaeda's Tracks Deepen in Europe," *Washington Post,* October 22, 2001, p. A1; Kamran Khan and Molly Moore, "2 Nuclear Experts Briefed Bin Laden, Pakistanis Say," *Washington Post,* December, 12, 2001, p. A1; James Risen and Judith Miller, "A Nation Challenged: Chemical Weapons—Al Qaeda Sites Point to Tests of Chemicals," *New York Times,* November 11, 2001, p. B1; Douglas Frantz and David Rohde, "A Nation Challenged: Biological Terror—2 Pakistanis Linked to Papers on Anthrax Weapons," *New York Times,* November 28, 2001; and David Rohde, "A Nation Challenged: The Evidence—Germ Weapons Plans Found at a Scientist's House in Kabul," *New York Times,* December 1, 2001.

36. Laqueur, *Terrorism,* pp. 112–116.

37. Ibid., pp. 115–116.

38. Groups with known or alleged connections to al-Qaeda include Jemaah Islamiyah (Indonesia, Malaysia, and Singapore), the Abu

Sayyaf group (Philippines), al-Gama'a al-Islamiyya (Egypt), Harakat ul-Mujahidin (Pakistan), the Islamic Movement of Uzbekistan (Central Asia), Jaish-e-Mohammed (India and Pakistan), and al-Jihad (Egypt).

39. For the purposes of this article, globalization is a gradually expanding process of interpenetration in the economic, political, social, and security realms, uncontrolled by (or apart from) traditional notions of state sovereignty. Victor D. Cha, "Globalization and the Study of International Security," *Journal of Peace Research,* Vol. 37, No. 3 (March 2000), pp. 391–393.

40. With respect to the Islamic world, there are numerous books and articles that point to the phenomenon of antipathy with the Western world, either because of broad cultural incompatibility or a specific conflict between Western consumerism and religious fundamentalism. Among the earliest and most notable are Samuel P. Huntington, "The Clash of Civilizations?" *Foreign Affairs,* Vol. 72, No. 3 (Summer 1993); Benjamin R. Barber, *Jihad vs. McWorld: Terrorism's Challenge to Democracy* (New York: Random House, 1995); and Samuel P. Huntington, *The Clash of Civilizations and the Remaking of World Order* (New York: Simon and Schuster, 1996).

41. For more on cyberterrorism, see Dorothy Denning, "Activism, Hacktivism, and Cyberterrorism: The Internet as a Tool for Influencing Foreign Policy," paper presented at Internet and International Systems: Information Technology and American Foreign Policy Decision-making Workshop at Georgetown University, http://www.nautilus.org/info-policy/workshop/papers/denning.html (accessed January 5, 2003); Dorothy Denning, "Cyberterrorism," testimony before the U.S. House Committee on Armed Services, Special Oversight Panel on Terrorism, 107th Cong., 1st sess., May 23, 2001, available on the Terrorism Research Center website, http://www.cs.georgetown.edu/?denning/infosec/cyberterror.html (accessed January 5, 2003); Jerold Post, Kevin Ruby, and Eric Shaw, "From Car Bombs to Logic Bombs: The Growing Threat of Information Terrorism," *Terrorism and Political Violence,* Vol. 12, No. 2 (Summer 2000), pp. 97–122; and Tom Regan, "When Terrorists Turn to the Internet," *Christian Science Monitor,* July 1, 1999, http://www.csmonitor.com (accessed January 5, 2003).

42. Ibid. Dorothy Denning cites numerous examples, among them: In 1989, hackers released a computer worm into the NASA Space Physics Analysis Network in an attempt to stop a shuttle launch; during Palestinian riots in October 2000, pro-Israeli hackers defaced the Hezbollah website; and in 1999, following the mistaken U.S. bombing of the Chinese embassy in Belgrade during the war in Kosovo, Chinese hackers attacked the websites of the U.S. Department of the Interior, showing images of the three journalists killed during the bombing.

43. Paul R. Pillar, *Terrorism and U.S. Foreign Policy* (Washington, D.C.: Brookings, 2001), p. 47.

44. Ibid.

45. Simon Reeve, *The New Jackals: Ramzi Yousef, Osama bin Laden, and the Future of Terrorism* (Boston: Northeastern University Press, 1999), p. 260.

46. Dorothy Denning, "Cyberwarriors: Activists and Terrorists Turn to Cyberspace," *Harvard International Review,* Vol. 23, No. 2 (Summer 2001), pp. 70–75. See also Brian J. Miller, "Terror.org: An Assessment of Terrorist Internet Sites," Georgetown University, December 6, 2000.

47. Miller, "Terror.org," pp. 9, 12.

48. Steganography is the embedding of messages usually in pictures, where the messages are disguised so that they cannot be seen with the naked eye. See Denning, "Cyberwarriors."

49. I am indebted to Dorothy Denning for all of this information. The Provisional IRA hired contract hackers to find the addresses of British intelligence and law enforcement officers. See Denning, "Cyberterrorism"; and Denning, "Cyberwarriors."

50. There are many recent sources on CBNR. Among the best are Jonathan B. Tucker, ed., *Toxic Terror: Assessing Terrorist Use of Chemical and Biological Weapons* (Cambridge, Mass.: MIT Press, 2000); Joshua Lederberg, *Biological Weapons: Limiting the Threat* (Cambridge, Mass.: MIT Press, 1999); Richard A. Falkenrath, Robert D. Newman, and Bradley A. Thayer, *America's Achilles' Heel: Nuclear, Biological, and Chemical Terrorism and Covert Attack* (Cambridge, Mass.: MIT Press, 1998); Gurr and Cole, *The New Face of Terrorism;* Jessica Stern, *The Ultimate Terrorists* (Cambridge, Mass.: Harvard University Press, 1999); and Brad Roberts, ed., *Terrorism with Chemical and Biological Weapons: Calibrating Risks and Responses* (Alexandria, Va.: Chemical and Biological Arms Control Institute, 1997).

51. See Falkenrath, Newman, and Thayer, *America's Achilles' Heel,* pp. 31–46.

52. A clear example of this phenomenon was the uncovering in December 2001 of a

multinational plot in Singapore by the international terrorist group Jemaah Islamiyah to blow up several Western targets, including the U.S. embassy. A videotape of the intended targets (including a description of the plans in Arabic) was discovered in Afghanistan after al-Qaeda members fled. Thus there are clear connections between these organizations, as well as evidence of cooperation and coordination of attacks. See, for example, Dan Murphy, "'Activated' Asian Terror Web Busted," *Christian Science Monitor,* January 23, 2002, http://www.csmonitor.com (accessed January 23, 2002); and Rajiv Changrasekaran, "Al Qaeda's Southeast Asian Reach," *Washington Post,* February 3, 2002, p. A1.

53. Rensselaer Lee and Raphael Perl, "Terrorism, the Future, and U.S. Foreign Policy," issue brief for Congress, received through the Congressional Research Service website, order code IB95112, Congressional Research Service, Library of Congress, July 10, 2002, p. CRS-6.

54. Roger G. Weiner, "The Financing of International Terrorism," Terrorism and Violence Crime Section, Criminal Division, U.S. Department of Justice, October 2001, p. 3. According to Weiner, the *hawala* (or *hundi*) system "relies entirely on trust that currency left with a particular service provider or merchant will be paid from bank accounts he controls overseas to the recipient specified by the party originating the transfer." Ibid. See also Douglas Frantz, "Ancient Secret System Moves Money Globally," *New York Times,* October 3, 2001, http://www.nytimes.com (accessed October 3, 2001).

55. International efforts to freeze bank accounts and block transactions between suspected terrorists have hindered, at least to some degree, al-Qaeda's ability to finance attacks; however, a proportion remains unaccounted for. "Cash Moves a Sign Al-Qaeda Is Regrouping," *Straits Times,* March 18, 2002, http://www.straitstimes.asia1.com.sg (accessed March 18, 2002).

56. U.S. Department of State, *Patterns of Global Terrorism, 2001.* According to the U.S. Department of State, Hezbollah also may have transferred resources by selling millions of dollars' worth of Congolese diamonds to finance operations in the Middle East.

57. Douglas Farah, "Al Qaeda's Road Paved with Gold," *Washington Post,* February 17, 2002, pp. A1, A32.

58. Pillar, *Terrorism and U.S. Foreign Policy,* p. 48.

59. Many in the United States focus on the technologies of terrorism, with a much less developed interest in the motivations of terrorists. Brian M. Jenkins, "Understanding the Link between Motives and Methods," in Roberts, *Terrorism with Chemical and Biological Weapons,* pp. 43–51. An example of a study that focuses on weapons and not motives is Sidney D. Drell, Abraham D. Sofaer, and George W. Wilson, eds., *The New Terror: Facing the Threat of Biological and Chemical Weapons* (Stanford, Calif.: Hoover Institution, 1999).

60. Christopher Coker, *Globalisation and Insecurity in the Twenty-first Century: NATO and the Management of Risk,* Adelphi Paper 345 (London: International Institute for Strategic Studies, June 2002), p. 40.

61. The indicators studied included respect for human rights and human freedoms, the empowerment of women, and broad access to and utilization of knowledge. See United Nations Development Programme, Arab Fund for Economic and Social Development, *Arab Human Development Report, 2002: Creating Opportunities for Future Generations* (New York: United Nations Development Programme, 2002).

62. Martha Crenshaw, "Why America? The Globalization of Civil War," *Current History,* December 2001, pp. 425–432.

63. A number of recent arguments have been put forth about the relationship between poverty and terrorism. See, for example, Anatol Lieven, "The Roots of Terrorism, and a Strategy against It," *Prospect* (London), October 2001, http://www.ceip.org/files/Publications/lieven-terrorism.asp?from=pubdate (accessed November 17, 2002); and Daniel Pipes, "God and Mammon: Does Poverty Cause Militant Islam?" *National Interest,* No. 66 (Winter 2001/02), pp. 14–21. This is an extremely complex question, however, and much work remains to be done. On the origins of the new religious terrorism, see Hoffman, *Inside Terrorism;* and Mark Juergensmeyer, *Terror in the Mind of God: The Global Rise of Religious Violence* (Berkeley: University of California Press, 2000). Important earlier studies on the sources of terrorism include Martha Crenshaw, "The Causes of Terrorism," *Comparative Politics,* July 1981, pp. 379–399; Martha Crenshaw, *Terrorism in Context* (University Park: Pennsylvania State University Press, 1995); and Walter Reich, ed., *Origins of Terrorism: Psychologies, Ideologies, Theologies, States of Mind,* 2d ed. (Washington, D.C.: Woodrow Wilson Center for International Scholars, 1998).

64. For more discussion on the traditional elements of U.S. grand strategy, especially mili-

tary strategy, see Barry R. Posen, "The Struggle against Terrorism: Grand Strategy, Strategy, and Tactics," *International Security,* Vol. 26, No. 3 (Winter 2001/02), pp. 39–55.

65. George F. Kennan, "The Sources of Soviet Conduct," *Foreign Affairs,* Vol. 25, No. 4 (July 1947), pp. 575–576.

66. See the extremely insightful article by Bruce W. Jentleson, "The Need for Praxis: Bringing Policy Relevance Back In," *International Security,* Vol. 26, No. 4 (Spring 2002), pp. 169–183.

67. I am indebted to Fiona Adamson for this observation.

68. Important terrorism scholars in the think tank community include Walter Laqueur (Center for Strategic and International Studies), Brian Jenkins (RAND), Bruce Hoffman (RAND), and, from the intelligence community, Paul Pillar. This list is illustrative, not comprehensive.

69. On these issues, see Cronin and Ludes, *The Campaign against International Terrorism.*

Reading 9-3

Constructing Post–Cold War Collective Security
Brian Frederking

Did September 11 fundamentally change world politics?[1] The global rift over the United States invasion of Iraq hinges on this question. The United States' "war on terrorism" presumes that new threats from terrorist groups and weapons of mass destruction have transformed the international system. Advocates of military intervention in Iraq argue that this fundamentally changed world justifies more aggressive, even preemptive policies. Critics of the United States invasion of Iraq, however, argue that existing collective security rules are still applicable even after the events of September 11. They prefer an international system where the use of force is justified only by explicit Security Council authorization or traditional standards of self-defense, neither of which applies to the U.S. intervention in Iraq. Healing this rift within the international community will require eventual agreement about the extent to which September 11 changed the rules of global security.

I argue that September 11 did not fundamentally change world politics. Using a rule-oriented constructivist approach, I argue that the dominant trend of the post–cold war world is the gradual institutionalization of global collective security rules. As in earlier struggles to punish states violating human rights rules, the international community is now struggling to punish both states and ruthless nonstate actors that violate terrorism and weapons proliferation rules. The pre–September 11 debate about intervening in Yugoslavia over human rights abuses in Kosovo is stunningly similar to the post–September 11 debates about the use of military force in Iraq. This analysis suggests that September 11 did not fundamentally change the rules governing global security; instead, it exacerbated already existing tensions about the appropriate implementation of fledgling collective security rules.

To analyze the Kosovo debate I use an interpretive method called *dialogical analysis* (Duffy, Frederking, and Tucker 1998; Frederking 2000). Dialogical analysis builds on

SOURCE: From "Constructing Post–Cold War Collective Security" by Brian Frederking, *American Political Science Review,* vol. 97, no. 3 (August 2003): 363–378. Copyright © 2003. Reprinted with the permission of The Cambridge University Press.

approaches that take the constitutive nature of language seriously, including Wittgenstein's (1968) latter philosophy of language, Habermas' (1984, 1987) notion of communicative rationality, and the speech act theories of Austin (1962) and Searle (1969). Dialogical analysis models a linguistic conception of social interaction capable of illustrating constructivist arguments. It assumes the existence of constitutive social rules and communicatively rational agents constructing those social rules through the performance of speech acts. The development of interpretive methods like dialogical analysis is important if we are to move beyond epistemological debates between advocates of Science and advocates of Anti-Science. Interpretive methods capable of yielding theoretical and practical insights can show both the positivist defenders of Science and the postmodern defenders of Anti-Science that one can accept the philosophical critiques of positivism and still engage in rigorous, replicable empirical research in the pursuit of knowledge.

I build on Onuf's rule-oriented constructivism to offer a tentative rule-oriented constructivist theory of global security. Onuf (1989) argues that agents are embedded in "social arrangements" of intersubjective rules. I posit four social arrangements constituting the security structures of world politics: war, rivalry, collective security, and security communities. The dominant post–cold war trend is movement away from cold war rivalry rules and (slowly) toward collective security rules. This trend is complicated because some rules in these social arrangements overlap. For example, the use of force is acceptable in war, rivalry, and collective security arrangements. How others interpret the use of force will depend on a dialogic consensus about which social arrangement governs the interaction. If others interpret force to invoke rules of war, then they will dismiss claims that collective security rules apply. I argue that a rule-oriented constructivist emphasis on language and rules shows the debates over Kosovo and Iraq to have tremendous similarities, casting doubt on arguments that September 11 fundamentally changed world politics.

CONSTRUCTIVISM

Constructivism[2] emerged in the 1990s as international relations scholars realized that the dominant approaches of neorealism and neoliberalism could not explain transformative events like the end of the cold war. Constructivism asserts the existence of social structures—including norms, beliefs, and identities—constituting world politics. All constructivists in some way assert the importance of what Searle calls "social facts": facts that exist because all the relevant actors agree they exist. Social facts like sovereignty, property, human rights, and collective security are for constructivists the stuff of world politics, and human agency constructs those social facts (Berger and Luckmann 1966; Searle 1995).

Within international relations, constructivism resembles English school arguments that the state system is embedded in a larger society in which states agree to certain rules and institutions (e.g., Bull 1977). However, leading constructivists cite many influences. Wendt (1999) cites Mead's symbolic interactionism and Bhaskar's scientific realism. Onuf (1989) cites Wittgenstein's latter philosophy of language, Giddens's structurationism, Habermas' theory of communicative action, and Searle's speech act theory. Campbell (1992) cites the postmodern arguments of Foucault and Derrida. Ruggie (1998) cites Durkheim's studies of the collective conscience and Weber's methods of *verstehen*. All emphasize the constitutive nature of language. Language not only represents the world but in many ways creates the world by making action possible. Language is not a neutral medium through which we study the world; language is itself action. Constructivism is thus part of the postpositivist "sociological turn" (Guzzini 2000) or "linguistic turn" (Palan 2000) in the social sciences.

Constructivists assert three common ontological positions (Finnemore and Sikkink 2001; Kubalkova 2001; Wendt 1999). First, social factors primarily influence human interaction. Constructivism opposes materialist ontology asserting material structures, like the balance of power in neorealism or markets in neoliberalism. Constructivists argue that material structures have meaning for human agents only within the context of social rules. For example, a state's military capability has different meanings depending on whether it belongs to an ally or an enemy. Second, social structures help constitute the interests and identities of purposive actors. Constructivism opposes individualist ontologies that explain social outcomes as the aggregate result of individual decisions. Human agency is enmeshed in a web of social rules that both constitute and regulate agency. Third, agents and structures construct each other. Rules make agents and agents make rules. The (social) world is made by people, who in turn are made by that (social) world.

Most categorizations of constructivist arguments are epistemological. For example, Hopf (1998) distinguishes between conventional and critical constructivists. Conventional constructivists adhere to standard positivist causal theorizing, using norms and ideas as independent variables that cause action (Katzenstein 1996; Wendt 1999). Critical constructivists, however, reject positivist epistemology and methods and the possibility of objective knowledge (Campbell 1992). Their goal is to demystify the discursive practices that constitute social rules in order to foster change.

Many constructivists do not consider themselves in either of these camps. Adler (1997) and Ruggie (1998) argue that constructivism offers an important middle ground between positivism and postmodernism. Indeed, Onuf (2002, 126) introduced constructivism to international relations to stake out such a middle ground:

> This third way holds that *ontology* is the key. . . . Constructivism challenges the positivist view that language serves *only* to represent the world as it is. Language also serves a constitutive function. By speaking, we make the world what it is. . . . Nevertheless, constructivism is not postmodern because it accepts, as a practical matter, the Enlightenment belief in the possibility of shared knowledge about the world we live in.

Many constructivists work within this middle ground, using a wide variety of methods to analyze the social world (Fierke 2001). Crawford (2002) uses linguistic methods similar to the dialogical analysis presented here to analyze the ethical arguments challenging colonialism. Hopf (2002) uses a phenomenological approach of inductively analyzing texts to recover identities influencing Soviet and Russian foreign policy. Mattern (2001) analyzes "friendship" narrative strategies in the Western security community. Fierke (2000) conceptualizes social interaction as a dialogue to analyze the interaction between Iraq and the United Nations (UN) in the 1990s. Doty (1993) uses a "discursive practices" approach to analyze U.S. counterinsurgency policy in the Philippines. Others not explicitly within constructivism also build such methods, including conversation analysis (Fetzer 2000) and event data analysis (Duffy 1994). Dialogical analysis, the method used in this article, is also intended to be within this middle ground.

Another way to categorize constructivism is to focus on ontology, emphasizing the type of social rule—beliefs, norms, or identities—constructivists argue influences world politics. Beliefs, norms, and identities are all types of rules that constitute the social structure of world politics. This categorization is consistent with Habermas' arguments (discussed in more detail below) for the existence of three fundamental validity claims: truth, appropriateness, and sincerity. Each type of constructivist argument emphasizes one of those fundamental validity claims. Beliefs are social rules that primarily make truth claims about the world. To criticize a belief is to say that it is untrue. Norms are social rules that primarily make appropriateness claims about relationships. To criticize a norm is to say that it is inappropriate. Identities are social rules that primarily make sincerity claims about agents. To criticize a conveyed identity is to say that it is insincere.

One type of constructivist argument emphasizes truth validity claims by studying the importance of beliefs, or ideas, in world politics. *Beliefs* are shared understandings of the world. For example, Adler (1992) argues that "epistemic communities" create shared interpretations that frame and structure human practices. Bukovansky (2001) analyzes how the ideas championed by the American and French revolutions influence world politics. Other examples include how economic ideas influence economic policy making (Jacobsen 1995) and Third World development policies (Sikkink 1991).

A second type of constructivist argument emphasizes the appropriateness validity claim by studying the importance of norms in world politics. *Norms* are shared understandings of appropriate action. Norms guide action and make action possible, enabling agents to criticize assertions and justify actions. Finnemore (1996) argues that states often follow a "logic of appropriateness" and adhere to existing norms. Kratochwil (1989) demonstrated how norms arise in rationalist environments to enable and guide action. Keck and Sikkink (1998) and Risse, Ropp, and Sikkink (1999) show the conditions under which "transnational advocacy networks" diffuse human rights and environmental norms and influence domestic institutional changes. Other examples include the role of norms in the collapse of the cold war (Kratochwil and Koslowski 1994) and sanctions against South Africa (Klotz 1995).

A third type of constructivist argument emphasizes the sincerity validity claim by studying the importance of identity in world politics. *Identities* tell agents who they are and who others are; they enable agents to make the actions of themselves and others intelligible. Constructivists argue that interests stem from a particular, constructed representation of the relationship between self and other. Wendt (1995) argues that 500 British nuclear weapons are less threatening to the United States than five North Korean nuclear weapons. A social concept of structure explains this, but a material concept of structure cannot. Other examples include the role of a liberal democratic identity in the North Atlantic Treaty Organization (Risse-Kappen 1997), the role of Arab nationalism in Middle East alliances (Barnett 1995), and the role of a friendship identity during the Suez Canal Crisis (Mattern 2001).

Many constructivists focus on the interconnections among ideas, norms, and/or identities. For example, Price and Tannenwald (1996) argue that the reproduction of norms is inseparable from the construction of identity: "Civilized" states adhere to chemical and nuclear weapons norms because only "barbaric" states violate those norms. Crawford (2002) explicitly analyzes all three validity claims in her analysis of how ethical argumentation influenced decolonization. Weldes (1999) also analyzes all three validity claims and how they influenced U.S. national interests in the Cuban Missile Crisis. Viewed through Habermas, constructivists illustrate how agents conveying validity claims of truth, appropriateness, and sincerity construct the rules governing world politics.

The rule-oriented constructivist approach presented here also includes all three constructivist arguments. Social arrangements include all three types of rules: beliefs, norms, and identities. Global security arrangements include beliefs about the world (e.g., the nature of security), norms about social relationships (e.g., the appropriateness of the use of force), and identities about self and other (e.g., enemy, rival, citizen, or friend). Finally, dialogical analysis illustrates these three arguments by analyzing the validity claims and counterclaims of the speech acts performed by communicatively rational agents.

RULE-ORIENTED CONSTRUCTIVISM

Rule-oriented constructivists make two fundamental claims (Kubalkova 2001; Onuf 1989, 1998). First, social arrangements, or stable patterns of rules, make up the structures of world politics. Social arrangements are constitutive (they tell us what is possible) and regulative (they tell us what to do). World politics is a complex set of interdependent and overlapping social arrangements. Rules constitute and regulate all aspects of world politics—even "anarchy" is a constitutive social arrangement. Rules make it possible for agents to act: They tell us how the world works, they tell us who we are and who others are, they tell us which social goals are appropriate, and they tell us what we should do. Rules, like language, are not reducible to the meanings that individuals attach to them; they exist in the shared meanings of their users and are reproduced through their practices (Guzzini 2000). And, as Onuf (1989) argues, rules create rule by inherently providing more benefits and privileges to some more than others.

Beliefs, norms, and identities are types of social rules that constitute and regulate world politics. For example, beliefs about whether security is based on military capability or political relationships help constitute the range of possible arms control practices and influence particular arms control negotiations (Frederking 2000). Norms about the appropriateness of weapons of mass destruction help constitute the range of possible war-fighting and deterrence practices and influence particular war and deterrence policies (Price and Tannenwald 1996). Identities about racial superiority help constitute the range of possible colonial practices and influence particular decolonization policies and even humanitarian interventions (Crawford 2002). For rule-oriented constructivists these rules explain world politics.

Onuf's concept of rules is based on Wittgenstein's (1968) critique of the mirror theory of language, which holds that language is meaningful to the extent that it accurately represents the real world. Wittgenstein argued that the meaning of a term is connected to its use in speech, not whether it corresponds exactly to things in the real world. Meaning resides in the everyday use of language as a "form of life"; that is, by context and/or convention. Shared background knowledge is necessary to interpret language. Wittgenstein argues that learning a language is like learning the rules of a game; they help you "go on" by acting in ways that make sense given the rules of the game. For example, the rules of chess enable one to participate in or to interpret a chess game. This also applies to the rules of global security. Hollis and Smith (1991, 179) put Wittgenstein's position this way: "*Social action can occur only when there is a rule followed,* thus identifying what is going on" (my emphasis). The task for rule-oriented constructivists, then, is to explicate a range of social arrangements and show how the rules within these social arrangements make action intelligible.

The second rule-oriented constructivist claim is that communicatively rational agents use speech acts to construct social rules. This claim builds on both speech act theory and Hebermas' notion of communicative rationality. Speech act theory begins with Austin's (1962) demonstration that many verbal statements constitute social action. For example, saying "I do" in a marriage ceremony is a meaningful social act because it invokes social rules of the institution of marriage. Speech act theory argues that language is action; speech acts (promising, declaring, apologizing, etc.) are both plentiful and central to social life. Searle (1995) argues that a touchdown creates six points and a promise creates an obligation because both are "social facts" based on the constitutive rules of football and promising. Onuf uses speech act theory to build his rule-oriented constructivism. Kubalkova (2001, 64) argues,

> Onuf's most important contribution to constructivism is his systematic effort to show that rules derive from, work like, and depend on speech acts, and that language and rules together (they can never be separated) are the medium through which agents and structures may be said to constitute each other. . . . To study international relations, or any other aspect of human existence, *is to study language and rules.* (my emphasis)

Onuf uses three types of speech acts to analyze world politics: assertions, directives, and commitments. These speech acts invoke and/or challenge social rules that have the form of speech acts. For example, *assertion rules* convey knowledge about the world. Liberalism, neoclassical economics, and neorealism, for example, all include assertions about world politics. Repeated and unchallenged assertions like "democratic governments do not go to war with one another," "free trade maximizes economic efficiency," and "unipolar systems are less stable than bipolar systems" both enable and justify democratization policies, trade agreements, and arms shipments. *Directive rules* tell us what we must or should do and often include consequences for disregarding them. Examples of speech acts invoking directive rules include the use of force, trade sanctions and International Monetary Fund structural adjustment programs. *Commitment rules* are promises to act in a particular way. Examples of speech acts invoking commitment rules are treaties, contracts, and international trade.

Habermas' notion of communicative rationality builds on speech act theory. Habermas argues that communicatively rational agents perform speech acts, convey validity claims, interpret and evaluate the claims of others, and act on the basis of mutually recognized validity claims. Rationality refers to linguistic competence; a rational act effectively conveys validity claims and invokes social rules so that others correctly interpret the speech act. This dialogic process of agents conveying and evaluating the validity claims of each other's speech acts constructs and reconstructs social rules. Rule-oriented constructivists rely on Habermas because only communicatively rational actors can achieve the interpretive accomplishments ascribed to them by constructivist arguments.

Habermas argues that communicatively rational speech acts convey implicit validity claims of truth, appropriateness, and sincerity.[3] Consider the three types of speech acts emphasized by Onuf. An assertion (X) conveys a truth claim (X is true), an appropriateness claim (It is right that I assert X), and a sincerity claim (I believe X is true). A directive (You must do X) conveys a truth claim (You can do X), an appropriateness claim (It is right that I direct you to do X), and a sincerity claim (I want you to do X). And a commitment (I promise to do X) conveys a truth claim (I can do X), an appropriateness claim (It is right that I promise to do X), and a sincerity claim (I want to do X). Others may accept or challenge the validity claims on the basis of reasons, requiring a "moment of insight" to justify the claim that goes beyond strategic rationality. All competent speakers intuitively know how to test claims and judge whether certain claims are warranted. The binding force of language comes from others' ability to say "yes" or "no" to the validity claims. When actors agree to the validity claims of a speech act, the binding effect of language motivates them to coordinate subsequent actions with the speaker.[4]

Focusing on the validity claims of speech acts enables constructivists to analyze the process through which speech acts construct and/or challenge social rules. When one performs a speech act and conveys the three validity claims, another can either accept all three claims or challenge one (or all) of the claims. For example, suppose that a teacher asserts the following to her class: "The United States Civil War occurred in the 1900s." The class may not challenge the speech act and add it to their notes(!). Or the class could challenge the sincerity claim: The teacher wanted to see if they were paying attention. Or the class could challenge the truth claim: The Civil War was not fought in the 1900s. Or the class could challenge the appropriateness claim: Teachers should not lie to their students. In each case the students construct and/or challenge the rules of the student-teacher social arrangement.

The same possibilities structure political interaction. Suppose that one country directs another to destroy its weapons of mass destruction within six months. The other country could accept the validity claims and comply, challenge the sincerity claim (you want a pretext to invade), challenge the normative rightness claim (it is not appropriate for you to determine our military capabilities), or challenge the truth claim (we cannot completely disarm within six months). This view of agency puts language at the heart of social life by emphasizing argumentation, a search for reasoned consensus, and the constitutive effects of an argumentative consensus on agents.

Using speech act theory and communicative rationality to inform a conception of social interaction enables analysts to treat physical, nonverbal acts as if they were speech acts. Of course, something unspoken is not literally a speech act. However, nonverbal acts are often communicatively rational—they make validity claims and invoke and/or challenge social rules—and are thus analyzable as speech acts. The use of force is an extremely important example of such a nonverbal, yet communicatively rational, act. How communicatively rational agents justify and interpret the use of force is central to the ongoing construction of global security rules. As the analysis below shows, how the world interpreted the NATO bombing campaign in Kosovo is central to that interaction, as is how the world interprets the use of force in Iraq. Treating nonverbal but communicative acts as speech acts makes a wide variety of social interaction amenable to dialogical analysis.

For example, during the cold war the superpowers understood each other's missile deployments to invoke the deterrence rules constituting the cold war rivalry (Frederking 2000). Missile deployments are intelligible only if they operated as speech acts within a particular social arrangement. Missile deployments are intelligible only if they operated as speech acts within a particular social arrangement. Missile deployments do not necessarily invoke deterrence rules; they could, for example, alter the strategic balance or expand a sphere of influence. Indeed, the superpowers criticized all missile deployments interpreted to invoke these latter rules. A missile deployment is understood as a deterrent only when all agree that a certain set of linguistically constructed rules govern their interaction. In this way speech acts, both verbal and nonverbal, are constitutive elements of social reality, and linguistically constructed rules provide meaning to both verbal and nonverbal speech acts.

Rule-oriented constructivism takes the constitutive nature of language and communicative agency seriously. Rule-oriented constructivists analyze the shared context that makes social action possible and meaningful. We make sense of action when there is coherence between the actions of agents (speech acts) and the meaning of their situation (existing social rules). Interpretive approaches like dialogical analysis explain in terms of intelligibility, not "expectability" (Dessler 1999). *To explain an act is to specify the rule(s) an agent is following.* Rule-oriented constructivism does not assume, as positivist causal arguments do, that language is a mirror and we compare our statements about the world with the world to see whether they correspond. As Kratochwil and Ruggie (1986) argue, in constructivist ontology language constitutes social interactions, while in positivist epistemology language is independent of social interactions. Constructivists who espouse positivism ignore the epistemological implications of their ontological arguments (Kratochwil 2000).

A RULE-ORIENTED CONSTRUCTIVIST THEORY
OF GLOBAL SECURITY

Constructivism is an ontology asserting the existence of social rules; it cannot tell us the content of those rules. This is an empirical question, and constructivists must demonstrate that their theoretical assertions about social rules cohere with the speech acts of real-world agents. This section is a first cut at a rule-oriented constructivist theory of global security. Many important social arrangements also constituting world politics—capitalism, globalization, postcolonialism, international law, and so on—fall outside the scope of this theory but are amenable to a rule-oriented constructivist analysis. The influence of other social arrangements (e.g., the position of Russia in the international economy, domestic politics) in the dispute over Kosovo also falls outside the scope of this analysis.

Wars, rivalries, collective security, and security communities are the "form of life" (Wittgenstein) or "life-world" (Habermas) or "social facts" (Searle) of global security. These social arrangements constitute global security in the way that the rules of chess constitute chess; participants use them to "go on" and act in intelligible ways. Sometimes one social arrangement is more institutionalized than the others; sometimes the social arrangements are contested and fluid; and sometimes social arrangements are more institutionalized in different geographic areas (e.g., war in the Middle East, rivalry in South Asia, security community in Europe). The operation of overlapping social arrangements constituting global security is similar to Fierke's (n.d.) argument that opposing "logics" may coexist within a historical context. What constitutes rational action depends on which logic is governing the particular interaction.

A first cut at stating ideal-typical rules in these social arrangements is in Table 1. Each social arrangement has six fundamental rules that constitute and regulate action: (1) identity, (2) autonomy, (3) the nature of security, (4) deterrence, (5) enforcement, and (6) the use of force. The identity rule establishes agent identities as enemies, rivals, citizens, or friends. The autonomy rule establishes the extent to which the autonomy of both state and nonstate agents is either threatened by others or limited by mutual obligations. The security rule establishes the belief that security is acquired by either relative military capability or friendly political relationships. The deterrence rule establishes a dominant normative expectation either to recognize the autonomy of others or to follow the rules of the community. The enforcement rule establishes the ultimate method of resolving conflict. The use of force rule establishes the extent to which force is required to resolve conflict. Variations of these rules constitute the ideal-typical social arrangements of war, rivalry, collective security, and security communities.

These rules are not intended to be a priori assertions of social reality. They comprise a tentative rule-oriented constructivist theory of global security. They may not

Table 1. Global Security Social Arrangements

	War	Rivalry	Collective Security	Security Community
Rule 1—Identity	We are enemies	We are rivals	We are fellow citizens	We are friends
Rule 2—Autonomy	We do not recognize the autonomy of others	We recognize the autonomy of others	Autonomy is limited by obligations to follow and enforce the community's rules	Autonomy is limited by obligations to follow the community's rules
Rule 3—Security	Survival is based on relative (alliance) military capability	Security is based on relative (alliance) military capability	Security is based on a multilateral commitment to use military capability	Security is based on political relationships
Rule 4—Deterrence	You must surrender	Do not attack me	Do not break the rules of our community	Do not break the rules of our community
Rule 5—Enforcement	We will attack until you surrender	We will retaliate if you violate our sovereignty	We will retaliate if you break the rules of our community	We will resolve conflicts peacefully
Rule 6—Use of force	The use of force is always necessary to resolve conflicts	The use of force is sometimes necessary	The use of force is sometimes necessary	The use of force is not acceptable

cohere with future empirical research and have to be abandoned. But they are a recognizable, plausible place to start. The contents of the rules are culled from major scholars of international politics, including Alker's (1996, 370) work on security systems, Onuf's (1989) "mutual insecurity system," Schelling's (1960) theories of deterrence and arms agreements, and Deutsch's (1957) work on security communities. Wendt's (1999) three cultures of world politics—Hobbesian war, Lockean rivalry, and Kantian security communities—heavily influence these rules. Wendt's characterization of Kantian culture, however, includes both collective security (in which the use of force is acceptable) and security communities (in which the use of force is not acceptable). I argue that this distinction warrants separate social arrangements; moreover, as I argue below, this distinction is essential to understand the construction of post–cold war collective security.

In war, agents identify each other as enemies (rule 1), perhaps even an enemy that threatens their existence. Agents do not recognize the autonomy of others or perhaps even the right of others to exist (rule 2). Survival demands a military capability greater than one's immediate enemies (rule 3) because the military capabilities of others are in-terpreted as a threat to one's existence. The directive rule in war is to surrender (rule 4), supported by the commitment to attack until the other does surrender (rule 5). Because others are enemies with the military capability to threaten one's existence, the use of force is considered inevitable, necessary, and appropriate (rule 6). War orients agents to act with great mistrust and hostility towards others, including interactions like tradi-tional nation-state warfare, Israeli-Palestinian relations, imperialism, and (perhaps) the ongoing "war" on terrorism.

In rivalries, agents identify each other as rivals (rule 1). They attempt to increase their security through joining alliances (rule 3) and performing classic deterrence threats (rules 4 and 5). Agents do recognize the autonomy of others (rule 2), but the rivalry con-stituting the system sometimes leads to violence to settle disputes (rule 6). War is thus an accepted but limited practice to end an attempt by any state to dominate world politics. Rivalry orients agents to act with mistrust and caution toward others, including inter-actions like power balancing, alliance systems, security dilemmas, arms races, and spheres of influence regimes. The cold war was a prototypical rivalry social arrangement.

In collective security arrangements, agents identify each other as citizens (rule 1) who are obliged to uphold agreed-upon rules of behavior (rule 2) and act collectively to punish those who do not uphold those rules (rule 3). There is no presumption that actors will universally agree to the directive rules (rule 4); an enforcement mechanism that includes military force is thus needed to punish any transgressors of the rules (rule 5). A collective security arrangement may enforce only the rule of state sovereignty, or it could enforce rules regarding weapons proliferation, terrorism, human rights, and so on. The use of force is considered to be sometimes necessary and acceptable to enforce community rules (rule 6). Collective security orients agents to act with a sense of duty to generate rules of peaceful behavior and punish those who break the rules. Through the explosion of multilateral treaties, Security Council resolutions, UN peacekeeping missions, and nongovernmental organizations, agents have been slowly institutionaliz-ing a global collective security arrangement in the post–cold war world.

In security communities, agents identify each other as friends committed to the peaceful resolution of conflict (rule 1). Agents in security communities have a strong consensus about the obligation to follow the rules of their community (rule 2), and they engage in peaceful, multilateral decision making to ensure security through political re-lationships (rule 3). The directive rule to follow the rules of community does exist in security communities (rule 4), but enforcement does not include the possibility of force (rules 5 and 6). Given the lower level of threat in these social arrangements, security of-ten refers to alternative security issues like the environment and the economy (Adler and Barnett 1998, Deutsch 1957). Security communities orient agents to act with great trust and "we-ness" toward others, as in the relations between members of the Euro-pean Union.

The first three rules—regarding the nature of identity, autonomy, and security in the world—are distinct across social arrangements. These rules constitute the core dif-ferences among the social arrangements. Agents establish which social arrangement is governing their interaction through speech acts implicitly conveying the validity of these rules. In war, agents are enemies that do not recognize the autonomy of others and must survive by acquiring greater relative military capability. In rivalries, agents are rivals that recognize autonomy but act to ensure security by acquiring, unilaterally or through alliances, greater relative military capability. In collective security arrange-ments, agents are citizens whose sovereignty is limited by obligations to follow com-munity rules and to use multilateral military force to ensure compliance with those rules. In security communities, agents are friends whose sovereignty is limited by obligations to peacefully follow the rules of the community.

However, rules 4–6—regarding deterrence, enforcement, and the use of force—overlap across social arrangements, and this overlap can lead to conflict between agents over the applicable social arrangement. For example, rule 4 is identical in collective security arrangements and security communities ("Do not break the rules of our community"). Rule 5 is similar—though not identical—in collective security arrangements and rivalries. In rivalries, the only agreed-upon rule of the community is state sovereignty, and alliance mechanisms enforce that rule. Collective security arrangements represent an alternative mechanism to enforce agreed-upon rules that often extend beyond state sovereignty to include human rights, etc. Most importantly, rule 6 justifies the use of force in war, collective security arrangements, and rivalries. The use of force in and of itself does not tell agents whether war, rivalry, or collective security rules govern their interaction; agents must justify and interpret which rules the use of force invokes at any particular time. Conflicts may develop if agents dispute which rules the use of force invokes. I argue that this overlap in the use of force rule helps explain the disputes over Kosovo and Iraq.

DIALOGICAL ANALYSIS

Dialogical analysis posits the existence of social rules communicatively rational agents, and the argumentation of validity claims. It is one method to illustrate constructivist arguments about the role of norms, beliefs, and identity in world politics. Dialogical analysis is an interpretive approach, explaining action by specifying the rules agents follow; that is, by showing the coherence between speech acts and rules within a particular social arrangement. Dialogical analysis proceeds in four steps (Duffy, Frederking, and Tucker 1998; Frederking 2000). First, one specifies the background knowledge necessary to understand the interaction. Second, one accumulates explicit speech acts that conveyed meaning during the interaction. Third, one conducts a pragmatic analysis of the speech acts, deriving the implicitly conveyed propositions during the interaction. Fourth, one constructs a formal argument analysis from the inventory of pragmatic propositions to isolate consensual and disputed claims during the interaction.

The analyst first specifies background knowledge, most importantly a set of rules governing the interaction. These rules are the theory asserted by the analyst; dialogical analysis is a methodological tool to provide empirical evidence for the existence of these rules. The social arrangements of war, rivalry, collective security, and security communities asserted in the section above are the background knowledge for the dialogic analysis of the veto power dispute over Kosovo. Other background knowledge used to support interpretive inferences is also in the narrative below.

The analyst next accumulates explicit speech acts during the interaction, including nonverbal acts that convey meaning, justifying the speech acts chosen with defensible selection criteria. The speech acts in the analysis are not, in the statistical sense, a random sample of all possible speech acts during the interaction. This step often requires a reconstruction of the dialogue from public sources. No algorithmic coding rules exist to transform textual data into analyzable speech acts. Perhaps such rules are even impossible to develop. The analyst simply generates the most relevant speech acts with the same interpretive ability of all communicatively rational agents.

The bulk of dialogical analysis is the pragmatic analysis. Pragmatics is the field of linguistics that relates the meaning of language to the context of its use. In the pragmatic analysis, one specifies the implicit propositions conveyed by speech acts given the context of the interaction.[5] Speakers convey and hearers infer more than uttered sentences; they make pragmatic inferences that enable them to understand one another and coordinate action. For example, Grice (1957) argues that speakers use rational principles of conversation in all exchanges, including the following maxims.[6] (1) *The maxim of quality*—Do not say what you believe to be false, and do not say anything for which you lack adequate evidence. (2) *The maxim of quantity*—Make your contribution as informative as is required for the current purposes of the exchange. (3) *The maxim of relevance*—Make your contributions relevant. (4) *The maxim of manner*—Avoid obscurity, avoid ambiguity, be brief and be orderly. Actors infer *conversational implicatures,* or the implicit contents of speech acts, by assuming that speakers adhere to these maxims.

The propositions generated by the pragmatic analysis convey validity claims of truth, appropriateness, and sincerity. When one agrees to a speech act, one concedes all three validity claims. When one disputes a speech act, one disputes (at least) one of these claims. As the interaction continues, the pragmatic analysis specifies all validity claims and counterclaims. For example, consider the following exchange between the United States and Afghanistan.

> *United States:*   Extradite the responsible parties immediately.
>
> *Afghanistan:*   We will try them under Islamic law.

The pragmatic analysis specifies truth, appropriateness, and sincerity claims conveyed by the speech acts. The United States directive toward Afghanistan conveys implicit claims of sincerity (The United States sincerely directs Afghanistan to extradite the responsible parties), normative rightness (It is appropriate that the United States direct Afghanistan to extradite the responsible parties), and truth (It is true that Afghanistan can extradite the responsible parties). The directive is coherent with collective security rules: The United States is directing Afghanistan to follow the community's rules against terrorism.

When Afghanistan refuses the directive, it disputes the United States' appropriateness claim and thus rejects the applicability of collective security rules. Instead, its claims of sincerity (Afghanistan sincerely intends to try them under Islamic law), appropriateness (It is appropriate that Afghanistan try them under Islamic law), and truth (It is true that Afghanistan can try them under Islamic law) are most coherent within a rivalry social arrangement. Afghanistan invokes the stronger sovereignty norms coherent in rivalries rather than the more limited sovereignty coherent with obligations to enforce collective security rules. Different understandings about which social arrangement is relevant generate the competing propositions in this dispute. Dialogical analysis is particularly appropriate to illustrate conflicts such as this in which agents invoke different social arrangements to justify their action.

The final step is an argument analysis that isolates and formalizes the disputed propositions and thus disputed social rules generated in the pragmatic analysis. The argument analysis extends Alker's (1988) approach in his dialectical analysis of the Melian Dialogue, which in turn builds on Rescher's (1977) model of argumentation. In Rescher's model, a proponent defends and an opponent challenges the truth of a thesis, and the argumentative stance is oriented toward winning the debate. In the argument analysis, agents instead negotiate the truth, appropriateness, and sincerity claims of speech acts, and the communicative stance is oriented toward constructing a valid social arrangement. Each claim in the argument analysis specifies (at least) one proposition in the pragmatic analysis. When one challenges the validity claim of another, the pragmatic analysis shows the dispute as contradictory propositions. When and if one "cancels" an earlier claim and ends a pragmatic dispute, the analyst updates the set of contested validity claims. Dialogical analysis can thus account for the changing construction of social rules both within and across social arrangements.

Constructivists can use dialogical analysis to illustrate their arguments about the importance of beliefs, norms, and identities in world politics. In the above example, constructivists interested in beliefs would focus on disputed truth claims about whether security is based on military capability or political commitments. Constructivists interested in norms would focus on the disputed appropriateness claims about whether Afghanistan is obligated to follow the rules of the international community. Constructivists interested in identity would focus on the disputed sincerity claims about whether the United States and Afghanistan are citizens or rivals. Dialogical analysis illustrates constructivist ontology by showing how communicatively rational agents convey validity claims that construct and/or challenge social rules.

Dialogical analysis takes the linguistic turn seriously. It is based on linguistics, and language (like the world) is ambiguous. Other analysts could use this method to analyze the Kosovo debate and assert different global security rules, select different speech acts, infer different pragmatic propositions, and reach contradictory conclusions. But dialogical analysis is rigorous enough that such disputes are transparent and explicit: We can then argue about the greater coherence of competing theory (background knowledge) and evidence (speech acts and pragmatic propositions). Dialogical analysis is deductive, is capable of replication, and relies on logic and empirical evidence for its conclusions. It is consistent with the notion that a community of interpreters can agree to the most coherent explanation and that those explanations can help us "go on" in that world and act in intelligible ways.

INTERPRETING KOSOVO: A DIALOGICAL ANALYSIS OF THE VETO POWER DISPUTE

Background Knowledge

The background knowledge for this analysis is the four ideal-typical global security social arrangements discussed above and more particularly a slow transition from a cold war rivalry arrangement to a post–cold war collective security arrangement. Many indicators of "global governance"—such as multilateral treaties, international organizations, Security Council resolutions, UN peacekeeping operations, nongovernmental organizations, and diffusion of human rights norms—have dramatically increased in number since the end of the cold war. Within this context, the international community has struggled to agree on the appropriate implementation of the fledgling collective security rules: Under what conditions should the international community use force to punish those who violate the rules?

When widespread evidence arose of human rights abuses by Serbs against Albanian Muslims in the Serbian province of Kosovo, many in the West advocated the punishment of Milosevic and the Serbs for violating the human rights rules of the international community. Russia and China, however, promised to veto any Security Council resolution that authorized the use of force. The dispute between the veto powers was whether the collective security rules emerging since the end of the cold war, together with emerging rules obligating states to limit human rights abuses, were sufficient to authorize NATO action. Critics of the use of force on the right (Waller, Drezov, and Gokay 2001), critics on the left (Chomsky 1999), and supporters (Daalder and

O'Hanlon 2000) all recognized the precedent-setting implications of Kosovo on the post–cold war construction of global security rules.

Speech Acts
The six speech acts in the analysis, as well as the narrative information in this section, are reconstructed from accounts of the dispute in the *New York Times*. The speech acts below were included because they represent official positions (all were conveyed by either the president or the top diplomat in each country) and focus on the relevant issue of how to implement collective security rules appropriately.

1. *United States:*   If Yugoslavia continues to violate the human rights of the Kosovo Albanians, NATO will use military force against Yugoslavia.[7]

2. *Russia/China:*   The Security Council has not authorized the use of force.[8]

3. *United States:*   Humanitarian concerns justify NATO use of force.[9]

4. *Russia/China:*   Any NATO use of force would threaten international order.[10]

5. *United States:*   NATO initiates a bombing campaign in Yugoslavia.

6. *Russia/China:*   NATO is engaging in unprovoked aggression against a sovereign state.[11]

The United States asserted speech act 1 when violence between Serbs and Kosovo Albanians escalated in early 1998. In September the Security Council demanded that Yugoslavia withdraw security forces from Kosovo, enable monitors to return to Kosovo, facilitate the return of refugees, and begin political negotiations with the Albanian Muslims. Russia voted for both resolutions but argued that there was no explicit authorization of the use of force and that further Security Council action was needed to authorize the use of force. China abstained on both resolutions, arguing that Kosovo was an internal matter and Yugoslavia was acting within its legitimate rights. Russia and China abstained on a third resolution in October 1998 endorsing the Holbrooke cease-fire agreement, arguing that they did not consider Resolution 1203 sufficient to authorize the use of force (speech act 2).

When Serb abuses in Kosovo increased in March 1999, the United States (speech act 3) argued that the overwhelming humanitarian crisis justified intervention even without explicit Security Council authorization. Clinton (1999) asserted a "moral imperative" for NATO to end the atrocities, arguing that "if the world community has the power to stop it, we ought to stop genocide and ethnic cleansing." Albright (1999) argued that human rights violations are not domestic matters but legitimate concerns of the international community; NATO has the right to defend the stability of Europe. State sovereignty in the post–cold war world is limited because "legitimate" states ensure basic human rights. States that perpetrate ethnic cleansing, thus, forfeit their right to territorial integrity.

Russia and China continued to criticize NATO policy (speech act 4). Yeltsin argued that NATO action would "destabilize the situation in the Balkans with unforeseeable consequences for all of Europe." Both argued that invoking a humanitarian crisis to justify unilateral armed intervention violated the UN charter. Nevertheless, NATO commenced the bombing campaign (speech act 5), which Russia and China denounced (speech act 6). Russian Foreign Minister Igor Ivan said, "Russia is deeply outraged by NATO's military action against sovereign Yugoslavia, an action that is nothing short of undisguised aggression. . . . Only the UN Security Council has the right to decide (if) the use of force should be taken to maintain or restore international peace and security. . . . The true aims are obvious. To impose on the world the political, military, and economic dictate of the United States."

Pragmatic Analysis

The pragmatic analysis generates all implicitly conveyed propositions during the interaction. These contextual propositions convey truth, appropriateness, and sincerity claims that invoke and/or challenge existing social rules. The pragmatic analysis specifies how each speech act conveyed validity claims and invoked social rules. Communicatively rational actors convey many implicit propositions during an interaction, and many are consensual and/or irrelevant to the specific issue of how to implement collective security rules. For reasons of space, then, the pragmatic analysis in Table 2 includes only the disputed propositions conveyed during the interaction.[12] Readers should refer to Table 2 throughout the discussion in this section.

The pragmatic analysis shows that throughout the interaction the United States invoked collective security rules, and Russia and China disputed the validity of those collective security rules. Within this overall pattern, however, each exchange in the interaction generated a set of escalated disputes. In speech acts 1 and 2, Russia and China disputed the appropriateness of United States–invoked collective security deterrence, enforcement, and use of force rules. Here all veto powers justified their speech acts with collective security rules, arguing that the other is inappropriately interpreting those rules. In speech acts 3 and 4, Russia and China disputed the truth of United States–invoked collective security identity, autonomy, and the nature of security rules. Here Russia and China began to dispute whether the United States would be actually invoking collective security rules with a use of force. And in speech acts 5 and 6, Russia and China disputed the sincerity of United States–invoked collective security identity, autonomy, and the nature of security rules. Here Russia and China argued that the United States indeed invoked war and/or rivalry rules with its use of force. By the end of the interaction, the veto powers had different understandings of which social arrangement governed their interaction. I discuss each exchange in turn.

In speech acts 1 and 2 the veto powers disagreed about whether the U.S. directive to Yugoslavia appropriately invoked collective security rules. With its directive to Yugoslavia in speech act 1, the United States invoked the collective security deterrence rule with proposition 1a; it invoked the collective security enforcement rule with proposition 1c; and it invoked the collective security use of force rule with proposition 1e. With their assertion that the Security Council did not authorize the use of force in speech act 2, Russia and China disputed the appropriateness of the United States invoking collective security rules to justify its directive to Yugoslavia. They disputed the appropriateness of the United States invoking the collective security deterrence rule with proposition 2a; they disputed the appropriateness of the United States invoking the collective security enforcement rule with proposition 2b; and they disputed the appropriateness of the United States invoking the collective security use of force rule with proposition 2c.

In this first exchange, the veto powers understood collective security rules to govern their interaction; all invoked collective security rules to justify their acts. However, Russia and China argued that the United States and NATO were not following those rules properly. One could interpret the Russian and Chinese criticism as intended to thwart the development of an emerging human rights norm that would justify humanitarian intervention given internal problems with Chechnya and Tibet (Carpenter 2000). While China did have these concerns, Russia had previously supported Security

Table 2. Pragmatic Analysis of the Great Power Interaction over Kosovo

Speech Act

1. *U.S.:* If Yugoslavia continues to violate the human rights of the Kosovar Albanians, NATO will use military force against Yugoslavia.

   Speech act: Directive

   Implicature:

   1a. Do not break the rules of our community. (CS4)
   1b. The NATO directive to Yugoslavia not to break the rules of our community is appropriate. (CS4N)
   1c. We will retaliate if you break the rules of our community. (CS5)
   1d. The NATO threat to retaliate against Yugoslavia is appropriate. (CS5N)
   1e. The use of force is acceptable to resolve the conflict. (CS6)

2. *Russia/China:* The Security Council has not authorized the use of force.

   Speech act: Assertion

   Implicatures:

   2a. The NATO directive to Yugoslavia not to break the rules of the international community is not appropriate. (~CS4N)
   2b. The NATO threat to retaliate against Yugoslavia is not appropriate. (~CS5N)
   2c. The use of force is not acceptable to resolve this conflict. (~CS6N)

3. *U.S.:* Humanitarian concerns justify NATO use of force.

   Speech act: Assertion

   Implicatures:

   3a. NATO countries are acting as citizens in our community. (CS1)
   3b. NATO is obligated to enforce the rules of our community. (CS2)
   3c. NATO is establishing security through a multilateral alliance commitment. (CS3)

4. *Russia/China:* Any NATO use of force would threaten international security.

   Speech act: Assertion

   Implicatures:

   4a. NATO countries are not acting as a citizen in our community. (~CS1T)
   4b. NATO is not obligated to enforce the rules of our community. (~CS2T)
   4c. NATO is not establishing security through an alliance commitment. (~CS3T)

5. *U.S.:* NATO initiates a bombing campaign in Yugoslavia.

   Speech act: Punishment (directive)

   Implicatures:

   5a. NATO is sincerely acting as a citizen in our community. (CS1S)
   5b. NATO is sincerely enforcing the rules of our community. (CS2S)
   5c. NATO is sincerely establishing security through an alliance commitment. (CS3)

6. *Russia/China:* NATO is engaged in unprovoked aggression against a sovereign state.

   Speech act: Assertion

   Implicatures:

   6a. NATO is a political rival (enemy?). (R1 or W1?)
   6b. NATO does not recognize Yugoslavia's sovereign rights to territorial integrity. (W2)
   6c. NATO is trying to increase its relative alliance military capability. (R3)

Note: The notation in parentheses after each proposition signifies the social rule and/or validity claim invoked by that proposition: CS = collective security, R = rivalry, W = war; 1 = identity rule, 2 = autonomy rule, 3 = nature of security rule, 4 = deterrence rule, 5 = enforcement rule, 6 = use of force rule; T = truth claim, S = sincerity claim, N = normative rightness or appropriateness claim. For example, (CS5) means that the preceding proposition invokes the collective security enforcement rule, and (CS5N) means that the preceding proposition claims that the collective security enforcement rule is normatively appropriate.

Council action regarding human rights. Of the 32 Security Council resolutions regarding Somalia, Haiti, Rwanda, and East Timor, Russia voted yes 31 times and abstained only once (Heinze and Borer 2002). Given this context, I interpret the criticism to stem from Russia's insistence that the collective security rules required a legal process based on Security Council action. Russia was preserving its role in world politics by asserting the primacy of the Security Council, not challenging the validity of an emerging human rights norm.

In speech acts 3 and 4 the veto powers deepened their dispute about whether NATO policy appropriately implements collective security rules. The U.S. assertion in speech act 3 conveyed a substantive, moral conception of collective security. NATO intervention was both legally and morally justified because it intended to avert humanitarian disaster and was consistent with Security Council Resolutions 1199 and 1203. Within the context of collective security, it argued for a rule enabling regional enforcement without explicit Security Council authorization. With these arguments, the United States invoked the collective security identity rule with proposition 3a; it invokes the collective security autonomy rule with proposition 3b; and it invokes the collective security nature of security rule with proposition 3c.

Russia and China countered the United States' moral and substantive conception of collective security with a procedural conception of collective security in speech act 4. Any use of force without Security Council authorization, they argued, threatened international peace and security. With this assertion, they challenged U.S. truth claims that NATO was acting as a citizen in the international community (proposition 4a), that NATO was enforcing the rules of the international community (proposition 4b), and that NATO was attempting to establish security through a multilateral commitment to use military capability (proposition 4c). Here the veto powers disputed truth claims about collective security rules 1–3; note that rules 1–3 are the core rules that differentiate the four global security social arrangements. With this exchange, then, Russia and China disputed that NATO policy invoked collective security rules. They began to suggest that perhaps the NATO use of force invoked a different social arrangement.

In speech acts 5 and 6 the conflict between the veto powers escalated dramatically. I treat the NATO bombing campaign as speech act 5. Within the context of the earlier interaction, the use of force defended the United States truth claims conveyed in speech act 3: NATO was indeed a citizen in our community (proposition 5a); NATO was indeed enforcing the rules of the community (proposition 5b); and NATO was indeed establishing security through an alliance commitment (proposition 5c). With speech act 6, Russia and China disputed the sincerity of U.S. claims that the NATO use of force invoked collective security rules. Instead they argued that NATO use of force is actually unprovoked aggression, invoking the rivalry (and perhaps war?) identity rule in proposition 6a, the war autonomy rule that NATO was violating Yugoslav sovereignty in proposition 6b, and the rivalry nature of security rule that NATO was trying to increase its relative alliance military capability.

With this exchange the veto powers completely disagreed about which social arrangement governed their interaction. While the United States continued to invoke collective security rules, Russia and China argued that it was trying to create a "NATO-centered Europe." They were no longer criticizing NATO for inappropriately implementing collective security rules; they now charged NATO with blatantly invoking rivalry and perhaps even war rules. For example, Russia charged the United States with violating the UN Charter, and China claimed that the United States was using pretexts like human rights to begin a new form of colonialism as part of a global strategy for world hegemony.

Table 3. Argument Analysis

Speech Act	U.S.	Russia/China
1. If Yugoslavia . . . , NATO will . . .	!1	
2. No SC authorization . . .		~N1/2 & !2
3. Humanitarian concerns . . .	N1/3 & !3	
4. Force would threaten order . . .		~T3/4 & !4
5. NATO bombing campaign	T3/!5 & !5	
6. NATO bombing threatens . . .		~S5/6 & !6

Disputed Social Rules	Disputed Validity Claim	Disputed Propositions
CS4, CS5, CS6	N1	1b–2a, 1d–2b, 1e–2c
CS1, CS2, CS3	T3	3a–4a, 3b–4b, 3c–4c
R1(W1?)/CS1, W2/CS2, W3/CS3	S5	5a–6a, 5b–6b, 5c–6c

Note: The notation in the argument analysis should be read as follows: An exclamation point signifies the performance of a speech act, S signifies the conveyance of a sincerity claim, N signifies the conveyance of a normative rightness or appropriateness claim, T signifies the conveyance of a truth claim, ~ signifies a negation, and / signifies a ceteris paribus argument, "All things being equal, this is normally the case. . . ."

Consistent with rivalry rules, Russia and China responded to the NATO use of force in Kosovo by attempting to increase their relative military capability. Russia sent a reconnaissance ship into the Mediterranean, revised its military doctrine to reinvigorate nuclear weapons capability, signed joint defense initiatives with Belarus and others, held war games in the Balkans, expelled NATO representatives from Moscow, suspended cooperation in the Partnership for Peace program, withdrew its mission and students from Brussels and NATO countries, and weakened communication between Russian and NATO forces in Bosnia. The Duma postponed ratification of the START II agreement (the December 1998 bombing in Iraq also caused a postponement of that vote). Although Russia never violated UN sanctions and sent direct military aid to Yugoslavia, the Duma voted 279 to 30 to send military aid and advisers. China suspended military ties with the United States and all negotiations with the United States over human rights issues. In June 1999, Russia and China announced that they would foster a "strategic partnership" to offset the global dominance of the United States. All of these responses invoked rivalry rules, particularly the rule that security is based on relative alliance military capability.

Argument Analysis

The argument analysis in Table 3 isolates and formalizes the disputes generated by the pragmatic analysis. It lists three sets of interconnected disputes discussed in the above section: disputed social rules, disputed validity claims, and disputed propositions. In speech acts 1 and 2, Russia and China contested the appropriateness of NATO's directive to Yugoslavia. Here the veto powers disagreed about how to implement the collective security rules regarding deterrence, enforcement, and the use of force. In speech acts 3 and 4, Russia and China disputed the truth of U.S. claims that NATO was enforcing collective security rules. Here the veto powers disagreed about the core rules of each social arrangement: the identity, sovereignty, and nature of security rules. In speech acts 5 and 6, Russia and China disputed NATO's sincerity that it was enforcing collective security. Here the agents disputed which social arrangement governed the interaction, with the United States citing collective security rules and Russia/China claiming that the United States is actually invoking rivalry and perhaps even war rules.

The overlap in rules between the social arrangements fueled this conflict. Specifically, the use of force rule—"the use of force is often necessary and acceptable to resolve conflicts"—holds in collective security arrangements, rivalry, and war. NATO's use of force was consistent with both U.S. justifications that NATO was invoking collective security rules and Russian and Chinese criticisms that NATO was invoking rivalry and/or rules. For the United States, NATO use of force was the appropriate way to enforce community rules regarding human rights. For Russia and China, NATO use of force was at least an attempt to dominate a global rivalry and at most an act of war consistent with imperialism. Both were rational interpretations from within the social arrangements each claimed were operative.

If interpretive methods explain action by specifying the rule(s) agents follow, then the dialogical analysis of the veto power conflict over Kosovo enables one to explain U.S. acts by specifying the collective security rules its speech acts invoked. Similarly, one can explain Russian and Chinese acts by specifying the rivalry and war rules their speech acts invoked. Finally, one can explain the entire conflict by specifying the difference and the overlap between the social arrangements.

Kosovo and Iraq

The debates about the use of force in Kosovo and Iraq do not seem similar on the surface. Kosovo was about human rights abuses and Iraq was about nonproliferation. But at the pragmatic level of the rules constituting global security, there are many stunning similarities. The three-stage Kosovo interaction occurred again regarding intervention in Iraq. First, there was a dispute about how to implement collective security given noncompliance with community rules: The United States (and Britain) advocated the use of force, and Russia and China (and France) advocated continued weapons inspections. Second, there was further debate about whether the use of force would actually invoke collective security rules: The United States and Britain argued that they would enforce the Security Council resolutions and disarm Iraq if the UN was unwilling to do so, with Russia, China, and France arguing that any use of force without Security Council authorization would violate international law and undermine international peace and security. Finally, there was a more fundamental disagreement about which social arrangement governed the interaction: The United States began the war in Iraq, and Russia, China, and France contended that the use of force deliberately invoked war rules because the United States never sincerely wanted a UN-centered enforcement of community rules.

The similarities between the two interactions also extend to the more detailed disputes. Table 4 lists both the disputed propositions generated by the pragmatic analysis of the Kosovo dispute and the restated propositions replacing "NATO" with "U.S." and "Yugoslavia" with "Iraq." The latter disputes reasonably characterize not only the global debate about the war in Iraq, but also the argumentative tasks facing the United States if it continues to widen its war on terrorism. The overall coherence of these disputed propositions regarding war in Iraq strongly suggests that the events of September 11 did not fundamentally change world politics. Instead, September 11 exacerbated already existing tensions prominently illustrated in the Kosovo interaction.

The reason for the similarities is the overlapping nature of the social arrangements constituting global security rules, particularly the use of force rule that exists in war, rivalry, and collective security arrangements. The United States was (again) trying to convince the international community that its use of force invokes collective security rules. Many in the international community were (again) interpreting the use of force to invoke war rules. Wittgenstein argues that the meaning of a term is defined by its

Table 4. Disputed Claims Over the Use of Force in Kosovo and Iraq

Security Rule	KOSOVO		IRAQ	
	United States	Russia/China	United States	Critics of War in Iraq
Identity	NATO countries are acting as citizens in our community	NATO countries are not acting as a citizen in our community	The U.S. is acting as a citizen in our community	The U.S. is not acting as a citizen in our community
Identity	NATO is sincerely acting as a citizen in our community	NATO is a rival (enemy?)	The U.S. is sincerely acting as a citizen in our community	The U.S. is a rival (enemy?)
Autonomy	NATO is obligated to enforce the rules of our community	NATO is not obligated to enforce the rules of our community	The U.S. is obligated to enforce the rules of our community	The U.S. is not obligated to enforce the rules of our community
Autonomy	NATO is sincerely enforcing the rules of our community	NATO does not recognize Yugoslav autonomy	The U.S. is sincerely enforcing the rules of our community	The U.S. does not recognize Iraqi autonomy
Nature of security	NATO is establishing security through an alliance commitment	NATO is not establishing security through an alliance commitment	The U.S. is establishing security through an alliance commitment	The U.S. is not establishing security through an alliance commitment
Nature of security	NATO is sincerely establishing security through an alliance commitment	NATO is trying to increase its relative alliance military capability	The U.S. is sincerely establishing security through an alliance commitment	The U.S. is trying to increase its relative alliance military capability
Deterrence	The NATO directive to Yugoslavia not to break the rules of our community is appropriate	The NATO directive to Yugoslavia not to break the rules of our community is not appropriate	The U.S. directive to Iraq not to break the rules of our community is appropriate	The U.S. directive to Iraq not to break the rules of our community is not appropriate
Enforcement	The NATO threat to retaliate against Yugoslavia is appropriate	The NATO threat to retaliate against Yugoslavia is not appropriate	The U.S. threat to retaliate against Iraq is appropriate	The U.S. threat to retaliate against Iraq is not appropriate
Use of force	The use of force is acceptable to resolve this conflict	The use of force is not acceptable to resolve this conflict	The use of force against Iraq is acceptable to resolve this conflict	The use of force against Iraq is not acceptable to resolve this conflict

use, by how speakers understand and use the term. In the post–cold war construction of collective security, the meaning of the use of force is defined by how agents understand the act. How will the international community interpret the use of force? Does it invoke collective security rules or war rules? In both the Kosovo and the Iraq debates, both sides asserted the validity of collective security rules but differed on whether U.S. use of force actually invoked those rules.

CONCLUSION

This paper makes three main contributions. First, it contributes to the constructivist research program by offering a tentative rule-oriented constructivist theory of global security asserting the existence of war, rivalry, collective security, and security community social arrangements. Second, it adds dialogical analysis to the growing toolkit of interpretive methods, using it to study the veto power debate over Kosovo. Third, it contributes to the policy debates about U.S. foreign policy after September 11, suggesting that preemption policies are premised on a flawed assumption that the events of September 11 fundamentally changed world politics. These three contributions are consistent with the tasks of rule-oriented constructivism: (1) assert the existence of social arrangements, (2) show how these rules make action intelligible, and (3) help agents "go on" in the world.

Within the context of constructivism, the rule-oriented theory of global security offered here modifies Wendt's argument for "three cultures" of world politics. Conceptualizing global security as constituted by four overlapping sets of social arrangements is necessary to understand the dominant security trends since the end of the cold war: movement away from the cold war rivalry and the gradual institutionalization of collective security rules. Wendt's Kantian culture includes both collective security and security communities, which are differentiated by (among other rules) the necessity and acceptability of the use of force. As the analysis above shows, however, the crux of the debates over Kosovo and Iraq is how the international community interprets the use of force in the post–cold war world. While the use of force is central to collective security, it is not conceivable in security communities. Wendt's Kantian culture hides this important distinction and thus cannot account for the argument presented here. Wendt's suggestions that world politics may be slowly moving toward a Kantian culture ignore the autonomy of collective security arrangements as an intermediate step in that process.

Dialogical analysis helps make the speech acts constructing post–cold war security intelligible by showing those acts to be logically consistent with the social rules—beliefs, norms, and identities—constituting global security structures. Dialogical analysis is one interpretive method capable of illustrating constructivist arguments because it adequately captures the social ontology of constructivism. It analyzes social interaction as a dialogue between communicatively rational actors who assert validity claims and evaluate others' validity claims. Through this interaction, linguistically competent agents challenge and/or perpetuate the rules constituting world politics. It does not assert causal explanations; instead, it explains action by specifying the (both regulative and constitutive) rule(s) that agents follow. It attempts to offer constructivists a nonrationalist, nonpositivist approach to analyze social interaction.

Finally, rule-oriented constructivism and dialogical analysis help provide practical insight into issues of global security. The analysis presented here casts doubt on justifications that a new post-9/11 world necessitates more aggressive, unilateral, and even preemptive U.S. policies. Instead, the war on terrorism is embedded within a larger post–cold war construction of global security rules. Tensions about the appropriate implementation of collective security rules to punish the global criminals who violate international rules existed before and after September 11. That the United States is now a direct victim of criminal acts does not change this larger context; instead it exacerbates already existing tensions because the United States is now that much more determined to enforce community rules against terrorism and nonproliferation.

This analysis suggests two broad trajectories for future global security rules. One possibility is that the international community will minimize these tensions, strengthen the post–cold war construction of collective security rules, and continue the "war" on terrorism through cooperative multilateral action. The other possibility is that U.S. use of force in Iraq, together with other likely uses of force in its "war" on terrorism, will break down the post–cold war construction of collective security rules and institutionalize some form of a war social arrangement.

The Bush administration is split about which direction it prefers. Of course, many in the administration are critical of "global governance" and prefer to weaken collective security rules because those rules limit the flexibility of U.S. foreign policy. Indeed, the Bush administration challenged emerging collective security rules in many ways prior to September 11 (e.g., rejection of the Anti-Ballistic Missile Treaty, the Kyoto Protocol, and the International Criminal Court). Constantly declaring a "war" on terrorism and using force in Iraq without Security Council authorization, at least on the surface, also weaken collective security rules and invoke a war social arrangement. Many in the administration continue to assert that September 11 fundamentally changed world politics, that the normal rules of collective security are no longer applicable, that a war social arrangement now governs global security, and that this new social arrangement justifies preemptive U.S. policies.

However, a terrorist event, even a horrific one, cannot automatically change the rules of global security. Even U.S. foreign policy, although tremendously important, cannot unilaterally construct a war social arrangement through declarations of a "war on terrorism" or even by invading Iraq. Social rules are constantly negotiated and mediated through the actions of many agents. Whether future global security rules are constituted by collective security rules or by war rules is always being negotiated and renegotiated. The analysis presented here suggests that the post–cold war rules governing global security remain strikingly similar after September 11. As in Kosovo, the United States sought Security Council authorization prior to intervention in Iraq. And as in Kosovo, the veto powers struggled with which rule violations should trigger multilateral intervention and how to appropriately implement collective security rules. The international community clearly prefers collective security rules over a unilateral U.S. war on terrorism.

The United States must consider this underlying context in which it is fighting its war on terrorism and how others will interpret its use of force. Continuing to claim that September 11 fundamentally changed world politics and advocating unilateralism may eventually convince others that global security is indeed constituted by rules of war. Such a world would only discourage many from cooperating with the United States in other areas of the war on terrorism. The United States is more likely to be successful in its war on terrorism by embracing rather than ignoring the emerging collective security norms and institutions.

NOTES

1. The final draft of this paper was written in April during the beginning of the war in Iraq.

2. For more comprehensive surveys see Checkel 1998, Farrell 2002, Finnemore and Sikkink 2001, and Hopf 1998.

3. A fourth validity claim of speech acts studied by linguists, but less useful for dialogic analysis, is "grammaticality."

4. Rule-oriented constructivism does not assume that Habermas' notion of communicative action within an ideal speech situation characterizes world politics. For Habermas, communicative action is action oriented toward mutual understanding and coordinated by a consensus on all validity claims. Risse (2000) analyzes whether Habermas' conditions for communicative action (lack of power relations, noncoerced consensus, etc.) resemble interactions in world politics. I do not assert the existence of communicative action in this sense. The Kosovo debate does not illustrate communicative action; the claims about whether intervention is consistent with existing security rules are constantly disputed. What is important, though, is that the agents invoke collective security rules to justify their acts. Their action is meaningful only within the context of (albeit disputed) collective security rules.

5. Pragmatically conveyed propositions include reflexive intentions, implicatures, presuppositions, and logical entailments. For reasons of space, the analysis presented here includes only implicatures. See Duffy, Frederking, and Tucker (1998) and Frederking (2000) for a discussion of how to generate a full-fledged pragmatic analysis.

6. Future work on this method will explore whether these maxims apply to all political rhetoric. More generally constructivists must deal with rationalist critics who emphasize "cheap talk" and realist critics who emphasize "uncertainty" as reasons not to rely on a linguistic conception of social interaction.

7. Myers, Steven Lee, and Steven Erlanger, "U.S. Is Stepping Up Military Threats Against the Serbs," *New York Times,* 7 October 1998, sec. A1.

8. Bohlen, Celestine, "Russia Vows to Block the UN from Backing Attack on Serbs," *New York Times,* 7 October 1998, sec. A10.

9. See Clinton 1999.

10. Gordon, Michael, "Conflict in the Balkans: Russian Anger Tempered by the Need for Cash," *New York Times,* 25 March 1999, sec. A1.

11. Eckholm, Eric, "Conflict in the Balkans: Bombing May Have Hardened China's Line," *New York Times,* 18 May 1999, sec. A11.

12. A more complete analysis, including reflexive intentions, implicatures, and presuppositions, as well as explanations for each reference, is at http://faculty.mckendree.edu/brian_frederking/kosovo.htm.

REFERENCES

Adler, Emanuel. 1992. "The Emergence of Cooperation: National Epistemic Communities and the International Evolution of the Idea of Nuclear Arms Control." *International Organization* 46 (Winter): 367–90.

Adler, Emanuel. 1997. "Seizing the Middle Ground: Constructivism and World Politics." *European Journal of International Politics* 3 (September): 319–63.

Adler, Emanuel, and Michael Barnett, eds. 1998. *Security Communities.* Cambridge: Cambridge University Press.

Albright, Madeline. 1999. "After Kosovo: Building a Lasting Peace." U.S. State Department, June 28; secretary.state.gov/www/statements/1999/990628.html.

Alker, Hayward. 1988. "The Dialectical Logic of Thucydides' Melian Dialogue." *American Political Science Review* 82 (September): 3–27.

Alker, Hayward. 1996. *Rediscoveries and Reformulations.* Cambridge: Cambridge University Press.

Austin, John L. 1962. *How to Do Things with Words.* Cambridge, MA: MIT Press.

Barnett, Michael. 1995. "Sovereignty, Nationalism, and Regional Order in the Arab States System." *International Organization* 49 (Summer): 479–510.

Berger, Peter L., and Thomas Luckmann. 1966. *The Social Construction of Reality: A Treatise in the Sociology of Knowledge.* New York: Anchor Books.

Bukovansky, Mlada. 2001. *Ideas and Power Politics: The American and French Revolutions in International Political Culture.* Princeton, NJ: Princeton University Press.

Bull, Hedley. 1977. *Anarchical Society.* London: Macmillan.

Campbell, David. 1992. *Writing Security: United States Foreign Policy and the Politics of Identity.* Minneapolis: University of Minnesota Press.

Carpenter, Ted Galen. 2000. "Damage to Relations with Russia and China." In *NATO's Empty Victory,* ed. Ted Galen Carpenter. Washington, DC: Cato, 77–91.

Checkel, Jeffrey. 1998. "The Constructivist Turn in International Relations Theory." *World Politics* 50 (2): 324–48.

Chomsky, Noam. 1999. *The New Military Humanism.* London: Pluto Press.

Clinton, William J. 1999. "Address to the Nation." *Washington Post,* June 11: A31.

Crawford, Neta C. 2002. *Argument and Change in World Politics: Ethics, Decolonization and Humanitarian Intervention.* Cambridge: Cambridge University Press.

Daalder, Ivo, and Michael O'Hanlon. 2000. *Winning Ugly.* Washington, DC: Brookings Institution.

Dessler, David. 1999. "Constructivism within a Positivist Social Science." *Review of International Studies* 25 (1): 123–37.

Deutsch, Karl. 1957. *Political Community and the North Atlantic Area.* Princeton, NJ: Princeton University Press.

Doty, Roxanne Lynn. 1993. "Foreign Policy as Social Construction: A Post-Positivist Analysis of US Counterinsurgency Policy in the Philippines." *International Studies Quarterly* 37 (September): 297–320.

Duffy, Gavan, ed. 1994. "New Directions in Event Data Analysis." *International Interactions* 20 (1): 1–167.

Duffy, Gavan, Brian Frederking, and Seth Tucker. 1998. "Language Games: Analyzing the INF Treaty Negotiations." *International Studies Quarterly* 42 (2): 271–94.

Farrell, Theo. 2002. "Constructivist Security Studies: Portrait of a Research Program." *International Studies Review* 4 (1): 49–72.

Fetzer, Anita. 2000. "Negotiating Validity Claims in Political Interviews." *Text* 20 (4): 415–60.

Fierke, Karin. 2000. "Logics of Force and Dialogue: The Iraq/UNSCOM Crisis as Social Interaction." *European Journal of International Relations* 6 (3): 335–71.

Fierke, Karin M. 2001. "Critical Methodology and Constructivism." In *Constructing International Relations: The Next Generation,* ed. Karin M. Fierke and Knud Erik Jorgenson. New York: M. E. Sharpe.

Fierke, Karin M. N.d. "Beyond Agents and Structures: Logics, Rationality and the End of the Cold War." Unpublished manuscript.

Finnemore, Martha. 1996. *National Interests in International Society.* Ithaca, NY: Cornell University Press.

Finnemore, Martha, and Kathryn Sikkink. 2001. "Taking Stock: The Constructivist Research Program in International Relations and Comparative Politics." *Annual Reviews of Political Science* 4: 391–416.

Frederking, Brian. 2000. *Resolving Security Dilemmas: A Constructivist Interpretation of the INF Treaty.* London: Ashgate.

Grice, Herbert P. 1957. "Meaning." *Philosophical Review* 64 (3): 377–88.

Guzzini, Stefano. 2000. "A Reconstruction of Constructivism in International Relations." *European Journal of International Relations* 6 (2): 147–82.

Habermas, Jurgen. 1984. *Theory of Communicative Action.* New York: Beacon.

Habermas, Jurgen. 1987. *Theory of Communicative Action II.* New York: Beacon.

Heinze, Eric, and Douglas A. Borer. 2002. "The Chechen Exception: Rethinking Russia's Human Rights Policy." *Politics* 22 (2): 86–94.

Hollis, Martin, and Steve Smith. 1991. *Explaining and Understanding International Relations.* Oxford: Clarendon.

Hopf, Ted. 1998. "The Promise of Constructivism in International Relations Theory." *International Security* 23 (Summer): 171–200.

Hopf, Ted. 2002. *Social Construction of International Politics: Identities and Foreign Policies, Moscow, 1955 & 1999.* Ithaca, NY: Cornell University Press.

Jacobsen, John. 1995. "Much Ado About Ideas: The Cognitive Factor in Economic Policy." *World Politics* 47 (January): 283–310.

Katzenstein, Peter J., ed. 1996. *The Culture of National Security: Norms and Identity in World Politics*. New York: Columbia University Press.

Keck, Margaret, and Kathryn Sikkink. 1998. *Activists beyond Borders: Advocacy Networks in International Politics*. Ithaca, NY: Cornell University Press.

Klotz, Audie. 1995. *Norms in International Relations: The Struggle against Apartheid*. Ithaca, NY: Cornell University Press.

Kratochwil, Friedrich. 1989. *Norms, Rules and Decisions*. Cambridge: Cambridge University Press.

Kratochwil, Friedrich. 2000. "Constructing a New Orthodoxy? Wendt's 'Social Theory of International Politics' and the Constructivist Challenge." *Millennium* 29 (1): 73–101.

Kratochwil, Friedrich, and Rey Koslowski. 1994. "Understanding Change and International Politics: The Soviet Empire's Demise and the International System." *International Organization* 48 (Spring): 215–47.

Kubalkova, Vendulka. 2001. "The Twenty Years' Cartharsis," In *Constructing International Relations: The Next Generation,* ed. Karin M. Fierke and Knud Erik Jorgenson. New York: M. E. Sharpe, 37–69.

Mattern, Janice Bially. 2001. "The Power Politics of Identity," *European Journal of International Relations* 7 (3): 349–97.

Onuf, Nicholas Greenwood. 1989. *World of Our Making*. Columbia: University of South Carolina Press.

Onuf, Nicholas Greenwood. 1998. "Constructivism: A User's Manual." In *International Relations in a Constructed World,* ed. Vendulka Kubalkova et al. London: M. E. Sharpe, 58–78.

Onuf, Nicholas. 2002. "Worlds of Our Making: The Strange Career of Constructivism in International Relations." In *Visions of International Relations,* ed. Donald Puchala. Columbia: University of South Carolina Press, 119–41.

Palan, Ronen. 2000. "A World of Their Making: An Evaluation of the Constructivist Critique in International Relations." *Review of International Studies* 26 (4): 575–98.

Price, Richard, and Nina Tannenwald. 1996. "Constructing Norms of Humanitarian Intervention." In *The Culture of National Security,* ed. Peter J. Katzenstein. New York: Columbia University Press.

Rescher, Nicholas. 1977. *Dialectics*. Albany: State University of New York Press.

Risse, Thomas. 2000. "Let's Argue!: Communicative Action in World Politics." *International Organization* 54 (Winter): 1–39.

Risse, Thomas, Stephen C. Ropp, and Kathryn Sikkink, eds. 1999. *The Power of Human Rights: International Norms and Domestic Change*. Cambridge: Cambridge University Press.

Risse-Kappen, Thomas. 1997. *Cooperation among Democracies: The European Influence on US Foreign Policy*. Princeton, NJ: Princeton University Press.

Ruggie, John Gerard. 1998. *Constructing the World Polity*. New York: Routledge.

Ruggie, John Gerard, and Friedrich Kratochwil. 1986. "The State of the Art on the Art of the State." *International Organization* 40 (Autumn): 753–75.

Schelling, Thomas. 1960. *The Strategy of Conflict*. Cambridge: Harvard University Press.

Searle, John. 1969. *Speech Acts*. Cambridge: Cambridge University Press.

Searle, John. 1995. *The Social Construction of Reality*. New York: Free Press.

Sikkink, Kathryn. 1991. *Ideas and Institutions: Developmentalism in Brazil and Argentina*. Ithaca, NY: Cornell University Press.

Waller, Michael, Kyril Drezov, and Bulent Gokay, eds. 2001. *Kosovo: Politics of Delusion*. London: Frank Cass.

Weldes, Jutta. 1999. *Constructing National Interests: The United States and the Cuban Missile Crisis*. Minneapolis: University of Minnesota Press.

Wendt, Alexander. 1995. "Constructing International Politics." *International Security* 20 (1): 71–81.

Wendt, Alexander. 1999. *Social Theory of International Politics*. Cambridge: Cambridge University Press.

Wittgenstein, Ludwig. 1968. *Philosophical Investigations*. Oxford: Blackwell.

Reading 9-4

A New Security Landscape
The End of the Post–Cold War Era
François Heisbourg

The security landscape faced by the United States and its European and Asian allies is undergoing basic change which is bringing to a close both the legacy of the Cold War and the transition period of the 1990s. The scope and the depth of this transformation are due to the fact that basic elements of this landscape are shifting simultaneously:

- The threat situation is characterized *inter alia* by the ability of non-state actors to wreak mass destruction. What was a risk prior to 9/11 is now a clear and present danger which challenges the traditional categories of internal security and military defense;

- The nature and contents of the relationships between the United States and its European and Asian allies are undergoing a deep revision, which puts into question both the transatlantic institutions and the political and strategic rationale which has underpinned them for more than sixty years.

These categories of change naturally interact with each other, and are also heavily influenced by other factors, both external (for example, Russia, China, and the Middle East) and internal (for example, demographics, most notably in the form of ageing populations).

CONTINUITIES AND CHANGES IN INTER-STATE SECURITY RISKS

If one confines oneself to conflict between states, three major sources of insecurity represent ever clearer and more present dangers:

- The exacerbation of contradictions in the traditional Maghreb-to-Pakistan "arc of crisis";

- The spread of nuclear weapons and the attendant risk of a breakdown of the existing non-proliferation regime, together with a similar evolution in the biological arena;

- The possible use of nuclear weapons in Asia, and its consequences for Europe.

The "Arc of Crisis" under Strain

In the late 1970s, the expression "arc of crisis" was coined by Zbigniew Brzezinski (among others) to characterize the combination of political Islam (such as the Iranian revolution of 1979), poor (sometimes atrocious) governance, the Israeli-Arab confrontation, and the control of much of the world's oil.

Moreover, the level of crisis in the region is set to rise with the increase in social, economic, political, and military tensions and contradictions. The associated risks call for greater European and Asian involvement. These risks include:

SOURCE: From "A New Security Landscape: The End of the Post–Cold War Era" by François Heisbourg, *Asia-Pacific Review*, vol. 10, no. 1 (May 2003): 52–63. Copyright © 2003 by Taylor and Francis, Ltd. (www.tandf.co.uk/journals). Reprinted by permission.

- The runaway demography of the *"états-rentiers"* of the Persian Gulf, and notably of Saudi Arabia, means that "performance legitimacy" has decreased sharply, while democratic legitimacy is non-existent in many states. Although countries such as Tunisia, Algeria, and Iran are now entering into demographic transition, with rapidly falling birth rates, such is not the case in the Gulf states, where most of the oil lies. Internal stability can only suffer as a result, particularly when the economies of the region appear to be, with few exceptions (most prominently Dubai and Qatar), incapable of benefiting from the forces of globalization.

- The weakening of broad-based political Islam[1] and the rise of more narrowly based but ultra-violent—even apocalyptic—radical minorities such as the GIA and the Salafists in Algeria, and al-Qaeda and its affiliates in Saudi Arabia.

- The incentive of relatively poorer countries to go directly to the "bottom line" in terms of military power: for a country like Iran, the acquisition of ballistic missiles and nuclear weapons may be a cheaper alternative to a replication of the Shah's policy of acquiring enormously expensive arrays of conventional combat aircraft, helicopters, and armored vehicles. Proliferation is an equalizer of power.

All these trends are unfolding against the backdrop of a region in which many states do not appear to have struck deep roots in terms of national identity: ideocratic dictatorships such as Syria, Iraq, Libya, and Saudi Arabia have been in existence for a shorter time-span than the total lifetime of the USSR. This post-Ottoman order is inherently fragile. Naturally, outside action—such as a US military invasion of Iraq—could precipitate the violent collapse of these legacy states whose only success has been in the ruthless suppression of civil society. In the absence of the sort of democratic or liberal forces which existed in the European satellite states of the USSR (and even to some extent within the USSR itself), change in the greater Middle East will on average be considerably more violent and war-generating than was the case with the collapse of the former Soviet empire.

In this context, it is worth recalling that the world's dependence on Middle Eastern oil is not going to diminish in the near future. Today, as in the previous quarter of a century, more than half of the world's oil exports come from the Gulf states. Furthermore, there is approximate parity in the levels of American, European, and East Asian dependency in terms of oil imports, with each of the three regions importing approximately nine million barrels a day (Mbd). China's and India's rising oil imports will increase the role of the Middle East as the world's petrol station.

Proliferation of Weapons of Mass Destruction (WMD): From Comparative Success to Prospective Breakdown

If one compares the situation surrounding the proliferation of weapons of mass destruction today with that which prevailed a quarter of a century ago, one is struck by the relatively high degree of success achieved through non-proliferation efforts, particularly when contrasted with previously prevailing forecasts.[2]

In 2002 the list of states possessing (or close to possessing) nuclear weapons was shorter than it was in 1975. India, Pakistan, and Israel were already on the list. Brazil, Argentina, South Africa (which produced six Hiroshima-type bombs during the 1980s), Taiwan and South Korea have dropped off the list, while North Korea, Iraq, and possibly Iran have been added to it, at least for the time being. Furthermore, the Nuclear Non-Proliferation Treaty (NPT) has become a quasi-universal norm, with only four non-signatory states (India, Israel, Pakistan, and Cuba) out of 191. This is in marked contrast to the situation that existed a quarter of a century ago.[3] In the field of chemical weapons (CW), the 1995 treaty banning CW has laid the ground for the chemical disarmament of existing stockpiles (notably in Russia, the US, India, and South Korea). Ballistic missile proliferation is occurring in the three *de facto* nuclear states (Israel, India, and Pakistan) as well as in Iran and North Korea. However, during the 1970s and the 1980s, Scud, Frog, and SS-21 missiles were exported by the USSR to over 20 countries (ranging from Algeria to Vietnam), while China exported 2500 km-range CSS-2s to Saudi Arabia. Missile proliferation on this scale is no longer occurring.

However, this comparison does not provide a good indication of what is in store in the future. First, and most importantly, in Asia nuclear proliferation is on the brink of becoming the norm rather than the exception. Alongside the traditional Maghreb-to-Pakistan arc of crisis, there is an emerging nuclear arc of crisis extending from Israel to Northeast Asia; two of the five official nuclear powers (Russia and China), the three *de facto* nuclear powers (Israel, India, and Pakistan), the two nuclear "wannabes" (Iraq and North Korea, who both violated the NPT in their quest for nuclear power), and a suspected candidate for nuclear power (Iran) are all located in Asia. Countries which have renounced the nuclear option, either willingly (Japan) or under outside pressure (South Korea and Taiwan), could feel compelled to revisit the issue. And if the international NPT regime breaks down in Asia, it will break down elsewhere as well. This is one of the reasons why Iran—and therefore Europe's relationship with that country—has become pivotal. Up until now, the non-proliferation regime has held (albeit just barely in Asia), with Iraq being forcefully deprived of its nuclear program and with North Korea having been induced to put its own ambitions on hold. The three *de facto* nuclear powers could be considered to have not violated the norm, since they had never subscribed to it in the first place. However, if Iran—a fully-fledged NPT member—goes nuclear without having been convinced to do otherwise by effective international action, then the whole NPT edifice is likely to come crashing down. The recent revelations regarding North Korea's gas centrifuge uranium enrichment program are particularly disturbing in this context, all the more so since there is reason to believe that North Korea and Pakistan have engaged in two-way technology transfers in both the nuclear and missile arenas. The possession of nuclear weapons by all powers capable of acquiring them would then become commonplace. This would have serious consequences, not only for Asia but also for Europe, most of whose countries have foregone the nuclear military option.[4]

In parallel, research and production of biological weapons (BW), although renounced by 144[5] members of the international community under the 1972 Biological Weapons Treaty, is unfettered by any verification regime. As is now known, the treaty was massively and deliberately violated by the USSR from the day it was signed.[6] Iraq has also done so from the late 1980s onwards. It cannot be assumed that certain other countries (as yet unrevealed) have been any more respectful of the BW ban.

Naturally, the combination of enhanced WMD proliferation and the aggravation of tensions in the greater Middle East represents a particular challenge to the European nations. Their armed forces and defense strategies are not currently adapted to such an evolution, with the limited exception of the deterrence capability provided by the French and British nuclear forces.

In the case of all these types of weaponry (nuclear weapons included), proliferation carries with it an increased risk of their use. Doubtless there is some reassurance to be drawn from the strength of the factors which explain why nuclear weapons have not been used since 1945. However, the increase in the number of nuclear actors increases the inherent generic risks of their use (whether accidental, inadvertent, or deliberate) in geometrical progression; moreover, the specific danger of the use of nuclear weapons is greater in certain circumstances than in others. The India-Pakistan situation is in most ways (strategically, politically, and technically) ' more conductive to the use of nuclear weapons than was the East-West confrontation during the Cold War. The European and Asian allies all need to reflect on the consequences that the breaking of the nuclear taboo would have on international security, particularly in terms of their own strategic postures.

HYPER-TERRORISM: THE ACQUISITION OF WEAPONS OF MASS DESTRUCTION BY NON-STATE ACTORS

A New Level of Threat by Non-Deterrable Actors

The preceding security risks have been viewed entirely through the prism of traditional state-to-state interactions. Since 11 September 2001, non-state actors have demonstrated the will and the capability to wreak mass destruction (even though the tools used to obliterate two skyscrapers containing in excess of 60,000 workspaces were purely conventional). No doubt the risk had already been present, with operations such as the first al-Qaeda attack against the Twin Towers in 1993, the attempt by Algerian terrorists to crash an Air France Airbus into the Eiffel Tower in 1994, and the nerve gas attacks by the Aum Shinrikyo sect in Matsumoto and Tokyo in the mid-1990s. However, the threat became real with the 9/11 attacks, followed by the separate anthrax attacks a few weeks later (which were apparently intended to disrupt rather than destroy).

Naturally, this form of empowerment of non-state actors does not exist on a purely stand-alone basis: it interacts with the strategies of state actors, from the Taliban of Afghanistan to the adversaries in the India-Pakistan confrontation—analysis of which can no longer be carried out purely in terms of state-to-state relations, but must now also integrate the strategy of al-Qaeda and its regional affiliates.

However, the hyper-terrorist threat is highly specific in terms of its consequences for security policy.

Non-state actors attempting to wage mass destruction terrorism, such as Aum in Japan or al-Qaeda and its affiliates, cannot be countered using the same set of policies as those which apply to antagonists controlling a state, along with its territory and population. Thus, the following policy tools are essentially inoperative:

- Deterrence, through the possible use of weapons of mass destruction. Nuclear deterrence is irrelevant against groups whose operating bases are often in the heart of the targeted country;

- Containment of the threat by the deployment of military forces, as in Central Europe during the Cold War;

- Diplomatic and strategic balancing of the threat by a third power.

In the absence of such options, the tools available to policymakers are essentially the following:

- Detection of potential and actual perpetration, through accurate and relevant intelligence and analysis;

- Prevention, including upstream action (addressing so-called root causes by economic, political, and ideological means);

- Pre-emption, entailing operations (by police or military forces) against a group (and those who aid and abet it) while it is still preparing for action;

- Interception and repression of the perpetrators before or after their "hit";

- Damage limitation, through timely and effective "hardening" of the terrorists' objective;

- Damage confinement and "consequence management" (to use an American expression) after a terrorist attack, through identification of the nature of the attack and the efficient conduct of rescue operations.

This set of approaches lies in stark contrast with those—both military and political—which animate relations between potentially antagonistic states.

Dealing with these topics will require significant departures from existing defense policies and strategic cultures in all of the industrialized countries.

Internal Security and External Security: From Discontinuity to Convergence

One of the consequences which flow from the emergence of the threat of destruction by non-state actors, is the transformation of the "traditional" (or more accurately the "Westphalian") divide between the external and internal dimensions of state security. In practice, as well as in the popular perception, the discontinuity between these two realms is no longer tenable, since the non-state antagonist works from within the targeted society while also operating across borders. This new paradigm carries with it three basic and closely related international implications:

- Although the tools of military force projection will continue to be materially distinct from those of internal police action, the basic facets of counter-terrorism (prevention, pre-emption, repression, and damage limitation) will have to be considered in an integrated manner. Furthermore, domestic security and external defense machinery will have to be tightly coordinated, since counter-terrorism involves a broad array of fields (such as the economic, financial, diplomatic, political, judicial, police, intelligence, and defense fields) which often cut across the external/internal divide. In the French case, this is beginning to happen with the establishment, at the Presidential level, of a "Conseil de Sécurité Intérieure" alongside the "Conseil de Défense";

- Cross-border terrorism can only be met through cross-border counteraction;

- Cross-border non-state violence cannot be effectively countered without the cooperation of other cross-border non-state actors, such as the banking community and the transportation industry.

Taken together, these factors imply a transformation of pre-9/11 approaches to security and defense.

ALLIANCES AND PARTNERSHIPS

The US and Its Allies: Mission-Driven Coalitions versus Permanent Alliances

Along with the threat situation, the nature and content of strategic partnerships between the US and its European and Asian allies are also undergoing transformation.

In the aftermath of 9/11, US policy was officially encapsulated by Donald Rumsfeld's and Paul Wolfowitz's stark formula "It's the mission that makes the coalition." Although unobjectionable given the requirements of the time (war had to be waged swiftly and decisively with the means immediately at hand against the Taliban and the al-Qaeda bases in Afghanistan), this was a basic departure from pre-9/11 rhetoric. The Bush administration's propensity for avoiding legally binding foreign commitments had not hitherto openly extended to US military alliances.

In other words, there is a trend away from old-style alliances functioning as automatic defense pacts and war-machines: this evolution is particularly clear in the case of NATO, but also applies to East Asia.

This trend does not necessarily entail strategic decoupling between North America and its Asian and European allies. There are, however, two ways in which strategic solidarity could be undermined: one way would be the deliberate disregard of the basic interests of one's partners (for example, heedless protectionism versus free trade, or the systematic undermining of all rule-based attempts at regulating the international system); the other (more prosaic) way would be the display of a lack of interest in using the machinery which allows the forces of the allied countries to work together when the need arises.

The Limits of Power: Prevention and Pre-emption

In his State of the Union speech of 29 January 2002, President Bush outlined a new US strategy of prevention[8] for coping with the threat of mass destruction from terrorist groups and states supporting them. This major turning point drew little public attention at the time, given the *brouhaha* provoked by the "axis of evil" formula. However, the fundamental nature of the shift became more apparent with the prominence and detailed treatment given to pre-emption and prevention in President Bush's speech at the West Point Military Academy on 1 June 2002.[9] This raises several connected (but analytically distinct) questions, the answers to which each have potentially major consequences for the US-European relationship:

- Can self-defense, in the sense of Article 51 of the UN Charter,[10] be legitimately extended to first-strike policies? And, as a companion question, will the answer be the same if the strike is effected against a non-state actor rather than against a state?[11]

- Independently of international jurisprudence, is there any strategically viable alternative to prevention and pre-emption when facing non-state actors who cannot, by definition, be deterred, and who, if unchecked, could inflict an unacceptably high degree of damage on society (through the use of nuclear or biological weapons, for example)? If (and one is tempted to write "Since" instead of "If") the answer to this second question is: "No, there is no acceptable alternative.", what will be the effect of that answer on the previous question concerning Article 51? Even though pre-existing Article 51 jurisprudence does not cover actions such as Israel's preventive strike against the Osirak nuclear reactor in 1981,[12] given the emergence of non-state threats of mass destruction, it is possible that a new jurisprudence could be generated, if need be, via discussion in the UN Security Council.

- What kind of action does prevention cover? If pre-emption (striking the adversary before the adversary strikes) is clearly of a forceful nature (entailing military or police action), prevention can cover a much broader range of largely non-forceful actions. In this regard, not only will the European nations emphasize non-military prevention, through economic and political means, they will also be extraordinarily reticent towards forceful action which might use prevention as a pretext rather than as a demonstrable necessity against a clear and present danger;

- What would the primary geographical points of application of a pre-emptive strategy be? Along with Iraq, the tentative answers provided by the State of the Union speech are "North Korea and Iran." This approach drew vigorous negative reaction from European and Asian officials. However, such condemnations do not in themselves constitute an alternative strategy for dealing with the post-9/11 threat of non-state actors.

After 9/11, just as before, the evolution of China is America's most important long-term strategic concern. Although 9/11 has downgraded this concern in the public eye and has displaced the administration's day-to-day attention, the "China question" remains. Indeed, in some ways it has been exacerbated by the consequences of the fight against al-Qaeda: not only is the US now militarily present in Central Asia, but in addition it has tightened its overall relationship with Russia, while also flexing its diplomatic muscles in South Asia. This is another way of saying that US relations with its European and Japanese partners will be largely shaped by the manner in which America's allies act (or do not act) in a manner congruent with Washington's China policy.

Although China holds the key, Russia (by virtue of its location, size, population, energy resources, and nuclear status) is also an essential player—much more so than one might conclude from Russia's weak economic state.

Its unresolved territorial dispute with Japan notwithstanding, Russia no longer constitutes an adversary for the US and the Europeans. In terms of its conventional military means it is incapable of presenting a challenge. (Even a middle-sized state such as Poland is arguably more than capable of facing a hypothetical conventional Russian threat.) Furthermore, under President Putin's stewardship, Russia has clearly decided to avoid even the slightest hint of hostility, for instance in response to the enlargement of NATO to the Baltic states, or to the fate of the Anti-Ballistic Missile (ABM) Treaty. Even if Putin's "modernization first" policy were to be discarded in favor of an anti-western stance in geostrategic[13] or military terms, it can be assumed that Russia's GDP base would not allow it to reconstitute conventional forces of any significant power within ten years of any decision to do so. The nuclear dimension, however, represents a serious problem, less because of Russia's nuclear strength (which can readily be met by Western nuclear deterrence) than because of Russia's weakness. Indeed, given the basic interests of the EU and Japan, they should be investing at a level comparable with the United States in programs to reduce the risk of criminal or inadvertent dissemination of Russian nuclear, chemical, and biological weapons, material, and know-how. The US spends approximately $5.8 billion in the former Soviet Union within the framework of the Cooperative Threat Reduction program. Comparable spending by EU states and Japan represents less than 10 percent of the US figure—hence the G8 proposal for a so-called "10+10+10 program" ($10 billion from the US plus $10 billion from the other G7 partners spent over a 10-year period). This was underscored at the G7/G8 Summit in Canada in June 2002.

Irrespective of whether Russia moves closer to NATO, the industrialized world will face the indirect security consequences of Russia's positioning as a Eurasian power. These principally involve energy policy (and its Middle Eastern ramifications) and relations with China.

Russian prime minister Mikhail Kasyanov has suggested[14] that, over time, his country could become an alternative energy source which might alleviate the West's dependence on Saudi Arabia. Given that Russia's oil production has decreased by more than 25 percent since its Soviet-era peak in 1986 (7.06 Mbd in 2001 compared to 9.32 Mbd in 1991), this remains a highly theoretical objective. In 2001, oil exports from the former Soviet Union (75 percent of which come from Russia) stood at 4.7 Mbd—only

60 percent of the level of Saudi Arabia's oil exports; more significantly, however, Russia's proven oil reserves represent less than 5 percent of the world's total, compared to Saudi Arabia's 25 percent share.[15]

The fact remains that, given the prospect of heightened instability in the Middle East, the EU and Japan would be well advised to focus political, legal, and financial efforts on oil prospecting and the acquisition of investment rights in Russia, as well as on more traditional imports of Russian gas.

The Chinese dimension of the West's relationship with Russia is political and strategic in nature. Although for the moment this involves the US rather than America's allies (with the Western force presence in Central Asia seen by China as a US-led challenge), America's allies will have to pay close attention to the spin-off effects of US policies towards Russia. During the 1990s, notably under Prime Minister Primakov, the fashion in Moscow was to "threaten" the West with a countervailing strategic partnership between Russia and China (to which was added, with some audacity, India, which has excellent relations with Russia, but not with China). This would have been an unpleasant prospect, had it corresponded to a serious reality: as things were, there was no such axis in practice, although substantial transfers of Russian technology and arms to China were not helpful from the standpoint of US interests. This multipolar Russian balancing act is no longer invoked. Indeed, the risk could now run in the opposite direction, with an evolution whereby Russia might attempt to instrumentalize its European and Japanese neighbours as partners to counter the economical and demographic challenges posed in the Russian Far East by an emergent China. This is a prospect, not a reality. However, the allied European and Asian countries will want to think through this dimension of their relations with Russia, given what it might entail for their relationship with China.

From this overview of the new security landscape, several general implications can be drawn.

1. The intensity of risks and threats has risen substantially, necessitating new organizational and budgetary initiatives within each of the European and Asian allies.

2. Current security challenges erode the traditional Westphalian distinction between the external and internal aspects of security and defense policy. This must in turn lead to a much higher degree of institutional and organizational congruence between domestic and external security and defense policy.

3. Military alliances are not configured to cope with these challenges; indeed, the United States is not relying on NATO to do so in Europe. However, military alliances should continue to play an important role as a provider of interoperability between US forces and those of their European and Asian partners.

4. The US military effort will continue to focus heavily on the greater Asian region, in view of US energy interests in the Middle East and Central Asia, nuclear instability in South Asia, and US economic and strategic interests in the Asia-Pacific area.

NOTES

1. For more on this subject, see Gilles Kepel, *Jihad: The Trail of Political Islam* (Harvard University Press, 2003).

2. Typical of these was the statement by President John F. Kennedy in 1963 that 15 to 20 nations could acquire nuclear weapons within a decade.

3. In 1977 fifty-two UN member states were not parties to the NPT.

4. The nuclear option was most seriously

considered by Sweden (which had the full nuclear military fuel cycle in place by the end of the 1960s), and to a lesser extent by Switzerland (in the mid-1950s) and West Germany (in 1957–58, in cooperation with France and Italy).

5. Notable exceptions are Egypt, Israel, Kazakhstan, Sudan, and Syria.

6. See Ken Alibek [Alibekov] with Stephen Handelman, *Biohazard* (New York, 1998).

7. For more on this subject, see V. R. Raghavan, "Limited War and Nuclear Escalation in South Asia," *The New Proliferation Review* Vol. 8, No. 3 (Fall-Winter 2001), Monterrey Institute of International Studies.

8. "We must prevent the terrorists and the regimes who seek chemical, biological or nuclear weapons from threatening the United States and the world."

9. In the West Point speech, President Bush did not name Iraq, Iran, or North Korea, nor did he mention the "axis of evil."

10. Article 51 recognizes "the inherent right of individual or collective self-defense if an armed attack occurs against a member of the UN."

11. Article 51 does not raise the issue of the state or non-state nature of an armed attack. However, Resolution 1368 of the Security Council (12 September 2001) applied Article 51 to the (non-state) attacks against the Twin Towers and the Pentagon.

12. Israel invoked Article 51 at the time, but was condemned by the UN Security Council, including the US.

13. Such as an attempted *rapprochement* with China.

14. Speech at the World Economic Forum, New York, 2 February 2002.

15. Source for all energy figures: *BP 2002 Statistical Review.*

10

✵

Economy

Reading 10-1

Economic Interdependence and War
A Theory of Trade Expectations
Dale C. Copeland

Does economic interdependence increase or decrease the probability of war among states? With the Cold War over, this question is taking on importance as trade levels between established powers such as the United States and Russia and emerging powers such as Japan, China, and Western Europe grow to new heights. In this article, I provide a new dynamic theory to help overcome some of the theoretical and empirical problems with current liberal and realist views on the question.

The prolonged debate between realists and liberals on the causes of war has been largely a debate about the relative salience of different causal variables. Realists stress such factors as relative power, while liberals focus on the absence or presence of collective security regimes and the pervasiveness of democratic communities.[1] Economic interdependence is the only factor that plays an important causal role in the thinking of both camps, and their perspectives are diametrically opposed.

Liberals argue that economic interdependence lowers the likelihood of war by in-

SOURCE: From "Economic Interdependence and War: A Theory of Trade Expectations" by Dale C. Copeland, *International Security*, vol. 20, no. 4 (Spring 1996): 5–41. Copyright © 1996 President and Fellows of Harvard College and the Massachusetts Institute of Technology. Reprinted by permission of the MIT Press Journals.

creasing the value of trading over the alternative of aggression: interdependent states would rather trade than invade. As long as high levels of interdependence can be maintained, liberals assert, we have reason for optimism. Realists dismiss the liberal argument, arguing that high interdependence increases rather than decreases the probability of war. In anarchy, states must constantly worry about their security. Accordingly, interdependence—meaning mutual dependence and thus vulnerability—gives states an incentive to initiate war, if only to ensure continued access to necessary materials and goods.

The unsatisfactory nature of both liberal and realist theories is shown by their difficulties in explaining the run-ups to the two World Wars. The period up to World War I exposes a glaring anomaly for liberal theory: the European powers had reached unprecedented levels of trade, yet that did not prevent them from going to war. Realists certainly have the correlation right—the war was preceded by high interdependence—but trade levels had been high for the previous thirty years; hence, even if interdependence was a necessary condition for the war, it was not sufficient.

At first glance, the period from 1920 to 1940 seems to support liberalism over realism. In the 1920s, interdependence was high, and the world was essentially peaceful; in the 1930s, as entrenched protectionism caused interdependence to fall, international tension rose to the point of world war. Yet the two most aggressive states in the system during the 1930s, Germany and Japan, were also the most highly dependent despite their efforts towards autarchy, relying on other states, including other great powers, for critical raw materials. Realism thus seems correct in arguing that high dependence may lead to conflict, as states use war to ensure access to vital goods. Realism's problem with the interwar era, however, is that Germany and Japan had been even more dependent in the 1920s, yet they sought war only in the late 1930s when their dependence, although still significant, had fallen.

The theory presented in this article—the theory of trade expectations—helps to resolve these problems. The theory starts by clarifying the notion of economic interdependence, fusing the liberal insight that the benefits of trade give states an incentive to avoid war with the realist view that the potential costs of being cut off can push states to war to secure vital goods. The total of the benefits and potential costs of trade versus autarchy reveals the true level of dependence a state faces, for if trade is completely severed, the state not only loses the gains from trade but also suffers the costs of adjusting its economy to the new situation.

Trade expectations theory introduces a new causal variable, the expectations of future trade, examining its impact on the overall expected value of the trading option if a state decides to forgo war. This supplements the static consideration in liberalism and realism of the levels of interdependence at any point in time, with the importance of leaders' dynamic expectations into the future.

Levels of interdependence and expectations of future trade, considered simultaneously, lead to new predictions. Interdependence can foster peace, as liberals argue, but this will only be so when states expect that trade levels will be high into the foreseeable future. If highly interdependent states expect that trade will be severely restricted—that is, if their expectations for future trade are low—realists are likely to be right: the most highly dependent states will be the ones most likely to initiate war, for fear of losing the economic wealth that supports their long-term security. In short, high interdependence can be either peace-inducing or war-inducing, depending on the expectations of future trade.

This dynamic perspective helps bridge the gaps within and between current approaches. Separating levels of interdependence from expectations of future trade indicates that states may be pushed into war even if current trade levels are high, if leaders have good reason to suspect that others will cut them off in the future. In such a situation, the expected value of trade will likely be negative, and hence the value of continued peace is also negative, making war an attractive alternative. This insight helps resolve the liberal problem with World War I: despite high trade levels in 1913–14, declining expectations for future trade pushed German leaders to attack, to ensure long-term access to markets and raw materials.

Even when current trade is low or non-existent, positive expectations for future trade will produce a positive expected value for trade, and therefore an incentive for continued peace. This helps explain the two main periods of détente between the Cold War superpowers, from 1971 to 1973 and in the late 1980s: positive signs from U.S. leaders that trade would soon be significantly increased coaxed the Soviets into a more cooperative relationship, reducing the probability of war. But in situations of low trade where there is no prospect that high trade levels will be restored in the future, highly dependent states may be pushed into conflict. This was the German and Japanese dilemma before World War II.

The article is divided into three sections. The first section reviews liberal and realist theories on the relationship between economic interdependence and the probability of war, and provides a critique of both theories. The second section lays out trade expectations theory. The final section examines the diplomatic historical evidence for the new theory against two significant cases: Germany before World War I and Germany before World War II. The evidence indicates that the new variable, expectations of future trade, helps resolve the anomalies for current theories: in both cases, negative expectations for future trade, combined with high dependence, led leaders into total war out of fear for their long-term economic position and therefore security.

THE LIBERAL AND REALIST DEBATE ON ECONOMIC INTERDEPENDENCE AND WAR

The core liberal position is straightforward.[2] Trade provides valuable benefits, or "gains from trade," to any particular state. A dependent state should therefore seek to avoid war, since peaceful trading gives it all the benefits of close ties without any of the costs and risks of war. Trade pays more than war, so dependent states should prefer to trade not invade. This argument is often supported by the auxiliary proposition that modern technology greatly increases the costs and risks of aggression, making the trading option even more rational.

The argument was first made popular in the 1850s by Richard Cobden, who asserted that free trade "unites" states, "making each equally anxious for the prosperity and happiness of both."[3] This view was restated in *The Great Illusion* by Norman Angell just prior to World War I and again in 1933. Angell saw states having to choose between new ways of thinking, namely peaceful trade, and the "old method" of power politics. Even if war was once profitable, modernization now makes it impossible to "enrich" oneself through force; indeed, by destroying trading bonds, war is "commercially suicidal."[4]

Why do wars nevertheless occur? While the start of World War I just after *The Great Illusion*'s initial publication might seem to refute his thesis, Angell in the 1933 edition argued that the debacle simply confirmed the unprofitability of modern wars. He thus upheld the common liberal view that wars, especially major wars, result from the misperceptions of leaders caught up in the outmoded belief that war still pays. Accordingly, his is "not a plea for the impossibility of war . . . but for its futility," since "our ignorance on this matter makes war not only possible, but extremely likely."[5] In short, if leaders fail to see how unprofitable war is compared to the benefits of trade, they may still erroneously choose the former.

Richard Rosecrance provides the most extensive update of the Cobden-Angell thesis to the nuclear era. States must choose between being "trading states," concerned with promoting wealth through commerce, and "territorial states," obsessed with military expansion. Modern conditions push states towards a predominantly trading mode: wars are not only too costly, but with the peaceful trading option, "the benefits that one nation gains from trade can also be realized by others." When the system is highly interdependent, therefore, the "incentive to wage war is absent," since "trading states recognize that they can do *better* through internal economic development sustained by a worldwide market for their goods and services than by trying to conquer and assimilate large tracts of land."[6] Rosecrance thus neatly summarizes the liberal view that high interdependence fosters peace by making trading more profitable than invading.[7]

Realists turn the liberal argument on its head, arguing that economic interdependence not only fails to promote peace, but in fact heightens the likelihood of war.[8] States concerned about security will dislike dependence, since it means that crucial imported goods could be cut off during a crisis. This problem is particularly acute for imports like oil and raw materials; while they may be only a small percentage of the total import bill, without them most modern economies would collapse. Consequently, states dependent on others for vital goods have an increased incentive to go to war to assure themselves of continued access of supply.

Neorealist Kenneth Waltz puts the argument as follows: actors within a domestic polity have little reason to fear the dependence that goes with specialization. The anarchic structure of international politics, however, makes states worry about their vulnerability, thus compelling them "to control what they depend on or to lessen the extent of their dependency." For Waltz, it is this "simple thought" that explains, among other things, "their imperial thrusts to widen the scope of their control."[9] For John Mearsheimer, nations that "depend on others for critical economic supplies will fear cutoff or blackmail in time of crisis or war." Consequently, "they may try to extend political control to the source of supply, giving rise to conflict with the source or with its other customers." Interdependence, therefore, "will probably lead to greater security competition."[10]

This modern realist understanding of economic interdependence and war finds its roots in mercantilist writings dating from the seventeenth century. Mercantilists saw states as locked in a competition for relative power and for the wealth that underpins that power.[11] For mercantilists, imperial expansion—the acquisition of colonies—is driven by the state's need to secure greater control over sources of supply and markets for its goods, and to build relative power in the process. By allowing the metropole and the colonies to specialize in production and trade of complementary products (particularly manufactured goods for raw materials), while ensuring political control over the process, colonies "opened up the possibility of providing a system of supply within a self-contained empire."[12]

In this, we see the underpinning for the neorealist view that interdependence leads to war. Mercantilist imperialism represents a reaction to a state's dependence; states reduce their fears of external specialization by increasing *internal* specialization within a now larger political realm. The imperial state as it expands thus acquires more and more of the characteristics of Waltz's domestic polity, with its hierarchy of specialized functions secure from the unpredictable policies of others.

In sum, realists seek to emphasize one main point: political concerns driven by anarchy must be injected into the liberal calculus. Since states must be primarily concerned with security and therefore with control over resources and markets, one must discount the liberal optimism that great trading partners will always continue to be great trading partners simply because both states benefit absolutely. Accordingly, a state vulnerable to another's policies because of dependence will tend to use force to overcome that vulnerability.

A Comparison of the Liberal and Realist Perspectives

While the liberal and the realist arguments display critical differences, they possess one important similarity: the causal logic of both perspectives is founded on an individual state's decision-making process. That is, while the two camps freely use the term "interdependence," both derive predictions from how particular decision-making units—states—deal with their own specific dependence. This allows both theories to handle situations of "asymmetric interdependence," where one state in a dyad is more dependent than the other. Their predictions are internally consistent, but opposed: liberals argue that the more dependent state is less likely to initiate conflict, since it has more to lose from breaking economic ties;[13] realists maintain that this state is more likely to initiate conflict, to escape its vulnerability.

The main difference between liberals and realists has to do with their emphasis on the benefits versus the costs of interdependence. The realist argument highlights an aspect that is severely downplayed in the liberal argument, namely, consideration of the potential costs from the severing of a trading relationship. Most liberals, if pressed, would probably accept David Baldwin's conceptualization of dependence as the opportunity costs a state would experience should trade end. Yet Baldwin's opportunity costs are only the loss of the benefits from trade received after a state moves from autarchy.[14] It is this understanding of opportunity costs that is followed in the most comprehensive liberal argument for interdependence and peace, that of Rosecrance. There is little sense in Rosecrance's work that a state's decision to specialize and thus to restructure its economy radically can entail huge "costs of adjustment" should trade be later severed, nor that such costs can actually put the state in a far worse position than if it had never moved from autarchy in the first place.[15] This is the concern of realists when they talk about dependence on "vital goods" such as oil. A state that chooses not to buy oil from outsiders forgoes certain benefits of trade, but by operating on domestic energy sources, it avoids the heavy penalty experienced by a state that does base its industrial structure on imported oil, only to find itself cut off from supplies.

That Rosecrance minimizes this realist concern is evident. In an explicit effort to refute Waltz's definition of interdependence as "a trading link which 'is costly to break,'" Rosecrance contends that "to measure interdependence in this way misses the essence of the concept." His subsequent discussion emphasizes only the benefits that states give up if they choose not to trade (his "opportunity costs"), and makes no mention of any potentially severe costs of adjustment. In fact, he argues that dependence on such things as foreign sources of energy is really no different than relying on outsiders for "fashions" or different makes of cars; if trade is cut off, a state loses only "consumer choice." Recognition that the whole industrial structure of a state might be undermined or destroyed by an adversary's severing of vital trade is absent.[16]

Rosecrance is reluctant to acknowledge realist concerns, perhaps because to do so would imply that dependent states might be more willing to go to war, as realists maintain, while Rosecrance is arguing that they are less willing to do so.[17] This points to a critical distinction between liberalism and realism that illuminates the liberal understanding of why wars ultimately occur. For liberals, interdependence does not have a downside that might push states into war, as realists contend. Rather, interdependence is seen to operate as a restraint on aggressive tendencies arising from the domestic or individual levels. If interdependence becomes low, this restraint is taken away, allowing the aggressive tendencies to dominate. To borrow a metaphor from Plato: for liberals, interdependence operates like the reins on the dark horse of inner passions; it provides a material incentive to stay at peace, even when there are internal predispositions towards aggression. Remove the reins, however, and these passions are free to roam as they will.[18]

This point becomes clearer as one examines Rosecrance's explanations for the two World Wars. World War II, for Rosecrance, was ultimately domestically driven. The main aggressors saw war as a means to cope with the upheavals flowing from "social discontent and chaos" and the "danger of left-wing revolutions"; given these upheavals, it is "not surprising that the territorial and military-political system [i.e., war] emerged as an acceptable alternative to more than one state." Connecting the Second World War to causes arising from the unit level in the First World War, he continues: "If Germany, Italy, and Japan did not fulfill their territorial ambitions at the end of World War I, they might develop even more nationalistic and solidaristic regimes and try again."[19] With trade and therefore interdependence at low levels in the 1930s, "economics offered no alternative possibility"; it failed to provide what he later refers to as a "mitigat[ing]" or "restraining" influence on unit-level motives for war.[20]

World War I is a problematic case for Rosecrance, as it was for Angell, since the great powers went to war even though trade levels were still high. Like Angell, Rosecrance's main defense of liberalism is that leaders simply did not see how beneficial interdependence was, and how costly war would be. Due to outmoded ideas and unit-level pathologies, they misperceived the situation; hence, interdependence could not operate as it should, as a restraint on aggression. He talks about leaders' obsession with "nationalist ambitions" and "balance of power politics." He suggests that "no pre-1914 statesman or financier was fully aware of the damage that war would do to the European body economic" because of the irrational belief that "[war] would be over very quickly."[21] At one point, he even seems to cast doubt on the efficacy of interdependence as a restraint on aggression:

> One should not place too much emphasis upon the existence of interdependence per se. European nations in 1913 relied upon the trade and investment that flowed between them; that did not prevent the political crisis which led to . . . World War I. Interdependence only constrains national policy if leaders accept and agree to work within its limits.[22]

It thus appears that Rosecrance cannot really envision interdependence as being anything but a "constraint" or "restraint" on unit-level tendencies to aggress. This view is consistent with the general liberal perspective that all wars are ultimately driven by unit-level phenomena such as misperceptions, authoritarianism, ideology, and internal social conflict. Rosecrance's historical understanding of the World War II, for example, would fit nicely with the "democratic peace" literature: had all the states in 1939 been democratic, war would probably not have occurred despite the disrupted global economic situation, but since some states were not democratic, their aggressive domestic forces became unfettered once interdependence had declined. The idea that economic factors by themselves can push states to aggress—an argument consistent with neorealism and the alternative theory I will present below—is outside the realm of liberal thought, since it would imply that purely systemic forces can be responsible for war, largely regardless of unit-level phenomena.[23]

While liberal theory certainly downplays the realist concern for the potential costs of severed trade, it is also clear that realists slight the positive role the benefits of trade can have on a state's choice between peace and war. In the next section, I bring together the liberal emphasis on benefits with the realist emphasis on costs to create a framework for understanding the true level of dependence a state faces. This section also seeks to correct the most significant error in both liberal and realist theories, namely, their lack of theoretical attention to the dynamics of state expectations for the future.

TRADE OR INVADE? A THEORY OF TRADE EXPECTATIONS

This section introduces the theory of trade expectations. This theory extends liberal and realist views regarding interdependence and war, by synthesizing their strengths while formulating a dynamic perspective on state decision-making that is at best only implicit in current approaches. The strength of liberalism lies in its consideration of how the benefits or gains from trade give states a material incentive to avoid war, even when they have unit-level predispositions to favor it. The strength of realism is its recognition that states may be vulnerable to the potential costs of being cut off from trade on which they depend for wealth and ultimately security. Current theories, however, lack a way to fuse the benefits of trade and the costs of severed trade into one theoretical framework.

More significantly, these theories lack an understanding of how rational decisionmakers incorporate the future trading environment into their choice between peace and war. Both liberalism and realism often refer to the future trading environment, particularly in empirical analyses. But in constructing a theoretical logic, the two camps consider the future only within their own ideological presuppositions. Liberals, assuming that states seek to maximize absolute welfare, maintain that situations of high trade should continue into the foreseeable future as long as states are rational; such actors have no reason to forsake the benefits from trade, especially if defection from the trading arrangement will only lead to retaliation.[24] Given this presupposition, liberals can argue that interdependence—as reflected in high trade at any particular moment in time— will foster peace, given the benefits of trade over war. Realists, assuming states seek to maximize security, argue that concerns for relative power and autonomy will eventually push some states to sever trade ties (at least in the absence of a hegemon). Hence, realists can insist that interdependence, again manifest as high trade at any moment in time, drives dependent states to initiate war now to escape potential vulnerability later.

For the purposes of forging strong theories, however, trading patterns cannot be simply assumed *a priori* to match the stipulations of either liberalism or of realism. Trade levels fluctuate significantly over time, both for the system as a whole and particularly between specific trading partners, as the last two centuries demonstrate. Accordingly, we need a theory that incorporates how a state's expectations of its trading environment—either optimistic or pessimistic—affect its decision-calculus for war or peace. This is where the new theory makes its most significant departure. Liberalism and realism are theories of "comparative statics," drawing predictions from a snapshot of the level of interdependence at a single point in time. The new theory, on the other hand, is dynamic in its internal structure: it provides a new variable, the "expectations of future trade," that incorporates in the theoretical logic an actor's sense of the future trends and possibilities.[25] This variable is essential to any leader's determination not just of the immediate value of peace versus war at a particular moment in time, but of the overall expected value of peace and war over the foreseeable future.

From consideration of the expectations-of-future-trade variable along with a state's level of dependence, one can derive a consistent deductive theory of state decision-making showing the conditions under which high interdependence will lead to peace or to war. High interdependence can be peace-inducing, as liberals maintain, as long as states expect future trade levels to be high in the future: positive expectations for future trade will lead dependent states to assign a high expected value to a continuation of peaceful trade, making war the less appealing option. If, however, a highly dependent state expects future trade to be low due to the policy decisions of the other side, then realists are likely to be correct: the state will attach a low or even negative expected value to continued peace without trade, making war an attractive alternative if its expected value is greater than peace. Moreover, since a negative expected value of trade implies a long-term decline in power, even if war is not profitable *per se,* it may be chosen as the lesser of two evils.[26]

The deductive logic of the alternative theory, as with liberalism and realism, centers on an individual state's efforts to manage its own situation of dependence. Consider a two-actor scenario, where one state "A" may trade with another state "B." If state A moves away from the initial position of autarchy to begin trading, and trade is free and open, it will expect to receive the benefits of trade stressed by liberals, namely, the incremental increase in A's total welfare due to trade.[27] Note that a state can still be aware of the "benefits of trade" even if present trade is non-existent, since they represent the potential gains from trade that would accrue to the state should trade levels become high in the future.[28] It is a state's ability to foresee future potential benefits that allows it to attach a high expected value to the peaceful trading option even when current trade levels are low (as long as it expects current restrictions to be relaxed).

When a state trades, it specializes in and exports goods in which it enjoys a comparative advantage, while forgoing the production of other goods, which it then imports. This process of specialization, however, entails potentially large costs of adjustment if trade is subsequently cut off. This is especially so in the modern world if the state becomes dependent on foreign oil and certain raw materials. With the economy's capital infrastructure (machines, factories, transportation systems, etc.) geared to function only with such vital goods, a severing of trade would impose huge costs as the economy struggles to cope with the new no-trade situation.[29] In short, the severing of trade, as realists would argue, would put the state in a situation far worse than if it had never specialized in the first place.

This analysis leads to a clearer understanding of any particular state's total level of "dependence." On a bilateral basis, that level is represented by the sum of the benefits that the state would receive from free and open trade with another state (versus autarchy), and the costs to the state of being cut off from that trade after having specialized (versus autarchy). If state A started with an economy of 100 units of GNP before any trade with B (the autarchic position), and open trade with B would mean economic expansion to a level of 110 units of GNP on an ongoing basis, then the "benefits of trade" could be considered as 10 units. If the specialization that trade entails, however, would mean the economy would fall to 85 units should B sever trade ties, then the "costs of severed trade" would be 15 units versus autarchy. State A's total dependence level would thus be the benefits of trade plus the costs of severed trade after specialization, or 25 units.

The dependence level will itself be a function of such parameters as the overall compatibilities of the two economies for trade, the degree of A's need for vital goods such as oil and raw materials, and the availability of alternative suppliers and markets. Thus if A's need for trade with B is great because the economies are highly compatible (say, in terms of mutual comparative advantages), B has valuable natural resources that A lacks, and A has few other countries to turn to, then A's dependence can be considered high.[30]

In deciding between peace and war, however, a state can not refer simply to its dependence level. Rather, it must determine the overall expected value of trade and therefore the value of continued peace into the foreseeable future. The benefits of trade and the costs of severed trade on their own say nothing about this expected value. Dynamic expectations of future trade must be brought in. If the state has positive expectations that the other will maintain free and open trade over the long term, then the expected value of trade will be close to the value of the benefits of trade. On the other hand, if the state, after having specialized, comes to expect that trade will be severed by the trading partner, then the expected value of trade may be highly negative, that is, close to the value of the costs of severed trade. In essence, the expected value of trade may be anywhere between the two extremes, depending on a state's estimate of the expected probability of securing open trade, or of being cut off.[31]

This leads to a crucial hypothesis. For any given expected value of war, we can predict that the lower the expectations of future trade, the lower the expected value of trade, and therefore the more likely it is that war will be chosen.

It is important to note that the expected value of trade will not be based on the level of trade at a particular moment in time, but upon the stream of expected trade levels into the future. It really does not matter that trade is high today: if state A knows that B will cut all trade tomorrow and shows no signs of being willing to restore it later, the expected value of trade would be negative. Similarly, it does not matter if there is little or no trade at present: if state A is confident that B is committed to freer trade in the future, the expected value of trade would be positive.

The fact that the expected value of trade can be negative even if present trade is high, due to low expectations for future trade, goes a long way towards resolving such manifest anomalies for liberal theory as German aggression in World War I. Despite high levels of trade up to 1914, German leaders had good reason to believe that the other great powers would undermine this trade into the future; hence, a war to secure control over raw materials and markets was required for the long-term security of the German nation. Since the expected value of trade can be positive even though present trade is low, due to high expectations for future trade, we can also understand such phenomena as the periods of détente in U.S.-Soviet relations during the Cold War (1971–73 and after 1985). While East-West trade was still relatively low during these times, the Soviet need for Western technology, combined with a growing belief that large increases in trade with the West would be forthcoming, gave the Soviets a high enough expected value of trade to convince them to be more accommodating in superpower relations.[32]

In making the final decision between peace and war, however, a rational state will have to compare the expected value of trade to the expected value of going to war with the other state.

The expected value of war, as a realist would emphasize, cannot be ascertained without considering the relative power balance. As one state moves from a position of relative inferiority in economic and military power to relative superiority, the expected value of war will move from negative to positive or even highly positive. This proposition follows directly from the insights of deterrence theory: the larger the state in relative size, the higher the probability of winning a victory, while the lower the costs of fighting the war.[33] Hence, if victory entails occupying the other state and absorbing its economy, war can take on a very positive expected value when a large power attacks a small state.[34] For example, if Iraq had been allowed to hold on to Kuwait after its August 1990 invasion, war for Iraq would certainly have "paid." Similarly, Czechoslovakia was an easy and attractive target for Germany by 1938–39, as were the other smaller states of Europe, and evidence suggests that war against these nations was indeed profitable for the Nazis.[35] On the other hand, war between more equal great powers is likely to have a much lower or even negative expected value. The Spartan leadership took Sparta into war against Athens in 431 BC, for example, under no illusions that war would be a profitable venture.[36] While the Athenian economy presented a large prize should victory be attained, war with a near-equal adversary could be expected to be very costly, with a low likelihood of victory.

Where we would anticipate a low or negative expected value to the option of war, the expectations-of-future-trade variable should have a determinant effect on the likelihood of war. If state A has positive expectations for future trade with B, and A and B are roughly equal in relative power, then state A will assign a high expected value to continued peaceful trade, will compare this to the low or negative expected value for invasion, and will choose peace as the rational strategy. The higher A's dependence and the higher the expectations for future trade, the higher the expected value for peaceful trade, and therefore the more likely A is to avoid war. But if state A is dependent and has negative expectations for future trade with B, then the expected value of trade will be very low or negative. If the expected value for trade is lower than the expected value for invasion, war becomes the rational choice, and this is so even when the expected value of invasion is itself negative: war becomes the lesser of two evils.[37]

Until now, I have talked about state A's "expectations of future trade" as though they were essentially exogenous, that is, as though state B, in its willingness to trade with A, were not affected by A's behavior. If, however, state A, by making political, military, or economic concessions, can induce B to relax trading restrictions, then A's low expectations for future trade may be raised.

This suggests that the effects of diplomacy and bargaining need to be integrated into any extended historical analysis.[38] The probability of B trading with A is never completely independent of A's actions, since there is always some concession that A could make to get B to commit to higher trade levels over the long term. But the problem for A is that B's price for high trade may be unacceptable in that it undermines A's internal stability or its external power position. To take an extreme example, if B were to demand, as the price for higher trade, that A unilaterally disarm and allow B to occupy A with its army, it is hard to imagine A accepting such a deal. If B remains unwilling to budge from such an exorbitant demand, then it is fair to say that A's pessimistic expectation for future trade is exogenous; there is little A can do, short of national suicide, to improve the likelihood of trade.

Thus state A, in estimating B's probability of trading with A, will refer to many indicators suggesting how "reasonable" B will be into the future, that is, how willing B will be to trade, and at what price. One may think of these indicators simply as causal factors affecting the variable "expectations of future trade." Such systemic factors as B's economic competitiveness, B's rate of depletion of raw materials and energy reserves (affecting its future export ability), and military pressures constraining B's trade with A will be important. German leaders before World War I, for example, had good reason to believe that Britain would be forced to move to imperial preference to protect its empire from the German economic challenge and to lend support to its entente partners. Japanese leaders in the late 1930s recognized that the United States would have to cut back on oil and iron exports to Japan as U.S. reserves were depleted or needed to supply a military buildup (even one directed only at Germany). Such systemic pressures on B to reduce trade with A will foster negative expectations of future trade among A's leaders.

But domestic and personal factors can also play a significant role in the exogenous rise or decline in B's likelihood of trading with A, indicating that the assumption that B is a "unitary actor" must be relaxed to some degree when examining history.[39] In 1972, for example, the Soviets saw Nixon and Kissinger as firmly in control of American policy, and therefore able to carry through on commitments to increase East-West trade. Two years later, however, such a positive expectation for future trade could not be sustained in the wake of Watergate and the reassertion of Congressional power, at least at a price which was reasonable to the Soviets. This had much to do with the failure of détente, as I argue elsewhere.[40]

A comparison of the arguments of trade expectations theory with those of liberal and realist theory is presented in Table 1. To summarize: liberals contend that high economic dependence, as manifest in high trade levels, reduces a state's likelihood of initiating war by providing a material "constraint" on unit-level forces for aggression. Low dependence will increase this likelihood, since this constraint on unit-level motives for war is removed. Realists argue that high dependence heightens the probability of war as dependent states struggle to reduce their vulnerability. In the realist world, however, low dependence should have no impact on the likelihood of war or peace; that is, other factors should become causally determinant of war. Still, since economic interdependence is at least eliminated as a possible source of conflict, realists would predict that the overall likelihood of war should fall when mutual dependence is low.

In other words, both liberals and realists believe that a situation of low dependence eliminates "dependence" as a causal variable. But since liberals argue that unit-level forces are always ready to be let loose (in the absence of a community of democratic nations), the termination of high dependence takes away the previous restraint on such forces, and therefore the probability of war rises dramatically. For realists, the causes of war come from systemic factors, including a state's dependence (as well as relative power, etc.); therefore, since high dependence will tend to push a state into war, the absence of dependence gives the state one less systemic reason to aggress.

The new theory departs from the two other approaches by incorporating both the level of dependence and the dynamic expectations of future trade. It is somewhat consistent with realism in that low dependence implies little impact on the prospects for peace or war: if there are few benefits from trade and few costs if trade is cut off, then trade does not matter much in the state's decision to go to war. As with realism, however, the elimination of a factor that might otherwise push a state into war suggests that the probability of war should be less when dependence is low.[41]

When dependence is high, peace will be promoted only when the state has positive expectations of future trade. Here, the liberal logic applies, whereby the positive benefits of trade give the dependent state the incentive not to disrupt a profitable peace. If, however, expectations of future trade fall, then realist concerns about the downside of interdependence—the costs of being cut off—enter in, dramatically increasing the likelihood that the dependent state will initiate war. Importantly, the decision for war does not hinge on what the present trade levels are; rather, it is leaders' expectations for the future that drive whether the expected value of trade is positive and peace-inducing or negative and war-inducing.

Table 1 The Competing Theories

	Core Liberal Theory (e.g., Rosecrance)	Core Realist Theory (e.g., Waltz, Mearsheimer)	Trade Expectations Theory (Copeland)
Nature of the system	Anarchy	Anarchy	Anarchy
Nature of the state	Generally a rational, unitary calculator of costs/benefits, but may also have aggressive, unit-level drives	Rational, unitary actor seeking to reduce vulnerability to improve security	Rational, unitary actor calculating the *expected* stream of benefits and costs *over the foreseeable future*, to maximize wealth and therefore security
Analytical focus	The individual state's concern for its own dependence	The individual state's concern for its own dependence	The individual state's concern for its own dependence
State's decision for war or peace driven by	Benefits of trade (the "gains from trade" from specialization)	Costs of severed trade (the costs of adjustment after being cut off, due to specialization)	Benefits of trade *and* costs of severed trade, *plus* expectations of future trade
Ultimate reasons that state goes to war	If level of dependence low (i.e., trade is low), "restraint" on unit-level aggressive tendencies removed	High dependence creates a systemic incentive to use force to overcome vulnerability	High dependence and pessimistic expectations for future trade, creating a low or *negative* expected value for trade
Reason for state choosing to stay at peace	If level of dependence high (i.e., trade is high), then high dependence "restrains" by making benefits of trade greater than value of war	Low dependence removes another systemic incentive for war	High dependence and optimistic expectations for future trade, creating a high expected value for trade

Note: All three theories recognize that relative power affects the value of the "invade" option; hence, Table 1 focuses on aspects of the "trade" option that affect the decision for war or peace.

HISTORICAL EVIDENCE

This section explores how expectations of future trade affected the decisions for war in two cases: Germany and World War I, and Germany and World War II.[42] These cases were chosen for two reasons. First, total wars between great powers minimize the problem of overdetermination that occurs when cases of great powers attacking small powers are included.[43] Second, since Germany lost these wars, internal documents are available to reveal the decision-making processes of aggressing states. If we want to go beyond correlation to causation, we must test the causal mechanism linking variables; that is, we have to see if leaders took their nations into war for the reasons hypothesized.[44] Exploring internal decision-making in some detail, I show how trade expectations theory helps solve the empirical puzzles for liberalism and realism.

Germany and the Outbreak of World War I

Germany had been one of the few great powers trying to buck the trend towards protectionism in the early and mid-1890s. Recognizing that German industrial products could now match the goods of any state, Chancellor Caprivi set in place policies to expand German trade in Europe and overseas. Other great powers, however, indicated their opposition to any German *penetration pacifique*. Severe tariffs from the United States (McKinley tariff, 1890) and France (Meline tariff, 1892) were certainly worrisome. Even that bastion of free trade—Britain—indicated after 1895 that its fear of rising German commercial strength would soon lead to a reversal of policy. In 1896, the British had raided the Transvaal region of South Africa, jeopardizing German commercial interests. In mid-1897, Canada slapped a discriminatory tariff on non-British goods, contrary to the 1865 Most Favored Nation treaty between Germany and the British empire. Despite Germany's protest, the British, far from making amends, upheld the Canadian decision and then renounced the 1865 treaty in July 1897. Soon after this Joseph Chamberlain opened talks with British colonies on the possible formation a general imperial preference system.[45]

German expectations for future trade reflected these developments. On July 31, 1897, the Prussian minister in Munich informed Chancellor von Hohenlohe that public opinion saw the British "denunciation" of the 1865 treaty as "the prelude to a close trade relationship of England with her colonies." The kaiser's marginal comments indicated his agreement that "the denunciation is the beginning of a revolution in the whole system of British commercial policy." For the kaiser, any suggestion that the target of British action was the United States was "nonsense"; clearly "it is against Germany." He continued, "now that the superiority of German industry is recognized, [the British] will soon make efforts to destroy it."[46]

The "main worry" of German leaders during the late 1890s, as Fritz Fischer recounts, "remained . . . the extreme protectionist tariffs of the United States and the plans for a British customs association."[47] The German naval buildup after 1898 was partly designed to protect German trade, particularly imports of raw materials and food. Cecil notes that there was widespread recognition in Germany that with its fast growing population, Germany "could no longer subsist on native-grown foodstuffs" and that a strong navy was needed as "a necessary bulwark against starvation."[48]

German leaders had good reason to worry about the dependability of outside suppliers. In the decade and a half before the war, dependence on trade for vital goods increased dramatically, driven by phenomenal growth in both population and industrial size. Domestic oil production, for example, had gone up 140 percent from 1900 to

1913, but still accounted for only ten percent of total German oil needs. The state went from being a net exporter of iron ore as late as 1897 to relying on outsiders for close to 30 percent of its needs by 1913, despite domestic production increases of 120 percent. By 1913, over 57 percent of Germany's imports were in the form of raw materials, versus 44 percent in 1903 and 41 percent in 1893. All this was occurring at a time when Germany's ratio of trade to GNP was rising to new heights: from 32 percent in 1900, to 36 percent in 1910, to almost 40 percent in 1913.[49]

Of great concern as well were the growing French, Russian, and British efforts to obstruct German commerce. After 1897, Britain and the United States worked in tandem to preclude German colonial gains: despite Germany's efforts, for example, it received nothing from the dissolution of the Spanish empire. In both Moroccan crises, 1905 and 1911, Britain helped France thwart greater German economic penetration of Africa. In fact, from 1898 to 1913, the colonial territory Germany had been permitted to acquire was only one-seventh that acquired by the United States, a state less often thought of as "imperialist."[50]

In the Middle East, the British worked actively to minimize German economic penetration. In 1907, they agreed with Russia to divide Persia into spheres of influence as part of a campaign to restrict any extension of German power via the proposed Berlin-Baghdad Railway. The Russian ambassador reported to Moscow in August 1910, "England is less interested in what happens in Persia than in preventing any other Power, except England and Russia, from playing any role there. This applies particularly to Germany and Turkey."[51] Just before the war, England worked out a tacit deal with the Americans, giving them a sphere of influence over Latin American oil, in return for British domination of the Middle Eastern oil reserves.[52] By these means, the Germans were effectively denied control over oil imports at a time when only 10 percent of Germany's growing oil requirements was supplied by internal production.

Two other areas concerned the Germans: raw materials and food. With Germany becoming a net importer of iron ore after 1897, French ore became increasingly important: German ore imports from France had increased almost sixty-fold from 1900 to 1913 as Sweden, Germany's main supplier, moved to establish export quotas. German industry invested heavily in the mines of Northern France, and by 1913, directly controlled about 10 to 15 percent of French ore reserves.[53]

The French government took steps to stop this economic penetration, delaying further concessions to German companies in early 1912 and then halting them altogether in December 1913. This came at a time when German capital in general was being shut out of both the French and Russian markets. It is not surprising, therefore, that German industrialists in 1913 would openly speak to the Italian Minister of Commerce "of the need to lay their hands on the iron ore basin of French Lorraine; war seemed to them a matter for industry."[54]

Expectations for the critical food trade were also deteriorating in the last years before the war. Imports of foodstuffs from 1890 to 1913 grew at an average of 4.8 percent a year, well above the overall economic growth rate of 3.9 percent. The Anglo-German naval arms race reflected fears on each side that the other might blockade imports to starve the adversary into submission. British plans for such a blockade were well-advanced in the last decade before the war, and "[the] threat to Germany was a real one."[55]

Thus German leaders after 1897 were increasingly worried about great power economic as well as military encirclement. Their declining expectations of future trade on the eve of World War I are revealed by the extensive documentary work of Fischer.[56] His evidence shows a clear relation between initial German war aims and the increasing economic anxieties of a diverse group of individuals before July 1914. The shared fear was that German industry, increasingly dependent on outsiders for vital goods, would be strangled by the growing economic restrictions imposed by adversaries. Since these powers had extensive imperial possessions, they could afford to adopt closed economic policies; Germany lacked such an alternative. As neomercantilist Gustav Schmoller in 1900 put it, the Russian, British, and American world empires, "with their greed for land, their power at sea and on land, their trade," want to put all others "into an economic straitjacket and to smother them."[57]

By 1911, after the failures of the second Moroccan crisis and "in response to the protectionist trends in the United States, Britain, and Russia," Germany "turned again to the idea of a central European economic area as a defensive measure."[58] Concern for economic security was tangible, transcending ideological and party lines. Future chancellor and National Liberal Stresemann stated in early 1913 that Germany must seek to "create a self-sufficient economic area, so as to make sure of our raw material requirements and to protect our exports." Basserman of the Centre Party in mid-1912 stated that "our trade declines more and more in certain places where we are pushed out or where it keeps its end up only with difficulties." Even the Social Democrat Hildebrand would write in 1911, "from a socialist standpoint the acquisition of colonial domains has become an acute economic necessity for Germany." Indeed, Fischer shows that after 1906 the Social Democratic party moved from opposition to acceptance of German colonial expansion.[59]

These views paralleled those within the government. Walter Rathenau, who was the influential head of the department of military raw materials in the War Ministry in August 1914, was arguing by December 1913 that Germany's raw material base was too "narrow," and that it depended on "the mercy of the world market as long as [Germany] did not itself possess sufficient raw material sources." In April 1914, Albert Ballin noted that the "expansion of our foreign markets is increasingly threatened," and in the oil-rich Near East in particular, "we have been thrown out of the most important regions there."[60]

The declining expectations of future trade contributed to the pervasive sense of general decline felt by the German leadership in July 1914. Extensive evidence shows that German leaders brought on world war for "preventive" motives, namely to forestall the rise of powers such as Russia.[61] Economic factors reinforced these motives. If France and Russia could be defeated, valuable areas in Europe would be incorporated under German tutelage, guaranteeing the raw materials and markets needed for future German economic power and therefore security; without major war, the economic policies of German adversaries would push Germany further into decline over the long term.

These aims were revealed in the so-called "September Program," which was finalized by Chancellor Bethmann Hollweg on September 9. The plan stated that the "general aim of the war" was "security for the German Reich in west and east for all imaginable time." Russia "must be thrust back as far as possible," while France would become "economically dependent on Germany, secur[ing] the French market for our exports." France's "ore-field of Briey, which is necessary for the supply of ore for our industry, [would] be ceded," and a "central European economic association," including central Europe, France, Poland, and "perhaps Italy, Sweden, and Norway," would be formed. And while members would be "formally equal," "in practice [the association] will be under German leadership and must stabilize Germany's economic dominance over *Mitteleuropa*."[62]

This blunt programme for German economic hegemony in Europe was clearly consistent with the pre-war call for a *Mitteleuropa,* and it reflected the work of Bethmann and his associates through the months of July and August 1914. Rathenau, now in charge of raw materials for the Reich, was particularly influential. On August 1, 1914, he submitted to Bethmann a long memorandum arguing that "only a Germany rein forced by 'Mitteleuropa' would be in a position to maintain herself as an equal world power between the world powers of Britain and the United States on the one side and Russia on the other," and war, if necessary, would help to achieve this "essential objective."[63] The date shows that the report must have been prepared during the height of the July crisis, demonstrating that the September program reflected pre-war objectives, rather than a post-hoc scramble to justify the reality of war.

Of particular concern were German iron ore interests in France. On August 26, Bethmann sought information on the size of the ore deposits in French Lorraine, and soon after agreed to consider annexation of French mines "in a final peace treaty." Aware of pre-war French discrimination against German companies, in the September Program he wrote that any commercial treaty with a defeated France "must secure for us financial and industrial freedom of movement in France in such a fashion that German enterprises can no longer receive different treatment from [the] French."[64] Russian pre-war trade restrictions were also to be torn down. Bethmann noted in an October 22, 1914, memo to Delbrück, secretary of state in the Reich Interior Office, that after the war Russia "would have imposed on it a long-term commercial treaty which would mean a lowering of Russian industrial tariffs."[65]

It is important to note the widespread agreement during the September–October period that despite likely opposition from industrial and agricultural interests, Germany needed to create a free-trade zone within Europe after victory in order to compete against the remaining world powers. In a September 13 memo to Bethmann, Delbrück argued that "only a Europe without customs barriers [controlled by Germany] can effectively face the vast producing potential of the transatlantic world."[66] In October, von Falkenhausen, counsellor at the Prussian Ministry of Agriculture, wrote that economic hegemony in Europe was needed to "match the great, closed bodies of the United States, the British, and the Russian Empires," in order to compete "over the conditions of the admission of each to the markets of the others."[67] Also in October, an adviser to Delbrück, Schoenebeck, argued that the "final great aim" in the war was "to create a great central European economic area which allows us to maintain our place in the economic struggle of the nations and prevents us from declining into economic impotence in the face of the increasingly closed and assertive economic world empires—Great Britain with its colonies, the United States, Russia, Japan and China."[68]

Thus increasingly pessimistic German trade expectations had much to do with the German willingness to bring on a major war in July 1914. With Britain shutting Germany out of the oil-rich Middle East and resource-rich Africa, with France threatening Germany's access to iron ore, and with high French and Russian tariff levels limiting German economic growth versus "economic empires" like Britain and the United States, German leaders felt that only a major war would provide the economic dominance of Europe needed for long-term German survival.

Germany and the Start of World War II

There is great continuity between German decision-making up to World War I and up to World War II in terms of the causal role of economic factors.[69] This derives from one overriding fact: Germany in the 1930s, as before World War I, was a state capable of great military power, but its small territory possessed few natural resources compared with the great powers surrounding it. In consequence, Germany would always remain highly dependent on outsiders for the food and raw materials vital to its economic health, unless it expanded. Moreover, since the surrounding great powers were better able to fashion self-sustaining imperial realms, should they ever move in this direction by closing their borders to trade—as they began to do in the early 1930s—long-term German economic viability and therefore security would be threatened. These two realities implied that Germany's potential military superiority might have to be used, as in World War I, to generate the territorial mass needed for survival against what in 1914 were referred to as the "economic world empires."

The strategic obsessions of Adolf Hitler and the Nazi regime revolved around this dilemma which the first World War had failed to solve. In *Mein Kampf*, Hitler foresaw that, because Germany's small size constrained its "living space" (*Lebensraum*), its dependence on foreign states for food would only increase as the population grew faster than the yields on arable land.[70] By the mid-1930s, his anxiety shifted somewhat: Germany's problem was not simply the supply of food, but even more seriously, the supply of raw materials needed for industrial strength. This dual problem could be overcome by one strategy: war against the system, with the acquisition of Russian land west of the Urals as the prime territorial objective. By destroying Russia, in one stroke Germany could acquire the land needed for vital food and raw materials, while preventing the rise of the state most likely to overwhelm Germany in the future.[71]

Even if we question critical aspects of Hitler's worldview, it is important to note not only that his strategic objectives mirrored much of pre-1914 thinking, but that without his mass appeal and the loyalty of subordinates, Hitler could not have initiated world war. Would Hitler's arguments have made as much sense to his followers, if Germany had possessed the land mass of Russia or the British empire, or if world trade had not been disrupted by the Great Depression? Implicit in what follows is the argument that had Germany been less dependent on vital goods, and had expectations for future trade not been so pessimistic following U.S., British, and French efforts to create closed trading blocs, it would have been much more difficult for Hitler to pull Germany into war: the expected value of the trading option would have been much higher—or at least not as negative—thus dampening the necessity for war.

Immediately after Hitler's accession to power, Nazi economic policy was guided by the so-called "Reformers," a group of economists calling for the creation of a self-sufficient "large economic area" (*Grosswirtschaftsraum*) protected by tariff barriers.

> This campaign was prompted by the collapse of the international trading system in the wake of the slump, the revival of world-wide protectionism, and specifically, the creation of imperial or regional preference areas. . . . If Germany's economy was to compete with those of the United States, the British Empire, and Japan, it would need to create a rival economic bloc.[72]

This was akin to the pre–World War I concept of *Mitteleuropa,* an idea actively resuscitated by the Brüning and Papen governments after 1930 in response to the collapse of world trade.[73]

Nevertheless, from 1933 to 1936, when the economy was overseen by Hjalmar Schacht, the president of the Reichsbank, Germany did not proceed immediately towards greater self-sufficiency. Keynesian deficit spending, including mass rearmament, produced an immediate economic revival that required marked increases in the input of raw materials, which generally came from abroad. The massive wave of protectionism that followed the U.S. Smoot-Hawley tariffs of 1930, however, created a major constraint: since Germany could not sell its exports abroad, foreign currency could not be raised to pay for the imports of raw materials.

By June 1934, Hitler was being told that the "raw materials situation [was] becoming daily more acute," and that there was a "drain of foreign exchange."[74] The problem was particularly acute since much of Germany's raw material was coming from British colonies or dominions that had entered into the British imperial preference system. Part of the "New Plan" of September 1934 was to reorient German trade away from the British Empire and towards smaller European countries and South America, where supplies would be more secure.[75]

The New Plan solved the balance-of-payments problem for 1935, but by late 1935, world economic upheavals had shifted the terms of trade against Germany; import prices had risen 9 percent while export prices dropped by 9 percent. In other words, Germany had to sell 18 percent more just to import the same amount.[76] By 1936, Hitler decided to move towards greater autarchy in preparation for the war he saw as necessary for Germany's long-term economic viability. This decision was embodied in the "Four-year Plan" of August 1936. Imports were to be restricted to goods that could not be acquired within Germany, while a program to synthesize oil and later rubber was initiated.

Since the plan was opposed by Schacht and others, Hitler composed a lengthy memorandum to his key subordinates in August, explicating his rationale. Germany, he wrote, was engaged in a struggle for its very survival. Germany's situation was dire: "We are overpopulated and cannot feed ourselves from our own resources. . . . It is equally impossible for us at present to manufacture artificially certain raw materials which we lack in Germany or to find substitutes for them." Germany needed to act to relieve its dependence on "foodstuffs and raw materials," and the solution "lies in extending our living space, that is to say, extending the sources of raw materials and foodstuff of our people."[77]

Hitler recognized that Germany could try to satisfy its dependence by importing the necessary goods, yet this required selling exports to get imports. The world economic environment was not amenable to this strategy.

(a) Since the German people will be increasingly dependent on imports for their food and must similarly, whatever happens, import a proportion at least of certain raw materials from abroad, every effort must be made to facilitate these imports. (b) An increase in our own exports is possible in theory but in practice hardly likely. *Germany does not export to a political or economic vacuum, but to areas where competition is very intense.* . . . Since imports of food on the whole cannot be substantially reduced and are more likely to increase, an adjustment must be found in some other way.

Hitler's solution was therefore to seek "100 percent self-sufficiency . . . in every sphere where it is feasible," to save precious foreign currency for the importation of food and any raw materials that could not be found or synthesized within Germany.[78]

The problem of raw material dependence turned out to be more intractable than Hitler imagined. Through vast investments, Germany was able to increase production of synthetic fuel by 130 percent from 1936 to 1939. In 1938, however, still only about 10 percent of German petroleum need was met by domestic production; the other 90 percent was coming from outside, primarily the West Indies, the United States, and Rumania. In the same year, two-thirds of iron ore requirements came from outside. By the outbreak of war itself, Germany still relied on outsiders for fully one-third of all raw material needs.[79]

Expectations for future trade were not getting any better after 1935. British and French moves towards imperial preference solidified. The League of Nations' attempt to impose oil sanctions on Italy after its attack on Ethiopia, while ultimately unsuccessful, also suggested how the "have" great powers would react should the "have-nots" seek changes in the status quo. And sometimes vital imports were suddenly cut off for no apparent reason, or due to uncontrollable domestic factors in the supplying nation. In February 1936, for example, the Soviet Union stopped all oil deliveries to Germany, citing only "difficulties with foreign payments."[80] Such actions could only have further reduced Hitler's estimate of the value of the trading option.

By 1937, the critical decision for war had been made. On November 5, 1937, Hitler brought together his top four military leaders and the Foreign Minister for what is generally considered to be the most important "war council" meeting prior to the war.[81] The issue at hand was whether Germany's "space" problem could be solved by "means of autarchy" or by "increased participation in the world economy." The first was infeasible, since complete autarchy "could not be maintained." Hitler then launched into a discussion of the trading option as a means to German long-term security. To "participation in the world economy," he said, "there were limitations which we were unable to remove. The establishment of Germany's position on a secure and sound foundation was obstructed by market fluctuations, and commercial treaties afforded no guarantee for their actual observance." Countries that Germany formerly relied on for food were now industrializing, implying that they could no longer meet German food needs. Germany was also living in "an age of economic empires," and Hitler compared Germany to others with small territories, such as Japan and Italy, where "economic motives underlay the urge for expansion." Unfortunately, "for countries outside the great economic empires, opportunities for economic expansion were severely obstructed."

Admitting that the economic stimulus provided by rearmament "could never form the basis of a sound economy over a long period," Hitler elaborated the supply dilemma:

> There was a pronounced military weakness in those states which depend for their existence on foreign trade. As our foreign trade was carried on over the sea routes dominated by Britain, it was a question rather of security of transport than of foreign exchange, which revealed in time of war the full weakness of our food situation. The only remedy, and one which might seem to us visionary, lay in the acquisition of greater living space.[82]

This living space "can be sought only in Europe"; this was "not a matter of acquiring population but of gaining space for agricultural use. Moreover, areas producing raw materials can be more usefully sought in Europe, in immediate proximity to the Reich, than overseas."[83] Germany, he said, would have to acquire territory from others through force. He then laid out three possible contingency plans, all of which envisioned war by 1943–45 at the latest, before German military power would be past its peak.[84]

From this meeting, it is clear that the two conditions outlined by trade expectations theory as determinant of war—high dependence and low expectations for future trade—were present in the German case by the late 1930s.[85] In such a situation, even if the expected value of invasion is low or negative,[86] the value of the status quo trading option tends to be even lower; major war then becomes the lesser of two evils, especially when the negative expected value of trade only exacerbates anticipated decline. While no one would want to understate important unit-level reasons for the war (Hitler's personality, the nature of the Nazi regime, its racist ideology, etc.), Germany's systemic economic situation was a fundamental cause. Like Japan in 1930s, Germany's small territorial size, highly industrialized economy, and growing population meant that it would always be dependent on other great powers for goods vital to its long-term well-being. This would be so despite German efforts to achieve relative autarchy. With the world economy going through significant fluctuations, and with large economic empires like the United States and Britain shutting off trade with have-not nations like Germany, it was not surprising that "participation in the world economy" was not seen as the means to achieve Germany's long-term security.

Thus, Hitler's calculations contained a certain tragic rationality eerily similar to those of German decision-makers in 1914. Moreover, German military leaders, most of whom were in positions of authority before Hitler assumed power, also accepted his logic. Disagreements with the military were mostly over tactics, not grand-strategic objectives: there was almost universal acceptance of the notion that Germany, to survive as a nation, had to overcome its severe dependence on others by grabbing the raw materials and fertile territory of other states.

CONCLUSION

This article offers a new theory to build upon liberal and realist approaches to economic interdependence and war. The other two approaches highlight important causal elements of interdependence—liberalism, the benefits of trade, and realism, the potential costs of severed trade—but neither specifies the conditions under which these elements will operate. By introducing a dynamic factor, expectations of future trade, the new theory shows when high levels of dependence lead to peace or to war. When expectations for trade are positive, leaders expect to realize the benefits of trade into the future and therefore have less reason for war now; trade will indeed "constrain." If, however, leaders are pessimistic about future trade, fearing to be cut off from vital goods or believing that current restrictions will not be relaxed, then the negative expected value of peace may make war the rational strategic choice.

A few practical implications of this new theoretical framework for the post–Cold War world can be briefly noted. In anticipating likely areas of conflict, one should look for situations in which powers have both high levels of dependence on outsiders and low expectations for trade. Both China and Japan, as emerging great powers, may soon satisfy these conditions. China's economy is growing at a yearly rate many times that of most other powers, and its domestic sources of raw materials are struggling to keep pace; within the next couple of years, for example, China will have to begin importing oil.[87] As it continues to modernize its armed forces, it will gradually gain the strength necessary to press its territorial claims.[88]

Japan has never truly overcome the problem it faced before World War II, namely, its overwhelming dependence on others for the vital minerals and oil needed to sustain its modern industrial economy. While U.S. hegemony in the region has allowed Japan to flourish since 1945, one can imagine the fears that would arise in Tokyo should the United States ever reduce its naval and military presence in the Far East (for budgetary or other reasons). Japan would be compelled to try to defend its raw material supply routes, setting off a spiral of hostility with regional great powers like China, India, Russia, and perhaps the United States itself.[89]

Russia still has significant economic ties with the states of the former Soviet Union, and is, in particular dependent on pipelines through Ukraine and Belarus to sell its natural gas to Western European customers. These states in turn depend on Russia for their energy supplies.[90] Should Ukraine use threats to turn off the pipelines as political leverage, low expectations for future trade might push Russia to reoccupy its former possession in order to mitigate its economic vulnerability.

American and European dependence on Middle East oil exports, combined with plummeting expectations for future trade, were probably the key factors leading the United States and Europe to unite against Iraq in 1990–91. It is not hard to envision future scenarios in the Persian Gulf involving fundamentalist Iran or a resurgent Iraq that could dictate a repeat of the Gulf War, this time with perhaps far more devastating consequences.

The key to moderating these potential conflicts is to alter leaders' perceptions of the future trading environment in which they operate. As the Far Eastern situation of the late 1930s showed, the instrument of trade sanctions must be used with great care when dealing with states possessing manifest or latent military power. Economic sanctions by the United States against China for human rights violations, for example, if implemented, could push China toward expansion or naval power-projection in order to safeguard supplies and to ensure the penetration of Asian markets. Sanctions against Japan could produce the same effect, if they were made too strong, or if they appeared to reflect domestic hostility to Japan itself, not just a bargaining ploy to free up trade.

The value of maintaining an open trading system through the new World Trade Organization (WTO) is also clear: any significant trend to regionalization may force dependent great powers to use military force to protect their trading realms. In this regard, my analysis tends to support the liberal view that international institutions may help reinforce the chances for peace: insofar as these institutions solidify positive expectations about the future, they reduce the incentive for aggression. Yet trade expectations between great powers are usually improved without formal institutions being involved, simply as the result of smart bilateral diplomacy. Nixon and Kissinger achieved just that when they negotiated the 1972 trade treaty with the Soviets. Conversely, trade expectations can be shattered by poor bilateral diplomacy even within the context of an overarching international regime. American trade sanctions against China or Japan tomorrow, for example, might produce profound political-military tension, even under the new WTO framework. The existence of formal institutions, therefore, does not do away with the need for intelligent great power foreign policy between individual great powers.

This article began with the question of whether high economic interdependence between states after the Cold War might help preserve the peace. For liberals confident that a new day is dawning for the international system, this analysis sounds a strong note of caution. It is the very states that are the *most* dependent on others that are likely to lead the system into war, should their leaders become pessimistic about the continuation of trading relations that so determine their wealth and security. But my argument also rejects the stark view of realists who automatically equate continued high interdependence with conflict: if leaders can sustain positive expectations for the future, then trading will indeed seem more rational than invading. To a large degree, whether interdependence leads to war or to peace thus becomes a question of political foresight. Those leaders who understand that an adversary's decisions rest not on the static situation of the present, but on the dynamic expectations for the future, will be better able to avoid the tragedy of war.

NOTES

1. For a summary of the causal variables in the two schools, see John J. Mearsheimer, "Back to the Future: Instability in Europe After the Cold War," *International Security,* Vol. 15, No. 1 (Summer 1990), pp. 5–56; Robert O. Keohane,

"International Liberalism Reconsidered," in John Dunn, ed., *The Economic Limits to Modern Politics* (Cambridge: Cambridge University Press, 1990), pp. 165–194.

2. Four other subsidiary liberal arguments,

employing intervening variables, are not sufficiently compelling to discuss here. The first suggests that high trade levels promote domestic prosperity, thereby lessening the internal problems that push leaders into war. The second argues that interdependence helps to foster increased understanding between peoples, which reduces the misunderstandings that lead to war. The third asserts that trade alters the domestic structure of states, heightening the influence of groups with a vested interest in peaceful trade. The final argument contends that trade has the "spill-over" effect of increasing political ties between trading partners, thus improving the prospects for long-term cooperation. For a critical analysis of these views, see Dale Copeland, "Economic Interdependence and the Outbreak of War," paper presented to University of Virginia Department of Government's faculty workshop, March 1995.

3. Richard Cobden, *The Political Writings of Richard Cobden* (London: T. Fischer Unwin, 1903), p. 225.

4. Norman Angell, *The Great Illusion,* 2d ed. (New York: G. P. Putnam's Sons, 1933), pp. 33, 59–60, 87–89.

5. Ibid., pp. 59–62, 256.

6. Richard Rosecrance, *The Rise of the Trading State: Commerce and Conquest in the Modern World* (New York: Basic Books, 1986), pp. 13–14; 24–25 (emphasis added); see also Rosecrance, "War, Trade and Interdependence," in James N. Rosenau and Hylke Tromp, eds., *Interdependence and Conflict in World Politics* (Aldershot, U.K.: Avebury, 1989), pp. 48–57; Rosecrance, "A New Concert of Powers," *Foreign Affairs,* Vol. 71, No. 2 (Spring 1992), pp. 64–82.

7. A book often seen as a statement on the peace-inducing effects of interdependence — Robert O. Keohane and Joseph S. Nye, *Power and Interdependence* (Boston: Little, Brown, 1977)—actually contains no such causal argument. For Keohane and Nye, "complex interdependence" is more peaceful by definition: it is "a valuable concept for analyzing the political process" only when military force is "unthinkable" (pp. 29, 24). In the second edition: "since we *define* complex interdependence in terms of [policy] goals and instruments," arguments "about how goals and instruments are affected by the degree to which a situation approximates complex interdependence or realism will be tautological." Thus, "we are left essentially with two dependent variables: changes in agendas and

changes in the roles of international organizations." Keohane and Nye, *Power and Interdependence,* 2d ed. (Glenview, Ill.: Scott, Foresman, 1989), p. 255; emphasis in original. The dependent variable of this article—the likelihood of war—is nowhere to be found, which is not surprising, since it is assumed away. Other works on interdependence from the 1970s, which largely examined dependent variables other than war, are discussed in Copeland, "Economic Interdependence and the Outbreak of War."

8. One might contend that realists doubt the causal importance of economic interdependence, since relative gains concerns convince great powers to avoid becoming dependent in the first place. Aside from arguments showing why states may cooperate despite concerns for relative gains (see essays by Powell, Snidal, and Keohane in David A. Baldwin, ed., *Neorealism and Neoliberalism: The Contemporary Debate* [New York: Columbia University Press, 1993]; Dale Copeland, "Why Relative Gains Concerns May *Promote* Economic Cooperation: A Realist Explanation for Great Power Interdependence," presented at the annual meeting of the International Studies Association, San Diego, April 1996), the argument is empirically false. Periods of high interdependence have arisen even when the security competition between great powers was particularly intense, such as from 1880 to 1914, as Waltz acknowledges. Kenneth Waltz, "The Myth of Interdependence," in Ray Maghoori and Bennett Ramberg, *Globalism versus Realism* (Boulder, Colo.: Westview Press, 1982), p. 83. Since the reality of high interdependence cannot be argued or assumed away, I focus here on the core realist claim that whenever high levels of interdependence are reached, for whatever reason, war is more likely.

9. Kenneth Waltz, *Theory of International Politics* (New York: Random House, 1979), p. 106.

10. John J. Mearsheimer, "Disorder Restored," in Graham Allison and Gregory F. Treverton, eds., *Rethinking America's Security* (New York: W. W. Norton, 1992), p. 223; Mearsheimer, "Back to the Future," p. 45. See also Robert Gilpin, "Economic Interdependence and National Security in Historical Perspective," in Klaus Knorr and Frank N. Trager, eds., *Economic Issues and National Security* (Lawrence, Kan.: Allen, 1977), p. 29. Adopting the realist argument, but emphasizing how dependence leads states to adopt destabilizing offensive strategies, is

Anne Uchitel, "Interdependence and Instability," in Jack Snyder and Robert Jervis, eds., *Coping with Complexity in the International System* (Boulder, Colo.: Westview Press, 1993), pp. 243–264. For Barry Buzan, since liberal free-trading systems are dependent on a hegemon which invariably declines, such systems are destined to fall into "malevolent" mercantilist practices, as states scramble to control access to goods formerly safeguarded by the hegemon. Avoiding the liberal system altogether, through a "benign" mercantilist system of self-sufficient trading blocs, will be therefore preferred. Buzan, "Economic Structure and International Security: The Limits of the Liberal Case," *International Organization,* Vol. 38, No. 4 (Autumn 1984), esp. pp. 597, 609–623. For a similar argument, see Robert Gilpin, *U.S. Power and the Multinational Corporation* (New York: Basic Books), 1975, p. 259.

11. See Eli F. Heckscher, *Mercantilism,* vol. 2, trans. Mendel Shapiro (London: George Allen, 1931), p. 15; Jacob Viner, "Power Versus Plenty as Objectives of Foreign Policy in the Seventeenth and Eighteenth Centuries," *World Politics,* Vol. 1, No. 1 (October 1948), p. 10; David A. Baldwin, *Economic Statecraft* (Princeton, N.J.: Princeton University Press, 1985), chap. 5.

12. Heckscher, *Mercantilism,* Vol. 2, p. 40.

13. See Keohane and Nye, "World Politics and the International Economic System," in C. Fred Bergsten, ed., *The Future of the International Economic Order* (Lexington: D. C. Heath, 1973), pp. 121–122; Neil R. Richardson and Charles W. Kegley, "Trade Dependence and Foreign Policy Compliance," *International Studies Quarterly,* Vol. 24, No. 2 (June 1980), pp. 191–222.

14. David A. Baldwin, "Interdependence and Power: A Conceptual Analysis," *International Organization,* Vol. 34, No. 4 (Autumn 1980), pp. 478, 482–484, 489; Baldwin, "The Power of Positive Sanctions," *World Politics,* Vol. 24, No. 1 (October 1971), pp. 19–38; Albert O. Hirschman, *National Power and the Structure of Foreign Trade,* exp. ed. (Berkeley: University of California Press, 1980), chap. 2.

15. On the costs of adjustment, see Ruth Arad, Seev Hirsch, and Alfred Tovias, *The Economics of Peacemaking* (New York: St. Martin's Press, 1983), pp. 26–34. Keohane and Nye examine the "costs of adjusting" as an integral part of "vulnerability" interdependence (*Power and Interdependence,* p. 13). Yet they do not establish the original autarchic position as a baseline for examining these costs independently from the benefits of trade forgone; this baseline is incorporated later in building the new theory. Liberals also consider "costs" in terms of losses in "autonomy" due to trade ties; see Richard N. Cooper, *The Economics of Interdependence* (New York: McGraw Hill, 1968), pp. 4–12; Rosecrance, *Rise of the Trading State,* pp. 39–41, 235. Note, however, that these are costs that go hand in hand with high trade, not costs that are experienced if trade is cut off. Hence, these losses in autonomy are more accurately considered as a form of sensitivity interdependence—costs incurred when trade is ongoing—rather than as a form of "vulnerability" interdependence so worrying to realists. On this, see Keohane and Nye, "International Interdependence and Integration," in Fred I. Greenstein and Nelson W. Polsby, eds., *Handbook of Political Science,* Vol. 8 (Reading, Mass.: Addison-Wesley, 1975), pp. 368–370.

16. Rosecrance, *Rise of the Trading State,* pp. 144–145. In the appendix, an iterated prisoner's dilemma is used to show the "concrete benefits" from trade cooperation. If states decide not to cooperate, they simply "[do] not benefit"; pp. 233–236.

17. Rosecrance occasionally seems to accept that some goods are more vital than others, but even here he reiterates the liberal argument: "Countries dependent on the world economy for markets, assistance, and *critical raw materials are doubly hesitant* to embark on military adventures"; ibid., p. 133, emphasis added.

18. See Plato's *Phaedrus* in *Phaedrus and Letters VII and VIII,* trans. Walter Hamilton (Harmondsworth: Penguin, 1973), sections 246–256. The historical roots of this view are explicated in Albert O. Hirschman, *The Passions and the Interests: Political Arguments for Capitalism before its Triumph* (Princeton: Princeton University Press, 1977). He quotes Montesquieu (ibid., p. 73): "It is fortunate for men to be in a situation in which, though their passions may prompt them to be wicked, they have nevertheless an interest in not being so."

19. Rosecrance, *Rise of the Trading State,* pp. 102–103 (see also p. 111). Rosecrance does point out that Germany and Japan apparently went to war also to gain raw materials (ibid., p. 108). He does not argue, however, that these two states were more dependent than other states for such materials; to have done so would suggest the validity of the realist logic.

20. See ibid., pp. 106, 123, 150, 162.

21. See ibid., pp. 18–19, 88, 96–97, 99, 150.

22. Ibid., p. 141 (see also p. 150). The argument here borders on being non-falsifiable: disconfirming cases where war occurs despite high interdependence can be sidestepped by saying simply that states did not "accept" being peaceful traders. Note as well that if states have already decided to be peaceful, then interdependence is not needed as a restraint.

23. On liberalism's inherently unit-level orientation to conflict, see Andrew Moravcsik, "Liberalism and International Relations Theory," Working Paper, Center for International Affairs, Harvard University, 1992; Michael Howard, *War and the Liberal Conscience* (New Brunswick: Rutgers University Press, 1978). On the democratic peace argument, see Bruce Russett, *Grasping the Democratic Peace* (Princeton: Princeton University Press, 1993).

24. See Rosecrance, *Rise of the Trading State,* appendix.

25. On the differences between comparative statics and dynamic analyses that incorporate the future, see Eugene Silberberg, *The Structure of Economics,* 2d ed. (New York: McGraw-Hill, 1990), chaps. 1, 12, and 18.

26. That is, war is rational if it has either a higher net *positive* value or a lower net *negative* value. The theory thus works regardless of whether states are innately "greedy"—seeking positive gains from war—or simply security-seekers desiring to minimize long-term threats. See Charles L. Glaser, "Political Consequences of Military Strategy: Expanding and Refining the Spiral and Deterrence Models," *World Politics,* Vol. 44, No. 4 (July 1992), pp. 497–538. By connecting the trading environment to fears about relative decline, I draw upon the notion that declining states launch preventive wars to uphold their waning security. Elsewhere, I build a solely power-driven theory showing why states faced with deep and inevitable decline initiate major wars. Dale Copeland, "Neorealism and the Myth of Bipolar Stability: Toward a New Dynamic Realist Theory of Major War," *Security Studies,* Vol. 5, No. 3 (Spring 1996).

27. This is consistent with standard trade theory. See Richard E. Caves and Ronald W. Jones, *World Trade and Payments,* 4th ed. (Boston: Little Brown, 1985), chaps. 3–4.

28. I thank Andrew Moravcsik for discussions on the potential benefits of trade.

29. The capital investments represent "sunk costs" not easily recouped. See Arad, Hirsch, and Tovias, *The Economics of Peacemaking,* pp. 26–28.

30. On the importance of alternatives, see Baldwin, "Interdependence and Power," p. 482; Keohane and Nye, *Power and Interdependence,* p. 13. It is worth remembering that alternative suppliers and markets are only valuable in reducing A's dependence if A can get access to them. If B is able not only to sever bilateral trade, but also to blockade A to prevent third-party trading, then A effectively has no alternatives and is therefore dependent. This was the situation for Japan *vis-à-vis* the United States before 1941 regarding oil imports.

31. This line of reasoning is developed formally in Dale Copeland, "Modelling Economic Interdependence and War: A Theory of Trade Expectations," paper presented at the annual meeting of the American Political Science Association, Chicago, September 1995. It is consistent with consideration of the "probability of transaction" as a determinant of expected national income in Arad, Hirsch, and Tovias, *The Economic of Peacemaking,* pp. 37–43, although they do not employ expectations of future trade as a theoretical variable affecting the likelihood of war.

32. The U.S.-Soviet Cold War case is covered in Copeland, "Modelling Economic Interdependence and War."

33. See Alexander L. George and Richard Smoke, *Deterrence in American Foreign Policy: Theory and Practice* (New York: Columbia University Press, 1974), chaps. 2–3.

34. This is developed formally in Copeland, "Modelling Economic Interdependence and War."

35. See Peter Liberman, "Does Conquest Pay? The Exploitation of Occupied Industrial Economies" (Ph.D. diss., Massachusetts Institute of Technology, 1991).

36. Thucydides, *The Peloponnesian War,* trans. Rex Warner (Harmondsworth: Penguin, 1954), Book 1, lines 80–88.

37. When one state is very large and the other very small, it is harder to sort out the effects of interdependence from the effects of relative power, at least in actual cases of war. The expected value of war for the superior state is likely to be quite positive anyway, and thus will tend to overshadow the expected value of trade even when the state has positive expectations of future trade. Here, the superior state simply chooses war as the "greater of two goods." This choice would not be altered by any diminution

of trade expectations; indeed, war would simply be even more rational as the expected value of trade (and therefore peace) falls. War in such a situation of marked power imbalance and low expectations of future trade is thus overdetermined; it would be difficult to tell whether war occurred because of the positive expected value of war, the negative expected value of trade, or both. Thus, in my empirical analysis, I examine cases where great powers attacked great powers in long and costly total wars. While these cases do not cover the universe of wars, they do isolate the role of economic interdependence and changing expectations of future trade in the outbreak of war.

38. Given space constraints, my case studies in this article do not provide a full analysis of the bargaining dynamic. For an analysis of interstate economic bargaining, see Baldwin, *Economic Statecraft,* chap. 6; R. Harrison Wagner, "Economic Interdependence, Bargaining Power, and Political Influence," *International Organization,* Vol. 42, No. 3 (Summer 1988), pp. 461–483. Note also that there may be a causal feedback loop, whereby increasing fears of war lead others to reduce trade, which in turn heightens the incentive of dependent state to initiate war. These and other issues involving the endogeneity of trade expectations are addressed more fully in my book manuscript, "Economic Interdependence and War."

39. Note that state A, the decision-making unit in the theory, can still be treated as a rational unitary actor *responding* to the observed domestic forces on the other side.

40. See Copeland, "Modeling Economic Interdependence and War," pp. 62–66. International trade institutions such as the General Agreement on Tariffs and Trade (GATT), by lowering transaction costs and facilitating the punishment of cheaters, may be an additional means to build positive expectations for future trade. Indeed, for some liberals, peace may only be likely when both interdependence and effective global institutions co-exist and reinforce one another; Keohane, "International Liberalism Reconsidered," p. 183. While such institutions may indeed affect trade expectations, they are unlikely to be as significant in history as the systemic and domestic factors just discussed, for the simple reason that these institutions are a creation of the post–World War II era. Moreover, since concerns for war and peace revolve mostly around the great powers, and powers like Soviet Union and China have been historically ex-

cluded from trade institutions like GATT, such institutions cannot account for fluctuations in the levels of tension between the United States and these powers since 1945. Finally, the institutional approach overlooks *bilateral* diplomacy as the principal mechanism through which expectations of trade change; consider the United States and Japan up to December 1941, or the United States and Japan today. Accordingly, while my argument recognizes the contribution institutions can make to the improvement of future trade expectations, the focus both theoretically and empirically remains fundamentally non-institutional.

41. Trade expectations theory, like realism, is a systemic theory; it assumes no unit-level drives towards aggression. While expectations may seem like a unit-level factor, remember that these are expectations of an external phenomenon, namely, the other's propensity to trade into the future; the causal source of behavior comes from outside, not from within, the actor. See Waltz, *Theory of International Politics,* p. 60. One might also argue that domestic and individual level factors within a state can distort expectations, but I simply assume that such misperceptions are minimal for purposes of building a deductive theory; this assumption can be later relaxed if so desired.

42. Given space limitations, my "best case" among the major wars of this century, Japan and World War II, is covered elsewhere; Copeland, "Modelling Economic Interdependence and War." I show that Japanese leaders—military, civilian, and the emperor himself—reluctantly moved towards a consensus for war with the United States and Britain due to progressively more devastating U.S.-British trade sanctions. Japan, due to its small size, was almost completely dependent on outside sources for the raw materials and oil that supported its industrial structure. As American and British trade restrictions began to increase after 1930, and especially after a series of embargoes starting in 1939, Japan shifted from a primary concern with the Soviet threat to the need for control of raw materials in South East Asia. After the U.S., British, and Dutch severed all oil trade to Japan in July–August 1941, Japanese leaders agreed that unless oil imports were restored, economic decline would imperil long-term security. Hence, following the failure of desperate diplomatic initiatives in November 1941 to secure renewed trade, the plan for all-out war was accepted by the emperor. In short, Japan's extreme depend-

ence, coupled with very negative expectations for future trade, pushed the country into a war that almost all recognized would have great costs and a low probability of success. See Nobutaka Ike, trans. and ed., *Japan's Decision for War: Records of the 1941 Policy Conferences* (Stanford: Stanford University Press, 1967).

43. See note 37, above. To minimize the selection bias of focusing just on the wars themselves, I also look at the periods before the wars began, to see how incentives for aggression changed as independent variables did.

44. Empirical analyses so far have been primarily correlational studies, finding that high trade tends to be associated with lower conflict. Mark J. Gasiorowski, "Economic Interdependence and International Conflict: Some Cross-national Evidence," *International Studies Quarterly*, Vol. 30, No. 1 (March 1986), pp. 22–38; Mark J. Gasiorowski and Solomon W. Polachek, "Conflict and Interdependence: East-West Trade and Linkages in the Era of Detente," *Journal of Conflict Resolution*, Vol. 26, No. 4 (December 1982), pp. 709–729; Polachek, "Conflict and Trade," *Journal of Conflict Research*, Vol. 24, No. 1 (March 1980), pp. 55–78; William J. Domke, *War and the Changing Global System* (New Haven: Yale University Press, 1988), chap. 5; Edward D. Mansfield, *Power, Trade, and War* (Princeton: Princeton University Press, 1994), chap 4. These studies, however, provide no documentary evidence that leaders considered trade levels in deciding between war and peace. It is thus hard to know whether the correlation is spurious or illuminating. While the result seems to support liberalism over realism, it is also consistent with trade expectations theory: high trade should be associated with lower conflict in those instances where expectations for future trade are also positive. Given their suspect methodologies, one should also be cautious about quickly dismissing realism. The correlation of trade with less conflict in the first three studies is not surprising, since dyads of small states are included to build the sample. Such states tend to have very high trade/GNP ratios. See Stephen D. Krasner, "State Power and the Structure of International Trade," *World Politics*, Vol. 28, No. 3 (April 1976), p. 328. However, they are deterred from war by their very size. Note as well that all of these tests simply assume that the trade/GNP ratio alone is an adequate measure of the core concept, dependence. Given the concern of realism and trade expectations theory for the costs of severed trade, a proper test must also include such factors

as dependence on others for vital goods and availability of alternative sources of supply.

45. See Paul M. Kennedy, *The Rise of Anglo-German Antagonism, 1860–1914* (London: Ashfield, 1980), chaps. 12–14.

46. Quoted from *German Diplomatic Documents, 1871–1914*, vol. II, trans. E. T. S. Dugsdale (New York: Harper and Brothers, 1930), pp. 486–487.

47. Fritz Fischer, *War of Illusions: German Policies from 1911 to 1914*, trans. Marian Jackson (New York: W. W. Norton, 1975), p. 7.

48. Lamar Cecil, *Albert Ballin: Business and Politics in Imperial Germany* (Princeton: Princeton University Press, 1967), p. 149. It was at this time that German leaders implemented the concepts of *Weltpolitik* and *Mitteleuropa* as responses to growing foreign protectionism. *Weltpolitik* sought "the attainment of secure external supplies of raw materials at regulated prices," while *Mitteleuropa*, its continental counterpart, envisioned the development of "an organized and protected system of economic exchanges between an industrial Germany and an agricultural periphery in central and eastern Europe." See Woodruff D. Smith, *The Ideological Origins of Nazi Imperialism* (New York: Oxford University Press, 1986), pp. 65, 78.

49. See B. R. Mitchell, *European Historical Statistics, 1750–1975*, 2d rev. ed. (New York: Facte on File, 1981), pp. 514, 821 on trade/GNP; pp. 393, 439 on oil; pp. 409, 445–446 on iron ore. See W. F. Bruck, *Social and Economic History of Germany from William II to Hitler, 1888–1938* (Cardiff: Oxford University Press, 1938), p. 110 on raw materials.

50. Holger H. Herwig, *Politics of Frustration: The United States in German Naval Planning, 1889–1941* (Boston: Little, Brown, 1976), p. 9.

51. Quoted in G. Lowes Dickinson, *The International Anarchy, 1904–1914* (New York: Century, 1926), p. 261; see also chap. 10.

52. See Fiona Venn, *Oil Diplomacy in the Twentieth Century* (New York: St. Martin's, 1986), chap. 2; Daniel Yergin, *The Prize: The Epic Quest for Oil, Money, and Power* (New York: Simon and Schuster, 1991), pp. 153–163.

53. Fischer, *War of Illusions*, pp. 321–322; see also Hans W. Gatzke, *Germany's Drive to the West* (Baltimore: Johns Hopkins Press, 1950), pp. 30–38.

54. Quoted in Fischer, *War of Illusion*, p. 326; see also pp. 322–326.

55. Avner Offer, *The First World War: An Agrarian Interpretation* (Oxford: Oxford University Press, 1989), p. 322; chaps. 15–21; pp. 325–

326, 335. By 1906, Germany was importing about 20 per cent of its annual grain consumption (p. 230).

56. While Fischer's goal is to show that domestic causes for the war were predominant, much of his evidence actually indicates that German leaders were driven by systemic concerns, namely the safeguarding of German economic security. Fischer, *War of Illusions,* pp. viii–ix.

57. Quoted in ibid., p. 35.

58. Fischer's words, ibid., p. 10.

59. Quotations in ibid., pp. 234, 250–253.

60. Quoted in ibid., pp. 238, 450.

61. For a summary, see Dale Copeland, "Realism and the Origins of Major War" (Ph.D. diss., University of Chicago, 1993), chaps. 3 and 4.

62. Quoted in Fritz Fischer, *Germany's Aims in the First World War* (New York: W. W. Norton, 1967), pp. 103–104.

63. Ibid., pp. 101 and 11. The first part of the quote is Fischer's paraphrase from the document; the words "essential objective" Fischer takes from the document itself. Bethmann was clearly impressed by the memo; he circulated it throughout the department. Ibid., p. 101.

64. Quoted in Fischer, *War of Illusions,* p. 533; Fischer, *Germany's Aims,* p. 104.

65. Fischer's words summarizing the document, *War of Illusions,* p. 538.

66. Quoted in ibid., p. 540.

67. Quoted in ibid., p. 539.

68. Quoted in Fischer, *War of Illusions,* p. 539 and *Germany's Aims,* p. 251.

69. In showing this continuity, I do not mean to minimize the atrocities committed by the Nazi regime. Rather, while Hitler's *means* were far more evil than Wilhelmine Germany's, many of his *ends* in terms of economic and territorial security were essentially the same. The most important contribution to the "continuity" argument in modern historiography is Fritz Fischer's work and the work of his followers in the "Hamburg School." See also Smith, *Ideological Origins.*

70. Hitler, *Mein Kampf,* trans. Ralph Manheim (Boston: Houghton Mifflin, 1925), pp. 131–140. For the pre-1914 origins of the idea of *Lebensraum,* see Smith, *Ideological Origins,* chap. 5.

71. On Hitler's fears of the rise of Russia, see Hitler, *Mein Kampf,* chap. 24.

72. From J. Noakes and G. Pridham's summary notes, *Nazism 1919–1945: A Documentary Reader,* vols. 2 and 3 (Exeter, U.K.: University of Exeter, 1988), pp. 259–260.

73. Ibid., p. 260.

74. Ibid., Doc. No. 181, p. 270.

75. Ibid., p. 274. See also Hirschman, *National Power,* part II.

76. Noakes and Pridham, *Nazism, 1919–1945,* p. 277.

77. Ibid., Doc. No. 185, pp. 283–284.

78. Ibid., Doc. No. 185, pp. 284–286 (emphasis added).

79. Oil figures from Robert Goralski and Russell W. Freeburg, *Oil and War: How the Deadly Struggle for Fuel in WWII Meant Victory or Defeat* (New York: William Morrow, 1987), p. 26; iron ore from Mitchell, *European Historical Statistics,* pp. 446, 410; raw materials from Noakes and Pridham, *Nazism 1919–1945,* p. 291. On German efforts to reduce dependence through increased trade ties with China and Eastern Europe, and through intervention in the Spanish Civil War, see Gerhard L. Weinberg, *The Foreign Policy of Hitler's Germany: Starting World War II* (Chicago: University of Chicago Press, 1980), chaps. 1, 5 and 7; David E. Kaiser, *Economic Diplomacy and the Origins of the Second World War* (Princeton: Princeton University Press, 1980); Robert H. Whealey, *Hitler and Spain: The Nazi Role in the Spanish Civil War, 1936–1939* (Lexington: University Press of Kentucky, 1989); Berenice A. Carroll, *Design for Total War: Arms and Economics in the Third Reich* (The Hague: Mouton, 1968).

80. Yergin, *The Prize,* p. 332.

81. See Noakes and Pridham, *Nazism 1919–1945,* p. 680.

82. Ibid., Doc. No. 503, pp. 681–683.

83. Ibid., Doc. No. 503, pp. 682–683.

84. Ibid., Doc. No. 503, pp. 684–685.

85. One might discount Hitler's language as mere talk necessary to justify his true driving force, which was his lust to dominate others; see Hans J. Morgenthau, *Scientific Man Versus Power Politics* (Chicago: University of Chicago Press, 1946). Even if this were true, however, it begs the question of why he felt his four key military leaders would need to hear an elaborate economic rationale for war. We thus return to the point that without the support of his subordinates, Hitler could not have initiated war; calculated aggression, therefore, had to have a logical end. It is also clear that the majority of Hitler's military leaders were not simply brain-washed dupes of Nazi ideology, but accepted the necessity of major war on strategic grounds. See the essays in Correlli Barnett, ed., *Hitler's Generals* (New York: Quill, 1989); John J. Mearsheimer, *Conventional Deterrence* (Ithaca: Cornell Uni-

versity Press, 1983), chap. 4; Dale Copeland, "Deterrence, Reassurance, and Machiavellian Appeasement: Was the Second World War Inevitable?" paper presented at *Security Studies* conference on "Deterrence after the Cold War: Theoretical Perspectives and Policy Implications of Enduring Rivalries," Naval Postgraduate School, Monterey, Calif., September 1995.

86. On May 23, 1939, Hitler told his top military officials that while Germany must "aim at a short war," it "must also be prepared for a war of 10–15 years' duration." Noakes and Pridham, *Nazism 1919–1945,* Doc. No. 539, p. 738.

87. See Nicholas D. Kristof, "The Rise of China," *Foreign Affairs,* Vol. 72, No. 5 (November/December 1993), p. 64.

88. China has already staked a claim to the potentially oil rich and much disputed Spratly Islands in the South China Sea. See Gerald Segal, "East Asia and the 'Constrainment' of China," *International Security,* Vol. 20, No. 4 (Spring 1996), pp. 107–135. William H. Overholt, *The Rise of China: How Economic Reform Is Creating a New Superpower* (New York: Norton, 1993).

89. For an exaggerated but still insightful analysis of this, see George Friedman and Meredith Lebard, *The Coming War with Japan* (New York: St. Martin's Press, 1991).

90. See Erik Whitlock, "Ukrainian-Russian Trade: The Economics of Dependency," *Radio Free Europe/Radio Liberty Research Report,* Vol. 2, No. 43 (October 29, 1993), pp. 38–42.

Reading 10-2

Spreading the Wealth
David Dollar and Aart Kraay

A RISING TIDE

One of the main claims of the antiglobalization movement is that globalization is widening the gap between the haves and the have-nots. It benefits the rich and does little for the poor, perhaps even making their lot harder. As union leader Jay Mazur put it . . ., "globalization has dramatically increased inequality between and within nations." . . . The problem with this new conventional wisdom is that the best evidence available shows the exact opposite to be true. So far, the current wave of globalization, which started around 1980, has actually promoted economic equality and reduced poverty.

Global economic integration has complex effects on income, culture, society, and the environment. But in the debate over globalization's merits, its impact on poverty is particularly important. If international trade and investment primarily benefit the rich, many people will feel that restricting trade to protect jobs, culture, or the environment is worth the costs. But if restricting trade imposes further hardship on poor people in the developing world, many of the same people will think otherwise.

Three facts bear on this question. First, a long-term global trend toward greater inequality prevailed for at least 200 years; it peaked around 1975. But since then, it has stabilized and possibly even reversed. The chief reason for the change has been the accelerated growth of two large and initially poor countries: China and India.

Second, a strong correlation links increased participation in international trade and investment on the one hand and faster growth on the other. The developing world can

SOURCE: From "Spreading the Wealth" by David Dollar and Aart Kraay, *Foreign Affairs,* vol. 81, no. 1 (January/February 2002): 120–133. Copyright © 2002 by the Council on Foreign Relations. Reprinted by permission.

be divided into a "globalizing" group of countries that have seen rapid increases in trade and foreign investment over the last two decades—well above the rates for rich countries—and a "nonglobalizing" group that trades even less of its income today than it did 20 years ago. The aggregate annual per capita growth rate of the globalizing group accelerated steadily from one percent in the 1960s to five percent in the 1990s. During that latter decade, in contrast, rich countries grew at two percent and nonglobalizers at only one percent. Economists are cautious about drawing conclusions concerning causality, but they largely agree that openness to foreign trade and investment (along with complementary reforms) explains the faster growth of the globalizers.

Third, and contrary to popular perception, globalization has not resulted in higher inequality within economies. Inequality has indeed gone up in some countries (such as China) and down in others (such as the Philippines). But those changes are not systematically linked to globalization measures such as trade and investment flows, tariff rates, and the presence of capital controls. Instead, shifts in inequality stem more from domestic education, taxes, and social policies. In general, higher growth rates in globalizing developing countries have translated into higher incomes for the poor. Even with its increased inequality, for example, China has seen the most spectacular reduction of poverty in world history—which was supported by opening its economy to foreign trade and investment.

Although globalization can be a powerful force for poverty reduction, its beneficial results are not inevitable. If policymakers hope to tap the full potential of economic integration and sustain its benefits, they must address three critical challenges. A growing protectionist movement in rich countries that aims to limit integration with poor ones must be stopped in its tracks. Developing countries need to acquire the kinds of institutions and policies that will allow them to prosper under globalization, both of which may be different from place to place. And more migration, both domestic and international, must be permitted when geography limits the potential for development.

THE GREAT DIVIDE

Over the past 200 years, different local economies around the world have become more integrated while the growth rate of the global economy has accelerated dramatically. Although it is impossible to prove causal linkage between the two developments—since there are no other world economies to be tested against—evidence suggests the arrows run in both directions. As Adam Smith argued, a larger market permits a finer division of labor, which in turn facilitates innovation and learning by doing. Some of that innovation involves transportation and communications technologies that lower costs and increase integration. So it is easy to see how integration and innovation can be mutually supportive.

Different locations have become more integrated because of increased flows of goods, capital, and knowledge. From 1820 to 1914, international trade increased faster than the global economy. Trade rose from about 2 percent of world income in 1820 to 18 percent in 1914. The globalization of trade took a step backward during the protectionist period of the Great Depression and World War II, and by 1950 trade (in relation to income) was lower than it had been in 1914. But thanks to a series of multilateral trade liberalizations under the General Agreement on Tariffs and Trade (GATT), trade dramatically expanded among industrialized countries between 1960 and 1980. Most developing countries remained largely isolated from this trade because of their own inward-focused policies, but the success of such notable exceptions as Taiwan and

South Korea eventually helped encourage other developing economies to open themselves up to foreign trade and investment.

International capital flows, measured as foreign ownership of assets relative to world income, also grew during the first wave of globalization and declined during the Great Depression and World War II; they did not return to 1914 levels until 1980. But since then, such flows have increased markedly and changed their nature as well. One hundred years ago, foreign capital typically financed public infrastructure projects (such as canals and railroads) or direct investment related to natural resources. Today, in contrast, the bulk of capital flows to developing countries is direct investments tied to manufacturing and services.

The change in the nature of capital flows is clearly related to concurrent advances in economic integration, such as cheaper and faster transportation and revolutionary changes in telecommunications. Since 1920, seagoing freight charges have declined by about two-thirds and air travel costs by 84 percent; the cost of a three-minute call from New York City to London has dropped by 99 percent. Today, production in widely differing locations can be integrated in ways that simply were not possible before.

Another aspect of integration has been the movement of people. Yet here the trend is reversed: there is much more international travel than in the past but much less permanent migration. Between 1870 and 1910, about ten percent of the world's population relocated permanently from one country to another; over the past 25 years, only one to two percent have done so.

As economic integration has progressed, the annual growth rate of the world economy has accelerated, from 1 percent in the mid-nineteenth century to 3.5 percent in 1960–2000. Sustained over many years, such a jump in growth makes a huge difference in real living standards. It now takes only two to three years, for example, for the world economy to produce the same amount of goods and services that it did during the entire nineteenth century. Such a comparison is arguably a serious understatement of the true difference, since most of what is consumed today—airline travel, cars, televisions, synthetic fibers, life-extending drugs—did not exist 200 years ago. For any of these goods or services, therefore, the growth rate of output since 1820 is infinite. Human productivity has increased almost unimaginably.

All this tremendous growth in wealth was distributed very unequally up to about 1975, but since then growing equality has taken hold. One good measure of inequality among individuals worldwide is the mean log deviation—a measure of the gap between the income of any randomly selected person and a general average. It takes into account the fact that income distributions everywhere are skewed in favor of the rich, so that the typical person is poorer than the group average; the more skewed the distribution, the larger the gap. Per capita income in the world today, for example, is around $5,000, whereas a randomly selected person would most likely be living on close to $1,000—80 percent less. That gap translates into a mean log deviation of 0.8.

Taking this approach, an estimate of the world distribution of income among individuals shows rising inequality between 1820 and 1975. In that period, the gap between the typical person and world per capita income increased from about 40 percent to about 80 percent. Since changes in income inequality within countries were small, the increase in inequality was driven mostly by differences in growth rates across countries. Areas that were already relatively rich in 1820 (notably, Europe and the United States) grew faster than poor areas (notably, China and India). Global inequality peaked sometime in the 1970s, but it then stabilized and even began to decline, largely because growth in China and India began to accelerate.

Another way of looking at global inequality is to examine what is happening to the extreme poor—those people living on less than $1 per day. Although the percentage of the world's population living in poverty has declined over time, the absolute number rose fairly steadily until 1980. During the Great Depression and World War II, the number of poor increased particularly sharply, and it declined somewhat immediately thereafter. The world economy grew strongly between 1960 and 1980, but the number of poor rose because growth did not occur in the places where the worst-off live. But since then, the most rapid growth has occurred in poor locations. Consequently the number of poor has declined by 200 million since 1980. Again, this trend is explained primarily by the rapid income growth in China and India, which together in 1980 accounted for about one-third of the world's population and more than 60 percent of the world's extreme poor.

UPWARD BOUND

The shift in the trend in global inequality coincides with the shift in the economic strategies of several large developing countries. Following World War II, most developing regions chose strategies that focused inward and discouraged integration with the global economy. But these approaches were not particularly successful, and throughout the 1960s and 1970s developing countries on the whole grew less rapidly than industrialized ones. The oil shocks and U.S. inflation of the 1970s created severe problems for them, contributing to negative growth, high inflation, and debt crises over the next several years. Faced with these disappointing results, several developing countries began to alter their strategies starting in the 1980s.

For example, China had an extremely closed economy until the mid-1970s. Although Beijing's initial economic reform focused on agriculture, a key part of its approach since the 1980s has involved opening up foreign trade and investment, including a drop in its tariff rates by two-thirds and its nontariff barriers by even more. These reforms have led to unprecedented economic growth in the country's coastal provinces and more moderate growth in the interior. From 1978 to 1994 the Chinese economy grew annually by 9 percent, while exports grew by 14 percent and imports by 13 percent. Of course, China and other globalizing developing countries have pursued a wide range of reforms, not just economic openness. Beijing has strengthened property rights through land reform and moved from a planned economy toward a market-oriented one, and these measures have contributed to its integration as well as to its growth.

Other developing countries have also opened up as a part of broader reform programs. During the 1990s, India liberalized foreign trade and investment with good results; its annual per capita income growth now tops four percent. It too has pursued a broad agenda of reform and has moved away from a highly regulated, planned system. Meanwhile, Uganda and Vietnam are the best examples of very low-income countries that have increased their participation in trade and investment and prospered as a result. And in the western hemisphere, Mexico is noteworthy both for signing its free-trade agreement with the United States and Canada in 1993 and for its rapid growth since then, especially in the northern regions near the U.S. border.

These cases illustrate how openness to foreign trade and investment, coupled with complementary reforms, typically leads to faster growth. India, China, Vietnam, Uganda, and Mexico are not isolated examples; in general, countries that have become more open have grown faster. The best way to illustrate this trend is to rank developing countries in order of their increases in trade relative to national income over the past 20 years. The top third of this list can be thought of as the "globalizing" camp, and the bottom two-thirds as the "nonglobalizing" camp. The globalizers have increased their trade relative to income by 104 percent over the past two decades, compared to 71 percent for rich countries. The nonglobalizers, meanwhile, actually trade less today than they did 20 years ago. The globalizers have also cut their import tariffs by 22 percentage points on average, compared to only 11 percentage points for the nonglobalizers.

How have the globalizers fared in terms of growth? Their average annual growth rates accelerated from 1 percent in the 1960s to 3 percent in the 1970s, 4 percent in the 1980s, and 5 percent in the 1990s. Rich countries' annual growth rates, by comparison, slowed to about 2 percent in the 1990s, and the nonglobalizers saw their growth rates decline from 3 percent in the 1970s to 1 percent in the 1980s and 1990s.

The same pattern can be observed on a local level. Within both China and India, the locations that are integrating with the global economy are growing much more rapidly than the disconnected regions. Indian states, for example, vary significantly in the quality of their investment climates as measured by government efficiency, corruption, and infrastructure. Those states with better investment climates have integrated themselves more closely with outside markets and have experienced more investment (domestic and foreign) than their less-integrated counterparts. Moreover, states that were initially poor and then created good investment climates had stronger poverty reduction in the 1990s than those not integrating with the global economy. Such internal comparisons are important because, by holding national trade and macroeconomic policies constant, they reveal how important it is to complement trade liberalization with institutional reform so that integration can actually occur.

The accelerated growth rates of globalizing countries such as China, India, and Vietnam are consistent with cross-country comparisons that find openness going hand in hand with faster growth. The most that these studies can establish is that more trade and investment is highly correlated with higher growth, so one needs to be careful about drawing conclusions about causality. Still, the overall evidence from individual cases and cross-country correlation is persuasive. As economists Peter Lindert and Jeffrey Williamson have written, "even though no one study can establish that openness to trade has unambiguously helped the representative Third World economy, the preponderance of evidence supports this conclusion." They go on to note that "there are no antiglobal victories to report for the postwar Third World."

Contrary to the claims of the antiglobalization movement, therefore, greater openness to international trade and investment has in fact helped narrow the gap between rich and poor countries rather than widen it. During the 1990s, the economies of the globalizers, with a combined population of about 3 billion, grew more than twice as fast as the rich countries. The nonglobalizers, in contrast, grew only half as fast and nowadays lag further and further behind. Much of the discussion of global inequality assumes that there is growing divergence between the developing world and the rich world, but this is simply not true. The most important development in global inequality in recent decades is the growing divergence within the developing world, and it is directly related to whether countries take advantage of the economic benefits that globalization can offer.

THE PATH OUT OF POVERTY

The antiglobalization movement also claims that economic integration is worsening inequality within countries as well as between them. Until the mid-1980s, there was insufficient evidence to support strong conclusions on this important topic. But now more and more developing countries have begun to conduct household income and consumption surveys of reasonable quality. (In low-income countries, these surveys typically track what households actually consume because so much of their real income is self-produced and not part of the money economy.) Good surveys now exist for 137 countries, and many go back far enough to measure changes in inequality over time.

One way of looking at inequality within countries is to focus on what happens to the bottom 20 percent of households as globalization and growth proceed apace. Across all countries, incomes of the poor grow at around the same rate as GDP. Of course, there is a great deal of variation around that average relationship. In some countries, income distribution has shifted in favor of the poor; in others, against them. But these shifts cannot be explained by any globalization-related variable. So it simply cannot be said that inequality necessarily rises with more trade, more foreign investment, and lower tariffs. For many globalizers, the overall change in distribution was small, and in some cases (such as the Philippines and Malaysia) it was even in favor of the poor. What changes in inequality do reflect are country-specific policies on education, taxes, and social protection.

It is important not to misunderstand this finding. China is an important example of a country that has had a large increase in inequality in the past decade, when the income of the bottom 20 percent has risen much less rapidly than per capita income. This trend may be related to greater openness, although domestic liberalization is a more likely cause. China started out in the 1970s with a highly equal distribution of income, and part of its reform has deliberately aimed at increasing the returns on education, which financially reward the better schooled. But the Chinese case is not typical; inequality has not increased in most of the developing countries that have opened up to foreign trade and investment. Furthermore, income distribution in China may have become more unequal, but the income of the poor in China has still risen rapidly. In fact, the country's progress in reducing poverty has been one of the most dramatic successes in history.

Because increased trade usually accompanies more rapid growth and does not systematically change household-income distribution, it generally is associated with improved well-being of the poor. Vietnam nicely illustrates this finding. As the nation has opened up, it has experienced a large increase in per capita income and no significant change in inequality. Thus the income of the poor has risen dramatically, and the number of Vietnamese living in absolute poverty dropped sharply from 75 percent of the population in 1988 to 37 percent in 1998. Of the poorest 5 percent of households in 1992, 98 percent were better off six years later. And the improved well-being is not just a matter of income. Child labor has declined, and school enrollment has increased. It should be no surprise that the vast majority of poor households in Vietnam benefited immediately from a more liberalized trading system, since the country's opening has resulted in exports of rice (produced by most of the poor farmers) and labor-intensive products such as footwear. But the experience of China and Vietnam is not unique. India and Uganda also enjoyed rapid poverty reduction as they grew along with their integration into the global economy.

THE OPEN SOCIETIES

These findings have important implications for developing countries, for rich countries such as the United States, and for those who care about global poverty. All parties should recognize that the most recent wave of globalization has been a powerful force for equality and poverty reduction, and they should commit themselves to seeing that it continues despite the obstacles lying ahead.

It is not inevitable that globalization will proceed. In 1910, many believed globalization was unstoppable; they soon received a rude shock. History is not likely to repeat itself in the same way, but it is worth noting that antiglobalization sentiments are on the rise. A growing number of political leaders in the developing world realize that an open trading system is very much in their countries' interest. They would do well to heed Mexican President Vicente Fox, who said recently,

> We are convinced that globalization is good and it's good when you do your homework, . . . keep your fundamentals in line on the economy, build up high levels of education, respect the rule of law. . . . When you do your part, we are convinced that you get the benefit.

But today the narrow interests opposed to further integration—especially those in the rich countries—appear to be much more energetic than their opponents. In Québec City last spring and in Genoa last summer, a group of democratically elected leaders gathered to discuss how to pursue economic integration and improve the lives of their peoples. Antiglobalization demonstrators were quite effective in disrupting the meetings and drawing media attention to themselves. Leaders in developed and developing countries alike must make the proglobalization case more directly and effectively or risk having their opponents dominate the discussion and stall the process.

In addition, industrialized countries still raise protectionist measures against agricultural and labor-intensive products. Reducing those barriers would help developing countries significantly. The poorer areas of the world would benefit from further openings of their own markets as well, since 70 percent of the tariff barriers that developing countries face are from other developing countries.

If globalization proceeds, its potential to be an equalizing force will depend on whether poor countries manage to integrate themselves into the global economic system. True integration requires not just trade liberalization but wide-ranging institutional reform. Many of the nonglobalizing developing countries, such as Myanmar, Nigeria, Ukraine, and Pakistan, offer an unattractive investment climate. Even if they decide to open themselves up to trade, not much is likely to happen unless other reforms are also pursued. It is not easy to predict the reform paths of these countries; some of the relative successes in recent years, such as China, India, Uganda, and Vietnam, have come as quite a surprise. But as long as a location has weak institutions and policies, people living there are going to fall further behind the rest of the world.

Through their trade policies, rich countries can make it easier for those developing countries that do choose to open up and join the global trading club. But in recent years, the rich countries have been doing just the opposite. GATT was originally built around agreements concerning trade practices. Now, institutional harmonization, such as agreement on policies toward intellectual property rights, is a requirement for joining the WTO. Any sort of regulation of labor and environmental standards made under the threat of WTO sanctions would take this requirement for harmonization much further. Such measures would be neoprotectionist in effect, because they would thwart the integration of developing countries into the world economy and discourage trade between poor countries and rich ones.

The WTO meeting in Doha was an important step forward on trade integration. More forcefully than in Seattle, leaders of industrial countries were willing to make the case for further integration and put on the table issues of central concern to developing nations: access to pharmaceutical patents, use of antidumping measures against developing countries, and agricultural subsidies. The new round of trade negotiations launched at Doha has the potential to reverse the current trend, which makes it more difficult for poor countries to integrate with the world economy.

A final potential obstacle to successful and equitable globalization relates to geography. There is no inherent reason why coastal China should be poor; the same goes for southern India, northern Mexico, and Vietnam. All of these locations are near important markets or trade routes but were long held back by misguided policies. Now, with appropriate reforms, they are starting to grow rapidly and take their natural place in the world. But the same cannot be said for Mali, Chad, or other countries or regions cursed with "poor geography"—i.e., distance from markets, inherently high transport costs, and challenging health and agricultural problems. It would be naive to think that trade and investment alone can alleviate poverty in all locations. In fact, for those locations with poor geography, trade liberalization is less important than developing proper health care systems or providing basic infrastructure—or letting people move elsewhere.

Migration from poor locations is the missing factor in the current wave of globalization that could make a large contribution to reducing poverty. Each year, 83 million people are added to the world's population, 82 million of them in the developing world. In Europe and Japan, moreover, the population is aging and the labor force is set to shrink. Migration of relatively unskilled workers from South to North would thus offer clear economic benefits to both. Most migration from South to North is economically motivated, and it raises the living standard of the migrant while benefiting the sending country in three ways. First, it reduces the South's labor force and thus raises wages for those who remain behind. Second, migrants send remittances of hard currency back home. Finally, migration bolsters transnational trade and investment networks. In the case of Mexico, for example, ten percent of its citizens live and work in the United States, taking pressure off its own labor market and raising wages there. India gets six times as much in remittances from its workers overseas as it gets in foreign aid.

Unlike trade, however, migration remains highly restricted and controversial. Some critics perceive a disruptive impact on society and culture and fear downward pressure on wages and rising unemployment in the richer countries. Yet anti-immigration lobbies ignore the fact that geographical economic disparities are so strong that illegal immigration is growing rapidly anyway, despite restrictive policies. In a perverse irony, some of the worst abuses of globalization occur because there is not enough of it in key economic areas such as labor flows. Human traffic, for example, has become a highly lucrative, unregulated business in which illegal migrants are easy prey for exploitation.

Realistically, none of the industrialized countries is going to adopt open migration. But they should reconsider their migration policies. Some, for example, have a strong bias in their immigration rules toward highly skilled workers, which in fact spurs a "brain drain" from the developing world. Such policies do little to stop the flow of unskilled workers and instead push many of these people into the illegal category. If rich countries would legally accept more unskilled workers, they could address their own looming labor shortages, improve living standards in developing countries, and reduce illegal human traffic and its abuses.

In sum, the integration of poor economies with richer ones over the past two decades has provided many opportunities for poor people to improve their lives. Examples of the beneficiaries of globalization can be found among Mexican migrants, Chinese factory workers, Vietnamese peasants, and Ugandan farmers. Many of the better-off in developing and rich countries alike also benefit. After all the rhetoric about globalization is stripped away, many of the policy questions come down to whether the rich world will make integrating with the world economy easy for those poor communities that want to do so. The world's poor have a large stake in how the rich countries answer.

Reading 10-3

A Postscript to the Asian Financial Crisis
The Fragile International Economic Order
Robert Gilpin

The 1997–98 financial/economic crisis in East Asia, alongside the extraordinary growth of the American economy and the collapse of the 1999 World Trade Organization (WTO) meeting in Seattle, is one of the three signal economic events of the post–Cold-War era. These events left a mixed legacy for the 21st-century global economy. In singling them out, I am not ignoring the acceleration beginning in the mid-1980s of the movement toward Western European integration, the post-1991 troubles of the Soviet/Russian economy, or the serious economic troubles of Japan following the collapse of the "bubble" in the early 1990s. A full accounting of important economic events during the last decade of the 20th century would have to include these important developments. However, my focus here is the stability and governance of the global economy, an issue set forth in Donald Hellmann's comment that "what is needed is . . . a systematic effort to create institutions designed to bring East Asia into the interdependent but non-convergent world in which we live."

As Donald Hellmann points out . . . , many, if not most, American political leaders, business executives, and scholars, especially economists, believe that the global economy "can be effectively managed by modestly reforming international economic organizations now in place." Underlying this conviction is the belief that market forces and growing acceptance of the guiding principles of neoclassical economics are leading to a convergence of Asian and other national economies to the highly successful American free market model. What need is there for international rules and institutions if economic actors pursue rational economic strategies in the confines of a global market economy? In such a self-regulating economic system, the thinking goes, the market will punish improper and irrational behavior as it did in South Korea, Thailand, and the other East Asian economies for their imprudent economic policies prior to the onset of the 1997 financial crisis. Having learned their lesson, these errant economies now are abandoning past risky economic practices and moving toward the superior American market-oriented economy.

My argument is that this prevalent American faith in the guiding hand of the market is likely to be undermined by unexpected developments as the 21st century progresses. Moreover, likely developments suggest that it is illusory to believe that the world is converging toward the American model of a market economy. . . . It is doubtful that Japan and the other East Asian economies will develop that way. The world will not witness the complete triumph of the free market in the foreseeable future. Although many proponents of this position believe that the East Asian financial crisis has proven the superiority of the self-regulating market, this faith, to which the Bush administration has given its unqualified support, is not shared by many other governments. Moreover, it is dangerous to believe, as the Bush administration does, that the stability and functioning of the global economy can be achieved through reliance on self-regulating and self-correcting markets.

SOURCE: From "A Postscript to the Asian Financial Crisis: The Fragile International Economic Order" by Robert Gilpin, *Cambridge Review of International Affairs*, vol. 16, no. 1 (April 2003): 79–88. Copyright © 2003 by Taylor and Francis, Ltd. (www.tandf.co.uk/journals). Reprinted by permission of the author and the publisher.

The twin beliefs that economic convergence will occur and unregulated markets will effectively guide the world are very much a product of the outstanding success of the American economy in the 1990s. The rest of the world, proponents of this position argue, should emulate what they regard as the reasons for America's unprecedented growth, namely, deregulate markets and minimize the role of the government in the economy. Moreover, the Bush administration has a powerful faith in what it perceives to be the self-regulating and self-correcting nature of markets. As Treasury Secretary Paul O'Neill informed a meeting of the Group of Seven financial officials in February 2001, national governments should let markets work and avoid intervention in currency and other international markets. A financial or currency crisis such as that of East Asia in 1997, O'Neill informed his astonished, largely European audience, "doesn't have anything to [do] with the failure of capitalism. It's to do with an absence of capitalism." In a world economy based on self-regulating markets, according to this perspective, international cooperation and international institutions are largely unnecessary.

THE 1997–98 EAST ASIAN FINANCIAL/ECONOMIC CRISIS

The Bush administration accepts the interpretation of the East Asian financial crisis first set forth by former Secretary of State George Schultz, Milton Friedman, and other conservative economists. This position sees the underlying cause of the severity of the financial crisis and of the ensuing economic/political crisis as the problem of moral hazard; that is, if lenders and borrowers believe that the International Monetary Fund (IMF) or other official agency will rescue them from their folly, reckless economic behavior will be encouraged. The role played by the United States and the IMF in rescuing Mexico from its 1994–95 financial crisis led investors to believe that the debts of the East Asian economies were backed by government guarantees and that investors would be protected in the event of financial troubles. This situation created an incentive for excessive risk-taking in speculative real estate ventures and highly leveraged, ambitious corporate expansion. The inflated financial markets of these economies became a huge bubble that eventually burst. Thus, the East Asian financial/economic crisis was due to inherent features of the state-led economies and the encouragement of moral hazard by the IMF.

Many believed that, if the IMF and national governments were to stay out of financial markets, there would be no moral hazard and investors would make the rational decision to stay out of risky markets. What is required, therefore, to prevent future financial crises is a completely open, transparent, and unregulated international financial system. Any other approach necessarily raises the problem of "moral hazard." In an unregulated financial market, the market itself will punish those investors and borrowers who fail to pursue prudent economic behavior. Knowing that no one will rescue them if they get into trouble, international investors will become more cautious. The only reform necessary is the modest one of ensuring that all financial situations and transactions are "transparent," that is, every investor has the full and complete information to make a rational investment decision.

This market-oriented position rests on the assumption that investors are rational and will not invest in risky ventures if they know that they will not be bailed out by the IMF and the American government. Therefore, eliminate "moral hazard," and you eliminate the problem of serious international financial crises. That may be correct, but such an approach has never been tried, and there is no empirical evidence to support such a daring policy experiment. Indeed, the available evidence leads to the conclusions that investors are *not* consistently rational, that they *do* get caught up in financial "euphorias," and that, when the speculative bubble bursts, many innocent people get hurt. For this reason, few governments are willing to risk leaving international financial matters entirely up to the market and many governments have installed mechanisms at the domestic level to protect their citizens from financial instability. This crucially important issue involving the stability of the international economy is likely to be divisive between the United States and other major economies in Europe and East Asia.

Charles Kindleberger, Jagdish Bhagwati, and other prominent economists have emphasized that currency and financial crises are an inherent feature of international capitalism; these periodic and frequently costly upheavals are one price to be paid for what Joseph Schumpeter labelled the "process of creative destruction" that generates wealth in the ever-evolving capitalist system. It took the Great Depression of the 1930s for the United States and other capitalist countries to learn that domestic markets were not self-regulating and self-correcting; as John Maynard Keynes demonstrated, governments have a positive role to play in the functioning of the capitalist system. Unfortunately, this lesson has yet to be learned at the level of global capitalism. One can only hope that learning this lesson will not be too costly.

EXTRAORDINARY AMERICAN GROWTH IN THE 1990S

The other foundation of the faith in the market and belief in convergence was the extraordinary experience of the American economy in the 1990s; this was the most extended period of high economic growth in the history of the world. Productivity growth, the major determinant of economic growth and wealth, was much higher than most economists had thought possible, and the American stock market soared to an unprecedented level as a result. Although there were reasons to be concerned over the sustainability of what enthusiasts called the "New Economy," such skepticism was quickly dismissed. Few appeared concerned that Americans were living way beyond their means; in fact, they had been doing so for several decades. Nevertheless, in the 1990s, the American urge to consume accelerated and became a major factor propelling rapid economic growth.

The outstanding success of the American economy in the 1990s laid the basis for its proclaimed superiority over the Asian and European economies, both of which were in recession or slow growing. Deregulation, decreased government interventionism, and "letting markets work" were said to have unleashed a decade of innovation, entrepreneurship, and unprecedented growth. If other economies wanted equal success, then they had to follow the American example of a free market economy. Although there was much truth in this argument, it did not tell the whole story. Americans, to a disturbing extent, were financing their extraordinarily high level of consumption through drawing down their personal savings, borrowing heavily from abroad, and mining the appreciation of stocks and other assets. Moreover, the high dollar had made imports of oil, raw materials, and consumer goods relatively inexpensive and thereby contributed to a low inflation rate that enabled the Federal Reserve to pursue an expansionary economic policy. American economic success in the 1990s was due in part to good luck because the United States benefited from the fact that much of the rest of the world was in recession or experiencing low economic growth.

The consumption binge caused the personal savings rate of Americans to plunge to approximately zero. The low personal savings rate and the high corporate investment rate, financed in part by borrowing from abroad, resulted in an unprecedented trade and payments deficit. With huge trade/payments deficits year after year, the foreign debt of the United States has reached an all-time high. On the positive side of the national economic ledger, the rapid growth of the economy and a significant tax increase put through by the Clinton administration enabled the United States to reduce the federal budget deficit, begin repaying America's huge accumulated public debt, and pass on a large budget surplus to the next administration. Disposition of this budget surplus was the principal economic issue facing the country in the early months of the new Bush administration, which successfully pressed for a US$1.3 trillion tax cut in May 2001, further disposing the United States to a market driven approach *vis-à-vis* the national and global political economies.

However, beginning in early 2000, the New Economy began a Humpty Dumpty fall that not only exposed weaknesses in the United States economic power but cast doubt on the integrity of American capitalism. The implosion of the dot-com bubble, a severe collapse in the telecommunications industry, a precipitous and protracted decline in the stock market, especially in technology stocks, a modest recession and overall slowdown in growth and a series of major corporate bankruptcies rooted in corruption, fraud and criminal accounting practices all combined to make the posturing that charged that the Asian financial crisis was due to "crony capitalism" an embarrassing display of arrogance. Despite this economic reversal on the domestic front, the value of the dollar has continued to be strong against most major currencies. Due in part to the high dollar, the trade/payments deficit of the United States has continued to grow rapidly as has the country's international debt; in 2001, the American trade deficit grew an extraordinary 40% to approximately US$1 billion a day. As a percentage of gross domestic product (GDP), the trade deficit had increased from less than 1% in 1992 to not quite 4% in 2001. These deficits have made the foreign debt of the United States, by one estimate, rise to more than 20% of GDP.

This situation of Americans living beyond their means cannot last forever; they cannot indefinitely buy more than they sell. Americans cannot realistically expect others to make up the difference through investing forever in American stocks, bonds, and other assets. However, dollar-denominated assets will continue to be favoured over yen- or euro-denominated assets as long as the Japanese economy is in recession and the Western European economy has its own serious economic problems such as a high level of unemployment. Yet one day the tide must turn, and when it does, Americans will find themselves in a highly uncomfortable position. When the US$1 billion a day flowing into the United States dries up and the flight away from dollar-denominated assets begins, the dollar will weaken and the economy will suffer. Although the growth of imports would slow and exports would increase, the trade/payments deficit and the debt build-up would probably continue for some time. Such developments would cause employment and the American standard of living to fall, or at least to grow less rapidly than in the 1990s.

One great danger in this situation is that it could trigger a powerful protectionist reaction in the United States, and such a development would seriously damage the global economy. Although the United States is the world's largest exporter, it is also the importer of last resort for many countries around the world. An American recession and accompanying trade restrictions could set off a vicious circle of protectionism and trade contraction around the world. Even in the good times of the late 1990s and during the first two years of the Bush administration, a number of American economic sectors, notably steel, were demanding and receiving protection against imports. If protectionist demands were to increase and the American government were to lead the way in a global revival of trade protection, the threat to an open world economy would be severe and would test the commitment of the Bush administration to let the self-regulating market rule.

THE COLLAPSE OF THE SEATTLE WTO MEETING

The collapse in November 1999 of the World Trade Organization summit in Seattle was an especially worrisome development, since it challenged the stability of the political foundations of the world economy. The meeting was expected to deal with the many issues left unresolved in the Uruguay Round of trade negotiations and to launch the "Millennium Round." The ambitious agenda before the assembled trade ministers included such items as significant reduction in overall trade barriers, review of WTO anti-dumping and anti-subsidy rules to curb abuse (especially by the US) of these otherwise legitimate trade rules, and granting of duty-free access for the poorest countries to the markets of the industrial economies. Unfortunately, the trade summit was devastated by a number of unprecedented political developments. To understand the most dramatic aspect of the Seattle débâcle—the violent street protests—one must appreciate the importance, at least in the United States, of what has been labeled the "new trade agenda."

As the volume of world trade has expanded and trade has penetrated more and more deeply into national societies, it has become increasingly entwined with politically sensitive matters and has come into conflict with powerful domestic interests, especially in the United States. This development has produced the new trade agenda; that agenda includes such highly controversial issues as labour standards and human rights, the environment, and national sovereignty. Some proponents of the new trade agenda on both the political left and right are unalterably opposed to free trade and are even outright protectionists; indeed, large parts of American organized labour provide a prime example. Most advocates of one or another of the issues on the new trade agenda want radical changes in the WTO which would greatly weaken the effectiveness of that institution and would undermine the trade regime. Examination of the new trade agenda and the intense political controversy surrounding various items reveals serious threats to the trade regime which will be difficult to overcome.

There is considerable conflict about the question of whether the important and politically sensitive issues of "fair" labour standards, human rights, and environmental protection should be treated together with conventional trade issues or in a different venue. Powerful groups, especially in the United States and Western Europe, believe strongly that these matters should be incorporated into the international trade regime and that trade liberalization should be made subordinate to achievement of such specific objectives as human rights and environmental protection. On the other hand, most economists, governments, and business groups are strongly opposed to integrating these issues into international trade negotiations and fear that, however well intentioned some groups are, the important issues of labour standards, human rights, and environmental protection will be and are being exploited by outright protectionists. Indeed, the political stalemate generated by these clashing positions led to the 1997 defeat of President Clinton's request for "fast track" authority, an authority that could have greatly facilitated negotiation of trade agreements. The restoration of this authority to President Bush in 2002 involved a bruising political battle even in the midst of enhanced White House clout acquired through the War on Terrorism.

In the United States, the opposition of environmentalists to the trade regime has grown intense. American environmentalist critics of the trade regime fall into two major camps. One accepts the principle of free trade but argues that environmental protection should be incorporated into trade negotiations and be given equal, if not higher, priority than trade liberalization itself. This group also believes that the WTO and its dispute-settlement mechanism should be more open to the public. The other and more radical position maintains that free trade is a threat to the environment, and it rejects the WTO because it views the WTO as an instrument of powerful corporate interests. This group agrees with American neo-isolationist conservatives that WTO actions infringe upon American sovereignty. The environmentalists have become a formidable force in the political struggle over trade.

The issues initially raised by environmentalists in Seattle are serious and must be addressed by national governments. Yet, with a few particularly important exceptions such as global warming and pollution of the oceans, almost every environmental issue can be dealt with most effectively on a domestic or regional basis; the serious problems of nuclear and other hazardous wastes, water contamination, air pollution, toxic dumps, and CO_2 emissions have little or nothing to do with international trade. One of the most vehement groups of protesters in Seattle consisted of opponents of logging and especially of clear-cutting. That problem is primarily the result of high government subsidies to timber companies (as in Alaska) and to forest destruction caused by land-hungry farmers and the national development strategy in many Lesser Developed Countries (LDCs). Even though the primary responsibility for overcutting belongs to national governments, the WTO has been made the whipping-boy of the environmentalists in this and many other matters. Moreover, even when environmental issues do relate to international trade (as happens in the cases of ocean oil spills and trade in endangered species), the WTO does not have either the authority or the power to deal with such matters. However, these pressing problems can be dealt with effectively through such other mechanisms as international conventions. The international agreement on safety rules for genetically modified foods, despite its imperfections, provides a good example of such an alternative procedure.

The issue of labour standards has become a major impediment to trade liberalization, especially in the United States, where this issue has been raised forcefully by organized labour and, to a lesser extent, by human rights advocates genuinely concerned about child labour in less developed countries and in China in particular. In fact, a disproportionate number of the street protesters in Seattle were union members mobilized by the American AFL-CIO, whose President John Sweeney lauded the collapse of the meeting. Although the International Labour Organization (ILO) has established labour standards, most advocates of labour standards and opponents of child labour believe that the ILO is incapable of enforcing its standards; moreover, the United States and a number of other countries have not even ratified all ILO standards. Furthermore, even though some advocates of labour standards and of prohibitions against child labour are genuinely concerned about the oppressive conditions of labour in many countries, others use the issue as a protectionist device.

Most economists, businesses, and national governments reject the idea that labour standards and human rights should be incorporated into trade negotiations. Economists are concerned that consideration of labour standards in trade negotiations would unduly complicate the already horrendous task of achieving agreement on trade liberalization and would provide a convenient and effective rationale for protectionist measures against low-wage economies. Developing countries have strongly denounced efforts to impose "Western" standards on them. They have reason to believe that such proposals are frequently motivated by protectionist interests and would be used to reduce their comparative advantage based on low-wage labour and their provision of only minimum welfare benefits.

The closely related issues of labour standards, human rights, and child labour are legitimate and need to be addressed. Furthermore, some countries are undoubtedly guilty of "social dumping," that is, of gaining competitiveness through their denial of workers' fundamental rights and decent working conditions. However, remedying these problems will be extraordinarily difficult. As almost every LDC is strongly opposed to incorporating labour standards and human rights into the WTO, a concerted effort to do so would likely destroy the effectiveness of the organization. It is particularly ironic that many protestors at Seattle denounced the rulings of the WTO as an infringement of American sovereignty while protestors also advocated that the WTO impose labour and human rights standards on delinquent LDCs. Needless to say, it will be difficult to reconcile the positions of those who support and those who oppose incorporation of workers' rights within the trade regime.

Ultimately a combination of education and economic development is needed to provide a solution to the associated problems of labour standards, human rights, and child labour. In general, the countries with the highest labour standards and respect for human rights are the most developed countries; this is, at least partially, because they are wealthy and have a strong and concerned middle class. In societies with low per capita income where parents frequently need the wages of their children, outside interventions like trade sanctions are unlikely to succeed. In the short term, the best solution is to exert organized consumer pressure against those business firms that violate human rights, utilize child labour, and abuse other labour standards.

A particularly disturbing aspect of the new trade agenda is that the WTO and other international economic institutions have come under heated attack by an alliance of environmentalists and human rights advocates with protectionist trade unions and even ultra-conservative neo-isolationists. In the vehement protests surrounding the WTO's November 1999 meeting in Seattle, the April 2000 protests in Washington, DC, and the subsequent clashes in Pisa, the WTO and other international agencies became a lightning rod for concerned and frustrated groups around the globe who want the world to be different from its present unfortunate state. The impossible and contradictory demands of the Seattle protesters ranged from abolishing the WTO altogether because it is undemocratic and infringes on American sovereignty, to demands that it actively intervene in the sovereign affairs of many nations to eliminate such destructive practices as forest clear-cutting and pollution of streams, lakes, and rivers. Those groups and individuals who blame globalization for their own and the world's problems now view the WTO, the World Bank, and the IMF as symbols of feared globalization.

Although the Seattle street protestors attracted most of the attention at the November 1999 WTO meeting, primary responsibility for the abysmal failure of that meeting belongs to the major economic powers and the Clinton administration in particular. For domestic political reasons, President Clinton tried to force the conference to include the issue of "labour standards" on the agenda of future trade negotiations; his irresponsible reference in a newspaper interview to possible imposition of economic sanctions on countries that did not meet certain labour standards was especially infuriating to developing countries that, quite correctly, viewed the President's motives as protectionist. Another factor in the breakdown of the negotiations was the inexperience of the recently appointed WTO Director-General, Mike Moore. Still other factors were inadequate preparation for the meeting, no agreed agenda, and the unwieldiness of a meeting composed of 135 member nations.

The unwillingness of the major economic powers, especially the United States and the European Union, to contemplate serious trade liberalization was critical in the Seattle fiasco. All major economic powers had different agendas that conflicted with one another and precluded a successful outcome. High on the Clinton administration's formal agenda were such issues as elimination of European agricultural subsidies and protection of intellectual property rights. However, at the conference, the President subordinated even this formal agenda to the issue of labour standards. Furthermore, the administration refused to discuss the outrage in Japan and other countries over his administration's extensive and improper use of the WTO's anti-dumping provision as a protectionist device. The administration also opposed the EU's strong desire to put competition (e.g. anti-trust) policy on the programme, and instead supported a narrow agenda favoring American export interests—financial services, information technology, aircraft, and agriculture—and did so with little regard for the interests of others.

At Seattle both the Japanese and the Western Europeans, also for domestic political reasons, adamantly opposed opening their economies to American and other nations' agricultural exports. Within the EU, protection of agriculture through large subsidies to farmers is considered essential to the achievement of European economic and political integration. In Japan, the ruling Liberal Democratic Party, needing the votes of rural areas, opposed opening its market to imports of rice and other agricultural products. The inability of the major economic powers to find compromises for these fundamental differences doomed the conference. For all three major participants, domestic political objectives took precedence over trade liberalization.

As these issues have not yet been resolved or even seriously discussed, prospects for a major breakthrough in trade negotiations are not especially promising. Trade barriers in sectors such as textiles and agriculture have declined, but only to a level politically acceptable to powerful domestic constituencies. The United States and Western Europe—the two largest trading powers—are at odds over a number of difficult issues, including genetically modified food, European trade discrimination, and American corporate tax policies. Moreover, public opinion in the US and EU has grown increasingly concerned about the impact of imports, especially from low-wage economies. The industrializing countries have also become increasingly disillusioned about opening their markets. Experience of the East Asian economic crisis increased concerns about the dangers of this process. Re-energizing the process of trade liberalization will require strong political leadership and international cooperation.

Since the end of World War II, the United States has taken the lead in promoting trade liberalization, and every round of multilateral trade negotiations followed an American initiative. Although the Doha meeting of the WTO avoided the débâcle seen in Seattle, the WTO agenda was set by calculated avoidance of the basic issues discussed, with the United States in the role of broker more than leader. The Bush administration has displayed an ambiguous leadership role in the free trade arena. Secretary O'Neill rejected the Western European interest in continued international cooperation on economic matters, and President Bush proposed a Free Trade Area of the Americas (FTAA) without calling for a new round of multilateral trade negotiations within the World Trade Organization (WTO). The protectionist measures to protect the steel industry and passage of the largest agricultural subsidy in history belie the White House rhetoric of free trade.

CONCLUSION

The danger in the impasse over trade in the United States and the world more generally is that preferential bilateral and regional arrangements will be substituted for multilateral trade negotiations conducted under the auspices of the WTO. There is, in fact, evidence that the shift from multilateral trade negotiations to bilateral and regional negotiations has been accelerating since the collapse of the Seattle meeting. As trade expert Jagdish Bhagwati has pointed out, the number of preferential bilateral agreements has grown four-fold since the mid-1990s. The Western Europeans have taken the leadership in forging such discriminatory trading arrangements. These initiatives in turn have stimulated other countries in East Asia and elsewhere to launch bilateral and regional arrangements, and the prestigious Business Roundtable has proposed that the United States initiate its own preferential deals. Unless the United States takes international institutions more seriously and exerts its leadership in such institutions in the interest of multilateral trade liberalization, protectionism and preferential trading arrangements will undermine the open global economy upon which world prosperity and possibly peace depend. In the context of the threshold economic events of the post−Cold-War era, the 1997−98 Asian economic crisis underscores a basic paradox of the contemporary global political economy: the need for new international institutions at a time when market-centered neoclassical economics and unilateralism are embraced by the only superpower capable of creating the appropriate global multilateral mediating structures.

11

❀

International Law and Organizations

Reading 11-1

The Rise of Ethics in Foreign Policy
Reaching a Values Consensus
Leslie H. Gelb and Justine A. Rosenthal

In the space of a few weeks recently, here's what happened on the international morality and values front: Madeleine Albright testified at a Bosnian war crimes tribunal, the State Department's chief policy planner argued that promoting democracy was one of the most important reasons to go to war with Iraq, and a top Bush administration diplomat traveled to Xinjiang to examine China's treatment of its Muslim citizens. The news stories were routine and unremarkable—which is what was remarkable. A former secretary of state at a war crimes trial. Democracy for Iraq. Beijing allowing a U.S. human rights official to check out its domestic policies. Such events occur regularly now with little comment, no snickering from "realists," indeed with little disagreement.

Something quite important has happened in American foreign policymaking with little notice or digestion of its meaning. Morality, values, ethics, universal principles— the whole panoply of ideals in international affairs that were once almost the exclusive domain of preachers and scholars—have taken root in the hearts, or at least the minds,

SOURCE: From "The Rise of Ethics in Foreign Policy: Reaching a Values Consensus" by Leslie H. Gelb and Justine A. Rosenthal, *Foreign Affairs*, vol. 82, no. 3 (May/June 2003): 2–7. Copyright © 2003 by the Council on Foreign Relations. Reprinted by permission.

of the American foreign policy community. A new vocabulary has emerged in the rhetoric of senior government officials, Republicans and Democrats alike. It is laced with concepts dismissed for almost 100 years as "Wilsonian." The rhetoric comes in many forms, used to advocate regime change or humanitarian intervention or promote democracy and human rights, but almost always the ethical agenda has at its core the rights of the individual.

This development of morality cannot be seen simply as a postmodern version of the "white man's burden," although it has that tenor in some hands. These values are now widely shared around the world by different religions and cultures. Movements for democracy or justice for war crimes are no longer merely American or Western idiosyncrasies. And although some in America's foreign-policy community may still be using moral language to cloak a traditional national security agenda, one gets the sense that the trend is more than that. In the past, tyrants supported by Washington did not have to worry a lot about interference in their domestic affairs. Now, even if Washington needs their help, some price has to be exacted, if only sharp public criticism. Moral matters are now part of American politics and the politics of many other nations. They are rarely, even in this new age, the driving forces behind foreign policy, but they are now a constant force that cannot be overlooked when it comes to policy effectiveness abroad or political support at home.

THE EVOLUTION OF AN IDEA

The moral phenomenon we are now witnessing did not materialize out of whole cloth. It evolved over time, in fits and starts, solidifying only in the last 30 years.

From the dawn of human history, there have been laws about the initiation and conduct of war. The ancient Egyptians and the fourth century BC Chinese military strategist Sun Tzu set out rules on how and why to begin wars and how those wars should be fought. Saint Augustine argued that an act of war needs a just cause, and Saint Thomas Aquinas believed that battle requires the authority of a sovereign power and should be acted out with good intention. The sixteenth-century French jurist Jean Bodin held that war was a necessary evil and largely the domain of the sovereign. And the seventeenth-century legalist Hugo Grotius, after witnessing the atrocities of the Thirty Years' War, wrote on the protection of noncombatants and methods to promote and ensure peace.

These and many other figures played a role in creating the system of international law and a related kind of international morality that we witness today. But the debates often occurred on the periphery of international practice and related more to the rights of the aristocracy and the sovereign state than to a universal set of values.

The Hague Conventions of the late nineteenth and early twentieth centuries, the precursors of the Geneva Conventions, set out "laws of war" with the aim of protecting combatants and noncombatants alike and outlining rules for the treatment of prisoners and the wounded. These guidelines helped make war somewhat more humane but did not address the ethics of larger foreign policy questions. And some of these issues were taken up on a targeted basis by transnational organizations in the nineteenth century. Thus Quakers in the United Kingdom and the United States joined hands in an antislavery movement, and women from around the world united to champion women's suffrage. But not until Woodrow Wilson did a modern world leader step forward to put ethics and universal values at the heart of a nation's foreign policy.

Wilson called for making matters such as national self-determination and democracy equal to the rights of man. Yet the perceived failure of his efforts made his successors less bold. Franklin Roosevelt's Four Freedoms speech and his subsequent stewardship of the creation of the United Nations fell short of Wilson's lofty ideals. The UN at its core was based far more on great-power politics than on universal principles.

Perhaps the boldest single effort to enshrine human rights as a universal value came with the Nuremberg trials, which charged Nazi rulers and followers alike with war crimes and "crimes against humanity." But although the tribunals astonished, the precedents they set were soon put aside, viewed more as victor's justice than as a universal and shared symbol of morality.

The Cold War did not get high marks for morality either. It pitted an evil system against a far better one, but on both sides the moral gloves came off when it came time to fight. The left in the United States challenged what it saw as U.S. moral misdeeds: supporting dictators and the like. But none of these challenges struck home and prevailed in American politics until the presidencies of Richard Nixon and Jimmy Carter.

The realpolitik policies of Nixon and Henry Kissinger generated a backlash among both Republicans and Democrats on grounds of immorality. The Republican right attacked détente as acceptance of the evil Soviet empire. The Democrats, and soon their presidential standard-bearer Jimmy Carter, attacked Kissinger's approach as contrary to "American values." And Carter made morality in U.S. foreign policy a core issue in his presidential campaign.

Although as president Carter did alter policies toward numerous dictatorships—such as those of Argentina, Uruguay, and Ethiopia—he also hedged his moral bets in places such as the Philippines, Iran, and Saudi Arabia. These contradictions served as examples of the almost inevitable policy inconsistencies that result when leaders try to balance security priorities with an ethical agenda.

His successor, Ronald Reagan, maintained Carter's ethical rhetoric but changed the focus to address communist dictatorships. He aided indigenous foes of the Soviet Union in Afghanistan, Angola, Cambodia, and Nicaragua. Again, however, the impossibility of consistently applying morality became clear. Even as Reagan made moves to defeat communism, he was criticized for supporting right-wing death squads in El Salvador, mining the harbors of the "democratically" elected government in Nicaragua, and trading arms and Bibles for hostages with Iranian zealots.

Carter used ethical rhetoric to pummel dictatorships on the right, whereas Reagan pummeled those on the left. But both made agile use of ethics and values in their foreign policies.

They left behind something approaching a consensus among Democrats and Republicans that morality and values should play a bigger role in U.S. actions abroad. With the passing of the Cold War and America's emergence as the sole superpower, moreover, the tradeoffs between security and ethics became less stark, and a moral foreign policy seemed more affordable.

WHAT NOW?

Debates over right and wrong are now embedded both in the international arena and in domestic deliberations. Protecting individual rights, advancing the rule of law, preventing genocide, and the like have become an inescapable part of arguments over policy. This is so not only in the public circus, where what is said rightly sparks a modicum of cynicism, but in private counsels in and out of government, where such arguments used to be dismissed as "unrealistic" or simply ignored.

Just how much ethical rhetoric has permeated policymaking is almost nowhere more clearly evident than in the lead up to war with Iraq. The debate about whether and why to go to war has featured a value-laden rhetoric: freedom for the Iraqi people, democracy for Iraq if not for the whole region, and the use of the United Nations (even if grudgingly) to help justify invasion. And this language is often proffered even more by the traditional realists than by the traditional liberals. Even if, in the end, a U.S.-led war effort serves to strengthen American power in the region more than anything else, the use of ethical rhetoric will have been a necessary ingredient in furthering that national security agenda.

Values now count in virtually every foreign policy discussion, at times for good, at times for ill, and always as a complicating factor. The cases where ethics must be factored in these days are startling in number and complexity.

For the longest time, Americans engaged in a sterile debate over human rights. It was a debate between those who believed the United States had to fight the bad guys no matter what the security tradeoffs, and those who believed the United States had no business interfering with the internal affairs of other states. Dictators used this split to neutralize U.S. pressure. Now that left and right have largely joined forces on the issue, however, dictators have to bend their precious local values and pay more heed to American entreaties—all the more so when those entreaties are inextricably bound to military and financial inducements. Human rights probably never will be effective as a public battering ram. Countries are complicated beasts most resistant when directly challenged. But leaders around the world understand today that they cannot take American money, beg American protection, and consistently escape the acknowledgment of American values.

Humanitarian intervention, meanwhile, is perhaps the most dramatic example of the new power of morality in international affairs. The notion that states could invade the sovereign territory of other states to stop massive bloodshed (call it genocide or ethnic cleansing or whatever) was inconceivable until the 1990s. The right of states or groups within states to mutilate and kill fellow citizens on a mass scale seemed to have assumed God-given proportions. But in the space of a few years, this pillar of international politics was badly shaken. The UN approved interventions in Bosnia and Somalia. NATO took military action in Kosovo. And the Organization of American States blessed the U.S.-led intervention in Haiti. What is more, the international community was quite prepared to intervene militarily in Rwanda had the Clinton administration not prevented it. Just think of it: states endorsing the principle that morality trumps sovereignty.

Even the historic triumph of this trumping, however, does not eliminate the moral problems raised by doing good through humanitarian intervention. Who is to be saved? The ethics of choice here remain cloudy indeed. Not everyone will be saved, particularly not minorities within major powers. And who is to assume the burdens of repairing and bettering societies that intervention pulverizes? The costs are staggering and the list of funders is wanting.

Other checks on crimes against humanity exist now as well. The UN has established war crimes tribunals to prosecute those who committed atrocities in Yugoslavia and Rwanda, and British authorities arrested former Chilean dictator Augusto Pinochet on charges of mass executions, torture, and other crimes against humanity. Even though these prosecutions may not deter all would-be killers, some justice is better than no justice at all.

As for the promotion of democracy, who could imagine how far America's commitment to it would go after Wilson's flop on the international and domestic stages? Just look at the odd soulmates who have found common ground on this issue in recent years: Morton Halperin and Paul Wolfowitz, George Soros and George W. Bush, even "realists" such as Richard Haass.

To be sure, some who ridiculed Presidents Clinton and Carter and their clans for advocating democracy now adopt this ideal whole, without so much as a blush, and perhaps may revert to their original positions under international duress. Whether or not they do so, the realists' warnings about democracy as a double-edged sword are worth remembering. It can be used to justify actions that otherwise would require better explanations; in this way democracy protects weak arguments. And its advocacy could compel excesses, such as rushing to elections before the development of a liberal society to underpin those elections.

We may be better off now that so many leaders, good ones and bad ones, feel they must protest their yearning for democracy. These protestations might actually entrap them, forcing them to do more good than they had ever considered desirable for their own ends. Still, this democratic ideal contains so much power that some prudence about rushing its implementation seems wise. Even if done cautiously, however, implementing democratic ideals carries its own contradictions. The Clinton and Bush administrations have promoted democracy around the world yet said little or nothing about the need for it in places such as China, Egypt, and Saudi Arabia.

The counterterrorism agenda only heightens these inconsistencies. It further divides Americans and Muslims around the world, many of whom see terrorists as freedom fighters. And many now in the Bush administration condemned President Clinton's decision not to make major issues of Russia's treatment of the Chechens or China's treatment of Muslim Uighurs, but have more or less abandoned that brief in the name of a common front against al Qaeda and like organizations.

Then there is the fact that the United States is often on a different ethical and moral track from others. Most nations have approved of the genocide convention, the International Criminal Court, the treaty banning land mines, and the Kyoto Protocol on climate change, all of which they consider part of their moral stance. But the United States rejects these and other such agreements on grounds that it suffers disproportionately under their terms. Such conflicts between the ethical and the practical will not be sorted out easily and so will remain a source of tension. But it is better to dispute matters such as land mines and global warming than to go to war over traditional power issues.

Yes, it will remain very rare for ethical and moral concerns to dominate foreign policy, particularly when it comes to national security issues. Yes, nations will continue to dispute the merits of their respective ethical and moral systems. Yes, within nations, there will be battles over whether moral or practical concerns should come first and over which moral concerns should take precedence. Even as universal values become more a part of the foreign policies of nations, those policies will still be ridden with contradictions and hypocrisies. And yes, the morality of the strong will generally still prevail over that of the weak, and considerations of value almost inevitably will have to take second place. But they used to have no place. Second place means that leaders now have to be mindful of ignoring or abusing what are increasingly seen as universal values.

We have passed from an era in which ideals were always flatly opposed to self-interests into an era in which tension remains between the two, but the stark juxtaposition of the past has largely subsided. Now, ideals and self-interests are both generally considered necessary ingredients of the national interest. For all the old and new policy problems this entails, Americans and most of the world are better off.

Reading 11-2

From San Francisco to Sarajevo
The UN and the Use of Force
Adam Roberts

The United Nations, although it emerged and took its name from a successful military alliance, has hardly ever been united and effective in the use of force—and it has never managed such use in the manner prescribed in its Charter. The UN has organized peacekeeping operations, some of which have had a measure of success. However, the actual use of force, in the sense of military operations for such purposes as reversing acts of aggression or repressing cease-fire violations, has proved more problematic.

This has especially been the case in connection with UN peacekeeping operations, most notably in the Congo, Somalia and former Yugoslavia. At least until the beginning of NATO's *Operation Deliberate Force,* which commenced on 30 August 1995, the situation in Bosnia-Herzegovina repeatedly involved difficulties over the authorisation and employment of force. It also exposed the lack of a conceptual framework for uses of force which are distinct in their purposes and character from the two well-established UN frameworks for use of armed forces—namely enforcement (war by another name) against overt aggression on the one hand, and peacekeeping (often seen as permitting only very restricted uses of force) on the other.

This article analyses the main problems and challenges faced by the UN in the use of force, and discusses some proposals to make UN operations more effective. The aim is not to revive the excessively optimistic proposals, widely canvassed in 1992–93, for a new, more forceful, form of peacekeeping, less dependent on consent, and presumed to be able to tackle a wide range of situations. Rather, it is to re-examine a problem which has affected the UN since at least the early 1960s, including in some troubled peacekeeping operations: how the UN and its members can react in those relatively few situations where agreed cease-fires are violated; where there are massive atrocities; where the situation demands, or UN mandates seem to require, more forceful military action than peacekeeping on its own can provide; or where the credibility and impartiality of a UN peacekeeping force may be as much at risk from military inaction as from use of military force. Examining this problem necessarily involves considering whether a given peacekeeping operation may need fundamentally to modify its mission, its dispositions and its command structure to take into account the hostility from belligerents that may result from uses of force.

PROBLEMS IN IMPLEMENTING THE MAIN PROVISIONS OF THE UN CHARTER

The UN Conference on International Organisation, meeting at San Francisco in April–June 1945, was marked by a fruitful combination of internationalism and tough-minded realism. The UN Charter, finalised at the Conference, reflected this. Signed on

SOURCE: From "From San Francisco to Sarajevo: The UN and the Use of Force" by Adam Roberts, *Survival,* vol. 37, no. 4 (Winter 1995–1996): 7–28. Copyright © 1995 Oxford University Press. Reprinted by permission.

26 June in the Veterans' War Memorial Building, its provisions on the use of force resulted from the experience of the Second World War, then in its final phase: international aggression by powerful states was seen as the central problem which had to be countered; the mistakes and vacillations of the League of Nations system were to be avoided this time; and the achievements of the wartime alliance provided a basis, if not a model, for future international military cooperation.

The UN Charter provisions thus created have had a powerful influence on many subsequent uses of force, but never quite in the way envisaged at San Francisco: the actual practice of the UN in managing force since then has been more varied, muddled and complex than what was imagined in 1945. As indicated below, a few of the Charter provisions have been a dead letter; however, many of the gaps and inadequacies of the Charter system have been filled by creative interpretation and ingenious improvisation.

The UN Charter's overall approach to the use of force is to stress that it may be used only for fundamentally defensive purposes, and preferably on a collective basis. In Chapter VII (on "Action with Respect to Threats to the Peace," Articles 39–51) the Charter seeks to establish elements of a general system of collective security, but this aim is heavily qualified by Article 51, which preserves "the inherent right of states to individual or collective self-defence," at least until the Security Council has taken necessary measures. In Chapter VIII (on "Regional Arrangements," Articles 52–54), the Charter emphasises on the role of regional arrangements or agencies in maintaining peace; the UN was by no means intended to have a monopoly on collective-security efforts. The Charter's acceptance of the role of individual states and their armed forces is further indicated by the fact that it says less about disarmament than had the Covenant of the League of Nations. The framers of the Charter were anxious not to commit the UN to unrealisable goals in this sphere. As in some other matters, the UN Charter went with, rather than against, the grain of the anarchical society of states.

The key body for organising collective international enforcement action is the UN Security Council (UNSC). The Charter conferred on the Security Council a considerable degree of authority over other UN members. It was given responsibility for determining the existence of threats to the peace, on the basis of a less legalistic definition of the circumstances in which it could act than that in the League Covenant. Under Chapter VII the UN had the power to decide what military or other measures should be taken "to maintain or restore international peace and security" (Article 39). It was supposed to have military forces at its disposal; and to get advice and assistance from the Military Staff Committee, consisting of the Chiefs of Staff of the Permanent Five Members of the UNSC (Articles 43–48). However, the wording of even these provisions is cautious, and leaves many key questions to be determined. Thus Article 47(3) says of forces placed at the disposal of the Security Council: "Questions relating to the command of such forces shall be worked out subsequently."

The Security Council has never, in fact, had armed forces at its disposal in the manner apparently envisaged in Chapter VII of the UN Charter. In 1946–47, in accord with Articles 43–48, the UN's Military Staff Committee was set up and asked to examine the question of contributions of armed forces to the Security Council. It duly published a report which reflected significant disagreements among the Permanent Five about the size and composition of national contributions. The whole enterprise was abandoned.[1] This was part of a broader failure to implement those provisions of Chapter VII which appeared to provide for an ambitious scheme for collective security.[2] In the first 50 years of the UN, agreements under Article 43 of the Charter, necessary to place national forces at the general disposal of the UN, have never been concluded.

The most obvious reason for the failure to implement the Charter provisions in the early years of the UN was the inability of the permanent members of the Security Council to reach agreement across the Cold War divide. However, there also appears to have been an underlying reluctance on the part of all states to see their forces committed in advance to participate in what might prove to be distant, controversial and risky military operations without their express consent and command. Such reluctance may also have owed something to a suspicion that a Charter-based system of international command of military operations by a pre-ordained group of powers in the Security Council and the Military Staff Committee would not be effective. The use of the veto by the Permanent Five to prevent the passing of resolutions by the Security Council reinforced perceptions, especially during the Cold War years, that the UN was unlikely to be able initially to decide upon, or subsequently direct, military action.

The veto power in the hands of the Permanent Five helps to explain why the Security Council had a marginal role for many decades in respect of a wide range of international security issues. Yet the veto system, much criticised for preventing UN action in many cases, has had complex effects, not all undesirable. On the positive side, it has played a part in getting, and keeping, major powers within the UN; and it may have saved the UN from being saddled with commitments which the great powers were not willing to support in practice. However, it has contributed to perceptions of the UN as a mere talking-shop; and to the tendency of states, large and small, to seek reinsurance in other security arrangements, including regional ones, where there was less risk of being out-voted or vetoed. The substantial decline in use of the veto since the late 1980s has not, except in a minority of cases, opened the way to united and forceful policies in the field of security. The failure to introduce a system of collective security—or even, more modestly, to develop a coherent practice of use of force in situations other than defence of a state which is victim of aggression—has causes which go beyond the veto.

The failure to implement Articles 43–48 of the Charter did not lead to anything like a complete abandonment of efforts to develop collective uses of armed force. On the contrary, the UN era has seen three striking variations on the Charter's collective security theme: regional alliances; UN authorisations of the use of force; and international peacekeeping forces. Each of these variations responds to difficulties in the pure idea of collective security, and in the Charter provisions.

VARIATIONS ON THE UN CHARTER SCHEME
FOR COLLECTIVE SECURITY

Regional Alliances and Multilateral Military Interventions

The international security arrangements that emerged in the first decades of the UN's existence were centred less on the UN itself than on bilateral and regional security treaties. Many of these treaties referred to UN Charter principles and procedures and incorporated aspects of the Charter ethos, including emphasis on defence as the main legitimate use of force. These regional arrangements, which were often alliances against an external power rather than true cases of collective security, reflected the reality that states are generally willing to commit their forces for serious military action not on a universal basis, but in their own region, or in defence of countries with which there are ties of blood, commerce, religion, common culture and/or political system. The development of nuclear weapons in the hands of a few powers reinforced the existing tendency for alliances of one kind or another to take the place of the more ambitious UN scheme.

Many regional alliances and organisations were associated with a tendency for uses of military force to have a multilateral character. Time and again, when states engaged in military interventions they did so with authorisation by and assistance from a regional body. Such a tendency, not unknown in earlier decades and even centuries, became particularly marked in the decades after 1945. Examples include the 1968 Soviet intervention in Czechoslovakia, the 1976 Syrian intervention in Lebanon and the 1983 US intervention in Grenada: these were approved by the Warsaw Pact, the Arab League and the Organisation of Eastern Caribbean States respectively. In some cases the emphasis on collective purposes and multilateral participation probably helped to limit the aims and activities of interventionists to those which were reasonably presentable.

Regional security arrangements can be seen as building blocks for a general UN-based system of collective security, or as detracting from it. Since such a system was not a serious possibility anyway, perhaps the alliances that developed should be seen as the nearest approximation to collective security that was available in the harsh circumstances of international politics. Manifestly imperfect in many ways, they could never be a complete substitute for the idea of UN-based military force: an idea which was to assume two unanticipated forms.

UN Authorisations of Military Enforcement Activities

The UN's most explicit variation on the collective security theme has been its practice of authorising certain uses of force by states or groups of states. This is distinct from the Charter conception of the Security Council having forces more directly under its authority.

The Korean War (1950–53) marked the beginning of the UN practice of authorising the use of force by states. Following the invasion of South Korea by North Korean forces on 25 June 1950, the Security Council recommended that member-states "furnish such assistance to the Republic of Korea as may be necessary to repel the armed attack and to restore international peace and security in the area."[3] Two weeks later, the Council recommended "that all military forces and other assistance be under a unified command under the USA."[4] It also authorised the unified command to use the UN flag—something that has never been repeated in UN-authorised enforcement actions.

The initial Security Council resolutions on Korea could only be passed because, fortuitously, the USSR was boycotting the Security Council at the time for its refusal to seat the People's Republic of China. When, later in 1950, the Soviet Union resumed its Security Council place, it was able to use its veto to prevent the passing of any further substantive resolutions on Korea. The US and its allies, which at that time could still view the General Assembly as a pliant body, then secured the passage by 52 votes to five, with two abstentions, of General Assembly Resolution 377 ("Uniting for Peace") of 3 November 1950:

> If the Security Council, because of lack of unanimity of the permanent members, fails to exercise its primary responsibility for the maintenance of international peace and security in any case where there appears to be a threat to peace, breach of the peace, or act of aggression, the General Assembly shall consider the matter immediately with a view to making appropriate recommendations to Members for collective measures, including in the case of a breach of the peace or acts of aggression the use of armed force when necessary, to maintain or restore international peace and security. If not in session at the time the General Assembly may

meet in emergency special session within twenty-four hours of the request therefor. Such emergency special session may be called if requested by the Security Council on the vote of any seven members, or by a majority of the members of the United Nations.

This "Uniting for Peace" procedure, which constituted a significant change in UN Charter arrangements, indicated that the Security Council veto need not be an insuperable obstacle to UN action. However, it has seldom been invoked, largely because in most cases on which action was stalled in the Security Council there was not in fact enough consensus among General Assembly members about what action should be taken. It will be interesting to see whether there are any proposals for reviving it in current or future cases in which the Security Council is widely considered to have failed in its fundamental duties.

The *locus classicus* of UNSC authorisation of the use of force to repel an act of aggression was the response to the Iraqi invasion of Kuwait on 2 August 1990. After numerous resolutions had imposed sanctions on Iraq and demanded its withdrawal from Kuwait, Security Council Resolution 678 of 29 November 1990 authorised:

> Member States cooperating with the Government of Kuwait . . . to use all necessary means to uphold and implement resolution 660 (1990) and all subsequent relevant resolutions and to restore international peace and security in the area.

Significantly from the point of view of the theory of collective security, it did not call on all states to take military action (for which the term "all necessary means" was to become a standard euphemism), but only those states already cooperating with the Kuwaiti government in exile. Other states were simply requested to provide "appropriate support." This was a sensible recognition that, whatever Article 25 may say about states agreeing to carry out decisions of the Security Council, people in different countries perceive the world differently, and there remains a place for some form of neutrality even in respect of UN-authorised operations.

In some of its authorisations of force from 1991 onwards, especially in northern Iraq, Somalia, Haiti and Rwanda, the Security Council collectively, and its Western permanent members individually, were seen by many to be taking hesitant steps towards a new doctrine and practice of humanitarian intervention—that is, military intervention in a state, without the approval of its authorities, with the purpose of preventing widespread suffering or death among its inhabitants.[5] "Humanitarian intervention" in this sense was not explicitly provided for in the Charter, and remains controversial under it. The difficulties faced by all the post-1991 cases suggest that the very term "humanitarian intervention" is an oversimplification.

The case of Somalia illustrated most clearly some of the difficulties of UN control of military force. The original UN Operation in Somalia (UNOSOM I), a peacekeeping force authorised in April 1992, took more than three months to get established, and was ill-suited to tackle clan warfare and general violence.[6] In December, the Security Council authorised the Secretary-General, the US and cooperating states "to use all necessary means to establish as soon as possible a secure environment for humanitarian relief operations in Somalia."[7] An armed US-led military force, the Unified Task Force (UNITAF), then intervened, operating in Somalia between 9 December 1992 and 4 May 1993. It was subsequently partially absorbed into a UN peacekeeping force, United Nations Operations in Somalia (UNOSOM II). In subsequent months the security situation in the capital, Mogadishu, deteriorated. In June 1993, UN peacekeeping forces were involved in incidents in which they both suffered and inflicted severe casualties. On 3 October some US Rangers, deployed in Mogadishu in support of the UNOSOM II mandate but not under UN command or control, came under concentrated fire and 18 were killed. Shortly thereafter, US President Bill Clinton announced that US forces would withdraw by 31 March 1994. The remaining contingents in UNOSOM II were nervous about both their security and their ability to bring an end to the conflict in Somalia. They finally withdrew, under US protection, in March 1995. This hybrid of enforcement and peacekeeping achieved very mixed results, and was riddled with disagreements between different participants over the purposes of the operation and its command structure. Neither the US nor the UN systems of controlling the use of military force emerged with vast credit.

The case of Somalia has been frequently cited to support the proposition that it is fatal for a peacekeeping operation to be involved in, or associated with, the use of force and the loss of impartiality. It must be debatable whether so hard and fast a rule can be derived from the Somali experience alone. Many of the problems of the various UN and US forces in Somalia stemmed from the absence of a clear overall purpose, and from a weak system of coordinating of outside forces once the US-led phase of the operation had ended.

In addition to the above-mentioned cases, there have been several UN-based authorisations of force for more limited purposes: enforcing sanctions, air-exclusion zones and other restrictions on particular states and activities.

Despite the difficulties encountered, the arrangement whereby forces or missions are authorised by the Security Council but remain largely national or alliance-based in command has certain advantages. It is slightly different from what was envisaged in the Charter, but has similarities to the practice of the Allies in the Second World War. It reflects the reality that not all states feel equally involved in a given enforcement action. Moreover, military action requires an extremely close relation between intelligence-gathering and operations, a smoothly functioning decision-making machine and forces with some experience of working together to perform dangerous and complex tasks. These things are more likely to be achieved through existing national armed forces, alliances and military relationships than they are within the structure of a UN command. Furthermore, action by one state or a group of states can be a valuable stopgap while the UN slowly cobbles together an international peacekeeping or other force. Finally, for the UN there may be risks in too-direct involvement in the management of military force: when terrible mistakes occur, as they inevitably do in military operations, they could reflect badly on the organisation, and could threaten its universal character.

Peacekeeping Operations

Peacekeeping is another major UN variation on traditional UN Charter and collective-security ideas, and responds to a weakness at their heart. Most models of collective security are based on the idea of collective military enforcement actions in support of states which are victims of acts of aggression. However, in practice many international problems are not seen by most states or indeed individuals in simple terms of "aggression" versus "defence." In some cases they may be viewed as more suitable for treatment by impartial efforts of various kinds. In conformity with this view, peacekeeping operations have evolved as the international community's principal form of collective military activity. Peacekeeping forces generally consist of separate national contingents under a unified UN-appointed command. They must normally be authorised by the Security Council, but are directed on a day-to-day basis by the Secretary-General or his representative.

Peacekeeping is, notoriously, a very different type of activity from more belligerent or coercive uses of force, and the differences cause serious problems. The three principles on which peacekeeping operations have traditionally been based (impartiality, consent of host states and avoidance of use of force) are different from the principles on which other uses of force are based. Further, the dispersion of forces typical of peacekeeping missions, and their lightly armed character, mean that they are intensely vulnerable to reprisals in the event that force is used on their behalf. This problem, which has been particularly acute in Somalia and former Yugoslavia, is an objective one, which cannot be wished away.

In theory, peacekeeping has long been seen as compatible with the use of force by peacekeepers for their own self-defence. The definition of self-defence has on occasion been slightly stretched to encompass aspects of carrying out a mandate. In reporting on the setting up of the second UN Emergency Force (UNEF II) in the Suez Canal and Sinai areas in October 1973, then UN Secretary-General Kurt Waldheim wrote:

> The Force will be provided with weapons of a defensive character only. It shall not use force except in self-defence. Self-defence would include resistance to attempts by forceful means to prevent it from discharging its duties under the mandate of the Security Council.[8]

This formulation, which has been deemed to cover subsequent UN peacekeeping operations as well, did not in practice lead to a general pattern of more forceful response when UN forces were hampered by armed groups from performing their duties; nor did it lead to a general pattern of troop deployments and armament levels which might have been appropriate to the role implied in Waldheim's letter.

The use of UN peacekeeping forces in situations of endemic intra-state conflict, which has increased markedly since about 1989, was already significant in the Congo in 1960–64. There, as subsequently, extremely difficult problems concerning UN management of the use of force arose. The Security Council produced a classic case of contradictory mandates. A resolution of August 1960 reaffirmed that the UN force in the Congo "will not be a party to or in any way intervene in or be used to influence the outcome of any internal conflict, constitutional or otherwise."[9] Then in February 1961, concerned about Katangese secession, the killing of the Congolese leaders and the general threat of civil war, another Security Council resolution urged "that the United Nations take immediately all appropriate measures to prevent the occurrence of civil war in the Congo, including arrangements for cease-fires, the halting of all military operations, the prevention of clashes, and the use of force, if necessary, in the last resort." It further urged that "measures be taken for the immediate withdrawal and evacuation from the Congo of all Belgian and other foreign military and paramilitary personnel."[10]

The incoherent mixture of peacekeeping with elements of enforcement inherent in these two resolutions was followed by actions which led eventually to a respectable outcome, in that it maintained the unity of the Congo. Yet the whole episode, especially issues connected with the use of force, contributed to an atmosphere of acrimony unusual even for the UN. There was disagreement about the extent to which the February 1961 resolution constituted an authorisation to use force; and about the level of authority at which military actions of the UN forces were approved. There were many press reports of alleged UN involvement in killings of civilians. Important members of the Security Council, especially the UK and France, did not assist pursuit of a vigorous military policy. The Soviet Union and its allies refused to pay for the enterprise.

A curious feature of the Congo operation was that some military actions were dressed up as self-defence when in fact they were essentially proactive.[11] There was deep resistance in the UN, on a variety of grounds, to accepting the idea that the UN might ever have a policy of using force. This was true of Secretary-General Dag Hammarskjöld, who was especially anxious to avoid all appearance of the UN being an occupying power in the Congo. In what may well have been his last message, written to Moise Tshombe in the night of 16–17 September 1961 immediately before his fatal flight, Hammarskjöld quoted the terms of the February 1961 resolution cited above, but then said:

> A principle of the United Nations which is absolutely binding upon all is the maintenance of peace and, to that end and in order to protect human life, they are bound to cease all hostilities and to seek solutions to the conflict by means of negotiation, mediation and conciliation.[12]

Statements such as this confirm the idea that there is a UN culture which, while not being explicitly pacifist, is opposed to associating the UN with the management of force.

On rare occasions, peacekeeping has been associated with the effective use or threat of force—but not necessarily by the peacekeepers themselves. This was the case with the UN Transition Assistance Group (UNTAG) in Namibia at the start of its operations in April 1989. When members of the South West Africa People's Organisation infiltrated into Namibia in violation of cease-fire terms, UN representatives authorised, or at least tolerated, a South African use of force to stop the infiltration. The judgement of many of those involved is that this use of force (paradoxically, by the very South African forces that were at the time the subject of a UN arms embargo) was a necessary precondition for the successful completion of UNTAG's peacekeeping and election-monitoring operation.

While much has been achieved by UN peacekeeping, especially in helping resolve various conflicts at the time of the end of the Cold War, peacekeeping operations in many countries, from the Congo to the post–Cold War period, has exposed many problems. These include the huge number of crises which an international organisation may be asked to address; the reluctance of states to provide the necessary financial, material and human resources for many peacekeeping operations; the inherent limitations of a complex multinational system of decision-making and operational command; and the difficulty of engaging in enforcement at the same time as troops are widely dispersed in peacekeeping or humanitarian assistance mode.

All three variants to the UN Charter scheme (alliances, authorisation to use force and peacekeeping) which emerged in the organisation's first 50 years shared one feature. They constituted moves away from the Charter idea of the UN as a principal centre from which to take military action or (in the words of Article 45) "urgent military measures."

To many, especially in the 12–15 months following the 1991 Gulf War, the idea that the UN was at last operating in the military sphere in the way that its founders had intended was attractive. Yet ideas of this kind tended to underestimate two considerations. First, the 1991 Gulf War had been fought on the basis of an authorisation to a US-led coalition, an utterly different arrangement from what was in the UN Charter; and, second, it had only been possible to get a wide degree of international support for military action because Iraq's aggression was so blatant and extreme. Other more complex (and perhaps therefore more typical) cases would not find such a high level of agreement among states.

FORMER YUGOSLAVIA

The several interconnected wars in former Yugoslavia are of a kind which international organisations are ill-equipped to tackle. In the late nineteenth century and the early years of the twentieth century, war in the Balkans defeated the efforts of the Concert of Europe, and contributed to the undoing of the Habsburg, Turkish and Russian empires. The wars which broke out in 1991 quickly exposed the incapacity of states to respond effectively, including through the European Community and the Conference on Security and Cooperation in Europe (CSCE—now OSCE). The CSCE's members failed to make effective use of its newly established and inaptly named Conflict Prevention Centre.

Any fair assessment of the UN's performance in former Yugoslavia has to start by recognising the intractable and tragic nature of the problem and the historically unprecedented nature of the attempt to maintain a large international military presence in the middle of an ongoing war. In December 1991, the UNSC endorsed the Secretary-General's view that "the conditions for establishing a peace-keeping operation in Yugoslavia still do not exist." [13] There must be many, within and outside the UN, who suspect that they did not exist subsequently either.

Among the objective difficulties which prevent outside bodies from exercising an effective role in the conflicts in Croatia and Bosnia-Herzegovina are: the fact that stable cease-fires are extremely hard to achieve in this war; the lack of anything approaching a common public perception among the powers involved about the nature of the conflict; their different interests, instinctive political responses and national military styles; and the reluctance of the United States under two administrations to take a coalition leadership role, at least until the events of July and August 1995. The UN is not responsible for these and other difficulties, which have severely hampered its performance.

The UN, however, along with its major members, is vulnerable to many criticisms of its role in former Yugoslavia. Five critiques which bear directly on the question of use of force are:

- There has been a failure to develop anything like a political or strategic vision of what the UN is attempting in former Yugoslavia. The organisation, being little more than the sum of its parts, has proved better at agreeing relatively uncontroversial short-term measures, such as mediation efforts, humanitarian assistance and supporting cease-fires, than it has at developing a sense of purpose about the kind of settlement ultimately envisaged, and how that might be reached.

- The UN lacks unity of overall strategic command. A system in which the tasks of forces in the field are largely defined in resolutions drawn up by a multinational committee has obvious weaknesses if it has to respond to a situation which is both complex and fast-moving. The system leads inevitably to the complaint of officers in the field that they simply cannot carry out the bewildering variety of mandates they have been given.

- The UN seems to have been basically limited to only two types of troop-deploying action in response to threats to peace. Either it can authorise a major Chapter VII military enforcement operation, for example with the objective of supporting one party and removing aggressive armed forces from the territory in question; or it can engage in a peacekeeping operation, with its requirements of consent, impartiality and non-use of force. This crude choice between enforcement and peacekeeping does not correspond to the complexity and variety of conflicts in the world, especially in former Yugoslavia. Sometimes, indeed, it seems as if the problem is being simplified or redefined in order to fit the remedy.

- The numerous attempts in recent years to devise new categories of UN action, new terms and new doctrines (second-generation peacekeeping, wider peacekeeping, peace-support operations and so on) have by no means been complete failures, but in former Yugoslavia they have not, for the most part, overcome the problem that most actual or envisaged uses of force were likely to be seen by at least one of the belligerent parties as favouring another party; and were likely to lead to reprisals against peacekeepers, who, by the very nature of their tasks, are widely dispersed and extremely vulnerable.

- Peacekeeping forces which are prepared to engage in self-defence, but not in systematic defence of threatened communities in a peculiarly nasty and bitter war, must expect to incur odium.

Such a litany of problems should not obscure the accomplishments of the UN forces in former Yugoslavia since 1992. The work within Bosnia-Herzegovina in support of the Muslim-Croat Federation, the delivery of humanitarian relief to threatened communities and the many measures to reduce the military deployments and incidents in and around Sarajevo, are perhaps the principal achievements. The scale and effectiveness of much of this work is not widely known. It is no mean achievement that from the start of the humanitarian airlift to Sarajevo on 30 June 1992 until 17 October 1995 there were 12,625 sorties, delivering 156,557 tonnes, of which 141,285 were food and the rest non-food items (such as shelter materials and medical supplies). The fact that siege warfare is among the cruellest forms of warfare enhances the significance of such figures.

Threats and Uses of Force by or on Behalf of the UN

Yet in matters related to the threat or use of force by or on behalf of the UN, the operations in former Yugoslavia, at least before August 1995, were, for the most part, a failure. Perceptions of failure have been aggravated by misleading labelling. It was a serious mistake to call the UN forces in former Yugoslavia a UN "Protection" Force (UNPROFOR), when by their nature they could not offer serious military protection. It was also a mistake, though in terms of UN requirements a more forgivable one, for the force to be classified as a "peacekeeping" force, when there was very little peace to keep.

In the conflict in former Yugoslavia, threats and uses of force by or on behalf of UN forces have been made in many contexts. In some instances, certain contingents showed a willingness to use force to defend themselves and their mission, and won respect for so doing. Overall, however, the record of threatening and using force was mixed. Only three of the main instances are listed below.

Operation Sharp Guard This operation began on 16 July 1992, when NATO ships took up positions in the Adriatic Sea to monitor compliance with two UN resolutions: the embargo on the delivery of arms to Yugoslavia adopted by the Security Council the previous September, which was subsequently applied to all the republics of former Yugoslavia;[14] and the application of economic sanctions against the newly incarnated Federal Republic of Yugoslavia (Serbia and Montenegro).[15] Subsequently there was also Western European Union (WEU) involvement in this operation in the Adriatic. In April 1993, the Security Council strengthened the arms embargo and general sanctions: [16] thereafter, according to a Dutch study, "no ship at sea has reportedly been able to break the embargo, a little-noticed accomplishment." [17] In the Adriatic, the enforcement of general sanctions and, in particular, the stopping of oil tankers was a significant achievement.

However, the maintenance of the arms embargo in the Adriatic was less so. There were many other ways of getting arms into former Yugoslavia than via the Adriatic. There were also disagreements as to the value of the arms embargo. There have been persistent reports in 1995 of arms supplies reaching Bosnian government territory; some have suggested a degree of US government involvement in such deliveries. Within the United States there have been very strong objections to maintaining the arms embargo at all so far as Bosnia-Herzegovina is concerned: these were reflected in the Congressional resolutions passed in July 1995 calling for its termination. On 26 July 1995, Senator Bob Dole won a majority of 69–29 for a resolution requiring the US to lift the arms embargo on Bosnia within 12 weeks of a Bosnian government request to UNPROFOR to leave. This increased the pressure on President Clinton and his British and French allies to act in a manner enabling UNPROFOR to retain Bosnian government consent.

The "No-Fly Zone" In October 1992, the Security Council imposed a "ban on all military flights in the airspace of Bosnia and Herzegovina." [18] This was rightly seen as primarily directed against the Serbs, and as being of only limited relevance to the main problems posed by the war, in which air-power had not been a major instrument. NATO, in *Operation Sky Monitor,* promptly monitored action in the air. Various violations of the no-fly zone led to the passing of further Security Council resolutions, including, in March 1993, an authorisation to member-states:

> To take, under the authority of the Security Council and subject to close coordination with the Secretary-General and UNPROFOR, all necessary measures in the airspace of the Republic of Bosnia and Herzegovina, in the event of further violations, to ensure compliance with the ban on flights. [19]

On the basis of a North Atlantic Council decision on 8 April 1993, *Operation Deny Flight* began on 12 April. This involved close liaison and exchange of information between NATO and UNPROFOR.

Many problems arose with the no-fly zone. It proved extremely difficult, if not impossible, to prevent night flights by helicopters. Also, the UK and France were reportedly reluctant to back it up, because of concern about reprisals against their forces on the ground. On 28 February 1994 NATO aircraft shot down four Serbian aircraft. As Dutch analyst Dick Leurdijk observed: "It was the first time that NATO planes opened fire over Bosnia. They carried out the Alliance's first military action since it was founded 45 years ago." [20] While this incident had no immediate adverse consequences, subsequent experience of the no-fly zone was mixed, with Serb forces in spring and summer 1995 defying it, and also occasionally demanding its non-implementation.

"Safe Areas" In May 1993 the Security Council proclaimed six towns in Bosnia-Herzegovina "safe areas." Yet it did not at the time agree detailed rules about either Bosnian or UN military protection of such areas. [21] A resolution the following month provided a framework for the use of force in respect of the safe areas: UNPROFOR was authorised "to deter attacks against the safe areas"; and "acting in self-defence, to take the necessary measures, including the use of force, in reply to bombardments against the safe areas by any of the parties or to armed incursions into them"; while:

Member States, acting nationally or through regional organisations or arrangements, may take, under the authority of the Security Council and subject to close coordination with the Secretary-General and UNPROFOR, all necessary measures, through the use of air power, in and around the safe areas in the Republic of Bosnia and Herzegovina, to support UNPROFOR in the performance of its mandate.[22]

These resolutions seemed to promise much, but did not in the event unequivocally commit the UN to the defence of the "safe areas." The effect of the resolutions was undermined by the reluctance of states to provide the additional troop requirement of approximately 34,000 that UN Secretary-General Boutros Boutros-Ghali estimated was necessary. A Security Council decision in June 1993 to reinforce UNPROFOR contained no figure and had few, if any, results.[23]

Following the mortar attack on the Sarajevo central market on 5 February 1994, Boutros-Ghali, in a letter of 6 February, stressed the need for an early decision by the North Atlantic Council:

To authorise the Commander-in-Chief of NATO's Southern Command to launch air strikes, at the request of the United Nations, against artillery or mortar positions in or around Sarajevo which are determined by UNPROFOR to be responsible for attacks against civilian targets in that city. The arrangements for the coordination of such air strikes would be elaborated through direct contacts between UNPROFOR Headquarters and NATO's Southern Command, as has already been done in the case of close air support for the self-defence of United Nations personnel in Bosnia and Herzegovina.[24]

This was followed by the decisions taken by the North Atlantic Council on 9 February 1994, and by the purportedly separate and locally negotiated cease-fire agreement of the same day, for the demilitarisation of Sarajevo. The very public arrangements to use NATO force in association with the UN seemed to have produced some tangible results. These did not last, being followed by Serb attacks on Gorazde, which exposed the extreme vulnerability of UN forces; the erosion of the Sarajevo exclusion zone in 1995; the continued fighting around the Bihac safe area; and the fall, in July 1995, of the two safe areas of Srebrenica and Zepa. The fall of these towns—to the accompaniment of official claims that the UN forces were only there to deter attacks, not to defend against them—exposed the UN, and in some measure NATO, as incoherent, impotent and untrustworthy.[25]

Weakening of the UN-NATO Military Role

The rapid erosion in 1994–95 of the idea of a joint role for UNPROFOR and NATO as cease-fire enforcers and defenders of safe areas has been attributed to many causes: the reluctance of UNPROFOR commanders and UN officials, especially the Secretary-General's Special Representative, Yasushi Akashi, to authorise the use of air-power; the large number of people on both the UN and NATO sides who had to agree before any action could be taken; the inherent limits of air-power to affect the position on the ground; the hostage-takings of UNPROFOR personnel by Bosnian Serbs and their bombardments of safe areas, on the occasions when NATO air-power was used; UNPROFOR's need for Serb cooperation if its humanitarian flights and convoys were to reach besieged areas; the strong opposition of some powers, especially Russia, to extensive use of NATO force in former Yugoslavia; and the more subtle opposition of other powers, including many NATO members (not least the UK), to action which might entangle them further in Yugoslavia, or endanger their troops serving with UNPROFOR. All of these explanations contain an element of truth.

Both NATO and the UN appear to have badly underestimated the difficulty of combining peacekeeping with enforcement in the peculiarly difficult circumstances of former Yugoslavia. By their nature, peacekeeping and humanitarian work require forces to be widely dispersed, and hence vulnerable to hostage-taking: but when a peace-keeping force also includes, or is accompanied by, military observers and forward air controllers, the risks are increased, because belligerents, for whom strategic surprise is always a crucial asset, resent their presence. Furthermore, the lack of control over Bosnian government forces in some of the safe areas, including Bihac and Srebrenica, led to Serb accusations that the UN was protecting bases for assaults against Serb-held areas. Again, there was no clear vision as to how, in the long term, some of the safe areas could be expected to survive when surrounded by hostile Serbs.

Such criticisms of the unique combination of peacekeeping and enforcement attempted in Bosnia are probably justified, but they do not mean that the alternative commonly proposed, encapsulated in the phrase "lift and strike," would necessarily have worked better. The idea of abandoning a flawed peacekeeping effort and instead supplying arms to Bosnia-Herzegovina had many attractions, but quickly ran into difficulties, not the least of which were the apparent opening of a door to competitive national interventions; and the risk of having to close down the humanitarian relief effort for at least some of the besieged areas. Further, such a policy would have probably put those pursuing it in the uncomfortable position of openly violating a Security Council resolution for which they had voted, and which could not be rescinded.

In the event, developments on the ground in Bosnia-Herzegovina, and in Croatia, provided a basis for pursuing a different policy, which was in conformed with Security Council resolutions. The Bosnian Serb forces, encouraged no doubt by weak reactions by outside powers, overplayed their hand from April 1995 onwards by virtually stopping the humanitarian aid effort to besieged areas, and by taking UN personnel as hostages in response to NATO use of force. This led, especially in NATO countries, to consideration of more intensive use of force in Bosnia-Herzegovina.[26]

The case for such a move was strengthened by the loss of Srebrenica and Zepa in July 1995 and the Croat offensives of April–May (in Western Slavonia) and August 1995 (in Krajina). These events created a greater need, and also a greater opportunity, to implement the Security Council resolutions by robustly responding to attacks on the four remaining safe areas. The very factors that had previously inhibited the use of NATO force diminished: with the aid effort at a virtual standstill, and UN forces withdrawn from positions where they were vulnerable to Serb hostage-taking, two strong practical arguments against the use of NATO force were undermined. There was, in effect, a gradual transition from peacekeeping, with its obligation of impartiality, to a form of enforcement.

A development in this direction was the London Conference of July 1995, with its solemn promises to use air-power to protect at least Gorazde. It was also in the logic of the deployment outside Sarajevo of the new rapid-reaction force, established as part of UNPROFOR by France, the Netherlands and the UK. It was further presaged by the decision of the UN Secretary-General, reportedly bowing to US pressure, to cut Akashi out of the decision-making process on the use of force.[27]

The will to use force had clearly come more from outside powers and from NATO than from the UN Secretariat. Indeed, in January 1995, Secretary-General Boutros-Ghali had issued a "Supplement to an Agenda for Peace," which stressed that peacekeeping required the consent of the parties and could not be combined with the use of force. It also said: "It is necessary to resist the temptation to use military power" to speed up the resolution of conflicts.[28] At the end of May 1995, the Secretary-General's report on former Yugoslavia reiterated that peacekeeping and enforcement were basically incompatible—a view rejected by the Security Council.[29] The approach that stressed consent and opposed many uses of force was open to strong criticism, and made the UN a prisoner of events in Bosnia-Herzegovina.[30] Under the pressure of these events, in August and early September 1995 Boutros-Ghali expressed support for *Operation Deliberate Force*. However, his oft-repeated view that the UNSC had to make a fundamental choice between waging peace or waging war did not change, and was reflected in his letter to the UNSC on 18 September stating that it should end the peacekeeping operation in Bosnia and replace it with a multinational force—presumably under NATO auspices.[31] The huge costs of the UN forces in former Yugoslavia, aggravating the severe UN financial crisis, provided a further motive for this remarkable plea.

Operation Deliberate Force has changed the situation significantly, and was the necessary prelude to the cease-fire that came into effect in mid-October 1995. However, it has also raised some difficult questions. There has been a further move away from the old idea of impartiality between the belligerents, but there has not been a clear indication of a new conception. It could be one of impartiality in carrying out UNSC decisions;[32] or (which could be much the same thing in practice) one of legitimation in the sense of basing action on "the dynamics of the social compact between those in positions of authority and those subject to that authority."[33]

The air campaign of *Operation Deliberate Force* had complex interconnections with action on the ground. It was supported by the rapid-reaction force, but its effect also owed much to the fact that Bosnian government and Croat forces (including from Croatia proper) were already putting pressure on the Bosnian Serbs. However much the targeting of *Operation Deliberate Force* avoided any suggestion of direct battlefield assistance to the Bosnian government and Croat forces, it involved a form of co-belligerence with them. This posed dilemmas for the UN. In their September advances, the Croat and Bosnian government forces committed acts of anti-Serb "ethnic-cleansing," about which NATO and the UN could apparently do little. There was also the possibility that Croat forces might ultimately undermine or dominate Bosnia-Herzegovina. The unwillingness of UN member-states to allow risks to be taken with the lives of their own armed forces assigned to UN duties has not fundamentally changed, and still constitutes a constraint on the actions of UN forces on the ground.

Plainly, the creation of the rapid-reaction force, and the launching of *Operation Deliberate Force,* owed much to national decision-making, especially in Paris, London and Washington. If these developments were formally linked above all to the protection of Sarajevo, as mandated in Security Council resolutions, they also owed much to a larger political agenda of pressing the Bosnian Serbs to accept a peace settlement. Indeed, the day before the 28 August attack on Sarajevo, which provided the formal trigger for *Operation Deliberate Force,* US officials had threatened the Serbs with bombing if there was no progress on an accord.[34] US and allied actions confirmed the truism that the more force is used on behalf of the UN, the more central the role of individual states becomes.

What are the preliminary lessons of the Yugoslav experience so far as use of force under UN auspices is concerned? Force has been deployed quite effectively in situations where the tasks are relatively simple and there is very little danger, as in the Adriatic. The preventive deployment in the Former Yugoslav Republic of Macedonia (FYROM), not itself a use of force, but hinting at that possibility, has probably had a calming effect on a situation full of potential dangers. Elsewhere, the picture up to August 1995 was largely, though not entirely, one of vacillations, hesitations and failure. UN forces had been marginalised in both Bosnia-Herzegovina and Croatia. The greatest problem was not a UN culture hostile to uses of force, but something deeper, and harder to change: the absence of an overall strategy, of clear goals and of political leadership among the principal members of both the UN and NATO. A barnacle-like encrustation of UN Security Council resolutions had added to the difficulties of changing course and moving purposefully. Some such faults are inevitable in an international society where different states see things differently, and have varying interests. However, the weak leadership within, as well as between, states has been especially striking over former Yugoslavia. In this case, in contrast to the 1990–91 crisis over Kuwait, countries chose to act through the UN precisely because they were not keen to get directly involved themselves: this must always be a bad basis for coalition action. As a result, the UN, sadly, ended up by involuntarily teaching some of the new states in the region an ancient lesson: that they can only achieve results by their own efforts, not by those of the international community.

PROPOSALS TO ENABLE THE UN
TO USE FORCE MORE EFFECTIVELY

What general lessons emerge about how the UN might use force more effectively? The first requirement is some agreement on what the problems have been. Cases such as Somalia 1992–95, Rwanda 1994–95 and former Yugoslavia since 1991 confirm lessons which can also be drawn from earlier episodes, including some during the Cold War years. The main problems include: the failure to reach a clear and agreed view of the strategic and political purposes of involvements in complex and fast-changing situations; the persistent, but by now battered belief, that what the UN Security Council proclaims, others will respect and implement; the lack of an accepted mode of action beyond the two familiar nostrums of impartial peacekeeping and enforcement in favour of one side; the absence of an effective system of international command and control; and the difficulty of getting states to commit their forces to distant and dangerous operations.

Are the UN's problems peculiar to the UN, or do they exist in any large multilateral organisation, including NATO? It cannot be claimed that NATO is free from all the above problems, nor is it self-evident that the NATO Council is better at reaching decisions or at framing coherent strategies than the UN. Until a few years ago, NATO had a clear system of leadership, by the US, but that has been very much in question in recent years. NATO's greatest advantage over the UN, historically, has been agreement on some clearly defined defensive purposes, whereas the UN has an almost infinite range of responsibilities. Part of NATO's difficulty in former Yugoslavia has been that, until the fall of Srebrenica in July 1995, there was not general agreement within NATO, any more than within the UN, on exactly what the Alliance wished to achieve there.

While NATO came to favour the use of major force in connection with a peacekeeping operation, in the UN Secretariat opinion had been moving for some time in the opposite direction. Back in 1992, the UN Secretary-General's *An Agenda for Peace* had favoured "the utilisation of peace-enforcement units in clearly defined circumstances and with their terms of reference specified in advance."[35] It was envisaged that these forces, distinct from any constituted to deal with acts of aggression, might help to restore and maintain cease-fires. Events in Somalia in 1993, and in Bosnia-Herzegovina in 1994–95, left many at the UN understandably nervous about mixing peacekeeping and peace-enforcement, principally because of the vulnerability of peacekeepers when force was used. There was a marked tendency at the UN to oppose major uses of force that might jeopardise the perception of peacekeepers as impartial. This reversion to a traditional concept of peacekeeping was rejected by the major Western powers so far as Bosnia was concerned. In the event, it did prove possible, in Bosnia in summer 1995, to limit the exposure of peacekeepers to Serb reprisals, and even to resume humanitarian relief during and after major military action under UN and NATO auspices.

As to the more general question of how the problems connected with the UN and the use of force might be overcome, much discussion has centred on the many variants of the idea of creating a standing UN force. In 1993, Sir Brian Urquhart advocated a light-infantry force composed of 5,000 volunteers, not limited to peacekeeping as traditionally understood.[36] In 1995, Boutros Boutros-Ghali suggested creating a standing rapid-reaction force, formed of contingents from UN member-states, for situations where there was an emergency need for peacekeeping troops.[37] Also in 1995, the Netherlands government put forward a "non-paper" proposing a UN Rapid-Deployment Brigade with a wide variety of possible tasks, some of which go beyond an expanded definition of peacekeeping.[38] A further development this year is the Canadian study aimed in a general way at improving the UN's rapid-reaction capability.[39]

Such proposals for a standing UN force or rapid-reaction capability deserve to be taken seriously, because they address several important problems connected with the UN's ineffective responses to many crises. They pre-dated the emergence of a rapid-reaction force under UN auspices in Bosnia in June–August 1995, although that assumed a form and purpose different from anything previously envisaged.[40] Yet these proposals, to the extent that they imply that all that the UN needs is more "muscle," which states will hand over to its direction for use in a wide variety of situations, may deflect attention from other deficiencies which are as much conceptual as physical. These include a need to improve further the quality of military advice available to the Security Council and the Secretary-General; to work out some means of transforming an operation from peacekeeping to peace-enforcement mode; to develop a concept for UN operations which are distinct from both peacekeeping and enforcement against aggression; and generally to produce policies with some intellectual, strategic and moral coherence.

The UN retains considerable importance as a legitimiser of certain uses of force, and this may be among its most important roles. The UN and its leading members must remain prepared in particular instances to authorise operations led by one country or by a group of states, as distinct from staying with the basic pattern of UN control of most operations—states being by nature better than large multilateral organisations in reacting rapidly to fast-moving situations. Above all, the UN, including its leading members, needs to recognise openly that the Charter was right to provide for a balance between self-defence (whether by individual states or alliance-based) and collective military action under UN auspices; but wrong to imply that the UN could have a central role in more than a very small number of crises. If that role is to be exercised effectively by the UN and its member-states, they may need to recognise that occasionally there is a need for, and a possibility of, an approach which is conceptually distinct both from impartial peacekeeping based on consent of the parties and from a simple enforcement action on behalf of an attacked state.

NOTES

1. "General Principles Governing the Organization of the Armed Forces Made Available to the Security Council by Member Nations of the United Nations: Report of the Military Staff Committee," UN document S/336, 30 April 1947.

2. See, for example, Fernand van Langenhove, *La Crise du Système de Sécurité Collective des Nations Unies 1946–1957* (The Hague: Martinus Nijhoff for the Royal Institute for International Relations, Brussels, 1958).

3. UNSC Res. 83, 27 June 1950.

4. UNSC Res. 84, 7 July 1950.

5. For a general discussion of problems concerning the legitimacy of humanitarian intervention, see R. Lillich (ed.), *Humanitarian Intervention and the United Nations* (Charlottesville, VA: University Press of Virginia, 1973); Thomas Franck and Nigel Rodley, "After Bangladesh: The Law of Humanitarian Intervention by Military Force," *American Journal of International Law,* vol. 67, no. 2, April 1973, p. 275; Michael Akehurst, "Humanitarian Intervention," in Hedley Bull (ed.), *Intervention in World Politics* (Oxford: Clarendon Press, 1984), pp. 95–118; Nigel Rodley (ed.), *To Loose the Bands of Wickedness: International Intervention in Defence of Human Rights* (London: Brassey's, 1992); and Laura Reed and Carl Kaysen (eds.), *Emerging Norms of Justified Intervention* (Cambridge, MA: Committee on International Security Studies of the American Academy of Arts and Sciences, 1993).

6. UNSC Res. 751, 24 April 1992.

7. UNSC Res. 794, 3 December 1992.

8. UN doc. S/11052/Rev.1, 27 October 1973, para. 4 (a). UNEF II was set up on the basis of UNSC Res. 340, 25 October 1973.

9. UNSC Res. 146, 9 August 1960, para. 4.

10. UNSC Res. 161, 21 February 1961, paras. A(1) and (2).

11. For an example of the self-defence rationale of the use of force on behalf of the UN in the Congo, see the "Report of the Officer-in-Charge of the United Nations Operation in the Congo to the Secretary-General Relating to the Implementation of Paragraph A-2 of the Security Council Resolution of 21 February 1961," UN doc. S/4940, 14 September 1961; also the account by Conor Cruise O'Brien, representative of the United Nations in Katanga in 1961, *To Katanga and Back: A UN Case History* (London: Hutchinson, 1962), esp. chapter 15.

12. Hammarskjöld's message, trying to persuade Tshombe to agree to a firm cease-fire before the two leaders could begin talks, is contained within UN doc. S/4940/Add. 4, 17 September 1961.

13. UNSC Res. 724, 15 December 1991.

14. The arms embargo on former Yugoslavia had originally been adopted in UNSC Res. 713, 25 September 1991, which referred to Chapter VII. It was reaffirmed in subsequent resolutions in a manner which interpreted it as applying to the successor states of former Yugoslavia.

15. Sanctions were imposed on the Federal Republic of Yugoslavia (Serbia and Montenegro) by UNSC Res. 757, 30 May 1992, on account of its military involvement in support of the Serbs in Bosnia-Herzegovina.

16. UNSC Res. 820, 17 April 1993.

17. Dick A. Leurdijk, *The United Nations and NATO in Former Yugoslavia: Partners in International Cooperation* (The Hague: Netherlands Atlantic Commission, 1994), p. 28.

18. UNSC Res. 781, 9 October 1992.

19. UNSC Res. 816, 31 March 1993.

20. Leurdijk, *The UN and NATO in Former Yugoslavia*, p. 35.

21. The "safe areas" were proclaimed in UNSC Res. 824, 6 May 1993.

22. UNSC Res. 836, 4 June 1993.

23. UNSC Res. 844, 18 June 1993.

24. Boutros Boutros-Ghali, letter of 6 February 1994 to Manfred Wörner, NATO Secretary-General. See also his letters of the same date, and of 10 February, to the President of the UN Security Council. The 10 February letter delegated the authority to approve any request from the UNPROFOR force commander for close air support to his Special Representative, Yasushi Akashi.

25. "In Brussels, Yasushi Akashi, the UN chief in former Yugoslavia, told NATO officials yesterday that nothing could be done to help Zepa, and gave the green light for further Serb conquests by stating that the UN could not defend the UN-decreed safe areas for Muslim civilians. The UN Protection Force (UNPROFOR), he added, was not in Bosnia for protection purposes, but to deter." From a report by John Palmer and others, "All Safe Havens Under Attack," *The Guardian,* 20 July 1995, p. 10. Boutros-Ghali had similarly argued

two months earlier that "deterrence is the only means UNPROFOR is mandated to use against attacks on the safe areas." UN doc. S/1995/444 of 30 May 1995, para. 40.

26. For an exposition of the difficulties of moving towards enforcement by creating rapid-reaction forces, see "Bosnia: No Easy Options Left," *Strategic Comments* (London: IISS), no. 5, 8 June 1995.

27. On evidence of US pressure, see Andrew Marshall and Michael Sheridan, "US Wants Free Hand to Conquer the Skies with Massive Strikes," *The Independent,* 19 July 1995, p. 8. The UN Secretary-General's letter of 26 July 1995 to the President of the Security Council delegated to General Bernard Janvier, UN commander in the Balkans, the power to authorise uses of force. Janvier in turn was empowered to delegate it to Lt-Gen. Rupert Smith, the Commander of UNPROFOR in Bosnia, "when operational circumstances so require." Text in UN doc. S/1995/623, 1 August 1995.

28. "Supplement to An Agenda for Peace: Position Paper of the Secretary-General on the Occasion of the Fiftieth Anniversary of the United Nations," UN doc. A/50/60, 3 January 1995, paras 35 and 36.

29. Secretary-General's Report, UN doc. S/1995/444 of 30 May 1995, paras. 16, 38, 40, 41, 55, 56, 58, 60–65 and 80.

30. For a fine critique of UN (and to some extent UK) excessive attachment to consent in former Yugoslavia, see James Gow and Christopher Dandeker, "Peace Support Operations: The Problem of Legitimation," *The World Today,* vol. 51, nos. 8–9, August–September 1995, pp. 171–74.

31. "End Urged to UN Bosnia Role," *New York Times,* 19 September 1995, p. A10.

32. Suggested in Adam Roberts, "The Crisis in UN Peacekeeping," *Survival,* vol. 36, no. 3, Autumn 1994, p. 115.

33. Gow and Dandeker, "Peace Support Operations," p. 173.

34. See, for example, the news report by Steven Greenhouse, "US Warns of Air Strikes Unless Serbs Negotiate: NATO Will Intervene 'Heavily' if No Progress Is Made on an Accord," *International Herald Tribune,* 28 August 1995, p. 1. The Sarajevo attack which killed 37 took place later on the day that the report was published.

35. Boutros Boutros-Ghali, *An Agenda for Peace: Preventive Diplomacy, Peace-making and Peace-keeping* (New York: United Nations, 1992), para. 44.

36. Brian Urquhart, "For a UN Volunteer Military Force," *New York Review of Books,* 10 June 1993, p. 3. See also the comments in subsequent issues.

37. "Supplement to An Agenda for Peace," para. 44. See also the discussion of enforcement action in paras. 77–80.

38. The Netherlands non-paper, "A UN Rapid Deployment Brigade: A Preliminary Study," The Hague, revised version, April 1995, Section I.5, published in Dick A. Leurdjik (ed.), *A UN Rapid-Deployment Brigade: Strengthening the Capacity for Quick Response* (The Hague: Netherlands Institute of International Relations, 1995).

39. *Towards a Rapid-Reaction Capability for the United Nations,* Report of the Government of Canada, issued 26 September 1995.

40. The rapid-reaction force was envisaged as an integral part of the UN peacekeeping operation (UNPROFOR) in Bosnia-Herzegovina in the UN Secretary-General's letter of 9 June 1995 and its annex (S/1995/44 and Add. 1), and in UNSC Res. 998 of 16 June 1994.

12

❁

Social Issues

Reading 12-1

The Cartel of Good Intentions
William Easterly

The mere mention of a "cartel" usually strikes fear in the hearts and wallets of consumers and regulators around the globe. Though the term normally evokes images of greedy oil producers or murderous drug lords, a new, more well-intentioned cartel has emerged on the global scene. Its members are the world's leading foreign aid organizations, which constitute a near monopoly relative to the powerless poor.

This state of affairs helps explain why the global foreign aid bureaucracy has run amok in recent years. Consider the steps that beleaguered government officials in low-income countries must take to receive foreign aid. Among other things, they must prepare a participatory Poverty Reduction Strategy Paper (PRSP)—a detailed plan for uplifting the destitute that the World Bank and International Monetary Fund (IMF) require before granting debt forgiveness and new loans. This document in turn must adhere to the World Bank's Comprehensive Development Framework, a 14-point checklist covering everything from lumber policy to labor practices. And the list goes on: Policymakers seeking aid dollars must also prepare a Financial Information Management System report, a Report on Observance of Standards and Codes, a Medium Term Expenditure Framework, and a Debt Sustainability Analysis for the Enhanced

Heavily Indebted Poor Countries Initiative. Each document can run to hundreds of pages and consume months of preparation time. For example, Niger's recently completed PRSP is 187 pages long, took 15 months to prepare, and sets out spending for a 2002–05 poverty reduction plan with such detailed line items as $17,600 a year on "sensitizing population to traffic circulation."

Meanwhile, the U.N. International Conference on Financing for Development held in Monterrey, Mexico, in March 2002 produced a document—"the Monterrey Consensus"—that has a welcome emphasis on partnership between rich donor and poor recipient nations. But it's somewhat challenging for poor countries to carry out the 73 actions that the document recommends, including such ambitions as establishing democracy, equality between boys and girls, and peace on Earth.

Visitors to the World Bank Web site will find 31 major development topics listed there, each with multiple subtopics. For example, browsers can explore 13 subcategories under "Social Development," including indigenous peoples, resettlement, and culture in sustainable development. This last item in turn includes the music industry in Africa, the preservation of cultural artifacts, a seven-point framework for action, and— well, you get the idea.

It's not that aid bureaucrats are bad; in fact, many smart, hardworking, dedicated professionals toil away in the world's top aid agencies. But the perverse incentives they face explain the organizations' obtuse behavior. The international aid bureaucracy will never work properly under the conditions that make it operate like a cartel—the cartel of good intentions.

ALL TOGETHER NOW

Cartels thrive when customers have little opportunity to complain or to find alternative suppliers. In its heyday during the 1970s, for example, the Organization of the Petroleum Exporting Countries (OPEC) could dictate severe terms to customers; it was only when more non-OPEC oil exporters emerged that the cartel's power weakened. In the foreign aid business, customers (i.e., poor citizens in developing countries) have few chances to express their needs, yet they cannot exit the system. Meanwhile, rich nations paying the aid bills are clueless about what those customers want. Nongovernmental organizations (NGOs) can hold aid institutions to task on only a few high-visibility issues, such as conspicuous environmental destruction. Under these circumstances, even while foreign aid agencies make good-faith efforts to consult their clients, these agencies remain accountable mainly to themselves.

The typical aid agency forces governments seeking its money to work exclusively with that agency's own bureaucracy—its project appraisal and selection apparatus, its economic and social analysts, its procurement procedures, and its own interests and objectives. Each aid agency constitutes a mini-monopoly, and the collection of all such monopolies forms a cartel. The foreign aid community also resembles a cartel in that the IMF, World Bank, regional development banks, European Union, United Nations, and bilateral aid agencies all agree to "coordinate" their efforts [see Table 1]. The customers therefore have even less opportunity to find alternative aid suppliers. And the entry of new suppliers into the foreign assistance business is difficult because large aid agencies must be sponsored either by an individual government (as in the case of national agencies, such as the U.S. Agency for International Development) or by an international agreement (as in the case of multilateral agencies, such as the World Bank). Most NGOs are too small to make much of a difference.

Table 1 The Aid Cartel's Golden Oldies

Many of the "new" themes that the international aid agencies emphasize today have actually been around for several decades.

Donor Co-ordination	"[Foreign aid] should be a cooperative enterprise in which all nations work together through the United Nations and its specialized agencies." (U.S. President Harry Truman, 1949)	"Aid coordination . . . has been recognized as increasingly important." (World Bank, 1981)	"We should improve coherence through better coordination of efforts amongst international institutions and agencies, the donor community, the private sector, and civil society." (World Bank President James Wolfensohn, 2002)
Aid Selectivity	"Objective No. 1: To apply stricter standards of selectivity . . . in aiding developing countries." (President John F. Kennedy, 1963)	"The relief of poverty depends both on aid and on the policies of the recipient countries." (Cassen Development Committee Task Force, 1985)	"[The International Development Association] should increase its selectivity . . . by directing more assistance to borrowers with sound policy environments." (International Development Association, 2001)
Focus on Poverty	"[The aid community must] place far greater emphasis on policies and projects which will begin to attack the problems of absolute poverty." (World Bank President Robert McNamara, 1973)	"The Deputies encouraged an even stronger emphasis on poverty reduction in [the International Development Association's] programs." (Former World Bank Managing Director Ernest Stern, 1990)	"The Poverty Reduction Strategy Paper aims at . . . increasing the focus of . . . assistance on the overarching objective of poverty reduction." (International Development Association, 2001)
African Reforms	"Many African governments are more clearly aware of the need to take major steps to improve the efficiency . . . of their economies." (World Bank, 1983)	"African countries have made great strides in improving policies and restoring growth." (World Bank, 1994)	"Africa's leaders . . . have recognized the need to improve their policies, spelled out in the New Partnership for African Development." (World Bank, 2002)

SOURCES: William Easterly, "The Cartel of Good Intentions: Bureaucracy vs. Markets in Foreign Aid" (Washington: Center for Global Development, 2002); James Wolfensohn, "Note From the President of the World Bank" (April 12, 2002).

Of course, cartels always display fierce jostling for advantage and even mutual enmity among members. That explains why the aid community concludes that "to realize our increasingly reciprocal ambitions, a lot of hard work, compromises and true good will must come into play." Oops, wait, that's a quote from a recent OPEC meeting. The foreign aid community simply maintains that "better coordination among international financial institutions is needed." However, the difficulties of organizing parties with diverse objectives and interests and the inherent tensions in a cartel render such coordination forever elusive. Doomed attempts at coordination create the worst of all worlds—no central planner exists to tell each agency what to do, nor is there any market pressure from customers to reward successful agencies and discipline unsuccessful ones.

As a result, aid organizations mindlessly duplicate services for the world's poor. Some analysts see this duplication as a sign of competition to satisfy the customer—not so. True market competition should eliminate duplication: When you choose where to eat lunch, the restaurant next door usually doesn't force you to sit down for an extra meal. But things are different in the world of foreign aid, where a team from the U.S. Agency for International Development produced a report on corruption in Uganda in 2001, unaware that British analysts had produced a report on the same topic six months earlier. The Tanzanian government churns out more than 2,400 reports annually for its various donors, who send the poor country some 1,000 missions each year. (Borrowing terminology from missionaries who show the locals the one true path to heaven, "missions" are visits of aid agency staff to developing countries to discuss desirable government policy.) No wonder, then, that in the early 1990s, Tanzania was implementing 15 separate stand-alone health-sector projects funded by 15 different donors. Even small bilateral aid agencies plant their flags everywhere. Were the endless meetings and staff hours worth the effort for the Senegalese government to receive $38,957 from the Finnish Ministry for Foreign Affairs Development Cooperation in 2001?

By forming a united front and duplicating efforts, the aid cartel is also able to diffuse blame among its various members when economic conditions in recipient countries don't improve according to plan. Should observers blame the IMF for fiscal austerity that restricts funding for worthy programs, or should they fault the World Bank for failing to preserve high-return areas from public expenditure cuts? Are the IMF and World Bank too tough or too lax in enforcing conditions? Or are the regional development banks too inflexible (or too lenient) in their conditions for aid? Should bilateral aid agencies be criticized for succumbing to national and commercial interests, or should multilateral agencies be condemned for applying a "one size fits all" reform program to all countries? Like squabbling children, aid organizations find safety in numbers. Take Argentina. From 1980 to 2001, the Argentine government received 33 structural adjustment loans from the IMF and World Bank, all under the watchful eye of the U.S. Treasury. Ultimately, then, is Argentina's ongoing implosion the fault of the World Bank, the IMF, or the Treasury Department? The buck stops nowhere in the world of development assistance. Each party can point fingers at the others, and bewildered observers don't know whom to blame—making each agency less accountable.

THE $3,521 QUANDARY

Like any good monopoly, the cartel of good intentions seeks to maximize net revenues. Indeed, if any single objective has characterized the aid community since its inception, it is an obsession with increasing the total aid money mobilized. Traditionally, aid agencies justify this goal by identifying the aid "requirements" needed to achieve a target rate of economic growth, calculating the difference between existing aid and the requirements, and then advocating a commensurate aid increase. In 1951, the U.N. Group of Experts calculated exactly how much aid poor countries needed to achieve an annual growth rate of 2 percent per capita, coming up with an amount that would equal $20 billion in today's dollars. Similarly, the economist Walt Rostow calculated in 1960 the aid increase (roughly double the aid levels at the time) that would lift Asia, Africa, and Latin America into self-sustaining growth. ("Self-sustaining" meant that aid would no longer be necessary 10 to 15 years after the increase.) Despite the looming expiration of the 15-year aid window, then World Bank President Robert McNamara called for a doubling of aid in 1973. The call for doubling was repeated at the World Bank in its 1990 "World Development Report." Not to be outdone, current World Bank President James Wolfensohn is now advocating a doubling of aid.

The cartel's efforts have succeeded: Total assistance flows to developing countries have doubled several times since the early days of large-scale foreign aid. (Meanwhile, the World Bank's staff increased from 657 people in 1959–60 to some 10,000 today.) In fact, if all foreign aid given since 1950 had been invested in U.S. Treasury bills, the cumulative assets of poor countries by 2001 from foreign aid alone would have amounted to $2.3 trillion. This aid may have helped achieve such important accomplishments as lower infant mortality and rising literacy throughout the developing world. And high growth in aid-intensive countries like Botswana and Uganda is something to which aid agencies can (and do) point. The growth outcome in most aid recipients, however, has been extremely disappointing. For example, on average, aid-intensive African nations saw growth decline despite constant increases in aid as a percentage of their income. . . .

Aid agencies always claim that their main goal is to reduce the number of poor people in the world, with poverty defined as an annual income below $365. To this end, the World Bank's 2002 aid accounting estimates that an extra $1 billion in overseas development assistance would lift more than 284,000 people out of poverty. (This claim has appeared prominently in the press and has been repeated in other government reports on aid effectiveness.) If these figures are correct, however, then the additional annual aid spending per person lifted out of poverty (whose annual income is less than $365) comes to $3,521. Of course, aid agencies don't follow their own logic to this absurd conclusion—common sense says that aid should help everyone and not just target those who can stagger across the minimum poverty threshold. Regrettably, this claim for aid's effect on poverty has more to do with the aid bureaucracy's desperate need for good publicity than with sound economics.

A FRAMEWORK FOR FAILURE

To the extent that anyone monitors the performance of global aid agencies, it is the politicians and the public in rich nations. Aid agencies therefore strive to produce outputs (projects, loans, etc.) that these audiences can easily observe, even if such outputs provide low economic returns for recipient nations. Conversely, aid bureaucrats don't try as hard to produce less visible, high-return outputs. This emphasis on visibility results in shiny showcase projects, countless international meetings and summits, glossy reports for public consumption, and the proliferation of "frameworks" and strategy papers. Few are concerned about whether the showcase projects endure beyond the ribbon-cutting ceremony or if all those meetings, frameworks, and strategies produce anything of value.

This quest for visibility explains why donors like to finance new, high-profile capital investment projects yet seem reluctant to fund operating expenses and maintenance after high-profile projects are completed. The resulting problem is a recurrent theme in the World Bank's periodic reports on Africa. In 1981, the bank's Africa study concluded that "vehicles and equipment frequently lie idle for lack of spare parts, repairs, gasoline, or other necessities. Schools lack operating funds for salaries and teaching materials, and agricultural research stations have difficulty keeping up field trials. Roads, public buildings, and processing facilities suffer from lack of maintenance." Five years later, another study of Africa found that "road maintenance crews lack fuel and bitumen . . . teachers lack books . . . [and] health workers have no medicines to distribute." In 1986, the Word Bank declared that in Africa, "schools are now short of books, clinics lack medicines, and infrastructure maintenance is avoided." Meanwhile, a recent study for a number of different poor countries estimated that the return on spending on educational instructional materials was up to 14 times higher than the return on spending on physical facilities.

And then there are the frameworks. In 1999, World Bank President James Wolfensohn unveiled his Comprehensive Development Framework, a checklist of 14 items, each with multiple subitems. The framework covers clean government, property rights, finance, social safety nets, education, health, water, the environment, the spoken word and the arts, roads, cities, the countryside, microcredit, tax policy, and motherhood. (Somehow, macroeconomic policy was omitted.) Perhaps this framework explains why the World Bank says management has simultaneously "refocused and broadened the development agenda." Yet even Wolfensohn seems relatively restrained compared with the framework being readied for the forthcoming U.N. World Summit on Sustainable Development in Johannesburg in late August 2002, where 185 "action recommendations"—covering everything from efficient use of cow dung to harmonized labeling of chemicals—await unsuspecting delegates.

Of course, the Millennium Development Goals (MDGs) are the real 800-pound gorilla of foreign aid frameworks. The representatives of planet Earth agreed on these goals at yet another U.N. conference in September 2000. The MDGs call for the simultaneous achievement of multiple targets by 2015, involving poverty, hunger, infant and maternal mortality, primary education, clean water, contraceptive use, HIV/AIDS, gender equality, the environment, and an ill-defined "partnership for development" [see goals listed in box]. These are all worthy causes, of course, yet would the real development customers necessarily choose to spend their scarce resources to attain these particular objectives under this particular timetable? Economic principles dictate that greater effort should be devoted to goals with low costs and high benefits, and less effort to goals where the costs are prohibitive relative to the benefits. But the "do everything" approach of the MDGs suggests that the aid bureaucracy feels above such trade-offs. As a result, government officials in recipient countries and the foreign aid agency's own frontline workers gradually go insane trying to keep up with proliferating objectives—each of which is deemed Priority Number One.

A 2002 World Bank technical study found that a doubling of aid flows is required for the world to meet the U.N. goals. The logic is somewhat circular, however, since a World Bank guidebook also stipulates that increasing aid is undoubtedly "a primary function of targets set by the international donor community such as the [Millennium] Development Goals." Thus increased aid becomes self-perpetuating—both cause and effect.

FOREIGN AID AND ABET

Pity the poor aid bureaucracy that must maintain support for foreign assistance while bad news is breaking out everywhere. Aid agencies have thus perfected the art of smoothing over unpleasant realities with diplomatic language. A war is deemed a "conflict-related reallocation of resources." Countries run by homicidal warlords like those in Liberia or Somalia are "low-income countries under stress." Nations where presidents loot the treasury experience "governance issues." The meaning of other aid community jargon, like "investment climate," remains elusive. The investment climate will be stormy in the morning, gradually clearing in the afternoon with scattered expropriations.

Another typical spin-control technique is to answer any criticism by acknowledging that, "Indeed, we aid agencies used to make that mistake, but now we have corrected it." This defense is hard to refute, since it is much more difficult to evaluate the present than the past. (One only doubts that the sinner has now found true religion from the knowledge of many previous conversions.) Recent conversions supposedly include improved coordination among donors, a special focus on poverty alleviation, and renewed economic reform efforts in African countries. And among the most popular concepts the aid community has recently discovered is "selectivity"—the principle that aid will only work in countries with good economic policies and efficient, squeaky-clean institutions. The moment of aid donors' conversion on this point supposedly came with the end of the Cold War, but in truth, selectivity (and other "new" ideas) has been a recurrent aid theme over the last 40 years [see box].

Unfortunately, evidence of a true conversion on selectivity remains mixed. Take Kenya, where President Daniel arap Moi has mismanaged the economy since 1978. Moi has consistently failed to keep conditions on the 19 economic reform loans his government obtained from the World Bank and IMF (described by one NGO as "financing corruption and repression") since he took office. How might international aid organizations explain the selectivity guidelines that awarded President Moi yet another reform loan from the World Bank and another from the IMF in 2000, the same year prominent members of Moi's government appeared on a corruption "list of shame" issued by Kenya's parliament? Since then, Moi has again failed to deliver on his economic reform promises, and international rating agencies still rank the Kenyan government among the world's most corrupt and lawless. Ever delicate, a 2002 IMF report conceded that "efforts to bring the program back on track have been only partially successful" in Kenya. More systematically, however, a recent cross-country survey revealed no difference in government ratings on democracy, public service delivery, rule of law, and corruption between those countries that received IMF and World Bank reform loans in 2001 and those that did not. Perhaps the foreign aid community applies the selectivity principle a bit selectively.

DISMANTLING THE CARTEL

How can the cartel of good intentions be reformed so that foreign aid might actually reach and benefit the world's poor? Clearly, a good dose of humility is in order, considering all the bright ideas that have failed in the past. Moreover, those of us in the aid industry should not be so arrogant to think we are the main determinants of whether low-income countries develop—poor nations must accomplish that mainly on their own.

"Do Everything" Development

In September 2000, representatives of 189 countries met at the U.N. Millennium General Assembly in New York and adopted the Millennium Declaration concerning peace, security, and development issues. The Millennium Development Goals (MDGs), listed below, emerged from this gathering. Since then, virtually all the leading aid institutions have endorsed the MDGs, including the World Bank, International Monetary Fund, Organisation for Economic Co-operation and Development, and the Inter-American Development Bank.

Goal 1: Eradicate extreme poverty and hunger
Halve, between 1990 and 2015, the proportion of people whose income is less than $1 a day. Halve, between 1990 and 2015, the proportion of people who suffer from hunger.

Goal 2: Achieve universal primary education
Ensure that, by 2015, children everywhere, boys and girls alike, will be able to complete a full course of primary schooling.

Goal 3: Promote gender equality and empower women
Eliminate gender disparity in primary and secondary education preferably by 2005 and in all levels of education no later than 2015.

Goal 4: Reduce child mortality
Reduce by two-thirds, between 1990 and 2015, the under-five mortality rate.

Goal 5: Improve maternal health
Reduce by three-quarters, between 1990 and 2015, the maternal mortality ratio.

Goal 6: Combat HIV/AIDS, malaria, and other diseases
Have halted by 2015 and begun to reverse the spread of HIV/AIDS. Have halted by 2015 and begun to reverse the incidence of malaria and other major diseases.

Goal 7: Ensure environmental sustainability
Integrate the principles of sustainable development into country policies and programmes and reverse the loss of environmental resources. Halve, by 2015, the proportion of people without sustainable access to safe drinking water. Have achieved, by 2020, a significant improvement in the lives of at least 100 million slum dwellers.

Goal 8: Develop a global partnership for development
Develop further an open, rule-based, predictable, non-discriminatory trading and financial system. . . . Address the special needs of the least developed countries. . . . Address the special needs of landlocked countries and small island developing states. . . . Deal comprehensively with the debt problems of developing countries. . . . In cooperation with developing countries, develop and implement strategies for decent and productive work for youth. In cooperation with pharmaceutical companies, provide access to affordable, essential drugs in developing countries. In cooperation with the private sector, make available the benefits of new technologies, especially information and communications.

SOURCE: United Nations Development Programme and World Bank.

Still, if aid is to have some positive effect, the aid community cannot remain stuck in the same old bureaucratic rut. Perhaps using market mechanisms for foreign aid is a better approach. While bureaucratic cartels supply too many goods for which there is little demand and too few goods for which there is much demand, markets are about matching supply and demand. Cartels are all about "coordination," whereas markets are about the decentralized matching of customers and suppliers.

One option is to break the link between aid money and the obligatory use of a particular agency's bureaucracy. Foreign assistance agencies could put part of their resources into a common pool devoted to helping countries with acceptably pro-development governments. Governments would compete for the "pro-development" seal of approval, but donors should compete, too. Recipient nations could take the funds and work with any agency they choose. This scenario would minimize duplication and foster competition among aid agencies.

Another market-oriented step would be for the common pool to issue vouchers to poor individuals or communities, who could exchange them for development services at any aid agency, NGO, or domestic government agency. These service providers would in turn redeem the vouchers for cash out of the common pool. Aid agencies would be forced to compete to attract aid vouchers (and thus money) for their budgets. The vouchers could also trade in a secondary market; how far their price is below par would reflect the inefficiency of this aid scheme and would require remedial action. Most important, vouchers would provide real market power to the impoverished customers to express their true needs and desires.

Intermediaries such as a new Washington-based company called Development Space could help assemble the vouchers into blocks and identify aid suppliers; the intermediaries could even compete with each other to attract funding and find projects that satisfy the customers, much as venture capital firms do. (Development Space is a private Web-based company established last year by former World Bank staff members—kind of an eBay for foreign aid.) Aid agencies could establish their own intermediation units to add to the competition. An information bank could facilitate transparency and communication, posting news on projects searching for funding, donors searching for projects, and the reputation of various intermediaries.

Bureaucratic cartels probably last longer than private cartels, but they need not last forever. President George W. Bush's proposed Millennium Challenge Account (under which, to use Bush's words, "countries that live by these three broad standards—ruling justly, investing in their people, and encouraging economic freedom—will receive more aid from America") and the accompanying increase in U.S. aid dollars will challenge the IMF and World Bank's near monopoly over reform-related lending. Development Space may be the first of many market-oriented endeavors to compete with aid agencies, but private philanthropists such as Bill Gates and George Soros have entered the industry as well. NGOs and independent academic economists are also more aggressively entering the market for advice on aid to poor countries. Globalization protesters are not well informed in all areas, but they seem largely on target when it comes to the failure of international financial institutions to foment "adjustment with growth" in many poor countries. Even within the World Bank itself, a recent board of directors paper suggested experimenting with "output-based aid" in which assistance would compensate service providers only when services are actually delivered to the poor—sadly, a novel concept. Here again, private firms, NGOs, and government agencies could compete to serve as providers.

Now that rich countries again seem interested in foreign aid, pressure is growing to reform a global aid bureaucracy that is increasingly out of touch with good economics.

The high-income countries that finance aid and that genuinely want aid to reach the poor should subject the cartel of good intentions to the bracing wind of competition, markets, and accountability to the customers. Donors and recipients alike should not put up with $3,521 in aid to reduce the poverty head count by one, 185-point development frameworks, or an alphabet soup of bureaucratic fads. The poor deserve better.

Reading 12-2

Foreign Assistance in an Aging World
Susan Raymond

FROM MONTERREY TO MADRID

At the International Conference on Financing for Development held in Monterrey, Mexico, last March, the Bush administration promised it would request a $5 billion increase in the U.S. foreign assistance appropriations for those countries "making the strongest possible commitment to development." A month later, the UN Second World Assembly on Aging in Madrid, Spain, cast a spotlight on a global trend that has been accelerating for a decade: the graying of the world's population. Both a robust increase in money for development and an acknowledgement of what has long been the reality of population aging were major departures from past U.S. policy and recent global health priorities. Headlines did not link the two meetings, but they should have.

Fundamental changes in basic population trends and public health are transforming much of the developing world. Over the past four decades, discussions of health problems in developing nations have centered on communicable diseases and the needs of children and vulnerable women of childbearing age. Accordingly, these diseases and this limited population have been the focus of the health care programs supported by foreign assistance. But this focus needs to change. Over the next 20 years, fertility will drop sharply in the developing world, and the number of children under the age of five will decline both as a percentage of the population and in absolute numbers. Foreign assistance programs must recognize these new realities.

The growing challenge, in turn, will be managing adult health and the expanding ranks of the elderly. By 2020, there will be more people over 65 in the developing world than children under 5. Chronic conditions such as heart disease and diabetes, which are already more prevalent causes of disability and death than are communicable diseases in all regions except Africa, will become even more widespread. As this trend unfolds, the lifetime costs of treating these ailments will far outpace the costs of managing communicable diseases.

This changing pattern of disease and vulnerability will also make more obvious the intersection between health and the economic potential of the developing world. In the next several years, before the numbers of elderly start rising dramatically, falling birth rates will provide a window of opportunity for developing nations. Those economies

SOURCE: From "Foreign Assistance in an Aging World" by Susan Raymond, *Foreign Affairs*, vol. 82, no. 2 (March/April 2003): 91–105. Copyright © 2003 by the Council on Foreign Relations. Reprinted by permission.

will be responsible for fewer dependents, and health investments will potentially bear greater returns. Maintaining the health of working-age adults will therefore have a profound economic impact.

The implication for foreign assistance is clear. Donors must recast public health programs as part of an economic strategy targeted at the work force, not just as the provision of care to women and children. But implementing that shift will require both an expansion in the substance of health assistance and a more dramatic (and difficult) correction in the decades-old culture and traditions of foreign assistance itself.

INVESTMENT BEYOND CHARITY

The poor will always be with us, and disasters will always happen. The humanitarian impulse to help people must and will remain a core American value. But this discussion is not about charity. It is about strategies for health investment among nations that seek to foster economic growth and create mutually beneficial self-reliance.

This division between charity and investment bears further elaboration, because failure to make the distinction regularly muddies the waters of foreign assistance debates. Since the 1960s, foreign assistance has generally treated whole categories of nations and peoples as dependent. Magnanimous "donors" give; vulnerable "recipients" receive. The magnanimity of donors is questioned only in its quantity: Do donors give enough? Giving more is clearly more magnanimous than giving less, so giving more is meritorious and giving less is iniquitous. For their part, recipients have been largely passive: they simply receive and become grateful. This is charity, and it has its place.

The term "foreign assistance" itself reveals its underlying assumption: it is charity to foreigners. Recipients are residents of other nations, so from the point of view of the magnanimous donor, they are foreign. But the demographic and health changes in developing nations demand mutual investment, not charity. They call for collaboration among nations for whom there are no "foreigners." Rather, equal stakeholders need to agree on dismantling the critical barriers to economic progress, a course that would be mutually beneficial. All parties involved have joint capacity to tackle these challenges, and all parties should be ready to commit their own assets in relative proportion to their likely returns. "How much?" is no longer the standard by which resources must be judged. Increasing economic welfare, not piling on transfer payments, is the objective, and judgments on effectiveness must be made rigorously as the basis for continued investment.

BABY BUST

Health programs account for more than half the U.S. foreign assistance budget. But too few Americans pay attention to the startling new trends in the demographics of developing nations, even though demographics set the stage for health policies. First and foremost is declining fertility. The UN-designated "high fertility" nations (where birth rates are not expected to fall to two children per woman, or the replacement rate, by 2045–50) make up only 4.4 percent of the world's population today; given current population growth rates, they will represent only 5.2 percent in 2020. Even more striking are UN projections that fertility rates in the developed and developing worlds will converge by 2050. For the HIV-intense nations of Africa, the fertility decline will be even more dramatic. By 2020, the UN expects that fertility in these nations will decline by between 23 percent and 39 percent—compared to a 21 percent decline for Africa overall.

Except in the HIV-intense nations, moreover, people are living longer. In 1950, there was a 30-year difference between the life expectancy of a newborn in the developed world and that of a newborn in the developing world. By 2020, that gap will narrow to 10 years in all but the least developed nations.

The consequences are equally monumental. The very population structure of the developing world will shift as the numbers of old overtake the young. This crossover between aging and youth has already occurred in some developing nations, especially in the Caribbean and South America. Furthermore, by 2020 the absolute numbers of children under the age of five will begin to decline.

These changes will confront developing nations relatively rapidly. In the United States, for example, it took 70 years for the 65-and-over population to grow from 5 percent to 12 percent of the population. Latin America, by comparison, will have only 35 years to master this same growth of the elderly within its population. And the clock there started ticking in 1995.

This demographic shift has profound economic implications. Until 2025, a larger work force will be carrying a smaller social burden of the young and the elderly; investments to lift productivity will have higher economic payoffs because fewer resources are needed to care for dependents. Beginning in 2025, however, the pattern will shift toward greater dependency, as the ratio of the elderly to the work force doubles. At that point, the costs associated with high dependency ratios will return with a vengeance. The housing, living, and health care costs of the elderly far exceed those of the young. The less developed world will have greater numbers of elderly, and the old there will live longer. These elderly and their families will not escape the cost consequences. Hence, economic policymakers must take advantage of the demographic shift during the next 25 years—when dependency is at its lowest.

This approach assumes that the work force is healthy. But this assumption should be challenged as well. Overall, of course, there has been remarkable improvement in global public health. Infant mortality rates have been halved in the past two decades and are projected to drop by three-quarters by 2020. Global child mortality has dropped by 43 percent. Communicable disease control has also achieved notable successes. Since 1980, immunization coverage has risen from less than 20 percent of children to nearly 80 percent. But exceptions do exist, and where they exist they are striking. Ninety percent of malaria deaths occur in Africa. Among the very least developed nations, infant and child mortality rates remain at global highs, and significant declines, especially in HIV-intense nations, are not projected for the next several decades.

One way to maintain public health is through traditional measures such as continuing immunization and related efforts. Child survival has been the central objective of foreign assistance for several decades, and global health advocates have widely attributed progress purely to public health interventions such as immunization and oral rehydration. But important as these programs are, other measures may be equally important. Education, for example, is the central factor in reducing infant mortality—far more significant than the degree of poverty, family size, or the proximity of health facilities. Babies of mothers with six or more years of education are less likely to die compared with those of mothers with little or no education. The International Food Policy Research Institute has found that nearly half of the decline in malnutrition in the developing world in the last several decades is explained by female education alone. The UN projects that two-thirds of developing nations will have achieved female literacy rates of more than 75 percent by 2005. As education spreads, mortality will continue to decline.

Moreover, educational progress is spreading across generations. Not only are more girls literate, but more girls have mothers and grandmothers who are literate. As women's literacy becomes intergenerational, education will become the booster rocket for public health progress among mothers and children in the developing world.

DEATH AND DISABILITY

As a population ages and mortality declines, causes of death change. Most life expectancy estimates are based on either mortality models or on calculations of disability-adjusted life-years, commonly known as DALYs. Mortality rates take death as their endpoint, whereas DALYs measure the number of years lost to disability from any particular disease. These two approaches can result in widely different evaluations of the impact of disease. A head-on car collision at 70 miles an hour, for example, results in death, but zero years are lost to disability. A diagnosis of Alzheimer's disease will also result in death, but only after many years lost to disability. Thus the two methods can provide different rankings of various diseases in measuring their relative importance to health patterns.

Interestingly, this division is hardly distinguishable in data on the developing world. Research by the World Health Organization shows similar patterns regardless of which measure is used. But that same research shows that, with Africa excepted, the chief culprits of mortality are not communicable diseases. Rather, noncommunicable diseases—chronic conditions such as cardiovascular and hypertensive diseases, diabetes, and cancer—account for more deaths and more DALYs than do infectious and parasitic diseases such as measles or malaria. The WHO has also made disease-specific comparisons across regions for populations with similar overall mortality patterns. The upshot is that even among subpopulations with high mortality rates (usually the poor), noncommunicable diseases are more significant than infectious diseases as causes of either death or DALYs. This is a dramatic shift from the profile of a generation ago.

Another important factor is the stunning acceleration of urbanization in the developing world. By 2025, two-thirds of the population of the developing world will live in cities—a transition that will bring with it the associated sedentary lifestyle and nutrition changes. In India, for example, only two percent of the rural population has diabetes, whereas urban rates are five times that number. The WHO projects that the incidence of diabetes in the developing world will increase by 170 percent by 2025, which means that up to 30 percent of India's city dwellers will have diabetes.

How do lower mortality rates and changes in disease patterns affect the growing work force that will drive future economic progress? Here the indicators become troubling. Although overall death rates in developed countries are higher than those in many developing countries, death rates in prime labor-force years are higher in developing countries than in developed ones. For example, if death rates are compared for Portugal (a less well off developed country) with those of several developing countries, the contrast is stark. Portugal's overall death rate is higher than that of any of the developing nations, but the death rates in prime labor-force ages in all of the developing nations are higher than those for Portugal. This pattern is true for women as well as men, and for younger workers as well as older ones.

Specific chronic disease examples further illustrate the contrast and its implications for developing nations' economies. Among middle-aged workers in developing nations, death rates from circulatory diseases and diabetes are as much as seven times higher than Portugal's. Moreover, in nations with a history of vulnerability to communicable diseases, such as Thailand or the Philippines, death rates from circulatory diseases and diabetes in the labor force are between 10 and 100 times the death rates for infectious diseases such as pneumonia or malaria.

Even more striking are the economic implications of such death rates relative to the onset of disease. Unlike some infectious diseases such as pneumonia, chronic diseases usually kill many years after they are first detected. If men and women are dying of circulatory diseases in their mid-40s, then the onset of the disease probably occurred more than a decade earlier. Therefore, these labor-force death rates imply that people at the beginning of their productive ages (30 or 35 years of age) are further along the chronic disease curve than are their developed-nation counterparts—further along than they have any reason to be.

Here is where the convocations of Madrid and Monterrey passed each other silently in the night. Monterrey promised more money for foreign assistance, but it did not appreciate that this money must be spent on a new and emerging set of chronic-disease problems if it is to have an economic impact.

WHY CHANGE MATTERS

What are the consequences of these shifts in disease and mortality patterns? First, lower productivity and early death in the work force could reduce the opportunity for investment created by declining birth rates and reduced numbers of dependent children. At the very point at which economies can invest more of every unit of earnings, those who earn are dying. Justifiably, much has been made of this danger in discussions of the impact of HIV in Africa. But virtually nothing has been made of the very same danger regarding the growth of chronic diseases in the work forces of the less developed world.

Second, treating this changed health and disease pattern will get very expensive, very quickly. Chronic diseases build over many years. If treated when full-blown, they are costly. A full round of immunization costs about $30, whereas treating and rehabilitating a stroke victim costs exponentially more. Equally important, those cost burdens are nearly at hand. The early stages of chronic illness are hidden just below the surface in the lives of many workers in their 30s, especially in urban areas of developing nations. It may be too late for prevention in this generation. Only aggressive identification of risk factors such as smoking, poor diet, and obesity can delay the onset of chronic diseases already present in young workers and prevent the debilitating event (such as a stroke) that triggers high-cost care. Recurrent costs will also rise, because those with chronic diseases will need constant treatment.

This second category of costs—health resources—comes with an added dimension that has long been ignored as developing nations have fought health battles over nutrition, public education, and infectious-disease prevention. Diagnosing, managing, and treating chronic diseases will require capital. But capital financing has not been a concern of global health specialists for many years. Infrastructure was seen as the white elephant of health care, something to be elbowed aside by a more nimble strategy of cheap interventions. But budgeting for oral rehydration packets of sugar and salt to cure diarrhea must give way to finding the resources for rebuilding the laboratory and medical infrastructure needed to diagnose, monitor, and treat chronic diseases.

Productive economic enterprise and health care budgets will not be the only areas needing extra attention as health needs change. Given the scope of the problem, we should expect that at least some of the chronic disease burden will take the form of disability. A 50-year-old diabetic amputee may have 20 more years to live, but he or she has little remaining productive opportunity. Where social security systems are in place, the cost of supporting that life will fall on disability payments. But in many developing nations, such systems exist on paper only and remain largely unfunded. Where the systems are funded, costs will rise, perhaps further and more quickly than planned. Social security systems themselves will be threatened. In either event, the cost of disability will affect the recipient's family the most. In turn, families will find themselves with larger numbers of dependents, comprising not children but disabled relatives and a growing number of elderly. The cost of disability will reach its fingers into the only wallet left: the family. The ability to reinvest earnings in productive enterprise or consumption will decline—and once again, the window of economic opportunity created by a changing demographic structure will begin to close.

WHY CHANGE MATTERS TO AMERICANS

America faces its own dilemmas of aging, chronic diseases, health-care cost containment, and Social Security insolvency. Why should these same trends in developing nations vie for the attentions of foreign assistance strategists? The reasons are at least threefold.

First, compromised economic capacity is in no one's interests. With the exception of most of Africa, developing nations' economies have grown in the last decades; indeed, some of the highest growth rates in the 1990s occurred in the developing world. Maintaining and even increasing that growth is good for everyone, including those who produce and export goods and services in the United States. The global economy insulates few nations from the economic woes of others.

Second, the rising tide of chronic diseases and its financial undertow will exact a social price in the developing world. Supporting disabled adults will be economically expensive, but not supporting them will be politically volatile. Furthermore, changes in disease patterns will take place alongside striking changes in education in developing nations. According to the UN, roughly half of developing nations will have achieved literacy for 80 percent of their populations by 2005. In only 12 percent of developing nations will less than half of the population be literate. Knowledge and expectations will rise. Failure to meet adult health needs and the insolvency of social security for the work force will be recognized. Public reaction is not likely to be positive.

Third, the United States should pay attention because the changes represent opportunities as well as problems. Although Americans have long struggled with ways to implement systems for disease prevention, they know a great deal about disease management. Two decades of cost-containment pressure have forced them to learn how to identify and control risk factors, and how to address chronic diseases successfully using a combination of prevention, therapy, and management.

The United States has created a strong network of institutions and professional associations dedicated to managing and preventing chronic diseases. The additional value these institutions bring to the development table is not strictly medical; most developing-nation physicians know circulatory disease when they see it. Rather, these institutions bring decades of experience in managing the struggles among disease, aging, lifestyles, and money. The priority is to build strong professional relationships across borders in addressing these problems. In turn, these relationships will create bridges of a different type, fostering understanding and empathy between individuals who are also often leaders in their communities, and between institutions that often enjoy prestige. They build bridges not only in areas such as technical understanding but also in values regarding open societies, human rights, individual accountability, and institutional transparency. All of these are key to resolving the central barrier to progress in the developing world: good governance.

There is precedent for just such strategies. In eastern Europe and Russia, a series of such medical partnerships has been created with support from U.S. foreign assistance. These partnerships have linked U.S. physicians and nurses with their counterparts abroad to address a range of health needs. By and large, U.S. participation has been pro bono; participants share their insights not for contractual gain but because the ethic of the profession is to share skills and knowledge for the mutual gain of all providers and all patients.

THE VISION THING

Despite the successes of this small precedent, U.S. foreign assistance today is engineered to respond neither to changes in health patterns nor to their economic implications. Its policy priorities, human resources capacity, and professional networks are geared to address the past, not the future.

For a quarter of a century, U.S. foreign assistance in health has been focused on child survival and population control. Overall, health programs represent 52 percent of the U.S. foreign assistance budget, and child survival and population control account for nearly two-thirds of health expenditures. Such a concentration of resources and interests results in part from micromanagement by Congress. In part, it also stems from the aforementioned confusion between charity and development in foreign assistance thinking. And it is a result of organizational self-interest: repeated recipients of funds tend to have vested interest in the continued flow of those monies.

Whatever the causes, the result is a foreign assistance culture that does not encourage professionals to be attuned to changes in disease patterns, shifts in affected population groups, or emerging knowledge and capacity within the United States itself. Concentrating huge resources on narrow problems over long periods of time has created both tunnel vision and significant vested interests in those problems among those who disburse the funds and those who win the contracts to implement the programs.

More importantly, the past quarter-century of effort has not prepared U.S. foreign assistance experts to appreciate and act on the growing link between changed health patterns and economic development. "Health" has been seen as a matter of conveying vaccines, contraceptives, technical skills, and planning skills to ministries of health, government providers of health care, and community organizations focused on health care. Yet in traditional areas of foreign assistance concern such as child survival, long-standing research has shown that women's education matters as much as or even more than other factors in reducing infant mortality. Nonetheless, those findings resulted in neither resource shifts away from health inputs and into women's education nor widespread partnerships between education and health ministries.

The existing foreign assistance culture and traditional health program strategies map poorly onto the changes in the developing world. Chronic disease management will require more than individuals changing on a variety of nonhealth fronts such as diet and behavior. Governments will also have to reevaluate a variety of more complex public policies not directly in the control of ministries of health, such as taxes on alcohol or trade policies regarding tobacco. Better management will also mean working closely with leadership whose constituencies are not women of reproductive age and children but urban workers—employers, social security administrations, insurers, and organized labor. A sensible health strategy for future foreign assistance may, in fact, be to move money out of U.S. foreign assistance budgets dedicated solely to health and into other areas of economic investment and growth—where health can be a component of a multitiered U.S. initiative.

Finally, health care strategies have poorly prepared U.S. foreign assistance programs to recognize where money currently comes from—namely, the private sector. World Health Organization data on health-resource flows and World Bank data on income show that, on average, 52 percent of health expenditures in developing countries came from private resources, representing $120 billion each year. Only 16 percent of developing nations get less than a quarter of their health resources from the private sector. For the poorest nations, the private-sector average is even higher, at more than 60 percent of resource flows. In the future, affording the higher costs of the current health transition will require a deep understanding of private expenditures.

WHAT CAN BE DONE?

If demographic change is striking and its economic implications important, and if traditional assumptions and mandates impede an effective U.S. foreign assistance response, what can be done? Bureaucracies and vested interests do not change easily. When they are tied to congressional mandates, they do not change at all. Where will the needed leadership be found?

The Bush administration is to be applauded for beginning to think differently about old foreign assistance paradigms. The creation of the Millennium Challenge Account links new U.S. assistance to developing nations' performance based on good governance. This move is an important break with past "magnanimous donor, grateful recipient" approaches. Perhaps more important, the administration's recent announcement that the account will be administered by a new and independent government corporation provides hope that old ways will not entangle new ideas. Perhaps then, when women's literacy is shown to be the decisive factor in infant survival, women's literacy will be supported. For such new beginnings also to seed new disease priorities for new categories of people and overcome hide-bound approaches to health, however, the aid community should take three concrete steps to transform U.S. foreign assistance into development investment—rather than the charity-based approach of foreign assistance—and help tackle the emerging generation of health problems in the developing world.

First, all parties with operational responsibility or with concrete relevant experience should define the problems collaboratively. Rather than consult beltway contractors, development institutions should gather together the leaders of private associations (medical, insurance, business) from the United States and their counterparts from nations facing the most immediate health and disease transitions. These leaders should discuss face-to-face the coming priorities and share perspectives on how to collaborate on improving chronic disease management, work-force behavior, and the long-term financing problems that developing nations will face. U.S. development institutions must define what can be done by development investments through the leadership of those who know the problems and who will implement the solutions.

Second, these institutions must experiment and then evaluate. Using those deliberations, they should develop and fund experimental programs to address the new generation of health problems among men and women of working age, ranging as far beyond traditional health boundaries as logic dictates. If literacy is the barrier, for example, then let literacy be the solution. The experiments should have a fair but finite lifespan and a careful design, and they should be evaluated mercilessly. Chronic disease management is intimately interwoven with professional capacity, medical infrastructure, and human behavior. Program effectiveness is a matter not of mobilizing armies to vaccinate babies but of identifying health crises that are hidden until they kill, monitoring those problems over time in adults who have choices about whether they will cooperate, and getting people to change fundamental behaviors such as diet. The hardest problem for U.S. development investment is not gaining more understanding of the health care future of developing nations but using money to change that future. And the taxpayers footing this bill are owed honest and open evaluation of their money's effectiveness.

Third, more knowledge is needed. The data is poor. Apparent trends in chronic diseases are striking, but their details are elusive. U.S. development policymakers should establish a five-year "studies fund" along with experimental programs. The objective is not to fund dissertations but to pursue practical insights and questions that will illuminate the nature of current trends—or even disprove them altogether. The fund would seek to generate better information and seek it quickly. Anyone from anywhere could apply. Study parameters would be clear and funds would be limited; time frames would be relatively short. An outside peer-review panel, consisting of members with no past or current financial interests in any U.S. foreign assistance programs, would judge applications and determine awards. Awardees would present findings directly to development investment policymakers from both the United States and from the nations in which the work takes place. Perhaps as important, awardees would be encouraged to publish in professional journals any and all data generated. Over five years, such an accumulation of knowledge would lead to a better grasp of the problems of health transitions and a better understanding of effective program approaches cultivated through project experiments.

These three efforts together will create a new cohort of people with professional interests and experience in the health care changes that link the United States to developing nations. These people can then begin to move U.S. foreign assistance into a new age.

13

The Future of
World Politics

Reading 13-1

Images of the Coming
International System
Robert E. Harkavy

T he astonishing fact about the end of the cold war is that the events of 1989–92 ushered in a new international system, perhaps for the first time in history, without a
hegemonic war. The unraveling of the Soviet empire was, of course, the centerpiece of
this change, ending as it did forty-five years of bipolar, global ideologically driven
conflict and giving birth to—what? If indeed the present new era of history has any
defining feature it is surely the widespread confusion over how to characterize contemporary global politics and project trends and scenarios into the future. Thus, Henry
Kissinger recently stated that "never before have the components of world order, their
capacity to interact and their goals all changed quite so rapidly, so deeply, or so globally."[1] In the same vein, Stanley Hoffman has stated that we live today in "a completely
unprecedented world. It's very difficult to call this world anything . . . when you don't
know what a thing is, you call it post—something else."[2]

Nowadays, policymakers and academic theorists alike purvey a profuse variety of
clashing and contradictory classifications, theories, images, paradigms, and historical

SOURCE: From "Images of the Coming International System" by Robert E. Harkavy, *Orbis*, vol. 41, no. 4 (Fall 1997): 569–590.
Copyright © 1997. Reprinted with permission from the Foreign Policy Research Institute.

analogies, in every case bereft of the familiar signposts once provided by a clear ideo-logical spectrum.[3] Former political antagonists now often sing from the same page, while former cold war bedfellows have drifted apart and embraced new identifications and alignments. No two observers seem to agree on whether the present indefinable in-ternational system will itself exhibit more or less stability than did the bipolar system, or whether the current period will prove to be only a brief interregnum, and thus not really a "system" at all. Kissinger, for instance, has stated that the new world order "is still in a period of gestation, and its final form will not be visible until well into the next century."[4]

COMPETING IMAGES OF THE EMERGING SYSTEM

The profuse literature on the state of post–cold war international politics appears to of-fer seven discrete images, models, or paradigms which, their proponents assert, succeed in capturing the fundamentals of the emerging international reality. They include:

The three-bloc neo-mercantilist thesis, a.k.a., geoeconomics.

The multipolar balance of power model hinged on the traditional "realist" and/or neo-realist frameworks.

The controversial "clash of civilizations" thesis.

The unipolar dominance model, related to the traditional geopolitical "long cycle" theory and to theories of "hegemonic stability."

The "zones of peace" versus "zones of turmoil" model based on the apparently widening gulf between the developed and developing worlds.

The "global village" model based on the apparent shift of power and sovereignty from nation-states to international or non-governmental organizations, and the growth of functional global regimes.

The bipolar-redux model anticipating either a future challenge to U.S. domi-nance by China, Russia, Japan, or Europe, or a return to some sort of bipolar bloc structure.

These seven models do not exhaust the possibilities, nor are they necessarily mutu-ally exclusive. Samuel Huntington himself suggests that a world otherwise defined by the "clash of civilizations" might be alternatively characterized by (1) "One World: Euphoria and Harmony," (2) "Two Worlds: Us and Them," (3) "184 States, More or Less," or (4) "Sheer Chaos." The first parallels Francis Fukuyama's "end of history" the-sis predicated on the global acceptance of representative government and market eco-nomics. The second involves several possible bifurcations, i.e., between rich and poor, zones of peace and turmoil, or the West and the rest.[5] The third is derived from the classic "realist" theory of international relations, while the fourth is more or less con-gruent with the "zones of turmoil" thesis which predicts breakdowns of governmental authority, breakups of states, ethnic and tribal conflicts, refugee nightmares, prolifera-tion, and terrorism across much of the developing world. Alexander Nacht, meanwhile, offers a typology consisting of "the end of history," "the clash of civilizations," balance of power, the primacy of economics, and a final catch-all category of "humanitarian-ism and global trends" focusing on issues such as resource allocation, the environment, and world population.[6]

THE THREE-BLOC GEOECONOMICS MODEL

The theory that held sway in the early years of the Clinton administration posited a new international system in which geoeconomics replaced geopolitics as the most crucial determinant of the rise or decline of nations, and that military power was thus becoming increasingly less relevant, hence wasteful, in the context of global competition. Some writers have spied in this current shift an expression of a long-established historical cyclicality characterized by periods in which national security dominates the agendas of major powers and periods in which those same powers have tended, relatively speaking, to compete through trade and investment.[7] On the other hand, some analyses have claimed that traditional balance of power politics, stressing the primacy of national security, are never absent. Looking at the period since 1989, when the Soviet empire effectively collapsed, they would be inclined to predict that a temporary interregnum during which the major powers attempt to act in concert will inevitably give way to renewed discord among those powers and a return to a classic balance of power.[8]

Still other analysts, heralding the advent of geoeconomics as the central game of international politics, have abjured notions of cyclicality in favor of a linear view that borders on teleology. Hence the "end of history" thesis, which holds that the ideological conflicts that dominated the global stage since the 1930s, if not since the French Revolution, will now disappear, to be superseded by milder economic rivalries.[9] The assumption of this happy thesis is, of course, that modern democratic states with high levels of per capita income will not contemplate fighting each other, and instead embrace what Karl Deutsch first termed a "security community."[10]

Central to the geoeconomics imagery, as expressed in the writings of Walter Russell Mead, Jeffrey Garten, Edward Luttwak, Lester Thurow, and others, is the belief that the world is evolving into three competitive economic blocs including (1) a Japan-led Pacific Rim region including Korea, Southeast Asia, and presumably China; (2) a U.S.-led Western Hemisphere bloc centered on the North American Free Trade Agreement (NAFTA) and potentially encompassing Latin America; and (3) a German-centered European bloc, assumed to include Russia and other ex-Soviet states and perhaps also North Africa.[11] In this way, the less-developed expanses of Africa and South Asia, not to mention the Middle East, are relegated to the status of neocolonial resource zones to be courted by the three major blocs.[12]

The "three-bloc" image is fetching, but flies in the face of the presumed trend toward global interdependence, multinationalized industry, and free flows of investment, production, and marketing. In short, it may be too state-centric, too prone to viewing trade as occurring between nations rather than between firms operating in a complex global environment.[13] But Thurow brushes aside that caveat, predicting that:

> In the race ahead, one of the three great economic powers is apt to pull ahead of the other two. Whichever pulls ahead is apt to stay ahead. That country or region of the globe will own the twenty-first century in the sense that the United Kingdom owned the nineteenth century and the United States owned the twentieth century.[14]

Mead, Garten, and Thurow all attempt to analyze the inherent advantages, disadvantages, and trade-offs associated with each of the three blocs in the competitive struggle they assume will occur. These comparative advantages are seen as rooted variously in factors of size, location, demographics, culture, and political acumen. And, indeed, both Mead and Thurow seem to suspect that the U.S.-led bloc may ultimately be the weakest and the European bloc the strongest.

Mead believes that Europe has a vested interest in bloc politics rather than an open global economy. Hence as the former Soviet-bloc countries move toward market economies, they may serve as sources of low-wage industries for Europe, paralleling the respective roles of Mexico and Southeast Asia for the United States and Japan. Such a Europe could also import raw materials from Africa and Russia, and oil from the Middle East and the former USSR. Such a Euro-bloc would have large agricultural surpluses, especially as ex-Soviet-bloc agriculture was made more efficient. Europe would also move ahead rapidly to develop high-technology industries and thus have little need for goods or services from Asia or the Americas.

Thurow concurs, asserting that "While having been the slowest mover in the 1980s, Europe starts the 1990s with the strongest strategic position on the world economic chessboard," and that if it makes the right moves, it can become the dominant economic power in the twenty-first century, regardless of what Japan and the United States do.[15] As he points out, some 850 million people could come to comprise the "House of Europe," and that they are the "only 850 million people on the face of the globe that are both well educated and start out not poor."[16] He stresses the overall high levels of education in Europe, and notes the synergy among Germany's production capabilities, the science-oriented former Soviet educational system, the design flair of Italy and France, and the world-class London capital market.

Mead sees the Japan-led Asian bloc limiting U.S. technological exports and exploiting the Americas largely as a source of raw materials and market for industrial goods. Japan would move further toward the import of raw materials and low-end manufactured products from China and Southeast Asia, while trading manufactured goods for oil with the Middle East. It would also continue to export capital goods and high-technology products to all these markets plus NAFTA and Oceania in an (asymmetric) exchange for food, minerals, and entertainment products.

Thurow, writing before the bursting of the Japanese bubble, stresses the dominance of Japan's banks, its status as the world's largest net creditor, its world-record trade surplus, and its propensity to invest in plant and equipment (per employee) at a rate triple that of the United States and twice that of Europe. He also stresses Japan's educational levels, particularly its ability to educate the bottom half of its high school classes. To be sure, Japan has a smaller domestic market than the United States or Europe, but according to Thurow, "Cohesion and homogeneity give Japan an ability to focus its economic might that few others can rival. No nation can organize better to march toward well thought-out common goals."[17]

The U.S.-led NAFTA, by contrast, has serious disadvantages that Mead believes are likely to land it in third place. It has fewer real customers than Europe given the long-term economic stagnation of much of Latin America and the fact that much of Latin America is only weakly tied to the United States and loath to break its traditional ties to Europe and emerging ties to Japan. The U.S.-led bloc is also dangerously dependent on Middle Eastern oil and the U.S. dollar is vulnerable given its continuing role as the key international currency and the magnitude of the U.S. external debt. Mead even predicts that world trade will eventually shift out of dollars into yen and the new European currency.

Thurow grants that the United States will remain the world's military superpower into the next century, but notes that "To be a double superpower, [the United States] will have to be willing to invest what others invest in being economic superpowers and, on top of that, make whatever investments are necessary to remain a military super-power."[18] On the plus side, Thurow lists America's stock of real economic assets, its superior per capita income and average productivity, its universities, and a domestic market which is "far larger than that of Japan and far more homogeneous than that of Europe."[19] It also has cultural strengths as "the country where it is easiest for outsiders to become insiders" and one that historically responds magnificently to crises. On the negative side, he points to America's atrophied educational system, international debts, low levels of civilian R and D, and decaying infrastructure. The United States must therefore shift dramatically from consumption to investment, and solve the educational problems associated with its non-college workforce. Finally, Thurow agrees with Mead that Latin America is not much of an asset in global competition.

A number of general criticisms may be directed at this three-bloc thesis. Not only have its proponents underestimated the multinationalization of production and trade, they may have underestimated some of the political fault lines within the putative regional blocs. In Asia, for instance, it is far from clear that a rapidly rising China, or sullen but strong Korea, can be folded into a Japan-led Asia bloc. And despite rumors about huge oil and gas reserves in the South China Sea, Asia remains as dependent on Middle Eastern oil as the United States and Europe. (The three-bloc thesis also ignores the possibility that still grander economic blocs, such as that pursued by members of the Asia Pacific Economic Cooperation forum [APEC], may span the oceans.)

Europe, too, may suffer from political cleavages. German dominance is widely feared, Britain may not prove willing to throw in its lot completely with the continent, and Russia's future remains up for grabs, both with respect to its domestic political regime and its relations with the "near abroad." The European Union may or may not be on the road to full integration, and the specter of a growing fault line between Islam and the secularized West may raise questions about whether the incipient Eurobloc could achieve the preferential access to Middle East oil predicted by Mead.

Perhaps the most glaring weakness of the three-bloc thesis, however, is that some of its key assumptions have already been disproved by events. In the past few years the U.S. economy, far from exhibiting the traits of permanent decline, has rebounded sharply and is again the world's most efficient in terms of productivity. At the same time, Germany and most of Europe have been plagued by stagnation and unemployment born of the excesses and built-in inflexibilities of their social welfare states, their aging populations, and the fiscal austerity required to achieve the single European currency. Ironically, the costs of becoming the almighty "bloc" feared by Thurow are sapping Europe's strength. The Japanese, meanwhile, have not only seen their 1980s bubble burst, they are at a loss as to how to reform and revive their state-led economy. Growth remains low, their banks—far from indomitable as they seemed a few years ago—are in a state of crisis—and their financial markets are flat at a time when U.S. markets are at historic highs. Indeed, Japanese pundits who only a short time ago had viewed America's decadence and decline with more than a little condescension are now worrying out loud about that new Yankee phoenix, "Rising Sam."

Nothing, however, makes the three-bloc image seem dated more than its notion that China will function as a huge market and source of cheap labor for a Japan-led bloc. By the mid-1990s, forecasters in the Pentagon and think tanks, extrapolating from China's own dynamic growth rates, projected a Chinese GNP on a par with that of the United States and Japan early in the twenty-first century.[20] If anything like that is in the cards, it would certainly refute the notion of a Japanese-led Asian bloc and instead turn Japan into a crucial swing-state between a China-led bloc and NAFTA.

Joseph Nye has made three basic criticisms of the three-bloc thesis. First, he says it "runs counter to the thrust of global technological trends," and that "while regional trade will certainly grow, many firms would not want to be limited to one-third of the global market and would resist restrictive regionalism."[21] Secondly, "restrictive regional blocs run against nationalistic concerns of some of the lesser states that need a global system to protect themselves against domination by their large neighbors." Thirdly, the three-bloc vision is too dismissive of security concerns, for instance, the need of Germany and Japan for a continuing U.S. security umbrella in case Russia or China emerge as a threat.

THE REINVIGORATED BALANCE OF POWER MODEL

Traditionalists of the realist school of international relations envision a future that could not differ more sharply from that of the geoeconomists. According to them, security and brute power relationships always function as the most fundamental determinants of international systems, and the end of the cold war makes a return to multipolarity and balance of power almost inevitable. The *Economist* recently published a projection of an emerging global balance of power, noting that:

> each period of history has produced its own pattern of relations, settled or otherwise, among the world's powers, and that some in the past have been near monopolies in some corners of the world (the Roman Empire or the Chinese Middle Kingdom), but never on a global basis, while others such as the cold war have been temporary duopolies.[22]

More typically however:

> the order emerges from the interplay of three, four or five powers which create a shifting pattern of alliances and enmities among themselves. This is the dance of the dinosaurs. It is the way things were in most of Europe and Asia—the core of the historical world—for most of the time in the past few centuries, until 1945; and it is the way things are likely to be again now.[23]

Written in early 1994 during the panic over the rise of a "hegemonic China," this analysis argued that four powers were likely to define the emerging pattern of the twenty-first century: the United States, China, Russia, and Europe. The *Economist* then proceeded to compare the advantages and disadvantages of the four nations in the coming geopolitical competition. America it described as strong and resurgent, its main problem being not its economy, but its will to assert itself rather than choose to withdraw from the arena of world politics. The prospects for a cohesive European power are by comparison dubious, and Russia's "hope of being a force in the world ever again" is even dimmer than Europe's. Only China appears to be indisputably upwardly mobile, with a rapidly growing economy that can be translated into military power.

In stark contrast to the three-bloc mercantilist literature, the *Economist* considers Japan a longshot for global power status. Rather, Japan "will have trouble converting its splendidly high GDP-per-head into the more brutal currencies of international power. It is a small, vulnerable island lying between two great powers neither of which wishes to see it build up any very great armed strength."[24] The Muslim world is considered unlikely to spawn a contender for great power status, and India, often mentioned elsewhere as an emerging power and rival to China, is totally ignored in this analysis.

A major strength of the *Economist* essay is its effort to go beyond mere comparisons of emerging national power capabilities to examine the possibilities for alignments among the powers. Indeed, now that cold war ideological affinities no longer serve as a glue among nations, alignments are likely to shift rapidly in the coming era, with today's friend becoming tomorrow's antagonist, and vice versa.[25] What are the likeliest possibilities? According to the *Economist,* a Europe-China alliance to keep Russia under control is extremely unlikely, as is a U.S.-Chinese alliance directed at Europe or Russia. Rather, the most likely scenario is a loose alliance among Europe, America, and Russia for the containment of China, "while Japan—intimidated by China's growing power, and needing America's protection—stays modestly at sub-great power level." A second likely scenario is an alignment between rising China and the Islamic world, which would in turn push Russia and Europe closer together.

Other variants depict a rising China at odds with a containment alliance comprised of the United States, Japan (perhaps impelled toward large-scale rearmament), and India, with Korea tilting towards the latter combination and Russia playing a neutral role and selling arms and energy to China. Europe, in this scenario, remains on the sidelines, perhaps making the Americans unhappy by competing with the Russians for arms sales to China. Other scenarios broach the possibility of a China-Japan-Korea alliance aimed at driving U.S. influence out of Asia, with Russia and Europe remaining on the sidelines. Such a confrontation would bring the world close to the "clash of civilizations" model, discussed below.

Kissinger's analysis of a new, emerging balance of power is somewhat similar. He tends to assume a cohesive if not fully integrated Europe and is perhaps more inclined than the *Economist* to foresee a gradual decline of America's *relative* power. The United States would remain *primus inter pares* as "the greatest and most powerful nation, but a nation with peers." Harking back to earlier systems, Kissinger emphasizes that "The absence of both an overriding ideological or strategic threat frees nations to pursue foreign policies based increasingly on their immediate national interest."[26] Nye, in turn, criticizes this multipolar model as a false analogy with the nineteenth-century order that rested upon a balance of five roughly equal powers, i.e., Britain, France, Germany, Austria-Hungary, and Russia.[27] Russia's economic weakness, China's status as a developing country, Japan's limited military power, and Europe's lack of political unity suffice in his view to refute Kissinger's historical analogy.[28]

Finally, Richard Rosecrance questions the validity of traditional balance of power thinking in the present age. He agrees that the balance of power held sway during most of the nineteenth and the first part of the twentieth century, but it was an "inefficient mechanism at best, providing no automatic equilibration of power relationships," and gave rise to the world wars of this century.[29] Rosecrance sees nuclear deterrence and rule by a central coalition as alternative mechanisms for regulating the anarchic international system, the first having operated successfully if precariously from 1945 to 1989, and the second having operated for brief periods after the Napoleonic wars and World War I. He sees the current period as one in which a concert appears to be in operation. To be sure, a new concert system could crash should the United States, Russia, or the European Union withdraw from international responsibilities out of weariness or domestic priorities, but the prospects for a cooperative system transcending balance of power are real. What is more, unlike most forecasters, Rosecrance sees danger emanating from Japan rather than China.

> The most potent future antagonism the world could witness is a radical division between the United States and Japan. The Westernization of contemporary Japan

is as yet incomplete. Beneath the external policy of a Japanese trading state boil nationalist resentments directed at a half century of American tutelage and Western neglect　If current trends continue, it may not be too long before ideolog ical rationalizations of Confucian strength and vitality are propounded by Japan as antidotes to supposed Western decadence and lethargy.[30]

Rosecrance's warning about the possible revival of an aggressive Japanese nationalism calls to mind the fascist challenge to the "new world order" that emerged after World War I, and the division of the globe in the 1930s between revisionist and status quo powers. Indeed, Rosecrance's hopes for a concert of like-minded states would be dashed if one or more of its major members turned revisionist in pursuit of territorial aspirations or to erase a historical sense of humiliation or lost status. Thus Russia, humiliated by its loss of the cold war, near-collapse of its economy, and territorial dismemberment could well play the role of a disruptive expansionist.[31] China nurtures revisionist territorial aims with respect to some or all of the South China Sea islands, portions of Siberia, and perhaps of Kazakhstan—all of which were once in the Chinese orbit. China's long humiliation at the hands of western "barbarians" has also made it especially sensitive to perceived unequal treatment and desirous of "a place in the sun."[32] Japan's territorial ambitions do not appear to go beyond those Russian-occupied southern Kurile Islands, but, Japan, too, cannot forever repress its need to unburden itself of the legacy of defeat, occupation, and condescending treatment from its American mentor and protector. Given this potential for revisionist powers in Eurasia, a multipolar balance of power world may be a dangerous one indeed.

THE CLASH OF CIVILIZATIONS MODEL

A third image of the future, and the one that has dominated recent discussion is the "clash of civilizations" proposed by Samuel Huntington.[33]

> It is my hypothesis that the fundamental source of conflict in this new world will not be primarily ideological or primarily economic. The great divisions among humankind and the dominating source of conflict will be cultural. Nation states will remain the most powerful actors in world affairs, but the principal conflicts of global politics will occur between nations and groups of different civilizations. The clash of civilizations will dominate global politics. The fault lines between civilizations will be the battle lines of the future.[34]

Huntington sees in this the latest phase in evolution of international conflict over the past several centuries. For 150 years after the Peace of Westphalia (1648), the primary conflicts in the Western World "were largely among princes—emperors, absolute monarchs and constitutional monarchs attempting to expand their bureaucracies, their armies, their mercantilist economic strength and, most important, the territory they ruled."[35] In the next phase, ushered in by the French Revolution and lasting until World War I, the principal lines of conflict were between nation-states rather than princes. The third phase, triggered by the Bolshevik Revolution, and reaction against it, spawned ideological conflicts culminating in "the struggle between the two superpowers, neither of which was a nation state in the classical European sense and each of which defined its identity in terms of its ideology."[36] But in all the above phases, the world's great conflicts occurred among Western powers—they were in effect, Western civil wars. What makes the coming age unique is that henceforth the great conflicts may occur between, not within, civilizations.

Huntington defines civilization as "the highest cultural grouping and the broadest level of cultural identity people have short of that which distinguishes humans from other species,"[37] and identifies seven or eight major civilizations today: Western, Confucian (Sinic), Japanese, Islamic, Hindu, Slavic-Orthodox, Latin American, possibly the African. Stating that "fault lines between civilizations are replacing the political and ideological boundaries of the cold war as the flash points for crisis and bloodshed," Huntington focuses particularly on the cultural lines of demarcation between Western Christianity and Orthodox Christianity in Europe, and between the latter and Islam.[38] Like many other contemporary analysts, both in the West and Islam, he sees these two civilizations as potentially pitted against each other as a defining feature of an evolving world order.

Other fault lines that contain potential for large-scale future conflict include that between Arab Islamic civilization and the animist or Christian Africa to the south, and that between the Muslim and Hindu civilizations in South Asia. One might also interpret potential conflict between the United States and either Japan or China as a clash between Western and Confucian civilizations. With the recent conflicts in Bosnia, the Persian Gulf, and the Caucasus in mind, Huntington predicts that the next world war, if there is one, will be a war between civilizations.[39] A perceived Western hegemony exemplified by NATO, for instance, might engender a hostile Confucian-Islamic coalition (already presaged by transfers of military technology from China to Pakistan, Iran, and Syria). Such an alliance would be in a position to dominate most of the world's energy resources, and would be backed up by nuclear capability not only in China, but in Muslim countries assisted by China.

Huntington's thesis provoked such virulent criticism that he was compelled to pen a rejoinder.[40] But perhaps the most telling objection was that of the *Economist,* which pointed out that "it is striking that the new wave of self-awareness in the Muslim world has not produced any serious move towards a merger of Muslim states," that "in the Orthodox Christian part of the world, another arguably distinct culture-zone, the recent tendency has been for things to fall apart, not come together," and that "only in Western Europe is there any seriously conceived plan to dissolve existing nation-states into something bigger—and even this European experiment may now be running into the sands." None of this would suggest that the world is "heading for that fearful sounding 'clash of civilizations,'" but rather that global alignments would continue to be determined by the play of interests among nation-states of whatever civilization.[41]

THE UNIPOLAR MOMENT AND AMERICAN HEGEMONY

Contradicting the first three models of the emerging international system is the still-popular notion of an American unipolar dominance. The image was first suggested even before the impressive American performance in Desert Storm in an article by Charles Krauthammer.[42] But those who argued that the end of the cold war had left the United States in the position of sole superpower—and thus made the world unipolar—had first to contend with declinist theories that posited an exhausted America, the geoeconomic assumption that military power was passé, and the "chaos" theorists who saw America as incapable of dealing with the real problems that would define the next age of history, including proliferation of weapons of mass destruction, local famines and genocides, pollution, and resource depletion.

Krauthammer's thesis, echoed by others, is summed up in the following excerpt:

> The most striking feature of the post–Cold War world is its unipolarity. No doubt, multipolarity will come in time. In perhaps another generation or so there will be great powers coequal with the United States, and the world will, in structure, resemble the pre–World War I era. But we are not there yet, nor will we be for decades. Now is the unipolar moment.[43]

There is a noteworthy contrast here with the previously discussed and more or less contemporaneous article by Rosecrance. The latter posits a period in which a peaceful multipolar concert will prevail and regulate the world's high politics, after which it is likely there will be a return to a multipolar balance of power. Krauthammer is, in effect, forecasting the same outcome, but only after an interregnum marked by American hegemony. But in another sense, Krauthammer's article was a lineal descendant of one by Huntington, in which the latter criticized the widespread assumptions of American decline in the late 1980s, and observed that the anxieties over relative U.S. economic decline vis-à-vis Japan and Europe represented only the latest in a series of such bouts in anxiety.[44]

In refuting the declinist thesis Huntington stressed one point that was also basic to the arguments of Mead, Garten, and Thurow to the extent that they allow for the possibility of a superior U.S.-led economic bloc. That has to do with the versatile nature of American strength. Hence,

> In contrast to other countries, the United States ranks extraordinarily high in almost all the major sources of national power: population size and education, natural resources, economic development, social cohesion, political stability, military strength, ideological appeal, diplomatic alliances, technological achievement. It is, consequently, able to sustain reverses in any one area while maintaining its overall influence stemming from other sources.[45]

An American hegemony is also predicted by the "long cycle theory" advanced by George Modelski.[46] Seeking to explain global patterns of leadership since the Renaissance, he perceived five long cycles of about a century each:

1494–1580: Portugal is the leading power.

1580–1688: The Netherlands is the leading power.

1688–1792: Britain is the leading power.

1792–1914: Britain is again the leading power.

1914–1973 (and beyond): the United States is the leading power.

According to Modelski, each of these periods passed through four phases: global war; emergence of the world power; delegitimization of that power; and deconcentration of power. And it is important to note that Modelski believes that each of the previous world powers had dominant navies and acted as the world's commercial hub. Generally speaking, Modelski's analysis runs somewhat parallel to that of Captain A. T. Mahan, with its exposition of the long successive phases of maritime dominance by Portugal, the Netherlands, and Britain, to be followed by the United States.

Modelski, writing in the mid-1980s, believed that the United States' global dominance began to be challenged around 1973, citing the OPEC oil crisis of that year, the collapse of the Bretton Woods economic system, the rise of rival economic powers in Europe and Asia, Soviet achievement of nuclear parity with the ratification of SALT I in 1972, and the expansion of Soviet naval power.

Today Modelski would seem to have been unduly pessimistic. But America's ability to maintain its hegemony will depend greatly on the extent to which it is able to maintain leadership of the now widely heralded Military Technical Revolution or Revolution in Military Affairs (MTR/RMA) made manifest in the Gulf War. Observers differ as to American prospects. Some point out that leadership in new technology is never more than temporary because of rapid diffusion. Others insist that the quantum leap made by the United States in the "systems of systems" approach—integrating space technology, smart weapons, computers, and communications—is beyond the reach of any competitor today. In sum, the "unipolar moment" may last, but only so long as Russia, Europe, Japan, and China are unable or unwilling to replicate the sinews of high-technology warfare pioneered by the United States.[47]

ZONES OF PEACE AND TURMOIL, OR CHAOS THEORY

The one image of a new international system that dispenses entirely with the centrality of nation-state and traditional measurements of national power and interest is the "zones of peace" versus "zones of turmoil" dichotomy popularized by Max Singer and the late Aaron Wildavsky in *The Real World Order*.[48] The Singer/Wildavsky model holds that "the key to understanding the real world is to separate the world into two parts," one part of which, the zone of "peace, wealth, and democracy," includes Western Europe, the United States and Canada, Japan and the Antipodes, comprising some 15 percent of the world's population, and the other of which, the zone of "turmoil, war, and development," includes the lands of the former Soviet Empire, and most of Asia, Africa, and Latin America.[49] The book's primary thesis is simply stated:

> The political relations among the countries in the zones of peace and democracy will not be influenced by relative military power. Nor will those nations be divided into competing military blocs seeking to balance each other's power. There probably will be plenty of national and other conflict, but the decisive special characteristic of this conflict is that no one will believe that it can lead to war.[50]

The authors expect permanent peace in the first global zone because "a central pillar of the next world order is that modern democracies . . . do not even seriously imagine the possibility of being at war with one another."[51] After all, the relative wealth in the democratic areas give them a powerful stake in peace and stability—an argument notoriously made by Norman Angell on the eve of the First World War.[52]

"Zones of turmoil," by definition, are by comparison poor, overpopulated, disaster-prone, and virtually ungovernable. In the dire forecast of world-travelling author Robert D. Kaplan entitled "The Coming Anarchy," he sets out to show "how scarcity, crime, overpopulation, tribalism, and disease are rapidly destroying the social fabric of our planet."[53] Focusing on West Africa, which he considers a "symbol of worldwide demographic, environmental and societal stress, in which criminal anarchy emerges as the real 'strategic' danger, Kaplan points to a terrifying picture that would seem to give the lie to cheerful forecasts of a "global village."[54]

Perhaps the main points of Kaplan's work are that national and international borders are being eroded, and that private armies, transnational terrorist groups, and drug cartels are rising to challenge the authority of traditional states and international law. He notes Huntington's thesis about a coming "clash of civilizations," but adds to it a thesis of a more disaggregated world steeped in tribal as well as civilizational conflict. Much of contemporary political cartography is therefore little more than "the lies of mapmakers" in that they exaggerate the reality of national boundaries and government control over territories. What is in fact dawning, he warns, is "an epoch of themeless juxtapositions, in which the classificatory grid of nation-states is going to be replaced by a jagged-glass pattern of city-states, shanty-states, nebulous and anarchic regionalisms."[55]

Interestingly, neither Singer/Wildavsky nor Kaplan posit the specter of a north-south conflict *per se*. That thesis seems to have become passé in light of the political collapse of Marxist-Leninist regimes in the Third World and the intellectual collapse of dependency theorists who predicted north-south conflicts over resources, terms of trade, or immigration. The burden of the chaos theory, rather, is that the wealthy, peaceful nations will increasingly become gilded ghettos—or armed camps—in the midst of a sea of violent, suffering humanity, unable to help the "zone of turmoil" and ultimately unable to remain unaffected by it. Compared to such a vision of demographic and ecological collapse, the vanities of great power competition would seem beside the point.

THE GLOBAL VILLAGE

But perhaps the globe will not fracture, nor entropy dissolve the bonds of all civilization. Perhaps instead the coming age will be the one in which unity—the "global village"—is finally realized. That is the vision offered by theorists who identify the ongoing advances in telecommunications and data processing as the strongest forces in world affairs. They note that popular American television programs and rock music videocassettes can be found in the remotest villages of Africa and Latin America, and that the whole world is adopting the technologies, values, lifestyles, and aspirations of the West. They herald the Internet, stress global interdependence, not only in matters of trade, investment, and raw materials, but with regard to such global issues as environmental pollution, water shortages, weather, and population movements—solutions to which can only be found through global cooperation. Numerous political scientists highlight the evolution of global "regimes" to govern behavior in such crucial areas as nuclear proliferation, the environment, and international civil aviation, and suggest that such trends militate in the direction of world government.[56] Others identify the increasing dominance of multinational corporations in global affairs, and claim that they are on the verge of transcending the long-dominant nation-state.[57]

As Richard Barnet and John Cavanagh note:

> The emerging global order is spearheaded by a few hundred corporate giants, many of them bigger than most sovereign nations. Ford's economy is larger than Saudi Arabia's and Norway's. Philip Morris's annual sales exceed New Zealand's gross domestic product. The multinational corporation of twenty years ago carried on separate operations in many different countries and tailored its operations to local conditions. In the 1990s large business enterprises, even some smaller ones, have the technological means and strategic vision to burst old limits of time, space, national boundaries, language, custom and ideology.[58]

According to Barnet and Cavanagh, "the fundamental political conflict in the opening decades of the new century, we believe, will not be between nations or even between trading blocs but between the forces of globalization and the territorially based forces of local survival seeking to preserve and to redefine community." That image of the future provides, of course, a stark contrast to those previously discussed under the headings of balance of power, the three-bloc thesis, the clash of civilizations, and chaos theory, since it projects a world where the major fault lines lie not between civilizations, ethnic, religious, or national groups, but simply between those who are part of the new global "web" and those who are not. In a sense it provides an analogy with what has been hypothesized for the Europe of the eighteenth century, wherein it is claimed that the aristocratic elites of the various nations had more in common with each other than with the lower reaches of their respective societies.

INCIPIENT BIPOLARITY

Although the bulk of current commentators see the current international system trending from a concert and/or American unipolar dominance towards some form of multipolarity—either with or without serious security rivalries—the eventual possibility of a return to bipolarity cannot be discounted. A new U.S.-Russian rivalry could result from a reversal of current political trends in Russia and a successful attempt by the latter to reestablish some semblance of the old Soviet Union. Huntington's fears about a U.S.-Japan bipolarity have been noted. But above all, current analyses dwell upon a Chinese challenge to U.S. hegemony, a new cold war, and a new containment strategy.[59] What is more, a bipolar bloc system might well evolve from the current or anticipated multipolar one as a China-Russia bloc faces off against a U.S.-Europe combination, or an all-Asia bloc confronts a U.S.-Europe-Russian one, thus scotching the hopes of "global villagers" once and for all.

THE CURRENT CACOPHONY

The seven images or models of the emerging international system differ radically, but are not in all cases mutually exclusive. It may well turn out—indeed, the odds are it will turn out—that the forces and tendencies stressed by several or all of the models will coexist. For example, there is some overlap between the three-bloc economic model and that positing zones of peace and turmoil. Nor is there necessarily a contradiction between the balance of power multipolarity model and the clash of civilizations—Huntington himself speculates upon possible alliances across the divides of the civilizations. Some pairings of these models are, however, impossible to imagine. The global village and balance of power models provide altogether different interpretations of the emerging system, since they posit diametrically opposed predictions about the role of the nation-state. The global village and clash of civilizations models differ fundamentally in the importance they attribute to cultural divides and the power of technology to erase those divides. The zones of peace/zones of turmoil model projects the end of balance of power politics in the developed (wealthy and democratic) states, but may allow for the continuation of balance of power politics in regional contexts such as the Middle East and Africa.[60] As Nye concludes,

> No single hierarchy describes adequately a world politics with multiple structures. The distribution of power in world politics has become like a layer cake. The top military layer is largely unipolar, for there is no other military power comparable

to the United States. The economic middle layer is tripolar and has been for two decades. The bottom layer of transnational interdependence shows a diffusion of power.[61]

What then might be the implications of these competing models for U.S. foreign policy? Can American policy help to determine or shape the emerging system, and if so, what are the pluses and minuses of the alternative systems for the United States?

In the broadest sense, one might gauge the implications of the possible systems for such general criteria as American power and prestige (inevitably a relative matter), per capita wealth (an absolute matter mostly, but with a psychological component that involves transnational comparisons), security and stability as defined by the absence of wars and threats, and the progress of American values such as global democratization, human rights, and the market economy. For a long time during the cold war, it was a fairly simple matter to identify the basic interests American foreign policy was designed to advance, and thus who stood where on a range of issues. If one knew what the "hawks" thought about one issue, one could usually predict their position on others, and likewise for "doves." In the past few years, however, the literature on U.S. foreign-policy "schools of thought" has become diffuse and unpredictable as former political allies have fallen out and former cold war antagonists find themselves in agreement on such issues as interventionism abroad, immigration, trade policy, or NATO enlargement. As Alan Tonelson summed up,

> In foreign affairs, the old dividing lines are blurring or being ignored, and with good reason. As is clear from any recent op ed page, familiar classifications such as interventionist and isolationist, hawk and dove, realist and idealist, and multilateralist and unilateralist (at least as they have been used since the end of World War II) no longer make much sense, in the absence of the Cold War's defining conditions.[62]

Tonelson, George Weigel, and others have tried to make some sense of the emerging confusion by devising new typologies and subtypologies to characterize the current spectrum of foreign-policy thinking. Weigel divined a three-way division among "neo-isolationists," "democratic internationalists," and "realists."[63] His neoisolationists are a strange combination of the old McGovernite left and the new Buchananite right. His democratic internationalists include former Carterites such as Nye and neoconservatives such as Joshua Muravchik. The realists include other former "neo-cons" plus veteran internationalists of the Reagan and Bush variety. Robert Kagan instead perceives a two-way division between realists and internationalists, with the former seen as effectively indistinguishable from isolationists.[64]

Tonelson goes beyond the foregoing typologies to present a more complex "schools of thought" scheme that, in consonance with the new prominence of geoeconomics, involves a matrix of positions on national security and economics. He sees "American conservatism" as split into three principal factions—"conservative realists," "democratic crusaders," and "conservative minimalists"—that are roughly congruent with Weigel's categories. But each of these groups falls apart whenever economics (free trade vs. managed trade and economic nationalism) and security (interventionism versus isolationism) are at issue, resulting in at least six "boxes" on an implicit chart. On the left, "interventionists" and "laissez-faire liberals" also seem to comprise both ends of an economics policy spectrum, i.e., some of the former are free traders and others are not, and vice versa.

Daryl Press and Eugene Gholz, of the Defense and Arms Control Group at the

Massachusetts Institute of Technology also work with a matrix involving a three-way spectrum running from "military isolationism" to "selective engagement" to "collective security," and from "economic independence" (autarky), to "free trade," to "economic influence" (using such influence for leverage overseas).[65] That produces more possible pairings. Pat Buchanan and Ross Perot, for instance, want to combine economic independence and military isolationism. The Clinton administration (also Samuel Huntington and Richard Lugar) combine selective engagement and economic influence. Finally, Barry Posen and Andrew Ross have provided a spectrum of five general options for an emerging U.S. grand strategy: neoisolationism, selective engagement, collective security, containment, and primacy.[66] The last two appear to be add-ons to the Press-Gholz spectrum of options on the security side, while international economics policy is here subordinated.

However the current pundits sort themselves out, the question remains: what are the implications for U.S. foreign policy of the several possible new international system types, which models are advantageous, and to what extent might the United States be able to shape the emerging system?

The first, most clear-cut, option would be to attempt to maintain a unipolar dominance by which the United States, as Zbigniew Brzezinski put it, would be "perched on top of the world" with "no rivals capable of matching its comprehensive global power."[67] Such an America could presumably maximize its ability to promote its own interests and values, cajole the rest of the world into adopting or at least respecting them, and lead the world toward its preferred models of world order. Those, presumably, would be concert-style security regimes, open commercial regimes, and "global village" cooperation with respect to Third World chaos, the environment, proliferation, and terrorism. Critics, however, are quick to retort that such an American bid for hegemony would not only drain finite American resources, and will, but would also be the most powerful impetus to other great nations to balance American power through direct bilateral competition or the formation of opposing blocs.

A policy of primacy could, of course, be largely defensive. Modelski, seeing the United States as the successor to a line of world powers based on a combination of maritime and commercial predominance, advocates a fundamentally defensive strategy characterized as Periclean: "an attitude of watchful waiting, no conquests or interventions, the protection of the security of the home base through invulnerable deterrents, and the cultivation of the 'command' of sea, air, and space as the elements most strategic to a global position."[68] Such a defensive strategy would shun all "imperial presumption" lest it call forth a grand countercoalition.[69]

To the extent the United States resists the temptation to exploit its "unipolar moment," and accepts the ineluctable drift towards a multipolar system, it would presumably try to minimize the risks inherent in such an international system by nudging the other great powers to embrace diplomacy and eschew coercion. Kissinger concedes the inevitability of such a trend, and recommends that the United States conduct a subtle but forceful balancing diplomacy to prevent domination by a single power of either Europe or Asia.[70] Brzezinski, by contrast, sees the ongoing dilution of the primacy of the nation-state and predicts that increasingly, "world affairs are shaped by domestic trends that recognize no frontiers and require collective responses by governments less and less able to act in a 'sovereign' fashion."[71] He sees a coming ideological homogenization, and "with a bureaucratically controlled and supranational capitalism becoming the universal social system."[72] He seems to agree with the proponents of the global village model, albeit with a dominant United States playing the role of "catalytic nation" acting as the "agent of history."[73] His basic policy prescription is that Americans get their own (social, economic, cultural) house in order lest they lose the ability to lead the world into the coming universalist era.

In a policy sense, there is indeed little the United States can do to slow down the march towards a "global village." The U.S. government could hardly get into the business of reining in its major multinational corporations or stopping the diffusion of technology and associated global cultural change. Whether it can slow or halt a possible drift towards a three-bloc economic structure is more difficult to say. C. Fred Bergsten and others emphasize the need for the United States to continue pushing for a global free trade regime.[74] But American clout may not suffice to persuade Asia and Europe not to form regional trading blocs, in which case the United States will have to develop further a bloc of its own, whereupon Americans will be even less eager to maintain their security umbrella over East Asia and Europe.

The two models that would pose the most obvious threats to the United States are the clash of civilizations and incipient bipolar models, both of which raise the specter of arms races and large-scale conflict. In the former case, the main threats would appear to be a clash between the West and Islam, the West and a China-led Asian coalition, or a Sinic-Islamic coalition. These dire scenarios are what lurk behind the current debates over human rights and most-favored-nation status for China, the future of the American presence in the Gulf, and U.S. involvement in the Arab-Israeli peace process. For the United States to assume that civilizational conflict is coming and act prematurely would only hasten the clash it seeks to avoid. But to go out of its way to avoid such a clash might amount to appeasement and thus encourage aggressive challenges to American interests.

The zones of peace/zones of turmoil model presents less immediate problems of policy. To the extent it entails a low probability of major warfare with other major industrial nations it allows for modest defense budgets directed only against "regional" threats from an Iran, Iraq, or North Korea. However, smug acceptance of growing chaos, especially if it overtook Latin America, might in time invite serious threats to American security and prosperity in the form of armies of illegal immigrants, refugees, drug cartels, and terrorists. Hence the insistence of Kaplan, Paul Kennedy, and others that such regions cannot be ignored lest their agony overflow into the zones of peace.[75]

The paradox facing U.S. policy is that the more Americans assert their power in hopes of shaping the global environment, the more they may generate resentment, resistance, and results the opposite of those they intend. To do nothing, on the other hand, seems fatalistic, selfish, and short-sighted. What the United States can do is continue to promote democracy, free trade, and a balance of power politics among the major players, fight a rearguard action against the spread of weapons and mass destruction, and attempt to alleviate the suffering of "have-nots" in its own neighborhood. But the larger historical forces driven by technology and demography are beyond the power of any nation to shape. No doubt it is for that reason that while the Bush and Clinton administrations' foreign policy teams have shown little strategic vision, neither have their critics. Systems have their own logic and pace. Nor can one change systems from within.

NOTES

1. Henry Kissinger, "How to Achieve the New World Order," *Time,* Mar. 14, 1994, p. 73, an excerpt from a then-forthcoming book, *Diplomacy* (New York: Simon and Schuster, 1994).

2. Quoted in James Atlas, "Name That Era: Pinpointing a Moment on the Map of History," *The New York Times,* Mar. 19, 1995, p. E1.

3. The classic mapping of the relationship

between an ideological spectrum and a methodological one is in Gabriel Almond, "Separate Tables: Schools and Sects in Political Science," *PS*, Fall 1988, pp. 828–42. For analyses of the emerging post–Cold War spectrum of political/ ideological views on U.S. foreign policy, see Alan Tonelson, "Beyond Left and Right," *The National Interest*, Winter 1993/94, pp. 3–18; Charles Krauthammer, "The Poverty of Realism," *New Republic*, Feb. 17, 1986, pp. 14–22; George Weigel, "On the Road to Isolationism?" *Commentary*, Jan. 1992, pp. 36–42; and Alexander Nacht, "U.S. Foreign Policy Strategies," *The Washington Quarterly*, Summer 1995, pp. 195–210.

4. Kissinger, *Diplomacy*, p. 806. Kissinger sees the last several centuries as having had three long definable "systems" or eras: the order that grew out of the Peace of Westphalia that lasted for 150 years, the 100 years of the system created by the Congress of Vienna and (after the twenty-year-long Versailles "armistice") the forty-plus-years-long cold war.

5. Samuel Huntington, *The Clash of Civilizations and the Remaking of World Order* (New York: Simon and Schuster, 1996), pp. 29–35.

6. Nacht, "*U.S. Foreign Policy Strategies*," pp. 198–202; see also Council on Foreign Relations, *The New Shape of World Politics: Contending Paradigms in International Relations* (New York: Foreign Affairs, 1997).

7. Richard Rosecrance, *The Rise of the Trading State* (New York: Basic Books, 1986).

8. Richard Rosecrance, "A New Concert of Powers," *Foreign Affairs*, Spring 1992, pp. 64–82.

9. Francis Fukuyama, *The End of History and the Last Man* (New York: The Free Press, 1992).

10. Karl Deutsch, *Political Community and the North Atlantic Area* (Princeton, N.J.: Princeton University Press, 1957).

11. Walter Russell Mead, "On the Road to Ruin," *Harper's*, Mar. 1990, pp. 59–64; Jeffrey Garten, *A Cold Peace* (New York: Times Books, 1992); Edward Luttwak, *The Endangered American Dream* (New York: Simon and Schuster, 1993); and Lester Thurow, *Head to Head: The Coming Economic Battle Among Japan, Europe and America* (New York: Morrow, 1992).

12. The role of the Middle East as the strategic prize and high ground in the emerging system is discussed in Geoffrey Kemp and Robert E. Harkavy, *Strategic Geography and the Changing Middle East* (Washington D.C.: Carnegie Endowment for International Peace, 1997), esp. chap. 1.

13. Economist Paul Krugman has also criticized this model implicitly in faulting President Clinton's economic advisors for having overemphasized the role of competitiveness between the three blocs as a central cause of American economic problems. See Steven Pearlstein, "The Bad Boy of Economics," *The Washington Post National Weekly Edition*, Apr. 11–17, 1994, pp. 19–20.

14. Thurow, *Head to Head*, p. 246.

15. Ibid., p. 251.

16. Ibid., p. 252.

17. Ibid., p. 247.

18. Ibid., p. 254.

19. Ibid.

20. Among numerous sources, see Barber B. Conable Jr. and David M. Lampton, "China: The Coming Power," *Foreign Affairs*, Winter 1992–93, pp. 133–49; and Michael T. Klare, "The Next Great Arms Race," *Foreign Affairs*, Summer 1993, pp. 136–52.

21. Joseph Nye, "What New World Order?" *Foreign Affairs*, Spring 1992, pp. 83–96.

22. The New World Order: Back to the Future," *The Economist*, Jan. 8, 1994, pp. 21–23.

23. Ibid., p. 21.

24. Ibid.

25. For an analysis or projection of the possibilities for a return to a multipolar system in Europe featuring more rapidly shifting alliances, see John Mearsheimer, "Back to the Future: Instability in Europe After the Cold War," *International Security* 15, Summer 1990, pp. 5–56. The author sees such a system as inherently more unstable than the preceding bipolar one, and even recommends a degree of nuclear proliferation as an antidote via deterrence.

26. Kissinger, *Diplomacy*, p. 805.

27. Joseph Nye, "What New World Order?" *Foreign Affairs*, Spring 1992, pp. 83–96.

28. Ibid., p. 86.

29. Rosecrance, "Concert of Powers," p. 64.

30. Ibid., p. 78.

31. See, among others, Jim Hoagland, "Russia's Gaullist Phase," *The Washington Post Weekly Edition*, May 2, 1994, p. 28.

32. See James R. Lilley, "Nationalism Bites Back," *The New York Times*, Oct. 24, 1996, p. A27, which discusses the resulting Chinese xenophobia.

33. Samuel Huntington, "The Clash of Civilizations," *Foreign Affairs*, Summer 1993, pp. 22–49. See also Michael J. Mazaar, "Culture and International Relations," *The Washington Quarterly*, Spring 1996, pp. 177–97.

34. Huntington, "Clash of Civilizations," p. 22.

35. Ibid., p. 23.

36. Ibid.

37. Ibid., p. 24.

38. Ibid., p. 29.

39. Ibid., p. 39.

40. Fouad Ajami, "The Summoning," *Foreign Affairs,* Sept./Oct. 1993, pp. 2–9; Robert L. Bartley, "The Case for Optimism," ibid., pp. 15–18; Jeanne Kirkpatrick, et al. "The Modernizing Imperative," ibid., pp. 23–24: Albert Weeks, "Do Civilizations Hold?" ibid., pp. 24–25; and Lin Binyan, "Civilization Grafting," ibid., pp. 19–21.

41. "The Nation State Is Dead: Long Live the Nation-State," *The Economist,* Dec. 23, 1995–Jan. 6, 1996, pp. 15–18.

42. Charles Krauthammer, "The Unipolar Moment," *Foreign Affairs,* Vol. 70, No. 1 (1990–1991), pp. 23–33. A rebuttal to Krauthammer's thesis is offered in Ted Galen Carpenter, "The New World Disorder," *Foreign Policy,* Fall 1991, pp. 24–39.

43. Krauthammer, "Unipolar Moment," pp. 23–24.

44. Samuel P. Huntington, "The U.S.—Decline or Renewal?" *Foreign Affairs,* Winter 1988–89, pp. 76–96.

45. Huntington, "U.S.—Decline or Renewal?" p. 91.

46. See, in particular, the various writings of George Modelski, particularly his *Long Cycles in World Politics* (Seattle, Wash.: University of Washington Press, 1985), and also Joshua Goldstein, "Kondratieff Waves as War Cycles," *International Studies Quarterly* 29 (December 1985), pp. 411–44, and W. R. Thompson, ed., *Contending Approaches to World System Analysis* (Beverly Hills, Calif.: Sage, 1983). A good review of the long cycle literature is in Richard Rosecrance, "Long Cycle Theory and International Relations," *International Organization,* Spring 1987, pp. 283–301.

47. Amidst the massive, burgeoning literature on MTR/RMA, among the items most relevant to a discussion of the maintenance of American military predominance, in historical context, are Eliot Cohen, "A Revolution in Warfare," *Foreign Affairs,* Mar./Apr. 1996, pp. 37–54; Andrew Krepinevich, "From Cavalry to Computers," *The National Interest,* Fall 1994, pp. 30–42; William J. Perry, "Desert Storm and Deterrence," *Foreign Affairs,* Fall 1991, pp. 65–82; and William Owens, "Introduction," in Stuart E. Johnson and Martin C. Libicki, *Dominant Battlespace Knowledge* (Washington, D.C.: National Defense University Press, 1995).

48. Max Singer and Aaron Wildavsky, *The Real World Order* (Chatham, N.J.: Chatham House Publishers, 1993).

49. Ibid., p. 3.

50. Ibid. Some writers insist on a broader construction of these issues under the banner of what has come to be known as "endism." This is reviewed in Samuel Huntington, "No Exit: The Errors of Endism," *The National Interest,* Fall 1989, pp. 3–11. Herein, endism is seen to incorporate notions about the end of warfare among civilized and wealthy states, the "war proneness and democracy" thesis and the "end of history" thesis which celebrates the unabashed victory of economic and political liberalism.

51. The "war proneness and democracy" thesis now includes a fairly wide range of literature. See, in particular, Bruce Russett, *Grasping the Democratic Peace* (Princeton, N.J.: Princeton University Press, 1993); *Journal of Peace Research,* Nov. 1992, special section on "Democracy, War, and Peace," and Melvin Small and J. David Singer, "The War Proneness of Democratic Regimes," *Jerusalem Journal of International Relations,* Summer 1976, pp. 51–62. Russett, author of the most ambitious and rigorous study of this subject, concludes that the wealth factor is a subsidiary one in explaining the absence of wars between democratic states, overshadowed by the "norms and strategies characteristic of democracy-to-democracy relationships."

52. Norman Angell, *The Great Illusion: A Study of the Relation Between Military Power to National Advantage* (London: G. P. Putnam's Sons, 1913).

53. Robert D. Kaplan, "The Coming Anarchy," *Atlantic Monthly,* Feb. 1994, pp. 44–76. These themes are expanded upon in Kaplan, *The Ends of the Earth* (New York: Random House, 1996), on the basis of the author's travels in West Africa, the Middle East, and Central and South Asia. The theme of impending disintegration of many Third World nation-states due primarily to ethnic conflict is pursued in Daniel Patrick Moynihan, *Pandaemonium: Ethnicity in International Politics* (Oxford: Oxford University Press, 1993); and Zbigniew Brzezinski, *Out of Control: Global Turmoil on the Eve of the Twenty-First Century* (New York: Scribner's, 1993).

54. Ibid., p. 46.

55. Ibid., p. 72.

56. One definition is rendered by Ernst Haas, who refers to "the halting but steady development of convergent norms and rules of behavior in various domains of international activity deemed increasingly accepted as authoritative by many or most of the world's nations." See his "Why Collaborate? Issue Linkage and International Regimes," *World Politics*, Apr. 1980, p. 358.

57. Richard Barnet and John Cavanagh, *Global Dreams* (New York: Simon and Schuster, 1994). Similar themes but juxtaposed to the opposing possibilities for the resurgence of ethnic, religious, and civilizational identities, are purveyed in Benjamin Barber, *Jibad vs. McWorld* (New York: Times Books, 1995). Barber's work somewhat straddles, or goes back and forth between the basic themes of Huntington on the one hand, and Barnet and Cavanagh, on the other.

58. Barnet and Cavanagh, *Global Dreams,* p. 14.

59. This thesis has been popularized of late by Richard Bernstein and Ross H. Munro, *The Coming Conflict with China* (New York: Knopf, 1997).

60. For an analysis of the applicability—or lack of same—of the traditional Morgenthauian realist/balance of power model to the (pre-end of cold war) Third World, see Steven R. David, "Explaining Third World Alignment," *World Politics*, Jan. 1991, pp. 233–56.

61. Nye, "What New World Order?" p. 88.

62. Alan Tonelson, "Beyond Left and Right," *The National Interest*, Winter 1993/94, pp. 3–18 (3).

63. George Weigel, "On the Road to Isolationism?" *Commentary*, Jan. 1992, pp. 36–42.

64. Robert Kagan, "American Power—A Guide for the Perplexed," *Commentary*, Apr.

1996, pp. 21–31. See also Joshua Muravchik, "Clintonism Abroad," *Commentary*, Feb. 1995, pp. 36–40.

65. Daryl G. Press and Eugene Gholz, "Searching for that 'Vision Thing': America's Foreign Policy Choices," *Breakthroughs*, Spring 1996, pp. 4–10.

66. See Barry Posen and Andrew Ross, "Competing U.S. Grand Strategies," in Robert J. Lieber, ed., *Eagle Adrift* (New York: Longman, 1997), pp. 100–34. Still another "schools of thought" typology has recently been offered by Alexander Nacht, who in turn derives a matrix of sorts from the recent writings of former U.S. government luminaries Richard Haass, James Schlesinger, Zalmay Khalilzad, and William Maynes. This matrix crosses a "heavy involvement–selective involvement" spectrum with a "unilateral-multilateral" spectrum, focusing more on the security side, and with economics somewhat subordinated.

67. Zbigniew Brzezinski, *Out of Control: Global Turmoil on the Eve of the Twenty-First Century* (New York: Scribner's, 1993), p. 87.

68. George Modelski, "The Theory of Long Cycles and U.S. Strategic Policy," in Robert Harkavy and Edward Kolodziej, eds., *American Security Policy and Policy-Making* (Lexington, Mass.: D. C. Health, 1980), pp. 3–19 (15).

69. Ibid., pp. 15–16.

70. Kissinger, *Diplomacy*, p. 813.

71. Brzezinski, *Out of Control*, p. 92.

72. Ibid.

73. Ibid., p. 94.

74. C. Fred Bergsten, "Globalizing Free Trade," *Foreign Affairs*, May/June 1996, pp. 105–20.

75. Kaplan, *Ends of the Earth;* and Paul Kennedy, *Preparing for the Twenty-First Century* (New York: Random House, 1993).

Reading 13-2

The Clash of Civilizations?
Samuel P. Huntington

THE NEXT PATTERN OF CONFLICT

World politics is entering a new phase, and intellectuals have not hesitated to proliferate visions of what it will be—the end of history, the return of traditional rivalries between nation states, and the decline of the nation state from the conflicting pulls of tribalism and globalism, among others. Each of these visions catches aspects of the emerging reality. Yet they all miss a crucial, indeed a central, aspect of what global politics is likely to be in the coming years.

It is my hypothesis that the fundamental source of conflict in this new world will not be primarily ideological or primarily economic. The great divisions among humankind and the dominating source of conflict will be cultural. Nation states will remain the most powerful actors in world affairs, but the principal conflicts of global politics will occur between nations and groups of different civilizations. The clash of civilizations will dominate global politics. The fault lines between civilizations will be the battle lines of the future.

Conflict between civilizations will be the latest phase in the evolution of conflict in the modern world. For a century and a half after the emergence of the modern international system with the Peace of Westphalia, the conflicts of the Western world were largely among princes—emperors, absolute monarchs and constitutional monarchs attempting to expand their bureaucracies, their armies, their mercantilist economic strength and, most important, the territory they ruled. In the process they created nation states, and beginning with the French Revolution the principal lines of conflict were between nations rather than princes. In 1793, as R. R. Palmer put it, "The wars of kings were over; the wars of peoples had begun." This nineteenth-century pattern lasted until the end of World War I. Then, as a result of the Russian Revolution and the reaction against it, the conflict of nations yielded to the conflict of ideologies, first among communism, fascism-Nazism and liberal democracy, and then between communism and liberal democracy. During the Cold War, this latter conflict became embodied in the struggle between the two superpowers, neither of which was a nation state in the classical European sense and each of which defined its identity in terms of its ideology.

These conflicts between princes, nation states and ideologies were primarily conflicts within Western civilization, "Western civil wars," as William Lind has labeled them. This was as true of the Cold War as it was of the world wars and the earlier wars of the seventeenth, eighteenth and nineteenth centuries. With the end of the Cold War, international politics moves out of its Western phase, and its centerpiece becomes the interaction between the West and non-Western civilizations and among non-Western civilizations. In the politics of civilizations, the peoples and governments of non-Western civilizations no longer remain the objects of history as targets of Western colonialism but join the West as movers and shapers of history.

SOURCE: From "The Clash of Civilizations?" by Samuel P. Huntington, *Foreign Affairs*, vol. 72, no. 3 (Summer 1993): 22–49. Copyright © 1993 by the Council on Foreign Relations. Reprinted by permission.

THE NATURE OF CIVILIZATIONS

During the cold war the world was divided into the First, Second and Third Worlds. Those divisions are no longer relevant. It is far more meaningful now to group countries not in terms of their political or economic systems or in terms of their level of economic development but rather in terms of their culture and civilization.

What do we mean when we talk of a civilization? A civilization is a cultural entity. Villages, regions, ethnic groups, nationalities, religious groups, all have distinct cultures at different levels of cultural heterogeneity. The culture of a village in southern Italy may be different from that of a village in northern Italy, but both will share in a common Italian culture that distinguishes them from German villages. European communities, in turn, will share cultural features that distinguish them from Arab or Chinese communities. Arabs, Chinese and Westerners, however, are not part of any broader cultural entity. They constitute civilizations. A civilization is thus the highest cultural grouping of people and the broadest level of cultural identity people have short of that which distinguishes humans from other species. It is defined both by common objective elements, such as language, history, religion, customs, institutions, and by the subjective self-identification of people. People have levels of identity: a resident of Rome may define himself with varying degrees of intensity as a Roman, an Italian, a Catholic, a Christian, a European, a Westerner. The civilization to which he belongs is the broadest level of identification with which he intensely identifies. People can and do redefine their identities and, as a result, the composition and boundaries of civilizations change.

Civilizations may involve a large number of people, as with China ("a civilization pretending to be a state," as Lucian Pye put it), or a very small number of people, such as the Anglophone Caribbean. A civilization may include several nation states, as is the case with Western, Latin American and Arab civilizations, or only one, as is the case with Japanese civilization. Civilizations obviously blend and overlap, and may include subcivilizations. Western civilization has two major variants, European and North American, and Islam has its Arab, Turkic and Malay subdivisions. Civilizations are nonetheless meaningful entities, and while the lines between them are seldom sharp, they are real. Civilizations are dynamic; they rise and fall; they divide and merge. And, as any student of history knows, civilizations disappear and are buried in the sands of time.

Westerners tend to think of nation states as the principal actors in global affairs. They have been that, however, for only a few centuries. The broader reaches of human history have been the history of civilizations. In *A Study of History,* Arnold Toynbee identified 21 major civilizations; only six of them exist in the contemporary world.

WHY CIVILIZATIONS WILL CLASH

Civilization identity will be increasingly important in the future, and the world will be shaped in large measure by the interactions among seven or eight major civilizations. These include Western, Confucian, Japanese, Islamic, Hindu, Slavic-Orthodox, Latin American and possibly African civilization. The most important conflicts of the future will occur along the cultural fault lines separating these civilizations from one another.

Why will this be the case?

First, differences among civilizations are not only real; they are basic. Civilizations are differentiated from each other by history, language, culture, tradition and, most im-

portant, religion. The people of different civilizations have different views on the relations between God and man, the individual and the group, the citizen and the state,
parents and children, husband and wife, as well as differing views of the relative importance of rights and responsibilities, liberty and authority, equality and hierarchy.
These differences are the product of centuries. They will not soon disappear. They are
far more fundamental than differences among political ideologies and political regimes.
Differences do not necessarily mean conflict, and conflict does not necessarily mean violence. Over the centuries, however, differences among civilizations have generated the
most prolonged and the most violent conflicts.

Second, the world is becoming a smaller place. The interactions between peoples
of different civilizations are increasing; these increasing interactions intensify civilization consciousness and awareness of differences between civilizations and commonalities within civilizations. North African immigration to France generates hostility
among Frenchmen and at the same time increased receptivity to immigration by
"good" European Catholic Poles. Americans react far more negatively to Japanese investment than to larger investments from Canada and European countries. Similarly, as
Donald Horowitz has pointed out, "An Ibo may be . . . an Owerri Ibo or an Onitsha
Ibo in what was the Eastern region of Nigeria. In Lagos, he is simply an Ibo. In London, he is a Nigerian. In New York, he is an African." The interactions among peoples
of different civilizations enhance the civilization-consciousness of people that, in turn,
invigorates differences and animosities stretching or thought to stretch back deep into
history.

Third, the processes of economic modernization and social change throughout the
world are separating people from longstanding local identities. They also weaken the
nation state as a source of identity. In much of the world religion has moved in to fill
this gap, often in the form of movements that are labeled "fundamentalist." Such movements are found in Western Christianity, Judaism, Buddhism and Hinduism, as well as
in Islam. In most countries and most religions the people active in fundamentalist
movements are young, college-educated, middle-class technicians, professionals and
business persons. The "unsecularization of the world," George Weigel has remarked,
"is one of the dominant social facts of life in the late twentieth century." The revival of
religion, "la revanche de Dieu," as Gilles Kepel labeled it, provides a basis for identity
and commitment that transcends national boundaries and unites civilizations.

Fourth, the growth of civilization-consciousness is enhanced by the dual role of the
West. On the one hand, the West is at a peak of power. At the same time, however, and
perhaps as a result, a return to the roots phenomenon is occurring among non-Western
civilizations. Increasingly one hears references to trends toward a turning inward and
"Asianization" in Japan, the end of the Nehru legacy and the "Hinduization" of India,
the failure of Western ideas of socialism and nationalism and hence "re-Islamization" of
the Middle East, and now a debate over Westernization versus Russianization in Boris
Yeltsin's country. A West at the peak of its power confronts non-Wests that increasingly
have the desire, the will and the resources to shape the world in non-Western ways.

In the past, the elites of non-Western societies were usually the people who were
most involved with the West, had been educated at Oxford, the Sorbonne or Sandhurst,
and had absorbed Western attitudes and values. At the same time, the populace in non-
Western countries often remained deeply imbued with the indigenous culture. Now,
however, these relationships are being reversed. A de-Westernization and indigeniza-
tion of elites is occurring in many non-Western countries at the same time that Western, usually American, cultures, styles and habits become more popular among the mass
of the people.

Fifth, cultural characteristics and differences are less mutable and hence less easily compromised and resolved than political and economic ones. In the former Soviet Union, communists can become democrats, the rich can become poor and the poor rich, but Russians cannot become Estonians and Azeris cannot become Armenians. In class and ideological conflicts, the key question was "Which side are you on?" and people could and did choose sides and change sides. In conflicts between civilizations, the question is "What are you?" That is a given that cannot be changed. And as we know, from Bosnia to the Caucasus to the Sudan, the wrong answer to that question can mean a bullet in the head. Even more than ethnicity, religion discriminates sharply and exclusively among people. A person can be half-French and half-Arab and simultaneously even a citizen of two countries. It is more difficult to be half-Catholic and half-Muslim.

Finally, economic regionalism is increasing. The proportions of total trade that were intraregional rose between 1980 and 1989 from 51 percent to 59 percent in Europe, 33 percent to 37 percent in East Asia, and 32 percent to 36 percent in North America. The importance of regional economic blocs is likely to continue to increase in the future. On the one hand, successful economic regionalism will reinforce civilization-consciousness. On the other hand, economic regionalism may succeed only when it is rooted in a common civilization. The European Community rests on the shared foundation of European culture and Western Christianity. The success of the North American Free Trade Area depends on the convergence now underway of Mexican, Canadian and American cultures. Japan, in contrast, faces difficulties in creating a comparable economic entity in East Asia because Japan is a society and civilization unique to itself. However strong the trade and investment links Japan may develop with other East Asian countries, its cultural differences with those countries inhibit and perhaps preclude its promoting regional economic integration like that in Europe and North America.

Common culture, in contrast, is clearly facilitating the rapid expansion of the economic relations between the People's Republic of China and Hong Kong, Taiwan, Singapore and the overseas Chinese communities in other Asian countries. With the Cold War over, cultural commonalities increasingly overcome ideological differences, and mainland China and Taiwan move closer together. If cultural commonality is a prerequisite for economic integration, the principal East Asian economic bloc of the future is likely to be centered on China. This bloc is, in fact, already coming into existence. As Murray Weidenbaum has observed.

> Despite the current Japanese dominance of the region, the Chinese-based economy of Asia is rapidly emerging as a new epicenter for industry, commerce and finance. This strategic area contains substantial amounts of technology and manufacturing capability (Taiwan), outstanding entrepreneurial, marketing and services acumen (Hong Kong), a fine communications network (Singapore), a tremendous pool of financial capital (all three), and very large endowments of land, resources and labor (mainland China). . . . From Guangzhou to Singapore, from Kuala Lumpur to Manila, this influential network—often based on extensions of the traditional clans—has been described as the backbone of the East Asian economy.[1]

Culture and religion also form the basis of the Economic Cooperation Organization, which brings together ten non-Arab Muslim countries: Iran, Pakistan, Turkey, Azerbaijan, Kazakhstan, Kyrgyzstan, Turkmenistan, Tadjikistan, Uzbekistan and Afghanistan. One impetus to the revival and expansion of this organization, founded originally in the 1960s by Turkey, Pakistan and Iran, is the realization by the leaders of several of these countries that they had no chance of admission to the European Community. Similarly, Caricom, the Central American Common Market and Mercosur rest on common cultural foundations. Efforts to build a broader Caribbean–Central American economic entity bridging the Anglo–Latin divide, however, have to date failed.

As people define their identity in ethnic and religious terms, they are likely to see an "us" versus "them" relation existing between themselves and people of different ethnicity or religion. The end of ideologically defined states in Eastern Europe and the former Soviet Union permits traditional ethnic identities and animosities to come to the fore. Differences in culture and religion create differences over policy issues, ranging from human rights to immigration to trade and commerce to the environment. Geographical propinquity gives rise to conflicting territorial claims from Bosnia to Mindanao. Most important, the efforts of the West to promote its values of democracy and liberalism as universal values, to maintain its military predominance and to advance its economic interests engender countering responses from other civilizations. Decreasingly able to mobilize support and form coalitions on the basis of ideology, governments and groups will increasingly attempt to mobilize support by appealing to common religion and civilization identity.

The clash of civilizations thus occurs at two levels. At the micro-level, adjacent groups along the fault lines between civilizations struggle, often violently, over the control of territory and each other. At the macro-level, states from different civilizations compete for relative military and economic power, struggle over the control of international institutions and third parties, and competitively promote their particular political and religious values.

THE FAULT LINES BETWEEN CIVILIZATIONS

The fault lines between civilizations are replacing the political and ideological boundaries of the Cold War as the flash points for crisis and bloodshed. The Cold War began when the Iron Curtain divided Europe politically and ideologically. The Cold War ended with the end of the Iron Curtain. As the ideological division of Europe has disappeared, the cultural division of Europe between Western Christianity, on the one hand, and Orthodox Christianity and Islam, on the other, has reemerged. The most significant dividing line in Europe, as William Wallace has suggested, may well be the eastern boundary of Western Christianity in the year 1500. This line runs along what are now the boundaries between Finland and Russia and between the Baltic states and Russia, cuts through Belarus and Ukraine separating the more Catholic western Ukraine from Orthodox eastern Ukraine, swings westward separating Transylvania from the rest of Romania, and then goes through Yugoslavia almost exactly along the line now separating Croatia and Slovenia from the rest of Yugoslavia. In the Balkans this line, of course, coincides with the historic boundary between the Hapsburg and Ottoman empires. The peoples to the north and west of this line are Protestant or Catholic; they shared the common experiences of European history—feudalism, the Renaissance, the Reformation, the Enlightenment, the French Revolution, the Industrial Revolution; they are generally economically better off than the peoples to the east; and they may now look forward to increasing involvement in a common European economy and to the consolidation of democratic political systems. The peoples to the east and south of this line are Orthodox or Muslim; they historically belonged to the Ottoman or Tsarist empires and were only lightly touched by the shaping events in the rest of Europe; they are generally less advanced economically; they seem much less likely to develop stable democratic political systems. The Velvet Curtain of culture has replaced the Iron Curtain of ideology as the most significant dividing line in Europe. As the events in Yugoslavia show, it is not only a line of difference; it is also at times a line of bloody conflict.

Conflict along the fault line between Western and Islamic civilizations has been going on for 1,300 years. After the founding of Islam, the Arab and Moorish surge west and north only ended at Tours in 732. From the eleventh to the thirteenth century the Crusaders attempted with temporary success to bring Christianity and Christian rule to the Holy Land. From the fourteenth to the seventeenth century, the Ottoman Turks reversed the balance, extended their sway over the Middle East and the Balkans, captured Constantinople, and twice laid siege to Vienna. In the nineteenth and early twentieth centuries as Ottoman power declined Britain, France, and Italy established Western control over most of North Africa and the Middle East.

After World War II, the West, in turn, began to retreat; the colonial empires disappeared; first Arab nationalism and then Islamic fundamentalism manifested themselves; the West became heavily dependent on the Persian Gulf countries for its energy; the oil-rich Muslim countries became money-rich and, when they wished to, weapons-rich. Several wars occurred between Arabs and Israel (created by the West). France fought a bloody and ruthless war in Algeria for most of the 1950s; British and French forces invaded Egypt in 1956; American forces went into Lebanon in 1958; subsequently American forces returned to Lebanon, attacked Libya, and engaged in various military encounters with Iran; Arab and Islamic terrorists, supported by at least three Middle Eastern governments, employed the weapon of the weak and bombed Western planes and installations and seized Western hostages. This warfare between Arabs and the West culminated in 1990, when the United States sent a massive army to the Persian Gulf to defend some Arab countries against aggression by another. In its aftermath NATO planning is increasingly directed to potential threats and instability along its "southern tier."

This centuries-old military interaction between the West and Islam is unlikely to decline. It could become more virulent. The Gulf War left some Arabs feeling proud that Saddam Hussein had attacked Israel and stood up to the West. It also left many feeling humiliated and resentful of the West's military presence in the Persian Gulf, the West's overwhelming military dominance, and their apparent inability to shape their own destiny. Many Arab countries, in addition to the oil exporters, are reaching levels of economic and social development where autocratic forms of government become inappropriate and efforts to introduce democracy become stronger. Some openings in Arab political systems have already occurred. The principal beneficiaries of these openings have been Islamist movements. In the Arab world, in short, Western democracy strengthens anti-Western political forces. This may be a passing phenomenon, but it surely complicates relations between Islamic countries and the West.

Those relations are also complicated by demography. The spectacular population growth in Arab countries, particularly in North Africa, has led to increased migration to Western Europe. The movement within Western Europe toward minimizing internal boundaries has sharpened political sensitivities with respect to this development. In Italy, France and Germany, racism is increasingly open, and political reactions and violence against Arab and Turkish migrants have become more intense and more widespread since 1990.

On both sides the interaction between Islam and the West is seen as a clash of civilizations. The West's "next confrontation," observes M. J. Akbar, an Indian Muslim author, "is definitely going to come from the Muslim world. It is in the sweep of the Islamic nations from the Maghreb to Pakistan that the struggle for a new world order will begin." Bernard Lewis comes to a similar conclusion:

> We are facing a mood and a movement far transcending the level of issues and policies and the governments that pursue them. This is no less than a clash of civilizations—the perhaps irrational but surely historic reaction of an ancient rival against our Judeo-Christian heritage, our secular present, and the worldwide expansion of both.[2]

Historically, the other great antagonistic interaction of Arab Islamic civilization has been with the pagan, animist, and now increasingly Christian black peoples to the south. In the past, this antagonism was epitomized in the image of Arab slave dealers and black slaves. It has been reflected in the on-going civil war in the Sudan between Arabs and blacks, the fighting in Chad between Libyan-supported insurgents and the government, the tensions between Orthodox Christians and Muslims in the Horn of Africa, and the political conflicts, recurring riots and communal violence between Muslims and Christians in Nigeria. The modernization of Africa and the spread of Christianity are likely to enhance the probability of violence along this fault line. Symptomatic of the intensification of this conflict was the Pope John Paul II's speech in Khartoum in February 1993 attacking the actions of the Sudan's Islamist government against the Christian minority there.

On the northern border of Islam, conflict has increasingly erupted between Orthodox and Muslim peoples, including the carnage of Bosnia and Sarajevo, the simmering violence between Serb and Albanian, the tenuous relations between Bulgarians and their Turkish minority, the violence between Ossetians and Ingush, the unremitting slaughter of each other by Armenians and Azeris, the tense relations between Russians and Muslims in Central Asia, and the deployment of Russian troops to protect Russian interests in the Caucasus and Central Asia. Religion reinforces the revival of ethnic identities and restimulates Russian fears about the security of their southern borders. This concern is well captured by Archie Roosevelt:

> Much of Russian history concerns the struggle between the Slavs and the Turkic peoples on their borders, which dates back to the foundation of the Russian state more than a thousand years ago. In the Slavs' millennium-long confrontation with their eastern neighbors lies the key to an understanding not only of Russian history, but Russian character. To understand Russian realities today one has to have a concept of the great Turkic ethnic group that has preoccupied Russians through the centuries.[3]

The conflict of civilizations is deeply rooted elsewhere in Asia. The historic clash between Muslim and Hindu in the subcontinent manifests itself now not only in the rivalry between Pakistan and India but also in intensifying religious strife within India between increasingly militant Hindu groups and India's substantial Muslim minority. The destruction of the Ayodhya mosque in December 1992 brought to the fore the issue of whether India will remain a secular democratic state or become a Hindu one. In East Asia, China has outstanding territorial disputes with most of its neighbors. It has pursued a ruthless policy toward the Buddhist people of Tibet, and it is pursuing an increasingly ruthless policy toward its Turkic-Muslim minority. With the Cold War over, the underlying differences between China and the United States have reasserted themselves in areas such as human rights, trade and weapons proliferation. These differences are unlikely to moderate. A "new cold war," Deng Xaioping reportedly asserted in 1991, is under way between China and America.

The same phrase has been applied to the increasingly difficult relations between Japan and the United States. Here cultural difference exacerbates economic conflict. People on each side allege racism on the other, but at least on the American side the antipathies are not racial but cultural. The basic values, attitudes, behavioral patterns of the two societies could hardly be more different. The economic issues between the United States and Europe are no less serious than those between the United States and Japan, but they do not have the same political salience and emotional intensity because the differences between American culture and European culture are so much less than those between American civilization and Japanese civilization.

The interactions between civilizations vary greatly in the extent to which they are likely to be characterized by violence. Economic competition clearly predominates between the American and European subcivilizations of the West and between both of them and Japan. On the Eurasian continent, however, the proliferation of ethnic conflict, epitomized at the extreme in "ethnic cleansing," has not been totally random. It has been most frequent and most violent between groups belonging to different civilizations. In Eurasia the great historic fault lines between civilizations are once more aflame. This is particularly true along the boundaries of the crescent-shaped Islamic bloc of nations from the bulge of Africa to central Asia. Violence also occurs between Muslims, on the one hand, and Orthodox Serbs in the Balkans, Jews in Israel, Hindus in India, Buddhists in Burma and Catholics in the Philippines. Islam has bloody borders.

CIVILIZATION RALLYING: THE KIN-COUNTRY SYNDROME

Groups or states belonging to one civilization that become involved in war with people from a different civilization naturally try to rally support from other members of their own civilization. As the post–Cold War world evolves, civilization commonality, what H. D. S. Greenway has termed the "kin-country" syndrome, is replacing political ideology and traditional balance of power considerations as the principal basis for cooperation and coalitions. It can be seen gradually emerging in the post–Cold War conflicts in the Persian Gulf, the Caucasus and Bosnia. None of these was a full-scale war between civilizations, but each involved some elements of civilizational rallying, which seemed to become more important as the conflict continued and which may provide a foretaste of the future.

First, in the Gulf War one Arab state invaded another and then fought a coalition of Arab, Western and other states. While only a few Muslim governments overtly supported Saddam Hussein, many Arab elites privately cheered him on, and he was highly popular among large sections of the Arab publics. Islamic fundamentalist movements universally supported Iraq rather than the Western-backed governments of Kuwait and Saudi Arabia. Forswearing Arab nationalism, Saddam Hussein explicitly invoked an Islamic appeal. He and his supporters attempted to define the war as a war between civilizations. "It is not the world against Iraq," as Safar Al-Hawali, dean of Islamic Studies at the Umm Al-Qura University in Mecca, put it in a widely circulated tape. "It is the West against Islam." Ignoring the rivalry between Iran and Iraq, the chief Iranian religious leader, Ayatollah Ali Khamenei, called for a holy war against the West: "The struggle against American aggression, greed, plans and policies will be counted as a jihad, and anybody who is killed on that path is a martyr." "This is a war," King Hussein of Jordan argued, "against all Arabs and all Muslims and not against Iraq alone."

The rallying of substantial sections of Arab elites and publics behind Saddam Hussein caused those Arab governments in the anti-Iraq coalition to moderate their activities and temper their public statements. Arab governments opposed or distanced themselves from subsequent Western efforts to apply pressure on Iraq, including enforcement of a no-fly zone in the summer of 1992 and the bombing of Iraq in January 1993. The Western-Soviet-Turkish-Arab anti-Iraq coalition of 1990 had by 1993 become a coalition of almost only the West and Kuwait against Iraq.

Muslims contrasted Western actions against Iraq with the West's failure to protect Bosnians against Serbs and to impose sanctions on Israel for violating U.N. resolutions. The West, they alleged, was using a double standard. A world of clashing civilizations, however, is inevitably a world of double standards: people apply one standard to their kin-countries and a different standard to others.

Second, the kin-country syndrome also appeared in conflicts in the former Soviet Union. Armenian military successes in 1992 and 1993 stimulated Turkey to become increasingly supportive of its religious, ethnic and linguistic brethren in Azerbaijan. "We have a Turkish nation feeling the same sentiments as the Azerbaijanis," said one Turkish official in 1992. "We are under pressure. Our newspapers are full of the photos of atrocities and are asking us if we are still serious about pursuing our neutral policy. Maybe we should show Armenia that there's a big Turkey in the region." President Turgut Özal agreed, remarking that Turkey should at least "scare the Armenians a little bit." Turkey, Özal threatened again in 1993, would "show its fangs." Turkish Air Force jets flew reconnaissance flights along the Armenian border; Turkey suspended food shipments and air flights to Armenia; and Turkey and Iran announced they would not accept dismemberment of Azerbaijan. In the last years of its existence, the Soviet government supported Azerbaijan because its government was dominated by former communists. With the end of the Soviet Union, however, political considerations gave way to religious ones. Russian troops fought on the side of the Armenians, and Azerbaijan accused the "Russian government of turning 180 degrees" toward support for Christian Armenia.

Third, with respect to the fighting in the former Yugoslavia, Western publics manifested sympathy and support for the Bosnian Muslims and the horrors they suffered at the hands of the Serbs. Relatively little concern was expressed, however, over Croatian attacks on Muslims and participation in the dismemberment of Bosnia-Herzegovina. In the early stages of the Yugoslav breakup, Germany, in an unusual display of diplomatic initiative and muscle, induced the other 11 members of the European Community to follow its lead in recognizing Slovenia and Croatia. As a result of the pope's determination to provide strong backing to the two Catholic countries, the Vatican extended recognition even before the Community did. The United States followed the European lead. Thus the leading actors in Western civilization rallied behind their coreligionists. Subsequently Croatia was reported to be receiving substantial quantities of arms from Central European and other Western countries. Boris Yeltsin's government, on the other hand, attempted to pursue a middle course that would be sympathetic to the Orthodox Serbs but not alienate Russia from the West. Russian conservative and nationalist groups, however, including many legislators, attacked the government for not being more forthcoming in its support for the Serbs. By early 1993 several hundred Russians apparently were serving with the Serbian forces, and reports circulated of Russian arms being supplied to Serbia.

Islamic governments and groups, on the other hand, castigated the West for not coming to the defense of the Bosnians. Iranian leaders urged Muslims from all countries to provide help to Bosnia; in violation of the U.N. arms embargo, Iran supplied weapons and men for the Bosnians; Iranian-supported Lebanese groups sent guerrillas to train and organize the Bosnian forces. In 1993 up to 4,000 Muslims from over two dozen Islamic countries were reported to be fighting in Bosnia. The governments of Saudi Arabia and other countries felt under increasing pressure from fundamentalist groups in their own societies to provide more vigorous support for the Bosnians. By the end of 1992, Saudi Arabia had reportedly supplied substantial funding for weapons and supplies for the Bosnians, which significantly increased their military capabilities vis-à-vis the Serbs.

In the 1930s the Spanish Civil War provoked intervention from countries that politically were fascist, communist and democratic. In the 1990s the Yugoslav conflict is provoking intervention from countries that are Muslim, Orthodox and Western Christian. The parallel has not gone unnoticed. "The war in Bosnia-Herzegovina has become the emotional equivalent of the fight against fascism in the Spanish Civil War," one Saudi editor observed. "Those who died there are regarded as martyrs who tried to save their fellow Muslims."

Conflicts and violence will also occur between states and groups within the same civilization. Such conflicts, however, are likely to be less intense and less likely to expand than conflicts between civilizations. Common membership in a civilization reduces the probability of violence in situations where it might otherwise occur. In 1991 and 1992 many people were alarmed by the possibility of violent conflict between Russia and Ukraine over territory, particularly Crimea, the Black Sea fleet, nuclear weapons and economic issues. If civilization is what counts, however, the likelihood of violence between Ukrainians and Russians should be low. They are two Slavic, primarily Orthodox peoples who have had close relationships with each other for centuries. As of early 1993, despite all the reasons for conflict, the leaders of the two countries were effectively negotiating and defusing the issues between the two countries. While there has been serious fighting between Muslims and Christians elsewhere in the former Soviet Union and much tension and some fighting between Western and Orthodox Christians in the Baltic states, there has been virtually no violence between Russians and Ukrainians.

Civilization rallying to date has been limited, but it has been growing, and it clearly has the potential to spread much further. As the conflicts in the Persian Gulf, the Caucasus and Bosnia continued, the positions of nations and the cleavages between them increasingly were along civilizational lines. Populist politicians, religious leaders and the media have found it a potent means of arousing mass support and of pressuring hesitant governments. In the coming years, the local conflicts most likely to escalate into major wars will be those, as in Bosnia and the Caucasus, along the fault lines between civilizations. The next world war, if there is one, will be a war between civilizations.

THE WEST VERSUS THE REST

The West is now at an extraordinary peak of power in relation to other civilizations. Its superpower opponent has disappeared from the map. Military conflict among Western states is unthinkable, and Western military power is unrivaled. Apart from Japan, the West faces no economic challenge. It dominates international political and security institutions and with Japan international economic institutions. Global political and security issues are effectively settled by a directorate of the United States, Britain and France, world economic issues by a directorate of the United States, Germany and Japan, all of which maintain extraordinarily close relations with each other to the exclusion of lesser and largely non-Western countries. Decisions made at the U.N. Security Council or in the International Monetary Fund that reflect the interests of the West are presented to the world as reflecting the desires of the world community. The very phrase "the world community" has become the euphemistic collective noun (replacing "the Free World") to give global legitimacy to actions reflecting the interests of the United States and other Western powers.[4] Through the IMF and other international economic institutions, the West promotes its economic interests and imposes on other nations the economic policies it thinks appropriate. In any poll of non-Western peoples, the IMF undoubtedly would win the support of finance ministers and a few others, but get an overwhelmingly unfavorable rating from just about everyone else, who would agree with Georgy Arbatov's characterization of IMF officials as "neo-Bolsheviks who love expropriating other people's money, imposing undemocratic and alien rules of economic and political conduct and stifling economic freedom."

Western domination of the U.N. Security Council and its decisions, tempered only by occasional abstention by China, produced U.N. legitimation of the West's use of force to drive Iraq out of Kuwait and its elimination of Iraq's sophisticated weapons and capacity to produce such weapons. It also produced the quite unprecedented action by the United States, Britain and France in getting the Security Council to demand that Libya hand over the Pan Am 103 bombing suspects and then to impose sanctions when Libya refused. After defeating the largest Arab army, the West did not hesitate to throw its weight around in the Arab world. The West in effect is using international institutions, military power and economic resources to run the world in ways that will maintain Western predominance, protect Western interests and promote Western political and economic values.

That at least is the way in which non-Westerners see the new world, and there is a significant element of truth in their view. Differences in power and struggles for military, economic and institutional power are thus one source of conflict between the West and other civilizations. Differences in culture, that is basic values and beliefs, are a second source of conflict. V. S. Naipaul has argued that Western civilization is the "universal civilization" that "fits all men." At a superficial level much of Western culture has indeed permeated the rest of the world. At a more basic level, however, Western concepts differ fundamentally from those prevalent in other civilizations. Western ideas of individualism, liberalism, constitutionalism, human rights, equality, liberty, the rule of law, democracy, free markets, the separation of church and state, often have little resonance in Islamic, Confucian, Japanese, Hindu, Buddhist or Orthodox cultures. Western efforts to propagate such ideas produce instead a reaction against "human rights imperialism" and a reaffirmation of indigenous values, as can be seen in the support for religious fundamentalism by the younger generation in non-Western cultures. The very notion that there could be a "universal civilization" is a Western idea, directly at odds with the particularism of most Asian societies and their emphasis on what distinguishes one people from another. Indeed, the author of a review of 100 comparative studies of values in different societies concluded that "the values that are most important in the West are least important worldwide."[5] In the political realm, of course, these differences are most manifest in the efforts of the United States and other Western powers to induce other peoples to adopt Western ideas concerning democracy and human rights. Modern democratic government originated in the West. When it has developed in non-Western societies it has usually been the product of Western colonialism or imposition.

The central axis of world politics in the future is likely to be, in Kishore Mahbubani's phrase, the conflict between "the West and the Rest" and the responses of non-

Western civilizations to Western power and values.[6] Those responses generally take one or a combination of three forms. At one extreme, non-Western states can, like Burma and North Korea, attempt to pursue a course of isolation, to insulate their societies from penetration or "corruption" by the West, and, in effect, to opt out of participation in the Western-dominated global community. The costs of this course, however, are high, and few states have pursued it exclusively. A second alternative, the equivalent of "band-wagoning" in international relations theory, is to attempt to join the West and accept its values and institutions. The third alternative is to attempt to "balance" the West by developing economic and military power and cooperating with other non-Western societies against the West, while preserving indigenous values and institutions; in short, to modernize but not to Westernize.

THE TORN COUNTRIES

In the future, as people differentiate themselves by civilization, countries with large numbers of peoples of different civilizations, such as the Soviet Union and Yugoslavia, are candidates for dismemberment. Some other countries have a fair degree of cultural homogeneity but are divided over whether their society belongs to one civilization or another. These are torn countries. Their leaders typically wish to pursue a bandwagoning strategy and to make their countries members of the West, but the history, culture and traditions of their countries are non-Western. The most obvious and prototypical torn country is Turkey. The late twentieth-century leaders of Turkey have followed in the Attatürk tradition and defined Turkey as a modern, secular, Western nation state. They allied Turkey with the West in NATO and in the Gulf War; they applied for membership in the European Community. At the same time, however, elements in Turkish society have supported an Islamic revival and have argued that Turkey is basically a Middle Eastern Muslim society. In addition, while the elite of Turkey has defined Turkey as a Western society, the elite of the West refuses to accept Turkey as such. Turkey will not become a member of the European Community, and the real reason, as President Özal said, "is that we are Muslim and they are Christian and they don't say that." Having rejected Mecca, and then being rejected by Brussels, where does Turkey look? Tashkent may be the answer. The end of the Soviet Union gives Turkey the opportunity to become the leader of a revived Turkic civilization involving seven countries from the borders of Greece to those of China. Encouraged by the West, Turkey is making strenuous efforts to carve out this new identity for itself.

During the past decade Mexico has assumed a position somewhat similar to that of Turkey. Just as Turkey abandoned its historic opposition to Europe and attempted to join Europe, Mexico has stopped defining itself by its opposition to the United States and is instead attempting to imitate the United States and to join it in the North American Free Trade Area. Mexican leaders are engaged in the great task of redefining Mexican identity and have introduced fundamental economic reforms that eventually will lead to fundamental political change. In 1991 a top adviser to President Carlos Salinas de Gortari described at length to me all the changes the Salinas government was making. When he finished, I remarked: "That's most impressive. It seems to me that basically you want to change Mexico from a Latin American country into a North American country." He looked at me with surprise and exclaimed: "Exactly! That's precisely what we are trying to do, but of course we could never say so publicly." As his remark indicates, in Mexico as in Turkey, significant elements in society resist the redefinition of their country's identity. In Turkey, European-oriented leaders have to make gestures to Islam (Özal's pilgrimage to Mecca); so also Mexico's North American–oriented leaders have to make gestures to those who hold Mexico to be a Latin American country (Salinas' Ibero-American Guadalajara summit)

Historically Turkey has been the most profoundly torn country. For the United States, Mexico is the most immediate torn country. Globally the most important torn country is Russia. The question of whether Russia is part of the West or the leader of a distinct Slavic-Orthodox civilization has been a recurring one in Russian history. That issue was obscured by the communist victory in Russia, which imported a Western ideology, adapted it to Russian conditions and then challenged the West in the name of that ideology. The dominance of communism shut off the historic debate over Westernization versus Russification. With communism discredited Russians once again face that question.

President Yeltsin is adopting Western principles and goals and seeking to make Russia a "normal" country and a part of the West. Yet both the Russian elite and the Russian public are divided on this issue. Among the more moderate dissenters, Sergei Stankevich argues that Russia should reject the "Atlanticist" course, which would lead it "to become European, to become a part of the world economy in rapid and organized fashion, to become the eighth member of the Seven, and to put particular emphasis on Germany and the United States as the two dominant members of the Atlantic alliance." While also rejecting an exclusively Eurasian policy, Stankevich nonetheless argues that Russia should give priority to the protection of Russians in other countries, emphasize its Turkic and Muslim connections, and promote "an appreciable redistribution of our resources, our options, our ties, and our interests in favor of Asia, of the eastern direction." People of this persuasion criticize Yeltsin for subordinating Russia's interests to those of the West, for reducing Russian military strength, for failing to support traditional friends such as Serbia, and for pushing economic and political reform in ways injurious to the Russian people. Indicative of this trend is the new popularity of the ideas of Petr Savitsky, who in the 1920s argued that Russia was a unique Eurasian civilization.[7] More extreme dissidents voice much more blatantly nationalist, anti-Western and anti-Semitic views, and urge Russia to redevelop its military strength and to establish closer ties with China and Muslim countries. The people of Russia are as divided as the elite. An opinion survey in European Russia in the spring of 1992 revealed that 40 percent of the public had positive attitudes toward the West and 36 percent had negative attitudes. As it has been for much of its history, Russia in the early 1990s is truly a torn country.

To redefine its civilization identity, a torn country must meet three requirements. First, its political and economic elite has to be generally supportive of and enthusiastic about this move. Second, its public has to be willing to acquiesce in the redefinition. Third, the dominant groups in the recipient civilization have to be willing to embrace the convert. All three requirements in large part exist with respect to Mexico. The first two in large part exist with respect to Turkey. It is not clear that any of them exist with respect to Russia's joining the West. The conflict between liberal democracy and Marxism-Leninism was between ideologies which, despite their major differences, ostensibly shared ultimate goals of freedom, equality and prosperity. A traditional, authoritarian, nationalist Russia could have quite different goals. A Western democrat could carry on an intellectual debate with a Soviet Marxist. It would be virtually impossible for him to do that with a Russian traditionalist. If, as the Russians stop behaving like Marxists, they reject liberal democracy and begin behaving like Russians but not like Westerners, the relations between Russia and the West could again become distant and conflictual.[8]

THE CONFUCIAN-ISLAMIC CONNECTION

The obstacles to non-Western countries joining the West vary considerably. They are least for Latin American and East European countries. They are greater for the Orthodox countries of the former Soviet Union. They are still greater for Muslim, Confucian, Hindu and Buddhist societies. Japan has established a unique position for itself as an associate member of the West: it is in the West in some respects but clearly not of the West in important dimensions. Those countries that for reason of culture and power do not wish to, or cannot, join the West compete with the West by developing their own economic, military and political power. They do this by promoting their internal development and by cooperating with other non-Western countries. The most prominent form of this cooperation is the Confucian-Islamic connection that has emerged to challenge Western interests, values and power.

Almost without exception, Western countries are reducing their military power; under Yeltsin's leadership so also is Russia. China, North Korea and several Middle Eastern states, however, are significantly expanding their military capabilities. They are doing this by the import of arms from Western and non-Western sources and by the development of indigenous arms industries. One result is the emergence of what Charles Krauthammer has called "Weapon States," and the Weapon States are not Western states. Another result is the redefinition of arms control, which is a Western concept and a Western goal. During the Cold War the primary purpose of arms control was to establish a stable military balance between the United States and its allies and the Soviet Union and its allies. In the post–Cold War world the primary objective of arms control is to prevent the development by non-Western societies of military capabilities that could threaten Western interests. The West attempts to do this through international agreements, economic pressure and controls on the transfer of arms and weapons technologies.

The conflict between the West and the Confucian-Islamic states focuses largely, although not exclusively, on nuclear, chemical and biological weapons, ballistic missiles and other sophisticated means for delivering them, and the guidance, intelligence and other electronic capabilities for achieving that goal. The West promotes nonproliferation as a universal norm and nonproliferation treaties and inspections as means of realizing that norm. It also threatens a variety of sanctions against those who promote the spread of sophisticated weapons and proposes some benefits for those who do not. The attention of the West focuses, naturally, on nations that are actually or potentially hostile to the West.

The non-Western nations, on the other hand, assert their right to acquire and to deploy whatever weapons they think necessary for their security. They also have absorbed, to the full, the truth of the response of the Indian defense minister when asked what lesson he learned from the Gulf War: "Don't fight the United States unless you have nuclear weapons." Nuclear weapons, chemical weapons and missiles are viewed, probably erroneously, as the potential equalizer of superior Western conventional power. China, of course, already has nuclear weapons; Pakistan and India have the capability to deploy them. North Korea, Iran, Iraq, Libya and Algeria appear to be attempting to acquire them. A top Iranian official has declared that all Muslim states should acquire nuclear weapons, and in 1988 the president of Iran reportedly issued a directive calling for development of "offensive and defensive chemical, biological and radiological weapons."

Centrally important to the development of counter-West military capabilities is the sustained expansion of China's military power and its means to create military power.

Buoyed by spectacular economic development, China is rapidly increasing its military spending and vigorously moving forward with the modernization of its armed forces. It is purchasing weapons from the former Soviet states; it is developing long-range missiles; in 1992 it tested a one-megaton nuclear device. It is developing power-projection capabilities, acquiring aerial refueling technology, and trying to purchase an aircraft carrier. Its military buildup and assertion of sovereignty over the South China Sea are provoking a multilateral regional arms race in East Asia. China is also a major exporter of arms and weapons technology. It has exported materials to Libya and Iraq that could be used to manufacture nuclear weapons and nerve gas. It has helped Algeria build a reactor suitable for nuclear weapons research and production. China has sold to Iran nuclear technology that American officials believe could only be used to create weapons and apparently has shipped components of 300-mile-range missiles to Pakistan. North Korea has had a nuclear weapons program under way for some while and has sold advanced missiles and missile technology to Syria and Iran. The flow of weapons and weapons technology is generally from East Asia to the Middle East. There is, however, some movement in the reverse direction; China has received Stinger missiles from Pakistan.

A Confucian-Islamic military connection has thus come into being, designed to promote acquisition by its members of the weapons and weapons technologies needed to counter the military power of the West. It may or may not last. At present, however, it is, as Dave McCurdy has said, "a renegades' mutual support pact, run by the proliferators and their backers." A new form of arms competition is thus occurring between Islamic-Confucian states and the West. In an old-fashioned arms race, each side developed its own arms to balance or to achieve superiority against the other side. In this new form of arms competition, one side is developing its arms and the other side is attempting not to balance but to limit and prevent that arms build-up while at the same time reducing its own military capabilities.

IMPLICATIONS FOR THE WEST

This article does not argue that civilization identities will replace all other identities, that nation states will disappear, that each civilization will become a single coherent political entity, that groups within a civilization will not conflict with and even fight each other. This paper does set forth the hypotheses that differences between civilizations are real and important; civilization-consciousness is increasing; conflict between civilizations will supplant ideological and other forms of conflict as the dominant global form of conflict; international relations, historically a game played out within Western civilization, will increasingly be de-Westernized and become a game in which non-Western civilizations are actors and not simply objects; successful political, security and economic international institutions are more likely to develop within civilizations than across civilizations; conflicts between groups in different civilizations will be more frequent, more sustained and more violent than conflicts between groups in the same civilization; violent conflicts between groups in different civilizations are the most likely and most dangerous source of escalation that could lead to global wars; the paramount axis of world politics will be the relations between "the West and the Rest"; the elites in some torn non-Western countries will try to make their countries part of the West, but in most cases face major obstacles to accomplishing this; a central focus of conflict for the immediate future will be between the West and several Islamic-Confucian states.

This is not to advocate the desirability of conflicts between civilizations. It is to set forth descriptive hypotheses as to what the future may be like. If these are plausible hypotheses, however, it is necessary to consider their implications for Western policy. These implications should be divided between short-term advantage and long-term accommodation. In the short term it is clearly in the interest of the West to promote greater cooperation and unity within its own civilization, particularly between its European and North American components; to incorporate into the West societies in Eastern Europe and Latin America whose cultures are close to those of the West; to promote and maintain cooperative relations with Russia and Japan; to prevent escalation of local inter-civilization conflicts into major inter-civilization wars; to limit the expansion of the military strength of Confucian and Islamic states; to moderate the reduction of Western military capabilities and maintain military superiority in East and Southwest Asia; to exploit differences and conflicts among Confucian and Islamic states; to support in other civilizations groups sympathetic to Western values and interests; to strengthen international institutions that reflect and legitimate Western interests and values and to promote the involvement of non-Western states in those institutions.

In the longer term other measures would be called for. Western civilization is both Western and modern. Non-Western civilizations have attempted to become modern without becoming Western. To date only Japan has fully succeeded in this quest. Non-Western civilizations will continue to attempt to acquire the wealth, technology, skills, machines and weapons that are part of being modern. They will also attempt to reconcile this modernity with their traditional culture and values. Their economic and military strength relative to the West will increase. Hence the West will increasingly have to accommodate these non-Western modern civilizations whose power approaches that of the West but whose values and interests differ significantly from those of the West. This will require the West to maintain the economic and military power necessary to protect its interests in relation to these civilizations. It will also, however, require the West to develop a more profound understanding of the basic religious and philosophical assumptions underlying other civilizations and the ways in which people in those civilizations see their interests. It will require an effort to identify elements of commonality between Western and other civilizations. For the relevant future, there will be no universal civilization, but instead a world of different civilizations, each of which will have to learn to coexist with the others.

NOTES

1. Murray Weidenbaum, *Greater China: The Next Economic Superpower?* St. Louis: Washington University Center for the Study of American Business, Contemporary Issues, Series 57, February 1993, pp. 2–3.

2. Bernard Lewis, "The Roots of Muslim Rage," *The Atlantic Monthly,* vol. 266, September 1990, p. 60; *Time,* June 15, 1992, pp. 24–28.

3. Archie Roosevelt, *For Lust of Knowing,* Boston: Little, Brown, 1988, pp. 332–333.

4. Almost invariably Western leaders claim they are acting on behalf of "the world community." One minor lapse occurred during the run-up to the Gulf War. In an interview on "Good Morning America," Dec. 21, 1990, British

Prime Minister John Major referred to the actions "the West" was taking against Saddam Hussein. He quickly corrected himself and subsequently referred to "the world community." He was, however, right when he erred.

5. Harry C. Triandis, *The New York Times,* Dec. 25, 1990, p. 41, and "Cross-Cultural Studies of Individualism and Collectivism," Nebraska Symposium on Motivation, vol. 37, 1989, pp. 41–133.

6. Kishore Mahbubani, "The West and the Rest," *The National Interest,* Summer 1992, pp. 3–13.

7. Sergei Stankevich, "Russia in Search of Itself," *The National Interest,* Summer 1992,

pp. 47–51; Daniel Schneider, "A Russian Movement Rejects Western Tilt," *Christian Science Monitor,* Feb. 5, 1993, pp. 5–7.

8. Owen Harries has pointed out that Australia is trying (unwisely in his view) to become a torn country in reverse. Although it has been a full member not only of the West but also of the ABCA military and intelligence core of the West, its current leaders are in effect proposing that it defect from the West, redefine itself as an Asian country and cultivate close ties with its neighbors. Australia's future, they argue, is with the dynamic economies of East Asia. But, as I have suggested, close economic cooperation normally requires a common cultural base. In addition, none of the three conditions necessary for a torn country to join another civilization is likely to exist in Australia's case.